Long Rider 3-5   34.95

The
FRONTIER WAR
for AMERICAN
INDEPENDENCE

The
FRONTIER WAR
for AMERICAN
INDEPENDENCE

William R. Nester

STACKPOLE
BOOKS

Published by
STACKPOLE BOOKS
5067 Ritter Road
Mechanicsburg, PA 17055
www.stackpolebooks.com

Printed in the United States of America

10 9 8 7 6 5 4 3 2 1

FIRST EDITION

Library of Congress Cataloging-in-Publication Data

Nester, William R., 1956–
  The frontier war for American independence / by William R. Nester.—
1st ed.
     p. cm.
Includes bibliographical references and index.
  ISBN 0-8117-0077-1
    1. United States—History—Revolution, 1775–1783—Campaigns. 2.
Frontier and pioneer life—United States. 3. United States—History—Revolution,
1775–1783—Participation, Indian. 4. United States—Territorial expansion. 5.
Indians of North America—Wars—1775–1783. I. Title.
E230.N47 2004
973.3—dc22

                                                                                    2003018723

For Angela,
with deepest love

CONTENTS

INTRODUCTION

"To Extirpate Us from the Earth"

It is also your Business, Brothers, to exert yourselves in the Defense of this Road by which the King, our Father, so fully supplied our Wants. If this is once stopt we must be a miserable People, and be left exposed to the Resentment of the Rebels, who, notwithstanding their fair Speeches, wish for nothing more than to extirpate us from the Earth, that they may possess our Lands, the Desire of attaining which we are convinced is the Cause of our present War between the King and his disobedient Children.
                                            —Seneca Chief Sayenqueraghta

The frontier war for their nation's independence is little known to most Americans. That struggle is overshadowed by such stirring events as Lexington and Concord, Bunker Hill, the Declaration of Independence, the Delaware River crossing, Valley Forge, and Yorktown, and national icons like George Washington, Thomas Jefferson, and John Adams. But the largely conventional war along the eastern seaboard was paralleled and at times intersected by a racial war without mercy along the frontier.

Frontier warfare was vicious. Sometimes accompanied by British officers but more often acting alone, the Indians launched hundreds of raids along nearly the entire frontier, from Maine to Georgia, seeking to pillage, destroy, enslave, and kill. That viciousness was not one-sided. The Americans could be just as brutal as the "savages" they loathed and feared. Of the Indians killed during American campaigns into the wilderness, most were women, old men, and children who could not get away or believed that as noncombatants and, in at least one case, Christians, they would be spared. The Americans condemned atrocities by the British and their Indian allies while turning blind eyes and deaf ears to any rumors of those committed by their own side. Sayenqueraghta articulated the mingled defiance, dependence, and incomprehension with which Indians viewed that relentless American imperialism.

But the frontier war was more than a long, blood-soaked sideshow. The Americans won independence when and how they did because of three interrelated successes of diminishing yet vital importance. It was essential for American

1

conventional armies to stay in the field in every region along the eastern seaboard, evading and ideally defeating British offensives and shadowing the redcoats holed up in the cities they managed to capture. But the vitality of those patriot armies depended on foreign sources of money, munitions, and men, especially the last; the French alliance would eventually provide the fleet and army that would allow the Americans to win their independence sooner rather than later. First, however, the French had to be convinced that they would be backing a winning cause, which returns us to the frontier war.

Battles won or lost there could and did decide the Revolution's fate. Indeed, the most decisive campaign of not just the frontier but the entire war took place in 1777 when British armies embarked from Montreal, Oswego, and New York City to converge on Albany. In a half-dozen bloody wilderness battles and sieges, the Americans eventually forced the British and Indian army launched from Oswego to retreat and captured Gen. John Burgoyne's entire army of over 7,000 troops at Saratoga. Learning of Burgoyne's fate, the third expedition withdrew to New York City. Had those British offensives succeeded, there never would have been a French alliance and the decisive surrender of yet another British army at York-town in 1781.

But Yorktown depended on more than the 1777 wilderness victories. The crushing American destruction of British forces in the frontier battles of Kings Mountain in October 1780 and Cowpens in January 1781 drastically diminished the numbers and exposed the western flank of Gen. Charles Cornwallis's army, which had overrun Georgia and South Carolina. Had the British won those battles, they would have secured their rule over those two southern states with nothing more than small bands of patriot guerrillas to fight. Faced with overwhelming numbers, Gen. Nathanael Greene would undoubtedly have withdrawn into Virginia rather than stand at Guilford Courthouse in February 1781, where his troops destroyed a quarter of Cornwallis's army and forced the British to retreat to Wilmington. When Cornwallis did invade Virginia later that summer, he did so with an army sadly reduced in ranks and élan by three defeats. He also turned his back on Greene's army, which would eventually liberate the Carolinas and Georgia. While the French fleet ultimately allowed Washington to force the British surrender at Yorktown, Cornwallis never would have holed up there had he not suffered those earlier defeats at Kings Mountain and Cowpens.

The frontier campaigns and battles of 1777, 1780, and 1781 were decisive in determining the American Revolution's fate. Yet the importance of what happened along those thousands of miles of wilderness and scattered forts, hamlets, and homesteads does not end there. American failures there would mire the new nation in military, economic, and diplomatic conflicts that persisted for decades. The Americans would have captured Canada in 1775 had they not been so ineptly led on the Lake Champlain frontier; the subsequent expulsion of the British from all their colonies except Nova Scotia would at the very least have set back the attempted reconquest's timing and strategy and might have empowered the powerful peace faction in Parliament to determine policy. Likewise, a series of events favoring American interests would have accrued had General Sullivan's campaign taken Fort Niagara in 1779. Lightly defended, Detroit, Michilimackinac, and smaller posts would have surrendered to an American expedition moving up the Great Lakes. Most northwest tribes would have buried their hatchets, and raids against the Ohio valley settlers would have diminished to a trickle. With that region secure, diplomats could have been assertive in demanding trade rights down the Mississippi and at New Orleans. Those are just two of many "what ifs" that illuminate the frontier war's importance to subsequent American history.

The frontier war, at once genocidal and decisive, is obscured within the American Revolution's broader history and even more powerfully vivid and enduring myths. It is a story that has never before been comprehensively told, but it must be explored to better understand the American Revolution and the nation's history.

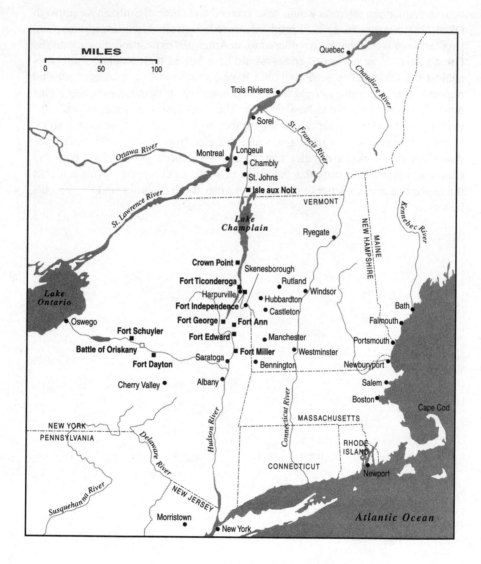

The Lake Champlain Valley–Canada Frontier

The Ohio Valley–Upper Mississippi Frontier

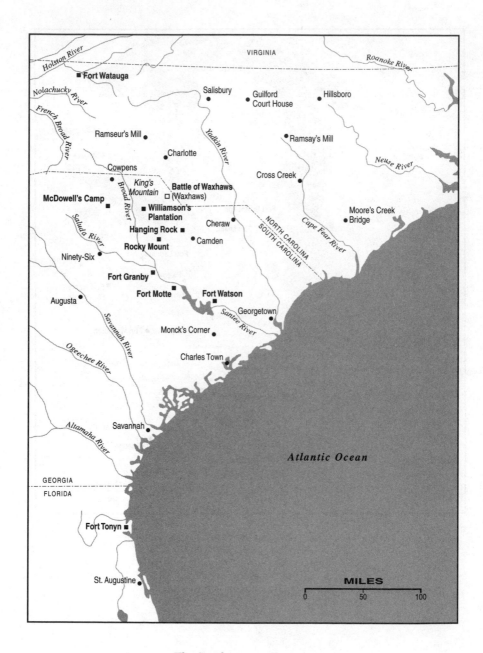

The Southeastern Frontier

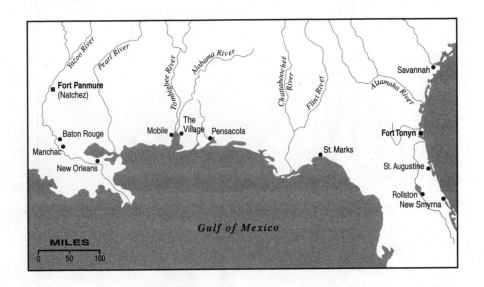

The Gulf Coast–Lower Mississippi Frontier

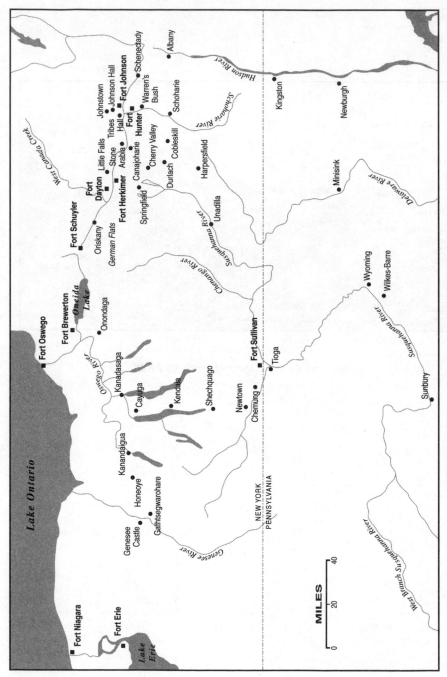

The Finger Lakes–Upper Susquehanna Valley Frontier

CHAPTER 1

"They May Possess Our Lands":
War, Revolution,
and Culture on the Frontier

*The Americans . . . acquire no attachment to Place: But wandering
about Seems engrafted to their Nature: and it is a weakness . . . that
they Should forever imagine the Lands further off are Still better than
those upon which they have already settled.*
                                                            —Lord Dunmore

*Why should I not go to war. I am old. I am too lame to be able to run
away. War is my vocation.*
                                                            —Chief Forgeron

"Great things have been affected by a few Men well Conducted." George
Rogers Clark penned those words in February 1779 upon learning that his
nemesis, Lt. Gov. Henry Hamilton, had recaptured Vincennes and intended to
march against him and his ragtag frontiersmen at Kaskaskia in the spring. To Virginia governor Patrick Henry, he admitted "being sensible that without a Reinforcement which at present I have hardly a right to Expect that I shall be obliged to
give up this Cuntrey to Mr. Hamilton without a turn of Fortune." Where most
would have wallowed in bleak despair, Clark had the genius and daring to see a
chance and gamble all in one roll of the dice. He "resolved to take the advantage of
his present Situation and Risque the whole on a Single Battle."[1]
    Clark won that desperate gamble. In the dead of winter he led 170 hardened
frontiersmen through 180 miles of forest and floodlands to capture Hamilton and
his command at Vincennes. Clark was not alone in his courage, fortitude, and
military and wilderness skills. For eight years during America's war for independence, hundreds of small and large groups of armed men "well conducted"
destroyed the lives and property of thousands along the frontier. Not all succeeded. Many a raid or campaign was poorly led and either never reached the
enemy or else suffered humiliating and bloody defeats and even massacre.
Indeed, the fortunes of that war fell most harshly upon the frontier.

During their Revolution, Americans fought for and against many vital issues and values. It was more than a huge tax revolt, more even than a nationalist bid for independence. It was as much about "freedom to" as "freedom from."

WHITHER THE FRONTIER?

A significant portion of the American Revolution was fought and thought over lands called the frontier, but what was the frontier during America's independence struggle? The frontier was any wilderness or sparsely peopled region where groups struggled for control. There was not one frontier but many, and they were determined as much by culture as by nature.

Amorphous frontiers thus should not be confused with clear-cut boundaries. Among other issues, that era's diplomats negotiated lines on maps that separated people. Nearly every treaty with Indians either reaffirmed or redrew boundaries. Yet it is one thing to scratch mutually accepted lines on maps and quite another to keep people from straying across or struggling for them.

Where then did the frontier begin or end? Was it that last hamlet or homestead or somewhere in the wilderness beyond? By definition, the frontier was fluid. It shifted with the fortunes of war, trade, diplomacy, harvest, or hunt, and the ambitions and fears that at once shaped and reflected those enterprises. Nothing punched back a frontier more swiftly than terror. Traumatized and enraged refugees stampeded from every frontier war. Many stayed away forever. Some threw experience and caution to the winds and headed west again along with hopeful others once the scalping knives were sheathed.

Geographically, the frontiers embraced the piedmont of the Carolinas and Virginia; the tidewater regions of East and West Florida; Georgia south and west of Sunbury; Maine north and east of Falmouth; the upper reaches of the St. Lawrence, Connecticut, Hudson, Mohawk, Delaware, Susquehanna, Ohio, Wabash, Illinois, Cumberland, Tennessee, Savannah, Broad, Catawba, Peedee, and Cape Fear Rivers; the Mississippi River valley from above New Orleans to its headwaters; the cluster of settlements in the hearts of Tennessee and Kentucky; the villages near Detroit, Michilimackinac, Niagara, Vincennes, Kaskaskia, St. Joseph, and other remote forts; the entire watersheds of Lake Champlain and the Great Lakes; most of Nova Scotia; and countless other lone villages and cabins buried within or near wilderness.

Culture was as important as geography in shaping passions and actions in the frontier war for American independence. Though most tribes sided with the British against the land-grabbing Americans, every tribe and village was split in varying degrees and ways over what to do about the war. The Americans were just as splintered by ethnicity, class, and, most importantly, the degree of loyalty or defiance to the king and all he symbolized. The frontier war was fought not just between settlers and Indians, but within each of those cultures.

Indians had fought Indians ever since they first arrived in the Western Hemisphere and continued to do so long after the Europeans joined them. They killed each other for the same reasons that have motivated war among all peoples at all times and places—greed, fear, pride, hatred, vengeance, and ignorance. What changed was the context. Tribal struggles became subordinated within the broader conflicts among the technologically and economically superior European powers and later with the Americans.

Indians were not the helpless victims or pawns of the Europeans. Tribal interests were just as clearly defined and followed as those of European states. To advance their interests, Indians were as adept at manipulating the power imbalance as the Europeans, perhaps more so. Indian diplomacy followed a time-honored maxim, "The enemy of my enemy is my friend." A tribe leaned toward the imperial power whose restless pioneers were the fewest, least intrusive, and farthest away.

Thus did most tribes tilt with varying degrees toward the weaker power, France, during its century-and-a-half struggle with Britain for mastery over North America's eastern half. In so doing, some tribes helped preserve and even enhance themselves, most merely slowed their decline, and a few were completely extirpated. The tribes lost this advantage when Britain drove the French from North America in 1763. Then a dozen years later America's independence struggle revived the Indian ability to play one power against the other. The American settlers posed the greater immediate threat, if not the greater military and economic power, so most tribes naturally favored the British.

But other forces complicated this seemingly clear-cut decision. Geography, trade, culture, and dependence were inseparable for all tribes. Relations with the British and Spanish empires were both a blessing and curse. The closer the Indians were to the settlements, the easier it was to trade and counsel in peace, or rip scalps and plunder in war. Or, conversely, the easier it was to suffer alcoholism, epidemics, poaching, squatting, and cultural leprosy at any time, along with the specter of enemy invasion in war.

A tribe's degree of economic dependence, more often than not, determined its allegiance. The Iroquois or Six Nations provide a good example. The prosperity of the Seneca, Cayuga, and Onondaga tribes was tied to Fort Niagara, while that of the Mohawk, Oneida, and Tuscarora tribes was anchored on Albany. Thus in war the western tribes leaned first toward France and then Britain, while the eastern tribes rallied around Britain first and then America.

Yet even here there were exceptions. During the American Revolution, the Mohawk Indians were mostly loyal to Britain despite the isolation of their two villages, Fort Hunter and Canajoharie, within a checkerboard of settlements. Their ties to their adopted sachem, Sir William Johnson, and after his death in 1774, to his son John and nephew Guy, kept them loyal despite their exposed position. A personal bond explains the Oneida Indians' allegiance as well. For the Oneida, it was the charisma and genuine love of their missionary Samuel Kirkland, rather than their proximity to the settlements, that knit them with the Americans against not just the British but also the other Iroquois tribes.

To use the word *tribe* is to substitute convenience for accuracy. Villages more than tribes shaped Indian identities. The idea of being a Shawnee or Iroquois was as abstract as living at Piqua or Genesee was concrete. Yet villages were little less diverse than tribes. Most were polyglot jumbles of not just clans but also dialects and even languages and races. Unlike whites, Indians saw strength in genetic and racial diversity rather than uniformity. Captives were adopted. Fragments of other peoples were enticed to join. Villages or even tribes depleted by disease or war meshed. In such social flux, individualism, democracy, equality, and tolerance became essential values that allowed Indians to get along with one another. There is certainly irony here. In the colonial world of religious conformity, class conceits, slavery, and steep slippery slopes for the ambitious up the economic, social, and political hierarchy, few Americans ever realized those very same abstract values that motivated and justified their own Revolution.

So what kept liberty from dissolving into anarchy? Indian society lacked (and did not want) such formal institutions as laws, courts, prisons, and police to keep order. Instead, a village modified behavior by socializing individuals into its values and reinforcing those teachings by wielding group approval or condemnation as appropriate. And each village or tribe had a government that made vital decisions on its behalf. The organization and power of those governments varied. Many tribes had separate chiefs for civil and military decisions. Some tribes had a head chief, others a council of chiefs with similar status.

How did one become a chief? More so than among the Europeans, Indians rose within their world by their merits. Those who became chiefs did so because they displayed outstanding diplomatic, political, oratorical, and war skills. As long as they stayed sober, most chiefs displayed highly sophisticated negotiating skills during councils with the whites.

Chiefs reigned rather than ruled. They gained status by giving away rather than amassing wealth, by forging consensus rather than issuing commands. Sir Guy Johnson explained that "the Authority of their Sachems . . . is not . . . coercive. . . . It consists in the Power of Convening the People, and proposing matters to them, for their Compliance, the Success of which much depends upon their Influence, and the Strengths and Reputation of their Connexions."[2] A consensus on even the simplest of issues could take days of debate and compromise to forge. Agreement was sometimes elusive, especially for tough questions of war or peace. When differences were unbridgeable, a chief might lead his followers away to join another village or form his own.

A village or tribal council declared war for the same general reasons that a European state would—the desire to defend or expand trade, territory, and honor, or take plunder and vengeance. Yet the similarities ended there. No chief could command the men to go to war. That was a purely individual choice shaped by the push of society and the pull of charismatic, skilled leaders. Indians trod the warpath as much for personal glory as village interests. Men rose or fell in status, wealth, and power by their relative feats or failures at war. War was so integral to many men's lives that they could do nothing else when it beckoned. Ouiatenon chief Forgeron explained: "War is my vocation, I had rather after my death have the flesh torn off the bones by wild beasts, than that it should lye to rot idly in the ground."[3]

Chief Forgeron was actually a rarity among Indians. Most warriors buried their hatchets after youth faded into middle age unless the enemy attacked their village. Perhaps 150,000 Indians lived between the Appalachians and Mississippi River and the Gulf Coast and Hudson Bay during the 1770s. Only a fraction of those peoples were active warriors at any one time. The best estimates at midcentury counted about 12,000 warriors north and 14,000 south of the Ohio and Potomac Rivers. Those warriors offered potentially decisive power to the side that could enlist them. But only a sliver of those men would actually tread the warpath at any one time. The number of men a village sent to war depended on its fighting strength, the charisma and previous war experiences of those calling for followers, how relatively unified or divided the council was on the war, its distance from the settlements, its relative prosperity or poverty, and whether it was hunting season.[4]

Indian participation in the war was not inevitable. When news spread that the American "sons" had revolted against their English "father," most Indians preferred to avoid that tragic family quarrel. And at first the Americans and British encouraged that neutrality. But with each failed attempt to crush the rebellion, ever more British officials recognized that Indian allies could be an enormous strategic asset. By late 1775, British officers and agents began presenting the war belt at Indian councils. Their American counterparts soon followed suit. Each warrior, village, and tribe had to make a very hard decision.

Most Americans were just as torn over which side to choose. In 1775, the rapid succession of news of Lexington and Concord, Boston's siege, the capture of Forts Ticonderoga and Crown Point, and Bunker Hill split asunder public sentiments like a burning sword thrust. Americans would fight not just British regulars and Indians, but often their neighbors as well. During the war, over 30,000 loyalists enlisted in the British army or various provincial companies and regiments; perhaps 80,000 loyalists eventually went into exile. Nonetheless, John Adams's belief that the American people divided into roughly equal thirds as supporters, opponents, and fence-sitters during the struggle understated the Revolution's actual support. Overall, active patriots comprised around 40 to 45 percent of white males, while loyalists were between 15 and 20 percent. Those proportions, however varied considerably among regions, religions, and ethnic groups.[5]

Loyalties among frontier settlers splintered as sharply as those along the eastern seaboard. The economic interests of most settlers tended to elbow aside sentiment in determining who was a rebel, who was a Tory, and who struggled to sidestep a decision. Frontier politics did not necessarily crack along traditional class lines. A successful rebellion would nullify the Proclamation of 1763 and other treaties restricting westward expansion. Those already holding secure titles to their land tended to be more conciliatory than those whose claims violated British law. Patriots flourished in counties and settlements with shakier or nonexistent land titles. One's relative voice in the colonial assembly, rather than one's wealth, was also important. Assemblies like Virginia's, which divvied out seats fairly equitably to the frontier settlers, preserved their loyalty; those like the Carolinas' and New York's, in which eastern landowners and merchants monopolized power, alienated a good portion of frontiersmen into neutrality or Tory ranks. Frontier communities dependent on the guns and pay of nearby British garrisons tended to stay loyal. Ancestry also played a role. The deeper the number of generations that a family was rooted in the New World, the more likely it identified itself as American rather than British. Newcomers to the frontier tended to settle with neighbors similar to those they left behind. The frontier resembled a tattered patchwork quilt of varying ethnic and religious communities, each with its own relative sentiments or animosities toward the Crown.

Aware that the Americans were developing a nationality and interests distinct from those of Britain, the Crown trapped itself in a dilemma from the 1763 Treaty of Paris ending French power in North America to the shots at Lexington Green in April 1775. Many prominent Britons were torn over the acquisition of Canada. For over 150 years the French threat had forced the ever more numerous and prosperous Americans to stay dependent on British protection. With the French threat destroyed, Britain's leaders worried that the Americans would eventually seek autonomy and perhaps even independence. But the measures Whitehall took to contain American nationalism actually nourished it.

Nonetheless, though inconvenienced or offended by the Crown's policies, many people were as lukewarm about the patriot as they were the Tory cause. They became ropes in a tug-of-war between fervent Americans and British. To favor one side would offend the other. Retaliation could follow. To avoid that, one had to be a political weathervane, shifting with the prevailing winds. Surrendering conviction to expediency meant toasting Congress or king, or even marching off into battle for a side that one might otherwise detest. With the patriots dominant in most places, loyalists tended to lie dormant unless a British army marched into the region. It took almost suicidal courage to go against one's community if it cheered a particular cause.

In all, the patriots enjoyed an advantage. By nature they were more aggressive and demanding than most loyalists bowed before the Crown. This often gave them an appearance of power initially larger than their numbers. Their ranks then swelled from those who wanted to join the winning side or feared suffering with the losers. Thus did perceptions of power create power. But those who wielded power unjustly could undermine their legitimacy. To wage war, Congress and the states had to requisition supplies, money, and men even more voraciously than the Crown whose yoke they had thrown off. This alienated many of the "sunshine patriots" that Thomas Paine despised, and forced even the most committed radicals to pause for thought.

That vicious and devastating civil war was engulfed by the broader conflict of settlers versus Indians, leading Lord Dunmore to lament American wanderlust.[6] Dunmore's insight into American character was profound. No government could dam or even for long channel that "restlessness." The greed or dream of virgin land and wealth had fueled the frontier's advance for more than a century and a half and would continue to do so for more than another hundred years. That restlessness would destroy the grip of one government on its colonies and convert its successor into a global power. Living in the way of that expanding frontier were, of course, the native peoples.

There is irony here because Indians and settlers shared more characteristics than most were willing to admit. A hybrid culture developed along the frontier. The economies of settlers and Indians alike depended on subsistence farming supplemented by hunting, fishing, and gathering, along with the manufacture and repair of tools, furniture, and weapons. What little they did not consume was traded for goods that they could not make themselves. Although most Indians and settlers retained their respective religions, their beliefs converged in many ways. Virtually all pioneers boasted their Christian faith in only one God while denouncing "savage" pantheism. Yet like the Indians, most settlers lived in a world shaped by the power of omens, dreams, healers, and spirits, and mingled many folktales and superstitions.

Imperialism loses some of its impetus in such a cultural dynamic. Though one people might be dominant, they must accommodate themselves to others on the frontier. In doing so, they transform themselves as well as their subjects. This cultural blending is more pronounced when a power balance checks two or more neighboring peoples. But those common practices and appearances should not be exaggerated. Ultimately, settlers and Indians superficially reflected each other from opposite edges of an unbridgeable cultural chasm.

THE NATURE OF FRONTIER WAR
The frontier war involved two distinct elements. Large-scale campaigns were mostly fought by regulars or volunteers, but often accompanied by Indians who served as guides, scouts, and flankers. Small-scale raids were mostly composed of Indians and sometimes joined by white officers and volunteers.

During that long war, the Americans and British each launched only one major campaign designed to burst through the frontier and conquer another province. Those campaigns were disasters. In the autumn of 1775, the Americans invaded Canada, with one prong under Gen. Richard Montgomery advancing on Montreal and the other under Gen. Benedict Arnold moving on Quebec. Montgomery captured Montreal and then joined Arnold before Quebec. But their New Year's Eve attack on that city was defeated and Montgomery was killed. Although the Americans gamely besieged Quebec that winter, they retreated back to New York before the 10,000 fresh redcoats who arrived in the spring. The Americans left behind nearly 5,000 dead and captured comrades. Britain's three-pronged invasion of New York in 1777 ended even more ignominiously. Checked at Oriskany and Fort Stanwix, Col. Barry St. Leger withdrew his army back to Fort Niagara, while Gen. John Burgoyne's 7,500-man army was defeated at Bennington and Saratoga, and finally surrendered in October. Word of defeats caused the third expedition up the Hudson River to turn back at Kingstown.

Those two massive invasions aside, neither the British nor the Americans ever launched a campaign that reached a more limited strategic objective—the enemy's supply bases. Along the long frontier, each side manned a few key forts that organized raids against the enemy and tried to protect the region's settlements. Of those strongholds, the British controlled Niagara, Detroit, Pensacola, and St. Augustine, and the Americans Fort Pitt, Fort Schuyler, Fort Ticonderoga, Sunbury, and Augusta.

Why did neither side make a serious attempt to take such prime targets? Each side's implementation of its strategies in North America nearly always fell short of its often grandiose goals. Warfare was tediously slow and laborious on the eastern seaboard. Those challenges were multiplied many times on the frontier. Logistics rather than gunfire defeated most wilderness expeditions. Gathering enough supplies and transport and hacking a road through the forest were Herculean challenges and sometimes Sisyphean traps. Packhorses had to carry their own fodder or perish on the trail. The longer the campaign, the more fodder the animals had to carry, and thus the less beans and bullets available for the troops. Low water or spring floods could retard an expedition by boat just as severely as a dearth of draft animals could doom one by land. When transport fell short of need, troops squatted in camp devouring provisions that were supposed to sustain them against the enemy.

The goal of most expeditions was modest: to destroy as much of the enemy frontier as possible and ideally push it back. Maj. Gen. John Sullivan led the largest American campaign—5,000 troops against the Iroquois in 1779. Although his army destroyed their villages, crops, and orchards, the inhabitants fled to fight, harvest, and procreate another day. In the Ohio valley the Americans embarked on a series of smaller expeditions. In distance if not manpower, no frontier campaign was more audacious than that of George Rogers Clark, who hoped eventually to capture Detroit and the upper Great Lakes after first taking British possessions in Illinois and along the Wabash River. But a shortage of men and supplies fouled Clark's grand design. Similar difficulties stymied the campaigns of Gen. Lachlan McIntosh in 1778 and William Crawford in 1782 against the Ohio tribes. The most successful American campaigns were against the Cherokee, whose villages were ravaged yearly from 1776 through 1781.

The British and Americans faced a dilemma regarding Indian allies. Nearly all frontier commanders and agents questioned whether warriors were worth the financial, diplomatic, emotional, and moral costs of enlisting and keeping them on raids and campaigns. Indians clearly provided advantages by performing such essential roles as guides, scouts, and flankers, ambushing enemy detachments, and capturing stray soldiers. Yet on the warpath, frontier commanders often found themselves forced to follow Indian strategies and tactics rather than their own. Gen. Frederick Haldimand complained in 1781 that "there is no dependence upon even those Indians who are declared in our favor, and there are a number in that country our avowed enemies . . . there has not been a single instance where the Indians have fulfilled their engagements but influenced by Caprice, a dream or a desire of protracting the war, to obtain presents, have dispersed and deserted the troops."[7] Under those conditions, the only thing worse than having Indians as allies was having them as enemies.

The decentralization and diversity of Indian politics bewildered and frustrated Europeans. They searched for a tribe that could make binding decisions for itself and others, and within each tribe tried to designate a head chief with whom to negotiate and forge binding agreements. Those efforts not only were often fruitless, but also provoked further animosities. Nearly all Americans and British alike just could not fathom the reality that, as White Mingo and countless others tried to explain, chiefs were powerless to "restrain or hold fast our young men against their will."[8]

Indian diplomacy involved elaborate rituals. Councils opened with a condolence ceremony for those who had recently died. One side would wipe away the other's tears by symbolically reburying the dead with gifts to the survivors. With their minds and hearts cleared, delegates could then debate the council's issues. Wampum was an essential part of diplomacy. Bits of white or purple shell were laboriously transformed into hollow cylinders and then strung into strings or belts in patterns that displayed a pictorial or symbolic message. During councils a speaker would present strings or belts to emphasize his key points. Wampum holders also enjoyed diplomatic immunity. Envoys traveling through enemy country would prominently display belts to avoid assassination. Wampum belts recorded a council's decisions or treaties.

Successful diplomats were those who had mastered the art of speaking the poetry of diplomatic language, enthusiastically and skillfully singing the songs and dancing the steps of war, listening carefully to the chiefs, gracefully accepting appropriate advice, acting decisively to prevent or compensate injustices committed both against and by Indians, and offering concessions to advance the long-term interests of one's nation.

But the most successful diplomats were usually those who were the most generous in distributing gifts. Indians were essentially practical people. Their loyalty usually went to the highest bidder. Gifts thus were essential to Indian diplomacy. The stronger always gave more to the weaker. Protocol demanded gifts on numerous occasions and situations. Gifts should be given annually, during any council, to cover the recent dead, to seal an alliance, to heal a rift, or to avert starvation and deprivation. A gift could come in many forms. The Indians not only expected goods, but also demanded interpreters, commissaries, military advisors, and blacksmiths.

The British and Americans rarely got a tangible return on their investments with the Indians. For instance, John Stuart, the British superintendent for the Southern District, gave away 7,500 pounds sterling worth of gifts in 1775, 14,500 in 1776, 33,000 in 1777, and 50,000 in 1778.[9] Just how many warriors did those ever-mounting piles of presents win for Britain? A pittance from the Crown's point of view. During those four years, only one tribe launched an all-out war against the Americans—the Cherokees in 1776—and it was defeated.

Truly great diplomats among the British or Americans were rare. The poison of British arrogance and American hatred seeped into diplomacy from all too many frontier officers and even agents charged with Indian affairs. As a diplomat, no one equaled let alone excelled Sir William Johnson, who died in 1774 on the war's eve. Unlike most diplomats, Johnson genuinely understood and sympathized with the Indians, mastered their psychology and culture, knew when to be tough or generous, and all along never wavered from advancing British interests. He would be irreplaceable.

Months and even years of painstaking expensive diplomacy that bought a tenuous peace could be shattered by an act of murderous rage. Impotent to retaliate against an elusive bloodthirsty foe, frontiersmen at times exploded their wrath on peaceful Indians. That usually just provoked the survivors' followers to swell the vicious cycle of death and destruction. The slaughter of Chief Logan's family and friends converted the Mingo into relentless avenging enemies. The butchering of Cornstalk united the Shawnee on the warpath. Less spectacularly but just as negatively, commanders tried to intimidate chiefs with threats and bluster. That might have cowed a few chiefs in the short run, but the Indians soon wised to the limits of American power. Over time the failure to respect Indian diplomatic etiquette swelled enemy ranks. American arrogance eliminated the most powerful Indian voices for neutrality—Cornstalk was murdered, Kayashuta seized the British hatchet, and White Eyes fell into a sullen acquiescence as ever more of his men joined war parties against the frontier and then was himself murdered.

But for the Americans, the worst handicap on Indian policy was financial. Congress and the state governments were bankrupt; inflation made their currencies worthless. Yet even if they had enough money, they lacked access to inexpensive, abundant well-made trade goods. Thus American diplomats and merchants alike were unable to do their jobs. As a result, nearly every tribe remained dependent on and thus allied with Britain rather than the United States.

But all that aside, the Indians understood that the ever-swelling and land-hungry American population posed a worsening threat that only alliance with Britain could stave off. After all, not just the Americans fought for their independence. Every native people that went to war from 1775 to 1783 also fought to be free or simply survive. With that understanding, most tribes contributed warriors or outright warred—enthusiastically or half-heartedly, consistently or sporadically—against the rebels between 1775 and 1783. Few tribes—Massachusetts' Mohican, New York's Oneida, and Maine's Penobscot, Maliseet, and Passamaquoddy Indians—openly allied with the United States during the war. No tribe on either side would emerge victorious over the long term. Sooner or later they would all be crushed, whether they fought or fled.

Guerrilla rather than conventional tactics dominated the frontier war. Though such tactics were not unknown in Europe at that time, conventional warfare by professional armies prevailed. Although some expeditions numbered in the hundreds and even thousands of men, the wilderness war was fought mostly by raids of a score or so. The object was not so much to conquer as to create "no man's lands" by destroying or driving off the enemy's settlers. Frontier wars have no real fronts, but sputter and burst into flames here and there, though never everywhere at once.[10]

This was a war in which the Indians enjoyed decided tactical and strategic advantages. Their warfare was adapted to the wilderness, which they and their ancestors had called home for thousands of years. They knew how to slip through the forest with little chance of detection, strike, and then disappear. Few Americans on the campaigns into Indian territory shared those skills, and their abilities were diluted by the hundreds of other armed men stumbling through the forest with them. With advance word of an approaching enemy, the Indians either prepared an ambush or, more commonly, withdrew before the Americans arrived. Only one American expedition, Clark's against Vincennes in early 1779, achieved surprise, and that was against a British garrison rather than an Indian village. Nonetheless, in addition to Clark, some masters of wilderness warfare emerged from the American and British ranks, like John Butler, Henry Bird, and Thomas Brown of the loyalists, and Daniel Boone, Evan Shelby, and John Sevier of the patriots, to cite only a few. Those men excelled because they created a hybrid of European and Indian tactics that gave them an edge.

Another Indian advantage stemmed from their relatively meager property and subsistence life. With less to lose, Indians tended to evade an approaching enemy. Unaware of just where the enemy was and weighed down with possessions, Americans preferred to fort up rather than flee. Thus, Indians were often able to destroy people along with their property, while the Americans could usually only burn houses and uproot crops.

But the glaring disparity in possessions was not always apparent. The troops in Sullivan's 1779 campaign against the Iroquois villages of the upper Susquehanna, Finger Lake, and Genesee valleys were astonished to find houses of squared logs with glass windows, stone fireplaces, and furniture, surrounded by orchards, fences, chickens and pigs rooting in the mud, and cattle lowing in the pasturelands. "Savages" were not supposed to enjoy such a lifestyle indistinguishable from that of Americans. Regardless, the ability to destroy as much as they had suffered made the looting and burning all the more gleeful to those invaders.

Forest battles between war parties and large bodies of troops were rare. War parties attacked the weak and evaded the strong. When it was decided to attack, the warriors carefully assessed the enemy. Were they militia or regulars innocent of forest warfare? Were they hardened frontiersmen or rangers? How many were there and how were they deployed? Were they rested or tired? Were they wary or complacent?

The most vulnerable opponents, of course, were raw, exhausted, fearful recruits caught in an ambush. Then a quick rush of screaming, tomahawk-swinging warriors might panic and overwhelm them. If the troops were alert and took cover, then steady sniping, creeping, and encirclement might pick them off until they broke or surrendered. Well-trained regulars commanded by courageous officers might order a bayonet charge before which Indians always fled, but then usually swarmed back like so many deadly bees. Unless the Indians suffered large losses, ammunition usually decided the battle. When their powder and ball ran out, so too did the warriors.

Contrary to popular belief, the Indians mastered not only wilderness tactics, but also obedience to their leaders to realize them. Col. James Smith, who spent four years as a captive with the Indians, revealed that on the warpath "they have all the essentials of discipline. They are under good command, and punctual in obeying orders; they can act in concert; and when their officers lay a plan and give orders, they will cheerfully unite in putting all their directions into immediate execution."[11] That discipline unraveled only when things went wrong. If the raiders suffered casualties or failed to overrun the enemy, warriors would lose heart and turn home.

Religion and warfare meshed for Indians. For protection, every warrior carried a medicine bundle that contained charms bestowed by the gods over the course of his lifetime. Each was different but might include "little figures of different kinds, some as Amulets, some as household Gods, these when they go to war they paint with vermillion." The most spiritually adept member of a war party guarded its medicine bundle with "heads, bones or skins of certain animals, preserved Birds in the feather, Snakes skins, Bows and arrows . . . to bundle up with the other valuable effects, Wolves teeth, Panthers claws, Eagles talons."[12]

Dreams were the most easily trod path within the spirit world, from which the gods gave messages: "Should any one have a dream which bodes something favorable, or the contrary, he relates it in the morning to his comrades, and their reliance on omens is such, as frequently to defeat the enterprise."[13] That seeming fickleness frustrated most white officers accompanying war parties.

A war party's goal was to kill or capture as many people and destroy or plunder as much property as possible while suffering minimal or no losses. That would seem an obvious strategy for any numerically weaker side. But steadily diminishing Indian populations reinforced that imperative. Disease and battle were killing off Indians faster than they could naturally replenish themselves.

That population crisis provoked a quandary for war parties. Was it better to kill or capture more of the enemy? Tactical circumstances, of course, ruled that question. How much the enemy resisted, how vulnerable they were to slaughter, and how violent the victors' blood lust determined the degree of carnage.

In all, it was obviously easier for triumphant warriors to bring home a scalp than a captive. Yet for various reasons, most war parties aimed for a mix of the two. Prisoners could be more valuable than scalps, and not just when British officials paid more for them. Some captives could be converted into Indians. Children were the best candidates, but Indian life held enormous appeal to free spirits of all ages. Over the preceding century and a half, interbreeding and converts considerably lightened the skin tone of warriors stalking the settlements. Women and children were usually automatically adopted to replenish the village's population. A captive male's life, however, hung in the balance.

Males were forced to run the gauntlet between two opposing lines of jeering villagers armed with clubs and sticks. Many an exhausted prisoner stumbled, fell, and was beaten to death. Trader John Leeth witnessed Indians hack off and impale on a pole a captive's head amidst "a scene of yelling, dancing, singing, and rioting, which, I suppose, represented something like demons from the infernal regions." When Leeth and some other traders asked permission to bury the remnants, Wyandot chief Half King replied, "They do not bury our dead when they kill them, and we will not bury theirs."[14]

Those who survived the gauntlet faced the judgment of the village elders, a grieving family, or the cries of the mob. The chiefs often allowed those families that had recently lost loved ones to decide the captive's fate. To assuage their loss, a family might tearfully embrace or fiendishly torture the prisoner, followed by the ritual cannibalism of organs and other body parts.

Those adopted rarely had it easy, at least initially. Captives struggled with mingled homesickness, rage, and terror. Villagers, including sometimes the adoptee's family, might bully the newcomer. Most men sought escape at the first opportunity. But for some men, many women, and nearly all children, the longer they remained the more they preferred Indian to white life. Many tearfully refused to return to the settlements when a peace treaty forced tribes to release their captives.

IMPORTANCE OF FRONTIER WAR

How did the frontier war shape the Revolution? Although the Americans ultimately won independence on battlefields along the eastern seaboard and at negotiations in Paris and London, the frontier struggle was more than a bloody sideshow. That remote war diverted huge amounts of men, money, supplies, and energies from the East Coast. It did so because both sides recognized the frontier's importance. The war's turning point, after all, took place on the frontier in 1777 when Burgoyne surrendered at Saratoga and St. Leger broke off his siege of Fort Stanwix. The ability of pioneers to cling to tiny settlements in Kentucky and Tennessee, Clark's seizure of the Illinois villages and Vincennes, and Spain's cap ture of West Florida helped force the British to concede a United States that ended at the Mississippi River rather than the Appalachian watershed.

For the United States, the frontier war not only helped win independence and expand the new nation's territory, but also accelerated the development of American nationalism. That identity was forged in part by consciously contrasting it with the "savages" who impeded the nation's destiny. That view of Indians was succinctly captured in the Declaration of Independence, which charged the king with, among other crimes, provoking against the frontier "the merciless Indian savages, whose known rule of warfare is an undistinguished destruction of all ages, sexes, and conditions."

That image not only promoted American national identity, but also justified a ruthless series of policies and military campaigns to evict or at times extirpate Indians from their land. As the savages were so "merciless," the Americans could only fight fire with fire. On the frontier, Americans and British alike often inflicted the same mayhem they condemned when committed by Indians.

The frontier war's most powerful immediate impact, of course, was on the people actually trying to survive there. For many of those settlers, the war was devastating and often deadly. Thousands of Americans and Indians alike were butchered or maimed; smallpox killed thousands more, mostly natives. Raiders from both sides destroyed an inestimable amount of the other's wealth—houses, livestock, crops, furniture, and various implements. To their dying days, untold numbers of people remained traumatized by the horrors and losses they survived.

Although they inflicted far more damage than they suffered, the Indians lost the war. That loss would become ever more crushing over the next generations as tens of thousands of settlers poured over the Appalachians and spread across the land, shouldering aside the natives, clear-cutting the forests, and provoking yet more wars. But all that lay ahead. The war's immediate impact varied from one tribe, village, and individual to another. When the killing stopped, the Indians received the abstract news that their "Great Father" across the sea had ceded his power to a new one much closer to their homes. The new "Great Father" would soon reveal his nature.

CHAPTER 2

"We Shall Not Yield an Inch": 1763 through 1774

Perhaps leaving them to the Mercy of the Indians may be the best if not the only Way to restrain them.
—Virginia governor
Francis Fauquier

Who is there to mourn for Logan? Not one.
—Chief Logan

No war is inevitable, only relatively likely or not depending on changing circumstances. Wars are rarely decisive. The issues resolved by one war usually exacerbate angers and ambitions that lead to others. While wars litter history, revolutions are rarer. Yet revolutions, like wars, break out in unique alignments of explosive forces. They often erupt when charismatic leaders, stirring ideologies, and efficient organizations combine to mobilize an enraged populace against a brutally exploitive, corrupt, and repressive but bumbling tyrant and cronies. A revolution is, of course, a type of war. While to varying degrees all wars change history, few tend to have greater impact than revolutions.

Neither the outbreak of the American Revolution nor its result was preordained. During the dozen years following Britain's conquest of Canada, King George III and his government pursued a series of related policies that inadvertently conceived and gave birth to the American Revolution. Those policies were hardly ruinous and repressive compared to what other peoples in other times and places, including Britain itself, have endured. But they provoked an assertive, hypersensitive American nationalism that had developed during 150 years of struggle and triumph in the New World. Different policies might have mollified rather than alienated the colonists. Likewise, after fighting broke out, the rival decisions of the Crown and rebels combined to decide the Revolution's fate.

Though most Crown policies largely squeezed the lives of people on the seaboard, where nine of ten Americans lived, some hurt the hardscrabble pioneers on the frontier and those merchants, land speculators, and hunters who strove to reap fortunes there. The Revolution would not have occurred had the Crown's policies hit only those exploiting the frontier. Still, policies like the 1763 proclamation and 1774 Quebec Act that crimped those ambitious for frontier land and trade fed bitter animosities.

War or its shadow had threatened Britain's American colonies from Jamestown's founding in 1607 until France's final official defeat with the Treaty of Paris in 1763. During that time, the British and French fought five frontier wars for mastery over North America's eastern third: Huguenot (1627–29), League of Augsburg or King William's (1689–97), Spanish Succession or Queen Anne's (1702–13), Austrian Succession or King George's (1745–48), and Seven Years' or French and Indian (1754–63). The first four were inconclusive, as was the fifth during its first several years.[1]

During those 156 years, the British had rarely stationed regular troops in the colonies and then only a few companies, nor did taxes ever more than lightly burden the colonists. During the first four frontier wars against New France, provincial troops provided the bulk of the forces and fighting. That changed during the last French and Indian War from 1754 to 1763, when Whitehall eventually dispatched nearly 35,000 troops to conquer Canada and destroy forever the French threat. Britain's hard-pressed taxpayers, however, would enjoy no genuine peace dividend.

Like dry rot, a truly profound paradox ate away the core of British policy toward its North American colonies from 1763 to 1775. With the French menace gone, Whitehall could have withdrawn all but a token number of troops from North America. Instead, the British not only stationed about 5,000 soldiers in the colonies, but also required the Americans to pay part of their upkeep. The troops and taxes provoked American protests, which Whitehall used to justify those very policies. Having eliminated the French threat, the British sought to contain a new and growing threat to their empire—American nationalism. But the very measures Britain took to contain that threat actually stimulated it.

It was not just higher and new taxes that alienated an ever-growing number of Americans. Whitehall's frontier and tax policies were thoroughly entwined. The relentless hunger of Americans for land had sparked all five wars with the French in the New World. The British had no sooner driven out the French and occupied their wilderness forts when a massive Indian revolt briefly drove them from most of the Great Lakes and Ohio valley. The influx of speculators and squatters along with the cutoff of gifts to the Indians combined to ignite that conflagration, popularly known as Pontiac's War, which raged in 1763 and 1764 before a shaky truce was negotiated.

Ironically, amidst that war but before understanding its gravity, King George III issued a proclamation in November 1763 that forbade any settlements west of the Appalachian divide unless they were on lands negotiated by the Crown's agents with the Indians. Speculators and squatters alike bristled at those restrictions and sought to evade them. Then in 1764, Whitehall issued strict regulations over the Indian trade that enraged frontier merchants. To restore peace, the British and Indian leaders agreed to separate their respective peoples. They hammered out a series of treaties, the most important of which were at Fort Stanwix and Hard Labor in 1768, that briefly delineated the northern and southern frontiers, respectively. Those treaties were effective little longer than it took the ink to dry. American merchants, hunters, land speculators, and farmers continued to nibble or gobble away at territory reserved for the Indians. Fearing another Indian war, the Crown issued the Quebec Act of 1774, which granted all lands north of the Ohio River to the colony of Quebec, thus eliminating the claims of other colonies to that region. All those measures simply angered ever more Americans and did little to stem the tide of frontier settlers, hunters, and surveyors, provoking yet another Indian war in 1774, known as Dunmore's, against the Ohio valley tribes.

By late 1774, the animosities between the Crown and colonies had reached a crisis. The first Continental Congress met to demand that the Crown repeal its coercive policies and to boycott British goods until it did. Cooler heads might have defused the crisis, but they were not in power. The crisis would explode in war with the fighting at Lexington and Concord the following year on April 19, 1775.

The frontier war for American independence cannot be understood without exploring the dynamic between the Crown's tax, trade, and frontier policies and the American reactions during the dozen years before that fatal gunfire on Lexington Green.

After fighting an ever more costly war in treasury and blood for nine years, one that rampaged across parts of North America, Europe, West Africa, India, Argentina, the Philippines, Caribbean and Mediterranean islands, and the connecting seas, Britain won a resounding victory. French power in North America was broken and forever buried. Under the Treaty of Paris, signed on February 10, 1763, Versailles ceded all of Canada and Louisiana east of the Mississippi River except for New Orleans to Britain. From France's ally Spain, the British took East and West Florida after restoring Cuba, which they conquered in 1762. In compensation for Spain's loss, Louis XV generously gave his cousin Charles III all of New France west of the Mississippi River along with New Orleans on the east bank.

To administer its conquests, Whitehall created three new colonies: Quebec, East Florida, and West Florida. Given the ambitious and conflicting claims of Britain's older American colonies for western territory, Whitehall kept the boundaries of those new colonies deliberately vague.

From a score of forts, British officers would reign rather than rule over that vast wilderness stretching from the Appalachians to the Mississippi, and the Gulf of Mexico to the Hudson Bay. A string of forts—Hunter, Stanwix, Brewerton, and Ontario—linked Albany with Lake Ontario. A similar string—Ligonier, Loudoun, Bedford, Lyttleton, and Pitt—knit Philadelphia with the upper Ohio valley. Three forts—Presque Isle, Le Boeuf, and Venango—guarded the portage between Lake Erie and the Allegeny River. Forts Crown Point, Ticonderoga, and Edward protected the corridor between Montreal and Albany. The British took over from the

French or built new forts at Niagara, Sandusky, Detroit, Michilimackinac, La Baye, St. Joseph, Miami, and Ouiatenon. They occupied Fort de Chartres and Kaskaskia in the upper Mississippi River valley. Along the central frontier, Fort Cumberland guarded the confluence of Wills Creek with the Potomac, Fort Loudoun protected Winchester, another Fort Loudoun stood on the Holston River, and Fort Chiswell sat atop the portage between the New and Holston Rivers. Fort Prince George on the Keowee River and Fort Charlotte and Fort Augusta on the upper Savannah River guarded the southern frontier. Along rivers flowing into the Gulf of Mexico across West and East Florida, forts stood at Natchez, Charlotte, Tombigbee, Toulouse, Apalachee, Pensacola, and St. Augustine. Impressive as that list may seem, those distant posts were undermanned, crumbling, expensive to maintain, and would soon be proven nearly impossible to defend. Soldiers might have won that immense wilderness for Britain, but only diplomats could hold it.

Britain's policy toward the Indians until 1755 had consisted of letting each colony determine its own policy. The results were colonial rivalries over securing trade and land from the Indians that alienated rather than pacified the tribes. In 1755, Whitehall wisely tried to alleviate this problem by appointing Indian super-intendents for the northern and southern Indians whose powers transcended those of the governors and were capped only by Whitehall and the commander in chief for British forces in North America. The superintendents, along with their deputies, agents, and interpreters, were responsible for advancing Britain's often conflicting goals of peace, trade, settlement, and alliance with scores of tribes. To its further credit, Whitehall then appointed as superintendents such brilliant diplo-mats and Indian experts as Sir William Johnson for all tribes roughly north of the Potomac, Monongahela, and Ohio Rivers, and John Stuart, who replaced a lack-luster Edmund Atkins in 1761, for those to the south. Unfortunately, those men had to serve under an inept commander in chief, Sir Jeffrey Amherst.

Britain had no sooner settled one North American frontier war when it pro-voked another. From the conquest of Canada in 1760 through 1763, Johnson, Atkins, and Stuart tried to consolidate British rule over those new territories. Suc-cessful diplomacy with Indians depended on many forces, with the diplomat's generosity perhaps the most important: peace and allies were bought with mounds of gifts. During those three years, Amherst was miserly in that essential diplo-matic lubricant, despite repeated warnings by the superintendents that the result could be catastrophic for the British empire. Amherst justified the severe cutback of gifts, especially gunpowder, in the interests of economy and containment. Forcing the Indians to revert to bows and arrows would divert their energies and drain their power while saving the Crown money.

In May 1763, nearly every northern tribe joined in a surprise assault on the British posts in their midst. They captured nine forts, besieged Detroit and Pitt, and killed an estimated 2,000 soldiers and civilians during two years of fighting. The uprising sputtered to a close by late 1764, ended more by a dearth of gun-powder and lead than the campaigns of Gen. John Bradstreet, who relieved Detroit, and Gen. Henry Bouquet, who marched into the Ohio country.

It was not just a want of gifts that had provoked those tribes to war against their British landlords. In the wake of Britain's conquest of New France swirled unscrupulous carpetbagger speculators and merchants who plied their "clients" with rum and took their furs, land, and women for a pittance. Some of these agents fronted partnerships of prominent colonial leaders who often invested in numerous speculative ventures. The Indians complained bitterly to the superintendents, who in turn repeatedly warned Amherst and Whitehall of the dangers.

While Amherst was deaf to those Cassandras, Whitehall listened. As early as May 15, 1761, the Crown ordered Amherst not to authorize any more land grants because "the settlements made in those parts on lands which the Indians conceived to have been reserved to them for Hunting Grounds, have been the principle Cause of those merciless Devastations which have greatly distressed the Western frontiers."[2] Those words were echoed by a government report of November 11, 1761, which condemned colonial land grabs as inimical to colonial security.[3] The privy council used that report as the basis for orders to the governors on December 3, 1761, that forbade any further land grants and announced that henceforth any applications for land should go to the Board of Trade.

Those rules were impossible to enforce. In early 1763, Johnson and Stuart warned Secretary of State for the Southern Department Charles Wyndham Egremont that the lack of gifts and influx of squatters, speculators, and conniving merchants onto Indian lands were straining relations to the breaking point. Egremont understood and acted. On May 5, 1763, he directed the Board of Trade to assess what was the most profitable and just policy for governing the latest addition to empire. Thirty-one select detailed reports accompanied his directive. Among those were "Hints Relative to the Division and Government of the Newly Acquired Countries in America."[4] Thus did Egremont essentially determine the policy he requested others to devise.

Reconciling profits and justice would be no easy task. Unjust rules that allowed cheating traders and speculators unlimited access to the Indians and their land might maximize profits in the short run but destroy them over time if the embittered tribes rebelled. On the other hand, a policy that emphasized protecting the Indians would likely raise the costs and lower the benefits of empire. But that calculation assumed an empire at peace. The cost of fighting Indian wars far exceeded that of preventing them.

The final policy emerged on October 7, 1763, when King George III issued a proclamation that forbade any new American settlements west of the Appalachian Mountains watershed and any land purchases from the Indians by anyone other than the superintendents. This was designed to stymie the cheating and squatting that provoked Indian wars. Alas, it came too late to prevent the uprising it was designed to avert.[5]

The unfolding disaster of the Indian uprising prompted Whitehall to reinforce the proclamation with its "Plan for the Future Management of Indian Affairs." On July 10, 1764, the Trade Board issued a circular letter to the commander in chief, Indian superintendents, and colonial governors that proclaimed that henceforth the superintendents along with their agents and commanders would strictly regulate trade. Licenses would be issued only to those who promised to follow the regulations and posted a bond, which would be forfeited should they violate their oath. Trade was allowed only at designated locations—forts in the north and villages in the south. Rum sales and credit of more than fifty shillings to any Indian was forbidden. Commanders and agents were empowered to uphold the law. As justices of the peace, they could arrest, judge, and punish any violators.[6]

That policy was never officially implemented. The Americans complained that those regulations stifled profits, revenues, and participants in the Indian trade and diverted them to French traders living in the region and supplied up the Mississippi River from New Orleans. Abolish the hated regulations and the British empire would prosper from the trade's easier profits and revenues. Bowing to colonial protests, the Crown rescinded the plan shortly after submitting it to the colonial officials. The superintendents did try to enforce the rules but lacked vital funds, personnel, and authority.

Whitehall then mulled two choices for managing its wilderness empire and the resentful natives who inhabited it. Neither was entirely palatable. The duty for conducting Indian diplomacy and, if necessary, warfare could be returned to the colonies. This was a troubling option to those familiar with recent history. Although withdrawing the troops and dismissing the Indian superintendencies would certainly save Whitehall money in the short run, it might well cost more over time if the British army once again had to save the Americans from their own follies. After all, the colonies had controlled Indian affairs before 1755 and generally made a mess of things. Chaos and animosities worsened as the colonies competed to carve away Indian lands. The French and Indian War had exploded partly because of colonial ambitions and ineptitude. The alternative was to maintain the present system of northern and southern Indian agencies accountable to the commander in chief and backed by Royal troops. This system theoretically promoted imperial rather than narrow colonial interests, but having one hand rather than many in charge of Indian affairs was no panacea. Amherst had blundered horribly when he was solely responsible. Direct imperial Indian diplomacy was only as good as its policies and the commander who devised and upheld them. As if that problem were not worrisome enough, the imperial system was brutally expensive to the Crown.

Unable to decide clearly between the two policies, the Crown acquiesced in the emergence of a hybrid. The commander in chief presided over the superintendents, deputies, and agents, while colonies asserted their traditional prerogatives and interests. The result alienated Indians and colonists alike.

The 1763 proclamation and 1764 plan were not the only Crown policies that irritated Americans. Whitehall would impose a series of taxes, regulations, and other burdens on the colonists that eventually would provoke a revolution. What was the justification for the taxes? Britain's national debt had nearly doubled from

73 million pounds sterling in 1754 to 137 million pounds sterling in 1764. Annual interest payments alone were 5 million pounds sterling, while the government budget was an additional 8 million pounds sterling. Of that, the official estimate of the military burden in North America in 1763 was 225,000 pounds; the actual average annual cost from 1763 to 1775 was 384,000 pounds. It was thought only fair that the Americans should partially pay for their own defense.[7]

Not just the British government owed money. The colonial governments and subjects owed ever more to British creditors. Inflation helped debtors and harmed creditors. Colonial governments partially caused inflation by issuing paper credit and currencies unbacked by gold. Whitehall first responded to this worsening problem in 1751 with a currency bill that forbade Massachusetts, New Hampshire, Rhode Island, and Connecticut to issue more paper money. The 1764 Currency Act extended the 1751 restrictions to all the colonies. Without paper money, the colonists had to amass scarce coin to pay for imported British goods. Deflation replaced inflation, and consumers and producers on both sides of the Atlantic suffered.

For Americans obsessed with their rights, cutting taxes could provoke as much controversy as raising them. The Molasses Act of 1733 had imposed a duty of six shillings on a gallon of foreign molasses, which was distilled into rum. Although the colonists protested the law, they had little cause for complaint. Smuggling and bribery meant that officials were only taxing a fraction of the molasses actually imported. Rather than the hoped for 200,000 pounds sterling, the annual revenue of 700 pounds did not even pay for the administrative costs. In 1764, Britain's government passed the Revenue or Sugar Act designed to increase revenues and cut smuggling. It was hoped that by cutting the tariff to three shillings a gallon, the incentive to smuggle would disappear and consumers would simply pay the fee. The annual boost to the treasury was optimistically estimated to be 78,000 pounds sterling. Actually, the Sugar Act produced only 5,200 pounds of revenue in 1764 and 4,090 pounds in 1765. The Sugar Act's most egregious tenets involved measures designed to stamp out smuggling. Officials could search suspected lairs like shops and warehouses without warrants. Those accused would appear before the admiralty court tribunal at Halifax rather than a jury of their peers. Distillers and smugglers deplored the law, which hit New England especially hard. Of 127 rum distilleries in the colonies, 64 were in Massachusetts and 40 split between Connecticut and Rhode Island. Leaders of those colonies howled in protest; leaders elsewhere were mostly silent. Parliament would have to impose taxes on all the colonies to provoke American unity. That tax was coming.[8]

No law to date provoked more outrage than the 1765 Stamp Act, which imposed a one-shilling stamp on newspapers and playing cards, a three-shilling stamp on all legal documents, a two-pound-sterling stamp on college diplomas, a four-pound-sterling stamp on appointments to public office and liquor licenses, and a ten-pound-sterling stamp on law licenses. Admiralty courts would judge anyone accused of violating that act. The Crown would appoint a stamp official in each colony. All proceeds would go to a fund devoted to colonial defense.

Contrary to popular belief, the Stamp Act was not hastily, arbitrarily, and harshly imposed on the Americans. It took more than two years from the Stamp Act's proposal to its implementation. All along, Whitehall was very sensitive to the potential colonial reaction against the amount and process of taxation. It tried to create a tax whereby the Americans would contribute one-third of the cost of defending the colonies while British taxpayers still bore the remaining two-thirds' burden. In all, the tax was relatively light and broadly distributed. It was thought only fair that the colonists should help pay for their own defense. Most Americans vehemently disagreed.

The Treasury Department ordered stamps created for the new tax as early as September 23, 1763. It was not until March 9, 1764, however, that Prime Minister George Grenville introduced the tax into Parliament. After Parliament approved, Grenville then delayed its implementation for a year so that the plan could circulate in the colonies and the legislatures could accept the tax or propose an alternative revenue source. On May 17, 1764, he issued to the colonies a circular letter repeating the act's justifications. After all this, Grenville still waited nearly another year before introducing to Parliament a bill that would implement the Stamp Act. The House of Commons voted 245 to 49 in favor of the bill on February 11, 1765; the House of Lords approved the measure unanimously. To ensure that all taxes collected in America would be spent there, the bill included a measure whereby the deputy paymaster for British forces in the colonies would receive all revenues.

What was the initial colonial reaction to the Stamp Act? Sporadic protests erupted and died amidst the general resignation. It was an incendiary speech by Patrick Henry in Virginia's House of Burgesses in late May that galvanized the movement against the Stamp Act. While conceding Parliament's right to impose "external" taxes like tariffs, he insisted that only the colonists could raise "internal" taxes like those of the Stamp Act. The assembly voted overwhelmingly in favor of Henry's "Virginia Resolves." The twenty-three colonial newspapers published the resolves and popularized Henry's stirring cry, "No taxation without representation." By early autumn, the assemblies of Rhode Island, Pennsylvania, Maryland, Connecticut, Massachusetts, South Carolina, New Jersey, and New York had issued their own protests. Starting in August, enraged mobs bullied those officials charged with administering the act; the Sons of Liberty tarred and feathered those appointees who did not immediately flee or resign, ransacked their homes, and destroyed their stamps. Various assemblies voted to boycott British goods, measures roughly enforced by the Sons of Liberty.

The most important reaction occurred from October 7 to 25, 1765, when twenty-seven delegates from nine colonies convened the Stamp Act Congress at New York City, responding to an appeal by Massachusetts' assembly in June. The congress asserted thirteen resolves, arguing that Parliament had repeatedly violated American rights as British subjects, that the various revenue acts were unconstitutional, that trials by a jury of one's peers must prevail, and that they would tolerate no taxation without representation. The assemblies of two nonattending colonies joined with the congress in ratifying those resolves and firing them off to King George III.

Colonial agents in London lobbied for the Stamp Act's repeal, none more vigorously than Benjamin Franklin. In a speech before the House of Commons in January 1766, he rejected the notion that the French and Indian War was fought for the colonies' behalf. The colonists did not need the redcoats and could have defended themselves. Whitehall had dispatched a huge army to North America to conquer Canada and the lands west of the Appalachians, access to which American merchants were restricted and settlers were denied altogether.

Parliamentarian Robert Nugent, Lord Clare, captured the bewilderment and indignation shared by most Britons at the protests: "We have fought, bled, and ruined ourselves, to conquer for them, and now they come and tell us to our noses . . . that they were not obliged to us."[9] How could the Americans be so ungrateful and selfish, they wondered? After all, the colonists paid but a fraction of the tax bill due those subjects in the British Isles.

Not all Britons concurred. The violent American reaction against the Stamp Act splintered the near unanimity on colonial policy that had hitherto prevailed. A growing minority within and beyond Parliament took the American position. John Wilkes, William Pitt, Charles Camden, and Edmund Burke would be the most prominent voices among a swelling chorus that sympathized with the American position.

For British leaders in Whitehall and Parliament, however, the primary issue with the colonies shifted when Americans resisted the Stamp Act. What was once a means of alleviating Britain's national debt and the costs of defending the empire would now be a test of parliamentary supremacy over the colonies. But money rather than principle would prevail in the short run. The boycott pushed the economy into depression. Ever more prominent British merchants and port officials petitioned the government to give in to the Americans. On March 18, 1766, after months of heatedly debating what to do, the government repealed the Stamp Act and issued the Declaratory Act, which asserted its right to tax as it pleased all subjects. In doing so, Whitehall made clear that it was yielding on policy rather than principle. To maintain the principle of parliamentary supremacy, Whitehall would soon impose other taxes. But rigidly adhering to principle was a self-destructive policy that would eventually provoke the American Revolution that British leaders feared and wanted desperately to avoid.

Almost lost in the tumult over the Stamp Act was another repressive policy imposed in 1765, the American Mutiny or Quartering Act. Adding insult to injury, the Mutiny Act required the colonies to help underwrite and house the troops that were deployed in their midst to enforce loathsome laws. However, contrary to popular belief, the Quartering Act did not force open American homes to loutish redcoats. It did require colonial governments to provide public buildings as barracks along with candles, bedding, firewood, and libations. The colonists viewed this as not only a new tax but a gross invasion of their privacy and rights as British subjects. In late 1765, New York became the first to resist when Gen. Thomas Gage tried to house his troops there. The dispute festered for a half year until June 1766, when New York's assembly bitterly agreed to issue the troops everything required except alcohol. Whitehall was in no mood to compromise and rejected New York's offer. When it learned of that decision in December, New York's assembly voted against any supplies for the troops. New Jersey issued a similar resolve that same month. But other assemblies did not join those protests for the practical reason that like the Sugar Act, the Quartering Act affected few colonies. Besides, the Stamp Act was a riveting enough issue. In July 1767, Parliament passed a harsh measure known as the New York Restraining Act, whereby the king would not sign any laws of that colony's assembly until it complied with the Quartering Act. But in June 1767, before that act could be imposed, New York's assembly voted to pay for all the army's needs according to the law. Whitehall and Parliament had triumphed in the Quartering Act. But ultimately it would prove to be a Pyrrhic victory.

The Stamp Act's repeal worsened Whitehall's financial crisis. All revenues from the colonies yielded only 80,000 pounds sterling, a fraction of the annual administrative costs. When Secretary of War William Wildman, the Viscount Barrington, presented that budget to Parliament on January 26, 1767, Grenville caustically noted the "greatest absurdity" that the Crown must "support and defend countrys who deny'd we had a right to tax them . . . [and] deny our sovereignty over them." Parliament debated just what to do about the conundrum. On February 18, Barrington reappeared with even worse news. Britain's North American empire actually cost 700,000 pounds sterling, of which the Indian superintendencies were a mere 20,000 pounds sterling. The political uproar was deafening. Parliament achieved near unanimity on the notion that the Americans must pay more to uphold the empire.[10]

But was that the most rational policy? The minuscule Indian Department budget was revealing. Whitehall's priorities were severely misplaced. Nearly every one of those 700,000 pounds sterling helped pay for a large British army in the colonies. That army had not existed in North America before 1754 despite a persistent French threat for the preceding century and a half. With Britain's conquest of New France in 1763, the army's continued presence could only serve to intimidate both the Indians and the Americans into meek submission. That army's rationale disappeared if both the Indians and Americans were satisfied with British rule. It was the army's presence and the taxes imposed to pay for that presence that angered ever more colonists. Removing the army and taxes would placate the Americans and thus maintain the empire. Part of the subsequent peace dividend could be invested in the Indian Department budget. A doubling or even tripling of that budget would allow the superintendents to employ more agents and money to keep the Indians happy, the traders honest, and the land-grabbers at bay, thus forestalling the chance of another frontier war. But only a minority saw it that way.

Whitehall and the overwhelming majority in Parliament believed that the empire's protection and very survival depended on imposing enough taxes to pay for it. In 1767, Exchequer Chancellor Charles Townshend sought a middle ground.

He proposed halving the number of troops in the colonies while raising import taxes on a range of nonessential products like paint, wine, paper, glass, lead, pasteboards, and tea. A Board of Commissioners of the Customs would be created at Boston to enforce all collections. Parliament passed the Townshend Act in June, and King George III signed it on July 2, 1767.

Like its predecessors, the Townshend Act backfired. The tax would annually yield at most 40,000 pounds sterling. Most of that would cover the tax's administrative costs. Thus was a tax imposed and justified to pay for itself. But even worse, the Townshend Act poured fuel on the political bonfire provoked by previous tax bills.

The Townshend Act's most articulate opponent was John Dickinson. In his dozen "Letters from a Farmer in Pennsylvania," he argued that the British army was not needed to defend the colonies during the recent war with France or against the Indians today. The Americans were fully capable of defending themselves. Any cost incurred by the Crown in keeping its army in America was more than offset by the profits made by British manufacturers in that huge and expanding market. But the taxes Whitehall imposed were not just unnecessary, they were unjust. While admitting that Parliament could impose external tariffs, he repeated the now well-established American arguments that there could and should be no internal taxation without representation. Dickinson concluded his arguments by calling for a boycott of British goods until the tax was lifted.[11]

Massachusetts' assembly was the first to act, passing in December a resolution condemning the Townshend Act and issuing a circular letter to the other colonies urging them to also follow with passive resistance "nonimportation." Eventually every colonial assembly would enforce the boycott.

Learning of the boycott, the hardliners prevailed at Whitehall. The king dissolved the assemblies of Massachusetts, Virginia, Maryland, Georgia, and North Carolina. The government tried to make a special example of firebrand Massachusetts by deploying the 14th, 29th, and 59th Regiments in Boston in late 1768, hoping that those troops would intimidate the resistance into compliance with British law. But once again the Crown had to retreat. Enforcement of the Townshend Act yielded only 295 pounds sterling the first year. Meanwhile, the boycott pushed Britain's economy into a worsening depression as exports to the colonies plummeted from 2,378,000 pounds sterling in 1768 to 1,634,000 pounds sterling in 1769. Whitehall rescinded the Townshend Act in April 1770, leaving only the tax on tea to symbolize Parliament's right. The decision to retain the tea tax passed by one vote. How different would history have been if that one vote had been nay.[12]

Tensions soared along the frontier. The worst problem was caused by the merchants who surged through the tribes, snatching all the furs they could. Though the competitive frenzy drove down prices for goods, the peddlers profited by selling alcohol. Rum-befuddled Indians gave away a season's worth of strenuous hunting and trapping to unscrupulous traders. That was bad enough. But in trying to meet the growing demand for southern deerskins and northern furs, the Indians destroyed those very resources. As the fur trade declined, horses stolen from the settlers and sold to the traders filled some of the gap in goods to take back east. But of course that traffic in their stolen horses incensed the frontiersmen against the merchants and Indians alike. The superintendents were supposed to regulate the trade but lacked the money and personnel to do so. Whitehall and the colonial governments turned a blind eye to this festering problem. Too many profits from too many prominent merchants were at stake.

Instead Whitehall tried to crack down on the least powerful interest group and most local problem—squatters. Whitehall condemned the illegal settlements along Redstone Creek and the Cheat River on August 27, 1765. On October 18, 1765, the Privy Council sent orders to Pennsylvania and Virginia to dismantle those settlements and severely prosecute anyone who committed crimes against the Indians. If necessary, the governors could apply to Gen. Thomas Gage for troops to carry out the orders.[13]

Would the governors obey Whitehall's bidding? Both Virginia governor Francis Fauquier and Pennsylvania governor John Penn issued but declined to enforce eviction notices. Trapped between the Crown and colonists over taxes and related issues, neither governor dared expel the squatters despite the danger they posed to relations with the tribes. Indeed, Fauquier suggested that "perhaps the leaving of them to the mercy of the Indians may be the best if not the only Way to restrain them."[14]

It was left to Gage himself to roust the squatters. The troops accomplished their mission nonviolently. But squatters sneaked back to their holdings as soon as the troops left, more bitter than ever against the government who evicted them and coddled the savages. Whitehall soon learned that even more squatters had popped up on Redstone Creek and elsewhere after the troops had briefly swept them away. In 1766, Secretary of State for the Southern Department William Petty, the earl of Shelburne, sent to the governors a circular letter urging them to enforce the 1763 proclamation. But once again the governors had more pressing issues to manage.[15]

Speculators were behind many squatter settlements. The land barons enticed tenants onto their claims with promises to forgo rents for the first few years and then gradually increased the rate afterward. Meanwhile, the land company agents lobbied incessantly in London to overturn the 1763 proclamation.

Subtly backing every land company were colonial officials and often the governors. Colonial governments and the land companies registered with them were incestuously linked. What more recently has been condemned as conflict of interest was then unashamedly rife. Many a colonial governor and assemblyman either pocketed bribes from or invested in land companies. Those august officials advanced their pecuniary interests by wielding the inside information, regulatory powers, and lobbying access to which they were privy.

Ironically, some of the most successful speculators were William Johnson, the Indian superintendent, and his deputy George Croghan, who cheerfully used their public powers to promote their private ambitions. They masked their takeover of Crown lands previously negotiated from the Indians by filing claims in the names of others and then purchasing them after the deeds were registered. Croghan dispatched thirty-eight men led by Alexander McKee to survey and claim 100,000 acres between Cherry Valley and the upper Susquehanna River in the late 1760s. Croghan then found ninety-nine people willing to file on his behalf. Johnson employed twenty-five confederates to buy up huge tracts of the upper Susquehanna River valley in 1770. Both Johnson and Croghan benefited from their close association with Goldsbow Banyar, the New York secretary for land patents.[16]

Speculators then as now varied in their skills and luck. Croghan's land empire was built of paper—patents and credit. By the early 1770s, he claimed over 250,000 acres in the upper Susquehanna valley and angled for similar holdings in the Vandalia stake between the Ohio and Greenbriar Rivers. To obtain the latter, he mortgaged the former. But when Whitehall refused to grant Vandalia, Croghan lost his other estate to his creditors. When the first shots were fired at Lexington in April 1775, Croghan was nearly as void of property as when he started his land grab a dozen years earlier.[17]

Croghan's most ambitious scheme was to create a new colony in the Illinois country. The idea first seized him in 1764 amidst the Indian uprising. In a letter to the Board of Trade, he argued that a colony there would help secure Indian loyalties, capture the fur trade, deter St. Louis merchants, and soon grow enough crops to sustain itself. That idea became an obsession after he returned from a diplomatic mission there in 1766. On March 20, 1766, he founded the Illinois Company, which then or soon included such prominent investors as his boss, William Johnson, Benjamin Franklin and his son, New Jersey governor William Franklin, and Philadelphia merchants John Baynton, Samuel Wharton, and George Morgan. Benjamin Franklin and Richard Jackson acted as the Illinois Company's London agents, lobbying for a colony.[18]

Croghan and his cronies were not the only group interested in carving an empire from Indian lands in the Mississippi valley. The Mississippi Company was founded in 1763 by some of Virginia's most prominent families, including the Washingtons, Lees, and Fitzhughs. In September 1763, it petitioned for a grant of 2.5 million acres where the Mississippi and Ohio River waters mingled. Thomas Cumming was its London agent.

Phineas Lyman petitioned for the same land claimed by the Mississippi Company but also requested land upstream as far as St. Anthony's Falls, all in return for a promise to bring in 10,000 settlers within four years. He envisioned that this upper Mississippi colony would be self-supporting, chase away the French, flourish from trading for furs and raising grain, and keep peace with the Indians.[19]

Each company petitioned Whitehall for its respective grant. The timing for submitting those requests could not have been worse. All of the petitions languished in Whitehall pigeonholes. No matter who was secretary of state or Trade Board president, all were either skeptical or adamantly opposed to the expense, vulnerability, and provocation of colonizing those remote regions, something no amount of articulated visions, investment shares, or outright bribes could alter. After all, the recent Indian uprising had destroyed nine forts, slaughtered perhaps 2,000 British subjects, and destroyed an incalculable amount of property. Diplomatic concessions rather than military might ended that rebellion. The 1763 proclamation prohibiting settlements west of the Appalachians would be strictly upheld. That edict precluded any new colonies. Even without an Indian threat, the viability of any colony along the upper Mississippi valley was questionable. Isolated tiny French settlements like Kaskaskia, Cahokia, and St. Louis were known liabilities before to France and now to Spain. It took at least three months to row supplies up the Mississippi River to those villages.

Only Secretary of State Shelburne toyed with the idea. On September 11, 1767, he submitted to the cabinet a proposal for a new colony in the Illinois country. Inspired by the example of Detroit, he questioned why Britons could not found similarly viable settlements in the upper Mississippi valley. He then outlined a plan for doing just that, to be financed by quitrents and the investments of those land companies eager to reap wealth by converting wilderness to civilization. Spurred by Shelburne's advocacy, the land companies upped their pressure on the cabinet. Though skeptical, the ministers agreed that the proposal was worthy of further consideration. When the proposal was submitted to the Trade Board on October 5, the land companies perched there like a flock of pigeons awaiting tossed bread crumbs.[20]

The Trade Board issued a preliminary judgment on December 23, 1767, authorizing Superintendent Johnson to renegotiate the 1763 boundary to accommodate existing settlements and land claims. Shelburne wrote Johnson to that effect on January 5, 1768. But on March 7, the Trade Board shot down the colony proposal with ironclad arguments about expenses, viability, and vulnerability.[21]

Shelburne accepted the board's decision with grace. He had always been lukewarm to the idea and reasoned that it was better to err on caution's side. All along the lack of solid information on the new lands frustrated him. Without it, he could hardly make a sensible policy. To Canada's governor Guy Carleton, he lamented the void of "accurate Knowledge of the Interior Parts of North America [which] would contribute much towards enabling . . . Ministers to judge soundly of the true Interests of the different Provinces. I cannot too strongly recommend to you the encouraging of such Adventurers as are willing to explore those Parts which have not hitherto been much frequented & consequently are scarcely, if at all known."[22]

Whitehall's rejection of these land petitions frustrated all the speculators and alienated more than a few. Not just money was at stake for most investors, but also rights to acquire property, invest wealth, and supplant savages as one chose. A government that restricted those rights lost legitimacy in the eyes of those who demanded them. Those most alienated were eager for alternatives. They would rally around the concepts of colonial legislative equality with Parliament and no taxation without representation. When those demands too were squelched, many would opt for outright American independence. Thus did stymied frontier ambitions stir a hunger for revolution.

Whitehall policy not only rejected any new colony, but even severed its tenuous links with that region by abandoning most of the military posts. From the time he took Amherst's place in November 1763, Maj. Gen. Thomas Gage struggled to act on an understanding that had escaped his mentally opaque predecessor. The wilderness garrisons were imperial liabilities rather than assets. Extremely expensive to maintain, the forts were not only incapable of enforcing the trade regulations, but also indefensible. Unscrupulous British or French merchants could easily slip around the forts and ply their trade unhindered. The only service the forts provided was to dispense gifts to the local tribes and thus help preserve a fragile peace. As early as May 1764, Gage planned to evacuate the most exposed forts as soon as the Indian uprising ended.[23]

The Stamp Act crisis made the withdrawal imperative. With his depleted regiments scattered across the wilderness of eastern North America, Gage struggled to gather enough troops to quell the rioters. Abandoning the most vulnerable frontier forts would free at least three regiments with which to cow the subversives. Thus the redeployment policy would at once save money, ease tensions with the Indians, and concentrate troops in the rebellious seaports where they were most needed.[24]

Gage eventually secured Whitehall's full support for this policy. After prolonged debate, the cabinet agreed in March 1768 to retain only Detroit, Michilimackinac, Fort Niagara, Fort Pitt, Fort Chartres, and either Crown Point or Fort Ticonderoga, and abandon all other posts. Gage was delighted when he got the order but pressed for scrapping Forts Chartres and Pitt as well. To War Secretary Barrington, he confided, "I wish most sincerely that there was neither Settler nor Soldier in any part of the Indian country." Whitehall would agree to evacuate Forts Pitt and Chartres on December 1, 1771. The word further boosted Gage's spirits. Let the colonists eat the bitter fruit of their own follies, he argued. If they provoke an Indian war, "let them feel the Consequences, we shall be out of the Scrapes."[25]

Wills Hill, the Viscount Hillsborough, secretary of state for the newly created American Department, firmly supported the policy of largely abandoning the country west of the Appalachians while concentrating troops on the eastern seaboard to quell the ever more defiant colonists. But that meant ordering the superintendents to desist from enforcing the 1764 plan, which had never been officially approved, by which troops at the scattered forts enforced strict trade rules and chased off squatters. With the army gone, it was each colony's duty to license and discipline its own traders. Given the fierce rivalry for furs and land among them, allowing the colonies to regulate themselves was a clear conflict of interest. The Crown was taking an enormous gamble with possibly tragic consequences. By abandoning the West to merchants, hunters, and settlers, Whitehall might inadvertently provoke another Indian war that deepened the empire's debts and death counts. Thus would an initial peace dividend become a financially crushing liability as military and diplomatic campaigns were sent to quell the uprising.

Whitehall was willing to take that chance. To dwarf the odds of war, the frontier had to be clearly demarcated. But with that done, the colonies and Indians rather than the army would have to stave off the swelling tide of restless and ambitious Americans.

The commander in chief, Indian superintendents, and colonial governments would implement the policy. To all concerned Hillsborough issued the appropriate instructions. William Johnson received a map detailing how far west to push the Indian frontier. The new line would run from the Susquehanna River to the Ohio River and down it to the Great Kanawha River, where it would link with concessions already won by Southern Indian Superintendent John Stuart.[26]

During the five years following the 1763 proclamation, the Indian superintendents had negotiated a series of treaties that extended colonial control west of the Appalachian watershed. Stuart won eight treaties between 1763 and 1768, and Johnson eleven treaties from 1764 to 1766 alone. Those treaties nibbled and sometimes devoured Indian lands and rights. They culminated in 1768 when Johnson's Fort Stanwix and Stuart's Hard Labor treaties completed the 1763 proclamation's destruction by zigzagging the line far west of the Appalachian watershed to include existing and projected settlements.

Until then, Stuart's most important treaty was signed on November 10, 1763, during a council among Cherokee and Creek delegations and Governors James Wright of Georgia, Thomas Boone of South Carolina, Arthur Dobbs of North Carolina, and Francis Fauquier of Virginia. By the Treaty of Augusta, the Indians gave up a 2.5-million-acre wedge of land between the Savannah, Ogeechee, and Little Rivers, and recognized settlements as far west as the Kanawha and Holston Rivers. Subsequent treaties delineated segments of the frontier. The Treaty of Hard Labor, signed on October 17, 1768, linked and extended the final strands of the southern boundary, which would run from the Savannah River above Rock Creek, Dewitt's Corner, the Reedy River, Tryon's Mountain, Chiswell Mine, the Kanawha River, and the Ohio River. A joint party of Indians and whites would begin to mark the boundary on May 10, 1769.[27]

Unfortunately, the line that ended on the Kanawha's mouth with the Ohio did not mesh with the boundary designated by the Fort Stanwix treaty on October 24, 1768. Sir William Johnson talked the Iroquois into a frontier that ran down the Ohio River to its juncture with the Tennessee River mouth, several hundred twisting watery miles from the Kanawha River. Thus, nearly all of Kentucky was hacked away from the tribes who claimed it and donated to the British empire and its restless subjects. In return, the superintendent distributed 10,000 pounds sterling in goods to those Indians present, almost none of whom actually lived in the surrendered lands.

In doing so, Johnson exceeded his instructions and created a new set of problems that would eventually spark war. Why did he do so? Although he was a brilliant, tireless diplomat who mediated peaceful ends to numerous conflicts between and within the British and Indians worlds, Johnson was not above advancing his own interests along with those of others. By 1768, the Indians had given away 700,000 acres to Johnson's land empire alone. To say that Johnson was in the pocket of land companies and individual speculators would not be a gross exaggeration. As one of America's most ambitious speculators and an associate of others, he had a vested interest in wresting large concessions from the Indians. This he succeeded in doing at Fort Stanwix.

Johnson himself would not personally benefit from the Kentucky cession. His own lands were mostly in New York. But the Fort Stanwix treaty at once aided the "suffering traders," who demanded compensation for losses during the 1763 Indian uprising, the half-dozen land companies that had petitioned Whitehall for concessions west of the mountains, the veterans who were promised homesteads for their service against the French and Indians, and the squatters already violating previous agreements. It also benefited the Iroquois, who received a small hill of gifts for lands they did not truly own.

The only people hurt by the transfer were those tribes that actually claimed Kentucky but were not present at Fort Stanwix to negotiate the fate of that territory. At the time, tribes from north of the Ohio River and south of the Cumberland River hunted but did not inhabit Kentucky. How could the Iroquois sell those rich hunting grounds to the Crown, whose frontiersmen would swiftly pour over the mountains and settle that rich land? The Iroquois claimed sovereignty over the Ohio valley tribes and thus the right to negotiate on their behalf. To deny that claim would have not only scuttled any chance of an agreement, but also alienated the Six Nations.

Word that the Iroquois had sold out their land enraged the Ohio valley tribes and the Cherokee. They demanded that the treaty be renegotiated. Meanwhile, settlers poured into the region. Pennsylvania opened a land office on April 3, 1769. That first day 2,790 claim applications were filed. Within four months over a million acres of 300 acres each were sold at five pounds sterling for a hundred acres, with a penny quitrent and payment a year later after the harvest was done. Similar land rushes broke out on the other colonial frontiers.[28]

Whitehall's ministers bristled when they received Johnson's treaty. Indian wars drained the empire of blood and treasury. By allowing settlers to leap the Appalachians, the Fort Stanwix treaty made war more, rather than less, likely. The government faced a dilemma. Was it too late to force Johnson to impose his original instructions? Did the ministers dare to dash hopes among all those powerful and volatile speculators, many of whom represented the cream of the colonial elite?

The point man in this debate was Hillsborough, who served both as American secretary and Trade Board president. He adamantly opposed any more settlements west of the Appalachians. Let that vast realm stretching to the Mississippi River remain in Indian hands, which would trap and haul in a wealth of furs to the few traders licensed to journey among them. Scrap all but a few key forts or settlements—Detroit, Niagara, Michilimackinac. This was a relatively inexpensive, uncomplicated way to run an empire that maximized benefits, minimized costs, and above all avoided the horrors and expense of an Indian war.

Hillsborough won that debate by persuading Whitehall to put the interests of empire before those of speculators. On May 13, 1769, he ordered Johnson and Stuart to renegotiate the line so that settlements ended on the Kanawha rather than the Tennessee River. It would take more than a year to do so. Meanwhile, a half-dozen land companies lobbied Whitehall for huge concessions based on the Fort Stanwix treaty.[29]

The orders to revise the Fort Stanwix treaty came not a moment too soon. The Ohio valley tribes were incensed that the Iroquois not only had sold their lands without their permission to the British, but also gave the real owners not a shilling in compensation. War belts circulated and agreements to unite were forged among the Ohio valley Indians.[30]

The superintendents convened councils and distributed more presents, platitudes, and promises. Johnson got the Iroquois to agree to draw back the boundary during a July 1770 council. Stuart meanwhile negotiated the Treaty of Lochaber, signed on October 18, 1770, which drew the line between Virginia and North Carolina at a point six miles east of Long Island on the Holston River, and then cut north until it reached the Kanawha River and followed down it to the Ohio.[31]

The Lochaber boundary was as ephemeral as most treaties with the Indians. The man charged with surveying that boundary during the spring and summer of 1771, Col. John Donelson, was either extremely unskilled or very corrupt. Rather than respect the treaty's Kanawha River boundary, Donelson led his men to the headwaters of the Kentucky (Louisa) River and surveyed it to its junction with the Ohio River. In backing the new boundary, John Murray Dunmore, Virginia's new governor, allowed his self-interest as an investor in various land schemes to override his professional duty to uphold the treaty. Hillsborough was outraged at the news of the treaty violations.[32]

Although not all governors were as deeply invested in western land speculations as Dunmore, they faced similar dilemmas. Their duties included regulating trade and restraining squatters while promoting prosperity. The colonies competed fiercely for market share of the Indian trade and land. In such a Darwinian world, the incentive for each colony was to cut any hobbles on its traders and speculators. But that would sanction the ruthless business tactics that helped ignite the last war. The only way to minimize that chance would be for the colonies to agree on joint regulations and vigorously enforce them. Ever more prominent voices were raised for such a congress.

Colonial cooperation was a dilemma for Whitehall. Those ministers sought to avoid an Indian war at all costs but also feared the resentful colonists forging a common Indian policy. That success might spur them to joint action on other issues. To Whitehall's relief, the Stamp Act congress of 1765 had dissolved after accomplishing its mission. Would a future congress be as content to close shop? A united colonial front could just as easily face across the Atlantic as across the Appalachians.

A congress almost emerged in 1770. In January, New York's assembly took the lead by appointing delegates to any congress that the colonies would convene and then sending out letters calling for such a meeting. Eventually the governors of New York, Quebec, Pennsylvania, Maryland, and Virginia gave tentative approval for a congress at New York City in May. But then the plan swiftly unraveled. Quebec's governor Carleton wrote that his delegation could not attend until winter. Virginia's assembly did appoint delegates but waited so long to do so that other colonies also dragged their feet. Pennsylvania's assembly, discouraged at the seeming inaction of the other colonies, announced that it too would no longer bother. This discouraged others who were still debating the issue. In July, New York canceled the meeting in disgust. Virginia's delegates arrived before word reached them. The effort was a humiliating debacle. Colonial unity appeared as elusive as ever.[33]

News of the budding congress alarmed Whitehall. Citing "the dangerous use that has been made [of other] meetings of the commissioners from the several colonies," Hillsborough sternly rebuked New York governor Cadwallader Colden for initiating a congress. Colden and William Johnson replied that a congress was essential to managing Indians affairs; tensions had risen among the tribes once they learned that the Americans had failed to meet let alone forge a common policy to resolve the worsening problems. They implored Whitehall to take the initiative. But the cabinet wanted neither the expense of an Indian war nor the expense of preventing one. In November, after the usual prolonged and indecisive cabinet debate, Hillsborough sent a circular letter to the governors calling on them to take up the duties and costs of regulating the Indian trade.[34]

The governors protested, arguing that empowering each colony to regulate trade meant no regulations at all; self-interest dictated no other course. When Hillsborough was silent on that reality, Dunmore sought to prod him by calling another congress. In early 1771, the colonial assemblies began debating the issue. Whitehall followed the developments with trepidation and the desire to assert itself. When Virginia's assembly voted once again to send delegates to a congress, Whitehall disavowed the act. This intimidated Maryland's assembly from appointing its own delegates. Pennsylvania once again backed off. By late 1771, it was clear that no congress was possible that year or most likely the next. New York governor William Tryon admitted defeat to Hillsborough in January 1772.[35]

As if the conflicts over Indian boundaries, colonial unity, and a range of other divisive issues were not worrisome enough for Whitehall, there recently arrived in London the most ambitious and skilled lobbyist of the mid-eighteenth century. Philadelphia entrepreneur Samuel Wharton was obsessed with getting rich by nearly any means. He organized two "suffering traders" groups, one in 1754 and the other in 1763, to pressure Whitehall for land to make up for alleged wartime losses of merchandise. But then John Cox complicated Wharton's efforts by rallying a rival "suffering" group. Wharton handled this challenge in two ways. He had his associate, William Trent, dig up as much dirt as possible on the Cox group to discredit it, and then, armed with that evidence, he and Trent sailed for London in early 1769 to directly lobby Whitehall. Before leaving, however, Wharton enlisted three other partners, William Franklin, George Croghan, and Robert Callender.[36]

Once in London, Wharton embarked on a campaign to either buy out or discredit any land company rivals. On July 24, 1769, he formed with wealthy Thomas Walpole the Walpole or Grand Ohio Company to lobby for 2.4 million acres of land along the upper Ohio River valley ceded by the Fort Stanwix treaty. For that realm, Wharton offered 10,460 pounds sterling, the amount paid by the Crown to the treaty chiefs. The Privy Council received the petition in September 1769, eventually debated it, and referred it to the Trade Board on December 20, 1769.[37]

Hillsborough cleverly staved off the petition in two ways. First, he proposed that the Walpole Company enlarge its claim to 20 million acres for 100,000 pounds sterling. Hillsborough reckoned that the tenfold increase in price would either kill the petition or help underwrite the cost of buying the peace with the Indians that the influx of settlers would sorely strain. He then further fouled Wharton's net by requiring the Walpole Company to get Virginia's approval for this transaction since the lands were claimed by that colony. Virginian approval was virtually impossible since many of that colony's elite had invested in their own land companies, with claims overlapping Wharton's.

At first the conflicts unfolded as Hillsborough expected. Upon learning of the Walpole petition, Virginia's agent in London, Edward Montague, registered a protest with Whitehall on January 15, 1770. The respective agents for the Ohio and Mississippi Companies, George Mercer and William Lee, followed suit later that month.[38]

Undaunted, Wharton tried to steamroll the opposition. He sold seventy-two shares in the Walpole Company to Mercer on behalf of the Ohio Company. He sent a promise to the group of Virginian officers lobbying for 200,000 acres along the Monongahela that he would honor that claim if the Walpole Company received its grant. He sought to discredit the land claims of both Virginia and the Mississippi Company as fraudulent. He then tried to sweeten his own petition by agreeing to pay a quitrent of two shillings an acre on all plowed land, but only after it had been farmed for twenty years. This would have been a laughable gesture from anyone else, but Wharton's charisma and bribes made it palatable. Finally, he submitted a new petition calling for that 20-million-acre concession to be a new colony. Presumably, Wharton would serve as its first governor.[39]

Wharton was not everywhere victorious. Hillsborough's ploy of forcing the Walpole Company to seek Virginia's approval for its claim would take two years to resolve. When he learned of the Walpole Company's grandiose ambitions, Dunmore vigorously protested the creation of another colony hived off from Virginia's realm. The Loyal Company somehow escaped being bought out by Wharton and echoed Dunmore's protests.[40]

The colonies competed as fiercely for Indian lands as the companies. Virginia, Maryland, and Pennsylvania quarreled over the Ohio forks. New York and New Hampshire nearly came to blows over the New Hampshire Grants, which became Vermont. Pennsylvania and Connecticut battled over the Susquehanna River's Wyoming valley. To assert its stake, each colony negotiated treaties with Indians, authorized land grants to companies, and encouraged settlements in the disputed territories.

Conflicting and ambiguous charters contributed to a rivalry between Pennsylvania and Connecticut over the Wyoming valley of the upper Susquehanna River. Connecticut's Susquehanna Company bought the land in 1754 during the Albany congress from several Iroquois chiefs. It would spend the next three decades trying to legitimize that claim. Those settlers it sent into the region after the French and Indian War were driven out during the 1763 uprising. Some returned, reinforced by others. Pennsylvania meanwhile also sold lands in the region. Tensions grew as settlers claimed the same lands. The Susquehanna Company enlisted the Paxton Boys, a vigilante group that had massacred peaceful Indians during the 1763–64 uprising. In February 1770, the Paxton Boys took over Fort Durkee, manned by Pennsylvanians. The Susquehanna Company strengthened its hold on the valley the following year with a new influx of settlers that began clearing or claimed the valley's remaining lands. Led by Col. Zebulon Butler, the settlers built a series of blockhouses and drove out the last of the Pennsylvanians. That victory would be fleeting. British and Indians would butcher most of the settlers in the 1778 massacre.

However fierce the rivalry among the land companies vying for the Ohio, Illinois, and Wyoming Territory, none exploded into violence. When violence broke out in 1771, it was between settlers and colonial authorities rather than with Indians.

Just as the elite of the established seaboard cities tended to look down their noses at backcountry denizens, the landowning majority on the frontier disdained the landless minority in the adjacent wilderness who survived by hunting, trapping, trading, and sometimes stealing. That frontier fringe was lawless and licentious, more Indian than white in behavior and appearance, and an immoral mélange of largely whites peppered with blacks, Indians, and people of mixed race who lived together without fear of God or their social betters.

The ties between a colonial government and the frontier settlements were tenuous at best. In some regions that authority sometimes collapsed into anarchy and lawlessness. The Carolinas and Georgia piedmont experienced those horrors. Those colonies paid a terrible price both during and after the Cherokee war of 1759 to 1761, when the war's destruction and death were exceeded only by what followed. Gangs of marauders grew fat from looting abandoned or stray homesteads during the war and continued their crimes after peace with the Cherokees was restored. The governments of South Carolina, North Carolina, and Georgia, obsessed with the fear of slave revolt and higher taxes, refused to mount any military campaign that might have restored order to the frontier.

What their governments refused to do, those victims of the frontier terror had to do for themselves. They formed groups of "regulators," which by 1767 had ruthlessly wiped out or dispersed the outlaws. The regulators then literally turned their guns on the government that had abandoned them. They refused to pay taxes and drove out any officials. But in doing so, the regulators alienated many settlers they had once protected. In 1769, the "moderates" arose to help the government reimpose rule over the piedmont. The subjection of regulators by the moderates almost exploded into violence in Georgia and South Carolina.

War did break out in North Carolina. On September 24, 1770, regulators seized the Hillsboro court, viciously beat officials, and plundered the homes of moderates. The regulators would dominate the region for the next eight months. It was not until May 1771 that North Carolina's government condemned the revolt by passing the Bloody Johnston Act, named after its author, Samuel Johnston, and authorizing Gov. William Tryon to muster the militia and march against the rebels. The two sides squared off at Alamance Creek on May 16. After a brief exchange of shots, the moderates routed the regulators, pursued them, and hunted down their leaders. After a trial at Hillsboro, six ringleaders were hanged and the rest pardoned. The regulators were beaten but not destroyed. Many would reemerge with a vengeance during the Revolution. As elsewhere along the frontier, a civil war would burn within a larger struggle.

A similar regulator movement emerged around the same time from a vicious competition between New Hampshire and New York over land that would later become Vermont. New Hampshire had long claimed that land under its charter, but only with New France's conquest was that region safe to settle. By 1765, Gov. Benning Wentworth had issued 129 charters in the New Hampshire Grants, while buying 100,000 acres for himself.

But, characteristically, Whitehall could not leave well enough alone. On July 20, 1764, the ministers succumbed to years of persistent lobbying and accumulated bribes by issuing New York a charter granting land east of Lake Champlain as far as the Connecticut River. Waving the charter, New York's lieutenant governor Cadwallader Colden declared that the colony would honor all settlers in that territory as long as they registered their deeds and paid their fees at Albany's land office before May 23, 1765. New York would not, however, validate any towns chartered by Governor Wentworth. New York then began organizing that territory by creating Cumberland County in 1766 and Gloucester County in 1770, and splitting off Albany County's north half in 1772 to form Charlotte County. In all, New York sold off over 1 million acres of that territory by 1767.

Whitehall further fouled matters on July 24, 1767, when it ordered New York to halt any more sales. What turned Whitehall? Once again powerful lobbying shifted policy. Prominent New Hampshire landowners with stakes in that territory had dispatched Samuel Robinson as their agent to London. Robinson convinced the highly influential Society for the Propagation of the Gospel in Foreign Parts that, unlike New Hampshire, New York did not require its settlers to set aside church lands. Hot with indignation, the society succeeded in pressuring Whitehall to issue its restraining order.

New York defied the order. Both colonies continued to sell land. The Crown was powerless to implement its own commands, but New York provoked a crisis in 1770 that weakened its claims to that region. Gov. William Tryon succumbed to the pressure of New York land magnates that he enforce the high registration fees by bringing suit against those who refused to pay. By failing to distinguish between hardscrabble pioneers and absentee landlords, the policy united the two groups in opposition to New York. The Green Mountain Boys, led by the brothers Ethan, Heman, Heber, Levi, Zimir, and Ira Allen, their cousins Seth Warner and Remember Baker, and others like Jonas and Stephen Fay, and Thomas Crittenden, formed and unleashed a campaign of terror against all those officials and settlers aligned with New York. The Allens rejected a May 1772 compromise by Governor Tryon that would have eliminated the registration fees in return for recognizing New York as the proper government. Instead, the Allens joined with Thomas Crittenden and Abidad Pratt that winter to form the Onion (Winooski) River Land Company.

Whitehall tried to solve the dispute in 1773 by validating all claims made by New York and New Hampshire in the Grants since 1749; overlapping claims would be settled by granting the later settlers lands elsewhere in the territory. The Green Mountain Boys defied Whitehall as well. With his army stretched to the breaking point trying to suppress dissent in Boston and other defiant eastern seaports, General Gage refused to dispatch troops to impose the Crown's will.

The violence worsened, culminating with the Westminister "massacre" of 1774, when 100 settlers protesting debt collection took over the Cumberland County courthouse. The New York appointed sheriff and fifty deputies surrounded the courthouse and opened fire, killing two and wounding eight. When war broke out between the Americans and British the following year, the Grants would be split not just between patriots and loyalists, but among those aligned with New Hampshire, New York, and Vermont. One civil war was fought within another.

Meanwhile, a more insidious conflict had slowly built up farther west. As elsewhere along the frontier, hunters preceded settlers in the region beyond the Appalachians in Kentucky and Tennessee. For fifteen years starting in 1760, an intrepid handful of men like Daniel Boone and Samuel Tate, and several score from 1769 on, explored, hunted, and trapped that wilderness, penetrating farther each season as they exhausted one area's game and headed on to exploit the next. Those who survived death or robbery by Indians not only led back packhorses laden with deerskins, furs, and sacks of ginseng, but also spread tales of rich, uninhabited land for the taking.

Mostly Cherokee and Shawnee Indians, along with men from a dozen other tribes, hunted and occasionally warred over that region. By common consent the tribes agreed not to settle that land to preserve indefinitely the rich bounty of its game. The longhunter practice of stripping the skins from deer and leaving the carcasses to rot enraged the Indians, who utilized nearly every part of the animal and nurtured through rituals a sacred kinship between themselves and their prey. Several times Indians caught up to Boone and his companions and robbed them of all their furs, and they killed a half-dozen other longhunters during those years.

But the worse problem for the Indians was the whites who stole land rather than game. Squatters deeply penetrated the upper Tennessee River watershed, first along the Watauga River and down it to the Holston River, and in parallel valleys of the Nolachucky, Clinch, and Powell Rivers in what is now eastern Tennessee. Hundreds of settlers surged into that region following the regulator defeat in 1771. By 1772, pioneers who struggled over passes from North Carolina's upper Yadkin and Catawba Rivers had carved farms and hamlets from patches of wilderness fifty miles west of the 1763 proclamation line and thirty miles south of the 1770 Lochaber treaty line. In May 1772, delegates from those settlements formed the Watauga Association based on a written constitution to govern relations among themselves and with the tribes. Courts, magistrates, and a militia were created, and all freemen twenty-one years and older were allowed to vote. Although the Wataugans did not assert independence, they did not seek the approval of a higher authority and governed themselves for another dozen years. Neither the Crown nor North Carolina's subsequent colonial and state governments would recognize Wautauga's autonomy but were powerless to impose their own rule.

With Fort Pitt's garrison withdrawn to Philadelphia, the last vestige of imperial order in the upper Ohio disappeared. Virginia's mélange of settlers and squatters grew ever more numerous and defiant of those from Pennsylvania. In 1771, they asserted their independence when they drove out Pennsylvania's land officers and imposed a fifty-pound-sterling fine on anyone who refused to honor their authority. The following year they expelled Bedford sheriff Thomas Woods when he bravely tried to assert Pennsylvania's control. Two hundred twenty settlers signed a petition demanding that Pennsylvania agree to separate at the Appalachian watershed. For now Pennsylvania's government could do nothing to squash that rebel government.

Elsewhere, a land company did succeed in gaining official approval of its nefarious acquisitions. Phineas Lyman, a prominent Connecticut merchant and general in the French and Indian War, organized the Company of Military Adventurers in June 1763 to lobby Whitehall for their own colony. Lyman spent nine years in London, promoting one scheme after another. The setting was unimportant. Some large tract somewhere in the Mississippi, Ohio, Great Lakes, or Florida region would do. Lyman finally struck pay dirt in 1772, when he returned to his Connecticut stockholders with the lie that Whitehall had granted them a wedge of land between the Mississippi and Yazoo Rivers. An advance group sailed to Pensacola to demand lands for which they had no title. To their delight, Gov. Peter Chester and his council granted their wish. Over 400 families settled in the Yazoo valley during 1773 and 1774.

All along, the Indians complained eloquently, ceaselessly, and fruitlessly of American violations of the treaties. At a December 1771 council among the Delaware, Munsee, and Mahican Indians and the Pennsylvania, Virginia, and Maryland governors, Delaware Chief Killbuck warned: "Unless you can fall upon some method of governing your people who live between the Great Mountains and the Ohio River and who are now very numerous, it will be out of the Indians' power to govern their young men, for we assure you that the black clouds gather fast in the country."[41] The Indian superintendents echoed these warnings. Stuart patiently explained, "I know nothing so likely to interrupt and disturb our tranquility with the Indians as the incessant attempts to defraud them of their land by clandestine purchase."[42] But British and American leaders either turned a deaf ear or were powerless to do anything about the worsening relations.

Meanwhile, the conflict over the claims of Virginia and its land companies versus the Walpole Company for western territory climaxed in the spring of 1772. Both General Gage and Virginia governor Dunmore rejected the proposal for a new colony; any concession would be on Virginia claims and subject to Virginia law. Hillsborough heatedly argued against the Walpole petition. But the Walpole Company had its own allies within Whitehall, including Treasury secretaries Thomas Bradshaw and Grey Cooper, who received shares and undoubtedly less reputable inducements. It promoted its claims by publishing the Board of Trade report on the issue along with the company's rebuttal, most likely penned by Samuel Wharton or Benjamin Franklin. The gist of the argument for a new colony was that as many as 30,000 families had settled west of the Appalachians in the upper Ohio valley, with Pittsburgh lying 320 miles from Philadelphia and 400 miles from Williamsburg. That large, growing, and remote population now had no effective government and deserved to be a separate colony.[43]

Wharton's arguments, charisma, and, undoubtedly, bribes won out over Hillsborough's. On July 1, 1772, the commissioners of trade approved the Walpole Company's petition and forwarded it to the Privy Council. Over Hillsborough's vehement protests, the Privy Council favored the petition on August 14, 1772. Hillsborough resigned in disgust. Learning that the Privy Council's approval of the Walpole Company's petition was imminent, General Gage made one last appeal that it be rejected for fear that it might provoke yet another Indian war. War Minister Barrington backed his North American commander but admitted that the die had been cast.[44]

The victory of Wharton and the Walpole Company seemed complete. On May 6, 1773, the Trade Board finished its planning for the new colony. Initially the colony was to be called Pittsylvania to honor William Pitt, the earl of Chatham, but the name was changed to Vandalia to honor Queen Charlotte, whose family claimed descent from the Vandals. The name change from the champion of American rights to the descendant of the Germanic tribe that rampaged across Europe resulted from political rather than ironically poetic reasons, although given the subsequent blood-soaked history of American settlement in that region, one can richly appreciate the appropriateness of the latter. Vandalia would have included all lands between the connecting Ohio, Kanawha, Kentucky, and Greenbriar Rivers, with vague lines drawn from the last two rivers to the Holston River. But final approval of Vandalia proved to be elusive. The attorney general and solicitor general, who were supposed to certify the petition's legality, dithered. By the time they got around to deciding, events had overtaken them. The American Revolution had broken out.[45]

Complicating the politics of speculation in 1773 was a publication that argued that any land title from any Indian secured by any British subject was legal. The Crown's sovereignty then extended to that land whose ownership remained with its procurer. William Murray, an agent for the Philadelphia merchants Michael and Bernard Gratz, claimed to have a document written by the former lord chancellors Charles Priatt, Baron Camden, and Charles, Baron Morden Yorke, who made that argument in 1757.

Murray's document was spurious on several counts. It was of questionable authenticity, heavily edited, and based on natives in India rather than North America. In India the Crown had ceded those powers it still retained in North America to the East India Company—the powers of land acquisition, war, trade, and diplomacy. Finally, even if the document were authentic, the opinion of the lords chancellor or supreme court justices, however honored and carefully examined, was hardly the rule of law. Ignoring these flaws, the speculators cited Yorke-Camden to justify their own landgrabs.

A group of mostly Philadelphia merchants used Yorke-Camden to justify forming in the spring of 1773 the Illinois Company, composed of Murray, the Gratz brothers, David and Moses Franks, Andrew Levy, Joseph Simons, and Robert Callender. Murray journeyed to the Illinois country in late spring to buy that region from the Indians. Arriving at Kaskaskia, he informed an incredulous Capt. Hugh Lord, the local commander, that British subjects were free to buy and sell from whomever they wished. He then proceeded to open talks with the local chiefs. On July 3, Lord hastily wrote to Gage asking for instructions. Gage was in England for a conference with the government. Gen. Frederick Haldimand, his temporary replacement, did not act upon the letter or even forward it until October 6. Meanwhile, not only Murray but also two local Frenchmen were busy buying up huge land tracts. When the word finally reached Whitehall, American secretary William Legge, Earl of Dartmouth, fired back on December 1 orders to roust the speculators. On March 10, 1774, Haldimand issued a proclamation that prohibited all land sales from the Indians and instructed Lord to erase from the registry any new claims made by Murray or the Frenchmen.[46]

Nonplussed, the Illinois Company persuaded Governor Dunmore to take up its cause with claims that the land was part of Virginia. Dartmouth was incensed when Dunmore sided with the speculators over the Crown. He ordered Dunmore to fulfill his proper duty to the king rather than to his own selfish interests. By the time he got Dartmouth's letter, it was too late: Dunmore had already sent a surveying party of thirty men led by Thomas Bullitt down the Ohio valley as far as the falls.[47]

Hoping to gain safe passage, Bullitt, three of his men, and three Delaware guides journeyed to the Shawnee village at Chillicothe up the Scioto River. But Bullitt stupidly wielded bluster rather than tact before the council. He announced that Kentucky was now Virginian rather than Indian, and warned that Lord Dunmore would send an army to destroy the Ohio valley tribes if they disputed the transfer. He then tried to soften that message by promising many gifts for the land. Hoping to avoid war, Chief Cornstalk restrained his enraged warriors from butchering the arrogant Virginian. Instead, he sent six envoys to Fort Pitt to lodge a vigorous but impotent protest with Indian agent Alexander McKee, who was then meeting with Seneca chief Kayashuta. Unmolested, the surveyors continued downriver.

Pennsylvania speculators were hot on the Virginians' heels in surveying Kentucky. George Croghan sent his own surveying party led by William Thompson down the Ohio to claim lands for the Vandalia Company. Those men did not escape the Indians' wrath unscathed. A Mingo war party killed one of Thompson's men, but Thompson succeeded in completing his survey and thus opened the way for countless squatters eventually to follow.

George Washington played an intriguing double and triple game during this time. He was among those who violated the 1763 proclamation, which he dismissed as a "temporary expedient to quiet the minds of the Indians."[48] He and partners William Crawford and Thomas Walker surveyed lands in the Monongahela, Greenbriar, and New River valleys. The future "father of his country" was an eager investor in several land companies. He served as a partner in both the Ohio Company and Virginia Officers Association. In the autumn of 1770, he journeyed to the upper Ohio valley to survey on behalf of the officers. Upon his return to Virginia in November, he wrote to George Croghan, offering to buy his share in the proposed Walpole colony as long as Croghan continued to keep it in his name. Strapped for cash, Croghan finally agreed to do so in August 1771. In the summer of 1773, Washington further stirred the region's chaos when he offered his upper Ohio valley surveys to the highest bidder. Washington, a Virginian, joined with Pennsylvanian William Crawford to speculate in lands that they hoped would be independent of the authority of both their provinces.[49]

Pennsylvanian speculators tried to assert their own claims. In October and November 1773, George Croghan, Alexander McKee, and Kayashuta councived with over 400 Ohio valley Indians at Pittsburgh. The chiefs protested that the whites trampled the Indians' peaceful intentions "by their unfriendly and hostile behavior towards us. For we cannot cross on the side of the Ohio River which you call yours, but our People are ill treated, and even knocked in the Head and thrown into the River by yours, whereas when your People come on our side they have the liberty to walk peaceably and quietly wherever they please."[50] By generously distributing gifts, Croghan and McKee defused some of the explosive anger with the Delaware and Shawnee, but the Mingo stayed defiant.

Dunmore trumped any advantage that accrued to Pennsylvania following the 1773 council. Earlier that year, he had traveled to Pittsburgh and promised to honor all the claims of war veterans and other squatters in the region. Upon his return to Williamsburg, 400 settlers gathered at Fort Redstone and signed a petition to Dunmore asking for his protection against Pennsylvania. Dunmore was happy to comply. In January 1774, he sent John Connolly to Pittsburgh with orders to assert control as a militia captain and declare that region part of Virginia's West Augusta County. Learning of the coup, Pennsylvania magistrate Arthur St. Clair appeared on the scene and had his escort arrest Connolly. When Connolly was later released on his own recognizance, he fled to Fort Redstone, gathered the militia, and returned to Pittsburgh. On March 8, he once again declared the region part of Augusta County and installed himself in Fort Pitt, which he renamed Fort Dunmore. The plot would thicken in subsequent acts.

The tension and sporadic violence festering in segments of the frontier were mirrored on the seaboard. News of the Townshend Act's annulment did not mollify radicals. In any case, they would have vowed to maintain the boycott until the tea tax was also revoked. But "massacres" in New York and Boston in early 1770 ratcheted the resistance to higher levels of outrage, organization, mass support, and, curiously, moderation.

The troops packing the streets and taverns of New York and Boston insulted their reluctant hosts in many ways. True, the soldiers did pump money into the economy, but at the cost of increased crime, prostitution, and violations of privacy. Under the best conditions, tensions were high pitched wherever troops were deployed. But given the worsening conflicts between the Crown and colonies, a crisis was brewing.

In New York the crisis exploded on January 16, 1770, when several troops hacked down a liberty pole and tossed it before the Sons of Liberty headquarters. That act was akin to waving a cape before a maddened bull. Retaliation was all but inevitable. It happened three days later. Several patriots and soldiers squared off and brawled. A riot exploded as more subjects and soldiers waded in swinging fists and clubs. Three civilians were wounded and one was killed in what became known as the battle of Golden Hill of January 19, 1770. The following day, soldiers killed another civilian in a fight.

Then in Boston, on the night of March 5, 1770, a mob emerged from the dark narrow streets and converged on the custom house to taunt its lone sentinel. Hearing the commotion, Capt. Thomas Preston led out seven troops to form ranks with their comrade. Someone threw a stick. A soldier slipped on the ice. His musket discharged. Enraged, he shouted, "Fire!" Despite Preston's order to desist, one after another soldier lowered and discharged his musket into the milling, screaming crowd. The bullets killed three, mortally wounded two, and injured six others.

The outrage forced Gov. Thomas Hutchinson to withdraw the troops from Boston's streets and homes to Castle William in the harbor. He also agreed to have the soldiers accused of murder tried. To show their respect for the law, patriot leaders John Adams and Josiah Quincy defended the eight accused troops. Six were acquitted; the two found guilty of manslaughter had their thumbs branded and were released.

The Boston massacre and trial at once expanded, unified, and moderated the opposition to Parliament's taxes and restrictions. Hutchinson's prompt actions defused an explosive situation. The patriot leaders used the trial to promote autonomy through law and principle rather than rampaging mobs.

A lull followed the tornadoes of New York and Boston. The boycott dissolved over the next few years as one by one the colonies quietly resumed trade with Britain. But incidents flared here and there to remind Americans elsewhere of their disputes with Parliament. The most electrifying occurred on June 9, 1772, when Rhode Island Sons of Liberty boarded and torched the British war sloop *Gaspee,* which had run aground on a sandbar while pursuing smugglers in Narragansett Bay. Whitehall insisted that Rhode Island's government capture and turn over the arsonists for trial in London.

When that did not happen, Whitehall once again overreacted, goading an opposition that it hoped to suppress. The Crown appointed a commission composed of the supreme justices of New York, Massachusetts, and New Jersey, along with the judge of Boston's vice admiralty court and Rhode Island's governor, to investigate, apprehend, and send back any suspects to London for trial. No one claimed the 500-pound-sterling reward for information about the arsonists, who remained gleefully at large. Instead, patriots massed to protest that deportation would violate the cherished right of a jury trial by one's peers. Acting on a call by Samuel Adams, committees of correspondence mushroomed among radical leaders throughout the colonies to share information and strategy. The flickering ghost of colonial unity revived boldly.

In 1773, Whitehall granted a monopoly to the East India Company to sell tea in America while eliminating the tariff and imposing only a three-penny tax. In so doing, the ministers hoped at once to rescue the grossly mismanaged East India Company from bankruptcy's brink, ruin smugglers, delight consumers, and erode the rabble-rousers' boycott. In London warehouses alone, 17 million pounds of tea had accumulated because of the lingering boycott and competition among suppliers. The release of that tea on the market would cause prices to fall below those charged by smugglers. That bargain, Whitehall surmised, should be irresistible to nearly all Americans, thus collapsing the nonimportation movement.

Once again a seemingly good idea for reviving the Crown's authority ended up undermining it. While Sons of Liberty groups in all the colonies organized boycotts of tea, Boston's acted the most radically. The commander of three merchant ships packed with tea learned of the boycott only after dropping anchor. He wanted no trouble. Spoiling for a precedent to break the boycott, Governor Hutchinson denied the commander's request to return to Britain and asked him to unload the shipment. Fearing the mob's wrath, the commander respectfully declined. A law allowed the governor to use troops to unload any ship that lingered in harbor over three weeks. On December 16, 1773, the night before that deadline, the Sons of Liberty boarded the ships and dumped the tea into the harbor.

Upon hearing of the crime, Whitehall hastily wrote and got Parliament to pass the four Coercive or Intolerable Acts, two of which aimed to harshly punish Massachusetts, while the other two enhanced the Crown's powers with all the colonies. The Boston Port Bill of March 31 authorized Gen. Thomas Gage to shut down that city's trade until the destroyed tea was paid for and the king decided that commerce was safe in that port. Gage arrived in Boston on May 13 to replace Hutchinson as governor. The Massachusetts Government Act of May 20 revoked that colony's charter and thus eliminated the elected assembly, magistrates, sheriffs, and other local officials; henceforth, the governor would rule as a dictator. The Justice Act of May 20 allowed governors to change the venue of trials if they could not find an impartial jury in their colony. The Quartering Act of June 2 reinforced previous laws to force the king's subjects to underwrite the costs of and provide housing for troops garrisoned in their midst. With these bills, Whitehall hoped to crush resistance not only in Boston, but throughout the provinces.

As usual, harsh British policies inspired greater American unity. On June 17, Massachusetts' committee of correspondence called for a continental congress to be held at Philadelphia in September. All the colonies except Georgia began selecting delegates and debating what to debate there. As they did so, and as most Americans contemplated the implications of the Intolerable Acts for their lives, they received word of yet another egregious law.

The Quebec Act was not supposed to punish and intimidate the colonies, though the Americans loudly accused it of doing just that. Its genesis lay two years earlier on April 7, 1773, when the king and his Privy Council called on the Trade Board to draw up new frontier regulations that they hoped might stave off the eruption of another Indian war. The urgency to do so then dissipated in the bureaucratic maze. It took ten months for the Trade Board to comply. On February 5, 1774, Dartmouth circulated a letter to the governors ordering them to suspend all licenses for land grants, except those to veterans under the 1763 proclamation. That policy preceded an actual bill. On May 1, 1774, Dartmouth presented the Quebec Act to the House of Lords, who overwhelmingly approved. The House of Commons began debating the bill on June 6 and approved it by a vote of fifty-six to twenty on June 13. The Quebec Act would take effect on May 1, 1775.[51]

The Quebec Act extended Quebec's jurisdiction to all lands north of the Ohio River, west of the Allegeny Mountains, east of the Mississippi River, and south of the watershed with Hudson Bay. An appointed military governor and council with legislative powers would rule the province. English and French civil law were joined in one legal code. Catholics were granted full civil and religious rights. Any French Canadian settlements in the region west of the Appalachian watershed were legitimized; no new settlements would be allowed.

To Whitehall, the Quebec Act at once addressed several related and worsening problems. Extending Quebec's jurisdiction across that vast swath of land eliminated the claims of other colonies and their land companies. Anyone who wanted to trade there had to get a license from Quebec's governor, an inconvenient, time-consuming, and expensive process. The geographical containment of the American colonies east of the Appalachians simultaneously clipped their potential economic, population, and political power. Indians were better protected from rapacious speculators, traders, and squatters, and thus would be less likely to revolt. With full religious and civil rights, French Canadians would be more inclined to remain loyal to the British rather than their former French Crown. With the Indians and French Canadians quiescent and their lands secure, the garrisons in that region could be reduced or completely redeployed to the volatile eastern seaports. The more redcoats there were stationed amidst the Americans, the more the potential rebels would be cowed into submission to pay taxes and heed other regulations.

Most Americans, of course, did not see it that way. Indeed, the Quebec Act personified all that was arbitrary, exploitive, and repressive about British rule. The land companies howled the loudest in outrage. The Quebec Act swept away all their claims in that territory. Prominent Americans and British had invested years of time and enormous wealth with dreams of reaping untold fortunes from that land. What they had hoped was a sound investment instead turned out to be a chimera.

The Quebec Act both frustrated ambitions to carve land empires in the northwest and spurred events south of the Ohio River. In 1774, two Indian wars broke out on the frontier. The Lower Creek bands won, and the Ohio tribes lost their respective wars. Though they ended before news of the Quebec Act reached the colonies, those wars seemed to justify a stronger hand for the Crown in separating Americans from Indians.

Land companies defied the 1763 proclamation in many ways, most blatantly by negotiating their own purchases of territory from the tribes. On February 22, 1771, a group of Augusta merchants led by James Spalding signed an agreement with the Cherokee chiefs at their central village of Chote for a deed of sixty square miles on the central stretch of the Savannah River. They then petitioned Indian Superintendent John Stuart, Gov. James Wright of Georgia, and King George III to approve the transfer. Stuart firmly opposed and Wright approved the cession. On November 9, 1772, Whitehall granted permission for the sale, but the land would go to the Crown, not to the speculators, and would be used to liquidate the Indians' debt of 74,833 pounds sterling to about forty merchants. On August 3, 1773, Wright signed the Treaty of Augusta with Upper Creek and Cherokee chiefs whereby 2.1 million acres of Indian lands were transferred. In doing so, the signatories repeated the common landgrab tactic whereby territory bought from one tribe, band, or faction was actually possessed by another. That new purchase was Lower Creek territory.[52]

Governor Wright actually announced the first sales of the ceded lands on June 11, 1773, nearly two months before the official treaty. Within a half year, hundreds of settlers were clearing land and building rude shelters in that region. Wright undermined the debt reduction plan by selling the land in small lots to prevent speculators from taking over. The creditors got little money from the sales. The result was the further alienation of prominent merchants from the Crown.

The Lower Creek Indians were determined to drive off the squatters. They shed the first blood on Christmas when they murdered a family at the Ogeechee headwaters in the ceded lands. On January 14, 1774, a war party of Coweta Creek attacked a stockade near Wrightsborough, killing seven and wounding five while suffering five dead. Another war party ambushed and routed Col. James Grierson's 100 militia and 25 rangers from Georgia on January 25. The Creek Indians won their war. Their attacks stampeded settlers from the ceded lands.

The victorious Creek Indians then sought to win a satisfying peace. Upper Creek chief Mad Turkey journeyed alone to Augusta for negotiations. That mission died abruptly when a blacksmith named Thomas Fee bashed in his skull with an iron bar. Rather than resume their war, the Creek bands continued to try to negotiate. Chief Emistisiguo slipped into Savannah to meet with Governor Wright. The governor agreed to deploy Capt. Edward Barnard's rangers to curb the rum trade with the Creek Indians, since it provoked many warriors to excesses. He also agreed to a formal peace council in October. Crown and Georgia officials opened a council at Savannah on October 18 with Emistisiguo and about seventy Upper Creek Indians, along with Pumpkin King and Chehaw King, who led about fifty Lower Creek Indians. Under the Treaty of Savannah, signed on October 20, 1774, Wright agreed to prevent any squatters beyond the Ogeechee River and resume trade if the Creek tribes returned runaway slaves and punished those who attacked the settlers and soldiers. That treaty satisfied the Creek Indians but further alienated the settlers.

The Lower Creek bands had no sooner chased out squatters from part of their territory when a handful of those Indians gave away a huge amount of their land elsewhere. In the autumn of 1774, Georgian land speculator Jonathan Bryan initiated one of the more ambitious landgrabs. He persuaded twenty-one Lower Creek Indians near Apalachee to give him about 5 million acres of East Florida from the St. Mary's River's source to the Apalachicola River for ninety-nine years in return for 100 pounds sterling and an annual basket of Indian corn. Why would those Indians give away so much for so little? When Georgia officials asked them that, they were stunned and said Bryan had lied about what he wanted. The sale was canceled, but the animosities it aroused lingered.[53]

The Treaty of Augusta was the last officially sanctioned agreement with the Indians before the Revolution. Whitehall's ministers were determined not to approve any more landgrabs. In early 1773, the Crown issued a circular letter to the governors and superintendent forbidding them from issuing "any Warrant of Survey, or to pass any Patents for Lands in the said Colonies, or to grant any License for the purchase by Private Persons of any Lands from the Indians without especial Direction from his Majesty."[54]

Those starved for land dismissed such laws. As early as October 1773, the first attempt was made to settle in Kentucky when Daniel Boone led forty hunters and five families along the trail from the upper Clinch River over Kane Gap toward the upper Cumberland River. As fate would have it, they crossed paths with a diplomatic mission of fifteen Delaware, two Shawnee, and two Cherokee returning from counciling with the Overhill Cherokee for an alliance against the whites. On the night of October 9, the warriors crept up on a detached party and opened fire, killing six men. Bowing to the majority's reasonable fears, Boone reluctantly led the survivors back to the Clinch valley. He and others would soon return to Kentucky.

Three land companies vied to be the first to settle Kentucky in 1774. That year Judge William Henderson, William Johnston, John Williams, the brothers Thomas and Nathaniel Hart, and John Luttrell formed the Louisa Company and began to amass money with which to purchase lands from the Indians. Two other groups, both representing veterans, beat the Louisa Company to Kentucky. In 1774, Captains William Bullitt and James Wood led a group of Virginia officers, while Capt. William Thompson headed Pennsylvania veterans. However, these were surveying, not settling, parties. The plow would follow the compass the following year. Yet another speculator, William Russell, enlisted Daniel Boone and Michael Stoner to trek as far as the Ohio falls to survey land and warn other surveying parties of the outbreak of war with the Indians. That warning was too late for a party led by James Herrod. Indians killed two of his men on July 8 and killed two from another surveying party a few days later. Those parties were unaware that an Indian war had broken out while they were immersed in the wilderness.

Lord Dunmore's War exploded from a series of sporadic but ever bloodier murders by Indians and frontiersmen against each other in the upper Ohio valley. On April 14, four Cherokee waylaid two traders in a canoe forty miles downriver from Pittsburgh, killing one and wounding the other, and looted much of the merchandise. John Connolly, who commanded Fort Dunmore at Pittsburgh, learned of the attack, mustered the militia, and sent it downstream. They rescued the wounded man but failed to catch the raiders. Around the same time, Shawnee Indians robbed and beat seven Virginians engaged in land claims on the Ohio. No word arrived from another survey party of thirty men led by John Floyd, which had earlier descended the Ohio. Although they were safe, Connolly feared the worst and acted on that fear. On April 21, he issued a circular letter warning the settlers to ready themselves for an imminent war. That proved to be a self-fulfilling prophecy.

The warning reached Wheeling, where Michael Cresap and nearly ninety Virginians were staking claims in the region. They interpreted Connolly's declaration as open season on any Indians. On April 26, some of Cresap's men murdered two friendly Indians and sought other victims. The following day, they pursued and opened fire on a Wakatomica Shawnee peace delegation returning from Pittsburgh. While losing one man killed, they killed a chief, wounded another, and captured their canoes filled with gifts. A third atrocity four days later would be the most notorious of all. On April 30, Michael Greathouse and several other frontiersmen enticed a group of Mingo Indians from across the Ohio River to a cabin, besotted them with rum, and then murdered them all, including the mother, brother, and sister of Mingo war leader Logan. A few escaped to spread word of the massacre. A war now seemed inevitable.[55]

Indian deputy Alexander McKee tried to avert that war. He sent Simon Girty to the Indian villages near Pittsburgh asking them to join a council, had Connolly write Cresap to inquire what justified the attacks, and issued an order cutting off all liquor shipments to the Indians. In a council with Kayashuta, Chief White Mingo, and an Iroquois delegation, he promised compensation for the murders. On May 4, Girty arrived at the council with Delaware chiefs White Eyes and Captain Pipe, and their followers. The chiefs accepted McKee's promises. Word arrived from the Scioto Shawnee chiefs that they would restrain their warriors.

Only the Mingo and the Wakatomica Shawnee understandably remained defiant. War parties from those tribes haunted the upper Ohio. They ambushed a party of whites and killed one in mid-May. In early June, Mingo Indians killed eleven whites. More than 1,000 settlers fled the region. Connolly mobilized the militia and ordered forts built at Wheeling and opposite the Hocking River mouth on the Ohio. On June 11, forty militia heading to Wheeling collided with four Mingo who routed the Americans, killing the captain and wounding the lieutenant. Unable to retaliate, the settlers turned on friendly Indians, killing a Delaware and wounding Scioto Shawnee chief Silver Heels in separate attacks. The assault on Silver Heels provoked the Scioto Shawnee warriors, howling for vengeance, into the fray.

Who was at fault for the latest Indian war? Dunmore pointed the finger of blame firmly in a predictable direction: "The Indians have been the aggressors, and thereby the occasion of the fatal consequences."[56] McKee begged to differ: "To do the Indians justice, they have given great proofs of their pacific disposition, and have acted with more moderation . . . a few Mingoes and Shawaness excepted . . . There are more effectual means of chastising them for their insolence and perfidy, than by involving the defenseless country in a war."[57] Pennsylvanians saw Dunmore's war as a contrived landgrab by Virginians: "It appears that a scheming party in Virginia are making a tool of their Governor to execute the plans formed by them for their private emolument, who being mostly land jobbers, would wish to have those lands."[58]

The war was splendid for Dunmore. A successful campaign and land-grabbing treaty could overturn the government's earlier rebuff of his schemes. On June 10, he called out the militia of the frontier counties and ordered their officers to prepare the men for "Striking Such a Stroke as might prove decisive." On June 20, he ordered Connolly to remain in command at Fort Dunmore while helping Col. Andrew Lewis and Capt. William Crawford prepare to attack the Shawnee villages. In July, Connolly sent 250 militia under Captains William Crawford and Henry Hoagland to Wheeling, which would be the springboard for his attacks on the hostile villages. On July 12, Dunmore dispatched Maj. Angus MacDonald and his troops to Wheeling and Col. Andrew Lewis and his command to the Great Kanawha River mouth, where they would build a fort before crossing over and attacking the hostile villages.[59]

A circular letter by Col. William Preston publicly announced the war's implicit goal:

> We may Perhaps never have so fair an Opportunity of reducing our old Inveterate Enemies to Reason . . . it will be the only Method of Settling a lasting Peace with all the Indian tribes around us . . . This useless People may now at last be obliged to abandon their Country. Their Towns may be plundered & Burned, Their Cornfields Distroyed; & they Distressed in such a manner as will prevent them from giving us any future Trouble . . . Our cause is good; & theirfore we have the greatest Reason to hope & expect that Heaven will bless us with Success in the Defense of ourselves & families against a parcel of murdering Savages.[60]

The governor launched the first attack in August when Maj. Angus McDonald led 400 Virginians down the Ohio and up the Muskingum against the Shawnee at Wakatomica, Snake's Town, and three hamlets, all of which they burned. They lost two killed and six wounded while killing three Indians and capturing one.[61]

Although the casualties and destruction were light, the Scioto Shawnee convened a council at Chillicothe. The headmen deposed the war chief Hardman and replaced him with Black Hoof. Cornstalk continued as the Mekoce Shawnee civil chief. Runners returned from more distant tribes like the Miami and Wabash Confederacy; Iroquois, Delaware, and Lake tribes; and even the Chickasaw with word that those tribes would sit out this war.

Dunmore negotiated at Pittsburgh with tribal envoys from September 12 to 17. Each envoy proclaimed his tribe's commitment to or readiness for peace. Dunmore rewarded with presents and words the neutrals, but rebuffed any deals with the hostiles. The governor was determined to smite the Shawnee and Mingo Indians so mightily that they would never again resist westward expansion.[62]

On September 25, Dunmore set forth with 1,150 militia toward Wheeling. From there he sent Maj. William Crawford with 500 men to build a fort at the Hocking River mouth. Dunmore followed with the rest of the troops a few days later. There he would await Col. Andrew Lewis and 1,100 men who were then marching down the Kanawha River valley.[63]

Logan and his Mingo warriors were far away, burning and killing along the Clinch and Holston Rivers. They hit first around Fort Blackmore on September 23, capturing two black slaves and slaughtering livestock. A week later, they crept up near Moore's Fort and opened fire, killing a man before slipping off. Several days after that, they killed a sentinel at Fort Blackmore.

Meanwhile, Cornstalk and Blue Jacket amassed as many as 550 warriors between their villages and Dunmore's army. MacDonald's earlier campaign had caught them by surprise. Now the Shawnee and the handful of Mingo, Delaware, Ottawa, Wyandot, Cherokee, and Miami Indians who joined them were eager for vengeance. Rather than wait until Lewis's army joined Dunmore's, the chiefs chose to attack the weaker of the two.

The Indians slipped across the Ohio River on the morning of October 10 and just after sunrise attacked Lewis's pickets at Point Pleasant on the Kanawha River mouth. They then fell back, provoking Lewis to order two columns of about 150 troops each to advance after them; Col. Charles Lewis, Andrew's younger brother, commanded the Augusta County troops on the right wing and Col. William Fleming the Botetourt County men on the left. The Indians hit them about a mile from camp. The battle raged all day. Lewis ordered enough other companies up from the camp to hold his own line but not enough to break the enemy. Just before sunset he ordered a flank attack. The Indians blunted the assault until a shot killed the warrior who carried their sacred medicine bundle. When the charging Americans then captured the bundle, the Indians were so sickened and fearful at the loss that they swiftly withdrew across the Ohio. The losses were heavy for both sides. The Americans lost fifty-five dead and ninety-two wounded, while the Indians suffered about thirty Shawnee and three Mingo dead. Musket balls killed Charles Lewis and hit Fleming twice in his left arm and clipped his chest. The battle of Point Pleasant proved to be decisive.

On October 11, Dunmore marched his army from the Hocking River mouth toward the Shawnee villages where Cornstalk and most of his force had withdrawn to mourn their dead and prepare for defense. But the headmen soon agreed that the Americans were too numerous to fight and their people too weary to flee with winter fast approaching. When Dunmore's army was fifteen miles away on October 15, Cornstalk sent the trader Matthew Elliott to the governor with a call for negotiations. Dunmore agreed to talk but marched his army to within a half dozen miles of the villages before he halted and established the fortified Camp Charlotte. Cornstalk, White Fish, and Hardman began talks with Dunmore but nearly broke them off on October 24 when they learned that Lewis's army was marching between them and their village. Although Lewis had simply taken the wrong path, the Indians broke off the talks and hurried away. Dunmore ordered Lewis to withdraw to Point Pleasant. The negotiations reopened.

In signing the Treaty of Camp Charlotte, the Shawnee and their allies promised to surrender their claim to Kentucky and no longer hunt there; return all prisoners, horses, and loot they had seized since 1764; stop attacking boats on the Ohio River; and hand over four headmen as hostages. The signatories agreed that the Camp Charlotte treaty was to be only preliminary to a lasting treaty to be signed with the northern Indian superintendent the following year.

Although Logan had returned with his warriors to shelter at the Shawnee village, he refused to attend the council or sign the treaty. He did send word to Dunmore that "I have killed many. I have fully glutted my vengeance. For my country I rejoice at the beams of peace. But do not harbor a thought that mine is the joy of fear. Logan never felt fear. He will not turn his heel to save his life." Then to remind Dunmore what started the war, he demanded: "Who is there to mourn for Logan? Not one."[64]

Dunmore dispatched Maj. William Crawford and 240 troops against Logan on October 25. Crawford's troops almost trapped the Mingo Indians at Salt Lick

Town, but Logan and most of his followers slipped away after suffering six dead and fourteen captured. Crawford kept twelve Mingo as hostages and burned the town. That action embittered the Mingo chiefs Logan and Pluggy, who had been ready to bury the hatchet. Of all the Ohio tribes, none would war more relentlessly against the Americans than the Mingo in the coming war for independence.

In late October, Dunmore withdrew and disbanded his army, leaving only seventy-five men at Fort Blair, which Lewis's men constructed at Point Pleasant. In November, the governor left Pittsburgh with his Shawnee hostages for Williamsburg while the twelve Mingo hostages stayed under Maj. John Connolly's supervision at Fort Dunmore.

Dunmore's war infuriated General Gage and Whitehall, but there was little they could do. The governors were independent of the commander in chief while Dartmouth and the other ministers were an ocean away. Those officials could only sit in impotent fury as reports arrived detailing actions committed weeks or months earlier contrary to Crown policy. Gage angrily refused to commit any regulars to the fray—"the vagabonds must themselves support the Mischief they are creating."[65] Gage told Johnson to impress on the Indians that "this is no general War against the Indians . . . it is merely a contest betwixt the Virginians and Shawnese, and that therefore they shou'd avoid injuring those who are at Peace with them . . . [it would] bring on a general war, in which all Parties must suffer."[66] Dartmouth penned Dunmore a sharp protest and reminder that the king was adamantly opposed to new settlements beyond the Appalachians or violations of solemn treaties with the Indians. Dunmore risked igniting the entire frontier. While Dartmouth did not doubt that potential war's outcome, he deemed the financial and human costs unacceptable. By the time that message reached him, Dunmore had already won his war.[67]

Dunmore replied to this storm of criticism with an icy calm. To Dartmouth he wrote: "I do not perceive the Misconduct which . . . your Lordship communicated to me . . . neither do I discover the Justice of the heavy rebuke." Contrary to what Dartmouth and others might believe, Dunmore claimed he was in total agreement and compliance with the policy "against extending any Settlements to the Westward." But uncontrollable forces had instigated the unwanted war: "I have learnt from experience that the established Authority of any governments in America, and the policy of Government at home, are both insufficient to restrain the Americans, and that they do and will remove as their avidity and restlessness incite them."[68]

What did the war achieve? If the war was unwanted by the Crown, the results were not, at least for the restless Americans and their financial backers. On paper Dunmore had won a stunning victory. The Indians had promised to relinquish Kentucky and never trespass there again! That encouraged hundreds of settlers to hurry across the Cumberland Gap and down the Ohio over the next few years. But the Indians would soon recant that promise and try to exterminate the settlers. Dunmore did not, of course, mention that he personally stood to profit handsomely from the conquest. He did not have to do so; his investments in various land schemes were well known.

Militarily Dunmore's campaign was highly successful. Ironically, the Royal governor proved to be more adept at conducting an Indian war than the subsequent American states or Congress during their struggle for independence. Dunmore deserves credit for rapidly mobilizing troops and supplies, devising and implementing a strategy, defeating the Indians, and imposing a settlement that advanced the American frontier. No American commander would be as successful in the pending frontier war for independence.

Early in the summer of 1774, as Dunmore mobilized for war, Northern Indian Superintendent William Johnson tried to promote peace. Upon learning of the murders, he sent runners to the Six Nations and other tribes in the region to journey for a council at Johnson Hall. The first Indians arrived on June 19, and other groups trickled in until over 600 had gathered when the council formally opened on July 8. Johnson urged the Iroquois to restrain the Mingo and other Ohio valley tribes. That, of course, was easier said than done. On July 11, a Seneca chief captured the essence of the latest crisis: "We are sorry to observe that your People are as ungovernable, or more so, than ours . . . It seems, Brother, that your People entirely disregard and despise the settlement we agreed upon . . . and are come in vast numbers to the Ohio, and gave our people to understand that they wou'd settle wherever they pleas'd."[69]

The frontier crisis worsened that night when a heart attack killed Sir William Johnson. He had faced a tough dilemma in the years leading to his death in 1774—who could possibly fill his moccasins as the Indian superintendent for the Northern Department? Ever since he had migrated from Ireland in 1738, Johnson had climbed the colonial pyramid of power until he nestled in rustic baronial splendor near its apex. His uncle Peter Warren, famed for his merchant and naval exploits, had beckoned the eighteen-year-old to the Mohawk valley to tend his lands and peasants. Johnson was not content to pass his days managing someone else's wealth. Power wisely wielded begets yet more power. His gifts as a diplomat and speculator won him an ever expanding land empire accompanied by honors, duties, and wealth entrusted by Indian and British leaders alike. To the Mohawk he was Warraghiyagey or "Doer of Great Deeds," who was made a sachem in the Iroquois council. The colony named him militia colonel, justice of the peace, and New York council member, while the king made him a general, Indian superintendent, and baronet. During the Seven Years' War he led troops to victory at the battles of Lake George in 1755 and Niagara in 1759.

All along his ambitions joined his sentiments in pushing him constantly to bridge the Indian and colonial worlds. In this his private and public life meshed. He had indulged his passions with two wives—European Catherine Weissenberg and Mohawk Molly Brant—along with numerous other women. But among his considerable progeny, only his son John and his nephew and son-in-law Guy could legitimately contend for his title. Alas the weaknesses of both overwhelmed their strengths. Johnson feared that either one would fritter away the empire of land, money, political power, and elite social standing he had so laboriously created. The choice between his son and nephew was painful—which was the lesser mediocrity?

Sir William's attempts to groom his son to succeed him proved to be a gross disappointment. John served his father as an aide in both the 1755 Lake George and 1759 Niagara campaigns, and in numerous Indians councils during and after the war. He attended the Wheelock Academy and later the Philadelphia Academy. In 1760, he was named a militia captain for Albany County. In 1765, Sir William sent John to London for a year to complete his worldly education, attend the Royal court, find a rich aristocratic wife, and have his title confirmed by King George III. Back in New York he became a justice of the peace, provincial grand master of the Order of Freemasons, and major general of militia for New York's northern district. Those accomplishments came from connections rather than competence. He could be as petty, haughty, and aloof as his father was the opposite.

Like his cousin John, Guy was but a shadow of his uncle and father-in-law. If Sir William epitomized the diplomat—intelligent, self-assured, charismatic—Guy was just the opposite, hot tempered, foul mouthed, indolent, vengeful; those vices sullied his genuine gifts of wit and oratory. Perhaps all that William and Guy shared was a passion for strong drink and comely women of easy virtue. Yet, disappointed with his son, Sir William made the less disinterested Guy an apprentice Indian superintendent as deputy for the middle district, which embraced the Iroquois, and helped secure him such positions as Tryon County's militia adjutant general, justice of the peace, and representative to New York's assembly.

So with Sir William Johnson's death, John inherited his estate and Guy the superintendency. It was no loss to John; his heart was never in Indian affairs. With ambivalent feelings, Guy took the position but never lived up to his uncle's achievements. In April 1774, Sir William had written American secretary Dartmouth asking him to accept the succession. All that remained was for King George III to confirm Guy's nomination.[70]

Upon his uncle's death, Guy Johnson wrote both Dartmouth and Gage, asking that they speedily confirm the arrangements. Gage swiftly approved. The letters to and from Dartmouth took longer. To Guy's disappointment, Dartmouth only got the king to agree to his temporary appointment as Indian superintendent, and then only for the Iroquois and their dependent tribes. Quebec governor Guy Carleton would take over the Ohio valley and Great Lakes tribes.

Does man make history or history man? It depends, of course, on the history and the man. The question of Sir William Johnson's legacy mattered greatly. Had that brilliant diplomat lived another decade, the northern frontier war and fate of America's Revolution might have turned out quite differently.[71]

As that year's military campaigns, diplomatic councils, and William Johnson's death shaped the frontier's fate, the First Continental Congress convened in Philadelphia on September 5, 1774. For nearly two months the delegates debated and decided a plethora of procedural and substantive issues. The delegates split between moderates who wanted Whitehall to revoke its coercive laws and radicals who sought self-rule. On October 14, after more than a month of mulling over various proposals, Congress voted for a Declaration and Resolves that justified their meeting, asserted their rights as British subjects, demanded the repeal of eleven "coercive acts," and condemned taxation without representation. On October 20, Congress approved an association of the colonies that would boycott all imports from Britain until she agreed to the American demands. These were vital steps toward revolution and independence. But symbolically perhaps the most vivid gesture occurred during the first debate over whether the delegates should vote as individuals or colonies. Patrick Henry declared, "I am not a Virginian, but an American."

American defiance and demands increasingly exasperated the king. In September 1774, George III insisted to Baron Frederick North, then Treasury secretary, that "we must not retreat." Two months later he declared the Americans rebels and "blows must decide whether they are to be subject to this country or independent."[72] Then when he learned on December 13 of Congress's actions, the king reacted with fury rather than contemplation; with his advisors' approval, he dispatched four more regiments and 700 marines to Boston. The king and his ministers schemed even harsher measures, but for approval those would have to await Parliament's next session in January 1775.

Gen. Thomas Gage also advocated a hard line with the colonists. He already had 4,000 troops, including the 4th, 5th, 14th, 29th, 38th, 43rd, 59th, and parts of the 64th and 65th Regiments in Boston. But he feared that was not enough and wrote War Minister Barrington for another 20,000 troops to intimidate the radicals from revolt or crush any rebellion that exploded. Even then he worried that regulars alone would not suffice.

With ominous consequences for the frontier, Gage concluded that warriors could help thwart a rebellion as "the Indians at their backs will always keep them quiet."[73] He ordered his post commanders to keep peace with the Indians at all costs. In a circular letter to them, he expressed his satisfaction "that you will do every thing that is Necessary to keep all the Indians firm in their Love and Attachment to the King, and in a Temper to be always ready to Act in his Services."[74] Those services would soon be amply needed and rewarded.

CHAPTER 3

"Desperate Measures": 1775

We do not comprehend what all this quarreling is about. How comes it that Old England and new should Quarrel & come to blows? The Father & Son to fight is terrible—Old France and Canada did not do so. We cannot think of fighting ourselves till we know who is right and who is wrong.

—Micmac chief

As the rebels have got Indians to their assistance, we must make use of the same desperate measures.

—King George III

Was reconciliation still possible? At this late date that was unlikely. A dozen years of escalating conflicts, demands, insults, and crimes had embittered Americans and Britons alike. While cooler heads urged compromise, both sides' leaders fortified their principles and refused to yield an inch.

Hardliners dominated British politics. They rejected any notion of appeasement that would only encourage more American demands, with independence the ultimate concession. When Parliament convened in January, William Pitt led those who favored mollifying the colonists. But the majority approved sterner measures and shouted down his eloquence. No more successful were those merchants threatened with ruin by the American boycott. George III spurned their petitions for reconciliation as little short of treasonous. The king and his ministers agreed that all resistance to the Crown must be crushed before it burst into outright rebellion. William Legge, Earl of Dartmouth, the American secretary, penned a January 27 letter to Gen. Thomas Gage authorizing him to seize the rabble-rouser leaders.[1]

That, of course, was easier said than done. The radicals were preparing for rebellion under Gage's nose. Try as he might he could do nothing about it. With the British military ruling Boston by martial law, the Massachusetts assembly met illegally twenty miles west in Concord. In 1774, the legislators voted to collect munitions in Concord, establish arsenals at other key towns, and issue orders to the militia to organize the hardiest of every four into "minutemen" companies ready to rush at an instant's notice to a crisis. The assemblies of New Hampshire and Connecticut pursued similar policies.

With growing alarm, Gage contemplated reports of the colonial forces building all around him. Rather than try to defuse the passions, he gambled that decisive assertions of force would cow the mob into submission. But that policy only enraged the resistance.

His expeditions to seize munitions at Portsmouth on December 12, 1774, and Salem on February 27, 1775, failed miserably. At Portsmouth the militia spirited away most of the munitions before the redcoats arrived. At Salem the militia captain merely ordered a drawbridge raised before the advancing British column; shamefaced, the redcoats had no choice but to withdraw. Those attempts provoked both outrage and contempt among colonists.

Having been twice humiliated, Gage was determined not to fail again. On April 16, he received Dartmouth's orders to capture the provincial congress and learned that four more regiments were coming. But Dartmouth's mission was impossible. As Gage was reading his instructions, the provincial congress was adjourning so its delegates could prepare for the Continental Congress at Philadelphia in May. Samuel Adams and John Hancock, however, lingered in Lexington. Gage planned to seize those radicals along with the arsenal at Concord. He entrusted the mission to Lt. Colonel Francis Smith and a 900-man elite force composed of the grenadier and light infantry companies of the regiments occupying Boston.

That expedition could not long remain secret. Night riders galloped warnings to the militia and committees of safety throughout the region. Capt. John Parker and the 60 or 70 armed men of Lexington's militia company silently stood on their village green in the early morning light of April 19 when Maj. John Pitcairn marched with the advanced guard of 238 troops from six light infantry companies into town. The redcoats were weary and short-fused. They had been up all night, first waiting to be rowed across the harbor to Cambridge and then marching eleven miles to Lexington. As his troops deployed into a battle line, Pitcairn shouted at the militia to lay down their arms and disperse. Parker hesitated and then issued an ambiguous dismissal to his command. Some men drifted away but most remained defiant. As the two forces nervously eyeballed each other, someone fired a shot. Without orders the British troops lowered their muskets, fired, and then charged. After the smoke cleared, eight Americans lay dead or dying and nine were wounded; the others fled. A bullet slightly wounded a redcoat.

The British column marched on to Concord. Upon reaching the town, Smith split his force into three, with two respectively guarding the northwest and southwest bridges and the third searching houses for hidden munitions. Militias converged and massed on the town's outskirts. The northwest British column crossed the bridge and advanced up a hill toward the militia. The Americans slowly withdrew, their ranks swelling steadily as other companies joined them. Smoke was spotted rising from Concord where the British were burning supplies. Fearing the redcoats were torching the town, Col. James Barret ordered his troops to advance. The British withdrew across the bridge. Once again some regulars fired without orders. The Americans lowered their muskets and fired back. Leaving dead and wounded behind, the British column withdrew to Concord's center. Smith recalled the other column, assembled his entire force, and pointed them on the long march back to Boston.

All along those twenty miles, militia companies swarmed and sniped on the British flanks and rear. The Americans might have overwhelmed the entire British force had not Gage sent Gen. Hugh Percy with 1,200 troops to the rescue. Those fresh troops covered the retreat of the remnants of Smith's command. The rebels had inflicted 73 killed, 174 wounded, and 26 missing on the British while losing only 49 killed and 41 wounded. It was a humiliating defeat for the king's army.[2]

The war had begun. Like metal filings to a magnet, New England's militia regiments joined the siege lines ringing Boston. The Massachusetts assembly reconvened and agreed that its president, Joseph Warren, should supervise while Artemas Ward commanded as general the 15,000-man "Army of Observation."

THE LAKE CHAMPLAIN FRONTIER

Within three weeks of Lexington and Concord, the rebellion engulfed a portion of the frontier. Forts Ticonderoga and Crown Point, sixteen miles apart on Lake Champlain's west shore, guarded one of the continent's most strategic regions, the corridor of lakes, rivers, and portages linking Albany and Montreal. Those forts were the perfect advanced base for a campaign in either direction. As long as the British held those forts, they would cast an ominous shadow all the way to Albany 65 miles south, and then 120 miles beyond down the Hudson River to New York City. As word of the bloodshed around Boston spread, the ambition to seize those forts gripped many men, with two especially notorious for their egos, ambitions, and courage.[3]

Capt. Benedict Arnold of the Governor's Footguards of New Haven, Connecticut, was a jack of many trades—bookseller, merchant, shipowner, apothecary, and horse peddler. But greater passions than piling and dispersing wealth animated him. He craved adventure, fame, power, and the affections of beguiling women, and was brimmed with the confidence of his genius to win those dreams. All he lacked was the opportunity—until now. Arnold grasped Ticonderoga's importance for the rebellion and himself.

While leading his company toward Boston five days after the battles of Lexington and Concord, he shared his vision with Col. Samuel Parsons, who was returning to Hartford on a recruiting mission. The men agreed to seek official permission for the expedition. On April 30, Arnold presented his plan to two committees of safety, in person to Massachusetts' and by letter to New York's. On May 2, Massachusetts granted Arnold a colonel's commission and 100 pounds sterling to raise and lead 400 troops on that mission. Ironically, Benjamin Church, the man who commissioned Arnold, was a British spy. Somehow Arnold got word of another expedition forming at Bennington and rushed there with just a secretary to take command.

When Parsons appeared before Connecticut's committee of correspondence on April 27, John Hancock and John and Sam Adams were also present to coordinate plans between the two colonies. The assembly granted approval. Parsons passed the torch to Capt. Edward Mott, who by April 29 recruited sixteen men and began the long march to Ticonderoga. At Pittsfield, Massachusetts, he was joined by John Brown and forty volunteers led by Col. James Easton. Earlier that year, Massachusetts had dispatched Brown to Montreal to curry Canadian support for America's conflicts with the Crown. Brown found little sympathy but did recognize how vital those wilderness forts would be should a war break out. On his way back he shared that idea with Ethan Allen.

Ethan Allen shared Arnold's raging passions, intelligence, and ambitions. Though like Arnold, Allen was Connecticut born, in 1770 he moved to the New Hampshire Grants (now Vermont). With his commanding charisma, physique, and drive, Allen swiftly rose to lead the Green Mountain Boys, who sought independence from New York and the creation of their own colony with its capital at Bennington. When news of the fighting around Boston reached them, Allen and his men began scheming to take Ticonderoga, hoping that a successful coup would prompt the Continental Congress to recognize their bid for a separate province.

When Mott, Easton, Brown, and their men strode into Bennington, Allen not only joined in with his Green Mountain Boys but asserted command over the expedition. On May 8, Allen sent some of his men to capture loyalist landowner Maj. Philip Skene and his boats at Skenesborough, while he led the rest of the men toward Hand's Cove on Lake Champlain's east shore across from Fort Ticonderoga. Arnold caught up with Allen on May 9 as they neared Lake Champlain, presented his commission, and demanded the expedition's command. Fearing that rejecting Arnold's authority might jeopardize Vermont's separation bid, Allen swallowed a portion of his overweening pride and agreed to a joint command.

Allen, Arnold, and eighty-three men waited impatiently at Hand's Cove for the boats from Skenesborough, but they never arrived. The leaders found two large scows, packed the men into them, and rowed the mile across the lake. Ashore, they formed their men into a column three abreast and led them up the slope toward the fort. It was near dawn on the morning of May 10.

Fort Ticonderoga was in disrepair and held by only forty-four troops under Capt. William Delaplace. Gage recognized the fort's vulnerability. On April 19, he sent orders to Canadian governor Guy Carleton to reinforce the forts with a regiment. The orders arrived too late. Word of the fighting had not yet reached Delaplace when the rebels appeared before the fort. Only one guard was posted. Hearing the shuffling feet and spying the shadows surging toward him, the guard lowered his musket and pulled the trigger. The hammer clinked in a misfire. The guard fled into the fort, leaving the gate open behind him.

The rebels rushed through the gate and onto the parade ground. As their men pointed their muskets at the barracks, Allen and Arnold strode to Delaplace's headquarters. Allen pounded on the door and demanded surrender or else his troops would slaughter everyone. When Delaplace asked by what authority he issued his demand, Allen bellowed, "In the name of the Great Jehovah and the Continental Congress!"[4]

The startled commander quickly capitulated. It was a bloodless, decisive victory. After sunrise, Allen dispatched Seth Warner with fifty men north to take Crown Point, whose commander also swiftly gave up without a fight his nine troops. Those two strategically placed forts, their 201 cannons, and other munitions were now in rebel hands. Fort Ticonderoga's capture brought instant fame to the two American commanders. Ethan Allen's life peaked that early May 10 morning; setbacks and notoriety would dog his remaining years. For Benedict Arnold, it was the first daring act of a brilliant career that would end abruptly five years later with his name forever blackened, being synonymous with treason.

Arnold and Allen had no sooner captured Ticonderoga and Crown Point when they targeted a far more ambitious prize—Canada. Canada's conquest would sever British supplies to Indian war parties that might soon again bloody the frontier. Now dependent on American largesse, those Indian enemies or neutrals would be forced to convert to allies. American troops guarding that long frontier could march east to swell Washington's ranks against the British. American independence and expansion could be won in Canada.

Arnold was the first to reach Canada's frontier. He commandeered Philip Skene's schooner, armed it with four cannons, and rechristened it the *Liberty*. With thirty-five men aboard the *Liberty* and two bateaux, Arnold headed north on May 16. Two days later, they scrambled ashore and captured Fort St. John's thirteen-man garrison without firing a shot, and then surged on to board a sloop and take prisoner its seven-man crew along with nine bateaux. They packed the munitions and provisions aboard their flotilla and started back. That afternoon, they encountered Ethan Allen with 100 men in four bateaux and together they returned to Crown Point.

Learning of the attack, Montreal's commander Lt. Col. Dudley Templer quick-marched Maj. Charles Preston with 140 troops to St. John's, but the rebels were long gone. The Americans would return later that summer in far greater strength.

THE SECOND CONTINENTAL CONGRESS

When the delegates to the Second Continental Congress gathered on May 10, they were horrified to find the duty of running a war dumped in their laps. They accepted that duty reluctantly. Most still hoped for reconciliation and were sickened by news of the bloodshed at Lexington and Concord. Still, they could at least justify those actions as defensive. As the delegates mulled over what to do, they got word that patriots had committed naked aggression in capturing Forts Ticonderoga, Crown Point, and, briefly, St. John's. They split over the proper response, with some calling for returning the forts with an apology. After days of debate, the hardliners won. Congress voted on May 31 to defend the Lake Champlain frontier.[5]

Congress was now committed to war with Britain. That was easier resolved than done. The delegates somehow had to raise money, troops, and supplies; appoint generals to command the armies and diplomats to negotiate with Britain, scores of Indian tribes, and foreign countries; build, man, and arm a navy; provide overall strategic guidance; and organize a permanent union. They were not all novices at war. Many had served either in the field or as legislators during the French and Indian War. Nonetheless, fighting a war was burdensome enough. Rebelling against their mother country provoked varying surges of fear, regret, and exhilaration among the delegates.

The first step was to set up a high command, including a commanding general, four major generals, and eight brigadier generals. The choice of commander fell on the shoulders of the only delegate who attended in uniform. On June 16, Congress unanimously selected George Washington to command the Continental forces at Boston.[6] Then a forty-three-year-old veteran of the French and Indian War, Washington was lauded for his bravery, character, and military competence if not genius. The appointment made as much political as military sense. As a Virginian commanding the American army, Washington provided regional balance and helped stimulate nationalism. Before Washington left Philadelphia on June 23, he would get word of yet another devastating British defeat.

Amidst congressional debates and efforts, the bloodiest battle yet was fought. On May 25, Generals William Howe, Henry Clinton, and John Burgoyne had joined Gage in Boston. Howe would take operational command of British forces while Gage remained the Massachusetts governor and North American commander. Howe was eager to break the siege and disperse the rebels with a decisive attack. He planned a double envelopment of the American lines, with Howe himself leading the landing and assault on Dorchester Heights while Clinton commanded the landing at Charleston and swift march to capture Cambridge. Those forces would then roll up the American flanks and meet in the center. It was a good plan in theory. But Howe grossly underestimated American fighting abilities and sheer numbers, along with their spy network.

Word of the impending attack prompted Gen. Israel Putnum to send Col. William Prescott and 1,200 men to fortify Breed's Hill behind Charleston. The following morning, the British commanders were astonished to see that hill bristling with trenches and armed men. The four British generals hastily devised a plan to have the fleet bombard the hill and then land 2,300 troops ashore to sweep away the rebel remnants. The plan miscarried. The fleet's guns could not be elevated high enough to reach the hilltop. The troops marched straight up the steep grassy slope against the enemy trenches. The Americans repelled two assaults and withdrew before a third only after exhausting their ammunition.

The battle of Bunker Hill was a British disaster. The redcoats took the field but did nothing with it other than bury the heaps of dead. The losses were horrifying—226 killed and 828 wounded, nearly half of all British forces engaged, three times worse than the rebel casualties of 100 killed, 271 wounded, and 30 captured.[7] Once again ragtag rebel militia had defeated the pride of the British army. That electrifying news surged through the colonies, inspiring the belief that if Americans could repeatedly humble the redcoats around Boston, they could do it anywhere. Faced with this reality, surely the Crown would soon yield to America's just demands.

Upon reaching Cambridge, Washington immediately embarked on the Sisyphean labor of converting the mobs of armed men ringing Boston into the Continental army. The Army of Observation was well named. Without heavy cannons, all the Americans could do was hem in and watch the outnumbered British, who dared not risk another Bunker Hill by mounting another assault. The siege would last nine more dreary months before the British finally yielded. Meanwhile, the war ignited one distant frontier after another.

AMERICAN POLICY TOWARD THE INDIANS

Among the most vital of questions debated by Congress and every colonial assembly with an exposed frontier was what to do about the Indians. Should the tribes be enlisted as allies or merely encouraged to remain neutral? Either course, especially the first, would be costly. How could Indian neutrality or a much higher priced alliance be purchased?

Massachusetts was the first government to devise and implement an Indian policy. In early April, before fighting broke out, the assembly engaged in diplomacy with distant tribes. It sent envoys to negotiate with the Penobscot and Micmac to protect the Maine settlements. A Stockbridge Indian delegation journeyed to the Seven Tribes of Canada with a message explaining the American cause and requesting their sympathy. It engaged Samuel Kirkland, the missionary to the Oneida Indians, to "influence with them to join us in the defense of our rights." If he failed to "prevail with them to take an active part in this glorious cause . . . at least engage them to stand neutral, and not by any means to aid and assist our enemies." Kirkland circulated Massachusetts' message: "We think it our duty to inform you of our danger . . . we fear they will attempt to cut our throats, and if you should follow them to do that, there will nobody remain to keep them from you, we therefore earnestly desire you to whet your Hatchet, and be prepared with us to defend our liberties and lives."[8] After fighting broke out, the assembly recruited a company of Stockbridge Indians who joined the siege of Boston. General Gage would use the presence of those Stockbridge Indians in the American camp to justify his own Indian policy.

Congress established an Indian policy in two decisive steps. On July 1, it declared that the states were subordinate to Congress in Indian affairs. On July 12, it created Northern, Middle, and Southern Indian Departments patterned on those of Britain, appropriated funds, and appointed officials. The policy would be to keep the Indians neutral. Congress issued a message to the tribes explaining, "We don't wish you to take up the hatchet against the King's troops. We desire you to remain at home, and not join on either side, but keep the hatchet buried deep . . . we ask and desire you to love peace and maintain it, and to love and sympathise with us in our troubles; that the path may be kept open with all our people and yours, to pass and repass, without molestation."[9]

In June, Congress sent two agents, James Dean and Eleazar Wheelock, to the Seven Nations of the St. Lawrence valley to coax them into neutrality. They traveled largely unmolested among the tribes that summer and found sympathetic audiences everywhere. Many of those Indians were descendants of New England prisoners dragged back from a century and a half of previous wars. A half-dozen sons of prominent chiefs had studied at the Indian school that became Dartmouth College. The tribes traded eagerly with New England and New York. The American cultural and economic pull on the Seven Nations was strong. Adept diplomacy could cement those ties.

To that American pull, Canada's governor Guy Carleton added a shove. On May 24, Benedict Arnold and Ethan Allen sent a delegation of Stockbridge and Caughnawaga Indians led by Stockbridge chief and captain Abraham Nimham to curry favor with the Seven Nations. News of that brazen mission spread. A column of British troops captured the envoys. A military court convicted them of spying and condemned them to be hanged. Carleton approved the verdict. The Seven Nations fiercely protested; the Caughnawaga offered volunteers to be hanged instead of the delegation. Fearing a meltdown of relations, Carleton finally agreed to release the delegation with the warning never to return or they would be executed. But the diplomatic damage was severe. It might have been lasting had the Americans not ended up squandering it.

A succession of Seven Nation delegations headed south that summer to George Washington's headquarters at Boston, most to declare neutrality and a few like the Abenaki and Caughnawaga to actually seek enlistment in the American cause. Washington had no choice but to politely decline these offers. Congress had already decided on neutrality rather than alliance with the Indians. In doing so, Congress missed a golden opportunity, one that might have enabled the Americans to conquer and hold Canada later that year.[10]

BRITISH POLICY TOWARD THE INDIANS

As commander in chief for North America, it was Maj. Gen. Thomas Gage's duty to crush any rebellion. But he currently lacked enough regulars to do so. He was besieged in Boston by rebels three times more numerous than his own troops. He desperately needed auxiliaries. Loyalist militia certainly would help but were stranded behind enemy lines and thus dared not reveal their feelings let alone act for the Crown.

Thinking solely in military terms shorn of political or humanitarian concerns, Gage unblinkingly concluded that Indians should be unleashed against the rebels to divert the enemy's arms and aims. As early as April 21, he suggested to Gov. Guy Carleton that "a number of Canadians and Indians would be of great use on the Frontiers of the Province of Massachusetts Bay, under the command of a Judicious person."[11] As the situation grew more dismal, on May 10 Gage wrote Northern Indian Superintendent Guy Johnson "to concert with [Carleton] the Assembling of Indians and the proper means to be taken for the support of that part of the Country, and otherwise to act as His Majesty's Service shall require."[12] He issued similar instructions that same day to Col. John Caldwell at Fort Niagara.[13] As the southern colonies ignited with rebellion, Gage ordered Indian Superintendent John Stuart on September 12 to "hold a correspondence with the Indians, which I beg you may improve to the greatest advantage, and even when opportunity offers, to make them take Arms against His Majesty's Enemies, and to distress them all in their power, for no Terms is now to be kept with them . . . no time should be lost to distress a set of people so wantonly rebellious."[14]

Recognizing that his policy of hiring savages to murder British subjects would spark controversy, he sought explicit crown approval. On June 12, he wrote his friend and boss, War Secretary Barrington, arguing that "you may be tender of using Indians, but the Rebels have shewn us the Exemple, and brought all they could down upon us here."[15] That was a gross exaggeration. Though the war whoops and paint of that single Stockbridge Indian company in the rebel ranks might have sent chills down redcoat spines, they fought with European rather than native tactics. But Gage was eager for a precedent, and the Stockbridge company was all he could find.

After news of the fighting reached London, the question of what to do with the Indians arose naturally in the general policy debate. It was essential to isolate the rebels and avoid alienating the general population. To that end Whitehall's initial policy was to restrain rather than unleash the Indians. On July 5, Dartmouth sent Gage instructions simply to hold the Indians in "a state of affection and detachment to the King."[16]

But that policy would change as the news from America worsened coupled with the receipt of Gage's convincing arguments. The fiction that the rebels had first used Indians appealed to the government's hardliners, especially the king. On July 17, George III told Dartmouth that "as the rebels have got Indians to their assistance, we must make use of the same desperate weapons."[17] Dartmouth passed on the command to Gage, Johnson, and Carleton: "The unfortunate rebellion now raging . . . calls for every effort to suppress it . . . It is, therefore, His Majesty's pleasure that you do lose no time in taking such steps as may induce [the Indians] to take up the hatchet against His Majesty's rebellious subjects."[18]

Whitehall's decision was unambiguous. Yet that policy of wielding Indians to help crush the rebellion would not be implemented for another two years. For some reason, Dartmouth's letters never reached Gage, Johnson, or Carleton. By such whims, history shifts in ways unintended by its leaders.

THE NEW YORK FRONTIER
Few frontier regions were as bitterly split between patriots and loyalists as upper New York. The rich landowners Philip Schuyler and Guy Johnson headed the

patriot and loyalist cliques, respectively. That rivalry was as much about the differences between old and new wealth, Dutch and English ancestry, Hudson and Mohawk valley fiefs, and squabbles over divvying up the spoils of public office as it was about disputes with the mother country.

The Johnson clique was ascendant when the war broke out. After settling in the Mohawk valley in 1738, Sir William Johnson had steadily amassed an empire in land, tenants, trade, prestige, political office, influence with the Indians, and royal favors. His son Sir John and nephew Sir Guy inherited that empire when the patriarch died in 1774. The Johnson political machine controlled all the leading civil and military positions of Tryon County, which encompassed most of the Mohawk valley. Tentacles of Johnson power extended throughout upper New York, enabling John to beat Philip Schuyler in the 1774 New York assembly election. But from 1774 a shadow government emerged as patriots formed committees of safety in Albany, Schenectady, the Palatine District, and Tryon County; Schuyler was the most prominent patriot leader. Although the patriots and loyalists formed militias to back their positions with muskets, violence would not explode until the summer. Until then, each side used its institutions and interpretations of the law to undermine and check the other.[19]

The year opened with a feud between the loyalist and patriot factions over Indian policy. In the tense months that led to the gunfire at Lexington Green, Samuel Kirkland, a patriot and missionary to the Oneida, challenged Indian Superintendent Guy Johnson for influence over the Iroquois. Perhaps no American Indian agent during the Revolution would contribute more to the cause than Kirkland. When the war broke out, he was thirty-four and an expert on Iroquois language and culture. That lifelong study began when he was eleven and his father enrolled him in Eleazar Wheelock's Indian Charity School in Lebanon, Connecticut. It was there that Kirkland met the Mohawk Joseph Brant, who would later become his fiercest rival for native loyalties. Inspired by the Great Awakening that swept the colonies during his youth, Kirkland proselytized for two years among the Seneca and then among the Oneida with an unrelenting fervor that captured the hearts and minds of his congregation. Once he was so animated by "these important truths" that he "spoke for four hours without intermission. None appeared weary or scarce willing to disperse." Yet even then his efforts fell short in his mind of what he wanted to convey. He often rebuked himself "with the view of my own stupidity & insensitivity to the grand & all important prospects that lie before us . . . I feel as if I had done nothing . . . When light & truth begin to break & operate in the minds of these poor beknight'd Indian creatures, they need a most skilful hand."[20]

But throughout the early 1770s, Kirkland increasingly mingled pleas for American salvation from British oppression with spiritual salvation from an evil world. Reports that the missionary was mixing radical politics with religion worried and angered Guy Johnson. On February 14, he wrote Kirkland of complaints by Oneida sachem Conoghquieson that he not only had "been accused of meddling in matters of a political nature" but had violated his sacred mission as well when "a considerable number of infants have died without Baptism as you refused them this sacrament on account of the misconduct of their parents."[21]

These were serious charges, and Johnson asked Kirkland to journey to his mansion called Guy Park to explain them. Spurning Johnson's order to do so, Kirkland fired off a long, powerful letter exonerating himself through his own reasoned arguments and testimonials of three Oneida sachems. He defended as Reform Church policy the practice of not baptizing children whose parents had not themselves received holy water; besides, he added, baptism was no guarantee of salvation. He flatly denied charges that he ran a store that profited off his congregation or had ordered burned a letter from Guy Johnson to the Oneida. As for his "telling strange matters of the white people," the minister replied that he answered all questions from his flock, including those concerning the growing conflicts between the Crown and colonies. Johnson's challenge provoked Kirkland into redoubling his efforts to convince the Indians of British wrongs and American rights.[22] A lull between the two men followed that exchange as Johnson found himself facing serious charges.

The feud between Kirkland and Johnson was part of the larger struggle. A precarious power balance teetered in New York province and especially Tryon County. In January, New York's legislative assembly rejected by the slender margin of eleven to ten a motion to endorse the measures of the Continental Congress. In March, the Johnson clique tried to reinforce their position by getting Johnstown's grand jury to pass a resolution of loyalty to the Crown. That provoked the region's committees of public safety to demand loyalty oaths to Congress. Those Tories who refused suffered imprisonment and the seizure of their property. Some of the more prominent loyalists fled to Canada; most reluctantly raised their hands and mumbled oaths before well-armed patriots. The committee of public safety fired off letters to the Johnsons on various issues but did not yet dare to demand an oath from them. Although he could muster more than 300 militia, Guy Johnson was outgunned by the rebels. He hoped to even the odds through his Indian superintendent powers. On March 31, he wrote Canadian governor Guy Carleton for permission to mobilize the Indians against the malcontents. Carleton adamantly rejected the proposal.[23]

That precarious political standoff would soon shift with the dramatic news of Lexington and Concord. Tensions soared. In mid-May, Guy Johnson felt he was strong enough to assert the king's authority. He led his militia to confront about 300 patriots erecting a liberty pole in Caughnawaga and berated the crowd for its treasonous sentiments. When one Jacob Sammons protested, Johnson and several of his guards beat him senseless while his militia leveled their muskets and kept the mob at bay. Then on May 14, Johnson arrested Samuel Kirkland and ordered all missionaries to leave the Iroquois "until the difficulties between Britain and the Colonies are settled."[24]

The Palatine committee of public safety complained on May 18 to the Albany committee that Johnson not only had broken up their meeting, but also was defying Congress, mobilizing the Indians against the patriots, and fortifying

Johnson Hall with 150 of his militia. The Albany committee exchanged several letters with Johnson, politely but firmly inquiring whether the charges were true. Johnson denied all, most heatedly the accusation of stirring up the Indians: "Men of sense and character know that my office is of the highest importance to promote peace among the Six Nations and prevent their entering into any such dispute." But then he added ominously: "And all men must allow that if the Indians find their council fires disturbed and their Superintendent insulted, they will take a dreadful revenge."[25] Johnson's threat could hardly have been more clear. If the committee did not back off, he would launch his Indians against them.

The committee expressed its hope that Johnson would fairly present both sides of the dispute at an upcoming Indian council, disperse his guards, and stop interfering with public meetings. But worried whether Johnson could be trusted, the committee assigned five commissioners to negotiate directly with the tribes. On May 23, those commissioners met with Mohawk chief Little Abraham, who warned: "We shall support and defend our Superintendent and not see our council fire extinguished. We have no inclination or purpose of interfering in the dispute between Old England and Boston; the white people may settle their own quarrels . . . we shall never meddle in those matters or be the aggressors, if we are let alone." The commissioners replied: "We are extremely well satisfied to learn that you have no inclination or purpose to interfere in the dispute between Old England and America . . . They intend no hostilities against you, do you continue peaceable, and you need apprehend no danger."[26]

The standoff between the loyalists and patriots in the Mohawk valley finally ended on May 31, when Guy Johnson headed west to Canada with about 120 whites and 90 Mohawks, along with his pregnant wife and children. En route, Johnson convened a council at Fort Stanwix's ruin with 260 Oneidas and a mélange from Oquaga. But Johnson failed to rally them against the rebels. His earlier harrassment and then arrest and release of their beloved missionary Samuel Kirkland had alienated most of those Indians. He had better luck at Oswego, where he opened a council officially attended by 1,458 Indians in July. He asked for their continued loyalty and readiness to join him on the warpath when he called them. Then tragedy struck: on July 11, Johnson's wife died during childbirth. A grieving Johnson and his entourage of 220 whites and Indians left by sloop for Montreal that same day. Upon meeting the governor, Johnson once again implored him to loose the Indians against the rebels. Carleton firmly refused.[27]

Guy Johnson's departure weakened but did not eliminate the loyalists in the Mohawk valley. His cousin Sir John Johnson and his family remained holed up nervously at their mansion, Johnson Hall. Guy's desire to inflict Indian atrocities against the patriots was well known. It was assumed that Sir John shared that desire. At the very least, he had to be watched like a hawk and arrested should he commit even the hint of a crime. On July 15, General Schuyler wrote the Albany committee asking that they inform him "the Moment you get an intelligence from Tryon County and inform me what Part Sir John Johnson takes or means to take should the Savages attack us as is apprehended."[28]

Violence almost exploded that month when Tory sheriff Alexander White arrested patriot John Fonda of Caughnawaga. A hundred sympathizers marched on the jail. Shots were fired; no one was hit. The patriot crowd swelled to nearly 600 as word spread. With the patriots on their heels, White and his men somehow managed to escape to Johnson Hall around which Sir John massed about 400 of his own militia. The patriots demanded that Johnson hand over White or face attack. White magically slipped through again, this time bound for Canada. But his luck ran out; he was caught near Fort Ticonderoga. The two enemy mobs dispersed but the incident only worsened their mutual hatreds.

Despite Guy Johnson's entreaties, the Iroquois kept off the warpath. The American rebellion worried the Iroquois as it did most other Indians. Not only were they ignorant of the revolt's causes, but they also feared being trampled by rampaging enemy armies. The Oneida expressed their own dismay in a circular letter to the New England governors: "Brothers! . . . We cannot intermeddle in this dispute between two brothers. The quarrel seems to be unnatural; you are two brothers of one blood. We are unwilling to join either side."[29] The Oneida led the Iroquois into neutrality. From June 28 to July 2, Oneida and Tuscarora envoys counciled with Tryon, Albany, and Schenectady committees of safety at the German Flats. Those Indians promised friendship, intelligence, and the blockade of any British advance through Fort Stanwix's ruins.[30] The chiefs hurried back to the Onondaga council, where in July they forged an Iroquois policy not only to embrace a policy of neutrality for themselves, but also to insist that the Ohio valley tribes follow. Wyandot and Shawnee envoys present at Onondaga carried that message back to the villages in their regions.

The Six Nations elaborated this policy when 389 members met with congressional commissioners Philip Schuyler, Oliver Wolcott, Turbutt Francis, and Volkert Douw at German Flats from August 14 through 16. That meeting was the prelude to a larger council at Albany from August 23 to September 2 attended by over 500 Iroquois. Schuyler opened the talks by thanking the Iroquois for rekindling the ancient council fire at Albany that was extinguished when Sir William Johnson moved it to his home. He then explained that the war "is a family quarrel between us and Old England. You Indians are not concerned in it. We don't wish you to take up the hatchet against the King's troops. We desire you to remain at home and not join on either side." The chiefs reiterated their neutrality pledge but demanded munitions, blacksmiths, the expulsion of squatters, and the promise of the Americans to not traverse their country against the British. The commissioners agreed to all but the last demand.[31]

THE NORTHWEST FRONTIER

A similar tug-of-war between the British and Americans broke out for the hearts, minds, and potentially the arms of the Ohio valley and upper Great Lake Indians that summer. Both sides sought neutrality and understanding from the tribes. Congress and the colonies were united on that policy. Carleton and Gage were split, but the governor's view prevailed over the general's.

The first major British council opened in June at Detroit among Capt. Richard Lernoult and chiefs of the four local tribes—Huron, Potawatomi, Chippewa, and Ottawa. Lernoult warned those Indians that the Americans were determined to first overthrow British rule and then drive off the Indians, but he obeyed Carleton's order to refrain from presenting them the war hatchet and instead simply elicited a pledge to join the king's forces when requested. When the council ended, Lernoult sent runners to seventeen tribes with wampum belts conveying his message. He then organized Detroit's inhabitants into militia companies.

Elsewhere, as Americans fought British, Indians fought Indians. At Fort Michilimackinac Capt. C. Arent de Peyster was able to end a war between the Chippewa and Sioux that had raged sporadically for decades. He did so by persuading the tribes to accept the Mississippi River as their boundary. With peace between them, those tribes were now available as potential allies against the Americans.[32]

But British diplomacy failed to end wars lower down the Mississippi and Wabash valleys. On June 2, 145 Sauk and Fox warriors swarmed through Kaskaskia and burned the Illinois village whose inhabitants had fled. Capt. Hugh Lord and his small garrison at Fort Gage refused to take sides. The raiders caught up to the Illinois a few days later, killed forty-four and captured six others, at a loss of six dead and six wounded. A similar war had sputtered for years between Wabash tribes and the Chickasaw and Cherokee. During the first half of 1775, seven parties of Miami, Wea, Mascouten, Kickapoo, and Potawatomi headed south. At least two of these turned their weapons on whites. Chief Pacane and his Kickapoo ambushed four traders and killed all but one, who escaped. A Wea party killed two Canadians and their slave. After a lull in late summer and early autumn, the war resumed as five war parties of twenty to fifty men, each composed of a mélange of Potawatomi, Mascouten, Kickapoo, and Piankeshaw, headed south against the Chickasaw and Cherokee from October through December.[33]

In the upper Mississippi valley, the threat to British rule came from the Spanish rather than the Americans. At St. Louis Lt. Gov. Pedro Piernas, followed by Francisco Cruzat when he took over in 1775, implemented a policy of enticing Indian migrants and the fur trade west of the Mississippi. The policy was successful. Small bands of Delaware, Shawnee, and Kickapoo had recently settled in the region, and the fur trade in upper Louisiana soared in value. The total amount of furs gathered in upper Louisiana reached 14,155 packs in 1775, four times larger than the 3,545 packs during the two previous years together.[34]

The upper Ohio valley Indians posed no immediate threat to the Americans. Their defeat in Dunmore's war cowed them for now as they mourned their dead, burnt villages, and destroyed crops. They would have been reluctant to raise their scalping knives even if British officials had asked. But that official call would not come for another three years. Until then, they nursed their hatreds while only a few sought vengeance. A British envoy to the Shawnee received this blunt reply to his appeal: "God gave us the Earth and everything that is on it . . . the English and Virginia brothers are killing our deer and destroying our trees and you call us fools but we think you are fools. We . . . hope you will not come further on our Land but let us live in friendship as long as we live."[35]

That year the rebellion provoked a struggle for control that included the British garrisons, the Virginia and Pennsylvania rebels, loyalists, and Virginia governor John Murray Dunmore, who was determined at once to intimidate any rebels and advance his province's claims to the Ohio valley against those of Pennsylvania. On April 20, he ordered gunpowder stored at the magazine in Williamsburg to be secreted aboard a British warship anchored in the James River. The patriots got wind of Dunmore's plot. Patrick Henry rallied the Hanover County militia and marched on Williamsburg. Dunmore defused the crisis by agreeing to pay for the powder. But he unwittingly committed an act with frightful symbolism for those living along the frontier. Fearing for his life, he converted the Shawnee hostages that were supposed to guarantee the peace into his personal bodyguard. That fall, Dunmore would take an even more decisive step when he sought to "raise such a force from among Indians, Negroes, and other persons as would soon reduce the refractory people of this colony to obedience."[36] Rumors of Dunmore's intentions spread swiftly.

Though the Americans in the upper Ohio valley recognized that an Indian war was unlikely for now, they nonetheless prepared for that possibility. Learning of Lexington and Concord, patriots in Virginia's West Augusta County gathered at Pittsburgh and formed a committee of safety on May 16. They drafted and sent to Congress a petition expressing their fears of an Indian war provoked by Governor Dunmore. That same day, those loyal to Pennsylvania's Westmoreland County convened their own committee of correspondence at Hannastown thirty miles east of Pittsburgh. Congress referred the petition to the Virginia and Pennsylvania delegates. After conferring with their respective state assemblies, those delegates jointly agreed to send commissioners to an Indian council at Pittsburgh in September.

The loyalists would convene their own Indian council at Pittsburgh well before the Americans. Many loyalists populated the Ohio valley, but nearly all kept a low profile in the flush of patriot enthusiasm following the outbreak of fighting. Alexander McKee remained the region's Indian agent but received no instructions from Johnson or Gage. He cooperated with local officials from all factions—Virginian, Pennsylvanian, congressional, and loyalist. The region's most overt Tory was John Connolly, Dunmore's agent at Pittsburgh. The Hannastown militia arrested him on June 19, the day before he was to preside over an Indian council. But the Pennsylvanians bowed to arguments that the arrest might provoke the Indians and freed him a few days later.

Scrutinized by patriots, Connolly opened the council on June 29 with the Seneca Indians led by Kayashuta and the Delaware Indians by White Eyes and Killbuck; the Mingo predictably spurned the meeting; the Shawnee arrived late. The council was disrupted on July 16: when "Cornstalk, Nimwha, Wryneck, Blue

Jacket, Silver Heels, and about fifteen other Shawanese arrived . . . immediately got drunk and Continued in that fashion for two days."[37] On July 18, those Indians, most likely with pounding hangovers, joined the others.

Throughout the talks, Connolly implored the chiefs "to put an End to all differences between your People and ours so effectually that your Children and ours may live in the Strictest friendship till the Sun Shall shine no more or the Waters run in the Ohio."[38] Although a lack of gifts undercut his diplomacy, all the chiefs present promised to remain neutral. Naturally they would do so, since in most Indian councils Connolly was preaching to the converted. The chiefs were but dimly aware of the fighting that had broken out between some Americans and the Great Father. When White Eyes informed Virginian commissioner James Woods that he wanted to accompany Connolly to met the governor in Williamsburg, the agent felt "the Necessity of Acquainting him with the disputes subsisting between Lord Dunmore and the People of Virginia." Practicing the timeless strategy of playing off opponents against each other, the Delaware declared their loyalty to the king on July 6. Connolly hoped to gain other pledges. As a goodwill gesture, he released the Mingo hostages, although with the secret message to remain true to the king. In between councils with the Indians, Connolly confided a plan with loyalists for a future revolt against the rebels. These machinations went unobserved by the patriots. Woods concluded of Connolly that even "his most inveterate Enemies all agree that he conducted this Affair in the Most Open and Candid Manner."[39] On July 25, Connolly set off for Williamsburg accompanied by White Eyes, Cornstalk, and other chiefs.

On July 18, Woods departed with Simon Girty for the Ohio tribes to invite them all to the council in September. That mission was fraught with danger. Only a few of the villages were represented at the July council. The rest were suspicious and a few outright hostile. After only two days on the trail, Woods got word from a trader, Garret Pendergrass, that British agent Duperon Baby had just concluded a council at the Sandusky Wyandot village, where he instilled them with the fear "that the White People intended to strike them very soon . . . to drive us off and to take our lands that we must be constantly on our Guard and not to give any Credit to whatever you said as you were a people not to be depended upon."[40]

At one Mingo town Woods discovered "the Indians were very angry Many of them Painted themselves black we Encamped near the Town . . . at night one of the Indians came and Stamped upon my head as I lay a Sleep waked and saw several Indians with Knives and Tomahawks a Squaw informed us privately that they intended to kill us advised us to hide ourselves in the Woods which we did."[41] Nonplussed, Woods entered the village the next morning for a council and endured a barrage of grievances and taunts. But he was allowed to proceed unharmed after inviting them to the council. At Pluggy's Town, Wood found "all the Indians drunk and very troublesome left a String of Wampum and Speech for Pluggy purchased some dried Meat from an Indian and then set off."[42] In another village he was similarly ignored as the Indians were "Conjuring the whole night during which they kept up a Constant howling like Wolves till day light."[43] He was received in some villages with puzzlement over the dispute with Britain and concern over which side they should take. Woods always reassured them "that we did not stand in need of or desire any Assistance from them or any other Nation but that we wished them to Continue in peace and friendliness with us by Observing a Strict neutrality as we had not the least doubt that all differences between ourselves would be soon accommodated." But he emphasized "the great Unanimity among the Americans and that they were now become so strong as not to fear any power on the face of the earth."[44]

He finally returned to Fort Pitt on August 11, after having completed a circular trek linking the clusters of villages along the Muskingum, Tuscaroras, and Scioto Rivers. After a mere day's rest, he hurried to Virginia with a full report of his mission. In tag-team diplomacy, Congress's Indian agent Richard Butler, Seneca chief Kayashuta, several aides, and gift-laden packhorses departed Pittsburgh on August 22 to carry the same message to the region's council fires. That mission returned safely on September 20.[45]

Getting word of the two rebel missions, Detroit commander Capt. Richard Lernoult called the four local tribes to council and warned them not to aid the Americans. Then to the Ohio tribes he sent a message explaining that Americans "were a bad people; that by the indulgence of their Protector they had grown a numerous and saucy people . . . they . . . propose to cut off the few regulars in this country, and then you Indians, and have all America to themselves . . . which if [you] refuse, you will all be massacred."[46] This was Britain's essential argument to the Indians, repeated at countless council fires during the American Revolution and beyond until 1815.

The tribes split between the American and British lures. The Detroit tribes, most Wyandot, Mingo, and the Kispoki, Pekowi, and Calaka Shawnee spurned the American invitation while the Delaware, Mekoce Shawnee, and Half King's Wyandot accepted the invitation to council.

Not all the Americans with a direct stake in the proceedings would be represented either. On September 11, Capt. John Neville and 100 militia marched into abandoned Fort Dunmore, renamed it Fort Pitt, and claimed it and all that region's lands for the state of Virginia. The Virginians then arrested or chased off anyone who claimed to represent Pennsylvania's authority. James Wilson, Lewis Morris, and Thomas Walker represented Congress, while Thomas Walker (again), John Walker, James Wood, Andrew Lewis, and Adam Stephen fronted Virginia. Simon Girty and John Montour interpreted. The war would drag those two interpreters in very different directions.

Although the council was supposed to open on September 10, the first Indians did not arrive until September 15. The Americans delayed opening the council until most of those who promised to attend did so. Groups large and small straggled in over the next two weeks. The Americans counciled and feasted with each delegation as it appeared. When the council officially began on October 7, more than 400 Indians were present, with about 100 Delaware under head chief White Eyes, accompanied by Wolf clan chiefs Captain Pipe and Custalog, and Turkey clan chief Captain Johnny; 70 Munsee; 50 Allegheny Seneca led by Kayashuta, White Mingo, and Flying Crow; 55 Shawnee led by Chiefs Cornstalk, Nimwha, White Fish, and Half King; and 10 Wyandot.[47]

The council met for the next two weeks. White Eyes took the lead in trying to persuade the other tribes, especially the Wyandot, to bury their hatchets. That message was not surprising; the Delaware had long been peace proponents. But then White Eyes dropped a bombshell on the council. He issued a declaration of Delaware independence from the Iroquois: "The petticoat I have thrown away, and have put on my proper dress!—the corn hoe and pounder I have exchanged for these fire arms and I declare I am a man!"[48]

To this bold assertion, Kayashuta could only fume in silence until it was his turn to speak. When he arose, Kayashuta angrily denounced White Eyes' declaration and insisted that the Delaware would remain subordinate. The Americans could not sidestep this awkward conflict. Whatever they did would alienate one or both tribes. Although the Americans did not openly endorse the Delaware declaration, they implicitly did so by not rejecting it. This disillusioned Kayashuta to the point where he would eventually turn against the Americans and embrace the British.

Instead, the Americans tried to steer the council back to the central concern— peace. In their speeches, the Americans mingled repeated calls on the Indians to remain neutral with the message that "the thirteen great colonies" had "at least One Million of Fighting Men, are now firmly United and Inseparably bound together by one lasting Chain of friendship, that we are no more to be Considered as Distinct Nations, but as one great and Strong Man, who if Molested in any one of his Members, will not fail to Exert the Combined force of his whole Body to Punish the Offender."[49]

Each chief stood and recited his tribe's ever lengthening list of grievances against the squatters, cheaters, poachers, and murderers infiltrating Indian lands. Embittered as they might have been, the chiefs still preferred to bury the hatchet. Dummore's war had bloodied those tribes that joined and intimidated all but the Mingo. Still, there were limits to what the chiefs were prepared to concede. Cornstalk and Half King denied that they retained any prisoners, horses, and slaves, and rejected the demand that they seal the peace by handing over hostages. The Americans were adamant.

Kayashuta broke the impasse by declaring that he would lead an Indian delegation to investigate and return any lingering prisoners or property, but in return the Americans must drop their demand for hostages. Both sides grudgingly accepted the compromise. More importantly, the Indians agreed to accept the Ohio River as the boundary between them. These tenets were codified when the envoys signed the Treaty of Pittsburgh on October 21. The commissioners then distributed 2,000 pounds sterling worth of gifts.

The Treaty of Pittsburgh advanced American interests. The frontier settlers could disgorge some of its best riflemen to join the siege of Boston, confident that an Indian onslaught would not explode against the families and neighbors they left behind. But the treaty encouraged a far larger tide of humanity to surge west. With the Ohio boundary confirmed, thousands of pioneers crossed the Appalachians during the American Revolution to escape the fighting and carve farms, hamlets, and forts from rich bottomland in Kentucky and Tennessee. Of course, many discovered to their horror that they had jumped from the proverbial frying pan into the fire. The hope that they would only have to struggle with each other rather than hostile Indians for land titles was soon stolen, along with hundreds of lives and vast wealth.

Like virtually all treaties with the Indians, that of Pittsburgh produced a shaky truce rather than lasting peace. The treaty failed to dampen the smoldering Indian hatreds toward the Americans. After receiving reports of the council and Indian sentiments, newly arrived Lt. Gov. Henry Hamilton at Detroit concluded that "any Peace between the people and any of the savage nations is liable to frequent interruptions . . . The [Americans] are haughty Violent and bloody, the savages have a high opinion of them as Warriors, but are jealous of their encroachments, and very suspicious of their faith in treaties . . . In the inroads of the [Americans] upon the savages, the former have plundered, burnt, and murdered without mercy."[50] That was a partly accurate description. The man who the Americans would dub the "hair buyer" would soon bloody Britain's hands in that frontier war.

The eruption of war did not deter those greedy for land. The Grand Ohio Company still awaited the issue of its patent for the new colony of Indiana. In 1775, the partners' patience finally broke. They dispatched William Trent back to Philadelphia from London with instructions that the title to lands occupied by squatters be sold to them at a price of fifty Spanish dollars for 400 acres. Politics stymied Trent. Virginia and Pennsylvania had not relinquished their conflicting claims to that same territory. After all, Virginia had just fought Dunmore's war with the Indians to defend its stake there. Those governments protested and declared invalid any such Grand Ohio Company sales.

That same year, William Murray, who had helped found the Illinois Company, founded yet another venture, the Wabash Company, to buy lands along that river from Piankashaw chief Old Tobacco. The Illinois and Wabash Companies joined to form the United Illinois and Wabash Land Company, and dispatched Louis Viviat to buy land. On October 17, Viviat purchased 37,497,000 acres on the lower Wabash River from the Piankashaw chiefs Old Tobacco and Le Grand Coete, and eleven other headmen at Vincennes. Viviat then hurried to Kaskaskia to register the deed.

No group of speculators seemingly advanced their ambitions as boldly that year as the Transylvania Company, the new name for the Louisa Company, which was formed on August 27, 1774. Its president, Judge Richard Henderson, met with 1,000 Cherokee led by Attakullakulla (Little Carpenter), Oconostota, and Savanukah (Raven) at Sycamore Shoals on the Watauga River on March 1. Initially the chiefs offered Henderson all lands between the Kentucky and Kanawha Rivers. Henderson pointed out that the Cherokee had already sold that land to Virginia with the 1770 Lochaber treaty. He countered by offering to buy all lands between the Kentucky and Cumberland Rivers, with a "path" or right of passage between the Holston River and Cumberland Mountains. The offer split the Cherokee. On March 17, after weeks of wrangling, Little Carpenter and most of the chiefs sold title to that land in return for what Henderson claimed was 10,000 pounds sterling worth of goods. His son Tsi'yugusi'ny, or Dragging Canoe, vehemently protested the sale and stalked away from the council with his followers. The settlers would not hear the last of him. Dragging Canoe and his people were not the only protesters. Upon learning of Henderson's deal, squatters in the region feared for their plots. The subsequent conflicts between new and old squatters would last for decades.

Having secured his land, Henderson did not hesitate to exploit it. On March 20, 1775, he sent Daniel Boone and thirty axmen to carve a road from Long Island on the Holston over the Cumberland Gap to the Kentucky River. They cut a wagon road only as far as Powell's Valley. From there they blazed a trail that often zigzagged from one buffalo trace to the next. Weeks of punishing labor bedeviled the road builders. On the night of March 25, a war party of Pekowi Shawnee and Cherokee crept up on the camp and opened fire. Shots killed Capt. William Twitty and his slave and wounded Felix Walker. Two nights later, that same war party killed two men from a different group led by Samuel Tate. On April 20, the trailblazers reached the Kentucky River, where they began clearing land and erecting cabins for the settlement named Boonesborough.

To attract settlers, Henderson offered 100 acres of land for twenty shillings if the farmer could raise a corn crop on his claim before September 1. A couple of weeks after Boone set out, Henderson followed at the head of about sixty settlers and slaves, forty packhorses, a cattle herd, and several wagons. Upon arriving at what would become Boonesborough, Henderson organized a lottery for plots. The men then dispersed to clear their land while the proposed stockade languished. After burning, clearing, and sowing a patch, most of the men then scattered to hunt. A score of fainthearts headed back to the settlements.[51]

Other settlements sprouted in Kentucky that year. A few weeks before Boonesborough arose, a party led by James Harrod founded Harrodsburg. In May, John Floyd led thirty men to erect St. Asaph's or Logan's Fort on the Dick's River. A dispute between Thomas Slaughter and Harrod caused the latter to split off with his followers and found Boiling Spring, six miles south. About 300 settlers altogether reached Kentucky that spring. They came from different states with different claims to the territory. Virginians dominated Harrodsburg and St. Asaph's, North Carolinians Boonesborough, and Monongahela men Boiling Spring. Tensions rose among the settlements.

To resolve the overlapping land claims, Henderson called for a convention of delegates from all four settlements. They met on May 23 beneath the Great Elm Tree before Boonesborough's unfinished stockade. The stakes were high. If Virginia's authority prevailed, homesteaders could get their land for free. If the Sycamore Shoals treaty was valid, then all land sales filtered through Henderson's hands. They discovered much common ground on many issues, agreeing to form their own government, which would collect taxes of two shillings per 100 acres, form a militia, create a court system that would punish criminals and collect debts, improve the breed of horses, and regulate hunting. It was an extraordinary session. But the delegates deadlocked over the most important question: what ultimate authority should prevail? Whatever elation they felt dissipated on May 29 when the disturbing and puzzling news arrived of the battles of Lexington and Concord. Few could foresee how it might eventually shape their own fates.

The legitimacy of Henderson's claim was increasingly challenged, with George Rogers Clark spearheading the movement against him. During a June 6 meeting at Harrodsburg, Clark and the land jobber and lawyer Gabriel Jones were elected as delegates to Williamsburg to present a petition critical of Henderson and another requesting the creation of a separate Virginia county for Kentucky known as West Fincastle County. Henderson countered by convening a meeting of the Transylvania Company at Boonesborough in September, when they called for an independent colony. But he lost support when he and his partners doubled the land price, while selling land at a discount to their cronies. Ever more Boonesborough settlers saw Virginian government as potentially less meddlesome and exploitative than rule by the Transylvania Company.

Clark and Jones reached Williamsburg on October 8 and presented their petitions to Virginia's assembly. A few days later, Henderson appeared to plead his case. The legislators decided on December 7, when they passed a law abolishing Fincastle County, which spread over Virginia's southwestern frontier, and split it into three new counties: Montgomery, Washington, and Kentucky.

With his bid to own Kentucky, Henderson hurried to Philadelphia to make the Transylvania Company's case before the Continental Congress. Congress rejected the bid and told Henderson to assert the legality of his petition before the governments of North Carolina and Virginia, which themselves claimed the territories that would become Tennessee and Kentucky. North Carolina joined Virginia in condemning as illegal Henderson's Treaty of Sycamore Shoals and all claims that followed. Settlers there, including Transylvania Company partners, would have to file claim with the appropriate colonial government.

The excitement about Kentucky puzzled those who had never been there. To Col. William Preston at Fincastle, the preacher John Brown wondered: "What a Buzzel is amongst People about Kentuck? to hear people speak of it one Would think it was a new found Paradise."[52]

Many of those who reached that promised land would share that skepticism. Hundreds of those who arrived during the war fled or were killed or captured. The year in Kentucky ended in violence. On December 23, two Wyandot and two Shawnee led by Mingo chief Pluggy's son, whose name strangely goes unrecorded despite his consistent prowess, killed one boy and captured another near Boonesborough.[53]

Unbeknownst then to the settlers along the upper Ohio valley and in Kentucky, a shadow descended on the region and would eventually haunt them. Henry

Hamilton is notorious in popular American history as the "hair buyer" who financed the slaughter of hundreds of pioneers. Is that condemnation justified? It is certainly no more appropriate for Hamilton than any other frontier commander. When a war party strode into Detroit with scalps and prisoners, he would give them gifts, at times in exchange, at times in reward. Yet Hamilton was one of the most fervent proponents of wielding Indians against the frontier. Shortly after reaching Detroit on November 9, he proposed to Carleton that he do just that. The appalled governor bluntly rejected the proposal. Hamilton reluctantly complied. For now his immediate challenge was not to dampen too much the enthusiasm of those Indians who implored him to equip war parties to stalk the American frontier.

THE CONNOLLY CONSPIRACY

When John Connolly departed Pittsburgh on July 25, most settlers must have sighed with relief, but they had not heard the last of him. The doctor's notoriety would soon spread through the colonies. Connolly reached Dunmore aboard the HMS *Royal William*, anchored off Portsmouth around August 8, and eagerly told the governor his plan. To the governor exiled by rebels, the scheme seemed as plausible as it was bold. Connolly envisioned trekking to Detroit, raising a force of regulars and volunteers from the western posts and Indians, and marching on Forts Fincastle and Pitt. After capturing and securing them with some of his force, he would cut across with the rest of his men to Alexandria, where they would rendezvous with Dunmore and a squadron of warships on April 20, 1776. What happened then, of course, depended on the fortunes of war there and elsewhere.

Dunmore bought this fantastic scheme and sent Connolly by frigate to Boston. Upon his arrival on September 6, he was ushered before the commander in chief. With his army besieged by rebels, Gage was as susceptible as Dunmore to any scheme that promised victory. He issued Connolly appropriate requisition powers and a major's commission, and dispatched letters to Carleton, the post commanders, and Indian agent Alexander McKee at Pittsburgh ordering them to cooperate. Word of an American invasion of Canada, however, forced a change in the plan. With the St. Lawrence route presumably severed, Connolly would return to Dunmore and attempt to reach Detroit via the upper Ohio valley. Connolly's seemingly impossible mission had become more so.

Reaching Dunmore on October 12, Connolly hoped to set forth immediately, but a severe sickness locked him in bed for weeks. It was not until November 13 that he and three companions set sail up Chesapeake Bay on the first leg of a long early winter journey to Detroit. They never made it. A servant betrayed Connolly's plan. American officials nabbed the conspirators five miles from Hagerstown on November 20. A search revealed Connolly's written plan. The conspirators would languish in jail until their exchange in 1780.

Such was the ignominious but likely end to Connolly's fantastic caper. It had no chance, at least given the timetable and skimpy numbers of troops and supplies available. But by highlighting a potential threat to the frontier, it aided the patriot rather than loyalist cause. For the war's duration, Congress would remain alert to attacks on the western settlements despite being hard-pressed by British campaigns rampaging through regions of the eastern seaboard.[54]

THE SOUTHEAST FRONTIER

As elsewhere, news of the rebellion split the Carolinas and Georgia between patriots, loyalists, and fence-sitters. The congressional call to form associations prompted the loyalists to create counterassociations. While the patriots swiftly secured most of the eastern seaboard towns and surrounding countryside, the frontier was up for grabs but was so politically fluid that neither side could long grasp it. With muskets ready, opposing bands of armed men eyeballed each other, exchanged warnings, and negotiated. Those that fielded the most muskets usually prevailed, forcing the others to disperse or sign some loyalty oath to Congress or Crown. But in many districts that shift in allegiance was fleeting. The other side would rally even more men and overrun the area for a while. Astonishingly, violence this year was rare. Aside from the notorious rebel torture of Thomas Brown, no one was seriously hurt.

Both sides sought the Indians as allies to be held ready should war engulf the region. The Crown's Southern Department deputies and Congress's newly appointed agents journeyed among the villages, convening councils, dispensing presents, and humbly requesting friendship. The chiefs complained of the trickle of gifts that year from both sides and maintained their neutrality for now.

Meanwhile, the colonial governments dissolved as provisional governments formed in their wakes. In June 1775, Gov. William Campbell arrived to rule South Carolina. He would briefly preside over the worsening chaos before fleeing aboard a British warship. North Carolina governor Josiah Martin and Georgia governor James Wright also escaped into exile.

Southern Indian Superintendent John Stuart would soon follow. Rumors swirled that the British were going to use the Indians against the rebels. The patriot leaders were determined to hold Stuart hostage to ensure peace on the frontier. Henry Laurens and the committee of intelligence warned Stuart that his Charles Town home was valued at 20,000 pounds sterling and would serve as "a Security for the good behaviour of the Indians in the Southern Department."[55] But Stuart slipped their grasp, sneaking from Savannah by ship on June 20. Learning of his flight, Captain Joyner, John Barnwell, and eighty others galloped to the Savannah River mouth, but the ship glided past beyond musket shot. Stuart safely reached St. Augustine a few days later. His wife and daughter, however, remained under house arrest in Charles Town.

Stuart's flight worsened fears that he would provoke the Indians against the frontier settlers and slaves against their masters. Stuart complained that the rebels "endeavored to blacken my Character & render me obnoxious to the people; giving out that my having called down the Indians was proved before the Congress, that great Quantities of Arms and Ammunition were shipped for me to arm the Negroes and Indians that it was now discovered that I had sold fort Loudoun and was the Instrument of getting the Garrison Massacred" during the 1760 Cherokee war.[56] But Stuart was quite willing to realize that dread when he boasted that "the Indians were very well disposed, and Mr. Cameron particularly had acquainted me that he could lead the Cherokees if necessary."[57] To Dartmouth he complained that the rebels had stolen gunpowder of which he had "intended sending a large supply to all my Deputies to keep up their Influence and weight when there may be great Occasion for an Exertion of them."[58]

Rebel leaders feared Stuart's flight was the prelude to an Indian war. On June 26, the South Carolina council of safety dispatched Andrew Williamson to seek out Cherokee agent Alexander Cameron, determine his intentions, and entice him to the patriot cause, with money if need be. Disdaining the bribe, Cameron denied any budding conspiracy with the Indians. Williamson warned him to either leave the region or remain at his peril.

Meanwhile, the rebels were sending their own diplomatic missions to the Indians. In July, South Carolina's government appointed and dispatched Commissioners George Galphin, LeRoy Hammond, and David Zubly to the Creek Indians, and Edward Wilkinson, Andrew Williamson, and John Bowie to the Cherokee. Of these men, Galphin was the most experienced in Indian affairs. Much like Sir William Johnson with the Mohawk Indians, Galphin had traded with them since the 1740s, married a Creek woman with whom he fathered several children, and made his home at Silver Bluff into a trading and council center.

In the south, no region was more fiercely contested that year than the Ninety-Sixth District of South Carolina's frontier. Most of the inhabitants either enthusiastically or reluctantly supported the Crown. On July 13, loyalist colonel Thomas Fletchal, assisted by Maj. Joseph Robinson and Captains Robert and Joseph Cunningham, mustered the militia and dared anyone to join the local rebel association if he wished. Not surprisingly, no one publicly took the dare. Robinson then presented a petition of loyalty to Governor Campbell that the militia to a man endorsed.

Patriot leader Maj. James Mayson tried to pull off a coup in that same district. In July, he led the Carolina rangers to seize munitions stored at Fort Charlotte and then holed up at Fort Ninety-Six. Major Robinson, the Cunningham brothers, and 200 loyalists pursued, surrounded Fort Ninety-Six, and forced Mayson to surrender.

Rebel forces elsewhere were more successful. In late July, they seized at Savannah a ship carrying gunpowder and other gifts bound for the Indians. The patriots confiscated and split most of the spoils between the Georgia and South Carolina militias. They delivered the rest of the shipment to the Indians, saying the gifts flowed from the generosity of the new state governments and Congress.

Having consolidated their rule on the seaboard, the patriots launched a diplomatic offensive backed by force to win the frontier. On August 2, Charles Town's council of safety dispatched William Drayton, Presbyterian minister William Tennett, and Baptist minister Oliver Hart to Augusta to mobilize the frontier people. Drayton mustered 120 Carolinians, 84 Georgians, and four cannons, and marched from Snow Hill to Ninety-Six commanded by Capt. Moses Kirkland. Learning of Drayton's advance, the loyalists dispersed and Kirkland fled to St. Augustine.

Drayton then marched on Fletchal, whose men also scattered. On September 16, Drayton persuaded Fletchal to sign an oath in which he promised not to aid the British or resist Congress. Despite all this, the patriot hold on the region was fleeting.

That nonviolent campaign was marred when Thomas Graham's militia beat, tarred, and feathered outspoken loyalist Thomas Brown at Augusta. Two of Brown's toes were burned off, and he suffered a concussion that would plague him with headaches for the rest of his life. Rather than intimidate him, that atrocity enraged him with a desire for vengeance that combined with charisma and military skills to make him the most feared and successful loyalist leader on the southern frontier. Upon his release, Brown made his way to St. Augustine.

Drayton returned to Charles Town, leaving 500 militia at Fort Ninety-Six commanded by Majors James Mayson and Andrew Williamson. In late November, Patrick Cunningham and Maj. Joseph Robinson rallied 2,000 loyalists and marched on Ninety-Six. Once again negotiations rather than gunfire ensued. Under the Treaty of Ninety-Six on November 22, the rebels were allowed to go home while the loyalists would withdraw beyond the Saluda River. Not long after the loyalists departed, the rebels broke the treaty's spirit if not letter by harassing lingering Crown sympathizers.

Though the colony of East Florida was a refuge for loyalists, for now it presented no threat to its rebellious neighbor Georgia. A skeleton force defended East Florida. Only a score of Royal Artillerymen and 122 troops of the 14th Regiment remained after 160 men were shipped north in July and September to reinforce Dunmore at Portsmouth. In December, three companies of the 16th Regiment disembarked at St. Augustine. Supporting the regulars were several hundred ill-trained and motivated militia.[59]

Germain and Gage saw East Florida as a secure base for eventually launching an offensive against the rebellious colonies northward. The British could substitute Indians for their dearth of regulars in the region. Most British minds met over the Indian role in crushing the rebellion. Nearly all the officials at St. Augustine had already reached that same conclusion. East Florida governor Tonyn, John Stuart, Thomas Brown, Robert Cunningham, and Moses Kirkland debated a scheme that involved a British invasion of the south with loyalist and Indian uprisings against the rebels. All but one of them agreed that trapping the rebels between Indians on the frontier and regulars on the coast was the best means of squelching the rebellion.

The sole holdout was the Indian superintendent. Like Quebec governor Guy Carleton, Stuart sought to keep the Indians loyal but peaceful. His primary goal that year was to end the war between the Creek and Choctaw Indians that had festered since 1765. To lubricate peace between those tribes and allegiance to the king from all the southern Indians, he distributed 7,500 pounds sterling worth of gifts that year.[60]

Though disappointed by Stuart's refusal to unleash the Indians, Tonyn simply bypassed the superintendent. The governor dispatched Kirkland to share the plan with Gage and seek the desired army. But much like John Connolly, Kirkland was captured and the conspiracy revealed. The result was a propaganda coup, as many a man wavering in loyalty to the Crown was enticed to the rebel cause. Most back-country folks held little understanding of or sympathy with the rabble-rousers in the faraway seaports protesting the government's policies, but wielding Indians against colonists was all too vivid a nightmare for those on the frontier.[61]

At this point, the settlers had little to fear from their neighbors. Puzzled by the rebellion, most southern Indians, like their northern brothers, preferred to sit on the fence. The rebels did whatever they could to keep them there. The American Southern Department's commissioners, George Galphin, John Walker, Willie Jones, and Robert Rae, met on November 13 at Salisbury, North Carolina. They agreed to council with the Cherokee at Fort Charlotte, South Carolina, on April 15 and the Creek Indians at Augusta, Georgia, on May 1. They deemed the Choctaw and Chickasaw too remote to bother with.

THE MAINE FRONTIER

Of all the frontiers, few were more forlorn than Maine, the colony of the province of Massachusetts. East of Falmouth the scattered clusters of settlements had stalled at the tidewater, venturing no farther into the wilderness than the falls of the Androscoggin, Kennebec, Penobscot, Machias, and Passamaquoddy Rivers and elsewhere along the wild rugged coast. Less than 1,000 pioneers and 3,000 Indians endured that region's long harsh winters broken by fleeting stretches of growing season. Farming supplemented incomes wrought mostly from exploiting forests and fish.

Maine would be largely a forgotten front throughout the war. The British made no effort to capture it, nor did the Americans use it as an invasion stepping stone against Nova Scotia. Maine was mostly the haunt of privateers that sheltered in the myriad of bays and inlets and then sailed forth to chase down merchant ships. The region's pockets of settlers and Indians alike mostly leaned toward the Americans. In contrast to other frontiers, no major landgrabs had accompanied the colonial intrusion. The fur trade enriched both colonists and tribes. Thus, the two peoples lived apart yet near in relative concord. Nonetheless, throughout the war, raids and skirmishes sporadically sizzled through portions of that frontier against a background of rival agents constantly jockeying for Indian loyalties.

Shortly after the fighting began, the Massachusetts assembly tried to cement these amiable relations. On May 15, the assemblymen sent a letter to all that region's tribes explaining the reasons for the conflict with Britain and calling for Indian support. American and Indian interests, they argued, were united against British exploitation: "The colonies from Nova Scotia to Georgia have firmly resolved to stand together and oppose them, we are Brothers and what is for our good is for your good. And we by standing together shall make them wicked men afraid & overcome them and all be free men."[62] The assembly sent another letter on June 21, reassuring the Indians that the Americans would "disdain to make use of unjustifiable force or artifice to rob their unsuspecting brethern [sic] of their rights, and are heartily disposed to prevent any injuries and encroachments."[63]

As strategic ropes torn between the British and Americans, the Penobscot Indians living at the Penobscot River, the Maliseet at the Passamaquoddy River, and the Micmac at the St. Johns River were understandably sullen and bewildered. The Micmac did delight that year in receiving a letter from George Washington requesting their allegiance but begged to remain aloof from the struggle. The Micmac chief conveyed his people's dilemma to a respected local figure, John Allen: "We do not comprehend what all this quarreling is about. How comes it that Old England and new should Quarrel & come to blows? The Father & Son to fight is terrible—Old France and Canada did not do so. We cannot think of fighting ourselves till we know who is right and who is wrong." Like other Indians, the Micmac realistically assessed their interests and the necessary means to uphold them. As a weak tribe, they had little choice but to bow to the stronger power, but whether that would be the Americans or British was as yet unclear: "When we see a sufficient Power in this Country we will tell you what we will do . . . We know we must submit to the strongest Power."[64]

The first violence occurred in June 1775. On June 2, two sloops and a cutter owned by the loyalist captain Ichabod Jones dropped anchor in Machias Bay. Word soon filtered out that Jones was commissioned by Vice Adm. Samuel Graves, commander of the Atlantic fleet, to gather supplies and return to besieged Boston. As protection, Graves dispatched the four-gun sloop HMS *Margaretta*, commanded by Midshipman James Moore, which reached Machias Bay around the same time.

Led by militia colonel Benjamin Foster, patriots demanded that Jones respect the Nonintercourse Act. Emboldened by the *Margaretta*'s presence, Jones replied with resentful ambivalence that sparked fear among the patriots that as soon as loading was done, he would spread sail. Foster concocted a scheme to seize the *Margaretta*'s officers after they emerged from Sunday church service on June 11, but the officers managed to flee back to their ship. From the *Margaretta*'s quarterdeck, Midshipman Moore threatened to bombard Machias if the rebels did not disperse and allow the king's officials to restore order. He then ordered his ship to sail down the bay. The rebels seized Jones's ships and prepared them to set out against the *Margaretta* the next day. On June 12, Foster could muster only enough men for the two sloops. As they sailed down Machias Bay, Foster's ship ran aground. Undaunted, Jeremiah O'Brien, commanding the sloop *Unity*, continued after the fleeing *Margaretta,* gained, and closed. The troops aboard both ships opened fire with muskets. After losing four dead and Moore mortally wounded, the *Margaretta*'s survivors struck her colors. That prize was costly—the rebels lost two dead and three wounded of their forty men. The patriots then seized a British schooner and cutter that appeared within days of the battle.

The capture of those ships gave the Machias patriots a small privateer fleet with which to protect Maine's frontier coast and raid British shipping in the sea-lanes. The battle for the *Margaretta* was a decisive local victory that kept Maine in American hands throughout the war. Falmouth, however, paid a harsh price for the Machias rebels. On October 18, a British squadron bombarded the town to rubble and sank eleven ships at anchor after its patriots refused a supply requisition order.[65]

THE FRONTIER AND INTERNATIONAL DIPLOMACY

Congress was willing to make a final attempt at reconciliation with the Crown. On July 8, it sent the Olive Branch Petition to the king. In November, word arrived that George III had not only snubbed the petition, but also declared on August 23 that the colonies were in a state of rebellion and would be crushed by force. Congress responded on November 29 by resolving to create a five-man committee of secret correspondence to conduct foreign policy. Until then, American diplomacy was limited to the colonies engaging agents in London to lobby Whitehall and Parliament. But having been spurned by the Crown, the Americans had no choice but to turn to other nations for help. Within days after the committee began to meet, it received its first unofficial diplomatic mission when secret envoy Julien-Alexandre Achard de Bonvouloir arrived in Philadelphia to determine whether the Americans wanted help and, if so, what they needed.

What explains that happy coincidence for the United States? French foreign minister Charles Gravier de Vergennes harbored no sympathy for the American rebels. Indeed, the rebellion against a sovereign provoked dread rather than admiration. Instead, he saw that revolt solely in terms of international power politics whereby an opportunity had arisen for France to elevate itself by diminishing its nemesis, Britain. If any nation should be willing to aid, trade, recognize, and even ally with the United States, it was France. For half a millennium, no kingdom had threatened, attacked, and humiliated France more than Britain. The 1763 Treaty of Paris ending the Seven Years' War was especially painful as France's North American empire was split between Britain and Spain, and many of its colonies in India, the Caribbean, and West Africa were transferred to London. The French were eager for revenge and any chance to erode British power and pride. Thus, shortly after receiving news of the fighting in America, Vergennes sent Bonvouloir on his secret mission. That French envoy's reports to Vergennes formed the basis for French foreign policy during the war. It would be French power that enabled the Americans to win their war for independence and the frontiers they demanded when and how they did.[66]

THE INVASION OF CANADA

America's greatest frontier campaign of the war would be launched late that summer. Having seized Forts Ticonderoga and Crown Point, rebel leaders felt that the next logical step was to invade Canada. Ethan Allen and Benedict Arnold led a growing chorus of those advocating the conquest of the "fourteenth colony." Those plans along with the reports filtering back from American and Indian envoys revealed that Canada was ripe for the plucking. On June 27, Congress authorized an invasion and appointed Gen. Philip Schuyler to command that expedition.[67]

Arnold's raid on St. Johns and subsequent rumors of an invasion prompted Gov. Guy Carleton to organize Quebec Province for defense. He declared martial law on June 9 and ordered all able-bodied men into militia companies that had atrophied from disuse. As for regulars, he had only about 700 troops of the 7th and 26th Regiments and 85 gunners of the Royal Artillery. Of these, he deployed about two-thirds on the Richelieu River flowing north from Lake Champlain, placing 341 troops at Fort St. Johns and 92 at Fort Chambly below.

What Carleton did not do was convene a council of the tribes, deliver an impassioned speech, ply the warriors with gifts and munitions, and point them south. He rejected the idea of using Indians against the rebels on both moral and practical grounds. Given the Seven Nations' tilt toward the Americans, it is unlikely that many warriors would have rallied to the Union Jack even if he had tried to inspire them. Still, Carleton's defense did not have to be static and passive. Even a handful of Indians and rangers could have brought back scalps, prisoners, and intelligence from Ticonderoga. He did agree to employ Indian scouts with the troops at Fort St. Jean, but only if they were strictly supervised by officers to prevent any atrocities. When he tried to rally the Seven Nations, as expected, they balked. The diplomatic efforts by the Americans and Oneida had persuaded those tribes to stay neutral for now.[68]

In early July, Carleton received two orders from General Gage: "I am to beg you to Collect a Body of Troops, Canadians, and Indians, to secure Lake Champlain and to fall upon the Frontiers of this Province, and that of Connecticut in order to make a Diversion of their forces."[69] But the general offered the governor an escape clause when he admitted, "Ignorant of your real situation it's impossible to send you positive instructions." Regardless, Carleton lacked the means to implement the order. Not only were his troops outnumbered by the swelling American army at Ticonderoga, but they also lacked supplies and bateaux.

The British defense of Canada was bolstered on July 17, when Guy Johnson and his entourage of 220 Indians and loyalists reached Montreal. Johnson and Carleton soon tangled heatedly over Indian policy. Thirsting for vengeance, the superintendent advocated loosing war parties on the American frontier. The governor adamantly rejected that notion, arguing that an unbridled Indian war against the frontier might destroy many lives and much property, but would exacerbate American alienation from the Crown. "What is or can be expected of them further," the governor argued, "than cutting off a few unfortunate Families whose Destruction will be but of little avail towards a Decision of the present contest."[70] Indians would be rallied only if the Americans invaded Canada, and then the warriors would be deployed only in firmly controlled light infantry-type companies under British or Canadian officers.

Those humanitarian sentiments undermined Britain's war effort. As Gage, Johnson, and other advocates vociferously argued, Indian raids on the enemy's supply lines or farms diverted troops from the front, killed them in the rear, and destroyed desperately needed provisions, wealth, workers, and moral. But Carleton was unmoved. That almost cost the British Canada.

Johnson hoped to sidestep the policy with a direct appeal to the chiefs. He sent runners to the tribes to council at Lachine in late July. Carleton protested and won his insistence that the council be held at Montreal, where he would preside. Johnson had no choice but to yield.

The council opened on July 26. Crowding into Montreal were 1,664 Indians, mostly of the Seven and Six Nations, along with knots of Great Lakes and Ohio valley tribes. While Carleton headed the council and was seconded by Johnson, the protocol and details were organized by Daniel Claus, who had served as Indian agent in Quebec for fifteen years. To Johnson's anger, Carleton's message prevailed that the Indians must remain at peace and faithful to the Great Father while he and the misguided colonists worked out their differences.[71] The Indians should fight alongside the British only if Canada itself was invaded. The governor did recruit 30 Indians under British officers to be deployed as scouts at Fort St. Johns. Those scouts would soon see action.

So far, both the Americans and the British had restrained the Indians on the Canadian front. In all, the Seven Nations tilted slightly toward the Americans. That tilt could mean the difference between victory and defeat when the Americans invaded Canada.

A fatal collision began to tip the balance of the Seven Nations' sentiments back toward Britain. On August 22, American captain Remember Baker and five rangers were patrolling the shore of Lake Champlain's Missisquoi Bay when they spotted Chevalier de Lorimier and four Algonquin Indians paddling south in a canoe. Baker warned them to return or his men would shoot. The Algonquin refused. The rangers fired a volley, killing two. The survivors squeezed off rounds and then paddled away. Balls shattered Baker's forehead and wounded another ranger. The rangers fled, leaving Baker's body behind. The following day, Maj. Charles Preston led thirty-three troops and twenty-five Indians to the site. The Indians butchered Baker, hacking off his scalp, head, and hands. The head was displayed on a pole at Fort St. Johns, while the scalp and hands were paraded through the villages. Blood had been drawn from a Seven Nations tribe, and that demanded vengeance. Baker's death and gruesome mutilation were not enough compensation. Other victims must be found. They soon arrived in abundance. Scores more Indians headed south to Fort St. Johns. They would prove to be decisive in the subsequent fighting.[72]

An American army was about to journey into that hornet's nest. On August 30, Schuyler ordered his 1,500 troops to embark in bateaux and row north. Upon landing a mile above St. John's on September 6, Schuyler immediately marched his troops toward the fort. Major Preston ordered the nearly 100 Seven and Six Nations warriors led by Capt. Gilbert Tice to delay Schuyler's advance. They attacked the Americans' left flank. The Americans stood and returned fire. After fifteen minutes, both sides withdrew. The Americans lost eight dead and six wounded, the Indians eight dead and five wounded, including the injured Tice.

That minor skirmish spooked Schuyler. He reembarked his army and rowed back up the Richelieu River to Isle aux Noix. On September 10, he sent Gen. Richard Montgomery and 800 troops back to Fort St. Johns. Montgomery ordered Col. Rudolphus Ritzema to lead 500 men around the fort. A small enemy force again routed the Americans. An Abenaki and five Canadians opened fire on Ritzema's troops in the dark. Many Americans fled; a few returned fire, killing the Abenaki and a Canadian. Inexplicably, Montgomery panicked and ordered a retreat to Isle aux Noix the next day. On two occasions, a small mélange of Indians and Canadians had routed the Americans.[73]

The Americans lay idle for another week as summer faded into autumn and ill-defended Fort St. Johns was reinforced. Then Schuyler proved to be a better diplomat than general. On September 6, he dispatched Maj. John Brown and Ethan Allen on a mission behind enemy lines to Chambly with a "Declaration to the Inhabitants of Canada" and promises to the Indians to cover their dead with gifts. Six days later, Schuyler sent an Iroquois delegation of mostly Oneida north. The Iroquois met a war party of 100 warriors heading toward St. Johns and persuaded them to return home and spread the word that the Seven Nations should follow the Six Nations' policy of neutrality. Word reached the Indians inside Fort St. Johns, and all but six deserted.

But Schuyler would be unable to follow up this coup. Debilitated by illness, he turned over command to Montgomery on September 16 and returned to Albany. The following day, Montgomery ordered his men to make a third march against Fort St. Johns. Preston ordered a sortie that drove off the American advance guard and then withdrew as the rest of Montgomery's army appeared. Montgomery deployed his troops around the fort and sent sixty troops under Maj. John Brown north to occupy La Prairie. Two days later, he reinforced Brown with 200 troops led by Col. Seth Warner.

Ethan Allen talked Brown into a reckless scheme that set back the campaign. Reports revealed that Montreal was poorly defended and Canadian loyalties were shifting to the Americans. Allen swore he could capture the city with forty-five frontiersmen leavened by eighty Canadians. Brown would then march to reinforce Allen. On the night of September 24, Allen and his men advanced toward Montreal's outskirts. A spy revealed Allen's plan. Carleton sprang a trap of 234 troops and a half-dozen Caughnawaga against him. Allen's troops fled at the first shots. The British and Indians pursued and eventually bagged Allen and thirty-five of his men, killed five, wounded ten, and scattered the rest at a loss of four dead and three wounded.[74]

The string of British victories inspired more Indians and Canadians to flock to the Union Jack—nearly 200 Indians and 1,800 militia gathered at Montreal during late September. Yet rather than loose the Indians on American pickets and supply lines, Carleton restrained them. He played a waiting game, hoping winter would bog down the lumbering timid enemy and force it to withdraw. That strategy went unchallenged when Guy Johnson chose to set sail with his entourage on October 21 for the long voyage to London. There Johnson would petition Whitehall for an aggressive Indian war against the American frontier. Johnson's departure ended the brief eclipse of Canada's own Indian superintendent, Capt. John Campbell, and Deputy La Corne St. Luc. Before the rivers froze, the year's last canoe caravans set forth carrying Carleton's orders for post commanders to retain at once Indian loyalty and passivity.

The British were not yet aware that a second expedition was approaching Canada. It took most of the summer to do so, but Benedict Arnold finally realized his dream of a commission to command an army. He had petulantly resigned on June 23 after Congress passed him over for command of the Lake Champlain front.[75] He then traveled to the American siege lines around Boston, secured an audience with George Washington, and presented his plan for an invasion of Canada via the Kennebec and Chaudiere Rivers. Washington saw the wisdom in aiding Schuyler's invasion by another route and authorized Arnold to organize and lead that expedition.

Arnold got to work. On August 21, he wrote a requisition order to Reuben Colburn at Pittstown, Maine, at the Kennebec River mouth to build 200 bateaux and gather supplies. It was not until September 5 that Washington issued a call for volunteers to join Arnold's expedition, whose destination was kept secret. Within two days, 786 troops were split into two regiments of five companies, each commanded by Lieutenant Colonels Roger Enos and Christopher Greene. To these troops Capt. Daniel Morgan added his several hundred Virginia and Pennsylvania riflemen. In all, Arnold commanded about 1,050 troops when they departed on September 11 for Newburyport and headed from there by ship on September 19 for Pittstown, which they reached on September 22.[76]

The expedition left Pittstown on September 25. The troops were packed into over 250 badly constructed leaking bateaux. Ahead of them was an epic, grueling six-week 340-mile trek to Quebec. En route, they would portage dozens of miles, be pounded by rainstorms and buried by snowstorms, endure frostbite, deplete their supplies, and resort to eating their moccasins, belts, cartridge boxes, and anything else leather. On October 25, Enos deserted with his regiment from the rear he was supposed to defend. With his troops scattered for over twenty miles along the route, Arnold could not organize a pursuit. Instead, he pressed onward with his army's exhausted, starving remnants. Perhaps as many as fifty perished along the way.

On November 6, Arnold reached Point Levy on the south side of the St. Lawrence directly across from Quebec. With him were only 650 men. Arnold had displayed extraordinary courage and leadership in getting most of his army through that wilderness to Quebec, but he committed two indiscretions that may have lost the Americans Canada. The British intercepted both of the letters he sent to General Montgomery. That gave Lt. Gov. Hector Cramahe several weeks to prepare Quebec for defense by gathering troops and supplies and shoring up the city's crumbling walls.

It took a week for Arnold to gather enough boats to carry his army across the St. Lawrence. Triumphantly, he and his men crossed the night of November 13, ground ashore at Wolfe's Cove, and climbed up to the Plains of Abraham. The following morning, November 14, the ragged American army paraded defiantly before Quebec's west wall. Without artillery Arnold could only hope to taunt out Lt. Col. Allan Maclean, who had arrived with 150 troops only two days earlier to command the garrison. But Maclean refused to budge. He feared defeat even though he had twice as many men, mostly regulars and militia, along with a few Indians of the region: Lorette Huron, Montagnais, and Abenaki. He was confident that the Canadian winter would vanquish the Americans. Arnold pulled his troops back on November 19 to Pointe-aux-Trembles twenty miles west and awaited Montgomery.

Where was Montgomery? On October 18, rebel troops captured Fort Chambly, Fort St. Johns supply post downriver at the foot of the Richelieu River rapids. It took another ten days before Carleton could concentrate enough militia to join his regulars for a counterattack. On October 30, he led 130 redcoats, 800 militia, and 80 Indians up the Richelieu. Col. Seth Warner and 350 Americans blocked his advance at Longueuil. Faced with cannon and musket fire, Carleton ordered a retreat downstream. That failure prompted most of the remaining loyal Indians to return to their villages. On November 2, the 481-man British garrison at St. Johns finally capitulated. Montgomery slowly redeployed his troops for an advance on Montreal.

The governor bowed to the inevitable. On November 11, Carleton dismissed most of the militia, packed his redcoats, supplies, and a couple hundred Canadians aboard eleven vessels, and abandoned Montreal for Quebec 160 miles down the St. Lawrence. Montgomery's army entered Montreal the following day, on November 12.

Carleton would not get away so easily. An American force under Col. James Easton reached the St. Lawrence at Sorel and hastily emplaced cannons that commanded the river. Easton demanded Carleton's surrender when his flotilla appeared on November 15. As if the cannons were not threatening enough, the winds blew steadily up the St. Lawrence, trapping Carleton's vessels. The governor left his men under Gen. Richard Prescott to their fate and escaped downstream in a whaleboat. Hoping the winds would change, Prescott held out for four more days. The winds refused to cooperate. Prescott finally surrendered on November 19, the same day Carleton reached Quebec. Among those who went into captivity were John Campbell and La Corne St. Luc.

The American victory over the British Indian superintendency seemed complete. Johnson and most of his deputies had sailed to England. Campbell and St. Luc were prisoners. Carleton would soon be besieged at Quebec. Alexander McKee was isolated and watched at Pittsburgh. Only John Butler was free to rally Indian support at Niagara. With an American army straddling the St. Lawrence, no British supplies to its forts or trade goods and gifts to the tribes could reach the Great Lakes or Ohio valley. Indeed, the Americans could empty Montreal's warehouses of such goods and place them into the hands of Indians at various councils. Montgomery named Col. Timothy Bedel to be the American Indian agent for Canada. A shift in the balance of Indian loyalties seemed inevitable. Shorn of supplies, replacements, and instructions, the frontier forts would wither on the vine and be plucked by American expeditions. Americans could even take over the fur trade from Canadians and British, as effects of the Quebec Act were reversed and the flow shifted from Montreal to Albany and Pittsburgh. Dazzling as those prospects seemed, everything depended on how the Americans capitalized on their advantages. This they failed to do. The American eclipse of the British would be brief.

So much depended on Quebec's fate. After a brief respite in Montreal, Montgomery embarked most of his army on November 28 to join Arnold at Pointe-aux-Tremble on December 1. Together they mustered only 1,325 soldiers, along with a half-dozen Penobscots who served as guides, scouts, and messengers. Many of the troops would be heading home on New Year's Day when their enlistments ran out. The Americans had to take Quebec before then or they probably never would.[77]

Montgomery and Arnold led their scarecrow army to Quebec on December 4. The ground was too frozen to dig batteries and entrenchments, and the light cannons Montgomery brought were too weak to breach Quebec's walls. The leaders debated various schemes for attacking the city. They finally decided that a night attack during a snowstorm might offer them a chance to place scaling ladders against the wall.

That opportunity did not arise until the night of December 31. Four units would simultaneously assault the city: two would make diversionary attacks across the Plains of Abraham against St. John's Gate and the Cape Diamond Bastion, while Arnold led a column against the north gate along the St. Charles River and Montgomery against the south gate on the St. Lawrence River. The hope was that Maclean would concentrate his regulars against the feints while Arnold and Montgomery broke through in his rear.

The result was a disaster. The British were ready and poured cannon and musket fire into the American columns. Montgomery was shot dead, a bullet smashed into Arnold's knee, 51 Americans were killed, 36 were wounded, and over 400 were captured, while the British lost 7 dead and 11 wounded. The remnants retreated to the entrenchments to carry out a desultory siege through the seemingly endless Canadian winter.[78]

In all, the Canadian campaign severely damaged the American cause. Mountains of supplies, hundreds of bateaux, and thousands of men were diverted from defense or production elsewhere. Bullets and germs had killed a couple thousand men who otherwise might have survived to arm less voracious fronts. Despite all this, the dream of adding Canada to the United States would not die. Throughout the war, other invasion schemes would be ventured only to be tabled for lack of means. The reason for that persistence was simple. Canada's seizure would end the frontier war from Maine to Kentucky.

CHAPTER 4

"The Will of the Supreme Being": 1776

I will Loose the Last Drop of My Blood in Defense of My Country when fighting for that Blessed Enjoyment called Liberty and Should all the Indian Nations Join in Confederacy and attack me here tho I had But Twenty men I would Defend it with My Latest Breath, and Glory in the Cause.

—Matthew Arbuckle

We must die when it is the will of the supreme being.

—Miami Chief Waspikingua

Shortly after taking office, George Sackville, Viscount Germain, became the policy point man for crushing the rebellion. It was important not only that the bright articulate Germain rather than some mediocrity filled the ministry for North American colonial affairs, but also that Prime Minister Frederick North was reticent to take the job and George III highly regarded Germain. The American secretary and the king enjoyed a meeting of minds on the rebellion. Germain championed smothering the rebellion by violence rather than the compromise, kindness, and sympathy preferred by his predecessor, William Legge, Earl of Dartmouth. In fulfilling that strategy, Germain was ably assisted by William Knox, the undersecretary for American affairs.[1]

The planning for 1776 had begun the previous autumn and continued that winter. Germain's first major step was to change commanders. In September 1776, Thomas Gage, who had served as America's commander in chief since 1763, was recalled. Maj. Gen. William Howe was ordered to replace Gage as commander in chief, seconded by Sir Henry Clinton and then John Burgoyne. Though Germain increasingly despised cautious humane Guy Carleton, he retained him as Quebec's governor; Carleton enjoyed powerful patrons in London.

The strategy that Howe and his subordinates would implement was bold and ambitious. The army would launch three offensives—Howe with 32,000 troops to invade New York City, Carleton with 10,000 to retake Canada through Quebec and advance south through Lake Champlain, and Clinton with 2,800 through Wilmington—while armed loyalists rose throughout the colonies and Indians attacked all along the frontier. Trapped in the cross fire, the rebel forces in New York and North Carolina would be overwhelmed and crushed. From secure bases in New York City, Albany, and Wilmington, the Royal Army could march on the remnants of rebel forces in adjacent colonies.[2]

Regulars, not Indians, would crush the rebellion. Nonetheless, Indians would play an important secondary role either on the warpath or just staying out of the way. Neutral tribes were valued nearly as much as allied tribes. As for those that supplied warriors, officers would accompany war parties in conjuncture with British forces. Terrorism against the frontier was condemned. This was essentially Carleton's policy, accepted by Germain, the other ministers, and the commanders in North America.

Perhaps with a twinge of guilt, Whitehall justified using Indians by claiming that they were simply emulating rebel strategy. As Lord North explained, "There was never any raising or employing the negroes or the Indians, until the Americans themselves had first applied to them."[3] That assertion was false. Congressional and state policy sought Indian neutrality rather than alliance. The domesticated Stockbridge Indians were enlisted and fought as regulars. Free blacks served voluntarily in the ranks; slaves accompanied or substituted for their masters in the field.

But Germain and the other leaders perceived otherwise, based on the lurid rumors they heard and what they wanted to believe. The view that the rebels first used Indians was most vigorously propounded by Guy Johnson, who met with Germain on December 28, 1775, the day after he arrived in London. But Johnson called for more than a tit-for-tat retaliation. Carleton's policy of inhibiting Indians was an abject failure and almost lost Canada, he argued. Untying all constraints on their warfare all along the frontier would divert or destroy men and supplies that the rebels would otherwise deploy against the British army on the seaboard.

An intrigued Germain asked Johnson to put his thoughts onto paper in a detailed policy analysis. Johnson completed his task by January 26, 1776, and submitted two documents to Germain, a narrative of the key events from May to November 1775, which he called a "journal," and an introductory letter summing up his proposals.[4] Upon pondering Johnson's arguments, Germain agreed in principle. But for now the policy of wielding Indians as army auxiliaries would stand. The regulars should stamp out the rebellion by the year's end. Waving the threat of unrestricted Indian warfare over the scalps of the settlers would hasten that end: "The Dread the People . . . have of a War with the Savages proves the expediency of our holding that Scourge over them."[5] Ideally, dread alone would suffice. In the unlikely event that the rebellion somehow persisted, Germain intended to use those sterner measures.

Though his strategy was stymied, Johnson did achieve one goal. Germain made his temporary title as Indian superintendent and colonel of the Six Nations and their dependent tribes official on March 8. Johnson would be subordinate only to Whitehall and the commander in chief. Rather than send Johnson back to the Iroquois via the back door of Canada, Germain ordered him to join Howe's campaign against New York. Just how Johnson would contact, let alone rally, the Six Nations from New York City was unclear. The order to turn his back on the wilderness and immerse himself at the commander in chief's urbane headquarters must have delighted Johnson as much as being freed of Carleton.

Johnson was not the only prominent person in London promoting Indian policy. The Mohawk Joseph Brant, or Thayendanegea, cut a swath through London's political and social circles.[6] Although he was not a formal Iroquois chief, no war leader on either side during the American Revolution would prove to be more daring, persistent, and brilliant than Brant. He was a remarkable man by any measure. He spoke not only all the Iroquois dialects, but also fluent English, having been educated at Ebenezar Wheelock's Indian school and having as a sister Sir William Johnson's wife, Molly. Powerfully charismatic, he stirred hearts and minds in Indian and Royal councils alike. He was a devout Christian and mason, and would later translate the Bible into Mohawk. When the war broke out, he was in his early thirties and living with his wife and children on a 100-acre farm near Canajoharie. He had followed Johnson to Canada and then to London.

Brant and Johnson received an audience with George III on April 30. Dressed as a Mohawk, Brant refused to kneel before the king since the Six Nations did not believe themselves subject to British sovereignty. He then asked the king as he had other officials for redress of a long list of Iroquois grievances. George III promised to look into them. That Royal audience capped several months where the dashing articulate Brant was the center of a swirl of London social events. Much was expected of the "noble savage" when he returned to America. Brant would not let them down.

Johnson, Brant, and the entourage departed London on May 20 for Falmouth, where they set sail aboard the packet *Lord Hyde* on June 2. En route near Bermuda, a privateer skimmed in for an attack. The two ships exchanged cannon shots for an hour and a half before the *Lord Hyde* outdistanced the privateer. Few warriors could boast like Brant of having fought in a sea battle. Shortly after reaching Staten Island on July 29, Johnson and Brant met with Lord Howe to see how they could fit into his campaign. To their dismay, they learned that they had no role to play.

AMERICAN OBJECTIVES

As the year opened, the Americans also had an ambitious strategy—expel the British from Boston, capture Quebec, and repel any enemy attacks elsewhere. To those ends, Congress worked with the states to mobilize enough money, men, and munitions. As they did so, a debate naturally arose over the role of Indians in America's unfolding Revolution. Was a policy of nurturing Indian allies or neutrality the wiser course? John Hancock, George Washington, and Philip Schuyler forged a consensus that Indian allies were more trouble than they were worth—they cost a fortune to recruit and then were unmanageable on campaign and undependable in battle. Yet the Americans could not afford to spurn the tribes altogether. To do so would most likely push ambitious warriors onto Britain's warpath. Congress and the states agreed to spend a portion of their meager and diminishing coin on trying to purchase Indian neutrality.[7]

In its eagerness to raise troops, Congress undercut that policy. Money alone was not enough enticement. Along with the rest of the population, potential recruits scorned the worthless scrip peeled off Congress's printing presses. The only tangible inducement that Congress could offer was land—land that it did not then control legally or militarily. But that did not stop Congress from making the promise. Here Congress competed with the states, most of which offered their own claims to western lands as recruitment bonuses. Any new settlements needed some form of government. On May 10, Congress issued a resolution that dramatically legitimized the bids for autonomy or outright independence of frontier regions. The resolution's author, John Adams, recommended that "where no government sufficient to the exigencies of their affairs has been hitherto established [the inhabitants should] . . . adopt such governments as shall in the opinion of the Representatives of the people best conduce to the happiness and safety of their constituents."[8] The promise of land and self-rule on the advancing frontier would inevitably be at the expense of the Indians who would naturally favor the lesser threat to their existence, the British.

Liberating Boston turned out to be surprisingly easy. During the winter, Gen. Henry Knox supervised the transport of cannons captured at Fort Ticonderoga by sleigh to a battery on Dorchester Heights 600 yards from Boston's south side. By March 4, the cannons were emplaced and opened fire. On March 7, Howe sailed away with 9,000 troops and 1,100 loyalists aboard 125 ships to Halifax. He would return later that summer.

But where would the British strike next? New York was the obvious answer. In April, Washington marched there with the bulk of the army.

In the lull following Boston's evacuation, America's leaders could debate at length the central issue—for what were they fighting? The war with Britain had lasted for over a year now. During that time, the Americans had squeezed the British from Boston and almost taken Canada. King George III had rejected the Olive Branch Petition of Congress and declared the colonies in a state of rebellion to be crushed with brutal force. Ever more delegates to Congress and the provincial governments along with the general population agreed that reconciliation was now impossible and the only course left was an outright declaration of independence.

The political momentum for independence mounted rapidly through the year's first half. Thomas Paine's *Common Sense* was published on January 10 and sold over 100,000 copies that year alone. With very vivid and clear prose, Paine presented the spectrum of philosophical and practical arguments for independence. On May 15, Congress reinforced its May 10 resolution that the colonies form their own governments by calling on them to eliminate the last vestiges of the Crown's rule. That same day, Virginia's government resolved that its delegates would lead Congress to declare independence. On June 7, Virginian Richard Henry Lee did just that. Congress agreed to postpone debate on the resolution for several weeks so that the delegates could vote unanimously for independence. On June 11, Congress created a committee of Benjamin Franklin, Thomas Jefferson, John Adams, Roger Sherman, and Robert Livingston to draw up an independence declaration. The committee asked Jefferson to do so. On July 2, Congress finally voted on Lee's resolution, with twelve favoring independence and New York's delegation abstaining. Congress then considered Jefferson's document line by line, made minor changes, and voted unanimously for that Declaration of Independence on July 4, 1776. American patriots had proclaimed their freedom. But they still had to win it.[9]

THE MOHAWK VALLEY FRONTIER

During all those months that Guy Johnson loitered in London or at Howe's headquarters, his cousin prepared to follow him into exile. Fears that Sir John Johnson was organizing a counterrevolution in their midst haunted the Mohawk valley patriots. Those fears were well founded. On January 5, Johnson wrote to Gov. William Tryon, then exiled aboard a British ship in New York's harbor, asking for a commission to form a Tory regiment with which he hoped to crush the rebels in the Mohawk valley. Tryon forwarded it to Whitehall for approval. Meanwhile, Johnson began secretly organizing a regiment.

These preparations and rumors of Johnson's letter to Tryon did not escape the surveillance of the Tryon committee. They wrote Gen. Philip Schuyler on January 11 that Sir John had amassed nearly 700 militia, munitions, and supplies around Johnstown. Schuyler agreed that the time had come to arrest Sir John. Though he mustered 3,000 troops of his own, the general hoped to avoid any violence. His troops faced not just the Tories, but also the Mohawks, whose chief Little Abraham had implored Schuyler to resolve the dispute peacefully and offered to serve as mediator. Although he politely declined Little Abraham's offer, Schuyler agreed to halt his march and open negotiations. At Schenectady he wrote Johnson of the reasons for his approach and asked him to give up: "Influenced, Sir, by the motives of humanity . . . [for you] to comply with my order in a manner the most peaceable, that no blood may be shed; I, therefore, request that you will please to meet me tomorrow at any place on my way to Johnstown, to which I propose to march."[10] Laudable though this move was, it ruined any chance of surprise Schuyler may have had and risked allowing Johnson time to flee to Canada.

Johnson too wished to avoid violence that might destroy his family and home. Schuyler's troops outgunned his own by four to one. Escape was possible but treacherous in the dead of a snowbound winter. Any chance of a successful flight would mean leaving behind his pregnant wife and small children. Upon mulling over these grim choices, Johnson accepted Schuyler's humiliating demand.

They met at Guy Park on January 17. Johnson agreed to surrender all his arms, disperse his militia, turn over all stores intended for the Indians, accept house arrest, post a 1,600-pound-sterling bond, promise to remain neutral, and hand over six of his men as hostages. On January 19, Schuyler and his army marched into Johnstown with Sir John to implement the agreement. Two days later, the patriot army headed back to Schenectady. While the immediate crisis was defused, its underlying causes still smoldered.

The crisis flared anew in March when rumors reached the Tryon County committee that Sir John had boasted of calling on the Indians to attack the rebels. Schuyler asked Johnson to met him in Albany and discuss the charges. Johnson denied the rumors and refused to meet. Schuyler accepted his word, but the whispers of conspiracy persisted. It would be another two months before the crisis was resolved.

The Six Nations and their affiliated tribes were the rope in a tug-of-war between two rival agents, John Butler at Niagara and John Dean at Albany. Both men counciled with the Iroquois and tried to entice them into a "neutrality" that was one step from outright alliance with his side. Dean attended the league council at Onondaga from March 28 to April 2. To his relief, the sachems agreed to continue their policy of neutrality. The league sent delegations to Albany and Niagara to explain their position and demand redress of problems and gifts.[11]

It was in the league's interests, of course, to sit on the war's sidelines and see who was winning and just what that meant. To that nearly all sachems agreed. But the neutral stance masked deep divisions among and within the tribes. Economic dependence explains some of the differences. The Seneca and Cayuga naturally leaned toward the British at Fort Niagara just as the Tuscarora and Oneida tended more toward Albany. But sentiment for two of the tribes was even more powerful. Despite being tiny islands in an American sea, the Mohawk villages of Fort Hunter and Canajoharie were devoted to their revered deceased sachem Sir William Johnson and his loyalist family, and thus sided with the Crown. The charismatic missionary Samuel Kirkland asserted just as firm an emotional hold on the Oneida, thus swinging them to the American cause. The factions within each tribe and village have as many explanations as the individuals who composed them.

The composition of councils at Niagara, Albany, and elsewhere reflects these divisions. No Seneca or Cayuga were among the 230 Iroquois who attended a council in Albany from April 29 to May 10 to meet with Commissioners Philip Schuyler, Timothy Edwards, and Volkert Douw. Samuel Kirkland's influence with the Oneida Indians was revealed when they demanded that an American fort be established at Fort Stanwix's ruins. That fort would protect both the nearby Oneida and the backdoor to the Mohawk valley. Schuyler promised to get New York's approval. Following the council, twenty-four Iroquois envoys journeyed to New York City and Philadelphia, where they met congressional leaders and George Washington. Those American leaders lauded the Iroquois choice of neutrality and sent back those envoys laden with gifts.[12]

John Butler convened his own councils with mostly Seneca and a sprinkling of other Iroquois and Great Lakes tribes at Fort Niagara in May and June. Most Iroquois rebuffed Butler's calls to seize the war hatchet. At the latter council, Seneca war chief Cawconcaucawheteda, or Flying Crow, pointed out: "It is true [the Americans] have encroached on our Lands, but of this we shall speak to them. If you are so strong a Brother, and they but as a weak Boy, why ask our assistance. It is true that I am tall and strong but I will reserve my strength to strike those who injure us . . . You say they are all mad, foolish, wicked and deceitful—I say you are so and they are wise for you want us to destroy ourselves in your War and they advise us to live in Peace."[13]

Kayashuta was even more blunt. After blasting Butler as a "mad, foolish, crazy, and deceitful person," he bluntly explained that the call for war was backfiring: "The Americans on the contrary are the wise people so far as they have yet spoke to us—for what they advise us . . . is in our interest to follow—they tell us your quarrel is between yourselves & desire us to sit still & they tell us right—But you want us to assist you which we cannot do. . . . I tell you brother you are foolish & we will not allow you to pluck up the Tree of Peace nor raise the hatchet—We are strong & able to do it ourselves when we are hurt."[14]

Yet despite the resistance of the chiefs, many young men eagerly snatched up the hatchet. Butler was able to recruit about fifty warriors, mostly Seneca Indians, along with a few Cayuga, Onondaga, Mohawk, Chippewa, and Ottawa, to leave with Capt. John Johnstone on May 10 for Fort La Galette at Oswegatchie. There Butler rallied another fifty warriors at the June council. But in doing so, he turned the young men against their chiefs' wishes. Kayashuta rebuked him for his "wicked intentions," but admitted that "we could not all be united & we are separated."

Worried that their unity was indeed cracking, the Iroquois left Fort Niagara for a hastily called council at Onondaga starting on June 15. Once again the sachems agreed on neutrality. When the council ended on June 22, runners carried that message to the Seven Nations, Ohio, and Great Lakes tribes and encouraged them to follow.[15]

Not only the Iroquois were torn by Hamlet-like indecision. The question of whether to arrest Tory leader Sir John Johnson continued to plague New York's leaders. Rumors persisted that Johnson was preparing his followers for civil war. On May 10, Schuyler warned Johnson of his imminent arrest for breaking their January agreement. Yet for another week, Schuyler did nothing; it was as if he tarried deliberately, seemingly wishing that the problem would disappear to Canada.[16]

Johnson did not squander his chance. When Col. Elias Dayton finally arrived with 300 troops at Johnstown late on May 19, 1776, Johnson was nowhere to be found. Just hours earlier, Sir John led 170 relatives, friends, tenants, and servants north through the Adirondacks toward Oswegatchie on the St. Lawrence River. That route was the least dangerous. American troops dominated both the Mohawk and Lake Champlain corridors. Angst-ridden, he left behind his pregnant wife and two small children.

Dayton found more than Johnson's abandoned family. Fifty Mohawk warriors led by Chief Little Abraham blocked Johnson's pursuit. Though Dayton backed away, he had strong words for Little Abraham, warning him that if the Mohawks "take up the hatchet . . . he would break the covenant chain; he would burn their upper and lower castles . . . would burn all their houses, destroy their towns, and cast all the Mohawks with their wives and children off the face of the earth."[17] Dayton ordered his troops to round up about 100 suspected loyalists and herded them back to Albany for internment.

Johnson's escape seemed to free Schuyler from indecision. He took a bold step toward the western New York frontier and the Iroquois. He accepted the Oneida request and ordered Colonel Dayton to march his regiment to ruined Fort Stanwix at the strategic portage between the Mohawk and Oneida watersheds. The rebuilt fort would be named Schuyler. The Oneida Indians were the only Iroquois tribe that supported Fort Schuyler. The others angrily condemned it as an aggressive act of trespass. Schuyler dismissed those protests. He and the other commissioners were convinced that a strong stance would best deter the Iroquois.[18]

Schuyler would sternly defend that fort on August 7 when he welcomed over 2,000 Iroquois and their satellite tribes, Delaware, and Mahican to a council at German Flats. He did so in a long speech filled with issues and assertions, the most dramatic of which was his announcement confirming word that the United States had declared its independence from Britain. He then cited six Iroquois violations of their neutrality policy, urged them to stay away from the warpath, and warned that the Americans would punish any Indians who joined the British. Speaking for the Six Nations, Mohawk chief Little Abraham reaffirmed their neutrality but then presented the familiar litany of complaints about squatters and cheaters on Indian lands. He also expressed a common fear that a plague that had burned through the Six Nations and other tribes that summer was the Great Spirit's anger for not joining the king against the rebels. Schuyler belittled the belief. What he did not mention was that various diseases were afflicting the American troops in the region. Despite the differences and fears, the council broke up with both sides relieved that they had preserved neutrality.[19]

At Fort Niagara, John Butler persisted in trying to destroy that neutrality. He convened his own council in late August and once again asked the Six Nations to join the British against the Americans. During the council, a delegation of Detroit chiefs arrived. Their enthusiasm for joining the British caused the Iroquois to waver and some eventually to break with their tribe's neutrality. Nearly all the Seneca chiefs and many of the Cayuga and Onondaga chiefs seized Butler's war belt, along with some Mohawk, Oneida, and Tuscarora warriors. But the absence of chiefs from the last three tribes belied Butler's assertion that the Six Nations now fully supported Britain. To the warriors' disgust, Butler obeyed Carleton's orders that the Indians be kept from the warpath. The council ended on September 10. Butler had won the Iroquois alliance while still restraining their actual arms.[20]

Iroquois neutrality was fraying rapidly. Fort Schuyler became a magnet for those warriors who had rallied to the Union Jack. In late August, a war party of Mohawk, Mississauga, and others ambushed six soldiers who were scouting toward Oswego, wounding three and murdering two that they captured. The same war party killed one man of a group of deserters heading toward Niagara. They escorted the survivors to Butler. A Seneca, Onondaga, and two Mississauga Indians captured two soldiers fishing in Wood Creek and hustled them off to Niagara. On the nights of September 19 and 20, Mohawk or Mississauga Indians attacked the fort's pickets but did not hurt or capture anyone. The sporadic killings and captures around the fort had only just begun.[21]

The most decisive event on the New York frontier that year was the arrival of Joseph Brant. He had spent the summer and fall with Maj. Gen. William Howe's army. On the night of November 16, Brant and Capt. Gilbert Tice slipped from New York City for their long trek as General Howe's emissaries to enlist the Six Nations for the British cause; Iroquois Superintendent Guy Johnson stayed behind to enjoy New York luxuries. Ten days later, they reached Oquaga on the Susquehanna River's eastern branch. Oquaga had a mixed population of Mohawk, Oneida, and Mahican tribes who had followed the Six Nations' policy of neutrality. Brant was not a chief, and his war leadership skills were as yet largely untested. At the village council, however, his powerful charisma and arguments swung most of the assembled chiefs and warriors to either sympathy or outright support. Periodically throughout the war, Brant would use Oquaga for his headquarters, shelter, supply depot, recruitment ground, and launching pad for raids against the frontier. From there, Brant, Tice, Mohawk chief Old Issac, and a score of warriors headed to the Delaware towns on the Chemung River. He gathered more men there and then pushed on to Genesee Castle or Chenussio, the central town for the western Seneca, and then with Tice and two others on to Fort Niagara, which they reached on December 19.

Indian agent Capt. John Butler warily greeted Howe's envoys. Antagonism arose between Butler and Brant. The Mohawk's call for an Indian war against the frontier challenged Butler's authority and policies. Butler cited Governor Carleton's orders to keep the Six Nations at once loyal and at peace. Brant countered with the orders of Howe and Johnson to rally the Six Nations against the rebels. As Johnson's subordinate, Butler would have to follow those orders. He asked for written proof. Brant explained the madness of carrying incriminating written orders through enemy lines. Butler organized his resistance around that technicality. Brant rebuffed Butler's assertion of rank and thus control.

After resting at Niagara for two weeks, Brant departed on New Year's Eve for the Six Nations. As he moved from one village to another, he inspired scores of Iroquois warriors to join him on the warpath in 1777.

THE CANADIAN FRONTIER
Following the disastrous attack on Quebec, the remnants of the American army withdrew to its frozen camps and awaited a counterattack that never came. Rather than disintegrate, the army swelled with reinforcements to 2,505 troops by late March.[22] The muster rolls did not reflect the army's true strength; smallpox infected half those men and killed hundreds. Without heavy artillery, the healthy troops could do nothing more than stare glumly at Quebec's walls. On April 12, Gen. David Wooster replaced Benedict Arnold as the army's commander and canceled a plan for another assault. On May 1, Wooster's place in turn was taken by

Gen. William Thompson, who did prepare another attack. But he was a week too late. On May 6, reinforcements had arrived with the spring supply fleet, rendering Carleton's army 900 strong. Thompson withdrew his army to Deschambault and then Trois Rivieres. Rather than pursue, Carleton was content to await more troops and supplies.

One enterprising courageous man can change the flow of history. The first attack on the Americans came not from British forces in Quebec, but from down the St. Lawrence from Oswegatchie. Capt. George Forster departed on May 12 with 210 men, including 38 regulars, 11 Canadians, and about 200 warriors in bateaux. Learning of the advance, General Arnold, now commanding at Montreal, dispatched Col. Timothy Bedel with 400 New Hampshire and Connecticut regulars along with two cannons to the Cedars, a village on the St. Lawrence's north bank upstream of the Ottawa River mouth. Arriving on May 18, Forster sent forward about ninety warriors under Chevalier de Lorimier to scout the American fortifications, now commanded by Maj. Isaac Butterfield. Shots were exchanged, killing an Indian and an American, while another was captured. Forster then sent in Lt. Henry Bird under a truce flag to demand that Butterfield capitulate or else suffer the consequences of an Indian assault. When Bird returned with Butterfield's request that his troops be allowed to withdraw, Forster ordered his men to open fire. Thirty Canadians joined Forster that night. The following day, Butterfield surrendered to Forster, who promised to protect the Americans from the Indians. A relief force of 140 Massachusetts troops under Maj. Henry Shelburne landed at Quinze Chiens four miles east of the Cedars on May 20. Hearing of their approach, Forster sprang an ambush that killed or wounded about ten Americans and terrified the rest. After his troops fired a volley that killed Seneca chief Kanughsgawiat and wounded three others, Shelburne promptly surrendered his command. In two days, Forster's audacity had bagged 500 American troops, but Forster was not yet done.

Reinforcements brought his force to 200 Canadians and 250 Indians. On May 23, he rowed his command to Lachine, nine miles from Montreal. That American defense, however, was too strong. When Forster ordered a withdrawal to Quinze Chiens, most of his Canadians deserted, leaving him with only eighty troops and the Indians. Arnold pursued with 600 troops. On May 27, as Arnold prepared to attack, Shelburne appeared with a British officer to inform the American commander that Butterfield and Forster had signed a prisoner exchange and truce. Shelburne added that if Arnold attacked, the Indians would massacre their prisoners. Arnold agreed to honor the exchange along with a six-day truce. The agreement required the 500 paroled troops to depart for the United States and not take up arms until they were formally exchanged. After Forster released the captives, Arnold withdrew to Montreal.

The Cedars was an important British victory. Not only did the Americans lose over 500 men, but also their morale plummeted and the bulk of Indian sentiments shifted toward Britain. It could have turned out differently. Had Butterfield held out, the Cedars might have been celebrated as an American victory rather than mourned as a humiliating defeat. Forster might well have retreated rather than opposed Shelburne's landing.[23]

News of the Cedars encouraged a timid Carleton to advance up the St. Lawrence. On May 22, he sailed with 940 troops of the 29th and 47th to Trois Rivieres, where a rebel force blocked his ascent. There he left his men aboard ship and returned once again to Quebec for the promised 10,000 troops. Most of them soon arrived. By early June, Carleton commanded 8,000 troops from seven British regiments under Gen. John Burgoyne and five Hessian and Brunswick regiments under Gen. Fredrich von Riedesel. Carleton convened a council of Lorette Huron, Micmac, Abenaki, Algonkian, and Iroquois on June 5, and persuaded 300 warriors to join his expedition.

Thompson meanwhile withdrew to Sorel. There Gen. John Sullivan arrived with 2,000 fresh troops on May 30 and took command of American forces in Canada. He ordered Thompson to lead his army against the reported 800 British troops at Trois Rivieres. Actually, Carleton had arrived there with 6,000 troops. When an unsuspecting Thompson attacked, his army was routed, leaving nearly 200 dead and 200 captives, including the general, on the field. Once again, Carleton failed to follow up his victory with a decisive thrust. Only after receiving nearly 3,000 more troops did he order an advance on June 14, deploying 1,200 troops under Brig. Gen. Simon Fraser to march along shore, while 8,000 others sailed aboard the fleet. The British reached the American position at Sorel that evening, but Sullivan retreated up the Richelieu River to St. Johns. While Burgoyne's 4,000-man brigade marched after Sullivan, Carleton sailed up the St. Lawrence to cut off Arnold at Montreal. Arnold escaped and joined Sullivan at St. Johns on June 17. Leaving a rear guard at Isle aux Noix, they withdrew with the bulk of their army to Crown Point.[24]

Carleton called off his pursuit. Though he commanded a superb army, he had no way to bring it against the enemy. To do so, he needed a fleet to sail his army down Lake Champlain. He set a portion of his army to work building vessels at St. Johns above the Richelieu River rapids. Warships were dismantled below, portaged in pieces around the white water, and reassembled. That Herculean task would take months to realize. With luck, the fleet might sail before the snow fell in autumn.

Until then, Carleton scattered most of his army in camps from Montreal to St. Johns. He received a surprise reinforcement on June 17, when Sir John Johnson and his followers reached Montreal. Carleton complied with Johnson's fervent request to avenge his humiliating losses by issuing him a commission as the lieutenant colonel of a regiment of loyalists he vowed to raise. To spearhead his campaign, Carleton created a special 1,500-man brigade at St. Johns composed of all the light and grenadier companies and commanded by General Fraser. The elite of that elite was a ranger company of 100 crack shots armed with rifles; each of the army's ten regiments had to contribute a sergeant, corporal, and eight privates. Those troops would be in the thick of the region's fighting until Burgoyne's surrender sixteen months later.[25]

His Indians were not content to idly wait. Fed up with their incessant demands for action, Carleton finally gave in. On June 20, he sent Capt. Joseph Marie LaMothe with a war party up the Richelieu. They captured or killed a couple dozen American stragglers before reaching Isle aux Noix. There they ambushed twelve troops from the 6th Pennsylvania, killing four and capturing six, while two officers managed to escape. Another Indian party jumped two bateaux that had fallen behind Sullivan's retreat, killing nine and capturing five. The governor was appalled when the warriors proudly paraded their scalps through Montreal. He forbade the taking of any more trophies and offered a reward for prisoners at a council with about 300 Indians, mostly Seven Nations, on June 24. The Indian enthusiasm for the British, which had swelled as the redcoat tide swept the rebels from Canada, now subsided. To Carleton's relief, most departed for their homes. He would reluctantly recall them in the fall.

THE NORTHWEST FRONTIER
Britain's economic and military hold on the northwest frontier weakened slightly in 1776. The American occupation of Montreal and siege of Quebec had disrupted British communications, trade, and supply with the Great Lakes. But after expelling the Americans, Governor Carleton swiftly reestablished those links. He issued licenses to forty-one traders to ascend into the high country, but those men would get a late start and would lose a portion of the trade to the Spanish in the upper Mississippi River valley.[26]

Faced with the American threat, Carleton tried to concentrate all available troops for Canada's defense. He ordered Captain Lernoult at Detroit to transfer two companies of the 8th to Fort Niagara, where they arrived in late May. To replace those troops, he ordered Capt. Hugh Lord to withdraw with his seventy troops of the 18th garrisoning Fort Gage at Kaskaskia to Detroit. Lord left in April and counciled with various tribes en route. At Vincennes in May, he met with Kickapoo, Piankeshaw, and White River Delaware chiefs to ensure their loyalty and safe passage for his troops. In late May, he held a council with the Miami chiefs at the Wabash portage. Rumors reached the Kentucky settlers that Lord was actually rallying those tribes to war across the Ohio, prompting them to dispatch James Herrod and Garrett Pendergrass to parley with the Delaware Indians in June. Meanwhile, Lord and his troops reached Detroit on June 3. There they remained until September, when they embarked for Niagara.[27]

Before leaving, Lord authorized local merchant Philippe Francois de Rastel, Sieur de Rocheblave, to act as the region's sole British agent. Lord's choice was as interesting as it was favorable to British interests under the circumstances. Rocheblave was French born, emigrated to Canada in 1751, fought at the 1755 Monongahela battle and 1759 Fort Niagara siege, emigrated to St. Louis after the conquest to serve Spain, and only recently, in 1773, settled in Kaskaskia under the Union Jack. He not only was an expert in Canadian and Indian ways, but also would loyally serve British imperial if not mercantile interests there for the next two years. Rocheblave's tendency to favor Canadian over British traders and the region's remoteness caused Carleton to refuse to reimburse him for any expenses.[28]

The only northwest fort where the British actively recruited warriors was at Michilimackinac. In councils from June 5 through July 14, Capt. Arent Schuyler De Peyster rallied over 500 warriors to head with British officers to Montreal. The first party numbered 140, mostly Ottawa Indians, and left on June 17, followed by 350 mostly Chippewa, Menominee, Fox, and Sioux Indians on July 4. Shortly after De Peyster saw the last war party off, he received a June 13 letter from Carleton ordering him not to send any Indians since the British had driven the rebels from Canada. All that work and satisfaction were for naught, the captain must have rued.[29]

A rumor circulating in Pittsburgh that Lt. Gov. Henry Hamilton was recruiting war parties at Detroit against the Ohio valley settlements was false. The rumor's main source was trader John Dodge, who had returned from Detroit to report that Hamilton "was urging the Western Indians to war upon the American frontier settlements."[30] This was the first account of Hamilton, whose notoriety would soon pervade the Ohio valley frontier. Actually, Hamilton was continually sought out for council from various delegations but did not know how to employ them other than to beseech their continued loyalty. The only attack that spring occurred when Indians killed one surveyor and wounded another from Richard Henderson's party at the falls of the Ohio. Those warriors most likely came from the only village openly hostile to the Americans that year—Pluggy's Mingo band on the Olentangy River, a branch of the Scioto.

An anonymous report offered a more accurate view, describing Detroit as

> garrisoned by 120 Soldiers of the 8th regiment commanded by Captain Richard Berenger Lernoult, the soldiers seem indifferent about the present unhappy Disputes . . . The Savages are wavering and divided . . . There is two armed Schooners On the Lake . . . mounting 12 Six pounders each . . . Besides these, there is two Schooners and two Sloops . . . To man the whole there is 30 Seamen . . . and not one gunner, they are generally dissatisfied with the Service and will make a poor resistance. The Vessels command the Fort, which is only defended by a Stockade of Picquets about 9 Feet out of the earth, without frize or ditch.[31]

This was a Detroit vulnerable to an American campaign, if a bold enough commander could be found backed by enough men and supplies. On April 23, Congress authorized an expedition against Detroit. That plan would die for lack of an enterprising enough leader and proper funding, along with the fear that carrying it out would provoke a general Indian war.

Fears of attack and subversion permeated Pittsburgh that spring. Alexander McKee, the king's Indian agent at Pittsburgh, had avoided arrest the previous year despite being implicated in Connolly's conspiracy. Then in April, a letter from

John Butler to McKee was intercepted. Once again, the American officials accepted McKee's explanation that the call on him to promote British policies was unsolicited. Though he promised to remain faithful to the new government, suspicion of McKee and other possible secret enemy agents lingered.

Diplomacy rather than arms preoccupied American policy in the Ohio valley that year. In April, Congress appointed John Morgan to replace Richard Butler as its Middle Indian Department superintendent. Morgan was an excellent choice. Then thirty-three years old, he was a former partner in the Philadelphia firm Baynton and Wharton, a relationship he sealed by marrying Baynton's daughter in 1764. As that firm's field officer, Morgan journeyed among the tribes to cut deals and distribute goods. He spent much of 1768 living in the Illinois country and was thoroughly familiar with Indian diplomacy.

Morgan embarked on a diplomatic tour through the friendly Ohio Delaware and Shawnee villages in May and June. Doing so, he simply preached to the converted, though he undoubtedly shored up some sagging sentiments. En route, he penned an extraordinary letter to his rival Henry Hamilton at Detroit, calling for him to "contribute toward a general Peace, good understanding, & happy Reconciliation" between Britain and America. To that he suggested that they regularly correspond and exchange information. He also denied that any American army would march against Detroit that year, although he reserved the right to do so if Indian depredations worsened. Essentially Morgan was calling for a demilitarized zone in the Ohio country preliminary to some sort of hazy peace settlement. What was Morgan thinking? Most likely he wanted to lull Hamilton into a false sense of security, while he pulled the tribes toward the United States. He also used his messenger, merchant James Heron, to spy on Detroit's defenses. In a July 20 reply, Hamilton denied rallying the Indians to war but rejected any notion of cooperating with the enemy.[32]

Accompanied by Alexander McKee and a few assistants, Morgan made a second diplomatic trip from June 4 to July 22, visiting Coshocton, the Moravian villages, Chillicothe, Kiskapo Town, and Wakatomica. Among these Indians, Delaware chief White Eyes and Shawnee chief Cornstalk led the peace factions of their respective tribes. Morgan's mission's most important accomplishment was to convince the Moravian missionary David Zeisberger to forward to him in Pittsburgh secret intelligence reports on the region. Morgan headed on to Philadelphia to report on his mission.[33]

While Morgan was gone, important envoys and news reached Pittsburgh. Seneca chief Kayashuta remained a stalwart champion of peace. He persuaded Shawnee chief The Shade and Munsee chief Pemetamah to join him in council with Delaware chief Captain Pipe on July 6. Worried about a rumored American campaign, Kayashuta warned that the Ohio Indians would resist any invasion of their lands by either side: "We will not suffer either the English or the Americans to march an army through our country."[34] Simon Girty and an Iroquois delegation reached Pittsburgh a few days later to report the Niagara council and the Six Nations' policy of neutrality.

William Wilson and Joseph Nicolson, eight Shawnee, three Delaware, and three Mingo conducted their own diplomatic mission through the Ohio tribes in July. They boldly entered Pluggy's Town on July 19 but were lucky to escape with their lives when an informant warned them they would be captured and carried off to Detroit. At Coshocton, Wilson sent out runners to call the tribes to a council at Pittsburgh in September. When most of the chiefs sent noncommittal or defiant replies, Wilson decided on a reckless course. He, interpreter John Montour, and Delaware chief White Eyes traveled all the way to the Wyandot village opposite Detroit to plead for peace before Half King, Cornstalk, the Hardman, and other Wyandot and Shawnee chiefs. He arrived on September 2, just when his rival Hamilton was conducting his own diplomacy across the river.[35]

Hamilton still reluctantly complied with Carleton's instructions to curry friendship, not warriors, among the tribes. On August 29, he convened a council of 200 Wyandot, Ottawa, Chippewa, Potawatomi, Shawnee, Mingo, Delaware, and Cherokee. He urged them to reject Morgan's entreaties and sit tight until he asked them to seize the war hatchet. Then, to his astonishment, he was told of Wilson's nearby presence. Hamilton invited the Americans to join his council. Wilson, Montour, and White Eyes appeared on September 3. As all eyes bore upon him, Hamilton tore up the American commissioner's written speech and the Delaware's wampum. He then asked that Wilson and Montour be allowed safe passage to Pittsburgh. Privately he was more conciliatory with Wilson, asking him to convey to the other rebels the Indian alliance against them and "the dreadful consequences of going to war with so terrible an enemy, and accept the King's pardon while it could be obtained."[36] While Hamilton treated Wilson in a way that discredited his mission, he inadvertently insulted White Eyes. In doing so, he created an enduring enemy.

The summer of 1776 was bloody and horrifying for Kentucky's settlers as war parties converged from north and south. The population ebbed and flowed as raids chased some out and others greedy for land poured in. On June 23, around eighty Mingo from Pluggy's Town wounded a settler and captured two boys outside Leestown. A Shawnee and Mohawk delegation to the Cherokee killed two settlers on the way north through Kentucky. A Kickapoo war party captured several settlers in July.[37]

The most famous attack occurred on July 14, when four Shawnee and the Cherokee Hanging Maw captured Jemimah Boone and Elizabeth and Frances Calloway as they foolishly paddled a canoe on the Kentucky River within sight and hearing but beyond rifle shot of Boonesborough. The girls' cries for help alerted the settlement. After the men gathered, Daniel Boone quickly organized a pursuit. Fearing the capture might be a decoy to lure the militia into an ambush, he told most men to defend the settlement. He then split the pursuit into two groups, one to head upstream while he led the other downstream.

The abduction was well timed. Having taken the girls an hour before twilight, the Indians had all night to prod their captives toward the Ohio River and the safety beyond, while the pursuers stalled as the trail dissolved in darkness. Boone and his men anxiously awaited daylight and then hurried forward, but the Indians and girls were about ten miles ahead. After crossing their trail several times, Boone guessed that they were heading toward a ford on the Licking River and spurred his men toward it. Darkness fell again and both parties holed up for the night, this time, unbeknownst to both, only an hour's strides apart. The next morning, Boone and his men caught up to the Indian camp, crept near, and opened fire. Two Indians were mortally wounded, and the rest fled into the brush. The girls were unhurt, and after a joyful reunion, Boone led them and his men back home.

That August, the Declaration of Independence arrived at the Kentucky settlements. Whatever their measure of enthusiasm or disdain for that act, most settlers went along with the celebrations. Their views aside, all understood that a bloody wilderness would soon engulf them as the British rallied the Indians against them. Indeed, around 820 Kentuckians would die violent deaths during the war.[38]

Virginia's government did what it could to ready Kentucky for that onslaught. In March, it appointed George Rogers Clark the major in command of Kentucky's militia; issued captains' commissions to Daniel Boone, Benjamin Logan, John Todd, and James Herrod over the militia in their respective settlements; and sent them a convoy of gunpowder, lead, and other supplies. Virginia then reasserted its claim to the western lands by citing its 1609 charter and denouncing all private deals that acquired those lands from the Indians. Only Virginia's government could buy that territory and then resell it to companies or individuals.

The assembly had in mind such speculators as Richard Henderson and his Transylvania Company. But Henderson's persistent lobbying of the Virginia and North Carolina legislatures paid off that year. Each state granted his Transylvania Company 200,000 acres—Virginia in the Ohio and Green River valleys and North Carolina in the Powell and Clinch River valleys. This would seem legally to seal his stake, but frontier land claims were rarely that straightforward. Conflicting claims would tie up Henderson's legal possession of various tracts for years and sometimes decades. The conflict over land among the Americans would frustrate the participants long after they had resolved the issue with the tribes.[39]

Despite scattered killings in Kentucky and along the upper Ohio, war was not inevitable between the Americans and tribes. Skilled diplomacy could divert that possibility. The Americans prepared for a peace council at Pittsburgh with its official opening date of September 25. There 400 militia gathered to prevent any disruptions and impress the envoys with American might. Gifts were gathered. The commissioners prepared and rehearsed their speeches. But the first Indian delegates would not arrive until three weeks after the council was to begin. Eventually 644 Iroquois, Shawnee, Delaware, Munsee, and Mahican Indians gathered. Among the most prominent chiefs were the Seneca Kayashuta and White Mingo, the Shawnee Cornstalk and Ninewha, and the Delaware White Eyes and Captain Pipe. The Mingo Indians were conspicuously absent.

During the proceedings from October 15 to November 7, the Americans offered their usual promises while the Indians replied with their usual complaints. Cornstalk eloquently explained the Indian position: "When God created this

World he gave this Island to the red people . . . Now we . . . see your people seated on our Land which all Nations esteem as their . . . heart—all our Lands are covered by the white people, & we are jealous that you still intend to make larger strides—We never sold you our Lands which you now possess."[40]

While all Indians shared that view, tensions sizzled among and within some of the tribes. White Eyes rejected Kayashuta's attempts to act as the Indian spokesman and taunted the Iroquois with the Delaware assertion of independence. Captain Pipe spurned White Eyes' tilt toward the Americans. When word arrived that their ancient Chief Netawatwees had died, the Delaware went into a prolonged council that finally approved the younger Captain John Killbuck as the proper hereditary successor. This was good news for the Americans—Killbuck strongly favored their cause. Despite all these animosities and conflicts, in the end the chiefs promised "inviolable peace with the United States and neutrality with Great Britain."[41]

While some Indians counciled, others warred against the frontier. In late September, a party of eighteen Wyandot, two Mingo, and an Ottawa crossed the Ohio and spread a reign of terror across the upper Monongahela valley. Col. Dorsey Pentecost reported to Gov. Patrick Henry the subsequent carnage:

On the 9th of October two women were killed at the mouth of Fish Creek & a little boy taken prisoner. The husbands of the women were in canoes moving home from the fort at Grave Creek; one of the men upon hearing the women fired on, ran ashore & discharged his gun at one of the Indians, & it is thought wounded him, as the party that went to bury the dead the next day found . . . three bags of paint, a hoppus, a pair of moccasons, a looking glass, & a head dress. On the 11th of the same month, seven men on their return from Caintuck were fired on in their camp nearly opposite the mouth of the Hockhocking; one was killed on the spot & scalped; one shot through with two bullets, of which he died the next day; two of the men had an arm broke each, one slightly wounded, the other two not hurt. When the men awaked the Indians were amongst them with their tomahawks and war club; a scuffle ensued, but the Indians being prepared & having the advantage the men were obliged to run, one was cut with a tomahawk by the side of his back bone to the hollow of his body, another cut under the shoulder to the ribs. After plundering the camp, they crossed the river.[42]

By late October, those warriors were swaggering with their scalps and loot through the Moravian and Delaware villages.

The frontier's respite was short. In December, Chief Pluggy and thirty Mingo plunged beyond the Ohio and up the Licking River to search and destroy. On Christmas Day, they ambushed ten men led by John Todd and John Gabriel Jones who were heading down the valley toward the Ohio where George Rogers Clark and Jones had cached 500 pounds of gunpowder. The fusillade killed Jones and another man; the warriors' charge netted four others. The survivors fled to tell the grim tale. The Mingo strode to McClelland's Station and attacked on December 29. Musket balls killed John McClelland and another man, but a rifle shot shattered Pluggy's life.

Pluggy won in death what he failed to achieve in life—the destruction of a fort. McClelland Station's settlers abandoned their homes and crowded into nearby Harrodsburg. That fort and Boonesborough were the only settlements left in all of Kentucky. Over 300 pioneers had fled back over the mountains. Two score others had been slain or captured.

Meanwhile, filled with goodwill from the Pittsburgh council, Cornstalk and his delegation stopped at Fort Randolph. The timing could hardly have been worse. A war party of three Mingo and a Wyandot joined their camp outside the fort. The warriors captured and carried off a stray soldier. Cornstalk sent White Fish and five others to liberate the soldier and bring him back on December 19. That rescue should have reinforced the peace status of Cornstalk and his people in the eyes of the frontiersmen. It did not.[43]

THE SOUTHEAST FRONTIER

After the tense standoffs and maneuverings of different factions in 1775, war would explode across the southeast frontier in 1776. The British attempted the first blow, but it miscarried. The plan was for 2,800 troops under Maj. Gen. Henry Clinton and thousands of loyalists gathered by Col. Donald McDonald in the Carolina piedmont to rendezvous at the Cape Fear River mouth below Wilmington in late February. That scheme was shaped by North Carolina governor Josiah Martin, who claimed that at least 10,000 loyalist militia merely awaited the word to serve the king. It was not until January 6 that Clinton received the plan. Within three weeks, he set sail with two companies of regulars to the Cape Fear River, where he would be joined by Gen. Charles Cornwallis and five regiments crammed aboard a flotilla commanded by Adm. Peter Parker.

By February 20, only 1,600 regulars and highlanders had rallied around McDonald at Cross Creek. Though far fewer had enlisted in return for promises of western land and tax relief than what Governor Martin had promised, McDonald had no choice but to march them to join Clinton's invasion force. Awaiting the loyalist advance were 1,200 militia and two cannons commanded by Col. Richard Caswell at Moore's Creek Bridge seventeen miles from Wilmington. McDonald's force arrived on February 27. Caswell feigned a retreat into the surrounding woods. McDonald ordered his men across the bridge. The Americans opened fire and charged. Within minutes, the battle was over, with as many as 70 loyalists killed or wounded and 850 captured. That victory decisively tipped the balance toward the rebels in that region where patriots and loyalists had been fairly evenly split.

Clinton and his small contingent, meanwhile, sat at anchor at the Cape Fear River mouth from late February until the ships of Parker's storm-scattered fleet arrived from April 18 through May 31. With North Carolina lost to the rebels, where could the invasion force land? Clinton, Cornwallis, and Parker decided that Charles Town was the best target.

What had become of the Indian war? According to Whitehall's strategy, the British invasion and loyalist uprising were supposed to be aided by Creek and Cherokee war parties attacking along the frontier. Here too the British would be disappointed. That strategy dated back to September 12, 1775, when Gen. Thomas Gage penned an order to Southern Indian Superintendent John Stuart to mobilize the tribes for a grand offensive in 1776. Gage had arrived at that strategy simultaneously with East Florida governor Peter Tonyn and prominent southern loyalists. Those men were ecstatic when they learned of their meeting of distant minds. Tonyn informed Gen. Henry Clinton that "nothing could have been more easy than to have had the Indians in action . . . the King's Loyal Subjects could be easily separated from the Rebels, and the attack, which would doubtless be cruel and wrong, but there are ways to do it distinguishably. It is cruel to continue doing nothing. It is always a losing game."[44] Tonyn and his subordinates set aside those qualms and worked feverishly to implement Gage's strategy.

But a major obstacle blocked the plan's fulfillment—John Stuart. Like Canadian governor Guy Carleton, Stuart expressed his abhorrence at wielding warriors against British subjects. The proper policy, he argued, should seek Indian neutrality rather than alliance. Were those views guided more by morality, ego, or inertia? After all, he had seemed to call for Indian alliances the previous year. Was his independent stance a peevish reaction to Governor Tonyn's assertion of power over Indian and military affairs on that front? Were the burdens of war too much for an overweight, sickly, rapidly aging man? How much did fear of retaliation against his family and property in Charles Town shape his position? Regardless, while Stuart did not outright disobey, he dragged his feet in following Gage's orders. An exasperated Tonyn complained to Gen. Henry Clinton of Stuart's lethargy, which "stands in need of a strong spur."[45]

Stuart was not entirely to blame. Germain and Howe assisted Stuart's inertia by forgetting to send him appropriate orders. Germain did not write at all, while Howe simply instructed him to "inculcate into the minds of the Indians how much it is in their Interest to remain Steady in their attachment to the King . . . Pursue every means to secure them by engagements to be always in readiness to assist his Majesty's arms when called upon, they must not be incited to Indiscriminate acts of Hostilities upon the Inhabitants of the Province in Rebellion."[46]

Maj. Gen. Henry Clinton also questioned the morality of sending Indians against British subjects. After months of wrestling with the question, he sent the superintendent orders in May to hold the Indians until further notice. Stuart was happy to oblige and had the means to do so. That year, he and his deputies dispensed 14,500 pounds sterling worth of gifts to the Indians, mostly to forge peace between the Creek and Choctaw.[47]

Learning of the shift in strategy, Tonyn vigorously protested: "The Americans are a thousand times more in dread of the Savages than of any European troops. Why not avail them of their help. A few months ago the whole Creek nation would have acted with very good Will. They may not be so well inclined now. The Cherokees the same."[48]

With the southern superintendent standing in his way, Tonyn simply sidestepped him. He sent Thomas Brown with an escort and twenty horseloads of gunpowder to distribute to those Creek and Cherokee willing to seize the war hatchet. In April, Brown reached the Lower Creek village of Chiaha, where in council he urged the chiefs to war against the frontier. There he was joined by Stuart's deputy David Tait with gifts and the same message. But then in June, the two agents received conflicting orders. Tait got Clinton's order via Stuart to hold rather than unleash the Creek. On June 1, Tonyn sent Brown a lieutenant colonel's commission and authority to raise the East Florida Rangers.

The Americans, meanwhile, tried to use diplomacy to stave off a rumored war with the Cherokee. On April 15, George Galphin, Willie Jones, John Walker, Edward Wilkinson, and Robert Rae arrived at Fort Charlotte for a council they had called the previous autumn. It would be another week before the first Cherokee trickled in. No prominent chiefs arrived. The council concluded with platitudes. Where were the chiefs and their followers?

Most Cherokee had flocked to Chota for a council with the British. The previous October, John Stuart had sent his brother and deputy Henry to Pensacola to organize supplies for the Cherokee. Early in 1776, Cherokee chief Dragging Canoe met with Henry Stuart at Mobile and sought aid for attacking the Watauga settlements. Stuart received 3,000 pounds of gunpowder from Gov. Peter Chester, packed it on twenty-one horses, and embarked with Dragging Canoe, Alexander Cameron, and an escort on a fifty-five-day trek north to the Overhill Cherokee village of Chota, arriving on April 24. Runners were sent out to the other villages for a council. Stuart opened the proceedings on May 2 with over 700 Indians present. Around that time, a fourteen-man delegation of Shawnee, Delaware, and Mohawk visited the Overhill Cherokee villages to form an alliance against the Americans. The Cherokee chiefs announced they had targeted the Watauga settlements.[49]

Stuart and Cameron privately debated the ethics of launching Indian attacks against British subjects, even if they were rebels. They finally decided to delay Dragging Canoe for twenty days, while on May 7 they signed and sent the Watauga settlers a letter. The message was blunt—the Wataugans were trespassers and an Indian assault was imminent. The British agents implored the Wataugans to resettle under the king's protection in West Florida, where they would be given free land. Trying to buy time, the Wataugans replied ambiguously on May 13 by declaring their loyalty and reluctance to move. Stuart fired off a letter on May 23 asserting that loyalty was not enough; those settlements were illegal and must be evacuated.

Meanwhile, the Wataugans applied to Virginia's Fincastle County to send them militia and supplies. Jesse Benton, a Wataugan, forged a letter from Stuart and Cameron stating that a British force was to march against them via the Creek and Cherokee villages. This provoked indignation and defiance among the frontier settlers. However moved the Fincastle and Williamsburg officials may have been, they could spare nothing for the Wataugans. Virginia's government not only refused to help, but actually hindered the Wataugans' defense and claims when it recognized the Lochaber line as the legal boundary with the Cherokee, a ruling that meant that in Virginia's eyes, the Wataugan settlements were illegal.

However appealing it was in the abstract, self-government was proving to be too costly in money, men, supplies, and stress for the Wataugans. On July 5, they bowed to political reality when they signed and sent off a petition to North Carolina's government humbly requesting annexation. It would be weeks before the state could receive, investigate, debate, and then rule on that request. For now, the Wataugans had to face the Cherokee onslaught alone.

War parties from the Lower and Middle villages were the first to strike, killing thirty-seven settlers along the Catawba River in South Carolina in late June. Satiated with scalps, mayhem, and destruction, they withdrew to their villages. The Overhill Cherokee were just then embarking on the warpath.

Word that several hundred warriors were heading their way may have prevented a massacre but sparked a panic. Lt. John Sevier had to abandon Fort Lee protecting the Nolichucky settlements when fifteen of its thirty defenders fled with their families. Most of the settlers who remained in the region crowded into Fort Watauga (Caswell) at Sycamore Shoals, whose seventy-five men were led by Col. John Carter, Capt. James Robertson, and Sevier.

The Cherokee burned Fort Lee and then split up, with Dragging Canoe leading his men toward Long Island, Old Abram and his warriors striding toward Sycamore Shoals, and Raven and his followers heading toward Carter's Valley. Raven's men would neither suffer nor inflict casualties as they looted and burned their way across the abandoned region, but the parties of Dragging Canoe and Abram would be repulsed with heavy losses.

Scouts brought back word on June 19 to Eaton's Station of the approaching Cherokee. Fearing the Indians would bypass their fort and burn their homes, the leader, James Shelby, decided to strike first. On June 20, he split his seventy men into two divisions, each with flankers and scouts, and advanced toward the enemy. Four miles from the fort, they encountered about twenty Cherokee, opened fire, charged, and scattered them. They then deployed atop a wooded hill and waited. Dragging Canoe and his men attacked later that day but suffered fourteen dead and many wounded, including the chief himself with his thigh broken. Only four frontiersmen were wounded. Dragging Canoe and his men retreated to their villages.[50]

Old Abram and his party attacked Fort Watauga on June 21 but were repulsed with unrecorded losses. They hovered around the fort for several more weeks, but succeeded only in killing two men and capturing two others. Relief was on the way. Colonels Evan Shelby and William Russell led their men from their respective forts into Watauga in late July, but the Cherokee had already disappeared.

The Creek almost joined the Cherokee in warring against the southeast frontier. George Galphin convened a council with the Creek at Augusta on May 16.

The chiefs demanded presents, the expulsion of squatters from their lands, and justice for the murder of a Coweta by Thomas Fee earlier that year. Galphin was impotent to address any of those reasonable demands. That failure caused the Coweta and other Creek to shift their allegiance to Britain and begin killing stray settlers and traders in the disputed ceded lands. On July 31, the squatters there sent a petition to Maj. Gen. Charles Lee, the newly appointed American commander for the southern region, urging him to bring the army "to exterminate and rout those savages."[51] The squatters would have to protect themselves for now. Lee had no troops to spare from more vital fronts.

Lee had his hands full elsewhere. Clinton's armada dropped anchor just beyond the entrance to Charles Town bay on June 7. The Americans were ready for them with nearly 3,600 armed men split among forts ringing the bay. Lee and several hundred Continentals had arrived just three days earlier and stirred passions by demanding that the 1,200 troops in Fort Sullivan on Sullivan's Island be withdrawn into Charles Town itself. South Carolina president John Rutledge and Fort Sullivan's commander Col. William Moultrie adamantly rejected the notion. On June 16, Clinton landed his 1,800 regulars, 500 armed sailors, and artillery on Long Island next to Sullivan's Island. On June 28, the fleet's guns and the batteries on Long Island opened fire on Fort Sullivan. When the smoke cleared after eight hours of cannon fire, the British had lost 225 men, the Americans 12 killed and 25 wounded. Short of supplies, munitions, and will, Clinton and Parker chose to sail away to New York.[52]

By midsummer, the initiative on the southeast coast and frontier had passed to the Americans. Having repulsed the British at Charles Town, Lee planned simultaneous offensives against East Florida and the Cherokee. The first venture failed abjectly, but the second was overwhelmingly successful. In July, Lee marched with his Continentals from Charles Town to Savannah, where he gathered supplies and troops. With high hopes, he led 2,000 men south toward St. Augustine on August 19. To defend East Florida, Governor Tonyn had less than half that number of troops. He deployed the newly arrived seven companies of the 60th Regiment in reserve at St. Augustine and small posts along the St. Johns River, while he sent Thomas Brown's four ranger companies of about 130 men to harass Lee on the Georgia frontier. Guarding the St. Mary's River were seventy troops and three small warships. By early September, American raiders captured all three ships and a newly arrived brig. With the Americans now enjoying naval as well as troop superiority, East Florida's conquest seemed inevitable.[53]

Then everything went wrong. British victories elsewhere shadowed by disease, inertia, and hunger halted Lee's advance at Sunbury. The war was going badly up north. Howe had beaten Washington on Long Island and driven him from Manhattan. Congress agreed to recall the experienced Charles Lee to bolster and perhaps save the army. When Lee departed, he took with him the Virginian and North Carolina Continentals. The command passed to Brig. Gen. Lachlan McIntosh, who sat tight before that seemingly impassable maze of swamplands ahead. A cocktail of ailments killed or sickened hundreds of his men. The survivors devoured supplies. South Carolina called home its troops. McIntosh's invasion army dwindled into a mere frontier guard.

While the Americans clung with an ever more feeble grip to that frontier, they mustered mighty thrusts against another. Virginia, North Carolina, South Carolina, and Georgia, with congressional assistance, coordinated a series of offensives against the Cherokee. The failure of American diplomacy with that tribe had hardened formerly conciliatory hearts. Commissioner William Drayton advocated a ruthless military campaign: "Cut up every Indian corn field, and burn every Indian town—and . . . every Indian taken shall be the slave and property of the taker; that the nation be extirpated, and the lands become the property of the public . . . I shall never give my voice for a peace with the Cherokee Nation upon any other terms than their removal beyond the mountains."[54] Thomas Jefferson called for taking all Cherokee land: "I hope that the Cherokees will now be driven beyond the Mississippi and that this in the future will be declared to the Indians as the invariable consequence of their beginning a war."[55] The three North Carolina congressional delegates most succinctly summed up the policy: "Mercy to the warriors is cruelty to ourselves."[56]

The first assault was launched in late July by Maj. Samuel Jack, who led 200 Georgia militia to burn two Cherokee villages on the upper Savannah and Chattahoochee Rivers. In August, Col. Andrew Williamson marched 1,200 South Carolina militia against the Middle Towns. That army was joined in September by Gen. Griffith Rutherford and 2,400 North Carolina militia. Together they burned their way through the region. On September 21, Col. William Christian led 1,800 Virginia and 300 North Carolina militia into newly built Fort Patrick Henry on Long Island. A dozen Cherokee skulking around the fort killed a soldier. After Capt. John Sevier and several score horsemen joined the expedition on October 1, the Americans marched through the Overhill villages, torching five of them. The destruction was total, but the invaders caught no more than glimpses of their human prey.

Before such overwhelming odds, the Cherokee disappeared into the thick forested mountains. Once the soldiers had tramped away, the refugees filed back to stare in stunned silence at the charred ruins of their homes. Calls for vengeance were muted. Only Dragging Canoe and his followers remained defiant. The elders reasoned it was time to talk. Led by Chief Raven, they met with Christian at Fort Patrick Henry the first week of November. Christian elicited their promise to a truce, the handover of hostages, the surrender of a portion of their land, and the return of all captives and property. A formal council and treaty next spring would formalize the promises.

Word of the victorious campaign against the Cherokee wrung jubilation from all frontier inhabitants no matter what their political leanings. They shared Thomas Jefferson's view that the "contest with Britain is too serious and too great to permit any possibility of avocation from the Indians. This then is the reason for driving them off, and our Southern colonies are happily rid of every other enemy and may exert their whole force in that quarter."[57]

Yet the southeast was not entirely secure despite the repulse of the British attack on Charles Town and the destruction of the Cherokee villages. Thomas Brown was the most energetic and successful British commander on the southern frontier. By year's end, he had raised six ranger companies and sent them rampaging along the borderlands between Florida and Georgia, mostly rustling cattle and looting suspected rebel homes. Defying David Tait's contrary efforts, he spent that year trying to rally the Upper Creek Indians to war against the rebels.

Two hundred warriors were about to follow Brown when an invitation arrived from John Stuart for a council at Pensacola in October. The Creek, like other Indians, tended to follow the most generous leader. Brown was clearly a warrior but had few gifts to give. Stuart, in contrast, was a wealthy peace chief. Over 500 Upper and Lower Creek and Choctaw Indians flocked to the council. Stuart distributed presents in return for their promise to stay off the warpath against both each other and the Americans. The tribes were eager for peace. Stuart reported that "all the Southern Tribes are greatly dispirited by the unopposed successes of the Rebels, and no appearance of any Support from Government to His Majesty's distressed subjects in the interior parts of the Provinces, or to the Indians who have engaged in His Majesty's cause."[58]

A personal success accompanied Stuart's official accomplishment. During the summer, a Creek delegation journeyed all the way to Charles Town to demand the release of Stuart's wife, Sarah, and daughter. The officials complied. The Stuart family was finally reunited.

Suffering from a painful boil that kept him off horseback, Thomas Brown meanwhile had holed up at the Upper Creek village of Chiaha. Although he could not personally lead them, he was able to talk a war party into heading east against the settlements. In mid-November, the Creek ambushed a Georgia ranger patrol near Fort Barrington, killing four and wounding two. That attack sparked a panic along that hitherto quiescent frontier. Gen. Lachlan McIntosh tried to coordinate a retaliatory attack on Chiaha, but the militia commanders refused to budge from protecting their own vulnerable settlements. The Creek Indians struck again and killed another four Georgia rangers on the Altamaha River in December.

In all, Britain's southern strategy failed miserably in 1776. The Americans defeated the loyalist uprising at Moore's Creek in February and repulsed Clinton's attack on Charles Town in June. Clinton undercut his own offensive by sending Stuart a last-minute order to restrain the Indians. After David Tait and Thomas Brown had rallied them to war's brink, the deputy then held back the Creek Indians. The Cherokee attacked anyway. The Americans fought off the raids and then counterattacked. With no British threat to the coast or Creek war parties ravaging the Georgia frontier, the Americans could concentrate their forces into a series of coordinated offensives that burned their way through all the Cherokee villages. Dazed and homeless, the Cherokee sued for peace. Elsewhere, Chiaha Creek war parties killed or wounded a dozen rangers while loyalists stole cattle along the Georgia frontier. But those were mere pinpricks that incensed the Georgians to vengeance. The effect of all these British efforts was to harden American resolve and unity. While American arms were primarily responsible for their victories, British disunity over Indian policy and the failure to coordinate far-flung attacks contributed to their defeats.

A more quiet American victory involved sorting out boundaries and asserting administration over a swath of frontier. Virginia and North Carolina finally resolved their overlapping claims and split the jurisdiction over the eastern Tennessee settlements with those north of the Holston River, west of Donelson's 1771 line, and in Carter Valley to the former and the rest to the latter. With the Wataugans officially part of their state, North Carolina's assembly could act on their petition, which reached Halifax on August 23. The government invited the Wataugans to send five delegates in November and formally present their petition to the state assembly. North Carolina's government voted in favor of annexation on November 19. The region would be incorporated into the state as Washington County.

THE FRONTIER AND INTERNATIONAL DIPLOMACY

Congress overwhelmingly agreed with its committee of secret correspondence that the United States desperately needed French aid, trade, recognition, and, ideally, alliance.[59] To that end, the committee appointed Silas Deane as America's first diplomat. It was a poor choice. Shortly after Deane reached Paris in July, negative reports began to filter back to Philadelphia. Deane had exceeded his instructions by indiscriminately handing out generals' commissions to nobles while annoying the French, who found him pompous, insensitive, and demanding.

Congress decided to send over to Paris two seasoned colonial agents to dilute Deane's brashness with their diplomatic skills. Benjamin Franklin had served as a colonial agent for fifteen years but was currently a delegate to Congress. Arthur Lee was still serving in London. Congress wrote Lee of his appointment and asked him to reach Paris by December. When Franklin departed on October 26, he carried with him a shopping list that included 25,000 muskets, 100 cannons, and other military supplies and a "model treaty" of commerce that had taken the committee from June to September to hammer out. To entice French support, the Americans would dangle that free trade treaty along with promises to share Newfoundland's fisheries and allow a free French hand to Britain's Caribbean islands and colonies anywhere but in North America, whose pickings the new republic reserved for itself. On September 17, Congress had agreed on its war aims. The United States would try to incorporate all British colonies to the north, including Canada, Nova Scotia, and Newfoundland. Would the French buy those offers?

Fortunately, despite Deane's blunders, the French had already set up a secret military aid program for the United States and were debating whether to war against Britain. Foreign Minister Charles Gravier de Vergennes had eagerly received reports from his secret envoy to Congress, Joseph Hamon de Bonvouloir. In March, Vergennes presented to King Louis XVI and his council of state two reports: "Considerations," which he wrote himself, and "Reflections," prepared by his undersecretary of state Joseph-Mathias Gerard. Together, they argued for a dramatic shift in French foreign policy.[60] As always, Britain remained the worst threat to France's national security. The American Revolution posed both opportunities and dangers for France. The worst-case scenario was for Britain and its colonies to reconcile and then attack France's Caribbean sugar islands. Vergennes offered no evidence to support this fear, but it was contagious, as it played on the importance attached to those few profitable colonies in the French empire. To counter that "threat," Vergennes advocated for France to revive its Bourbon family compact or alliance with Spain. Those countries would build up their fleets and Caribbean forces while supplying the Americans with enough munitions and weapons to keep their Revolution alive indefinitely. War would be declared when the combined fleets outnumbered Britain's. What would be Versailles' war aims? Vergennes was adamantly opposed to any attempt to reconquer Canada and Louisiana, which had been nothing but economic and strategic liabilities. Instead, France could avenge 1763 by taking trade and fisheries from Britain and nurturing American independence. Britain's loss of its North American empire would weaken it in its global struggle with France. Ideally, the French would play off a future weak United States against a future weakened Britain.

When the king asked for objections, the only major voice raised was predictably from Comptroller General Anne-Robert-Jacques Turgot. Aiding the Americans and war with Britain would bankrupt France, the finance minister argued. After two months of pretended reflection, Louis XVI issued his pronouncement. It was His Majesty's wish to defer to Vergennes; shortly thereafter, he dismissed the bourgeois Turgot, whose blunt manner he had always found distasteful. Turgot, of course, was prescient. France would ruin itself for American independence and then experience a revolution of its own, one immeasurably more destructive, and bringing but a sliver of the progress achieved by the American Revolution.

Versailles set up the front Roderique Hortalez and Company and funded it with 1 million livres tournois to pay for arms to the Americans. The king chose Pierre-Augustin Caron de Beaumarchais, best known as the *Barber of Seville*'s author, to head that front company.

America's first diplomatic mission gathered in Paris in mid-December. The three envoys promptly requested an audience with Vergennes, who agreed to meet on December 23. The Americans anxiously presented their nation's official position. The foreign minister replied that France would sooner than later officially welcome American trade, but recognition and alliance would be deferred for now. Versailles would need time to rebuild its fleet and secure an alliance with Spain before it could dare challenge Britain. He reassured them that France had no eye for retaking Canada or Louisiana. The Americans could indulge themselves in North America as they wished. As for the Mississippi navigation issue, that was for the United States and Spain to decide. He promised to introduce them soon to the Spanish ambassador, to whom they could present their proposal.

As these preliminary negotiations unfolded in Paris, Americans issued a direct appeal for aid from Spanish officials. That encounter took place not in Madrid but in New Orleans. Maj. Gen. Charles Lee initiated that policy. While serving as southern district commander, he recognized that Spain could provide essential aid to the American Revolution as supplier and ally. That relationship had to be initiated and nurtured. Lee did just that. He wrote to Louisiana's governor, appealing to the "generosity of Spaniards" that the Americans in their plight "flatter themselves that not only humanity and generosity but also interest, honor, and the security of your sovereign will dictate to your excellency the means to supply us the articles we lack, which consist of muskets, blankets, and medicinal drugs, particularly quinine."[61] Upon being informed by Lee of his intentions, Virginia governor Patrick Henry penned his own plea to the Spanish governor.

Lee chose Capt. George Gibson to deliver those letters and then gather and convey supplies back to the United States. In July, Gibson, Lt. William Linn, and sixteen men set out from Pittsburgh in bateaux for the long 2,000-mile row down to New Orleans. Arriving safely in late August, Gibson delivered to Gov. Luis de Unzaga y Amezaga the letters from Henry and Lee requesting aid, and then sweetened the plea by rhetorically asking if it was in Spain's interests to either take over West Florida or enjoy it as a present from the United States after the Americans overran it. Unzaga was eager to help. Oliver Pollack, who became the American agent at New Orleans, recalled that "Unzaga . . . privately delivered me gunpowder out of the King's store which I delivered to Colonel Gibson."[62] For this, Gibson presented a Virginia note for 1,850 Spanish dollars.

The plan was for Linn to take three-fourths of the powder upriver, while Gibson took the rest by ship outfitted by Pollack directly to Philadelphia. To allay British suspicions that Unzaga was violating Spanish neutrality, Gibson submitted to a mock arrest and imprisonment.

On September 22, Linn and forty-three men embarked in several boats for the long, hard row up the Mississippi and Ohio Rivers to Fort Pitt. Packed into the boats were ninety-eight barrels or 9,000 pounds of gunpowder. It took them two months just to reach Arkansas Post on November 26. Having exhausted nearly all their food, they decided to winter there, hunting and resting until spring. Meanwhile, Unzaga released Gibson, who sailed with his load of gunpowder to Philadelphia.

As for the question of West Florida's fate, an intrigued Unzaga forwarded a report to Jose de Galvez, the minister of the Indies. Would it be in Spanish interests to take West Florida? The wheels of Spanish bureaucracy ground slowly. It was not until December 1777 that Madrid sent an affirmative reply.[63]

THE LAKE CHAMPLAIN FRONTIER

When Gen. Horatio Gates took over the army from Philip Schuyler on July 11, he discovered only "the wretched remains of what was once a very respectable body of troops."[64] Those shards from Canada joined with reinforcements to number some 5,500 sickly, malnourished, and poorly armed men in squalid camps around Crown Point and Fort Ticonderoga. From that horde, Gates desperately tried to forge an army. Benedict Arnold, meanwhile, was assigned the challenge of building a fleet at Skenesborough to block Carleton's advance down Lake Champlain.

The British were coming, but when? A series of patrols up Lake Champlain tried to answer that question. Not anytime soon, concluded those scouts after slipping through the scattered enemy camps and spying the rising skeletons of vessels on the riverbank near St. Johns.

During one such scout on July 25, Benjamin Whitcomb assassinated Brig. Patrick Gordon as he rode alone from St. Johns toward La Prairie. That provoked a British condemnation and an advance. To curtail similar American forays, Gen. Simon Fraser led his brigade up the Richelieu to occupy Isle aux Noix. On July 29, he ordered Capt. Rene-Amable Boucher, Sieur de Boucherville, 36 troops, about 100 Indians, and some Canadians to patrol toward Crown Point. They returned six days later without spotting a soul.[65]

The way south seemed clear, but the fleet to carry Carleton's army there was far from complete. If the governor could not engage the rebels in battle, he sought to win them over with psychology. In early August, he paroled and sent back all his prisoners. That humanitarian gesture actually packaged a practical policy of imposing the cost of feeding nearly 2,000 noncombatants on the rebels while sowing among them scores who despised the war.

But Carleton adamantly rejected another strategy of psychological warfare at his command: he bluntly dismissed all advice from General Burgoyne, John Johnson, and other officers to turn loose his warriors in a reign of terror against the enemy's pickets and supply trains. Instead, he kept a tight rein on those few Indians attached to his army and told the others to stay home until further notice. He filled the arms of the Ottawa and Chippewa with gifts and turned them back when they arrived in mid-July, along with the Menominee, Sauk, Fox, Winnebago, Sioux, and a second group of Chippewa, who reached Montreal in August. Thus did one Crown official squander the enormous cost, effort, and time it took another to recruit all those Indians.[66]

General Burgoyne grew ever more frustrated during those idle months. He got a fleeting chance to do something when Carleton departed for Quebec on July 20 and left him in charge. Burgoyne promptly ordered the 9th's Capt. Alexander Fraser and the 24th's Lt. Thomas Scott to lead fourteen light infantry volunteers and thirty Indians in a scout around Crown Point. They left St. Johns on July 23. Two days later, they flushed thirty-five Americans commanded by Capt. James Wilson near Isle aux Noix. The British and Indians swarmed around the Americans, killing two while suffering two Canadians, a Briton, and an Indian wounded. When his troops appeared to be cut off, Wilson surrendered. The British and Indians returned in triumph with their captives.[67]

By mid-August, Carleton had finished his affairs at Quebec and returned to Montreal. There he began rallying warriors through councils and runners. He recognized that his campaign's success would depend on employing Indians as scouts and flankers, but he was determined to keep them on a short leash. He hoped the mere presence of Indians would terrorize rebel imaginations rather than their lives and property, and hasten their retreat or subjection to the Crown's rule. By September's first week, he had rallied to the Union Jack a mélange of 641 warriors, of which 561 were from the Seven Nations and most of the rest Iroquois, Abenaki, and Ottawa.[68] Capt. Christopher Carleton, the governor's nephew, took charge of the Seven Nations warriors while General Fraser commanded the Iroquois and Ottawa. They camped on Isle aux Noix, impatiently awaiting the word to advance.

Though his fleet was far from finished, Carleton ordered General Fraser to advance with his light brigade and the Indians from Isle aux Noix toward Isle la Motte near where Lake Champlain empties itself into the Richelieu River. There Fraser halted and hastily ordered his brigade to the Richelieu's shore. Guarding those waters was Arnold's fleet of seven warships and eight gundalows or gunboats.

Indians drew the campaign's first blood. On the night of September 5, Lt. Thomas Scott and seven warriors paddled their canoe quietly through Arnold's fleet and set up an ambush on Windmill Point. The next morning, twenty American troops rowed ashore from the *Enterprise* to cut wood. From cover, Scott called on them to surrender. They refused. The Indians killed three and wounded six, while the rest escaped in their bateaux. The *Enterprise*'s captain ordered his cannon fired into the woods. Scott and his warriors slipped away without harm.[69]

On September 19, a party of warriors, troops, and Canadians crept through the forest to Lake Champlain's brushy shore near where the schooner *Liberty* would soon cruise past. A Canadian waded into the lake and called for help. The *Liberty*'s captain ordered his men to trim sails and sent troops in a whaleboat to investigate. The whaleboat was slowly rowed backward and then stopped, unfortunately within musket shot of shore. The officer in charge asked the Canadian to swim. He claimed to be unable to do so. As he waded back to shelter, the British force rose and fired a volley, wounding five Americans. Gunners touched off the whaleboat's swivel and the *Liberty*'s cannon. The shots tore through the forest and wounded several. Both sides then withdrew.

Ever more Indians and elite infantry slipped through the forests parallel to the American fleet. On September 23, Arnold ordered his captains to sail south twenty miles from Isle la Motte to Valcour Island's west side. There he anchored his sixteen vessels in a crescent facing southeast toward the tip of Valcour Island, where the British fleet would pass. He did not worry about his rear, since the northern channel between the island and mainland was too narrow for a fleet's passage. By holing up in Valcour Bay, Arnold took an epic gamble. He hoped that the British fleet would sail past without spotting him. Then he could descend like a hawk on the hundreds of bateaux packed with troops trailing in the fleet's wake. After reaping havoc on those troops, he could sail on to the enemy's fleet as it turned into the wind to face him.

The autumn leaves shimmered at their glorious height when Carleton finally felt his fleet was powerful enough to sweep away Arnold's. Carleton set sail aboard his flagship, the *Maria,* from St. Johns on October 4 with four other warships, twenty gunboats, four armed longboats, and twenty-four supply bateaux, all crewed by 670 men along with 100 troops acting as marines. Capt. Thomas

Pringle commanded the fleet. The army followed in 400 bateaux and scores of canoes, with the Indians and Fraser's brigade leading. The season was so late that Carleton could at best try to seek out and destroy Arnold's fleet and then sail south to take Crown Point and Ticonderoga. This was but a whisper of the spring's grandiose plan to sail and march all the way to New York City.

The British flotilla did not spot Arnold's until October 11, when it sailed past Valcour Island. Carleton ordered his armed vessels to reverse course and head for the Americans, while Fraser's brigade and half the Indians headed toward the western forested shore of the half-mile-wide channel, and Charles Tarieu De Lanaudiere's Canadians and Indians landed on Valcour Island. With the wind in their face, only the gunboats could be rowed straight ahead. Of the warships, only the flagship was able to tack into range with the gunboats. The *Inflexible* did not reach the line until twilight, while the others straggled in during the early night.[70]

Carleton spent most of the morning of October 12 positioning his warships and slowly moving them toward Arnold's crescent. It was not until noon that the first cannon shots exploded. The artillery duel continued throughout the afternoon as the British vessels inched toward the American flotilla. The skilled British gunners sank two ships and killed or wounded over sixty men. American cannon shots splintered several of the British vessels, inflicted about forty casualties, and sank a gunboat. As the sun neared the southwest horizon, Pringle ordered his vessels to withdraw beyond cannon shot and anchor.

Arnold had won a tactical victory but faced certain destruction the next day as the entire British fleet closed for the kill. Hemmed in from three sides, many a commander would have surrendered with the dawn. Not Arnold. The autumn night was foggy and prolonged. Arnold ordered his men to muffle their oars and row past the British fleet.

Carleton discovered the escape shortly after sunrise and ordered his fleet to pursue. The British nearly caught up to the battered Americans late that day near Split Rock. To avoid capture, two American ships ground ashore and their crews disappeared into the forest. The British overtook only one vessel and forced its captain to surrender. The other five American ships reached Buttonmould Bay on the eastern shore that night. With escape impossible, Arnold ordered his 200 men to torch the ships and then head to safety down the lake. At Chimney Point, they crossed over the narrows to Crown Point.

Not a rebel was to be found when Carleton's fleet anchored off Crown Point on October 14. All the Americans had withdrawn to Fort Ticonderoga sixteen miles south. Only the Indians and Fraser's brigade had kept pace with the warships. The rest of the army trickled in over the next three days. Carleton sent Capt. Alexander Fraser, the general's son, with 60 rangers, 100 Indians, and 30 Canadians, to reconnoiter Ticonderoga. Word that Indians stalked the forests kept the Americans within their entrenchments. Fraser's party did round up 130 cattle and drive them north to the British camp.

Carleton also ordered detachments of Indians and Fraser's light brigade to scour the surrounding countryside of its rebel inhabitants. The redcoats and warriors burned, looted, killed, and captured their way through hamlets and homesteads along Lake Champlain's shores and far up its creeks. Lt. John Enys of the 29th recalled "how quietly all these Yankees take any distresses, so much so they appear to have lost all sort of feeling. They expressed no Sort of Surprise or Grief at our Coming and only Said very coolly they did not Suppose we Should have come so far into their Country. One of them appeared a little distressed however when She was told that her Husband was to be carried into Canada and that She herself must return to . . . friends."[71] The prevalence of death and destruction along the frontier must have emotionally numbed many of its inhabitants, especially among the culturally reserved New Englanders.

Like Europeans, Indians were capable of committing the most vicious of crimes and most tender of mercies. Enys witnessed the generosity of an Upper Lakes Indian who donated all his loot to an old woman who suffered "the destruction of everything She had in the world . . . [and] began to make a most dreadful outcry that She was totally ruined."[72]

The two armies faced each other for the next two and a half weeks. In all, Carleton had about 4,000 troops, while Gates commanded about 12,000. Outnumbered three to one, Carleton could only hope to lure the enemy into an attack. But Gates, for better or worse, did not take the bait. In a typical act of kindness, Carleton paroled about 100 men captured from Arnold's fleet. The nights steadily got colder and longer. The men awoke with frost on their blankets. Carleton feared early snows and ice trapping his army. The governor made a last belligerent gesture on October 28, sending five gunboats and thirteen canoes packed with four light infantry companies and Indians to Three Mile Point, where they swarmed ashore. But Gates still refused to fight, despite the chance to wipe out that British detachment. The British and Indians crept forward, fired a few shots, and then slipped away. That was enough for Carleton. On November 2, he set out with his army on the frigid lake from Crown Point and several days later reached St. Johns. From there, he marched his regiments into winter quarters and dispersed his Indians.

The Indians had turned out in large numbers for the campaign and behaved well, but they had little loot and even fewer scalps and tales of valor to display to their people. How many would turn out for next year's campaign? That question was complicated by the loss of Canada's Indian superintendent John Campbell, who remained an American prisoner. In his place, Carleton named Captain Fraser, who was a skilled wilderness fighter. No one doubted Fraser's courage or intelligence. The trouble was that he dismissed Indians as "the most treacherous worthless and ungrateful race of men on the face of the earth."[73] That poisonous attitude would seep into his relations with them and keep many a warrior home the next year who might otherwise have trod south with the army.

THE EASTERN MAINE FRONTIER

As elsewhere, the war disrupted trade and diplomacy with the Maine Indians. The tribes petitioned the Massachusetts government for relief from starvation caused by diminishing ammunition and other essential supplies. Lacking the power to mobilize all the necessary resources to fight a war and conduct diplomacy, Massachusetts could do little but convey its sympathy.[74]

George Washington had nothing to give but much to ask. He appealed to the Maine Indians to war against the British. They replied, "Our natural inclination being Peace, only accustomed to hunt for the subsistence of our family, We could not Comply with the Terms—Our numbers being not sufficient among other objections . . . we hope & trust no offense in sending [the appeal] back."[75] Upon receiving the Indian reply, Washington responded with another letter, this one urging them to keep the "chain of Friendship . . . bright & unbroken" and resist any British appeals to war against the Americans. He cited the fate of "the Cherokees and southern tribes [which] were foolish enough to . . . take up the hatchet against us, upon which our Warriors went into their Country burnt their Houses destroyed their corn and obliged them to sue for peace and to give Hostages for their future good behavour."[76] The Indians would heed his words. They were too impoverished to fight even if they so desired.

That year's war on the Maine frontier would be fought almost entirely by Americans and British, with merely a sprinkling of Indians. Col. Jonathan Eddy was a Machias Bay version of Ethan Allen, fiery, ambitious, fearless, and charismatic. While in the siege lines of Boston, he was inspired by the American victories and capture of Fort Ticonderoga. There Eddy concocted a scheme to take Fort Cumberland. He returned to Machias in the summer and recruited seventy-two Americans and Indians, who set forth in a tiny flotilla of whaleboats and canoes. At Shepody, they captured Captain Walker and thirteen troops, gained valuable intelligence and supplies, and then pushed on to Memrancok, where most French residents rallied to the Americans. They rowed on to Fort Cumberland and during the night captured a sloop and its thirteen-man crew. The next morning, the garrison discovered the capture and opened fire with the fort's cannon. Eddy and his men sailed off to Fort Lawrence and looted supplies from the warehouses at the landing. Local recruits swelled Eddy's force to 180 men, a score of whom guarded nearly 80 redcoat prisoners. On November 10, Eddy sent a surrender summons to Col. Joseph Gorham, Fort Cumberland's commander. Gorham replied with an appeal for the rebels to lay down their arms. Both letters stressed the war's tragedy and hopes that their differences could be resolved. On the evening of November 12, Eddy led an assault on the fort but lacked means to hurdle the wide moat or high walls. The rebels withdrew with one Indian slightly wounded. For the next two weeks, the Americans continued to pop away with their muskets at the fort and rally the locals to their cause. But on November 27, a warship arrived with 400 fresh troops who reinforced the 100-man garrison. At sunrise on November 30, Gorham ordered 200 troops to surge out and rush the rebel camp. The Americans mustered and fired several volleys, killing or wounding fifteen redcoats, and then retreated, leaving only one dead man behind. When the British withdrew into the fort, the Americans reoccupied their camp. The stalemate continued for several months as the outnumbered Americans continued to harass Fort Cumberland. Eddy would finally withdraw to Maine in the new year.[77]

THE SEABOARD WAR

The battles on those remote frontiers were crucial to those who fought and lived there, but the Revolution's fate depended decisively on whether Washington's army could evade capture and inflict stinging defeats on the British. After Howe withdrew his army from Boston, Washington accurately predicted his next move.

After refitting at Halifax, the Howe brothers, with William commanding the army and Richard the fleet, departed on June 10 for New York City. The first ships arrived off Staten Island on June 29. Howe spent six weeks slowly building up his army there as other flotillas arrived, including Clinton's from Charles Town. When the last contingent arrived on August 15, Howe commanded 73 warships and nearly 300 transports manned by 13,000 sailors, as well as 32,000 troops, the largest army yet gathered in America.[78]

New York City was nearly impossible to defend. Three islands—Manhattan, Staten, and Long—converged at the Hudson River mouth. Washington did not have enough troops to spread along all the scores of miles of beach where the British army could ground ashore. Instead, he fortified 9,000 troops on Brooklyn Heights, a mile across the water from New York City on Manhattan's south tip.

On August 22, the British army was rowed over from Staten Island to Gravesend Bay on Long Island's southwest end. Washington screened his army with small units that harassed the British advance from Gravesend Bay to just beyond cannon shot of his front line. Like Arnold, Washington took a suicidal gamble. With the sea at his back and an open left flank, he squared off against an enemy thrice as numerous and disciplined.

Howe soon learned of that open flank. On August 27, he sent Clinton's division on a long arching march toward the American left flank, while his artillery bombarded and troops feinted toward the enemy-entrenched front across Brooklyn Heights. Clinton's troops smashed into and rolled up the enemy's flank. The Americans retreated, leaving behind 970 dead and wounded and 1,079 prisoners, compared with 58 British dead, 316 wounded, and 26 missing. Howe rested his army on the battlefield for the knockout attack the next morning. But that night, Washington managed to evacuate the remnants of his army from Brooklyn to New York City.[79]

Howe failed to follow up his victory by ordering his brother to sail immediately toward New York City and cover the landing of his army on an undefended stretch of Manhattan shore. What explains that lost opportunity? It was partly a reflection of the leisurely pace of eighteenth-century warfare; his own methodical, conciliatory character; and the conflicts between his two roles of general and diplomat.

The Crown had invested Howe with the power not just to fight the rebels, but to negotiate with them as well. Having beaten them in battle, Howe hoped to forge a reconciliation with the misguided colonists. He released captured Gen. John Sullivan with a message to Congress for negotiations. After four days of debate, Congress decided to send Benjamin Franklin, John Adams, and Henry Rutledge to hear what Howe had to say. The delegation arrived at Howe's headquarters on Staten Island on September 11. The rebellion saddened Howe, who genuinely liked the Americans and the wondrous new world in which they lived. But all he could offer besides regret were pardons that the Americans politely declined. Howe would have to dangle far more tempting concessions than that to win the Americans back from independence. The meeting did help the American cause—it delayed Howe's pursuit of Washington's demoralized and disintegrating army.

It was not until September 15, two and a half weeks after the battle of Brooklyn Heights, that Howe launched his next attack. He landed 4,000 troops at Kip's Bay, halfway up Manhattan's east side, and routed the defenders, killing 70 and capturing 200. Washington withdrew his army to Harlem Heights, where the Americans repelled a British advance on September 16. As would happen time after frustrating time throughout the war, the inefficient command system, which delayed or derailed attack orders, prevented Washington from turning a minor into a major victory. Howe's advance was delayed for weeks after a mysterious fire engulfed New York City and many of his supplies on September 20. Howe tried a double envelopment on October 12, simultaneously sending a portion of his army up the Hudson while landing troops at Throg's Neck. When the Americans stymied the redcoat advance beyond Throg's Neck, Howe withdrew those troops and then landed them with reinforcements at Pell's Point farther up the coast. Washington retreated his army north across the Harlem River and up the Bronx River to White Plains by October 22. Howe gathered his army at New Rochelle, two miles distant from White Plains. He launched yet another flank attack on October 27 against American troops on Chatterton Hill, and finally dislodged them after losing 230 dead and wounded to the American losses of 130. Washington withdrew five miles to North Castle Heights and fortified the position.[80]

After a thorough reconnaissance revealed the American position to be near impregnable, Howe decided to halt his advance and consolidate his gains. He next turned his guns against Fort Washington on Manhattan's west side overlooking the Hudson and across to Fort Lee on New Jersey. Washington moved his army across the Hudson River and encamped it at Hackensack, New Jersey. He ordered Fort Washington's defenders to withdraw across the Hudson to Fort Lee, but the order was never carried out. On November 2, Howe besieged Fort Washington and bombarded it for two weeks. On November 16, its commander, Col. Robert McGraw, surrendered 2,900 troops, 161 cannons, and mountains of desperately needed supplies. That defeat would be the worst until the British captured 5,000 troops at Charles Town in 1780. The following day, Howe occupied an abandoned Fort Lee and its rich horde of supplies. His advance guard probed toward Hackensack and captured several thousand cattle that were being driven north to Washington's starving army.[81]

By eighteenth-century standards, Howe had fought a brilliant campaign. All along, he took his time, methodically maneuvering, probing, planning, and then executing set-piece battles that defeated the Americans with flank attacks and his troops' professionalism. He repeatedly outgeneraled Washington, who succeeded only in escaping from traps with an army that ebbed steadily in numbers, cohesion, and morale.

Howe now had several options. He could have made a last stab to trap Washington's army, militarily the optimum strategy. He could have rested on his ample laurels and sent his army into winter quarters. Instead, he split his army into three parts with different missions. While he and the bulk of his men watched Washington, he sent 10,000 troops under Clinton to take a poorly defended Newport, while 4,000 troops under Cornwallis marched across New Jersey and rallied loyalists to the colors.

Washington sidestepped Howe and withdrew before Cornwallis. On December 8, he led his army's remnants beyond the Delaware River into Pennsylvania as Cornwallis's troops marched unopposed into Trenton, New Jersey's capital. All but 2,000 of Washington's 4,700-man army would go home when their enlistments expired on New Year's Day.

In his desperation, Washington devised a plan that would restore the collapsing fortunes of the United States and himself. On Christmas Eve, he recrossed the Delaware River, marched his army into Trenton, and in a sharp skirmish, killed 29, wounded 84, and captured 918 of the enemy while 507 fled toward Princeton, at a cost of 3 wounded and none killed.[82] He then withdrew his army triumphantly back to Pennsylvania. But Washington and his army would soon return to battle and beat the British again.

CHAPTER 5

"Indiscriminate Attack": 1777

True policy as well as humanity forbids an indiscriminate attack, such as is intended by the Savages, wherein Women and Children, aged and infirm, the innocent as well as the guilty, will be equally exposed to their fury.

— Guy Carleton

We now tell you . . . to quit our Lands . . . or to blame yourselves for whatever may happen.

— Iroquois to American settlers

The year opened with a glorious American victory. With four-fifths of his army's enlistments due to expire on New Year's Day, Washington offered ten dollars of his own money to anyone who would stay another six weeks. About 3,000 troops agreed to remain with the 1,000 who had longer terms. On December 30, Washington led his 4,000 troops back across the Delaware River to Trenton.

Gen. Charles Cornwallis commanded 7,000 regulars at Princeton eight miles away. Learning of Washington's crossing, he quick-marched his army toward the enemy and encamped the evening of January 2 outside of Trenton. Once again, Washington had his back to deep water, faced an enemy twice as numerous, and gambled even more boldly. During the night, he left his campfires burning, marched his army around the enemy, and headed toward the supply depot at Princeton. The next morning, Cornwallis was astonished to find the enemy camp deserted and even more so to learn that Washington was threatening to capture his supplies and cut off his retreat. He hurried his army back to Princeton, where the two armies collided on January 3. The Americans repelled an attack and charged, driving the enemy from a field littered with 273 British dead or wounded mingled with 40 American dead and 100 wounded. Washington was tempted to push on toward the larger supply base at New Brunswick, but his officers talked him out of it. Instead, he withdrew his army to winter quarters in Morristown, New Jersey, and from there sent out detachments to harass the British around New Brunswick. Rather than preside over its collapse, Washington reinvigorated the Revolution with his Trenton and Princeton campaigns.[1]

Though the battle of Princeton was a minor defeat, it was a humiliating reminder that Britain was little closer to victory at the year's beginning than it was twelve months earlier. New York City and the lands surrounding the bay had been gained, but Boston had been lost. The Americans had been driven from Canada, but Carleton had withdrawn up Lake Champlain. The rebel grip on the southern colonies was firm following the loyalist defeat at Moore's Creek and Clinton's repulse at Charles Town. All along, the war's financial and human costs mounted steadily with no end in sight. What could be done to crush the rebellion once and for all?

The strategy for 1777 evolved during frequent meetings among the key ministers and generals at Whitehall from December through March.[2] But the most powerful initial voice shaping that plan was that of the North American commander in chief. William Howe recommended four separate campaigns that included 35,000 troops, of which 8,000 troops in New Jersey would pin down Washington's army and threaten Philadelphia, 10,000 troops now in Newport would capture Providence, and 10,000 troops would advance up the Hudson while 7,000 troops from Canada advanced south to meet in Albany. Howe's proposal was sent on November 30, received on December 30, and tentatively approved not long after.

But other important perspectives shaped the planning, including letters from those who had served or were then in North America, along with meetings with generals and former governors in London. Guy Carleton and John Burgoyne sent separate recommendations and then somehow forged a consensus and penned a joint letter. Germain tapped especially deep into the mind of his friend Gen. James Murray, Carleton's predecessor at Quebec. Former Virginia governor Lord John Murray, Lord Dunmore, contributed an impassioned defense of his own tenure and a plea for a ruthless campaign to crush the rebellion.[3]

What role would the Indians play in the war? Dunmore was the fiercest advocate of loosing the Indians against the frontier, a view reinforced by a letter from Lt. Gov. Henry Hamilton at Detroit. Once an apostle of restraint, Southern Indian Superintendent John Stuart now offered similar advice. Strangely, two men who should have had strong thoughts on the matter, Gen. William Howe and Guy Johnson, said little about Indians.[4]

The debate over how the Indians should be used in the pending campaign was shaped by an evaluation of their use the previous year. In mulling over those setbacks, Germain not only singled out Carleton for special blame for failing to wield the Indians more effectively, but also blasted him for letting the rebels escape from Canada and not capturing Ticonderoga. Germain decided that while Carleton could stay as governor, another general should take the field. What better choice was there than Maj. Gen. John Burgoyne, who had served as Carleton's second and was familiar with the challenges of campaigning in Canada and the Lake Champlain region?[5]

The debate over strategy shifted on February 23 when a letter arrived that was penned by Howe on December 20. Sir William announced that he would march with 10,000 troops on Philadelphia, leaving 4,000 men to defend New York, 2,000 men to defend Newport, and 3,000 troops to operate on the lower Hudson River. No British army would advance up the Hudson as far as Albany. The army marching south from Canada would be on its own.[6]

Howe's letter provoked another round of debate and planning. Here John Burgoyne articulated what became the decisive elements. Three armies would converge on Albany, at once conquering New York and cleaving New England from the other rebel colonies. Along the way the British armies would either drive like cattle the rebel forces before them or crush them if they made a stand. The campaign's three pincers included Burgoyne's 7,200-man army advancing down Lake Champlain, whatever troops Howe could spare after taking Philadelphia for a thrust up the Hudson, and Lt. Col. Barry St. Leger's 625 troops and hundreds of Indians striding east from Oswego.

The role of Indians in this grand strategy would be important if not decisive. Burgoyne wanted as many as possible led by British or Canadian officers to oper-ate against the enemy's pickets, flanks, and supply lines. Though he eschewed using the Indians to terrorize civilians, he appreciated the psychological erosion they inflicted on the minds of soldiers and settlers alike. "Gentleman Johnny," as Burgoyne was known, would later inflate the Indians' role, blaming their aban-donment of his campaign for his humiliating surrender. That was grossly untrue, but it helped polish the tarnished reputation of a once esteemed general.[7]

The plan had one crucial weakness. So much of life, including the gravest of government decisions, substitutes wishful sentiments for hard thinking. Howe made it clear in two letters, one received by Germain the same day that Burgoyne submitted his plan, that he was pointing his army toward Philadelphia rather than Albany. In a classic case of what psychologists call cognitive dissonance, Germain crumpled Howe's letter in his mind and celebrated Burgoyne's. The war was going badly, with its financial and human costs steadily mounting and no end in sight. Time had already eaten away a quarter of the year. Something had to be done. Bur-goyne's plan offered the distinct chance that the war would be won by autumn.[8]

Germain swiftly circulated the plan and got the approval of key advisors and the king. Then, in their persistent "dialogue of the deaf," Germain wrote Howe explaining the plan and the latter's expected role in it. Not only would Sir William head up the Hudson to join Burgoyne and St. Leger, but he would command all three armies. Thus did Germain pile an absurdity upon a misunderstanding. It was bad enough that two explicit statements of Howe's intentions failed to penetrate Germain's rigid mind, but even if Howe obeyed his orders, how could he possibly communicate with, let alone command, armies months distant via sea and then river routes? To this, Germain added one last surreal touch—he approved Howe's plan to take Philadelphia. It seems the American secretary believed the general could mount a major campaign that would defeat Washington and capture Philadelphia, and then return with his army in time to ascend to Albany. Nothing in the history of warfare in North America warranted such a belief, but that did not stop Germain from fervently wishing it even after Howe patiently explained that he intended "to invade Pennsylvania by sea" but had "little expectation that I shall be able, from the want of sufficient strength in this army, to detach a corps in the beginning of the campaign to act up the Hudson's River, consistent with the operations already determined upon." Clinging to his illusions, Germain seized the statement "the beginning of the campaign." If not then, surely Howe could achieve that critical junction later. In that, Germain would be sorely disappointed.[9]

Britain's use of Indians changed dramatically in early 1777. The policy of enlisting them solely as supervised allies against enemy forces changed. Now the Indians could operate either with or free of British arms, and either under the direct supervision of officers or on their own using their own strategies and tactics.

Germain was determined that Carleton not undermine the strategy with his humanitarian sentiments. He sent the governor explicit instructions that could be disobeyed only at the peril of Carleton's career. The governor was ordered to remain in Canada while he transferred to Burgoyne's campaign 7,200 troops, including 4,000 British and 3,200 Germans. If Carleton's removal from field command was insulting, his orders that the Indians be rallied by himself and his lieutenant governors for war against the enemy's forces and frontiers was morally repugnant. Germain was especially eager to enlist the Ohio Indians: "It is the King's Command that you should direct Lieut. Governor Hamilton to assemble as many of the Indians of his District as he conveniently can, and placing proper persons at their Head . . . to conduct their Parties, and restrain them from committing violence on the well affected and inoffensive Inhabitants, employ them in making a Diversion and exciting an alarm upon the frontiers of Virginia and Pennsylvania."[10] The American secretary also hoped to rally loyalists to the Union Jack, offering 200 acres of land to any who joined the companies at Niagara, Detroit, or other frontier posts. Adding insult to injury, Carleton's enemy, former Deputy Indian Superintendent Daniel Claus, would not only deliver the orders, but also command the Indians for Burgoyne's campaign.[11]

How would Carleton juggle his official duties and morals? As a good soldier, he followed orders, but having confined his own role to messenger, he washed his hands of any blood flowing from the policy. When Hamilton later asked for an elaboration of the instructions, Carleton stated: "The conduct of the War has been taken entirely out of my hands and the management of it, upon your Frontier has been assigned to you, as you have seen by a Letter from Lord George . . . I can therefore only refer you to that."[12]

Earlier that year, before receiving Germain's orders, Carleton had acted on his convictions. Learning that Joseph Brant was enlisting warriors for an Indian-style war against the frontier, he protested that "true policy as well as humanity forbids an indiscriminate attack, such as is intended by the Savages, wherein Women and Children, aged and infirm, the innocent as well as the guilty, will be equally exposed to their fury." He then ordered both Captains Richard Lernoult and John Butler at Fort Niagara "that all means may be used to prevent this and to turn the force of the Indians to the use which will be most for the Kings interest and their own good, by acting in concert with the Troops."[13] For nearly two years,

Carleton had largely succeeded in forcing his subordinates to follow that humanitarian policy. This year, that policy of restraint would be forced aside by unrestricted warfare on the frontiers.

THE FRONTIER AND INTERNATIONAL DIPLOMACY

The Americans had succeeded in winning French aid the previous year and in
early 1777 made a strong bid for Spanish aid. Spain would be a far harder diplomatic nut than France for the Americans to crack. The court of Carlos III sneered
with horror at the American rebels. Even more than the French, the Spanish
feared the specter of revolution. The conquistadores' descendants in the colonies
had become more Mexican, Peruvian, or some other Creole nationality than
Spanish. Would the American plague of natural rights and nationalism poison
New Spain? That would surely be more likely if thousands of restless American
settlers imbued with radical notions of free enterprise and elections, rather than
scattered British officials, ruled the land between the Appalachian Mountains and
Mississippi River.

Nonetheless, Spain's foreign policy, like that of France, logically followed
the balance-of-power principle, whereby the weaker naturally combined against
the stronger. Britain's sea power could be diminished by aiding the Americans.
France not only was supplying credit, munitions, and supplies to the rebels but
even mulling war with Britain. For now that was unthinkable for Spain. Its fleet
and army were even less ready for combat than France's, while Spain's empire
had much more to lose. The British had already ripped away most of France's foreign conquests; since 1763, Versailles had bolstered the defenses of its shards.
Spain's empire lay mostly supine to the attacks of a British navy far superior in
numbers, skills, and initiative. During Spain's brief year of fighting in the Seven
Years' War—it entered in 1762 and sued for peace in 1763—it suffered a series of
military humiliations. The British captured Cuba and the Philippines, picked off
scores of Spanish war and merchant ships, and just missed nabbing the biggest
prize of all, the annual silver fleet, which still sailed from the New World to the
Old, albeit with a lighter load than in previous centuries. Like filings to a magnet,
much of the navy was drawn from distant ports to protect that convoy so vital to
propping up Spain's sagging power. Could that treasure fleet run the gauntlet of
prowling British squadrons? Undoubtedly, Britain's sea dogs would be as voracious in a future war as they had been in the last.

Still, victory was not impossible. The combined French and Spanish fleets
outnumbered Britain's. Spain, like France, lusted for vengeance. It sought to
reconquer Gilbraltar, Minorca, and Jamaica, those three jewels of its imperial
crown that the British had stolen in previous wars, as well as to have another go
at overrunning Portugal. After all, despite its defeats, Spain had actually emerged
from the last war with more territory. What it lost on the battlefield, it more than
made up for at the negotiating table. All its colonies were restored except the
Floridas, a loss that King Louis XV graciously compensated by granting his distant cousin Louisiana and New Orleans.

Ever more ministers in Madrid and Louisiana leaned toward a war to restore Spain's eroded honor and power, but the ministers agreed that for now, patience was the best policy. Spain must bide its time and rebuild its fleet for the moment that British power tottered from defeats by the rebels, France, and perhaps other belligerents, a moment, of course, that might never come.

The most powerful opponent to this strategy was the new foreign minister, Jose Monimo y Redondo Floridablanca, who would repeatedly spurn French entreaties to revive the family compact alliance of 1762. But Floridablanca alone did not make Spanish foreign policy. Don Jose de Galvez, the president of Spain's American ministry, the Council for the Indies, and his brilliant nephew Bernardo de Galvez, who would become Louisiana's governor that year, championed and succored the American cause as much as possible, just short of presenting Britain with a casus belli.

Well aware that Spain would be much less receptive than France to its requests, the Americans were willing to make some major concessions. Originally Congress counted the acquisition of West and East Florida among its war aims, but for a Spanish alliance, they were willing to concede that territory as long as they were assured free navigation of the Mississippi River and the right to deposit goods at New Orleans. Surely, the Americans reasoned, Madrid would not spurn a chance to make the Caribbean a Spanish lake ringed by its colonies. They would soon be disillusioned.

The Americans tried a two-pronged diplomatic offensive. In Paris, Benjamin Franklin lobbied Spanish ambassador Pedro Pablo Abarca de Bloca de Aranda, asking for an alliance and free navigation of the Mississippi in return for the Floridas. Aranda forwarded the letter to his superiors. Meanwhile, Arthur Lee set out from Paris for Madrid with a wish list for the American cause. He never made it to the capital. Learning of his mission, Madrid dispatched envoy Geronimo de Grimaldi to intercept the rebel in Burgos far from the prying eyes of British diplomats and spies. To Grimaldi's astonishment, Lee requested not just military aid, but also recognition of American independence and even an alliance.

Madrid mulled over the petition for months and then passed on word of its decision to the Americans in Paris. Recognition and an alliance were unthinkable, along with free navigation of the Mississippi through Spanish territory. Left unsaid was the Spanish policy to bottle up the Americans in the upper Ohio and Tennessee River hinterlands. Yet the Americans should not feel slighted. King Carlos III in his magnanimity had agreed secretly to supply arms and credit to the rebels.

Spain was good to its word. Madrid set up its own front company, Diego de Gardoqui and Sons of Bilbao, and funneled shiploads of muskets, gunpowder, cannons, and other supplies to the United States by way of French and Spanish colonies in the Caribbean and New Orleans. Like France, Spain allowed American privateers to shelter and refit at ports in both its kingdom and colonies. In addition, Madrid dispatched Don Juan de Miralles to Philadelphia to serve as a secret, uncredited liaison with the American government. His mission was to ensure that the Americans conceded the Floridas to Spain while abandoning their demand for free navigation of the Mississippi River. Finally, orders were sent to Louisiana governor Bernardo de Galvez to aid the Americans and prepare for possible war with Britain. Galvez would brilliantly fulfill both policies.

France meanwhile readied for war and aided the United States. That year alone, Pierre-Augustin Caron de Beaumarchais, the head of the front Roderique Hortalez and Company, chartered nine ships, packed them with supplies, and sent them to America. By the year's end, the French would funnel through that firm an additional 3 million livres worth of supplies atop their initial 1 million livres contribution.

THE VERMONT FRONTIER

A new state joined the rebellion and enacted its own extraordinary political revolution in January 1777, although it would not be officially recognized and accepted by the United States until 1791.[14] Among the more acrimonious overlapping claims among colonies involved the New Hampshire Grants, in what is now Vermont. New York claimed that its eastern border extended to the Connecticut River, while New Hampshire asserted that its western border rested twenty miles east of the Hudson River. Connecticut and Massachusetts also insisted on rights to portions of that wilderness. All four colonies justified their claims by citing their vaguely worded charters. Until 1749, the dispute was an abstraction, since none of the colonies had tried to settle the region. But that year New Hampshire governor Benning Wentworth, acting on the Crown's authority, issued the first land grant in that region for a town to be called Bennington. From then until 1764, Wentworth sold off 129 townships as governors of the other three colonies protested vainly to the Crown. Then, in a 1764 proclamation, King George III reversed his grandfather's position and accepted New York's assertion to land to the Connecticut River north of the forty-fifth parallel. Massachusetts and Connecticut reluctantly shelved their claims, but New Hampshire persisted along with New York in issuing land grants. By 1775, nearly 16,000 people lived in the region, mostly on grants issued by New Hampshire.

Fearing they would lose their homes to those granted the same land by New York, the settlers organized the Green Mountain Boys militia in 1769 to defend themselves. Shortly after the charismatic Ethan Allen migrated to Bennington in 1770, he rose to leadership of the Green Mountain Boys, who wielded the law and intimidation in thwarting periodic bids by New York to assert control. By 1775, committees of safety emerged to govern the territory. The Green Mountain Boys captured Forts Ticonderoga and Crown Point and joined the Canada campaign. From 1775 through 1777, the New Hampshire Grants held six conventions to debate their political future.

Though the New Hampshire Grants was clearly self-governing, it lacked legitimacy in the eyes of other governments. Led by New York, Congress and the other states rejected any notion of Vermont's independence. Though that policy would seem to violate the Revolution's principles, it made political sense. Most states claimed regions whose settlers demanded autonomy or outright independence.

Vermont was not declared an independent republic until January 15, 1777, during a convention at Westminster. The delegates justified their action by citing New York's abuse of power since 1765; the May 10, 1776, congressional resolution allowing governments to form where none now existed; the overwhelming majority of Vermonters who favored independence; and the general principles for which the revolution was fought. Those seemingly ironclad arguments were rejected once again by Congress and the other states when Vermont applied for admission to the United States. On June 30, Congress called on Vermonters to dismantle their government and accept New York's rule.

That hardly dampened Vermont's revolution. As Burgoyne's army surged down Lake Champlain, fifty delegates convened a constitutional convention at Windsor on July 2. On July 8, they voted overwhelmingly for a constitution that, among other liberal measures, was the first to outlaw slavery and grant universal manhood suffrage for those twenty-one years and older, a unicameral legislature, and other elected state positions. The frontier realm of Vermont truly ignited a revolution within a revolution.

THE NEW YORK FRONTIER
An event of enormous symbolic importance struck the Iroquois in the new year. As if the psychological strain of being yanked in two diplomatic directions were not wearying enough, an epidemic had burned through the Onondaga in 1776, leaving ninety corpses, including three head sachems, in its wake. The survivors debated their future that winter. In mid-January, they sent a stunning announcement to their brother Iroquois tribes—the Grand Council fire at Onondaga was extinguished![15]

How significant was this gesture? Did it really end the league's two centuries of history? While this declaration was certainly unprecedented, it was not the first time that discord had broken the Six Nations. At times the Iroquois had simply chosen not to meet when they could not forge a consensus. That way they could at least maintain the structure if not substance of union.[16]

The Iroquois council's ashes would not be cold for long. In April, a council was reconvened. Although any details of what transpired have been lost, Samuel Kirkland's diplomacy may have played an essential role in rekindling that fire. When he learned of the Onondaga's dramatic action, he advised Gen. Philip Schuyler immediately to send three large wampum belts of condolence, gifts to bury the dead, and words of encouragement to reestablish the covenant chain and neutrality. Schuyler did so. The Onondaga responded favorably. Yet despite these American efforts, the steady swelling of British forces by Iroquois warriors would continue.[17]

That was only one of Schuyler's diplomatic initiatives. In the new year, he ordered John Dean at Fort Schuyler and Col. Timothy Bedel on the upper Connecticut River to send agents among the Seven Tribes and gather information and possibly allies for the year's campaigning. Upon accomplishing those missions, the agents reported that most of the Seven Nations either favored the Americans or had wearied of supporting the unreliable British. Those sentiments, of course, were volatile. Charismatic British leadership, the generous distribution of gifts, and word of America defeats could dramatically shift the balance.[18]

Kirkland, meanwhile, nurtured ties with the Oneida, the one frontier tribe in all of North America openly allied with the United States. On January 31, he, Chief Kayendalongwa, and five warriors departed from Fort Schuyler on a four-month journey that would take them to Albany, Boston, and Washington's army at Morristown, New Jersey. En route, officials feted and impressed them with the might and justice of America's independence struggle.[19] Yet no matter how strenuous his efforts, Kirkland would never wield more than a fraction of the influence of Joseph Brant.

Only a month after Joseph Brant lingered in their villages to harangue their men into warring that spring against the Americans, the chiefs of Oquaga and other villages along the Susquehanna's eastern branch had second thoughts. They sent for their longtime friend militia colonel John Harper, from nearby Cherry Valley, for talks. On February 27, Harper met with Mohawk, Oneida, and Tuscarora chiefs, along with several prominent Onondaga and Mahican residents. The headmen promised to stay off the warpath if New York would favor them in land disputes with squatters and speculators. Harper eagerly agreed to carry their message back to Albany. Then, en route, he and his escort of troops camped with a group of Indians led by Chief Nicholas, who admitted that they planned to attack a nearby hamlet. Harper had his men disarm the Indians and marched them off to jail at Albany. When news of the capture reached Oquaga in April, the chiefs sent word asking the officials to release Nicholas and keep the peace road open. Inexplicably, that message was ignored. At this critical point, Joseph Brant and his warriors reappeared at Oquaga. It took little for Brant to swing the chiefs of Oquaga, Unadilla, and other villages in the valley against the Americans.[20]

Oquaga was only the latest village that Joseph Brant had visited. After leaving Niagara around the first of the year, he and his followers traveled through first the Seneca and then the Onondaga villages. From Onondaga, he corresponded with his sister Molly at Canajoharie and requested a safe conduct pass from Philip Schuyler to visit her. Schuyler was well aware of Brant's alliance with the British and knew he would use any visit to rally the Mohawk Indians to the Union Jack. He forbade Brant to enter the region. With their villages of Canajoharie and Fort Hunter islands amidst settler seas, those Mohawk Indians were unofficial American hostages, of which Molly Brant was the most important. So far, her brother had only heatedly called for war but not waged it. Would Brant stay put, Schuyler and other officials nervously wondered?[21]

Brant returned to Niagara in March for a council convened by John Butler with several hundred Iroquois, Mississauga, and small groups from other tribes. Whitehall's new policy of enlisting the tribes for war had not yet reached North America, so the Indians heard Butler's familiar message to remain allies and at peace for now. It was after the council broke up in mid-April that Brant and his entourage headed back to Oquaga. While the British may have urged peace, Brant was ready for war. And Oquaga would be the headquarters and supply base for his campaigns that would terrorize the New York and Pennsylvania frontiers.[22]

It was not Brant who drew first blood that year on the New York frontier, but Gov. Guy Carleton, who sought intelligence of rebel intentions. He ordered raids by Indians and British to nab as many stray soldiers as possible. A war party to the Kennebec River brought back four prisoners in February. In March, Capt. Samuel Mackay and Chevalier de Lorimier headed down icebound Lake Champlain with about 25 Iroquois and Ottawa, three British, and three Canadians. Near their quarry, they broke up into three parties that skulked around Forts Crown Point, Ticonderoga, and George. A party captured two soldiers and a loyalist near Ticonderoga, and learned that twenty-six troops commanded by Capt. Alexander Baldwin would soon appear on their grueling march from Fort George at Lake George's southern end. Runners trudged to the other two parties. They united on March 20 near Sabbath Day Point where the Americans were encamped. The Indians shot down five troops and captured Baldwin and nineteen others. Learning of the raiders, Capt. Benjamin Whitcomb set out with his rangers in pursuit, but Mackay, Lorimier, and their men reached Montreal safely with the prisoners on March 30.[23]

Schuyler, meanwhile, blundered badly in Indian policy. He forbade any traders to peddle their goods west of Fort Schuyler. The edict was supposed to prevent the murder of any merchants that could sever the already frayed relations between the Americans and the Six Nations, but the effect was to push the western Iroquois, the Seneca, Cayuga, and Onondaga, into British arms. The British eagerly confirmed the Indian fear that the American policy aimed first to weaken and then attack the Iroquois. The more trade dependent a tribe was, the less likely that it would bite the hand that fed it. The collapse of trade made the Iroquois' eventual decision for war all the easier.[24]

The Iroquois tilt toward the British became clear to the Americans early that summer. Schuyler ordered agent James Dean at Fort Schuyler to gather as many Iroquois as possible for a July 15 council at Albany. Dean dispatched Thomas Spencer with five Oneida on June 18 through the Six Nations. The Iroquois received the envoy cordially enough, but most were noncommittal about the council and the question of neutrality. Only a handful would appear at Albany. Nearly all the rest would be enticed to John Butler's councils at Iroquois Bay and Three Rivers in late July. The Seneca en masse and most or many of the other Iroquois except the Oneida would join St. Leger's expedition.[25]

Schuyler's attempt to stymie Joseph Brant's spring recruiting at Oquaga and Unadilla was no more successful. The 150 mostly Mohawk and Mahican warriors Brant had gathered at Unadilla threatened settlements in the Mohawk and Cherry valleys. Schuyler hoped to neutralize that threat with diplomacy backed by overwhelming force. On June 14, he ordered Col. Goose Van Schaick to lead 150 militia into Cherry Valley and Gen. Nicolas Herkimer to confront Brant at Unadilla. Herkimer arrived with 380 militia at Unadilla on June 19 and requested a meeting with Joseph Brant.[26]

The request posed a dilemma for Brant. Not only did Herkimer's force outnumber his 150 warriors, but his men also had little gunpowder. If a fight broke out, he and his men would have to flee, and if he did so, he would lose face. Brant did not flinch. He agreed to meet with Herkimer, gambling that bold resolve would make up for other deficiencies.

When they met, Brant paraded his 136 men and boasted that he had 500 within hailing distance; Herkimer miscounted 200 warriors before him. With haughty disdain, Brant denounced the theft of Indian lands and the American rebellion. He proclaimed himself the king's loyal subject. Herkimer stayed calm, but Brant's words enraged Col. Ebenezer Cox, who rose and shouted, "Let the fight begin now." Brant translated the challenge to his men, who war whooped, dashed back to their weapons, and fired several shots skyward.

As long as the militia held its ground, that Indian spirit would have counted for little in an open-field battle. But Herkimer grasped hands with Brant and assured him that he had not come to fight. Brant sent a runner to calm his men. He then stated the terms for preventing violence, including allowing the Mohawk Indians at Canajoharie and Fort Hunter to travel freely and the loyalists at Unadilla and Oquaga to remain unmolested. Herkimer first requested that Brant turn over the loyalists, but then agreed to leave them be. In return for Brant's promise to avoid the warpath for now, Herkimer shared with him several cattle and other provisions. Then both sides marched away. Herkimer believed that he had persuaded Brant to keep the peace. Instead, he had unwittingly boosted Brant's prestige. Had he tried to seize rather than appease Brant, Herkimer might have spared the lives of hundreds of Americans in the following years.[27]

THE NORTHWEST FRONTIER: FIRST PHASE

The Seneca committed the year's first killings west of the Appalachian divide. Warriors from the upper Allegheny River villages broke through the winter snows to raid the nearest settlement downstream, Kittanning. On February 14, a war party captured a militia lieutenant and took him to Niagara. In March, thirteen Seneca killed a soldier and captured a civilian near Kittanning. On the corpse, they left a war club, hatchet, and pouch with a message that condemned and warned the Americans for having "feloniously taken Possession of part of our Country . . . we have sometimes since sent you word to quit our lands . . . we now tell you . . . to quit our Lands . . . or blame yourselves for whatever may happen."[28]

Those raids most likely took place because their most prominent chief, who had struggled for peace for years, abandoned the cause early that year. Kayashuta's fruitless labors had left him exhausted and embittered. The Delaware assertion of independence the previous year seemed to have finally broken him. He moved his family up the Allegheny to the Seneca town of Conwango, where he nodded grimly to war parties striding away.[29]

Not all Iroquois had given up on peace. In January, the Seneca chiefs Big Tree and Captain Johnston, Cayuga King Iaasguah, Nanticoke chief Amatenica, Conoy chief Wilakuko, and Munsee chiefs Mytakawha and Kakwah led 70 warriors and 100 women and children on the long, frigid journey from the upper Susquehanna to Easton on the Delaware River. There they met with congressional and Pennsylvania envoys from January 30 through February 6. A sincere desire for good relations animated the talks. The chiefs presented their list of grievances along with their desire for peace. The Americans promised to resolve all problems and heaped gifts upon their guests. The two sides parted, convinced that war would not divide them. Within two years, an American army would be burning the villages and uprooting the crops of those very people.

Ever more warriors of the Ohio and Detroit tribes were eager to join the warpath. In late January, the Sandusky Wyandot held a council with the Mingo and the four Detroit tribes. They agreed jointly to war against the frontier that spring and swing the other tribes behind them. The Shawnee and Delaware lay between the belligerent tribes and the Americans. Those villages were an obvious source of recruits, shelter, and supply. To implicate them in the war, the Mingo took two gunpowder kegs and distributed one among the Shawnee villages and the other to Delaware chief Wyondochella's village on the Waldhonding River.

That gunpowder diplomacy worked. Most of the Shawnee and Chief Wyondochella's Delaware seized up the war hatchet. Although all the other Delaware villages remained neutral, Cornstalk's Mekoce and some Kispoko were the sole Shawnee that favored peace. Calaka chief Blackfish now rose to lead the Shawnee war faction. In March, Wyandot chief Half King attended the Delaware council at Coshocton and urged them to follow their Chief Wyondochella and join the British. The Delaware chiefs politely demurred. Despite the declaration of neutrality, Delaware chief Captain Pipe and his village on the Little Beaver River and the Munsee villages tilted increasingly toward the Union Jack.[30]

The hostile tribes even targeted for conversion the Moravian Delaware towns of Schonbrunn, Gnaddenhutten, and Lichtenau, whose 500 people espoused an unconditional pacifism, although their missionaries John Heckewelder and David Zeisberger secretly spied for the Americans. Pacifists tend to attract bullies. The Moravians would suffer from both sides during the war. Hostile Munsee Indians pressured Munsee converts to renounce their faith. In February, Moravian chief Augustin Newalike did just that and led his people to a Munsee village on the Walhonding River. War parties of Mingo and Wyandot invaded Schonbrunn to loot and intimidate those people with impunity. Heckewelder and Zeisberger counciled with their flock and on April 19 decided to turn the other cheek—they abandoned Schonbrunn to the hostiles and concentrated at Lichtenau only a mile and a half from the Delaware council town of Coshocton.[31]

When the war parties crossed the Ohio into Kentucky that year, they would find few targets for their wrath. Only three settlements remained: Boonesborough with thirty men, Harrodsburg with ninety men, and Logan's Fort or St. Asaph's with twenty men. In March, Chief Blackfish's Shawnee and Chief Logan's Mingo were the first war parties to arrive. Blackfish struck a maple syrup party near Harrodsburg on March 6, killing one man and capturing another, while two men sprinted off to sound the alarm. The next morning, the Shawnee fired a cabin, hoping to provoke a sally by the frontiersmen. Sure enough, they did. The Shawnee killed one settler and wounded three while losing one dead and several wounded. Among the mutilated corpses was the stepson of Hugh McGary. The grief-deranged father vowed to exact a bloody vengeance. Five years later, that lust would lead to the war's bloodiest debacle for Kentuckians. Meanwhile, Chief Logan and his men headed toward Boonesborough. They opened fire on March 7, killing one man and wounding another. Unable to take either fort, the two war parties lingered for weeks, burning outlying cabins and butchering stray livestock. The Shawnee killed a man near Harrodsburg on March 18, and killed one and captured another on March 28. Having wreaked all the available havoc, the raiders retired beyond the Ohio; Blackfish and his men would soon return.[32]

Other war parties harassed the upper Ohio region. On April 6 and 7 alone, militia colonel William Crawford reported at Fort Pitt that Indians had

> killed and scalped one man at Raccoon Creek, about twenty-five miles from this place; at Muchmore's plantation, about forty-five miles down the Ohio, they killed and scalped one man, and burnt a woman and her four children; at Wheeling they killed and scalped one man, the body of whom was so mangled with tomahawks and other instruments suitable for their barbarity; at Dunkard's Creek . . . they killed and scalped one man and a woman and took three children; and at each of the above places they burned houses, killed cattle, hoggs &c . . . I am at a great loss for arms; two thirds of my battalion have none . . . this together with my bad health . . . I only await further directions.[33]

After repleneshing his munitions, provisions, and men, Blackfish led 100 mostly Shawnee along with 20 Miami and a sprinkling of Wyandot and Mingo back to Kentucky. On April 24, they slipped up to Boonesborough and lay in wait. Daniel Boone sensed their presence when the cows balked at being let out to pasture. He sent out two scouts, who were fired on at the clearing's edge. A bullet struck down one, while the other dashed away. Boone, Simon Kenton, and Michael Stoner led a half-dozen other men to the rescue. Kenton killed a warrior about to finish off the wounded scout. A bullet hit Boone's ankle. Kenton killed two more rushing Indians, slung Boone over his shoulder, and dashed back to the fort with the others.[34]

Discouraged at their losses, Blackfish led his men to Harrodsburg, but the alarm raced ahead of them. The Indians arrived on April 29, and for a month, they sniped and burned but hit no one. Frustrated, they decided to haunt Boonesborough again. They began peppering the walls with musket balls on May 23 and kept this up for two days; they succeeded only in wounding three men. Restless for a decisive coup, they stalked back to Harrodsburg and jumped a scouting party, but their prey escaped without harm. Striding on to Logan's Fort, they killed one man and wounded two others who were out milking the cows on May 30. After slaughtering the livestock, they departed for home on June 1.[35]

Pluggy's son sought bloody vengeance for his father's death. He led eight Mingo, Mahican, and Munsee to Wheeling and attacked several soldiers outside the fort on June 7, killing one and stampeding the others. They stalked on toward Pittsburgh and killed two men a week later. Then they turned home to replenish their munitions. They would be back.[36]

These Indian raids were not directly instigated by the British. Across the northwest, British officials were more concerned with administrative worries than provoking war parties. Forts Niagara and Detroit experienced a shuffling of commanders. Illness killed Fort Niagara's commander, Col. John Caldwall, on October 31, 1776. The word soon reached Detroit, and Capt. Richard Lernoult hurried to Niagara to command the post that winter. Upon reaching Niagara, Lernoult sent Capt.-Lt. John Mompesson back to Detroit to head that garrison. Governor Carleton did not learn of Caldwall's death until late the following January, when he promptly promoted Maj. Mason Bolton of the 9th Regiment to lieutenant colonel of the 8th Regiment and ordered him to Fort Niagara once the river ice had melted. When Bolton arrived, Lernoult sailed back to Detroit.

His return was not soon enough for the lieutenant governor. Henry Hamilton and the prickly Mompesson had clashed harshly over policy and ego from their first meeting. Hamilton also sparred with Lt. Gov. Edward Abbott, who lingered in Detroit with his wife's family for months before finally departing for his Vincennes post. Abbott had served at Detroit for a decade, married a local women, and thought himself superior in understanding the Canadians and Indians to the relative novice Hamilton.

Hamilton's squabbles with his fellow officers were briefly overshadowed by spy scares. Who were the spies? Profit solely drove most merchants, but a few counted information among the goods they peddled. The Indian trade flourished despite the war, providing merchant spies with cover, profits, and intelligence. In 1777, Governor Carleton issued 121 licenses, three times more than any previous year, and 1,670 men headed west packed in 312 bateaux and 155 canoes with 176,665 pounds sterling worth of goods, including 68,436 gallons of rum and brandy, 9,326 gallons of wine, 2,589 trade guns, 1,866 hundredweight of lead, and 122,910 pounds of gunpowder.[37]

Merchants competed fiercely with no holds barred. Accusing a rival of spying could eliminate a pesky competitor. In mid-March, acting on a tip-off, Hamilton had Matthew Elliot arrested and sent in chains to Montreal on spy charges. Elliot actually not only was innocent, but also would later openly declare for the British despite his unjust treatment. Daniel Sullivan was a genuine spy sent by George Morgan to ferret out the secrets of Detroit and its four outlying Indian villages. Getting wind of Sullivan's espionage, Hamilton had him arrested. But after interrogating him at length, Hamilton pronounced Sullivan innocent and released him. Sullivan might have escaped had not Chief Pluggy's son then been in Detroit. The son accused Sullivan of killing one of his warriors during a raid on the Kanawha the previous autumn. Hamilton had Sullivan rearrested and this time shackled and conveyed to Montreal. Hamilton's relations with much of Detroit's population soured that summer. In June, he had the popular James Sterling arrested for treason for his refusal to help rally the Indians against the settlers. Sterling was sent to Quebec for trial, where he was acquitted.[38]

The richest source of Indian recruitment for the warpath was not at Detroit but at Michilimackinac. In February, Charles de Langlade arrived after an arduous journey from Montreal with a mission to gather 200 warriors for that year's campaign in New York. The fort's commander, Capt. Arent De Peyster, counciled with the several hundred Ottawa and Chippewa who had wintered at the fort. With their ranks thinned by smallpox, those warriors who survived were eager to appease their anguish with vengeance and replenish their families with captives.

But De Peyster's work was hardly done. Rumors trickled in that the Spanish were enticing the tribes of the upper lakes and upper Mississippi valley. De Peyster sent his own belts to those tribes, asking them to journey to Michilimackinac. He then sent Langlade to La Baye to rally the Indians of that region. Langlade brought back sixty warriors in early June. On June 4, Langlade set off for Montreal with about 200 Ottawa, Chippewa, and Menominee. During the next several weeks, other parties arrived, including Winnebago, Potawatomi, Sauk, Fox, and even Sioux led by Chief Wabasha. In all, De Peyster dispatched over 400 warriors to the distant front on the upper Hudson. Those allies did not come cheap—De Peyster spent 23,982 pounds sterling that year alone.[39]

Like his counterparts elsewhere, Philip Rocheblave, the lone British agent in the Illinois country, was beset by seemingly endless and unsolvable problems. Canadian and British traders were bitter rivals. The latter issued a petition accusing Rocheblave of favoring the former. As if these animosities were not distracting enough, rumor had it that the Spanish across the river were inciting the Kickapoo, Mascouten, and Peoria of the upper Illinois River to sack St. Joseph. Warriors from those tribes robbed four traders in January. In February, a party of Potawatomi opened fire on five British hunters opposite the Missouri River mouth, but no one was hurt in the exchange.[40]

Whether distant Spanish intrigues instigated those attacks will never be known. But Lt. Gov. Don Francisco Cruzat at St. Louis sent belts requesting councils to all the tribes up the Mississippi watershed and even over into Lakes Michigan and Superior. Those invitations worked. Indian delegations arrived at St. Louis all year long. Cruzat counciled with tribes on both sides of the Mississippi along with Canadians in Illinois, trying to seduce them into trade and allegiance with Spain. Along with distributing gifts, he promised that the French king would soon awaken from his long sleep and return to nurture his neglected children. Francois Valle, the Spanish commander at St. Genevieve across the Mississippi from Kaskaskia, conducted the same diplomacy.[41]

Adding to worries about tribes defecting to Spain were troubles with those that returned. A band of Peoria crossed over after having lived near St. Louis for a dozen years. A group of Kaskaskia who had migrated to the Arkansas River valley in 1774 also reappeared. Rocheblave feared those tribes would infect local villages with Spanish sentiments.[42]

In late May and early June, Rocheblave hosted a council at Fort Gage with Mascouten, Kickapoo, Potawatomi, and White River Delaware Indians. Buying and keeping friendships was as expensive as it was tedious and endless. Rocheblave ran up 685 pounds sterling worth of charges for that council alone. Meanwhile, Carleton received orders to pare his colony's expenses. The governor targeted the Illinois as expendable strategically and thus fiscally, and sent word on May 16 to Rocheblave to stop spending. Rocheblave promptly did so when he received the letter in July. But that fall, he would receive another letter from Carleton announcing that the Crown would disavow all his expenses. That decision financially ruined Rocheblave, who had carefully tended British interests on the empire's fringe.[43]

Lt. Gov. Edward Abbott would have little better luck rallying the Wabash Indians to the Union Jack. He would be the first British official to occupy Vincennes since France ceded that region fourteen years earlier. It was essential that he make a strong, favorable impression. On April 15, Abbott left Detroit for Vincennes accompanied by his wife, children, thirty-five Canadians, and three Piankashaw chiefs. At Miamis Town on April 30, he counciled with a mélange of 500 Miami, Kickapoo, Wea, Piankashaw, Mascouten, Shawnee, and Delaware, who happily snatched up more than their share of gifts and supplies. Even more showed up at Ouiatenon on May 14. When he finally reached Vincennes a week later, he had little left to hand out. His goodwill tour had briefly animated the thousand or so Indians who had attended his words and grabbed his handouts, but nearly all remained indifferent to the British cause. Most of those who would stalk south of the Ohio were young braves eager for glory who most likely would have done so anyway. In all, Abbott could point to little that the 7,500 pounds sterling worth of goods he gave away en route accomplished for the king. Such were the excesses and frustrations of Indian diplomacy.[44]

That spring, the Americans could count only one achievement on the northwest frontier, but it was essential. What was the fate of the 9,000 pounds of gunpowder that Lt. William Linn and his men were rowing up the Mississippi? The Americans were desperate for that powder and feared the enemy might have captured it. Virginia governor Patrick Henry ordered a force sent down the Ohio River to escort the expedition back to Pittsburgh. That mission fell on the shoulders of Capt. William Harrod, who was ordered in the dead of winter to embark with fifty men down the Ohio, "taking all possible Care to examine Strickly the mouth of all Creeks and Rivers which you pass, & when you arrive at the Mouth of Kentucke or at the Falls of Ohio . . . send to Harrod's Burgh and make inquiry after Captain Linn & the said Cargo . . . If you should not fall in with Captain Linn . . . before you reach the Mouth of Ohio . . . it will be necessary that you pass up the Mississippi to the Kaskaskias village where you will make inquiry."[45]

After wintering at Arkansas Post, Linn and his men resumed the hard, tedious row upstream with their gunpowder in January. On March 3, they reached the Ohio River mouth. Hearing rumor of the expedition, Rocheblave tried to rally first Kickapoo and then Canadians to intercept Linn but got no takers. A war party of

Kickapoo independently learned of the shipment and set off for the Ohio Falls to ambush it. By the time the warriors straggled up to the falls, the Americans had long since passed. On May 1, the expedition reached the relative safety of Wheeling. Had that gunpowder fallen into enemy hands, the war in the northwest might have shifted decisively to the British and Indians. Instead, the frontiersmen would burn most of that powder defending their settlements or attacking the enemy.[46]

BURGOYNE'S CAMPAIGN: FIRST PHASE

What manner of general and man had Whitehall tapped to command the campaign from Montreal to Albany? Though he was not known as Gentleman Johnny for nothing, Burgoyne's surrender at Saratoga obscures the fact that he was actually a good general, by the era's standards. His defeat stemmed as much from bad luck and that epoch's leisurely approach to warfare as his own mistakes. He deserves high marks for spearheading his advance with Gen. Simon Fraser's elite corps and the Indians and emphasizing light infantry tactics and flank attacks on the battlefield. He was also adept at psychological warfare. The murder of Jane McCrea aside, he kept a tight rein on the Indians while spreading word to the Americans to flee or perish beneath their tomahawks. He even wielded that fear to terrify his own soldiers not to straggle, desert, or plunder. But ultimately he defeated himself by failing to push south as swiftly as possible and concentrate his forces to encircle and destroy the American army blocking the road to Albany. Instead, he frittered away his time in inaction and troops in diversions against Vermont.[47]

Burgoyne's first task after stepping ashore at Quebec on May 6 was to assert command of that year's campaign. Germain's letter to Carleton relieving him of the campaign and ordering him to rally and loose the Indians against the frontier was gleefully blunt and even sarcastic. Carleton returned fire with letters blasting Germain and Crown policy, culminating with his June 27 offer to resign. Nonetheless, as Burgoyne readied his army, Carleton swallowed his venom and dutifully followed his orders to rally the Indians.[48]

The governor's diplomacy was bolstered on May 26, when Sir John Johnson, Canadian Indian superintendent John Campbell, and veteran diplomat and military leader to the Indians La Corne St. Luc arrived. Campbell and St. Luc were recently exchanged from a year's imprisonment at Reading, Pennsylvania. The two men were very close; Campbell was St. Luc's son-in-law and carefully followed his father-in-law's advice. Johnson had met with Campbell and St. Luc in New York, where they boarded the same ship to Quebec.

Conspicuously absent from that voyage was Guy Johnson, the superintendent for the Iroquois and their dependent tribes. Although the three had met with Sir Guy and urged him to join them, he stayed attached to Gen. William Howe's cozy headquarters. Howe caused Johnson's inaction by refusing to issue definitive orders. Yet Johnson dared not press the matter lest he get an unpleasant posting. Indians generally disinterested Howe; he tried to put them out of his mind and grew irritated when the distasteful subject intruded. The most he could tell Johnson was the standard line "to pursue the most effectual means for maintaining the present friendly disposition of the Indians, and for keeping them in Readiness to joyn & act with the King's troops where ever and whenever it may be thought most requisite. This is a Point which, from your own judgement & knowledge of the Indians entrusted to your Superintendency must be determined."[49] In other words, that unseemly Indian issue was Johnson's problem alone and one he should keep to himself. When Johnson timidly suggested that fulfilling his duty might require going to Canada, Howe dismissed the notion as unnecessary. So Sir Guy tarried at New York carrying on his pantomime of superintending Indians who lived several hundred miles away. The most he did was send word to John Butler at Fort Niagara to cut loose the warriors against the frontier.[50]

Howe was just as maddenly vague about whether he would eventually trouble himself with sailing up the Hudson to join hands with Burgoyne at Albany. Although Campbell and St. Luc met with Howe when they passed through New York, the general was cagey about his plans. He clearly intended to strike Philadelphia first. What he did next, of course, depended on the fortunes of war on that campaign. Howe clearly preferred fighting in such civilized regions as the mid-Atlantic colonies to risking his army even on the thinly settled portion of the Hudson up to Albany, let alone that wild, mysterious land beyond. Surely Burgoyne, his large Regular army, and hundreds of painted savages could traverse that dark region on their own, scattering the hordes of ill-trained and ill-equipped Americans as they marched. At most, Howe offered the vague idea to send "a corps upon the lower part of Hudson's River sufficient to open the communication for shipping through the Highlands."[51] When that would occur, how far it would advance, who would command it, and how many men would accompany it were left hanging.

What then was Burgoyne to do? He could only carry on his campaign and hope that Howe or a proxy awaited him in Albany. He certainly commanded a formidable army: 3,725 British regulars, 3,025 Brunswicker regulars, and 650 gunners, whose ranks increased by hundreds when officers, sergeants, and musicians were included. His auxiliaries included about 150 Canadian militia and two skeleton loyalist regiments led by Lieutenant Colonels Ebeneser Jessup and John Peters, who would recruit in New York. Tough veteran commanders led his brigades. Gen. William Phillips commanded the British regulars; Gen. Friedrich von Riedesel the Brunswickers; Lt. Col. Heinrich Breymann the reserve corps of Brunswick grenadier, light, and dragoon companies; and Brig. Gen. Simon Fraser the 24th Regiment and British grenadier and light infantry companies, the Canadian militia, loyalist regiments, Capt. Alexander Fraser's fifty rangers, and nearly 500 Indians, along with women and children, when the campaign opened. Most were from the Seven Nations, leavened by Iroquois and small numbers from many other tribes.[52]

The extended march and row began on May 29 when Fraser's corps set forth, trailed in the following days by other regiments. The campaign's first blood was shed on June 17, when Indians killed two soldiers and captured two others on the road from Fort Ticonderoga to Lake George. As they hurried north, the war party evaded Capt. Benjamin Whitcomb and his rangers but ambushed Lt. Taylor's scouting party near Putnam's Creek, killing two and capturing two, while losing one.[53]

Burgoyne counciled with his Indians on June 21 at the Bouquet River. He admonished them to follow his orders strictly and the officers he assigned them "to regulate your passions when they overbear, to point out where it is nobler to suspend the uplifted stroke, to chastise and not to destroy." In all, the Indians should adhere to "the dictates of our religion, the laws of our warfare, and the principles and interests of our policy." Most importantly, he warned: "I positively forbid bloodshed when you are not opposed in arms. Aged men, women, children, and prisoners must be held secure from the knife or hatchet, even in the time of actual conflict. You shall receive compensation for the prisoners you take, but you will be called to account for scalps" taken from prisoners, although the practice was allowed from dead on the battlefield. What was the Indian response to such an affront to their way of war? As usual, they mouthed diplomatic platitudes then did as they pleased.[54]

On June 22, Burgoyne sent Fraser's corps to scour the lower reaches of Otter Creek on Lake Champlain's central eastern side. With his rangers, 20 light infantry volunteers, the Canadians, and 400 Indians, Fraser pushed southeast up Otter Creek from June 23 to 26. Fraser kept tight control over his Indians. Nothing was plundered or burned, and no one was hurt. Nine patriots were arrested, while most other settlers declared for Britain or fled. Fraser then marched west to Chimney Point, where he rejoined the army. Burgoyne then split his command again, sending Riedesel's Brunswickers down the eastern shore against Fort Independence and Phillips's British brigade led by Fraser's corps down the western shore to Fort Ticonderoga.

Awaiting the British advance were 3,000 troops split between Forts Ticonderoga and Independence straddling Lake Champlain. Their general, Arthur St. Clair, did nothing to delay the enemy and little to determine Burgoyne's intentions other than send out Whitcomb's rangers. Three never returned. He ordered the garrisons at the Lake George blockhouse and Sawmill fortifications withdrawn into Fort Ticonderoga. Mostly, he prepared to withdraw south.[55]

Fraser advanced with his 560 troops a mile from the American lines on July 2. A probe by Indians of the enemy pickets cost the Americans a half-dozen dead and eight wounded, while two Indians were killed and four wounded. The rest of Burgoyne's army arrived later that day. Riedesel meanwhile had marched just beyond cannon shot of Fort Independence. Burgoyne hoped at once to besiege and capture both rebel forts. He sent Fraser's light corps across the lake to encircle Fort Independence while Riedesel pinned them down. But Fraser arrived too late to cut off the arrival of Col. Seth Warner with 1,000 troops of the 11th Massachusetts and 2nd New Hampshire, along with a cattle herd, to Fort Independence on July 4.

That same day, Burgoyne dispatched Chevalier de Lorimier and some Canadians and Indians to scout atop Sugar Loaf Mountain (Mount Defiance) overlooking Fort Ticonderoga 1,500 yards away. They returned to report that it was possible to plant cannons on the summit. The general put his engineers to work. By late afternoon, they were dragging a battery of 24-pounders, 12-pounders, and 8-inch howitzers up the steep slope.

When St. Clair spotted those guns atop Mount Defiance, he knew the game was up. That night, his troops quietly withdrew from Fort Ticonderoga across the bridge to Fort Independence and joined that garrison in withdrawal toward the Hudson River. They left behind huge amounts of munitions and provisions.

With the rest of the army trailing by boat and on foot, Fraser's corps and those Indians not busy plundering the forts spearheaded the pursuit. Burgoyne pushed the main American army south with his redcoats while Fraser and Riedesel quick-marched in an arc toward the enemy rear. But the American army also was split, with its bulk on the road along Lake Champlain's east shore and Warner's brigade withdrawing on a parallel road farther inland. On July 5, Fraser's advanced guard caught up with Warner's rear guard. The Americans held their ground and then charged and routed the weary redcoats, capturing eight troops and forty cattle. Those victorious Americans withdrew south the next morning to rejoin Warner's brigade at nearby Hubbardton. Fraser's troops camped a few miles away with Riedesel's Germans a few miles beyond. Indians spotted the Americans and hurried back with word to their aggressive commander.

After calling on Riedesel to follow, Fraser roused his men early on the morning of July 6 and marched them through the dark. With fixed bayonets, they emerged from the dawn and attacked. The 2nd New Hampshire fled; the 11th Massachusetts stood steady and counterattacked. Fraser's left was about to snap when Riedesel's column marched onto the field. The Massachusetts advance hesitated. The British line stiffened, charged, and routed the Americans. In all, the Americans lost 325 killed or captured while killing 50 redcoats and wounding 140. Had not the New Hampshire troops fled and Germans arrived, the Americans would have celebrated the Hubbarton battle as a decisive victory.[56]

Gen. Philip Schuyler took over the field command from St. Clair and established his headquarters at Fort Edward, where he gathered most of the army. The northernmost American position was fourteen miles away at Fort Anne, commanded by Colonel Long. Reinforcements had swelled the ranks to 6,359 troops, 3,925 Continentals, and 2,434 militia, nearly as strong in numbers, if not discipline, as the enemy.[57]

Burgoyne's redcoats reached Skenesborough on July 6; Fraser and Riedesel appeared the following day. Indian war parties surged on ahead to harass the rebel pickets. They collided with an American patrol on July 7, killing three, wounding four, and scattering the rest. Learning the Americans were not far off, Burgoyne ordered Col. John Hill to probe them with the 150 troops of his 9th Regiment on July 8. That same day, Colonel Long sent 100 militia up the road to haul in supplies abandoned during the retreat. The two columns clashed on the road, deployed in lines through the thick forest, and exchanged shots for a couple of hours. The 9th's ammunition was running low and the rebels pressed their flanks;

Hill was just about to order a withdrawal when Indians and Fraser's corps double-timed into sight. Screaming war cries, the Indians fanned out and charged. Faced with overwhelming odds, the militia retreated in good order. The exhausted British did not pursue.[58]

It seemed that once again an American victory was dashed when enemy reinforcements arrived at the last moment, but those ragged, tough farmers actually scored an important triumph. They had squared off with and battered professional British troops, killing thirteen, wounding twenty-five, and capturing two, while suffering only ten casualties. Even more significantly, Burgoyne ordered Fraser and Hill to withdraw back to Skenesborough. The militia's aggressive attack, the thick forest concealing the enemy, scouting reports of a troop buildup at Fort Anne, and a shortage of draft animals and wagons caused Burgoyne to hesitate and regroup for the next two weeks rather than hurry his army toward the Hudson, a mere twenty-eight miles or leisurely two days' stroll south.

Schuyler put that reprieve to good use. He withdrew his garrisons from Forts Anne and George to Fort Edward. On July 9, he sent Brig. Gen. John Fellows with 1,000 New York and New England militia north to fell trees along the road to Fort Anne. A few days later, he reinforced Fellows with Brig. Gen. John Nixon's understrength 600-man Massachusetts brigade of the 3rd, 5th, 6th, and 7th Regiments. A scouting party of Stockbridge Indians captured two regulars and three loyalists near Skenesborough on July 20. Those prisoners revealed that the British army was resting and a day's march away, but Nixon took no extra precautions to forestall a surprise attack.

With Fraser's light corps camped between, Burgoyne and his redcoats were bivouacked at Skenesborough while Riedesel's Brunswickers were at Castleton ten miles east. On July 17, Canadian Indian superintendent John Campbell and Charles Langlade joined Burgoyne with 400 upper lakes Indians, boosting the army's total from 900 to 1,000 warriors from seventeen different tribes. Accompanying those western Indians were La Corne St. Luc and Charles de Lanaudiere leading 170 Canadian volunteers. On July 20, Burgoyne sent the Indians and Canadians to Fraser, who would then push them toward Fort Anne.[59]

The first blow was struck on July 21, when western warriors surrounded Captain Lane and thirty-four Massachusetts regulars a quarter mile from Fort Anne. Twelve troops escaped; the Indians killed two and took twenty prisoners back to Burgoyne. Nixon withdrew his force eight miles south and sent out fifty-man patrols to scour the forests. In early afternoon on July 22, the western and Canadian Indians evaded those patrols and attacked Nixon's pickets. Nixon charged his brigade against the Indians. After a half-hour fight, the Indians disappeared with fourteen wounded, having killed ten and wounded ten Americans. Nixon withdrew his force to Fort Edward on July 23. Fraser's brigade entered Fort Anne on July 24. Burgoyne ordered the rest of his army forward, and it reached Fort Anne two days later.

Leaving 600 troops at Fort Edward, Schuyler withdrew his army to Moses Creek four miles south on July 24. An Indian war party shadowed the Americans, took two scalps, and slipped away from a 200-man pursuit. The Americans enjoyed a minor vengeance the following day, when militia killed several Indians near Salem fifteen miles southeast of Fort Edward. Schuyler reduced his rear guard at Fort Edward to 150 troops from the 7th Massachusetts and New York militia under Maj. Daniel Whiting. On July 26, Indians murdered all eight members of the loyalist family of John Allen at their home near Moses Creek, the first clear violation of Burgoyne's strict orders against atrocities by his warriors. That same day, most of the western Indians attacked Whiting's pickets, killing five and capturing five others. Word was sent to Schuyler, who immediately ordered Gen. Abraham Ten Broeck with his militia and Gen. Ebenezer Learned with his 500 regulars to encircle the Indians, but they arrived too late.

As the Indians withdrew, they captured two women from their house near Fort Edward. Ironically, one was fifty-something Sarah Fraser McNeil, a distant cousin of General Fraser, and the other was beautiful young Jane McCrea, who was engaged to New York loyalist Lt. David Jones with the King's Loyal Americans. Two Indians quarreled over McCrea, each hoping to win the reward for bringing in a prisoner; one of them, apparently the loser, murdered her, leaving the scalp to the victor.

The murder appalled Burgoyne, who gathered all the chiefs of the seventeen tribes, "reprimanded them in very severe terms, for their late behaviour," and ordered them to hand over the murderer, who would be hanged. Now it was the Indians' turn to be appalled. They protested Burgoyne's severity for such a common act of Indian warfare and promised not to kill other civilians if he would pardon the murderer. When Burgoyne appeared ready to reject that plea, La Corne St. Luc persuaded him to issue a pardon, arguing that to do otherwise would alienate his Indians, most of whom would abandon the British for their distant homes, while some might even join the rebels. Burgoyne reluctantly gave in, but the damage was done, to both Burgoyne's army and his reputation. The Indians would stay with the campaign a bit longer, but the incident atop Burgoyne's cautious advance deflated their enthusiasm.

More importantly, Americans resurrected a national heroine and martyr from Jane McCrea's tragic death, one that would stiffen the beliefs of patriots in the justice of their struggle while sowing doubt in the minds of countless fence-sitters and loyalists alike. In a public letter written on September 2, Gen. Horatio Gates issued the first condemnation of Burgoyne for the outrage that would be echoed by newspapers, speeches, engravings, pamphlets, poems, and paintings: "Miss McCrea, a young lady lovely to the sight, of virtuous character and amiable disposition, engaged to be married to an officer in your Army, was . . . carried into the woods and there scalped and mangled in a most shocking manner . . . The miserable fate of Miss McCrea was . . . aggravated by her being dressed to receive her promised husband, but met her murderer employed by you. Upwards of one hundred men, women, and children have perished by the hands of the ruffians to whom it is assured you have paid the price of blood."[60]

Schuyler withdrew all his troops from Fort Edward to Moses Creek on July 28. Two days later he withdrew his army west across the Hudson to Fort Miller. Burgoyne's Indians hung about Schuyler's army, slipped around to ambush supply convoys and galloping couriers, and fanned out east of the Hudson to loot, burn, and occasionally murder, despite Burgoyne's order. That same day, Burgoyne's army entered Fort Edward. It was twenty-four days since the British had first marched into Skenesborough, a mere twenty-eight miles north. Valuable time had been lost, which would only become apparent later. With Fraser's brigade and the Indians in hot pursuit, Schuyler brought his army farther down the Hudson to below the Fishkill River mouth near Saratoga. Indians took the scalps of five stragglers and captured three more. But Burgoyne kept his main army at Fort Edward for now. Gen. John Glover led 1,200 Massachusetts troops along with several hundred New York militia into Schuyler's camp on July 31. The Americans now outnumbered the British, but that would not be immediately obvious.

Patrols skirmished in the woods between the two armies for the next several days. On August 4, Fraser demonstrated before the American advanced guard, commanded by Maj. William Hull, while sending a force around the enemy's left flank. Hull's troops broke, leaving twenty dead and seven captured behind. That same morning, Indians ambushed a forty-man picket two miles southwest of Saratoga, killing a dozen. Another war party slipped below the army and fired on troops guarding a hospital and swimming in the river, killing eleven and wounding more. Schuyler ordered yet another retreat, this time to Stillwater twelve miles south. There the Americans would take their stand.

As week followed frustrating week of thrashing through the wilderness after the elusive Americans, a question loomed ever darker in the minds of Burgoyne and his army—where was Howe? Burgoyne knew that Howe intended a campaign toward Philadelphia, but he also seemed to promise linking up with Burgoyne after he completed that excursion. Just when would word arrive that Howe awaited him in Albany?

THE SEABOARD WAR

As Burgoyne's soldiers marched, Howe's troops, after a jaunt into New Jersey, spent most of the summer squatting in reeking, sweltering transport ships. Howe's quixotic strategy for the summer of 1777 baffled both his army and the enemy, along with historians ever since. He did not begin his campaign until June 12, when he marched 17,000 troops from New Brunswick toward Princeton in hopes of provoking Washington to descend from the Morristown highlands for a showdown battle. It did not work. With only 8,000 poorly trained and equipped troops, Washington did not dare risk a field battle with a professional army twice as numerous. Less than a week after setting out and advancing no farther than Middlebrook, Howe gave up. Why he did not simply march with the army and supply train from Middlebrook to Philadelphia sixty miles away while the fleet packed with supplies sailed to meet him there remains a mystery. Even more puzzling is why Howe fancied Philadelphia's occupation rather than the rebel army's destruction as his primary objective.

Regardless, on June 19, he ordered his army to about-face and march all the way back to Staten Island. Along the way, he dropped off enough troops to defend New Brunswick and Perth Amboy. At Staten Island, he squeezed 13,000 troops into 260 transports bound for Philadelphia. But once aboard, Howe did not immediately set sail. The general's indecision mixed with adverse winds to keep the troop-packed fleet rocking at anchor for two weeks. Howe finally ordered the anchors weighed on July 23. Contrary winds delayed his arrival at the Delaware River mouth until July 31 and a reconnaissance of the forts guarding its mouth deterred him from advancing farther. Howe then sailed all the way down to Chesapeake Bay and up it to the Elk River, where he finally disembarked his troops on August 24. Those men had been pent up in those vile, cramped transports for six weeks. In all, Howe had squandered two and a half months of campaign weather and was still short of Philadelphia, which his army could have reached by foot in mid-June.

Howe's flounderings were a godsend to the American cause. Washington led his army of 8,000 regulars and 3,000 militia in gentle marches first to Philadelphia and then the Brandywine River valley to block Howe's advance. Alas, Washington and his generals seemed to have learned nothing about Howe's penchant for flank attacks. On September 11, Howe once again defeated Washington by overrunning his army's exposed right end and inflicting 1,000 casualties while losing half that number. The Americans retreated through Philadelphia and on to Germantown six miles north. On September 15, Washington led his army into the Schuylkill River valley northwest of Philadelphia. Howe occupied Philadelphia and sent forward a detachment of light troops that attacked Gen. Anthony Wayne's advanced position at Paoli on September 20, killing fifty-three, capturing seventy-one, and driving off the rest.[61]

Washington was eager for vengeance. Though outnumbered two to one, he devised an elaborate plan to double envelop Howe's army at Germantown on October 4. As usual, poor staff work defeated a bold strategy. When the smoke cleared, the Americans had inflicted 535 casualties on the British, but suffered 673 dead and wounded and nearly 400 captured. Washington withdrew his army a few miles north to Whitemarsh and by his presence taunted Howe to another fight.[62]

But as usual, Howe was not eager to try a knockout blow. Instead, he turned toward two forts, Mifflin and Mercer, that blocked the fleet from ascending the Delaware River to succor his army at Philadelphia. On October 9, he deployed a portion of his army in twin sieges of the forts. Fort Mifflin at the Schuylkill's River mouth capitulated on November 16, and Mercer's defenders slipped away to safety two days later. The British occupied those forts at a cost of over 500 casualties and two scuttled warships.[63]

That task done, Howe wasted another two weeks before sending his army toward Washington on December 4. The Americans stood their ground before the

British. After a sharp skirmish at Edge Hill on December 6, the armies glared at each other for two days. Then Howe withdrew his army into winter quarters, while Washington led his troops to Valley Forge twenty-one miles west of Philadelphia. All along, Howe seems to have forgotten his role in Burgoyne's fate.

THE NORTHWEST FRONTIER: SECOND PHASE
Hamilton's fervent wish came true on June 16. On that day, he opened Germain's order, sent via Carleton, to mobilize the tribes for war. He sent runners to the local tribes to council the following day. Before 350 Ottawa, Chippewa, Wyandot, Potawatomi, Shawnee, Miami, and Delaware, Hamilton displayed the war belt and hatchet, sang the war song, and urged them to attack the American frontier. That set off a prolonged debate among and within the tribes. By the council's third day, most of the chiefs had embraced Hamilton's call. Having stirred their blood lust, Hamilton then tried to temper it. On the fifth day, he cautioned the Indians that "they were men, & were desired to make war against men, and not against women or Children, and to forbear to dip their hands in blood."[64] Another week of drunken feasts, dances, and speeches followed. The council formally ended on June 24 with the distribution of gifts. War belts were sent to all Lake, Ohio, and Wabash tribes.

Hamilton raised a company of about forty volunteers among Detroit's militia to provide advisors and restraints for the Indians. Capt. Guillaume Pierre LaMothe commanded the company. Hamilton's recruiting tactics could be heavy-handed. He used his power to grant trade licenses to pressure reluctant merchants into enlisting.[65]

Once Hamilton released the genie of war, events unfolded swiftly. By July 4, the lieutenant governor had equipped and bade farewell to six war parties composed of 128 warriors and 18 volunteers. Within a month, that total had risen to 289 warriors and 30 officers. By September, Hamilton boasted that he had furnished seven hundred of the "eleven hundred and fifty warriors . . . now dispersed over the frontiers."[66] But all those warriors cost the Crown many a pretty penny. Hamilton spent 18,000 pounds sterling in 1777's first half alone and 11,220 pounds sterling in the second half to harvest 129 scalps and 73 prisoners that year.[67]

The lieutenant governor was not content just to inspire raids. Those alone could not crush the rebellion. For that he had a far more grandiose plan in mind, whose vision he shared with Carleton and Germain. An expedition would march from Detroit against Fort Pitt. Upon capturing the Ohio forks, the victors would then descend the Ohio and Mississippi Rivers to take New Orleans. Meanwhile, another British detachment would reach the Illinois settlements, rally the militia and Indians there, cross the Mississippi, and capture all of upper Louisiana. Hamilton's plan so excited him that after dispatching all those war parties, he traveled to Quebec to present it personally to the governor.[68]

Shortly after arriving there on September 18, Hamilton's enthusiasm would be sharply punctured. Carleton dismissed the plan as impractical at best, but more likely disastrous diplomatically and probably militarily. The lieutenant governor seemed to have overlooked the crucial reality that Britain and Spain were not then at war, although an attack on Louisiana surely would have changed that. Besides, all available forces and supplies had been committed to the Burgoyne, St. Leger, and Howe campaigns, which either had failed or appeared to be faltering. The barrel was scraped dry for an expedition against Pittsburgh let alone New Orleans this year and most likely the next.[69]

But all that aside, Carleton washed his hands of as much blood as possible from the frontier war. That war was Germain's moral and political responsibility. Carleton had simply performed the administrative task of relaying the American secretary's March 26 orders to its executors. He had bluntly told that to his boss in an August 11 letter: "You have also taken the conduct of the war entirely out of my commission; and . . . entrusted it to Lieut.-General Burgoyne, to Lieutenant Colonel St. Leger, and to Captain Hamilton."[70]

Meanwhile, for the Americans, Gen. Edward Hand's arrival at Fort Pitt on June 1, 1777, represented a watershed in frontier strategy. From now on, Congress would try to lead in defending the frontier. This would strengthen the movement among "landless" states within Congress to acquire all western lands as a trust for the new nation.

Shortly after arriving, Hand reassured Congress that "we here had nothing to apprehend from Detroit."[71] Indeed, the reputed sixty redcoats at Detroit—350 miles of wilderness away from Fort Pitt—did not seem terribly menacing. But the Americans in turn posed no threat to Detroit. Hand brought no troops with him. All available regulars were mobilized against the British offensives in the east. The general relied on his skimpy diplomatic rather than more pronounced military skills to defend the frontier. By mid-July, he had collected nearly fifty Indians of various tribes at Fort Pitt. But fearing the Mingo and Seneca present were spies, he had them thrown into jail. That incensed not only those victims, but the other Indians as well.

Indian commissioner George Morgan arrived on July 24 to sort out the mess. The internees were heaped with presents and set free. Morgan then promised gifts and trade to the delegates if they stayed at peace and destruction if they went to war. No Indian present was more important than Mekoce Shawnee chief Cornstalk. Morgan spent considerable time alone with him, trying to bolster his neutrality. But his attempts to dam diplomatically the stream of Indians visiting Pittsburgh could not stem the tidal wave of attacks elsewhere.

This year, the Indian raids on Kentucky began in earnest. In July, Shawnee chief Blackfish led over 200 Shawnee along with Mingo, Wyandot, and Delaware Indians across the Ohio against the three surviving Kentucky posts: Boonesborough with twenty-two riflemen, Harrodsburg with sixty-five, and St. Asaph's (Logan's Fort) with fourteen. Maj. George Rogers Clark commanded those militia. The warriors struck first at Boonesborough on July 2, killing one and wounding two of the defenders and burning everything beyond the palisade. But they dared not assault the fort and grew discouraged after marksmen killed several warriors. Blackfish led his men to St. Asaph's. They attacked it on July 19, killing two and wounding one defender, but again they did not rush the tiny but vigilant garrison. They headed on to harass Harrodsburg during August's first week. On August 5 a militia patrol ambushed a dozen warriors, killing three and wounding several more; the survivors fled, abandoning loot they had taken at the other two forts. Any discouragement Blackfish and his men may have felt was lifted when Great Lake Indians reinforced him about that same time. However, word soon arrived that Col. John Bowman had reached Boonesborough on August 1 with 100 fresh men from the Holston River settlements. Bowman marched toward St. Asaph's on August 25. Indians ambushed his six scouts, killing one and wounding two others. Those militia shored up the fort's defense and then pushed on to Harrodsburg in early September. On September 11, Indians jumped thirty-seven militia who had gingerly emerged from the fort to harvest cornfields, killed one, and wounded a half dozen others. On September 13, Capt. William Smith arrived with forty-eight militia at Boonesborough. Most of the warriors departed Kentucky by this time. The raids would shift to the upper Ohio.[72]

Four forts guarded that region—Pitt at Pittsburgh, Henry at Wheeling, Randolph at Point Pleasant, and Kittanning—while every settlement had its own blockhouse or palisade. As elsewhere on the frontier, those forts offered shelter, but the defenders could do nothing to prevent raiders from burning houses and murdering any laggards from the surrounding hamlets and farms. The region suffered its first raid on July 13, when Indians rounded up livestock and horses from the Grave Creek settlement ten miles downriver from Fort Henry. The next day, Indians butchered two men and a boy and captured three children near Statler's Fort on Dunkard Creek. The following day, about thirty warriors fired on seventy militia rowing upriver, but hit no one. On July 31, Indians killed the wife and a child and took another prisoner of the Grigsby family on Elm Creek of the Little Kanawha River. That same day, a Chippewa war party captured all six members of the Baker family from their home at Little Beaver Creek on the Ohio forty miles below Fort Pitt. An ambush on five militia near Logstown on August 1 left a man and boy dead and a second youth captured. On August 16, fifteen Wyandot attacked Col. John Carnahan's fortified house forty miles east of Pittsburgh and killed a man, but they lost two dead and another wounded in the assault. Twenty Chippewa killed three of six militia herding cattle just beyond Kittanning's walls on August 19.

While warriors from all other Ohio and Lake tribes stalked south or east against the settlements, most Delaware Indians clung to a tenuous neutrality. Their villages clustered along the upper Muskingum River and its tributaries halfway between the Sandusky Wyandot and Fort Pitt. Vulnerability to retaliation and genuine pacifist yearnings inspired by the neighboring Moravian converts explain much of their policy. The pressures and temptations for war were near constant in their lives. War parties eager for glory strode past and later back with scalps, captives, loot, wounds, and stirring tales. Although the Delaware fed and sheltered the warriors, ever more tribal councils angrily mulled over the question of why they did not do more.

That summer, Wyandot chief Half King began what would become years of pushing the Delaware ever harder to join their brothers in war against the Americans. On July 20, he led nineteen men into Coshocton, the Delaware head village, and met with the tribe's chiefs until July 28. The Delaware politely spurned all of his eloquent and reasoned arguments. Those most steadfast were Chief White Eyes; Killbuck, head of the Turtle phratry and paramount tribal chief; and Captain Johnny, head of the Turkey phratry. Wolf phratry head Captain Pipe, who leaned toward war, was absent. Half King would not depart until he thrust a war belt into their reluctant hands. They sent a runner with the belt back to Sandusky after Half King led his men toward the Ohio. News of that gesture would disappoint him. Yet his diplomatic mission fared better luck with the Walhonding River band of Wolf Delaware and the related Munsee and Mahican who lived farther north in Ohio. Their councils opted for war.

An unyielding pacifism may have been a central Moravian teaching, but that did not prevent the leading Moravian missionaries, David Zeisberger and John Heckewelder, from aiding the Americans by all nonviolent means. Throughout the war, trusted runners carried secret reports of war parties and tribal politics to Fort Pitt commanders. They also did what they could to keep the Delaware neutral.

Spying was dangerous for anyone, especially white people deep in Indian territory. Rumors of their activities inevitably spread. On the return from their raid, Half King and eighty-five warriors stopped at Lichtenau, two miles from Coshocton. There Half King asked Zeisberger about the rumors. Zeisberger responded by asking for Half King's protection. The chief readily granted it and spread the word that the Moravians should not be harmed. Yet that protection came at a price. Half King set up a war camp between Lichtenau and Coshocton, and there collected 210 warriors from a mélange of tribes by mid-August. On August 22, Half King led those men toward Wheeling, but Zeisberger sent a courier warning of the raid to General Hand, who reinforced Fort Henry with four militia companies led by Col. David Shepherd. When no attack occurred, three companies were withdrawn to Fort Pitt, leaving only sixty to defend Fort Henry.

As September 1 dawned, Half King's warriors lay in wait near Fort Henry. Six warriors rose and fired on four men who emerged from the fort to tend the cattle herd. The ambush would, they hoped, provoke the fort's commander to sortie against what were thought to be only a few warriors. Shepherd took the bait. He ordered Captain Mason and fourteen men to pursue the attackers. Half King signaled his warriors to open fire. Shepherd sent Captain Ogle and a dozen other militia to rescue Mason's troops, who were pinned down. Fifteen militia died and five suffered wounds before Mason and Ogle could flee to the fort with the survivors. The warriors peppered the distant fort with musket fire that day and the next. They killed three other men who blundered into the siege. When they withdrew on September 3, they had taken scalps and loot while suffering only eight wounds.[73]

Many more people would die in the upper Ohio that year. On September 11, Shawnee Indians killed three males and captured a daughter of the Graham family on Greenbriar River. In late September, Seneca chiefs Kayashuta and White Mingo led a war party that killed four, took several captives, and gathered horses near Fort Ligonier. Sixteen Wyandot captured five militia near Ligonier on September 25.

The most spectacular Indian coup that year in the region was yet to come, and Half King led it. On September 26, Capt. William Foreman led thirty-four militia from Fort Henry down the Ohio River's eastern shore for a two-day patrol. The following day, they were wearily trudging back and reached a point eight miles below Fort Henry when Half King's forty Wyandot opened fire and then rushed the survivors, killing twenty-one, wounding several, and capturing one.

As if all these raids were not dispiriting and destructive enough to the Americans, the settlers near Redstone Creek on the Monongahela River gathered in August and declared for King George. Militia colonels Zackwell Morgan and Thomas Gaddis led 500 men to the settlements to reassert American control. The Tories either fled or gave an oath of allegiance to the United States. Paranoia about secret loyalists among the American patriots spread, especially to Fort Pitt, where rumors targeted Indian Agent George Morgan for his friendship with former Crown agent Alexander McKee and Simon Girty, a former Seneca captive who resigned as militia lieutenant in August. Bowing to the pressure, General Hand actually jailed the three for several days, but then released them on the strength of testimony by character witnesses.

Delaware neutrality came under ever more pressure. After his warriors slaughtered twenty-one militia on the Ohio, Half King then led them back to Coshocton, where he displayed the scalps before the tribal council and claimed that he had defeated the Americans on their way to attack the Delaware. Many initially believed that propaganda, which Chiefs White Eyes and Killbuck dispelled only after considerable effort. At Pittsburgh, Indian Agent George Morgan was well aware of how fragile the Delaware neutrality was. He helped the peace chiefs with letters detailing that year's British defeats. In November, the Coshocton council decided to assuage both the Americans and British. White Eyes traveled to Pittsburgh to meet with Morgan, while Captain Pipe and Killbuck journeyed to Detroit to council with Hamilton.[74]

Though not formally part of the tribe, the Munsee were a Delaware people often influenced by Coshocton council decisions. In late 1777, the Munsee chose to break completely with Coshocton and join the British against the Americans. To escape Coshocton, they moved from the Muskingum valley to live among and raid with the upper Allegheny Seneca. About thirty Munsee stayed behind for either pacifist or practical reasons.

Raids into Pennsylvania continued well into early winter. In early November, a war party fired on a militia company en route from Pittsburgh to Wheeling when it tried to land near Logstown, killing one and wounding another. Later that month, Indians killed a father and two children five miles downstream from Pittsburgh. A party of fourteen Wyandot, two Mingo, two Canadians, and a Delaware killed two and took a prisoner near Wheeling. That prisoner was tortured to death at the Sandusky village.

Captain LaMothe led the year's largest war party, 132 men including 75 Lake Indians and 57 Canadians, from Detroit on September 20. They journeyed first to the Indian village at the Cuyahoga River mouth on Lake Erie. There they constructed a storehouse large enough to pack munitions for the region's raiders, and LaMothe counciled with the chiefs to muster more warriors to his party. Not everyone appreciated his efforts. Captain Pipe stalked from his nearby Delaware village on the Mahoning River to reproach LaMothe for undercutting his authority with his men. Although Captain Pipe and his people leaned toward the British, they had not yet seized the war hatchet. That grave decision was for the village elders to decide, not young men befuddled by British rum and gifts. Captain Pipe's protests persuaded nearly half of LaMothe's recruits to drop out. When LaMothe led his party out in late October, it numbered only about fifty Indians and Canadians. On November 4, they crept up to Wallace's Fort on Conemaugh Creek in western Pennsylvania and opened fire. Although their shots splintered wood rather than bodies, they did kill two stray men outside the fort, but they also lost one of the Canadians. LaMothe's first raid was hardly a ringing success.[75]

That same day, another party, most likely of Allegheny Seneca, surrounded Palmer's Fort seven miles from Ligonier and killed eleven people as they frantically tried to reach its safety. Those warriors had little time to savor their victory. Colonels James Smith and James Perry led a pursuit that caught up to a raiding party near Kittanning, killing five and recovering much stolen loot.[76]

The raids might have ended as winter worsened and warriors turned from hunting people for security to hunting animals for sustenance. But then something happened that sparked another round of raids and deepened hatreds. Among the Shawnee, only Chief Cornstalk of the Mekoce branch remained neutral. In late summer, he informed Coshocton of his people's desire to live in peace among the Delaware. The Coshocton council warmly accepted his petition and invited him to join them as soon as possible. Had that happened, the mingled strength of peaceful Moravians, Delaware, and Mekoce Shawnee on the upper Muskingum might have influenced other villages and tribes in the region. A vicious murder would destroy that chance.

In early September, some Delaware brought Cornstalk a black wampum belt said to have been sent by George Morgan. The belt puzzled Cornstalk, who sent envoys to Fort Randolph on September 19 to ask its commander Capt. Matthew Arbuckle just what it meant. Arbuckle had the envoys arrested as spies. Cornstalk then sent his son Elinipsico to persuade Arbuckle to release the envoys. Arbuckle told Elinipsico that he would only negotiate directly with Cornstalk. In late October, Cornstalk appeared at the fort. Arbuckle promptly had the chief and son jailed. Completely ignorant of Shawnee politics and Cornstalk's sincerity, Arbuckle wanted to use his four hostages as bargaining chips with the rest of the tribe. That gross violation of diplomacy alone would have alienated the Mekoce from peace to war, but an infinitely worse crime would be committed. When two soldiers were killed outside the fort on November 10, militia captain James Hall led his men to the jail, shoved aside the guards, and slaughtered Cornstalk, his son, and the two envoys. A jury later acquitted those involved of murder charges.[77]

Once again, a horrible atrocity wiped out years of careful diplomacy. The only Shawnee chief committed to peace was murdered by the people with whom he had buried the hatchet. That news spread rapidly, overwhelming the word favorable to Americans of Burgoyne's surrender and St. Leger's retreat. The murder swelled the ranks of warriors warring against the Americans and discredited those who called for peace. The propaganda effect on Indians was comparable to that of Jane McCrea's murder on Americans. How could any Indian trust any American?

The first blow struck to avenge Cornstalk's murder occurred in December when a Shawnee war party provoked a sortie from Fort Randolph and killed three soldiers. Many more raids and deaths would follow in the new year and the years beyond.

THE SOUTHEAST FRONTIER

In the southeast, with their diplomatic and military efforts blunted on the Carolina and Georgia frontiers, the British could only operate from St. Augustine.[78] Guarding southern Georgia on the Satilla River was Fort McIntosh, with its forty-eight Carolina rangers and twenty-two Georgia troops commanded by Col. Richard Winn. On February 17, Lt. Col. Thomas Brown, 100 rangers, and 50 Creek and Seminole led by Cowkeeper, Hycutt, and Philotougi deployed in the thick woods around Fort McIntosh. Brown hoped to nab prisoners for interrogation, but the Indians opened fire too soon on a woodcutting party, which sprinted to the fort's safety. The British and Indians inflicted four casualties as they sniped at the fort, but they dared not rush it. As it happened, that was not necessary. A rider got through to Gen. Lachlan McIntosh at Savannah. McIntosh immediately gathered most of his men and marched south while dispatching Col. John Screven and his men to reinforce Fort Howe, commanded by Capt. Chesley Bostick. McIntosh was too late. On February 18, Winn surrendered in return for parole. McIntosh met them on the road to Fort Howe. Determined to catch Brown, McIntosh pushed his command onward, but Brown caught the Americans in an ambush while they were crossing the Altamaha River. McIntosh lost twelve dead and was himself wounded. Brown retired to round up 2,000 cattle south of the river and herd them back to St. Augustine's grateful inhabitants.

Georgia general Button Gwinnett gathered troops and supplies at Sunbury for a campaign against St. Augustine. Although he opposed the plan because he feared the expedition would be too weak to take St. Augustine and would drain Georgia's defenses, the south's Continental commander, Maj. Gen. Robert Howe, sent Gwinnett a regiment of South Carolina cavalry and a battalion of foot soldiers, along with General McIntosh. Gwinnett and McIntosh bickered over strategy and command. To resolve the impasse, Howe and Georgia's council of safety recalled their respective leaders and jointly agreed to replace them with Col. Samuel Elbert. That did not end the dispute. With their honor deeply offended, McIntosh and Gwinnett dueled with pistols. Balls plowed into both men. Gwinnett died of gangrene three days later; McIntosh survived.

Elbert launched his expedition on May 1. Thomas Brown and his men hit one of Elbert's detachments, a regiment of mounted Georgia militia led by Col. John Baker at Cowford twelve miles above the St. Johns River on May 12. Fifteen of Brown's Creek drove off Baker's horses. Sixty Georgians pursued, recovered the horses, killed a Creek, and then retreated. That was enough of a scare for the Georgians. They retreated toward Elbert. Brown managed to slip around, ambush, and rout them on May 15. The fleeing Georgians then ran into Maj. James Prevost and his regulars advancing by another road on May 17. Prevost's troops and Indians captured forty Georgians at the battle of Thomas Creek. Ignoring the major's protests, the Indians tortured to death thirty-four prisoners in vengeance for the Creek killed five days earlier. When Baker and the remnants of his command reached Elbert, he chose to retreat. Prevost and Brown returned to their posts along the St. Mary's River. That frontier remained quiet until the summer.

Meanwhile, in early March, Southern Indian Superintendent John Stuart at Pensacola received Lord Germain's orders to wield Indians against the southern colonial frontier to divert troops and supplies from being sent to the northern rebel armies: "The distress and alarm so general an attack upon the frontiers . . . must occasion cannot fail of greatly assisting Sir William Howe's operations to the northward during the summer and of giving facility to any enterprise he may direct against the Carolinas and Georgia in the winter."[79] He was also told to guard against rebel incursions against British settlements on the lower Mississippi River and Gulf Coast.

Having previously registered his protest at such a policy, Stuart would do his best to realize that command. He, like most British officials and officers, assumed that the Crown's interests and ethics were interchangeable. But while now willing, he and his deputies lacked the means of rallying the southern tribes to the warpath that year. Those Indians had become the king's wards rather than warriors. The American devastation of the Cherokee villages the previous autumn cowed and impoverished most of that tribe. Few southern Indians would dare raise their hatchets against such a relentless foe. But more palpable than fear was poverty. The British blockade of the southern colonies had rendered moribund the deerskin trade. The colonists had neither the goods nor the desire to trade with the Indians. Pensacola displaced Augusta as the region's entrepôt, yet the trade there was little more lively. Stuart reported that the "Cherokees & Creeks having been so long destitute of Trade, and the former prevented from hunting by the incursions of the Rebells to their Country, being incapable of purchasing; the Creeks have hitherto been and the Cherokees still continue to be entirely depending upon his Majesty's Bounty."[80]

That year, Stuart handed out to the Indians over 33,000 pounds sterling worth of gifts to prop up their drooping loyalties and relieve their pinched stomachs.[81] Alas, many of those gifts and trade goods were kegs of rum that left the recipients drooping even more, sometimes permanently. With deep disgust, Choctaw deputy Charles Stuart revealed "nothing but Rum Drinking and Women crying over the Dead bodies of their relations who have died by Rum." He concluded that "unless some Step is taken to put a Stop to this abuse we need not look for any assistance from this nation, for at the very time they may be wanted they may be all drunk and Rum flows into their land from all quarters and is in my Opinion the only source of all abuses and complaints."[82]

On May 1, John Stuart met with the chiefs and over 2,800 mostly Creek and Choctaw, along with several score Chickasaw at Mobile. In response to his request to war against the Americans, most chiefs demurred or promised to send out war parties later that year, but only if a British expedition landed in the region. An exasperated Stuart concluded: "We court Indian help, we do not command it."[83]

That year, the tug-of-war for Indian hearts, minds, and weapons began to shift noticeably toward the Americans. Stuart reported that the "Rebels have their Emissaries in all the Indian Nations, which whilst the Management of the Trade is upon the present Footing cannot be prevented, for [by] the King's Proclamation of 1763 every person who can give Security for the Observance of Regulations, has a right to a License to Trade in any Nation of Indians, which gives the Rebels an Opportunity of sending their Emissaries under the Character of Traders, Packhorse Men or Servants without Danger of being detected. By such means the Rebel Agents have gained over some of the Creeks to their Interest."[84]

Most Cherokee reasoned it was best to ally with a people they could not beat. When Virginia colonel Nathaniel Gist and an escort arrived in the Overhill villages in March, several hundred warriors agreed to serve as rangers. Formal peace talks between the Americans and the Cherokee were scheduled to begin on April 15 at Long Island on the Holston River. Virginia governor Patrick Henry commissioned William Christian, William Preston, and Evan Shelby to negotiate. But only 100 Overhill Cherokee led by Old Tassel appeared on April 19. The commissioners persuaded Old Tassel and a delegation to journey to Williamsburg for further talks. Meanwhile, the representatives of South and North Carolina negotiated with the Middle, Valley, and Lower Cherokee. Preliminary talks were held by the chiefs with Col. Andrew Williamson at Charlestown early that year. A formal council opened at De Witt's Corner on May 7. On that date, commissioners Andrew Williamson, LeRoy Hammond, William Drayton, and Daniel Horry of South Carolina and Jonathan Bryan, Jonathan Cochran, and William Glascock met with 600 Cherokee. After two weeks of speeches, bargaining, feasts, and gifts, the delegates signed the Treaty of DeWitt's Corner on May 20, 1777. The Cherokee agreed to surrender all land east of the Unicoi Mountains, return all property and prisoners, and hand over any loyalists or British agents in their midst. That cession was confirmed by the Overhill Cherokee led by Raven, Little

Carpenter, and Old Tassel at Long Island on the Holston in July. Joseph Martin and James Robertson would serve respectively as the agents of Virginia and North Carolina to the Overhill Cherokee.

The treaties of Dewitt's Corner and Long Island sparked an influx of whites and an exodus of Indians from the territory. With the title in its pocket, North Carolina initiated a land rush into the Wataugan region, which it formally annexed and renamed Washington County, by offering up to 640 acres for each settler, and 100 acres for his wife and each child, for fifty shillings per 100 acres.

That giveaway broke the final tie between Little Carpenter and his son Dragging Canoe, who migrated with his followers to Chickamauga Creek just upstream of where it flows into the Tennessee River. From that stronghold, Dragging Canoe vowed to war against the settlers. Scores of Upper Creek Indians would join his Cherokee warriors there. That summer, about twenty-five of his warriors raided through the Holston River's north fork and killed several settlers. A party of militia tracked the warriors down, cornered them with the river to their back, and killed seven.

The Americans had less luck with the Creek Indians. Congressional commissioner George Galphin opened a council with some 400 Lower Creek on June 17 at his home, Silver Bluff, on the Ogeechee River. Assisted by Jonathan Bryce and Robert Rae, Galphin tried to persuade the Creek to bury the hatchet in return for ample goods. As one of them admitted, the Creek were definitely eager to resume trade: "We have been used so long to wrap our Children up as soon as they are born to Goods procured of the white People that we cannot do without" them.[85] Just how the merchants would get their hands on those goods was not clear, but it was essential to establish a rock solid peace now and worry about winning back the trade from their Pensacola and Mobile loyalist rivals later. One thing the Americans did have in abundance was rum. They rolled out one barrel after another to their ever drunker guests. That expedient worked until the imbibers awakened with splitting hangovers and either demanded more or staggered off in disgust.

How could the Americans counter the British advantage in enjoying nearly unlimited access to cheap, well-made goods? The most viable option was to literally kill off the opposition. In August, George Galpin and Samuel Elbert called on Creek chiefs to murder "those white Men in the Nation who set them" against the Americans.[86] About 120 warriors from Okfuskee stalked toward Hickory Ground to assassinate the British agents David Taitt, Alexander Cameron, and Jacob Moniac and to loot the gifts stored there. Had the assassination succeeded, British influence among the Creek Indians would have largely collapsed. It was Alexander McGillivray, half-Creek and Tait's agent, who single-handedly thwarted the plot. He met the war party, debated for hours with the chiefs, and finally persuaded them to return home. Nonetheless, the near-death experience spooked the agents to flee to Pensacola. The diplomatic field was left to the Americans.

Before leaving, Tait had talked several Coweta Lower Creek chiefs into leading war parties against the frontier while Lt. Col. Thomas Brown dispatched his Florida scout companies on various raids. Along the Ogeechee River, the Coweta

Indians murdered the wife and daughter of militia captain Elijah Clark at their home and killed Capt. Thomas Dooley as he led a patrol of Georgia Continentals. The ranger patrols scouted and looted more than killed, skirting Savannah and Augusta and invading St. Simons Island before heading back with cattle herds and other plunder to St. Augustine.

Capt. John Dooley sought to avenge his brother's death but picked the wrong target. He ordered his troops to capture at Galphin's Silver Bluff home Lower Creek chief Handsome Fellow and his delegation, who were returning from talks with Gov. John Rutledge in Charles Town. The incident almost provoked a war not just with the Creek, but between South Carolina and Georgia. Tensions between the states were already tense. First William Henry Drayton had publicly exhorted South Carolinians to annex Georgia. Then Georgia's government posted a reward for Drayton's arrest for sedition. Upon learning that the Creek envoys were Georgian prisoners, Rutledge ordered South Carolina troops to liberate them. A war within a broader war seemed inevitable. George Galphin defused the crisis by persuading Dooley to free the Creek Indians to his deputy Lt. Robert Rae, who would escort them back to their homes. One of Brown's ranger companies ambushed the delegation en route, killing Capt. John Gerard, whom they mistook for Galphin. Col. Samuel Elbert ordered Col. John Baker to march his regiment after the raiders. But Baker's troops refused to budge, fearing to leave while Creek war parties lurked near their homes. Then Handsome Fellow died of an illness just short of his home.

As if these tragic-comic events were not debilitating enough to the frontier's defense, a bad loser form of Georgian pride had petitioned Congress to recall Continental general Lachlan McIntosh for killing state militia general Button Gwinnett in a duel earlier that year. McIntosh was transferred to the northern front. Then the Georgian government and militia leaders pressured Howe to launch a campaign against the Creek. Howe wisely resisted the entreaties, which naively made the Georgians dupes for British strategy.

Despite the fumbling diplomacy, conflicting interests, rival egos, and military ineptness plaguing the American camp, try as they might the British just could not provoke the Indians and loyalists to rise and sweep away the rebels along the frontier. The Americans had crushed the Cherokee, intimidated the loyalists, and kept most Creek Indians off the warpath. The Creek villages were split among those favoring the British, Americans, or neutrality, with those of Okfuskee, Tallassee, and Cusseta leaning the farthest toward the rebels.

At an October council with the Lower Creek, John Stuart appealed to Indian interests to talk them into seizing the war hatchet. Contrasting how the British helped and Americans hurt the Indians, he reminded them: "I for many years have . . . been employed in seeing Justice done you in settling boundaries to your reserved Lands that your hunting Grounds might not be encroached upon and spoilt. I likewise sent emissaries into your Nation to take Care that you should not be imposed upon . . . and bad Men should not poison your Minds with bad Talks & Forgeries . . . if the Rebels should prove victorious you may be certainly assured that they would immediately endeavour to possess themselves of all your Land and extirpate you."[87] Few Indians were blind to that reality, yet they were unwilling to go to war to prevent it. At most, Stuart succeeded in persuadng them to allow British agents to return to their villages with gifts that winter.

As elsewhere, the members of the British high command in the south did not command as one but squabbled incessantly and often acted at cross-purposes. In April, Augustine Prevost was promoted to brigadier general and given command over East Florida's regulars, while Gov. Patrick Tonyn retained control of the militia and loyalist volunteers. Thereafter, the general and governor debated strategy, with Tonyn strengthening his position by refusing to share his militia unless Prevost acquiesced. In December, the general politely requested the governor to grant him command over all armed men in the province. Tonyn just as politely denied the request. Afraid that Prevost would go over his head, Tonyn preempted him with letters to Germain and Howe, asking them to confirm his control over the rangers and other loyalists units. Just as Tonyn feared, Prevost issued his own protests to his superiors.[88]

ST. LEGER'S CAMPAIGN

The western arm of New York's invasion was entrusted to forty-four-year-old Barry St. Leger.[89] He was a seasoned soldier, having joined the army as an ensign in 1756, and fought in the 1758 Louisbourg, 1759 Quebec, and 1760 Montreal campaigns. He mustered out on half pay as a major in 1763 and spent the next dozen years as a civilian. War and marriage into a rich family coincided in 1775. St. Leger bought the lieutenant colonelcy of the 34th in 1776 and sailed off to Canada. The 1777 expedition would be his first independent command. St. Leger was far from the best choice. Three flaws were especially prominent. He knew nothing of substance about Indians, drank to excess, and tended to prefer lethargy to action.

Nonetheless, the campaign started out well enough. St. Leger was at Montreal when he received his orders from Germain and Carleton on May 22. He needed less than a month to organize the supplies, munitions, and transport. The first contingent left Lachine on June 21 for the hard paddle up the St. Lawrence to Deer Island (renamed Carleton Island in 1778), a dozen miles below Lake Ontario. There, from July 8 to 19, he tied up loose ends and awaited word on a scout toward Fort Schuyler he dispatched on June 16.[90]

Upon receiving St. Leger's orders, Mohawk chief John Deserontyon and Lt. John Hare gathered about forty men at Oswegathchie and headed south. They arrived near Fort Schuyler on June 25 and jumped two officers who had gone fishing on Wood Creek; the Americans fought to their death. The war party lingered, waiting for a chance to capture a stray soldier or two. That chance came on July 3 when they ambushed a sixteen-man sod-cutting detail three-quarters of a mile from the fort; they killed four and captured four. The information they extracted from their captives was bleak—at least 600 troops and several weeks of supplies were crammed within Fort Schuyler. They hurried back to Deer Island.[91]

There, all 630 troops had arrived by July 19. They included 100 of the 34th with Capt. Richard Lernoult, 100 of the 8th with Lt. Henry Bird, 80 Hanau Chasseurs with Lt. Jacob Hildebrand, 133 of the Royal Regiment of New York with Sir John Johnson, 50 Canadians with Capt. Hertel de Rouville, 67 rangers with Capt. Walter Butler, and 20 gunners manning two 6-pounders, two 3-pounders, and four coehorn mortars. With such few soldiers, of whom only 280 were regulars, St. Leger needed every available Indian. Three skilled agents led the recruiting, John Butler first among the Seneca and then other Iroquois, Daniel Claus among the Mississauga, and Joseph Brant among the Mohawk and other eastern Iroquois. They would eventually rally 50 Mohawk; 300 Seneca, Cayuga, and Onondaga; 250 various Iroquois; 150 Mississauga and St. Regis Indians; 50 Detroit Indians; and some Delaware to the expedition. Those Indians did not come cheap. Butler alone spent 22,483 pounds sterling in gifts between the time he received Germain's orders on June 6 and the expedition's departure.[92]

Butler focused on converting the Iroquois, especially the Seneca, from neutrality to alliance. He counciled with mostly Seneca chiefs from July 13 to 24 at Irondequoit Bay on Lake Ontario. That was the war's most decisive Iroquois council. Then and there, the Seneca firmly took to the warpath, followed with varying degrees of enthusiasm and numbers by the other Iroquois tribes. After three days of speeches, gifts, feasting, and rum, Butler offered the chiefs the war belt on July 17. At first the Seneca were split within and among their three divisions. Sayenqueraghta represented the Lake Seneca villages, which were most vulnerable to an American attack; they still tilted toward neutrality. The enemy was far from the clusters of villages along the Allegheny and Genesee Rivers. Their chiefs, Kayashuta and Cornplanter, expressed the warriors' enthusiasm for war. The Seneca Indians debated several days before hammering out a consensus. Not only would the Seneca go to war, but the nearly seventy-year-old Sayenqueraghta, or Old Smoke, of the Turtle Clan would lead all the Iroquois warriors, seconded by twenty-five-year-old Gayentwagha, or Cornplanter, of the Wolf Clan.

A triumphant Butler then hurried on to Three Rivers, the confluence of the Oswego, Seneca, and Oneida Rivers, where he met with representatives of the rest of the Six Nations from July 30 to August 4. Joseph Brant joined him and stirred the assembly with his oratory. Their mission was not only to recruit, but also to get permission for St. Leger's army to march through Iroquois territory. Most Oneida and Tuscarora adamantly rejected Brant's war belt, while most Cayuga and Onondaga embraced it.[93]

St. Leger's army reached Oswego on July 23. After three days' rest, the expedition embarked on July 26 in bateaux and canoes for the ten-day seventy-five-mile journey via Onondaga River, Oneida Lake, and Wood Creek route. St. Leger would deploy his army around Fort Schuyler piecemeal. A week earlier, he had ordered Captains John Hare and James Wilson to lead six rangers and some Mississauga and Seneca to prowl near the fort. Arriving on July 27, the Indians promptly killed two girls and wounded a third picking berries within sight of the defenders. It was hardly a glorious start to the campaign. On July 29, St. Leger sent ahead Lt. Henry Bird with 30 troops of the 34th and 200 Indians to prevent the Americans from clogging Wood Creek with felled trees. Nearly all the Indians stopped to butcher and feast off some stray oxen they found. Unable to entice them away, Bird pushed ahead with his troops and only twenty-seven Seneca and nine Mississauga, but a detachment from Fort Schuyler had arrived first, obstructing the stream with fallen trees on July 26 and 27. Those Indians who had gorged on the beef caught up with Bird on August 1. Bird urged them to hurry on to the fort, but they insisted on resting. Bird impatiently awaited the next morning, when they all strode off, reaching Fort Schuyler around noon on August 2. Had they arrived on July 30, Bird's force might have ambushed 200 troops that marched into the fort that day. Had they arrived just a few hours earlier on August 2, they might have captured five supply-filled bateaux. Instead, they killed a guard at the empty boats and wounded two others, who escaped to the fort.

Fort Schuyler was crammed with over 750 troops of the 3rd New York and 9th Massachusetts, thirteen cannons, and six weeks of supplies. As important to its defense was its indomitable commander, Col. Peter Gansevoort, who came from one of Albany's more venerable aristocratic families. In July 1775, Congress commissioned him a major in the 2nd New York, and he marched off to serve gallantly in Montgomery's Canada campaign. On March 1, 1776, he was named the 3rd New York's lieutenant colonel, and on November 21, its colonel. He was only twenty-eight when he received command of Fort Schuyler in April 1777.

When St. Leger arrived with the bulk of his army before Fort Schuyler on August 3, the sight discouraged him: "Instead of the insultable and unfinished work we were taught to expect I found it was a respectable Fortress strongly garrisoned with 700 men and demanding a train of artillery we were not master of for its speedy subjection."[94] He camped his regulars 1,000 yards northeast of the fort and sent the loyalists to bivouac to the south with Bird's troops, while the Indians scattered all around. Not all of his troops were up. He had left 110 men to clear Wood Creek; it would take them nine days to end that grueling task.

Just after dawn on August 4, most of the troops and Indians crawled within musket range of the fort and peppered its walls with lead. But a day's firing left only one American dead and seven wounded. The gunshots faded with the night but started again with the dawn and continued all day. All that burnt powder killed only one more defender.[95]

Relief was on its way to Fort Schuyler. Gen. Nicolas Herkimer commanded the upper Mohawk valley's militia. Upon receiving word from Gansevoort of St. Leger's approach, Herkimer called out his men to muster at Fort Dayton guarding German Flats, thirty miles east of Fort Schuyler. By the morning of August 4, about 760 had answered the call and marched west with their general and fifteen creaking ox carts piled high with provisions. They marched slowly that day and the next, camping the second night at the small Oneida village of Oriska. There Herkimer enlisted sixty warriors under Chiefs Thawengarakwen and Henry Cornelius. He also sent three men with a letter to Gansevoort revealing their advance and asking him to fire three cannon shots to signal that he received word. But the

British were the first to learn of Herkimer's advance when Molly Brant, William Johnson's widow, sent a runner to her brother Joseph.

St. Leger faced the dilemma of being crushed between two enemy forces, each of which equaled his own in size. That and word that the Oneida Indians had joined Herkimer caused the Seneca and John Butler to suggest negotiating with Herkimer. Joseph Brant, backed by Sir John Johnson, rejected the notion and called for an ambush of the enemy. St. Leger agreed.

When Herkimer's army approached on August 6, the British and Indians were ready. While St. Leger and the rest of his army pinned down the garrison, Johnson and about eighty loyalists, John Butler, and nearly 500 Indians lay hidden in the forest six miles east of Fort Schuyler and just west of the steep ravine where Oneida Creek gushes down to the Mohawk River. The plan was to attack the Americans after they had passed from the ravine. The loyalists would step onto the road to fire several volleys and retreat, thus goading the Americans into a fishhook of Indians, with the shank paralleling the road's south side, and Brant and his men at the eastern tip. The Indians at either flank would swiftly dash around the enemy's rear, cut off their retreat, and slaughter them. That plan was almost perfectly executed.

Herkimer was cautious and wanted to remain at Oriska until he heard the three cannon shots, but his hotheaded officers urged a rapid advance and he reluctantly agreed. The militia and carts were strung out for a mile. Though Herkimer had posted the Oneida and troops ahead in the woods, the forest was so thick that they squeezed back to the road. Around ten o'clock, they stumbled right into the trap.

The loyalists emerged from the trees, packed onto the road, and fired a volley. With the first shots, the Indians impatiently rushed forward rather than wait for the Americans to advance. About 200 militia fled, pursued by Brant and his warriors, who butchered them. That left the 80 loyalists and 200 Seneca and other Indians led by Sayenqueraghta and Cornplanter to battle about 500 militia who stayed to fight. A ball slammed into Herkimer's knee. Despite excruciating pain, he propped himself against a tree and continued to direct the battle, ordering the men to pair off with one man firing while the other reloaded. The battle raged for hours, dampened only by a passing thunderstorm. The Americans retreated into an ever more compact circle. After three hours, Brant and his warriors reappeared, carrying plenty of munitions looted from the carts and the dead littering the road and woods eastward. Around one o'clock, the British and Indians had prepared a final rush that would slaughter the enemy's remnants, when a runner brought word that the Americans were looting their camp.

Herkimer's couriers had finally managed to reach the fort. Gansevoort had three cannon shots fired and ordered Lt. Col. Marinus Willet to sally forth with 250 men. The Americans spilled through the gate and ran toward the nearly deserted British and Indian camps, scattered the score of guards, killed four loyalists and two Indians, captured four loyalists, and dragged back to the fort twenty-one wagon loads of supplies. Among the loot was the medicine bundle of the Seneca's Little Warrior Society, a coup that would deeply dishearten them.

Willet's sortie saved Herkimer from complete massacre. When the Indians heard about the attack, they dashed back to their camp, leaving the loyalists behind. Butler and Johnson withdrew their men in good order. So the Americans held the blood-soaked field known as Oriskany that day, but at a terrible cost. Only about 150 militia remained unhurt. They gathered about fifty wounded comrades and retreated. In all, the Americans lost about 500 killed, wounded, and captured; Herkimer died a few days later of gangrene after his leg was amputated. Six or seven troops of loyalists along with thirty-three Indians were killed and thirty-two wounded; of these losses, the Seneca suffered seventeen dead and sixteen wounded.[96]

Though the Indian losses were light compared with those of the Americans, they were heavy in proportion to their population. Even more ominously, the political split in the Iroquois was now seared with civil war—the Oneida had fought against warriors of all the other tribes. The British Iroquois would seek vengeance against the Americans and Oneida alike.

It could have been much worse for the Americans. The harvest of scalps from Oriskany could not appease the Indians' rage at losing so many of their finest warriors. At a council on August 7, the chiefs implored St. Leger, Johnson, and Butler to loose them down the valley on the heels of Herkimer's survivors. Johnson and Butler embraced the strategy, but St. Leger vetoed the idea, arguing that it made no sense to split his diminished army before an enemy superior in numbers. Without the Indians, the garrison could concentrate four or five times as many men in a rush against one of the two batteries then being emplaced. The Americans would not dare a sortie as long as the warriors lay vigilant nearby. Furthermore, St. Leger insisted that the Indians promise not to harm any soldiers once they gave up, though he permitted them to loot the fort. The chiefs consulted with their men and issued a response the next day. They would stay with St. Leger and not molest a single soldier as long as they suffered no more losses, but if any more of their men fell to enemy bullets, they would seek a terrible revenge.

The British and Indians had reason to be optimistic. After all, they had crushed Herkimer's rescue, slaughtering hundreds of American militia. It would be weeks before the enemy could mount another venture, if at all. Fort Schuyler should fall well before that. Then the victorious British army could sweep down the Mohawk and join triumphantly with Burgoyne in Albany, and from there perhaps all the way down the Hudson River to New York City itself.

St. Leger set his troops to work enfilading Fort Schuyler with two batteries, one for the 6-pounders to the northeast and another for the 3-pounders a half mile to the southeast. Abatis-spiked redoubts guarded both batteries and the nearby camps for the troops. The Indians scattered in a crescent on the fort's west side, where they impotently fired at the distant walls. The batteries were ready on August 8. St. Leger sent in Captains John Butler and William Ancrum under a truce flag with his surrender demand. The choice was stark—capitulate now and be spared or hold out longer and most likely be butchered if the Indians swarmed over the wall.

To this Colonel Gansevoort replied angrily: "Before I would consent to deliver this garrison to such a murdering set as your army, by your own account, consists of, I would suffer my body to be filled with splinters and set on fire, which as you know has at times been practiced by such hordes of women and children killers as belong to your army."[97] Having vented that fury, the colonel said that he and his officers would discuss the matter and reply the following morning. When that time came, early on August 9, Gansevoort sent word that they would respond only to written rather than oral demands. Clearly the rebels were playing for time.

St. Leger tried to hasten them with a letter that stated his terms and ended with the warning that "the Indians are extremely impatient; and if this proposal is rejected I am afraid it will be attended with very fatal consequences, not only to you and your garrison, but the whole country down the Mohawk river—such consequences as will be very repugnant to my sentiments of humanity, but after this entirely out of my power to prevent."[98]

Gansevoort and his officers did not flinch from the threat. They had played out the negotiation dance as long as they could. Now was the time for a defiant reply: "It is my determined resolution, with the force under my command, to defend this fort and garrison to the last extremity, in behalf of the United States of America, who have placed me here to defend it against all their enemies."[99]

The Americans had called St. Leger's bluff. The enemy's four cannons were too weak to breach the fort's low earthen walls. With at least a month's worth of provisions, the defenders could sit tight and await another rescue. Nonetheless, the barrage did kill or wound thirty-seven defenders. St. Leger ordered some of his men to zigzag a trench toward the fort while others diverted the stream that supplied water to the defenders. But the trenches could only be inched forward, while the Americans dug wells to reach fresh water.

To intimidate another rescue attempt, on August 13 St. Leger sent Ens. Walter Butler, ten troops, and two Indians with a letter to settlers down the valley warning that all who resisted would be slaughtered. Col. James Wesson, commanding companies of the 8th and 9th Massachusetts at Fort Dayton, ordered out 100 troops to arrest Butler's party on August 15. Butler claimed that his truce flag protected him. Wesson replied that nothing justified such blatantly subversive actions to rouse the Mohawk valley's loyalists and thwart its patriots. Butler and his men were sent to Albany to be tried as spies, with death by hanging the likely result. Wesson then ordered his troops to round up any confessed loyalists. St. Leger's ploy had grossly backfired in German Flats.

That effort, however, did inspire a village of whites and Indians on the Charlotte River. John MacDonell and Adam Crysler mustered about seventy loyalists and fifty Mohawk and marched east toward Schoharie valley on August 11. Learning of the advance, Col. John Harper led 20 cavalry and 200 militia from the valley against the approaching enemy. The two forces clashed at Flockey Swamp on August 13; shots killed one American and wounded three others before a cavalry charge scattered the loyalists into the woods. The next day, the loyalists retreated to join St. Leger's force at Fort Schuyler. That incursion prompted the patriots in the Schoharie valley to construct three forts, known as the Upper, Middle, and Lower.[100]

The defiance of Fort Schuyler's defenders sank any lingering Indian enthusiasm that St. Leger had buoyed with visions of a swift surrender and all that loot. Their dead and wounded at Oriskany, along with their plundered camp, weighed more heavily than ever upon their minds. Over the next two weeks, about 200 Indians drifted away to their villages. That infuriated St. Leger, who called a council to rally the rest. Instead, he had to listen in silent fury as they bluntly told him he "should retreat or they would abandon him."[101]

Meanwhile, another rescue was approaching. On August 12, Gen. Philip Schuyler dispatched Gen. Ebenezer Learned's Massachusett brigade and Col. Goose Van Schaick's 1st New York from Albany up the Mohawk valley; the following day, he sent Gen. Benedict Arnold to command those troops. That force reached Fort Dayton on August 20, where Arnold prepared his 933 regulars and 100 militia for the final push to Fort Schuyler.

But before marching, Arnold devised a fascinating bit of psychological warfare. Hans Yost Schuyler was an unusual loyalist, so feeble-minded the Indians believed he possessed great spiritual powers. Arnold threatened the entire Schuyler family with arrest if Hans did not carry a story to St. Leger that 2,000 crack American troops, twice their actual strength, were approaching. Hans set off on the evening of August 21, reached the British camp the next afternoon, and dutifully spread the tale among the Indians and British alike.

Ironically, the story spooked St. Leger most of all. After briefly consulting his officers and the chiefs, St. Leger departed with his regulars so hastily that he neglected to send word to about 200 loyalists and Canadians laboring in the trenches. Those men eventually heard and, like the regulars, abandoned most of their equipment and supplies, which the Indians happily began looting, especially the rum kegs. Gansevoort got wind of the retreat and sent a sixty-man patrol to investigate. In the British camp, the Americans scattered the drunken Indians, killing two and wounding and capturing one along with three loyalists. The enraged Indians caught up to St. Leger's fleeing troops and butchered several before they were persuaded to stop. St. Leger's army packed into the flotilla of boats and canoes. The army did not tarry after reaching Oswego on August 26. Awaiting St. Leger were orders from Burgoyne to join him with all possible speed by way of either Montreal or the Mohawk valley. With the latter route closed, St. Leger embarked most of his troops for the long row down Lake Ontario, the St. Lawrence, and then up the Lake Champlain route toward the Hudson. They would arrive too late to help Burgoyne.

Arnold's army reached Fort Schuyler on August 24 and sent out 100 Oneida on the British rear to take as many stragglers as possible. He readied 500 crack troops to pursue the following morning, but a steady downfall slowed their march. A handful reached Oneida Lake just as the last of St. Leger's boats were skimming away. The Americans did seize tons of abandoned supplies both in the camps outside Fort Schuyler and along the British retreat to Lake Oneida. His mission accomplished, Arnold headed east on August 26 for what would become his career's most decisive battle.

St. Leger's withdrawal brought not just relief, but also opportunity to the Mohawk valley's defenders. With danger gone for now, the settlers and Oneida who had lost loved ones at Oriskany and elsewhere sought vengeance. In August, mobs searched the Fort Hunter and Canajoharie Mohawk villages for Molly Brant and others who might have abetted the invaders. Molly and her children joined an exodus of all the Canajoharie and many Fort Hunter Mohawk to Onondaga, while more than 150 others, mostly warriors, headed north through the Adirondacks to join Burgoyne. Forty troops of the 3rd New Hampshire pursued those bound for the British, stumbled into an ambush on September 4, and lost nine dead while killing three Mohawk. That night, the Mohawk entered the British camp. Meanwhile, the Oneida stripped the Mohawk fields of their crops and livestock. A hard winter lay ahead for the half-dozen Fort Hunter families led by ancient Chief Little Abraham who clung to their homes. They were lucky to escape with their lives and houses. Eventually they too would be driven away.

BURGOYNE'S CAMPAIGN: SECOND PHASE

That same month that St. Leger's campaign stalled and then collapsed, Burgoyne's began a slower meltdown. As August opened, everything seemed to be going so well for the general. It was still summer and his army was only forty-five miles from Albany. His troops had swept all before them since the campaign began. He was building up his supplies at Fort Edward for a final push against the rebels that should carry him to Albany and a juncture with Howe and St. Leger. The army had plenty of provisions and munitions as heaps of supplies lay waiting at Skenesborough to be packed atop the rickety ox carts and rumbled down to Fort Edward. There seemed to be no need for hurry let alone haste. The summer heat distanced autumn's frost and winter's ice and snow.

But from August's first week, things started to go wrong. On August 3, Burgoyne got a discouraging letter from Howe. It was up to Burgoyne and St. Leger to take Albany on their own; Howe would send forces to meet them there later. That meant the Americans could concentrate their forces against the two British armies without worrying about a third attacking their rear. Then on August 5, chiefs of the western and Canadian Indians informed Burgoyne that they wished to go home with their scalps and plunder. The general tried to dissuade them with arguments sweetened by offers of rum and gifts. Most Indians agreed to stay, but the rest departed the next day. Most of those who remained searched for their version of glory. On August 7, war parties in separate skirmishes killed three soldiers near Stillwater, captured four officers several miles south, killed a major and two civilians, and lost a man shot by pursuing troops. With their honor satisfied from these coups, many of these warriors departed. Not just Burgoyne's Indians deserted. Silence greeted ever more names during the morning muster rolls. Burgoyne offered the Indians twenty dollars for every deserter they retrieved and the scalps of those who resisted. With 1,000 men deployed along his supply line and another 1,000 casualties from various battles and disease, only about 5,500 combat troops remained. As if all this were not worrisome enough, a potential threat began to loom on Burgoyne's eastern flank, where Gen. John Stark was mustering the militia of Vermont and New Hampshire.[102]

Strategically, it was time to concentrate his troops and crush Schuyler. But Gentleman Johnny did not do that. The pace of eighteenth-century warfare was relaxed. Campaigns unfolded methodically like chess games, and battles only after all the pieces were in place. Distracted by that militia massing to the east, an idea came to Burgoyne that made sense at the time but would prove to be his undoing. He decided to dispatch Fraser's light corps, 220 troopers from Lt. Col. Friedrich Baum's unmounted Brunswick Dragoon Regiment, and 160 Indians on a foraging raid to Vermont. There was rumor of a huge rebel supply depot at Bennington whose capture would at once deprive the enemy and enrich the British. Perhaps those dragoons could find horses to mount as well. And the enemy in Burgoyne's front might well weaken itself by detaching a large force to intercept Baum. The expedition set off on August 9, the officers and men alike confident that easy victories and good eating lay before them. That conceit would soon be shattered.[103]

When Burgoyne's army captured Fort Ticonderoga, the Vermont council of safety entrusted its defense to native son Gen. John Stark, a rugged canny wilderness fighter and veteran of Rogers' Rangers from the French and Indian War. By August 13, Stark had massed 1,500 New Hampshire regulars and 400 militia at Bennington, while Col. Seth Warner commanded 150 regulars and 200 militia at Manchester twenty miles north.

Baum's corps marched east, brushing aside small rebel detachments and rounding up cattle and loyalists. On August 14, the expedition paused briefly at the ruins of a bridge over Owl Kill, destroyed by Lieutenant Colonel Gregg and his 200 troops. The Americans withdrew as the Indians and rangers waded across, followed by the rest of Baum's troops. The rapid British pursuit came to a dead halt a few miles beyond and only a half-dozen miles from Bennington, where Stark's army straddled the road.

Stark hoped to provoke a British attack on his superior numbers and position. He sent out riflemen, who picked off two Indians and thirty loyalists, but Baum stood fast, confident his troops could repel any American attack. When Baum's intentions were clear, Stark left his skirmishers on the field and withdrew the bulk of his army a mile hoping to entice the enemy. But Baum was unyielding, merely awaiting promised reinforcements of Lieutenant Colonel Breymann with the 642 Brunswickers and two 6-pounders. Thunderclouds piled up and released a drenching storm that churned the roads to muck. As his troops took shelter around Cambridge a dozen miles away, Breymann sent a courier galloping to Baum with word that they would not arrive until at least noon the next day. Although he would march at noon, Breymann would arrive too late to save his countrymen.

The sky was clear early on August 16, when Stark executed a very carefully planned attack. While most of his army massed in Baum's front, four detachments of about 200 men each angled around the enemy rear. By midmorning, the Americans moved in for the kill. Firing and shouting, they squeezed the British in a giant nutcracker. Only about thirty Caughnawaga slipped the noose. An ammunition cart blew up within the German lines, killing several and briefly stunning all. The Americans charged, swarmed over hastily constructed breastworks, and shot, bayoneted, and clubbed their way through the enemy. A bullet mortally wounded Baum. The survivors threw down their muskets. Just then, Breymann's column appeared a mile down the road. The victorious Americans turned on the new enemy. Those closest fanned out across the road and opened fire. Breymann deployed his troops from column into line and sent out skirmishers to match the Americans. The gunfire died with dusk.

With their bodies and cartridge boxes exhausted from the previous day's battle, the Americans' attack the next morning was piecemeal and plodding. When Warner's corps finally arrived, Stark pushed them into the thick of the fighting. The British fell back, abandoning their two 6-pounders; night saved Breymann from suffering Baum's fate. He and his weary troops retreated through the dark to Cambridge. In all, the battle of Bennington cost the British over 900 troops, including 200 dead and nearly all the rest captured, while the Americans lost no more than 30 dead and 50 wounded.[104]

The battle of Bennington was the campaign's turning point. Burgoyne's offensive had already stalled at least a week earlier, deepened by his choice to send Baum on a foraging raid. The shock of losing a tenth of his army appeared to have mired Burgoyne in a fog of indecision that persisted until his surrender two months later. Should he attack the swelling American army before him before it got too large? Provoke it to attack him? Retreat?

As the general and his officers debated these questions, the Indians made their own choices. They invited Burgoyne to council on August 19 and once again asked permission to go home. The general implored them to stay and refused any provisions to those who deserted him. Despite this, about 200, largely westerners, headed north the next day, and most of the rest drifted away during the next week, depriving the British of desperately needed scouts and ambushers. Less than 50 Seven Nations warriors of the original 1,000 Indians would stay with Burgoyne to the bitter end, although war parties from the Mohawk valley and Montreal would bolster the total to 120 Indians.[105]

The initiative and numbers had shifted sharply toward the Americans. Yet the campaign's victor was still in doubt. A decisive battle would determine all. But for now, both sides avoided that and awaited the other's move. On August 19, Gen. Horatio Gates replaced Schuyler as the American army's commander, but he was just as passive as his predecessor.

Burgoyne concentrated all his troops west of the Hudson, but most stayed in camp. He ordered the creation of another ranger company, commanded by Capt. Alexander Fraser, who had lost all but a half-dozen men in various battles, most devastatingly at Bennington. Each of the five British regiments would supply one intrepid noncommissioned officer and its sixteen best marksmen. Good soldiers filled that ninety-man company, but hardly any knew anything about Indian-style fighting or wilderness survival.

On September 13, despite having lost from battle and desertion over a quarter of his army, the cavalryman, fierce British patriot, and, above all, gambler in Burgoyne won out over the prudent commander. He chose to make a final desperate lunge toward Albany. The remnants of Fraser's corps led, followed by the British brigade, the forty-eight artillery pieces and the supply train, and finally the German brigade. The army carried thirty days' rations and enough munitions for two or three battles. Declaring loudly that "Britons never retreat!" Burgoyne ordered the bridge dismantled rather than burned behind his army at Stillwater on the Hudson. He was determined to either conquer or perish.

As Burgoyne's army marched south toward Gates's swelling American tide in his front, another enemy force imperiled his rear. Colonels John Brown and Samuel Johnson led 1,000 militia past Fort Edward to Lake George, commandeered bateaux, and rowed north to the portage. On September 18, those troops captured four British companies of the 53rd atop Mount Defiance and drove in Fort Ticonderoga's pickets. Without artillery, they could not hope to force the fort's surrender. They withdrew on September 23, were repulsed from an attack on Diamond Island in Lake George, and eventually returned triumphant to the American lines. At that same time, a militia force under Col. Benjamin Woodbridge raided Skenesborough and Fort Anne before withdrawing.[106]

Gates found an excellent position to defend. He marched his army north on September 12 to Bemis Heights, a 300-foot-high plateau that begins about 500 yards west of the Hudson and stretches west into the forest. Batteries commanded the river road that ran through fields and patches of woods. Other batteries studded the lines westward, especially where two large ravines would channel attackers up the plateau. Gates's army numbered about 8,000 troops, including 6,500 regulars and 1,500 militia. The only potential weakness was the left flank, if the British could find a way through the forest around it. But Gates was clever enough to anchor the left with Benedict Arnold and Daniel Morgan's rifle brigade, along with the brigades of Poor and Learned.

The British army massed just beyond cannon shot of Bemis Heights on September 17. Burgoyne gleaned an accurate view of the American position from reports of his scouts, deserters, and captives. He ordered his army to attack early on September 19, sending General Riedesel's 1,700-man German brigade along the river road; Gen. James Hamilton's 9th, 20th, 21st, and 62nd Regiments of his 1,100-man British brigade against the center; and Fraser's 1,200-man corps of the light and grenadier companies, along with the 24th, the rangers, loyalists, Canadians, and 90 Indians, hooking around the American left flank. The Americans broke up all three attacks by noon. Arnold led his wing down from the plateau after Fraser's retreating corps and caught up at Freeman's Farm. Once again, reinforcements saved a British force from annihilation. Burgoyne sent Riedesel's brigade to Fraser's rescue. They beat off a final American attack late that afternoon. Arnold withdrew his men back onto the heights. The battle was tactically a draw, as both sides withdrew to their camps and each side suffered similar losses, with the American losses about 65 to 100 dead, 218 to 325 wounded, and 40 missing or captured, and the British losses about 560 dead, wounded, and captured. Strategically, however, the Americans scored a vital victory.[107]

Burgoyne compounded his defeat by ordering his troops to dig in rather than withdraw. Wishful thinking indeed led to that decision. On September 21, a courier somehow managed to pass through the lines with a September 12 letter from Gen. Henry Clinton, who promised soon to lead his 2,000 troops from New York City against the rebel positions in the Hudson Highlands. Of course, nothing guaranteed that Clinton would break through. Even if he could, it was another 100 miles from there to Saratoga, with more numerous American forces in between. Clinton understood all that and merely promised a diversion, not a deliverance, but Burgoyne read into Clinton's clearly written lines the latter. He also hoped that St. Leger's corps would reach him. That too would prove to be impossible.

St. Leger's expedition reached Montreal the first week of September. There Carleton provisioned them while John Butler and Daniel Claus competed with each other to rally Indians from the Seven Tribes. However, warriors returning from Burgoyne's campaign spread such discouraging tales that the rival agents mustered only a handful. Butler had more luck, talking the governor into granting him a major's commission on September 15 to create a special corps of crack frontiersmen to be known as Butler's Rangers. Butler set off for Niagara to begin recruiting.[108]

Carleton subordinated St. Leger's force to Brig. Gen. Allan McLean, and then added the 31st, several companies of the Royal Highland Emigrant Regiment, and 220 Brunswick recruits to flesh out Riedesel's regiments. McLean's command reached Fort Ticonderoga on September 29. With rebel militia forces haunting the fifty miles of wilderness south to Burgoyne, he dared not enter that land with his small force. Fort Ticonderoga was the closest the relief got to Burgoyne.

As for General Clinton, he more than fulfilled his guarded promise to mount a large-scale diversion. With 3,000 troops, he set sail up the Hudson on October 3, captured forts Montgomery and Clinton on October 6, and Fort Constitution on October 8. As he consolidated his position around Kingston, he sent upriver Gen. James Vaughan with 1,700 troops and six months of provisions for Burgoyne, but Vaughan got no farther than forty miles south of Albany on October 23. Word reached Clinton of Burgoyne's fate, and he ordered Vaughan to withdraw.

In sitting tight and awaiting salvation, Burgoyne surrendered the initiative to the Americans and thus sealed his own doom. His army dwindled daily from disease, desertion, and death, while the Americans swelled with confidence and fresh troops. On September 20, nearly 300 Oneida and Tuscarora joined the 100 Stockbridge Mahicans with Gates's army, although only about half were warriors. Gates sent them to Arnold's wing, where they skulked along the British lines for a week with the Mahican, bringing back thirty prisoners and three scalps. They left in high spirits on September 27, having suffered no losses and reaped some measure of vengeance for Oriskany.

By early October, Gates's army numbered more than 12,000, while Burgoyne's could mass little more than 5,000. From the battle of Bemis Heights, Gates began a slow encirclement of Burgoyne, dispatching the raids of Brown and Johnson against Ticonderoga, and Woodbridge against Skenesborough in late September, and sending Brig. Gen. John Fellows with 1,300 Massachusetts militia up the Hudson's eastern bank to a position opposite Burgoyne's left flank in early October.

The cavalryman in Burgoyne conceived an audacious plan to hold his front with 800 troops and encircle the American left flank with his other 4,200, but his officers shot down the idea as too reckless. Instead, they urged him to order an immediate withdrawal. That was not what the general wanted to hear. Burgoyne's conception of honor demanded no retreat, but he offered a compromise. He would have Fraser probe the American left on October 7, and if an opening was discovered, the army would attack the following day; otherwise, they would withdraw four days later.

But the Americans struck first. The crack troops of each regiment attacked and drove in Burgoyne's pickets on October 6. Burgoyne might have readied his army for a general enemy attack. Instead, he gathered 1,500 of his best troops under Fraser and sent them around the American left flank at noon on October 7. Gates ordered Morgan's brigade, covered by the brigades of Learned and Hand, to intercept Fraser at Fraser's Farm. Arnold was not initially with them, having been ordered by Gates to his tent for disputing his cautious commander, but when the guns sounded, Arnold dashed to the front and took command of the attack. Bullets mortally wounded Fraser and crippled Arnold's knee. Gates and Burgoyne fed in a few other regiments, each fearing the Freeman Farm battle was a diversion from a main attack on the other's front. Arnold's troops battled back the redcoats and in late afternoon overran Breymann's redoubt, which anchored the British right flank.

The Americans were in a position to roll up the entire enemy line—if Gates was sensible enough to attempt it and the British did not retreat. Burgoyne finally came to his senses, however, and ordered his army to withdraw that night. Gates's army pursued on October 8. While most of the army marched forward, reinforcements joined Fellows's militia east of the Hudson, and Morgan's riflemen angled through the forest in a huge double envelopment. Heavy rains turned the roads to mud soup. By October 10, Burgoyne's exhausted army straddled Fishkill Creek on the Hudson. Gates massed most of his army in the front and pushed the brigades of Morgan, Poor, Learned, and Patterson around the enemy's right flank. Fellows's brigade stood opposite Burgoyne's left flank across the Hudson. General Stark and his New Hampshire militia probed around Fort Edward.

Gentleman Johnny finally understood that he was almost completely cut off. He asked Gates for terms on October 13. In the subsequent negotiations, he proved a more adept diplomat than general, succeeding in getting the weak-willed Gates to agree to a convention whereby he could withdraw his army with a promise not to return to North America, rather than capitulation where they would become prisoners of war. Burgoyne signed the agreement on October 17. About 6,000 troops, civilians, and camp followers surrendered. The victorious American and humiliated British armies reached Albany on October 20.

What happened to the 200 Indians who stayed with Burgoyne until near the end? They slipped away. American troops did capture fifty-three Mohawk near Fort Edward and sent them to Albany under guard, where they were finally released to their homes at Fort Hunter with the promise to stay at peace. The rest escaped to Canada along with the garrison at Fort Ticonderoga.

Burgoyne's surrender was truly the American Revolution's turning point. The most important impact was to embolden France to ally with the United States and join the war the following spring. French troops and warships would tip the war's balance and win American independence sooner rather than later.

It also lessened the threat to the New York frontier. Those Indians who had marched with Burgoyne or St. Leger dispersed to their distant homes with hearts and minds embittered by all the frustrations, deaths, and humiliations they had suffered. In subsequent years, many would resist British blandishments to retake the warpath and instead nursed their alienation at home.

The Americans made the most of all this. Schuyler sent Samuel Kirkland with a huge wampum belt depicting Burgoyne's defeat to Oneida Castle. He arrived on October 27 for several days of jubilant council. Those allies agreed to dispatch envoys with word of the American victory and a request for peace to the Six and Seven Nations.[109]

In October, even before news of Burgoyne's surrender reached them, the Six Nations' sachems gathered at Onondaga to mull over the essential question of whether to continue the war. The council was as badly split as ever. The Seneca and Joseph Brant's Mohawk argued that the league's fate rested on allying with Britain against the Americans; if the Americans were victorious, they would eventually overrun and destroy the Iroquois as they had so many other tribes. The Oneida and Tuscarora pressured the council to ally with the Americans. Most of the Onondaga and many Cayuga preferred neutrality.[110]

Despite Burgoyne's surrender and St. Leger's withdrawal, most Iroquois understood that only a British victory guarded them from a future American conquest. Nearly 2,700 Iroquois along with other tribes counciled with John Butler at Fort Niagara in early December. Butler softened the sting of that year's defeats with promises and 14,000 pounds sterling worth of gifts. Then he and the chiefs hammered out the next year's strategy. It was decided that Sayenqueraghta would lead the western Iroquois against Wyoming valley, Kayashuta would rally the Allegheny Seneca and their allies against the western Pennsylvania settlements, and Brant would gather those Iroquois and other tribes living along the East Branch against the Mohawk and Cherry valleys. They would insist on warring with their own traditional strategy and tactics rather than remain yoked to Britain's. The council ended on December 14. War parties from Allegheny Seneca were the only ones to attack that winter, bringing back two captives and three scalps. The real harvest would not begin until spring.[111]

THE MISSISSIPPI FRONTIER

The future of the American Revolution and the Spanish empire alike became more secure when Don Bernardo de Galvez became Louisiana's governor on New Year's Day, 1777. Galvez was a tough, skilled leader who had fought against the British and Portugese in 1762, and the Apache in three campaigns on the Nueva Vizcaya frontier from 1769 to 1771. He then took an extended leave from Spanish service to join France's Cantaria Regiment, during which he was wounded in an assault on Algiers in 1775. When he returned to Spain to convalesce, he was promoted to lieutenant colonel and taught at the military school of Avila. In 1776, he was sent to Louisiana to command the troops. Those varied military experiences rendered him supple in grasping Spain's colonial and foreign threats, and the means of confronting them.

No greater threat to the Spanish empire loomed than Britain, the world's leading naval, commercial, and industrial power. Galvez reasoned that New Spain would be far more secure neighbored by the weak coalition of former colonies, which called itself the United States, than the British empire. While his predecessor, Unzaga, had sympathized with the rebels, Galvez began to take all steps short of war to weaken the British and strengthen the American cause.

On April 17, Galvez ordered eleven smuggling boats seized on the Mississippi River between Balize and Manchac. Nine of the boats were British and two American. Galvez also declared all British persona non grata, to be expelled within fifteen days. In doing so, he hoped to divert profits going to British merchants and manufacturers to Spanish subjects instead, even if it meant that Louisianans would have to pay more for less well made goods. He also hoped to help the Americans by turning a blind eye to their smugglers; the two seized boats were secretly released and no Americans were expelled. The British ships were sold at auction and fetched $53,000. When the British frigate *Atlanta* appeared below New Orleans, Galvez denied it permission to sail up to Manchac and Natchez. The captain sailed away, vowing to reappear with another frigate and force their way upstream. The governor dismissed commissioners dispatched from Gov. Peter Chester at Pensacola to negotiate for the British merchants. Finally, Galvez issued edicts that allowed Louisiana to trade with Cuba and Yucatan, reduced the export duty to 2 percent, and granted the slave trade to the French. These measures wiped out nearly all of Britain's trade with Louisiana. Galvez's initiatives accorded perfectly with instructions issued by Madrid on February 20, 1777, to secretly supply the Americans.

In all, Galvez sold $70,000 worth of desperately needed supplies to the Americans in 1777 alone. He did so by issuing credit to Oliver Pollack, who then purchased and dispatched the supplies. Hearing rumors of Spanish supplies to the Americans, Governor Chester issued several vigorous protests that Galvez studiously ignored.[112]

Meanwhile, an American plan had arisen for an attack on West Florida. In late 1776, George Morgan, the Indian commissioner at Pittsburgh, had circulated a scheme in Congress for 1,500 troops to descend to New Orleans and from there attack Mobile and Pensacola. In June 1777, Congress asked Gen. Benedict Arnold to assess the plan. Arnold submitted his elaboration of Morgan's ideas on July 11. Congress debated the proposal for two days, but with America's armies hard-pressed elsewhere, no troops, supplies, or money could be spared for the expedition. The plan died.

It was just as well. Earlier that year, on April 22, Morgan wrote Galvez a request for supplies, free trade, and permission to launch an attack on West Florida from New Orleans. In an August 9 reply, Galvez promised to "extend my permission and whatever assistance I can, but it must appear that I am ignorant of it all . . . The commerce that you desire with this province will be established . . . [be] assured that those who carry it on will be well received and protected by me, holding me responsible for all." As for assisting an attack on West Florida, Galvez replied that "although it would please me greatly, I cannot enter into it."[113]

Shortly after Congress wrote off Morgan's ambitious campaign, another proposal was aired that promised the same results with a far more modest investment. James Willing was a prominent member of the Philadelphia elite, a partner of Robert Morris, and a delegate to the Continental Congress of 1774. He was also a visionary, adventurer, and spendthrift. After finishing his congressional stint, he abruptly moved to Natchez, where he sought a fortune as a merchant and plantation owner. Things did not work out as he had hoped. His mounting debts, decadence, and bluster alienated Natchez society. In November 1777, he was back in Philadelphia with a plan that at once could advance America's cause and fulfill his own desire to avenge his humiliations. He promised the commerce committee of Congress that he could take West Florida's Mississippi settlements with a couple score men by inspiring a rebellion among the suppressed patriots there. Willing could hardly have bettered his timing. The confidence and ambitions of Congress had soared after the surrender of Burgoyne's army.

With little debate, the committee approved the scheme, authorized funds, commissioned Willing a navy captain, and sent him to Fort Pitt to raise supplies and men. His formal mission was to go to New Orleans and bring back supplies. Willing later claimed that the committee granted him permission to capture Natchez, Manchac, and any other British property on the Mississippi. That was quite likely, even though no committee documents on the expedition survive and Congress was never informed of the decision. The result may well have been one of America's first covert actions that soon became embarrassingly overt. Regardless, by late December, Willing had received from Gen. Edward Hand at Fort Pitt the keelboat *Rattletrap*, twenty-nine men, and enough supplies to get them to New Orleans. The expedition would depart shortly after New Year's.

As reports of various American schemes to conquer West Florida reached Madrid, the ministers wrestled over a question with enormous consequences for Spain. What if the Americans took West Florida and offered it to Spain? Galvez's predecessor, Unzaga, had posed that question to Madrid. Minister of the Indies Jose de Galvez wrote his nephew Bernardo de Galvez a reply on August 16, 1777, that Spain would be most happy to receive as a trust or outright grant any British lands conquered by the Americans. That was clear enough. But Galvez was cautioned to do so in a way that did not provoke British retaliation. How exactly the governor was supposed to avoid that conundrum Madrid did not say. As it happened, explicit instructions were unneeded. Bernardo de Galvez would brilliantly win West Florida for Spain.[114]

Just as brilliant a leader was George Rogers Clark, who was also among the Revolution's more tragic figures. Born in the Virginia tidewater, he first entered the Ohio country as an apprentice surveyor in 1772 and returned in 1773. In 1774, he was once again in the region, this time participating in Dunmore's war as an enthusiastic Indian hater and killer; he raided Shawnee towns on the Scioto River and fought at Point Pleasant. The Ohio Company employed him as a surveyor in 1775, and he spent that year and the next two helping organize and defend the Kentucky settlements. During those years, he earned a reputation for courage and leadership. Virginia governor Patrick Henry recognized those virtues on March 5, 1777, when he named Clark a major of militia.

It was obvious to Kentucky's settlers that their lives and property would never be secure unless they destroyed the Indian villages and British forts north of the Ohio. But how? There simply were not men, supplies, money, and leaders to do so. Clark promised to donate the leadership if the government helped him raise everything else.

By spring 1777, he was concocting a grand strategy to conquer the region. In May, he dispatched two spies, Benjamin Linn and Samuel Moore, to Kaskaskia. They returned on June 22 with word that there were no British regulars to back the militia, while the French population was largely indifferent to the war. Other hunters and merchants trickled back from that country with similar reports. Clark's vision of taking the Illinois country and then the Wabash settlements before marching on Detroit blossomed. That autumn, he trekked to Williamsburg to sell his plan to Virginia's government. Shortly after arriving on November 5, he met with Gov. Patrick Henry and his advisors. It took several weeks, but they finally embraced Clark's proposal. George Rogers Clark hurried back to the upper Ohio to organize the expedition that would win him immortal fame and the United States its first grip on the Mississippi.

CHAPTER 6

"How Vain Are Our Hopes": 1778

Before the water is again frozen there will not be an English soldier at Detroit or Niagara unless they are prisoners.
—Gen. Edward Hand

How vain are our hopes! How changeable are our fates, when we think ourselves most secure, we are most in danger.
—Col. John Allan

The exhilarating news of Burgoyne's surrender reached Paris on December 4, 1777. France enjoyed a rare and fleeting opportunity to war against its nemesis while it struggled to recover from a debacle. Yet, while diminished, British power remained formidable. To war victoriously, the French needed allies beyond ragtag American rebels. Foreign Minister Charles Gravier de Vergennes wrote his latest request to his counterpart at Madrid, Jose Monimo y Redondo Floridablanca, to revive their family compact into an outright alliance against Britain. While anxiously awaiting a reply, Vergennes presented a war plan and advocated negotiating treaties of trade and alliance with the United States to Louis XVI and his council of state on January 7. The king and council readily agreed to all of that persuasive minister's proposals.

Vergennes summoned the Americans and announced he was ready to deal. Over the next few weeks the diplomats worked out the details of both a Treaty of Amity and Commerce and a Treaty of Alliance, which they signed on February 6, 1777. The Americans got what they wanted. Vergennes granted the United States diplomatic recognition, most favored nation status in trade, a promise of several million livres worth of more military aid, and an alliance while disavowing any claims in North America. Both nations agreed to forgo a separate peace with Britain. That last promise seemed innocuous at the time but would cause some sticky diplomacy toward the war's end.

Versailles had allied with the United States not from altruism or idealism, but from a hard-nosed calculation of French interests. The alliance accorded with the timeless diplomatic maxim "the enemy of my enemy is my friend." For centuries, Britain had thwarted French ambitions. That perennial struggle culminated in 1763, when France surrendered Canada to Britain after losing a global war. For the foreseeable future, Britain would remain France's most indomitable economic and military rival. Thus, anything that weakened Britain strengthened France.

By mutual consent, the treaties were kept secret as Versailles feverishly prepared for war. It was not until March 13 that the French announced their commerce and amity treaty and officially accredited the American diplomats to the court of Versailles; they would not unveil the alliance until after the first blood was shed with the British. On April 13, Adm. Charles Hector d'Estaing led twelve ships of the line, three frigates, and a score of transports filled with 4,000 troops from Toulon toward America. Accompanying d'Estaing was Conrad-Alexandre Gerald, France's first minister to the United States. In sailing to America, the French took a bold and fearful gamble. Madrid held aloof from the war.

Spies passed on the dismal news of French ties with the United States to Whitehall on February 8. Until then, the failed attempts to crush the rebellion were disheartening enough, but at least the rest of the empire was largely immune from attack. That was no longer true. French expeditions could potentially sail against any colony and even the British Isles itself. War with France would stretch Britain's soldiers and sailors thin and quite possibly to the breaking point as the conflict in North America spread to anywhere in the world either side had colonies, along with the sea-lanes linking them.

That was only the latest blow to British morale after the previous year's defeats capped by Burgoyne's disaster. The two most successful generals in America, William Howe and Guy Carleton, wanted out. Whitehall reluctantly honored their requests and replaced them with Major Generals Henry Clinton and Frederick Haldimand, respectively. But what were the new leaders to do?

France's entrance into the war forced Britain to change its diplomatic and military strategy. Diplomatic relations with France were severed. Although with sixty-six ships of the line to France's fifty-two, Britain enjoyed overall naval superiority, its fleet was scattered in squadrons protecting the king's lands in North America, the Caribbean, India, the Mediterranean, and elsewhere as well as the home islands. With fewer overseas commitments, France could concentrate its fleet. Whitehall feared a more numerous French fleet could pounce on either Philadelphia or New York. Then word arrived that Versailles had dispatched a fleet to North America. France's first contribution to America's war for independence was bloodless. Germain ordered Gen. William Howe to withdraw from Philadelphia to New York.[1]

As for North America, Whitehall concluded that if the northern colonies remained immune to conquest, then perhaps the army would have a go at the South. The plan was to hold New York City and Canada while an army invaded Georgia and worked its way north, wiping out the rebels and rallying the loyalists as it went, while Indians attacked all along the frontier. A tightening blockade along the entire American coast combined with large-scale amphibious raids from

New York City against New England and middle colony ports would grind down resistance. Or so it was hoped. What else could be done?[2]

Desperate times demanded desperate measures. Whitehall grudgingly agreed to offer the rebels an olive branch. Parliament passed two conciliatory acts on March 16, one withdrawing its right to tax the colonies, pardoning all rebels, withdrawing its army, and accepting Congress as a permanent institution subject to Parliament, and another creating a peace commission led by Lord Carlisle to negotiate with Americans over their grievances. The only concession Britain refused to grant was independence. With these conciliatory bills, the British king, cabinet, and Parliament essentially admitted defeat. On April 16, the Carlisle commission embarked with its olive branch for America. On June 11, Congress received the commissioners' request for an interval. The timing of Britain's concessions could not have been worse. The commissioners reached Philadelphia nearly two years after the Americans declared independence, nine months after Burgoyne's surrender, four months after France allied with the United States, and just as Clinton was preparing to abandon that city. Though the offer tempted some prominent Americans, the majority of patriots remained welded to independence. Congress politely but firmly spurned the offer; the patriots demanded freedom and nothing less.

Ever more members of Parliament were sympathetic or resigned to that demand. The war's mounting costs in treasury and blood, with no light at the tunnel's end, caused ever more thoughtful observers to question whether conquering the colonies was worth the price. And atop that were the war's moral costs. Vivid accounts of Indian atrocities preyed on many a conscience. William Pitt, the earl of Chatham, had long championed American interests. In February, he rose in Parliament to condemn the government for setting "the savages of America loose upon their innocent inoffending brethern; loose upon the weak, the aged, the defenseless; on old men, women, and children; upon the very babes upon the breast to be cut, mangled, sacrificed, broiled, roasted, nay, to be liberally eaten."[3]

Whitehall defended its policies, including crushing the rebels with the tribes. The earl of Suffolk argued that "the alliance of the Indians is to be justified upon two grounds; one, as necessary in fact; the other, as allowable upon principle; for first, the Americans endeavored to raise them on their side, and would gain them, if we did not; and next, it was allowable, and perfectly justifiable, to use every means that God and nature had put into our hands."[4] The government's case was arguable on principle but not on fact. The American policy from the beginning was to promote neutrality rather than alliance with the Indians, but the government retained a powerful majority in Parliament and thwarted any challenges to its policies. The British would continue to encourage the Indians to war against the frontier.

THE SEABOARD WAR

Upon receiving orders to return to New York City, Clinton faced a choice: should he do so by land or by sea? Fearing interception by the French fleet, he organized an overland march. The British abandoned Philadelphia on June 18. Once Washington learned of Clinton's withdrawal, he sent a contingent to reoccupy Philadelphia while he crossed the Delaware River forty miles north and shadowed the enemy march with the bulk of his army. Clinton's regiments and wagon train stretched twelve miles long across New Jersey.

Washington decided to attack the enemy's rear guard encamped around Freehold. Ideally, he would not only crush those regiments, but also defeat others as they rushed piecemeal to the battle. Unfortunately, his bitter rival Maj. Gen. Charles Lee was the senior field officer and thus entitled to take charge of the battle. Whether from spite, ineptness, or Washington's unclear orders, Lee grossly mismanaged the attack on the morning of June 28. He probed when he should have launched an all-out assault. The British easily repelled those attacks, counterattacked, and routed the Americans. Washington galloped up, stemmed the stampede, fed his reserves into a makeshift line, and blunted the redcoat charges. The battle of Monmouth sputtered out in a withering heat of over 100 degrees. Each side suffered about 300 dead and wounded, many axed by sunstroke.

Washington shadowed Clinton until the British withdrew into New York City and then marched his army up the Hudson River, crossed over, entrenched at White Plains, and awaited the arrival of d'Estaing's fleet. Alas for the American cause, the French arrived a few days after the British fleet sailed into New York's harbor.

Washington and d'Estaing agreed that a campaign against Newport was more promising than a direct assault against the massed guns and troops at New York. But that venture also failed. D'Estaing sent his troops ashore to join Gen. John Sullivan's army, bringing their force to 10,000 armed men. The allied army and French fleet were supposed to simultaneously attack Gen. Robert Pigot's 6,000 troops entrenched around Newport on August 10. But when a British squadron appeared off the coast, d'Estaing called off the attack, withdrew his troops aboard his ships, and set off in pursuit. The French never caught up. A hurricane roared in and for three days battered the fleets. When it subsided, d'Estaing withdrew to Boston to refit. Meanwhile, near Newport, the Americans repelled an attack on their position at Butt's Hill on August 29. Sullivan withdrew to Providence to await d'Estaing's return. At Boston on September 17, a wild brawl exploded between French and American sailors during which a French officer was killed. A British fleet commanded by Adm. John Byron approached Boston. As d'Estaing readied his fleet for action, another storm blew up, this time hitting Byron's fleet so badly he withdrew to Newport. Thoroughly discouraged, d'Estaing set sail to winter in the Caribbean. The first joint Franco-American campaign had been a frustrating charade.

The inconclusive battle of Monmouth would be the last full-scale battle fought on the northern seaboard during the war. From now on, the focus of fighting on the seaboard would shift to the four southern states, Georgia, South Carolina, North Carolina, and, decisively in October 1781, Yorktown, Virginia. Meanwhile, the frontier war burned ceaselessly.

THE NEW YORK AND PENNSYLVANIA FRONTIER

American confidence soared following word of Burgoyne's surrender but would soon plummet just as far. In December 1777, Congress ordered Brig. Gen. John Stark to lead an expedition up Lake Champlain to burn the bateaux fleet at Fort St. John. Stark got to work organizing the venture. The following month on January 22, 1778, Congress approved an invasion of Canada by 2,500 troops under the Northern Department commander, Maj. Gen. Marie Joseph Yves Gilbert du Motier, Marquis de Lafayette. Reality, however, intruded. A lack of supplies and troops forced Congress to cancel both operations.

Then came the exciting news of the French alliance. Suddenly the rebel leaders could dream big again. Even then, the hope of conquering Canada proved to be as illusory as ever. By July, that province was defended by a formidable force—6,518 troops, of which two-thirds were British and the rest German, along with 17,714 French and 403 British Canadian militia. About 1,400 of the 4,000 regulars were loyalists. Blocking any American advance on Lake Champlain were thirty-six armed vessels with various tonnages and guns. It would take a year or two for the Americans to construct a fleet to match that of the British, assuming their enemy did not add to their own during that time. Even if an American fleet was able to clear the enemy from Lake Champlain, the army would face forts at Isle aux Noix, St. Johns, and Chambly on the Richelieu River guarding the approach to Montreal.[5]

Why did that large British army not march against New York as Burgoyne's had the previous year? The word of France's alliance with the United States strategically pinned the army in Canada to defending that province. One prominent British nightmare involved the appearance of a French fleet and army before Quebec to reclaim the empire it lost in 1763. That threat was not as great as it seemed. While an invasion was possible, a clause in the alliance forbade France to retake Canada, but the British did not know that.

If Canada could not be invaded, it could be harassed. To do so effectively demanded Indian allies. George Washington now embraced what for practical and moral reasons he formerly opposed. While testifying before a congressional committee on January 29, he recommended that "a body of Indians joined by some of our Woodsmen, would probably strike no small terror into the British and foreign troops, particularly the new comers. The good resulting from the measure, if these savages can be kept in the field at so great a distance from their native haunts, would more than compensate for the trouble and expence they might cost us."[6] No one could dispute that. The trouble was, of course, finding any large body of Indians willing to join the side that harbored the ill-concealed lust and means to conquer their lands.

Nonetheless, the Americans tried. Indian Commissioner Philip Schuyler and Northern Department commander Lafayette called a council at Johnstown for the Iroquois and other tribes in February. The Seneca bluntly rejected the invitation; only a handful of Cayuga, Onondaga, and Mohawk would attend. When the council finally opened on March 7, the Oneida and Tuscarora composed most of the 732 Indians present. The American goal was to cement the alliance with the Oneida and Tuscarora while enticing the other tribes back to neutrality. They succeeded in only the former. The Oneida persuaded the Americans to build a fort at Kawnowalohale, their central village, to help deter attacks from their enemies, who now included the four Iroquois tribes to their west.[7]

After the council, the commissioner and general worked hard to shore up the region's defenses. Lafayette inspected the New York frontier and ordered repairs to Fort Schuyler and the erection of forts in Cherry valley and Kawnowalohale. He assigned Col. Ichabod Alden's 7th Massachusetts to man the fort in Cherry valley and the Schoharie valley's three forts. Schuyler kept up his efforts to entice the western Iroquois off the warpath. In May, he had James Dean take word to the Oneida that France was now allied with the United States. The Oneida then passed that electrifying news to the other tribes along with a summons to council. Seneca chief Big Tree took up the offer. At Albany on June 5 and 6, he and a small delegation proclaimed their neutrality to Schuyler and other commissioners. After a visit to George Washington and his army, Big Tree returned to his village and did what he could to keep his young men off the warpath. But that was just one Seneca village of two score or more.

The initiative on the frontier usually lay with the side wielding Indian allies. It was the British rather than the Americans who struck the year's first blows. Taking the initiative, of course, did not guarantee victory. In January, Lt. James Secord led twenty-seven rangers to the Wyoming valley to round up loyalists and cattle. Learning of the raid, the militia mustered, marched, and captured the entire party. Astonishingly, the militia sent only eighteen off to prison; Secord and nine others were released for lack of evidence. The British suffered another setback on March 12, when a raiding party of forty-five troops and Indians attacked Shelburne on Lake Champlain's eastern shore. Capt. Thomas Sawyer and twenty militia defended a fortified house and then unexpectedly charged and routed the British, killing five, capturing six, and wounding eight.[8]

When Indians raided alone, they usually succeeded. Early that year, Seneca chief Sayenqueraghta sent war parties to scour the settlements between the Allegheny and Susquehanna Rivers. By April, those parties had carried back a gruesome harvest of over 170 scalps and several score captives. Then in April, four large parties of Seneca and Cayuga rampaged through that territory. On April 28, a war party rushed a twenty-man patrol near Fort Wallace and killed one as the rest fled into the fort. The defenders of nearby Fort Barr heard the firing, and Maj. James Wilson dashed with a score of men to the sound of the guns. Spotting the relief, the Indians broke off their siege and attacked. When the gunsmoke cleared, nine Americans and four Indians lay dead. Wilson and the survivors fled back to Fort Barr. Another party of 90 Seneca warriors took thirteen scalps and two prisoners while losing one killed and four wounded. A party of 150 warriors killed twenty and captured eighteen settlers along the Susquehanna's north branch. Another wave of raids struck in June. A war party ravaged the Susquehanna River's west bank on June 10 and 11, killing ten people and capturing five. By June's end, other parties had killed forty-five and captured forty-four. Those raids caused the "great runaway" that left most of the valley's homes and fields abandoned. Some refugees crowded into Fort Augusta at Sunbury, while others streamed farther east. But the worst calamity to the region was yet to come.[9]

In mid-April, an incident occurred that embarrassed and offended New York officials but would later have tragic consequences. Walter Butler broke his parole and fled west from Albany. By chance he met his father, who was counciling with Chief Sayenqueraghta and 400 warriors, mostly Seneca but including Cayuga, Onondaga, and Delaware, at Canadasaga. Upon their return to Fort Niagara on May 17, his father named him a captain in the Butler's Rangers. Captain Butler journeyed to Quebec to recruit his company.

Joseph Brant spent the year's first three months gathering men in Oquaga, Unadilla, and the other East Branch villages. By late May, he had over 350 men, two-thirds of whom were Indians and the rest loyalists. He led his force toward the Cobbleskill Creek valley, which flows east into the Schoharie.

Capt. Christopher Brown commanded the local militia company in the upper fort. Upon learning of Brant's approach, Brown sent word to Fort Clinton, Schoharie's middle fort. On May 26, Capt. William Patrick led thirty-three troops from the 7th Massachusetts into the upper fort.

Brant's force slipped into the woods near the fort on May 30. Brant baited a trap by concealing his main force and dispatching small parties to burn the homes. Dismissing Brown's warning, Captain Patrick took the bait. He quick-marched his regulars and the militia out after the Indians, who withdrew with shots and catcalls. The Americans blundered into Brant's trap. The fusillade and then charge killed twenty-two, wounded nine, and captured six Americans; the Indians lost only two killed. Patrick was among the dead; Brown made it to the fort with the other survivors. After plundering and burning the valley's homes, Brant led his men north toward German Flats in the upper Mohawk valley. The raid was Brant's first as a leader. It was an outstanding success, the first of many.[10]

Getting wind of Brant's intentions, Col. Jacob Klock led his Palatine District militia south to intercept him. But by chance, another enemy party approached the settlements in his rear. John Deserontyon and Isaac Hill had led 200 mostly Mohawk and loyalists from St. Regis through the Adirondacks to the valley. Their primary mission was not to destroy, but to rescue the Fort Hunter Mohawk and any remaining loyalists in the region. From June 3 through 6, they accomplished that as well as captured seventeen patriots and burned some homes. A detachment of Brant's force appeared farther up the valley on June 6 and destroyed the hamlet of Dillenburgh.

Where was Brant? He returned his force to Tioga to refit and council with Butler and Sayenqueraghta. For a week, the three leaders and other headmen debated their options. They finally decided to go their own ways, with Butler and Sayenqueraghta heading down the Susquehanna River to ravage the Wyoming valley, and Brant carrying on his raids against the Schoharie and Mohawk valleys.[11]

THE NORTHWEST FRONTIER

At Detroit, Lt. Gov. Henry Hamilton vigorously waged war against the upper Ohio River valley and Kentucky settlements. Psychological warfare was one way to diminish the enemy. On January 5, he issued a proclamation offering amnesty to all who sought refuge in Detroit and pledged loyalty to the Crown and death to those who did not. War parties left copies of the proclamation like calling cards in the wake of their raids, adorning bloating bodies and the charred ruins of cabins. The policy probably returned few openly to the British fold; the danger in traversing enemy Indian lands for Detroit's safety was too great to seriously contemplate. It did, however, ensure mild treatment for captives who happily fibbed about their affections for King George and were later able to escape through the lowered guard and return to defend Kentucky and the upper Ohio. The year's early raids were brutally successful. By midwinter, the Indians and their British advisors had hauled back to Detroit 129 scalps and 73 prisoners. In all, Hamilton concluded, "the parties sent from hence have been in general successfull, tho' the Indians have lost men enough to sharpen their resentment."[12]

The finest coup occurred when a war party captured the elusive Daniel Boone and twenty-six other Kentuckians.[13] Around Christmas, the Indian agent at Miamis Town, Charles Beaubien, and trader Louis Lorimier traveled first to Piqua on the Mad River and then Chillicothe on the Little Miami to recruit a war party. Blackfish, Blue Jacket, about eighty Shawnee, and a black man named Pompey were eager to avenge Cornstalk and joined Beaubien and Lorimier. They headed south from Chillicothe in late January. As snow fell on February 7, they were encamped on the Licking River about forty miles north of Boonesborough.

About midday, four scouts surprised a lone hunter who was packing buffalo meat on his horse beside Hinkston Creek off the Licking River. Earlier that day, he had shot the beast while checking his trapline along the creek. When the Indians appeared, the hunter tried to pull his skinning knife, cut the pack, mount his horse, and gallop away, but the bloody knife had frozen in the sheath. The hunter dashed away amid a flurry of shots. Determined to take a captive or scalp, the Shawnee sprinted after him. The forty-year-old hunter was in excellent shape, but his ankle was still weak after getting hit by a musket ball the previous summer. The young men tearing after him steadily gained. A lucky shot severed the strap of his powder horn, which fell to the ground. Without powder, he had only the shot in his rifle against four enemies. Winded, he propped his rifle against a tree, stepped behind it, and called out cheerfully in Shawnee that they had won the race and he was tired of running.

The warriors triumphantly escorted their captive back to the war party's camp three miles away. There the hunter, speaking through Pompey, identified himself to Captain Will, who had captured and released him during one of his hunting trips to Kentucky eight years earlier. The warriors whooped and laughed in joy when they learned they had nabbed Daniel Boone. Other scouts had discovered a party of twenty-seven men at the Lower Blue Licks a few miles away on the Licking River. Boone explained that they were his men and that they had left Boones-borough on January 8 for the Lower Blue Licks to boil enough salt to last them through the year. Salt boiling was time-consuming work. About 500 gallons boiled down to a 50-pound bushel of salt. That many men cutting logs and feeding fires beneath huge kettles produced about 10 bushels a day. By the end of February's first week, they had produced several hundred bushels, half of which they had sent back to Boonesborough. When the war party arrived, the men lounged around idle; the river's rise had flooded and diluted the spring's salt content.

Boone feared that an attack would kill many or all of the salt makers, and that a follow-up surprise assault on Boonesborough would carry that fort as well. Many of the women, children, and old men would perish from the cold as the Indians herded them north to their villages. Boone offered to surrender his salt makers if the Indians agreed to harm none of them then or back at their villages while leaving Boonesborough alone until the summer. At that time, Boone would secure his settlement's bloodless surrender as well. Blackfish, Blue Jacket, Captain Will, and the other chiefs mulled over Boone's offer and finally accepted it.

The next morning, February 8, the war party strode with Boone at their head to the salt makers' camp. The salt makers agreed to Boone's plea to surrender. While he had secured the Indians' promise not to harm his men, he forgot to do the same for himself. The Indians armed themselves with heavy sticks, formed two lines, and ordered Boone to run between them. Covering his head with his arms, Boone ran the gauntlet and emerged bruised and bloody. The gauntlet proved his courage and stamina not only to the Indians, but to his men as well. It would help dilute later claims that he had sold out to the British. It took ten days to hike the 100 miles north through the snow, crossing the swollen Ohio River en route, and reach Chillicothe. There the other men were forced to run the gauntlet. All survived. They were then given to families eager to adopt a son to replace loved ones killed in battle. Blackfish himself adopted Boone, who cheerfully seemed to embrace his new life.

On April 1, Blackfish and forty warriors escorted Boone and several other prisoners to Detroit to show them off to Hamilton. The lieutenant governor was moved by Boone's declaration of loyalty from himself and the beleaguered Ken-tuckians. He offered Blackfish 100 pounds sterling to free and send him back to Boonesborough to prepare the people for surrender and migration north to Detroit, but Blackfish loved his son too much to lose him. The Shawnee did sell four other captives to Hamilton, and then returned with Boone and the others in a triumphant procession through other villages back to Chillicothe. That proud parade would turn to tragedy for the Indians. Boone later explained that in doing so, the captives were "learning . . . the way to their towns and the geography of the Indian country."[14] Boone and others who escaped would guide expeditions against those villages.

April was a banner month not just for the news of the capture of Boone and his men. A week later, Hamilton dispatched a party of fifty Wea, Kickapoo, and Mascouten toward Kentucky. Late that month, he handed the war belt and gifts to about 125 Shawnee, Mingo, and Delaware. Forty Shawnees brought in four prisoners.[15]

Hamilton's ambitions exceeded merely inspiring and equipping war parties. In January he forwarded to Gov. Guy Carleton a plan to attack Pittsburgh. Prisoners revealed that Fort Pitt's structure was decrepit and its threadbare garrison ill-disciplined, malnourished, and homesick. A vigorous thrust could take it if the governor approved. Carleton dismissed the plan as beyond British power in the region to fulfill.[16]

Hamilton was not the only regional commander harboring grand ambitions. At Pittsburgh, Gen. Edward Hand was determined to strike a blow against the enemy tribes. In February, he set out with 500 militia to attack the Cuyahoga River villages and capture a British storehouse on Lake Erie. Guided by Simon Girty, the Americans slogged through the sodden wilderness with its rivers and streams swollen by rain and snow. They got no farther than a collection of huts at the forks of the Shenango River and Neshannock Creek. Scouts reported that it was a large village. Hand ordered his troops to encircle and capture the Indians. The "enemy" consisted of Captain Pipe's wife, brother, three other women, and a young boy. All were neutral Delaware, but when the soldiers appeared, the warrior bravely defended his family and killed one before being shot to death. Fired with blood lust and frustration, the troops slaughtered two women and the boy, and dragged away the other two women. With supplies diminishing, a disgusted Hand ordered his troops to return to Fort Pitt. There he asked Congress for a transfer. The "squaw campaign" was the first expedition into the Ohio country during the war. It was a shameful failure, the first of several.[17]

American atrocities, British enticements, and Indian pressure on the Delaware converted ever more of that tribe to the warpath. During March, George Morgan did what he could to limit that conversion by trying to bury the dead with gifts and letters of apology to the Delaware council at Coshocton. Captain Pipe and the other chiefs were at first inclined to remain neutral, but a plea from an unexpected source convinced at least Captain Pipe that vengeance rather than conciliation was the best path.[18]

The mindless murders committed during the "squaw campaign" were the last straw for three men who had sided with varying degrees of reluctance with the Americans over the previous three years. On March 28, 1778, Alexander McKee, who had served as the Northern Department's Indian agent at Pittsburgh since 1772, the interpreter Simon Girty, and trader Matthew Elliott slipped out of Pittsburgh with four others and headed first to Coshocton, arriving on April 4. At the council, they declared that "it was the determination of the American people, to kill and destroy the whole Indian race, be they friends or foes, and possess themselves of the entire country."[19] They then headed to Detroit, reaching it on April 20. Hamilton embraced them with open arms. Soon those men were either encouraging or leading Indian raids against the settlements.

The Coshocton council resumed its debate after the renegades' departure. White Eyes was able to have himself declared war chief and get most warriors to agree never to seize the hatchet without his permission, but he could not persuade a grieving Captain Pipe to remain with him. That startling renegade message had tipped the balance in his mind. Within weeks, Captain Pipe moved his people to the Sandusky River and there gave his blessing for his warriors to join forays against the Americans.[20]

The pressures on White Eyes and the Coshocton council to join the war rose ever higher that spring and beyond. War parties tarried at Coshocton and the other villages, feeding off Delaware hospitality, enticing their young men to join, and hoping the Americans would retaliate with another brutal attack. Yet most of the Delaware held firm to their neutrality and were joined by others. Despite the murder of Cornstalk, his son, and two other Mekoce Indians the previous November, some of that band remained devoted to their chief's plea for neutrality. They settled at Coshocton, while the rest of the Mekoce remained at their villages and sent warriors against the settlements.

Fired to avenge Cornstalk and exceed his previous year's victories, Half King led 200 Wyandot and Mingo across the Ohio and encircled Fort Randolph on May 20. The fort's commander, Capt. William McKee, was a man of not only fortitude and enterprise, but also humor. He recalled that "when it grew dark [Half King] . . . came near the garrison and talked as if they wanted peace. I observed to him, he had taken very odd measures to introduce anything of that nature, which he apologized for with their usual kind of sophistry."[21] McKee could play the "sophistry" game just as readily. Facing an acute water shortage, he asked if he could have a night "to dream" over the demanded capitulation. Half King readily agreed to this method of his own culture to seek answers to weighty questions. Under cloak of darkness, McKee deployed his men in a bucket brigade from the river to fill every possible vessel in the fort. The next morning, he sent Nonhelema, or Grenadier Squaw, Cornstalk's sister, with word that the Great Spirit had appeared in a dream and told him not to surrender.

The Indians besieged the fort for nearly a week but failed to shoot or starve out the defenders. All the lead splintering the palisade succeeded only in wounding Lieutenant Gilmore and killing a private. They did slaughter or round up all the nearly 150 cattle. About half of Half King's followers grew discouraged and withdrew across the Ohio. The rest followed Half King up the Kanawha River to the Greenbriar valley in search of easier prey.

Learning of their intentions, McKee sent John Inchminger and John Logan to circle around them and warn the distant settlements. The two men found their mission impossible as the Indians were dispersed hunting throughout the valley. Upon their return, McKee asked for two more volunteers. John Pryor and Philip Hammond stepped forward. When one of his friends remarked that he might not venture forth if he knew the danger that lay ahead, Hammond allegedly quoted Ossian's Cathmor: "The time of danger is the very season of my soul—it swells into a mighty stream, and rolls me on the foe."[22]

Dressed as Indians, Hammond and Pryor managed to pass through the enemy ranks and warn the settlers in the nick of time. By the evening of May 28, twenty-five men and sixty women and children crammed into Fort Donnelly. The tireless Hammond and the slave Dick Pointer stood watch while the others slept. The Indians did not wait until dawn. In the middle of the night, they tried to bash in the door with their tomahawks. Hammond yanked back the door, thrust his rifle against an Indian's chest, and pulled the trigger while Pointer fired a fowling piece packed with swan shot. The shots killed or wounded several and scared off the rest. The alarmed settlers manned the bastions. Four settlers were killed, two in the fort and the others in a dash to its safety. The next day, Col. Samuel Lewis led sixty-eight men to Fort Donnelly's relief. Lewis surprised the besiegers, killed eight, and drove off the others. The defeat unsettled Half King's confidence.[23]

At Fort Pitt, General Hand tried to keep the enemy at bay with diplomacy rather than arms. On June 11, he met with White Eyes and other headmen from the Coshocton Delware and a few Shawnee. He promised them that "before the Water is again frozen there will not be an English soldier at Detroit or Niagara unless they are prisoners."[24] Though their thoughts were unrecorded, the chiefs undoubtedly dismissed that boast as thoroughly as the promise of rewarding their neutrality with mountains of presents. Fort Pitt's storehouse remained as skimpy of gifts as its parapets were of soldiers. But the alternative to neutrality was worse. Death and destruction would join hunger at Coshocton.

At nearly the same time that Hand was blustering before White Eyes' Delaware, his counterpart, Gov. Henry Hamilton, was haranguing a much larger and more diverse crowd at Detroit from June 4 to 20, when 1,683 men, women, and children showed up. Most came from the four local tribes, the Wyandot, Ottawa, Potawatomi, and Chippewa, along with groups from those tribes from distant villages. Then there were delegations of Shawnee, Miami, Mingo, Munsee, and Delaware. Hamilton by now was a skilled player of Indian diplomacy, performing the rituals and words with gusto. After stirring the warriors into a frenzy, he cautioned them to spare any men who surrendered along with women and children. Unanimous enthusiasm for war against the American frontier animated every tribe except most Delaware Indians, who clung to neutrality as the British and other tribes tried to pry them loose. Hamilton and the war chiefs took turns castigating the Delaware for their reticence and warned darkly that they had better join the British or else risk retaliation. That council no sooner broke up than Hamilton convened another, this time with Mascouten, Wea, and Kickapoo Indians from June 29 to July 3.[25]

White Eyes soon learned of the Detroit council and passed on word to George Morgan. He promised to continue to "tell you all what passeth, when Warriors go by here . . . I am blamed by the Nations that I betray them, therefore keep all what I tell you secret. These two Messengers I send privately & none of my people knoweth of it but I, because I cannot trust them, but am glad that I can inform you . . . You can easily see that I am frightened & with my people in great danger, there consider & remember me for I rely now entirely on your help."[26] David Zeisberger sent a similar message to Morgan: "White Eyes and I are blamed & accus'd before the Governor at Detroit for giving you Intelligence of the Affairs in the Indian Country."[27] He then went on to give a detailed account of raiding parties and the disposition of various tribes, but there was little that Morgan, Hand, or any other frontier commanders could do when they got advance word of a raid but to send out scouts and keep the settlers close to the forts.

Over 200 warriors in a dozen parties strode toward settlements beyond the Ohio River in July alone. They hauled back to Detroit eighty scalps and thirty-three captives, while only eight Wyandot, one Ottawa, and one Potawatomi were killed and fourteen wounded. A Delaware war party was the most triumphant, bringing in fifteen scalps. One big prize got away. Hamilton pointed two war parties toward the upper and middle Ohio River to intercept the rumored return of Capt. James Willing and his gang aboard a keelboat packed with supplies. Chief Ouquandarong, or Old Baby, led eighty Wyandot to lie in wait along the Ohio; they lingered near Wheeling for three weeks without sighting their prey but did pluck two scalps and a prisoner. Potawatomi chief Paymamakituck and forty warriors captured a man on the river. As always, the bills for enlisting all those Indians or just keeping them in British arms was exorbitant—Hamilton alone spent 42,790 pounds sterling from December 1777 to August 1778.[28]

Despite the stream of scalps and captives being paraded through Detroit, Hamilton felt ever more pessimistic about the frontier war: "It is true the Indians continue to act with good temper, unanimity & success but . . . it is surprising considering the state of matters here, the coolness if not disaffection of numbers, the reports of a French and Spanish War . . . My authority has lately been so cramped, that it will shortly have very little force or influence."[29]

Britain's Indian allies did not unquestionably march where their "fathers" pointed them. Plenty of demands and complaints accompanied their services. No matter how many gifts the Crown's agents passed out at each council, the Indians harped on the paucity and stinginess of their hosts' generosity. This was mostly a ploy to extract larger concessions. Hamilton and others could only patiently explain the war's expensive complexity and the challenges of supplying such distant wilderness posts. In the spring, the Lake and Ohio Indians insisted that the king forever grant them any lands they retook from the Americans. International law fully codified such conquest rights. Hamilton swore off any power to grant such a concession and told the Indians he would defer the matter to Governor Carleton at Montreal. The Indians also sorely resented that they endured all the fighting and danger while the redcoat officers and troops remained safely billeted in their posts. Delaware chief Captain Pipe bluntly told Hamilton that "he & his captains were only fattening themselves & did nothing, that if he would not rise & send an army to Kanawha, & another to Wheeling this Spring they would help him no more & all the Nations should not go to war any more."[30] This threat, of course, was largely bluff. It was in Indian interests to war against any settlers west of the Appalachians regardless of the amount and type of British aid. Hamilton understood this. But it was in British interests to send at least token forces with the Indians, not only to encourage more to join the warpath, but also to restrain their hands from atrocities. However, the British, like the Americans, lacked enough troops, supplies, transport, and heavy guns to drive the enemy from the region. Nonetheless, the Indian questioning of British honor was one of many reasons that propelled Hamilton to head the force that would recapture Vincennes later that year.

While Hamilton reveled in the Indian war that he had long advocated and could finally command, not all the frontier officers agreed with him. Though Lt. Gov. Edward Abbott at Vincennes had once advocated using the Indians against the Americans, he had concluded that the strategy was self-defeating. On June 8, he wrote Governor Carleton that

> employing Indians on the Rebel frontiers has been of great hurt to the cause, for many hundreds would have put themselves under His Majesty's protection was there a possibility; that not being the case, these poor unhappy people are forced to take up arms against their Sovereign, or be pillaged & left to starve; cruel alternative. Your Excellency's known humanity will certainly put a stop if possible to such proceedings, as it is not people in arms that Indians will ever daringly attack; but the poor inoffensive families who . . . are inhumanely butchered sparing neither women nor children. It may be said that it is necessary to employ Indians to prevent their serving our enemies, I will be bold to say, their keeping a neutrality, will be equally (if not more) serviceable to us . . . & surely the presents they receive will prevent their acting against us.[31]

Of course, this was Carleton's position, as Abbott well knew, but the governor had received his orders from American secretary Germain to wield the Indians against the frontier and had passed them on in a manner that he hoped would morally wash his hands of the subsequent blood and other horrors. Such decisions would soon no longer be in Carleton's hands to make. To the very end, Indian duties filled his agenda. That spring, he had counciled at Montreal with delegations of Sioux, Chippewa, Ottawa, Fox, Sauk, Menominee, and Winnebago. Along with gifts, he distributed the message that the Great Father in London needed their friendship against the rebels, but he warned them not to prey on the innocent. The moral weight of rallying Indians for war against fellow British subjects wore down the governor. He could, however, hearten as trade with those distant tribes soared to a new height despite the war—152 canoes and 374 bateaux packed with 191,013 pounds sterling worth of goods headed west from Montreal that year.[32]

Most of the Indian delegations and trade passed through Michilimackinac. That year, the post's commander, Capt. Arent De Peyster, amply fulfilled his duty of recruiting Indians. He sent off to Montreal 110 Chippewa on May 30, 150 Ottawa on June 10, and 300 Winnebago, Menominee, Sauk, Fox, and Sioux on June 29, recruited by the strenuous efforts of Charles Gautier that spring. In all, the diplomacy of De Peyster and his agents netted over 550 warriors, although at a cost of 19,000 pounds sterling worth of goods. De Peyster's success was aided by the mountain of trade goods reaching the upper Lake Indians that year. Over 78,000 pounds sterling worth of goods passed through Michilimackinac, including 1,492 fusils, 55,775 pounds of gunpowder, 71,350 pounds of shot, and, to wash down various deals, 2,155 kegs of rum and 310 kegs of wine. Well-equipped Indians were more inclined for war. Ironically, the British army would not know what to do with all these western Indians when they arrived in July.[33]

Carleton's moral dilemma was finally lifted on June 27 when Maj. Gen. Frederick Haldimand stepped ashore at Quebec. Swiss-born Haldimand was a professional soldier, having fought with the Sardinian, Prussian, and Dutch armies before joining the British in 1756 as a lieutenant colonel of the 60th Royal American. He was wounded at the 1758 assault on Fort Ticonderoga (then called Carillon), defended Fort Ontario against a French and Indian attack in 1759, and joined Amherst's campaign, which took Montreal in 1760. He was Trois Rivieres' lieutenant governor from 1761 to 1765, enjoyed a year's leave, served as governor of East Florida from 1767 to 1773, and was then sent to New York as acting commander in chief while Gen. Thomas Gage was in England. When Gage returned, Haldimand retired to Canada for three years as the war raged. Satiated with inactivity, he went to London in 1777 and solicited a position. Whitehall awarded him Carleton's job as governor. Given his North American experiences, diligence, and courage, Haldimand was overall an excellent choice for the post. Strangely, though, Fort Pitt's strategic importance escaped the new governor. Upon perusing Hamilton's proposal to capture Pittsburgh, Haldimand expressed his extraordinary belief that "no essential point would be gained by reducing it."[34]

The year's largest raid on the Ohio frontier occurred in September, when Blackfish led 400 mostly Shawnee Indians along with Lt. Charles de Quindre, interpreter Pierre Drouillard, and nine of LaMothe's volunteers across the Ohio River. Blackfish entered Kentucky with mingled sorrow and anger—his adopted son Daniel Boone had escaped on June 16.

It had taken Boone only four days to thread the 120 miles of wilderness to Boonesborough. Upon arriving exhausted on June 20, he did not receive the warm homecoming he had imagined. Boone's wife, Rebecca, and all his children but Jemimah had fled east with scores of other frightened refugees. Mingling with that disheartening news were humiliation and frustration over the prevailing suspicion among his neighbors that he had betrayed the salt makers and was now about to sell them to the enemy. He convinced enough of them of his loyalty to place him in charge of the defense. Blockhouses and the stockade were completed and the clearing around the fort enlarged. With reinforcements from Harrodsburg and St. Asaph's, Boonesborough's defenders now numbered about sixty riflemen.

The summer dragged on with little sign of Indians, let alone the huge force that Boone and other escapees reported. Boone was determined to discover the enemy's intentions. On August 30, he and Simon Kenton led thirty men north. About a third of the men turned back at the Ohio River, but Boone and Kenton slipped across with eighteen stalwart followers. They skirmished with Indians on the Scioto River and advanced up that valley as far as the Paint Creek village. Not spotting any warriors or horses, they concluded that Blackfish and his party had already departed. They got back to Boonesborough on September 6 in the nick of time.

Blackfish and his men arrived the following day. The chief paraded his warriors and Canadians, then called for a talk. Boone and Blackfish met about sixty yards from the fort. With tears in his eyes, the father reproached his son for running off and then reminded him of his promise to surrender the fort. He then presented a pardon and safe conduct pass for the settlers. Boone asked to talk the offer over with his men and invited Blackfish and his men to enjoy all the cattle and corn they needed; it was hardly a concession to grant what would be stolen. The offer at first split the garrison, with some advocating surrender and others defiance, but an impassioned speech by Boone's brother Squire inspired a unanimous vote to resist.

Boone managed to stall two days before Blackfish insisted on another council. With riflemen on the ramparts covering them, Boone and several others met with a dozen Indian and British leaders beyond the fort on September 9. When the Kentuckians dismissed the demand to surrender, Blackfish then offered to divide their lands at the Ohio River, although each side could hunt on the other. When the settlers agreed, Blackfish insisted they shake hands. The Indians seized the delegates and dragged them toward the woods. The riflemen in the fort opened fire, killing one. Boone and the others broke free and dashed to the fort's safety. The siege had finally begun.

Without cannons, the enemy's large numbers were neutralized by the palisade. The riflemen turned back a rush on the first day, and from then a distant sniping continued until the siege ended; a bullet clipped Boone's shoulder and another grazed his daughter Jemimah. A sniper killed the black Tory Pompey, who had taunted the defenders from a treetop. The Indians and British tried tunneling under the fort, but rains caved in their effort. At night, warriors sprinted toward the fort and tossed firebrands over the wall. The defenders quickly doused the flames. The Indians tried a final assault on September 17 but were repulsed, with several killed and wounded. They disappeared the following day, having lost perhaps thirty-seven killed and many wounded, and expended 125 pounds of lead against the walls.[35]

After the enemy withdrew, did a grateful community celebrate Daniel Boone's daring escape to warn them of the pending invasion, followed by his skilled leadership that strengthened their defenses, scouted and raided the Scioto villages, and fought off the siege? No. They put him on trial for treason.

Richard Calloway and Benjamin Logan pressed four charges against Captain Boone in a military court, including surrendering the salt makers to save himself, conspiring with the enemy to hand over Boonesborough, weakening the fort's defense by the expedition across the Ohio, and agreeing to negotiate far from the palisade. Boone justified his actions as ways to buy time, save lives, and thwart the invasion. The jury unanimously acquitted him on all charges. Boone was promoted to major.

The trial was more than a humiliating episode in Daniel Boone's life or a controversial chapter in Boonesborough's fleeting history. Tens of thousands of other frontiersmen could have faced similar charges. Any war imposes agonizing moral dilemmas on those it engulfs, none more than a civil war. To what and whom should a man donate his ultimate loyalty? To Daniel Boone and countless others, the answer was clear. Neither undying patriots nor loyalists, they desired a government that ideally would shield them from their enemies while refraining from diminishing their own wealth and liberties. Thus they fought not for Crown or Congress, but for the survival and prosperity of their families and the communities in which they lived. Thousands would lose that struggle during the American Revolution.

THE SUSQUEHANNA AND NEW YORK FRONTIER
A stockade protected each of the eight townships of the Wyoming valley, which enveloped twenty-five miles of the Susquehanna River. Split among those forts was the 24th Connecticut militia, commanded by Col. Nathan Denison, and a company of sixty troops of the 3rd Connecticut led by Col. Zebulon Butler. Why was the valley defended by Connecticut rather than Pennsylvania men? Connecticut settlers had taken over the valley a dozen years earlier and held it against all attempts by Pennsylvania to evict them. Many of those settlers would soon rue the day they ever left Connecticut.

The 574 men of Maj. John Butler and Sayenqueraghta scrambled aboard a flotilla of rafts and canoes at Tioga on June 27. Butler's three ranger companies numbered 110 men, with John commanding one, his son Walter captaining another, and Capt. William Caldwell the third. With Cornplanter his right-hand man, Sayenqueraghta led 464 Indians, mostly Seneca, along with 40 Cayuga, and a sprinkling of Onondaga, Chemung Delaware, and Tuscarora.[36]

The British force struck their first coup on July 28 when they killed three men foolishly working a gristmill north of the valley. Reaching the valley's north end on June 30, they beached their flotilla on the west shore. Pushing down the valley, they killed four and captured four others nurturing a cornfield close to Wintermoot's Fort, the northernmost fort on the valley's west side. The following morning, July 1, Butler sent in a surrender demand to the fort's commander, Lt. Elisha Scovell, who was responsible for the lives of about forty men and their families. Scovell and his men agreed to give up and be neutral for the war's duration in return for amnesty. The next morning, Butler issued the same terms to Jenkins Fort, three miles south. Judge John Jenkins and his eight men quickly accepted.

Colonels Denison and Butler first learned of the raiders on July 1 and mulled over what to do the next two days. On July 3, they decided to march with 450 men across the river and up the valley's west side against the enemy. By about two o'clock that afternoon, word of the American approach reached the invaders' camp near Wintermoot's. Sayenqueraghta and Butler dispersed the rangers among the Indians along a ravine that ran down to the river and sent about fifty warriors through the woods to encircle the American left flank. The road cut straight through the heart of the Indian and British position. The trap was set. Would the Americans be so foolish as to blunder into it?

Denison and Butler halted the column at Abraham's Creek a mile south and pondered their next move with their junior officers. They all sensed the enemy was close but did not know where. The colonels favored sitting tight and sending out scouts. In a nightmarish repetition of the psychology that had contributed to other disasters, most notably Oriskany, the junior officers derided such timidity and urged a rapid march forward. The colonels succumbed to the assault on their pride.

The American column marched forward along the road through the grain-fields and clumps of trees. It was after four o'clock when they neared the enemy position. Someone spotted Indians and Tories among the trees ahead. The commanders ordered the column into line. The Americans advanced to within 200 yards, halted, and fired a volley. The Indians and British merely ducked as the balls splintered wood and shredded leaves above them. The Americans resumed their advance. Sayenqueraghta ordered his men to fire when the enemy got within 100 yards. Just then, the fifty detached warriors burst from the woods and sprinted, firing and screaming, around the American left flank. The mingled volleys cut down scores of Americans. The Indians and British charged forward from the ravine. The American line wavered and then broke. The fighting lasted only a few minutes, the slaughter another hour as the Indians ran down and tomahawked hundreds of fleeing militia.

Brother sometimes fought against brother in America's first civil war. At Wyoming this was literally true with a horribly tragic ending. Patriot Henry Pencel ran to the river and swam out to a small island. His loyalist brother John had spotted his escape during the butchering and followed. As John pointed his musket, "call'd him a damn'd rebel & threaten'd to kill him, Henry fell on his knees & begged for his life saying brother John I am in your hands I'll be your slave I'll go with you but pray my life we have differ'd in sentiment & have met on the field of Battle." Burning with hatred, Pencel shot, tomahawked, and scalped his brother. When some Indians appeared, he boasted to them of his murder, but they cursed this vilest of crimes and threatened to kill him. This tragedy never would have been known had not another patriot named Slocum been hiding in the bushes.[37]

It was another gruesomely lopsided British victory. The Americans suffered 302 dead, several dozen wounded, and 5 captives. Denison and Butler were among the 150 survivors who straggled back to Forty Fort. The British lost only two killed and five wounded, and the Indians one killed and eight wounded. Maj. John Butler recalled that though their casualties were light, "the Indians were so exasperated with their loss last year near Fort Stanwix that it was with the greatest difficulty I could save the lives of those few" captives.[38]

After a frenzied war dance that night to celebrate their harvest of scalps, the Indians and loyalists surged on to Forty Fort the next day. Butler sent in the familiar terms to capitulate or risk butchering by the Indians. The colonels agreed to abandon their fort, arms, and the entire valley for the war's duration. The troops and settlers streamed southeast along the mountain road to Easton or the river road south to Sunbury. Meanwhile, the Indians and British torched and looted their way through the valley behind them and then moved on to Lackawanna valley. By July 8, when their deed was done, they had destroyed over 1,000 dwellings and 11 forts in the two valleys, sparing only the homes of professed loyalists. Then, laden with plunder, the British and Indians staggered back to their flotilla and began poling upstream. Two days later, they reached Tioga.

That widespread destruction enabled the American colonels to declare that Butler had broken his promise, thus relieving them of their own. On August 4, Col. Zebulon Butler marched with 112 regulars back to the ruins of Wyoming Fort. All they could do was erect a stockade and bury the rotting corpses. Settlers drifted back, but it would be years before the valley recovered its population and prosperity. Many of those who first returned scavenged what the enemy failed to destroy or loot. Fifteen months after the raid, John Burrowes visited the valley to search for the remnants of a friend who was killed there, but "instead of finding the gentlemen whom I thought would take care of them, I met with robbers of the dead."[39]

As Sayenqueraghta and Butler returned with their triumphant men, Joseph Brant was leading yet another devastating raid. He and his men burned Springfield at Lake Otsego's north end and nearby Andrew's Town, killed eight men, and took fourteen prisoners. They then burned outlying houses in German Flats before striding back to Oquaga. But that prolonged raid was just a warm-up to what followed.[40]

In mid-September, Brant with 152 Indians and Capt. William Caldwell with 300 loyalists surged into the German Flats district. They captured a five-man Oneida scouting party and then on September 16 killed three of nine American scouts on the Unadilla River. The survivors hurried with word of the expedition to Fort Dayton, commanded by Col. Peter Bellinger. The alarm was sounded, and 719 local people squeezed into Fort Dayton and Fort Herkimer a half-dozen miles away. Bellinger sent riders galloping for help to Col. Jacob Klock and his militia regiment farther down the Mohawk valley and Col. Ichabod Alden's regiment at Cherry valley. Without cannons, the British and Indians could not besiege the forts. Instead, they looted and burned sixty-three homes and scores of outbuildings and drove off 235 horses, 229 cattle, and 269 sheep. Hoping to taunt the defenders of those forts into a sortie, the British and Indians crept close and sniped, but knowing they were grossly outnumbered, the commanders prudently kept their enraged troops within the stockades. Alden's regulars and Klock's militia arrived not long after the British and Indians disappeared.[41]

In retaliation for this destruction of lives and property, the Americans could launch only a few pinprick raids in New York that year. In July, Col. Peter Gansevoort authorized Lieutenant McClellan to lead a party of volunteers in a daring thrust to Oswego, where they burned the buildings and supplies before returning safely to Fort Schuyler. In mid-September, an Oneida and Tuscarora war party plundered Unadilla and Butternuts, and captured five men at each village. Later in September, Col. Thomas Hartley and 200 troops marched from Wyoming up the valley to destroy Sheshecunnunk and Tioga. They withdrew when they learned from prisoners that Capt. Walter Butler, his rangers, and warriors were gathering at Chemung a dozen miles north. Butler and his men caught up with them at Wyalusing but lost ten Indians while killing four and wounding ten Americans. On October 1, Col. William Butler led 500 troops of the 4th Pennsylvania from Schoharie to Oquaga; they burned the village, destroyed 4,000 bushels of corn, and raped and murdered an Oneida chief's wife.[42]

The destruction of those villages did not end enemy raids in the region that year, it just provoked the ferocity of the subsequent vengeance. In early November, Capt. Walter Butler led 150 rangers, 50 troops of the 8th Regiment, and 321 Indians, of which Joseph Brant commanded about 30 and Cornplanter most of the rest, toward Cherry valley. Col. Ichabod Alden commanded the 350 regulars and 150 militia there. He discarded reports of a pending attack and was himself lodged in a home about 400 yards from the fort. The British and Indian attack on the morning of November 11 caught the valley's defenders by surprise. Although the troops in the fort repulsed the assault, the British and Indians killed sixteen soldiers and thirty-two settlers, captured seventy-two others, and burned nearly all the homes before heading back.[43] The carnage sickened those who arrived to bury the dead. Capt. Benjamin Warren admitted that "such a shocking sight my eyes never beheld before of savage and brutal barbarity . . . To see the husband mourning over his dead wife with four dead children lying by her side, mangled, scalped, and some their heads, some their legs and arms cut off, some torn the flesh off their bones by the dogs—12 of one family killed and four of them burnt in his house."[44]

The war that year had devastated New York's frontier settlements. Gov. George Clinton noted that "the Public have lost by the Destruction of these settlements some of the principal Granaries in this State from whence alone the army might have drawn supplies sufficient at least to have prevented their present want . . . If the Enemy . . . continue their Depredations much longer, the Consequences may be fatal, as this state will be disabled from furnishing any supplies to the army & hitherto they have depended upon it for bread."[45] The only way to protect the frontier, Clinton concluded, was with "Offensive Operations, thereby carrying the War into the Enemy's Country." That belief would lead to the Sullivan campaign of the following year.

THE MAINE FRONTIER

No man was more vital to securing the Maine frontier than John Allan. His long-standing criticism of Whitehall policies became ever more vitriolic following news of Lexington and Concord. On January 4, 1777, he appeared at the Continental Congress in Baltimore and gave an in-depth report of the strategic situation in Maine and Nova Scotia. Impressed with Allan's keen intelligence, enterprise, and experiences, Congress appointed him Indian superintendent and colonel for the region, designated the Eastern Department. Departing Baltimore on February 3, he reached Machias Bay, where he established his headquarters and trading house. Like other Indian agents and frontier commanders, Allan's life was a bee-hive of endless councils, presentations of gifts, alarms, demands, scarcities, dispatches of scouts, reviews of intelligence reports, interrogations of prisoners, submissions of largely fruitless appeals to Massachusetts for more troops and supplies, sporadic receipts of provisions and news from privateer captains, courts-martial and punishments of thieves and deserters, and construction and repair of fortifications.[46]

While the neighboring Penobscot, Maliseet, and Passamaquoddy Indians remained allied to the United States for the war's duration, the more distant Micmac kept a sullen neutrality. Despite continual British entreaties to join them, Micmac weakness in numbers, disunity, fear of American retaliation, and Allan's adroit diplomacy combined to restrain them from the warpath.[47]

The Machias settlers received a frightening jolt on June 27. Two Indians in a canoe skimmed up to the landing, beached, and dashed to the trade house, where they handed to Allan a hastily scribbled letter from militia colonel Francis Shaw warning that the thirty-four-gun HMS *Vulture* had dropped anchor in Machias Bay that morning. The militia had fired on a forty-man British landing party crammed into whaleboats with swivel guns mounted on the bow. The militia fusil-lade of six rounds and swivel shots killed or wounded eight men among the sitting British ducks. The redcoats awkwardly returned fire but hit no one ashore; they retreated to the *Vulture*'s safety.

Allan immediately called the visiting Maliseet Indians to council and asked them to join the Americans. The warriors enthusiastically agreed, and Allan led them down to Machias Bay. The British tried another landing on June 30. This time they avoided the American breastworks and ground ashore at two unde-fended places. A pincer of the two British columns ambushed thirty militia, killed five, and scattered the rest while suffering ten casualties. With a landing secure, reinforcements swelled the British ashore to 150 troops conveyed in eight whale-boats. But the British were blind without information about where the settlements lay. They returned to the *Vulture* the next day.

On July 5, Chief Pierre Toma and four warriors boldly canoed to the *Vulture*, boarded, and harangued the likely startled and amused captain, crew, and soldiers for intruding on their lands. After hearing out the chief, the *Vulture*'s captain let him and his warriors go. The chief's speech combined with the inability to reach or even find the enemy caused the captain shortly thereafter to order the *Vulture*'s anchor weighed and sails spread for the journey to the open sea and reinforce-ments.

Rather than sit tight and await the next British foray, Captains Henry Dyer and Jabez West led an American raid against St. Johns where they found the *Vul-ture* and two small ships in the harbor. Learning of lurking rebels, the British sent 120 troops after them. While most of the Americans withdrew up the St. Johns River, Dyer and twelve men set an ambush. The British marched right into the trap. The Americans opened fire, killing six, and then withdrew before superior numbers. They crossed trails with a British flank guard that opened fire, killing three and wounding two Americans. Dyer and his survivors caught up with the main party and eventually reached safety.[48]

Allan opened a council with about fifty envoys from the Penobscot, Maliseet, and Passamaquoddy tribes on August 13. The timing was fortuitous. A runner disrupted the council with word that a brig, schooner, and sloop had sailed into the bay and exchanged cannon shots with the battery. The 350 militia and Indians rushed down to the bay and split among various fortifications. The following day, the British commander, Capt. George Collier, sent ashore a landing party that captured the battery, whose gunners and guards fled. After spiking the guns and burning two adjacent houses, they returned to their ships. Once aboard, the flotilla's eleven whaleboats were manned and slowly towed the ships up the bay. Near Libby's Hill, the British got within musket shot of militia hiding in the woods. Both sides opened fire. Because of the angle, the British gunners could only point their swivels and muskets toward the enemy. A shot killed an American. The brig ran aground. The fire continued for three hours until the brig was refloated and the flotilla withdrew down the bay. The standoff was broken on August 15, when the Americans dragged a cannon atop Manchester's Point and opened fire on the brig. The balls hulled the brig and smashed several whaleboats. The sloop warped the brig down the bay to shelter near Round Island. After the brig was repaired, Collier ordered the flotilla to put to sea the next day. In all, the British had suffered three dead and eighteen wounded, while killing one American and wounding another. The Americans and Indians celebrated their victory. Allan distributed gifts and sent home his charges.

The flotilla lingered off the coast. An American scouting party captured three men of an eight-man party that came ashore to replenish their water barrels. Allan sent one of the prisoners back to the flotilla with a letter requesting a prisoner exchange and a halt to British cruelties to their captives. The British ignored Allan's request. An order arrived from Massachusetts' General Court that provoked consternation amid the lingering danger—all state soldiers should be disbanded and the region's defense left on the militia's shoulders. On September 4, scouts reported that the flotilla had disappeared over the horizon. The community celebrated its latest victory. In mulling over the preceding months' routine, broken by the whirl of two separate attacks, Allan captured the frontier war's essence when he exclaimed: "How vain are our hopes! how changeable are our fates, when we think ourselves most secure, we are most in danger."[49]

Word arrived that the British were preparing a third attempt to destroy Machias, this time with a 700-man and thirteen-ship expedition to set sail from St. Johns. Allan called the militia and Indians. Some drifted away, but most lingered until October 5, when news was received that the expedition was canceled and troops sent to winter quarters. Allan then dispersed the militia and Indians back to their homes.

THE SOUTHEAST FRONTIER

With Britain's offensives destroyed, blunted, or withdrawn in the north, Lord George Germain hoped the southern colonies would be the rebellion's soft underbelly. On March 8, 1778, he wrote Maj. Gen. Henry Clinton to send 2,000 troops to seize Savannah while Maj. Gen. Augustine Prevost marched with his troops north from St. Augustine and John Stuart instigated an Indian war on the frontier with the goal of capturing Augusta. Using Georgia as a base, the British would then systematically march north over subsequent years, as loyalists flocked to the colors across the region and Indians attacked all along the frontier, crushing all resistance and reimposing governments until all rebel colonies were extinguished. That ambitious plan would not begin to unfold until December.[50]

The southern frontier was relatively quiet in 1778, the lull before the destructive storm of the following three years. Few Indians had any will to fight. Crop failures, the collapse of trade, disease, and war had brought them to starvation's brink. The chiefs could merely beg for relief from both sides. The abject conditions appalled Superintendent John Stuart, who reported, "The greatest part must have perished, but with the Assistance and Supplies with which I furnished them from time to time this and the preceding Year."[51] In all, he distributed 54,224 pounds sterling worth of presents that year, up from 19,000 just two years earlier. To disperse those goods, he sent his agents back to the field, but only after the Indians promised not to harm them. By spring, Alexander Cameron was with the Cherokee and David Tait and William McIntosh with the Creek. While Cameron could not rouse the Cherokee, Tait and McIntosh did instigate some sporadic Creek attacks that killed about twenty settlers and soldiers on Georgia's frontier. For now, most Indians were not allies but wards.[52]

American Indian policy that year was typically contradictory. George Washington authorized Nathaniel Gist to distribute $5,000 to recruit several hundred Cherokee and any frontiersmen for a $20 bounty each. Gist got no takers. Then in May, the North Carolina assembly voted to pay fifteen pounds for a prisoner and ten pounds for a scalp. Of course, that extra five pounds for a prisoner was good money, but a scalp was a lot easier to retrieve from the frontier to the bounty office.[53]

On the extreme southern frontier, rival forts glared at each other across fifty miles of mostly wilderness.[54] Fort Tonyn on the St. Mary's River protected East Florida's northern frontier, while Forts Howe and Barrington on the Altamaha guarded Georgia's southern approach. From Fort Tonyn, Lt. Col. Thomas Brown and his four companies of Florida Scouts ranged across the region garnering cattle, captives, and intelligence. Sometimes Brown sought larger prey.

On March 13, Brown led 100 rangers and ten Indians across the Altamaha River and crept up to Fort Barrington. They rushed the fort at dawn, killing two, wounding four, and capturing twenty-three men, while losing one killed and four wounded. The rangers destroyed the fort and hauled back the supplies and prisoners. It was a daring and brilliant coup with important consequences. News of Fort

Barrington's elimination atop recent laws in the Carolinas and Georgia requiring loyalty oaths emboldened hundreds of Tories in those states to flee south. A portion joined Brown's Florida Scouts, 350 filled the ranks of the newly formed South Carolina Royalists commanded by Col. Alexander Innes, and Col. Joseph Scophol led south 500 men from the Ninety-Six region. Those reinforcements arrived at just the right time.[55]

That spring, Congress submitted to Georgia's pressure and approved another expedition against St. Augustine. Maj. Gen. Robert Howe, the southern commander, was reluctant to do so. He knew all too well how formidable and far away his enemy was compared with the limited troops, supplies, money, and transport plaguing his own ghost of an army. But a dearth of cooperation was perhaps even more debilitating to the American cause on that frontier. Petty jealousies rooted in rival egos and states doomed the expedition's already unlikely chance of success.

By mid-May, four distant forces were ready to begin their separate marches against St. Augustine. At Savannah, Howe had gathered 600 South Carolina and 500 Georgia Continentals, while Gov. John Houston readied the Georgia militia for a different road south. Several hundred Georgia militia under Col. Samuel Elbert massed at Fort Howe. Gen. Andrew Williamson was preparing his South Carolina militia to join the campaign but had not bothered to inform Howe.

The campaign opened with a victory. Colonel Elbert with 300 militia and two cannons crammed aboard three large galleys captured three British gunboats near Frederica. With naval superiority in local waters, the American offensive could proceed. By May 26, Howe's 1,100 troops had joined Elbert at Fort Howe while Houston's were approaching. The next step was to march on Fort Tonyn, but it took nearly a month to accumulate enough supplies before the Americans could take that step. It was not until June 23 that Howe's army crossed the Satilla River.

With his 300 troops outgunned nearly six to one, Lt. Col. Thomas Brown had Fort Tonyn burned and sent Capt. James Moore with seventy-six rangers and a few Indians around the enemy rear. The raid failed. Some troops deserted to the American camp. Moore and his men rode into an ambush in which the captain and several of his men were killed and the rest scattered. Brown and his men, meanwhile, disappeared into Cabbage Swamp, from which they emerged to pick off stragglers.

When Gen. James Screven and 100 cavalry threatened to cut off his retreat, Brown led his men seventeen miles south to join Maj. James Mark Prevost and 450 regulars and South Carolina royalists encamped at the bridge over Alligator Creek. Learning that Brown's force was approaching on June 30, Prevost assumed it was safe to allow his men to loll about camp, but the American cavalry was hard on the heels of Brown's exhausted men when they stumbled across the bridge. The alarm was sounded in the British camp, and the troops hastily assembled around their colors. Brown's rangers filed through the British ranks into the camp's safety, but astonishingly, Brown did not halt there. After allowing a short breather, he led two ranger companies through a swamp and attacked the enemy's right flank. Screven called for his men to retreat, leaving nine dead behind among one dead and seven wounded British.

With this victory, the British seized the initiative. The following morning, Prevost, Brown, and their small army marched forward ten miles and scattered an advanced American detachment fixing a bridge. That was enough for Howe, encamped at Fort Tonyn's ruins. His army was wasting away. British bullets inflicted several score casualties, but disease would kill over 500 of his troops and sicken hundreds more before the season was over. On July 11, he ordered his skeleton of an army to retreat back to Savannah. The American campaign had failed ignominiously.

To Brown's disgust, Prevost refused to pursue. As a regular major, Prevost outranked the provincial lieutenant colonel and haughtily rejected his advice. That haughtiness was reinforced when Prevost was promoted to lieutenant colonel later that year. From June through November, a lull descended over the southeast frontier, broken only by bickering within each enemy camp.

Then the British mounted a large raid toward Sunbury. Lt. Col. Lewis Fuser and Brown led the 750-man army's advance under Lt. James Mark Prevost. Learning that General Screven and his cavalry were hurrying forward to intercept them, Fuser ordered Brown to set a trap. Brown deployed thirty-two men into a thicket embracing the road near Bulltown Swamp. The Americans trotted right into the ambush. The fusillade mortally wounded Screven, killed several others, and routed the survivors. Fuser and then Prevost joined their forces with Brown and then pushed forward. An American force stood at the Midway Meeting House. Brown's rangers led the attack, followed by Prevost's regulars. The Americans fled. Fuser hurried his troops to Fort Morris guarding Sunbury and on November 21 demanded that Lt. Col. John McIntosh surrender. McIntosh issued the celebrated reply, "Come and take it!"[56] Lacking artillery, Fuser withdrew to Prevost's main body, and together they herded over 2,000 cattle and other booty south to St. Augustine. They would soon return.

That raid was supposed to divert American attention from a far more ambitious British venture that, if successful, Prevost was supposed to join. Clinton only began to implement Germain's southern strategy that autumn. On November 27, Lt. Col. Archibald Campbell set sail from New York with 3,500 troops in a flotilla commanded by Comdr. Hyde Parker. It took nearly a month for them to drop anchor off Tybee Island at the Savannah River mouth on December 23.

The first troops did not land until Christmas day. Their mission was to scout Savannah and gather intelligence about the city's defenses. Learning that Gen. Robert Howe commanded only twice as many men in makeshift defenses, Campbell chose to attack the city before it could be reinforced. He disembarked his entire force and marched it toward Savannah on December 28. The following day, his army had reached the city's outskirts. From a slave, Campbell learned of a path that arced around to the rear of the American position. While he distracted the rebels with a demonstration on their front, he sent a detachment on that path.

That attack routed the Americans. The British troops joined in the pursuit with all the exhilaration of a fox hunt. They chased the rebels into Savannah and out the other side, and along the way captured 443, killed 83, and wounded 11 at a loss of 7 killed and 19 wounded. Savannah was a vital and inexpensive New Year's gift to the king and Britain's war effort.[57]

THE LOWER MISSISSIPPI VALLEY FRONTIER

While the British easily repelled Howe's blundering campaign against East Florida, they faced a far more daring enemy thrust against West Florida. On January 10, 1778, Capt. James Willing and twenty-nine volunteers embarked aboard a keelboat christened the *Rattletrap* from Fort Pitt on the swift current toward New Orleans. The British agent at Kaskaskia, Philip Francois Rastel de Rocheblave, got wind of Willing's expedition and feared it would target the upper Mississippi British settlements. Any relief he felt when word arrived that Willing had continued downriver would be short-lived; George Rogers Clark's expedition was soon on its way toward Kaskaskia.[58]

Willing's rowers made excellent time. On February 17, they ground ashore at militia colonel Anthony Hutchins's plantation just above Natchez. Willing gleefully led his men to capture that nemesis from his years in the district and confiscate his slaves. The next objective was Natchez itself, which they reached on February 19. Without firing a shot, they rounded up the inhabitants, occupied Fort Panmure, and on February 21 got the adult males to pledge neutrality in return for a guarantee that their property was secure from confiscation. Volunteers swelled Willing's ranks to nearly 200 men. They pushed downstream. Off Manchac on February 23, Willing's raiders scored their greatest coup when they suddenly emerged silently from a thick fog and swarmed aboard the sixteen-gun brig *Rebecca,* the only significant British naval vessel then on the Mississippi. The stunned captain and crew surrendered without a fight. The Americans almost captured Choctaw deputy Henry Stuart, who fled from Manchac across the river to a Spanish fort.

From Manchac, the adventurers extracted loot and loyalty oaths at Baton Rouge, Pointe Coupee, and plantations along the river's British east bank. Upon reaching Spanish territory, they descended swiftly to New Orleans. There, Willing handed Oliver Pollock a letter from Congress commissioning him an American agent. After recruiting another twenty-six men, he led his expedition downstream, where, near the Mississippi River's mouth, they captured yet another brig, the *Neptune,* along with the merchant ship *Despatch.* Willing and his men got a hero's welcome back in New Orleans and a warehouse to use as a barracks. The ships, slaves, and other plunder fetched $62,000 at auction. To Pollock's frustration, the adventurers spent most of that money on wild victory orgies in New Orleans' brothels and grogshops rather than more supplies for America's cause.[59]

As Willing and his men overindulged with women and rum, the tide slowly turned against them. A delegation of West Florida Tories appeared in New Orleans to petition Gov. Bernardo de Galvez for redress from Willing's vandalism and theft of their property. A three-man commission appointed by Galvez to investigate their claims ruled against Willing. The British frigate *Sylph,* captained by John Ferguson, dropped anchor at New Orleans. In a March 14 meeting with Galvez, Ferguson protested Willing's presence in the city and demanded compensation for his victims. He also complained about Willing's lieutenant, Thomas McIntyre, who gleefully shouted a torrent of invectives against the *Sylph*'s officers and King George.

Galvez dismissed Ferguson's entreaties with the timeworn practice of promising to do something and then doing nothing, but that might only have postponed a day of reckoning with the British. The governor tiptoed a precarious diplomatic tightrope. Officially Spain was still neutral. Word of Madrid's decision for war against Britain would not arrive until the next year. Ferguson argued that Galvez violated Spain's neutrality by aiding and abetting Willing. This truth Galvez vigorously denied, yet the governor feared handing the British a pretense for attacking poorly defended New Orleans with the 1,000 redcoats stationed in Pensacola and Mobile. In 1778, Louisiana's troops amounted to 437 regulars and 1,500 militia scattered in small clusters from New Orleans to St. Louis. But the British were no more eager for a showdown, as their army and navy were also stretched to the breaking point. Thus would Ferguson bluster his way to war's brink but would not step over. This Galvez understood and acted upon.[60]

A bold attitude and bolstered defenses could persuade the British to restrain their demands and, should war break out, deter an attack. Galvez strengthened with troops and fortifications the battery at Balize guarding the downriver approach to New Orleans. On April 14, he decreed that all British subjects either take a neutrality oath or leave Louisiana. On April 21, he ordered the commanding officer at Fort St. Johns on the bayou bypassing New Orleans to turn back three British warships attempting to reach the Mississippi. This latter action elicited from Pollock "the greatest applause to Govr. Galvez for his noble Spirit & behavior on this Occasion, for, tho' he had no Batteries erected, or even Men to defend the place against the Two Sloops of War, and at the same time a Small Sloop with a Hundred Men in the Lakes all coming against him with Demands & Threats, yet in this Situation he laughed at their Haughtiness and despised their attempts, and in short they returned as they came."[61]

Meanwhile, the British began to pry loose America's grip on the Mississippi. Daring and destructive as Willing's mission was, it provoked the opposite effect. In March, West Florida governor Peter Chester sent Lt. John Pearis, Indian Deputy Adam Chrystie, and thirty rangers overland. Those troops attacked Fort Bute at Manchac, killed two defenders and a woman, and captured fourteen others. Gaining word of the seizure, Willing dispatched Lt. Reuben Harrison and thirty-four men upstream. The British fled to the forest when the Americans arrived. Upon raising the flag again over Fort Bute, Harrison and his men continued upstream to quell a rebellion at Natchez led by Col. Anthony Hutchins, who had broken his oath and mustered the loyalists there and at White Cliffs below Natchez. Learning that Hutchins had set an ambush for him, Harrison sent word that his mission was peaceful and then approached Fort Panmore. The British opened fire, killing Harrison and four others and capturing the rest. Governor Chester sent reinforcements under Capt. Michael Jackson along with Indian Agent John McGillivray to Natchez and Manchac. There McGillivray presented the inhabitants with the choice to either rally to the Union Jack or else be treated as traitors. Not surprisingly, they chose the king over Congress.

The backdoor to the United States for Willing and his men had slammed shut. Willing lacked enough men to dare ascend the river and kick open that door once again. Stripped of his conquests, Willing's monstrous ego and extravagances became intolerable for Galvez and a gross embarrassment for Pollock. He and his cutthroats were now a liability rather than an asset. The British could use his continued presence as a pretext to block the Mississippi or even attack New Orleans. An increasingly alarmed Pollock complained to Congress that "the Small Party you sent here under Command of Captn. James Willing without any order or subordination has only thrown the whole river into Confusion and created a Number of Enemys and a heavy Expence."[62]

In May, the governor and financier politely but firmly informed Willing that it was well past time to move on. To reinforce his request, Pollock cut off Willing's allowance. Willing refused to budge. He acknowledged that difficulties had arisen, but blamed Pollock: "My Men and Officers are discontented, myself displeased and the Governor himself highly dissatisfied with your Conduct . . . My Men are deserting and the American bank as it is termed is become proverbially ridiculous. In a word the Service suffers and our Enemys rejoice—This therefore is to insist that You forthwith make out all your accounts so that the one half belonging to me and the Men be instantly divided."[63] To this Pollock lent a deaf ear.

Willing did make two halfhearted attempts to leave. He asked Pollock to refit the *Rebecca,* rechristened the *Morris.* But when this was done, the captain chose not to sail. Instead, he asked Galvez for permission to trek overland and bypass the British on the Mississippi. Galvez granted permission on July 14. Once again, Willing refused to trade the easy women and cheap liquor of New Orleans for the wilderness. But by August, the Americans had spent nearly the last of their credit. Capt. Robert George and about fifty robust patriots urged Willing to return to the fight. Willing refused and resigned his command. George led his men overland north through Louisiana to Arkansas Post and from there by boat up the Mississippi.

Pollock grew ever more exasperated. To the commerce committee, he fired off a letter in August, wondering rhetorically what Willing's "next Pretence for tarrying here will be God knows, but as there is a clear Passage for him and his Party to go up, part by Land and Part by Water through the Spanish territories . . . and join Col. Clark, I am determined to stop all Supplies in order to get him away."[64] Willing recognized his bargaining power and acted upon it. He shook down Pollock for another 919 pesos and 1 real for ship passage and expenses back to Philadelphia. For Pollock, it was a small price to pay to get rid of the miscreant.

It was not until November 15 that Willing finally set sail. En route he expended what little luck he still harbored. A British warship intercepted the ship, captured Willing, and hauled him in irons to New York. His charisma and connections extended even from a British prison. He persuaded Congress to send him 100 pounds for living expenses and finally got himself exchanged in 1781. Two years later, Willing was back in New Orleans, deeply enmeshed in get-rich schemes and decadence.

In the end, what had Willing's filibustering gained and lost for America's cause? Actually, it was not as bad as it seemed to Pollock, Galvez, and others at the time. The fear that Willing would provoke a British attack was rational but never realized. Britain and Spain were not yet officially at war. The seeming complicity of Galvez in Willing's violation of Spanish neutrality was serious but not quite a casus belli. Regardless, Whitehall was but dimly aware of the situation. The American Revolution and France's war declaration had stretched Britain's army, navy, and treasury to the snapping point. War with Spain would conjure up another horrid nightmare within the original. West Florida governor Peter Chester knew well Galvez's hand in aiding Willing and the American struggle. He lacked not only the authority, but also the troops, transports, and supplies to attack Louisiana. The reinforcements he received in late 1778 were insufficient to allow an offensive but, as will be seen, would not prevent Galvez from systematically conquering West Florida from 1779 to 1781.

Still, Willing did provoke the British to tighten their throttle on river traffic, thus cutting what was already a sporadic trickle of supplies from New Orleans to Pittsburgh. He also squandered the wealth his crew had looted on the Mississippi and Pollock's subsidies. At worst, Willing brought on sooner Pollock's inevitable bankruptcy. By late 1778, Pollock's once formidable credit had run dry. That was not the fault of Pollock or Willing, but of the impossibility of Congress and Virginia to arrest the plunge in value of their paper currencies.

MCINTOSH'S CAMPAIGN

Hard-pressed to counter British offensives, raise troops, money, and supplies, and often just evade capture, America's fledgling government could spare little time to the frontier war. At first the states seemed capable of containing the Indian threat. The militia of several states won a war with the Cherokee in 1776, but the Cherokee took to the warpath the following year, along with increasing numbers of warriors from other tribes along the frontier from East Florida to Canada. With each year, ever more and larger Indian raids scorched frontier regions. By 1778, the raids along the Ohio valley, Pennsylvania, and New York frontiers had become systematic. Unable to cope alone, the states issued increasingly desperate pleas to Congress to help them crush the Indians.

Congress first took up that challenge in November 1777, when it sent George Clymer and Sampson Matthews to Pittsburgh to study the situation and report their findings to the War Board. On April 27, 1778, they submitted an analysis that called for a force of 2,500 Virginia militia, 500 regulars, and a small artillery train to march from Pittsburgh to take Detroit. Congress debated the proposal and on June 11 resolved that "the cruelties lately exercised by the savages on the frontiers of New York, Pennsylvania, and Virginia, are the commencement of an Indian war, which threatens, with extensive devastation, the frontiers of these United States."[65] Congress appropriated $932,743 to equip and supply those 3,000 troops for the Detroit campaign.

Where would the troops come from and who would command them? At Pittsburgh, Gen. Edward Hand had thoroughly discredited himself for that role. He had failed utterly to stem Indian attacks in that region and committed diplomatic blunders that shoved erstwhile neutrals into the British camp. Though the Indians did not attack Fort Pitt directly, their raids elsewhere ate away its defenses. So many settlers had fled the frontier that Hand feared the only ones left would be loyalists. He offered to Gen. Horatio Gates his "sincere belief, that if a few men are not put here immediately to encourage the timorous . . . and overawe the Tory faction, this whole country will be abandoned or overrun by the enemy in a short time."[66] Hand left unexplained why he did not wield his own troops to that end. Nonetheless, those familiar with the frontier could echo Hand's worries. Timothy Pickering warned Washington that "in addition to the barbarous savages, the disaffected inhabitants are a terror to their neighbors, and some of them mingle with the Indians to committing these horrid cruelties. To repel the incursions of the Indians & reduce the disaffected to obedience, nothing . . . will be effectual but a regular force, under the direction of good officers. The inhabitants appear, many of them, to be a wild ungovernable race, little less savage than their tawny neighbors."[67]

As loyalist sentiments swelled, Fort Pitt's garrison diminished. In late April, Hand wrote Gates of

> the frequent desertion from the garrison & that 14 had eloped the night of the 20th [April] . . . & that a party of 40 men & 4 officers had been detached after them. I am pleased that I can now tell you they have been overtaken at the mouth of the Muskingum river; that Davis, two sergt . . . six soldiers, a Mr. Puzie lately assistant surgeon here, & one of the townsmen were secured. Six soldiers, a townsman, & Davis' servant escaped—the whole effected a landing before the party could close with them. One of the soldiers is since dead of his wounds he received before landing . . . Those who have escaped in their hurry deprived themselves of any probable means of subsisting, must undoubtedly perish or return to Wheeling, except the Indians meet with them.[68]

George Washington and Congress blamed Hand for his problems with loyalist deserters, renegades, and, most importantly, the failure to launch a crushing blow against the Indians. Congress readily accepted Hand's request to be recalled on May 2, but who should replace him? Congress allowed Washington to decide.

The frontier war was much on George Washington's mind. The Ohio valley's defense demanded a skilled decisive leader, but a dearth of such officers in his own hard-pressed, tattered army cautioned him from transferring one such elsewhere, no matter how vital and threatened the region. "After much consideration," Washington chose Gen. Lachlan McIntosh, with whom he would "part . . . with much reluctance, as I esteem him an officer of great worth and merit, and as I know his services here are and will be materially wanted. His firm disposition and equal justice, his assiduity and good understanding added to his being a stranger to all parties in that quarter, pointed him out as a proper person."[69] Washington informed McIntosh of his choice on May 26. That trust was misplaced. McIntosh would accomplish little more than his predecessor.

The frontier demanded not just a good commander, but also troops with professional discipline and wilderness skills. Washington transferred the 13th Virginia and 8th Pennsylvania from his army back to the upper Ohio, where they had been raised. Those troops would fight all the harder for their own homes. Colonels John Gibson of the 13th and Daniel Broadhead of the 8th were both energetic, veteran leaders. Gibson's years as a frontier settler and merchant had rendered him conversant with Indian tongues and ways.[70]

It might be thought that the frontier settlers and their governments would uniformly applaud the proposed Detroit campaign, but some hesitated, especially Virginia, which was asked to provide the bulk of the troops and supplies. On July 7, Virginia's governor Patrick Henry and the council offered the contradictory resolve to "advise against Gen. M'Intosh's expedition to Detroit but authorize him to call on" the militia of the frontier counties to march with him.[71] The Virginians feared stripping their defenses elsewhere to supply the campaign's militia.

George Morgan unequivocally supported the campaign. To America's War Board he argued that the road linking Pittsburgh and Detroit was "practicable," the Delaware and Shawnee would "remain quiet" though some "might be induced to join in a well ordered Expedition," no powerful tribes that might resist straddled the road, Detroit was "defenseless" but supplied the region's Indians, and thus taking it would "induce all the Tribes to enter into our Alliance through fear & interest."[72] At most during its march through Ohio, the expedition would encounter no more than 300 hostile warriors, including 200 Wyandot at Sandusky and Detroit, 60 Mingo on the Scioto, and 40 Ottawa and Chippewa who had mixed with the Wyandot.

Like most wilderness campaigns, the success of McIntosh's depended more on diplomacy than battle. It was essential to keep the Delaware and Shawnee at peace while deterring those already on the warpath. The Delaware were vital diplomatic intermediaries between the Americans and the hostile tribes. To the Coshocton council, George Morgan sent from Philadelphia news of America's war successes and a warning of McIntosh's campaign: "The United States still wishes to avoid sending an Army over the Ohio—and if the foolish People who have struck us so often, will grow wise immediately, they may yet avoid destruction—You know Brothers & I know that we are not to blame nor will it be our Fault if we cross the Ohio & trample them into dust as we will undoubtedly do if they continue their evil ways."[73] The Delaware passed on the message to the enemy tribes. Few if any hostiles were intimidated.

Six weeks after authorizing the Detroit campaign, Congress called it off. Instead, McIntosh was ordered to attack the hostile villages of central Ohio. The general would find even that more limited objective impossible to reach.[74]

The general did not arrive at Fort Pitt until August 6. Hand was not impressed with his replacement. To his wife, he confessed that McIntosh was "an entire stranger to the nature of the present command, has requested my remaining a few days to give him some necessary information. All my papers & letters on business are now in his hands for that purpose. The day after tomorrow I hope to set forth to Lancaster."[75]

It was not until August 27 that McIntosh sent orders to the commanders to send their militia and supplies to Fort Pitt. Meanwhile, he received intelligence reports revealing that the shift in the campaign's goal from capturing Detroit to attacking the Ohio Indian villages was a grave mistake. Detroit was poorly defended, while even many of Britain's Indian allies might not fight if their villages were spared. John Leith, a trader who was captured by Delaware Indians in 1774 and married a white woman, wrote that there were "only 70 or 80 Volunteers that has encamped . . . at Detroit & about that number of Regulars. The Inhabitants I am pretty well convinced will not at all assist the English at an Army's approaching. I there think you will find no difficulty at all without it be from the Indians, which has agreed to strike you as soon as you have cross'd the river."[76] But word of McIntosh's campaign had cowed at least some Indians. Wyandot chief Baubee met with Delaware chief White Eyes on August 16 and sent a message to George Morgan: "If you intend to go to Detroit . . . then I beg & desire of you to leave our Towns along the Road unmolested & they shall all come to you, shake hands with you, & make Peace."[77] David Zeisberger offered an even more optimistic assessment: "By the disposition of the Enemy Indian in general it is supposed if an Army comes out, that they will not offer to give them battle, they will fly & hide themselves where ever they can & sue for Peace."[78]

McIntosh took advantage of the dread among the Ohio tribes by getting Delaware chief White Eyes to sign the Fort Pitt treaty on September 12 that pledged their peoples to "our mutual good & happiness, on such principles that if faithfully adhered to, will secure our future peace whilst the Sun, Moon or the Earth endures."[79] On September 21, McIntosh named White Eyes a lieutenant colonel "of all Indian nations between the rivers Ohio, Mississippi, & the Lakes."[80]

The general's diplomacy would soon be skewered when its consequences became known. By placing a hatchet in White Eyes' hands during the council, he tried to convert the Delaware from neutrals to allies, but his failure to follow Indian etiquette made his gesture ambivalent. As a result, the Delaware lost credibility in the eyes of the hostile tribes. Formerly they could argue that the Americans desired only neutrality in the war.[81]

The Delaware wanted a friendship treaty that would protect them from the bullying of other tribes; they adamantly did not want to fight their powerful neighbors. Upon returning to Coshocton, White Eyes became eager to review the treaty council's transcripts after "I was looked upon as a warrior & was the cause of so much confusion among my People." What he found incensed him. He angrily reported that the transcripts "are wrote down false & as I did not understand the Interpreter what he spoke I could not contradict his Interpretation."[82] The Delaware angrily returned the war hatchet and wampum belt, but the damage was done. Over 200 Delaware fled toward Detroit to avoid getting dragged into a war with the other tribes. Many of those Delaware would join war parties against the American frontier.

McIntosh's most important task was to convert a mob into an army. The ranks wanted men, supplies, morale, and, above all, discipline. The officers were often no more orderly than their men. The general castigated the 13th Virginia's officers for their frequent absence for duty, their whereabouts undetermined, a behavior "not even known & would be inexcusable in militia."[83] The troops displayed an ignorance and ineptness in performing their manual of arms. McIntosh noted that the troops "form their lines very awkwardly and slow which is attended with many inconveniences, especially against such enterprising & vigilant enemies as the savages are who take every advantage & strike with savage fury."[84]

Parade ground drilling and strictly enforced regulations could combat these ills. Soldiers were court-martialed almost daily for a range of petty and serious offenses. Desertion was the most common crime, the penalty varying with whether the miscreant headed home or to the enemy, and if he tried to induce others to join him. Those worn down by the drudgery, fear, and homesickness usually got twenty-five lashes. Those who tried to desert to the enemy were hanged within a hollow square of the assembled army. Drunkenness, insubordination, looting, firing muskets, or wandering beyond 300 yards of camp without permission all met with fines or vigorous swings of cat-o'-nine-tails. Civilian sutlers who overcharged or cheated the soldiers could have their licenses revoked or forage withheld from their horses.[85]

McIntosh understood that attention to appearance and hygiene boosted morale and health. He required "both officers & men . . . to appear as clean as their circumstance will admit, with their hair powdered & green boughs in their hats."[86] To twenty-first-century minds, the era had curious medicinal notions. Fearing the morning dew "may be injurious to the soldiers' health, they are allowed to sit in their tents with their arms in their hands until reveille beating."[87] The general recognized that the long marches, parades, woodcutting, and camp and sentry duties, mingled with fear of sudden attack, were wearying enough for his troops without the officers exploiting them as personal servants. This latter practice McIntosh urged his officers to "restrain . . . to a moderate number."[88]

With battle, the ultimate purpose of soldiers, the condition of their arms was essential. Troops were issued fifty cartridges. Officers daily conducted morning and evening inspections of their troops, paying special attention to their muskets. Moisture deadens gunpowder, which in turn can corrode a barrel's innards. Charges thus should daily be pulled or fired and the barrel cleaned. The soldiers were forbidden from firing their muskets without orders. To supplement their larder and marksmen skills, soldiers were given permission to hunt but were admonished to make each shot count. Two or more shots heard in succession would provoke the army to beat to arms.

Apparently eighteenth-century soldiers were just as inclined to record for posterity that they passed through as the more recent "Kilroys." The general condemned those who "have presumed to mark trees in the woods with initial letters & their names at large, & thereby give great uneasiness to our friends and allies the Delaware nation or friend Indians."[89] Even more essential to maintaining the peace with the friendly Indians was distinguishing them in one's rifle sight from enemy Indians. All the expense and years of nurturing relations with the Delaware could dissolve with a nervous or vengeful soldier's musket shot. The Indian allies were encouraged to wear deer tails, leaves, white flannel, or white flags with thirteen red strips. Soldiers and sutlers alike were forbidden to trade with the Indians without permission, supervision, and strict price controls.

After each company was equipped and ready, the general sent it twenty miles down the Ohio River to the Beaver River mouth, where Fort McIntosh was erected. McIntosh arrived on October 25 and hurried his army's final preparations. The year's hourglass was fast running out. The militia's term would expire in January, leaving him with only several hundred regulars. Provisions were short. Complaining that the prices offered were too low, merchants sold little or nothing to the army. Winter assailed the region with frosty days and nights and freezing rains. McIntosh's campaign threatened to dissolve before it took a step into the forest.[90]

Finally, on November 4, McIntosh ordered 1,200 of his best troops to march west along the trail leading to the heart of the Ohio country. The column averaged only five miles daily along the sodden path. Much time was lost gathering forage for the packhorses, which steadily weakened and died one by one from exhaustion and starvation. On November 18, the expedition reached the Tuscaroras River, less than halfway to the Shawnee villages on the Scioto River. The campaign had reached its limit. There, seventy-seven miles due west of Fort McIntosh, Fort Laurens was laid out in a vast meadow on the west bank. It was constructed "mostly of large, hard-wood timber, splits, some six inches thick, bulletproof, planted in trenches three feet deep, solidly packed around, and extending fifteen feet above ground."[91]

The neighboring villages were friendly Delaware and Moravian Indians. During a November 22 council with the Delaware chiefs, McIntosh explained why his army had come and what it would do if the hostiles did not sue for peace. He swore he "will never . . . rest or leave this Country but pursue them while any of them remains upon the face of the earth for I can fill the woods with as many men as the Trees, or as the stones are on the Ground."[92] But that threat was mere bluster, as all could recognize. McIntosh could neither attack nor negotiate with the elusive enemy.

News arrived that Chief White Eyes had died at Fort Pitt. Though Morgan spread the story that smallpox was to blame, the chief was actually murdered by soldiers nearly a year after troops at Fort Randolph had slaughtered Shawnee chief Cornstalk, his son, and two other Indians. In one year, Americans had killed the two most influential Ohio valley chiefs friendly to their cause. McIntosh "buried" White Eyes with gifts to the chiefs in council.

The Delaware swallowed their suspicions and remained loyal. The general was able to resolve a Delaware complaint that the merchants gouged them for essential goods. McIntosh's solution was to impose strict price controls, with a horse costing thirty to fifty dollars depending on its quality, deerskins a dollar for bucks and a half dollar for does, corn a dollar a bushel, and so on. The Delaware remained "entirely peaceable; no attacks from them during the expedition remembered; frequently visited the camp, and brought fine haunches of venison, bear meat, and turkies, and presented to the officers who gave them some of their too beloved fire-water in return. The Indians, both men and women, would have frequent dances, a hundred or more together, the taller taking the lead, and others falling into the circle, according to their height . . . and dancing around the circle to the rude music derived from beating upon a kettle by an old Indian, intermingled with occasional yells."[93]

There was nothing more that McIntosh could do at Fort Laurens. He could not advance or even stay without his troops starving to death. All that remained was to withdraw to the upper Ohio valley. After garrisoning Fort Laurens with 152 troops of the 13th Virginia and 20 troops of the 8th Pennsylvania, and entrusting that command to Colonel Gibson, the general led the rest of the army on the long muddy trail east on December 9.

An award awaited the exhausted troops after they plodded into Fort McIntosh four days later. Capt. Jacob White recalled that their commander "ordered that every man should draw 2 days provision and half a pint of whiskey, and the men generally poor and emaciated, the liquor flew to their heads, and some 2000 (of about 25 or 26 hundred) were quite inebriated in a few minutes. General M[cIntosh] said 'a hair of the same dog was good for the bite; & tomorrow morning you shall all have double rations & another half pint.' But none were seen drunk the next day."[94] After that grand debauch, McIntosh released all his six-month volunteers and settled his regulars into winter quarters, with the 8th Pennsylvania at Fort McIntosh and the 13th Virginia at Fort Pitt and other minor posts.[95]

Other than throw a drinking party for his men that they would never forget, just what did McIntosh achieve? The general flatly failed to attack let alone crush the Ohio tribes. Was it a want of talent or overwhelming circumstances that explain that failure? His campaign was defeated by the late start, short-term enlistments, and dearth of supplies, packhorses, forage, and, above all, daring.[96]

CLARK'S CAMPAIGN

If George Rogers Clark was endowed with any special gift, it was daring. With never more than 200 men, he would wrest the Illinois and lower Wabash territory from Britain and capture the infamous "hair buyer" Hamilton himself. But Clark would find that daring would not be enough to seize faraway Detroit.

On January 2, 1778, Gov. Patrick Henry issued Clark a lieutenant colonel's commission and authorized him to spend 1,200 pounds sterling to raise 350 troops, publicly for Kentucky's defense, but actually for the Illinois campaign. To achieve surprise, those who volunteered in return for promises of 300 acres of land would be not be told where they were heading until they were far down the Ohio River. Henry insisted on secrecy: "You are to take special care to keep the true destination of your forces secret. Its success depends upon this." As for conquering the region, Clark was to "show humanity" to those who submitted and "the miseries of war" to those who resisted.[97]

Two days later, Clark set off to the upper Ohio valley to recruit. Pickings were slim as Virginia and Pennsylvania had already thoroughly combed the region for volunteers. Try as he might, Clark had mustered only about 150 men when he departed from Redstone Creek on the Monongahela River on May 12. A few others signed up at Pittsburgh and Wheeling when he stopped to requisition supplies. The expedition reached Fort Randolph a day after Half King and his warriors broke off their siege and strode up the Kanawha valley. There, Clark's men were joined by twenty families bound for Kentucky and a detachment commanded by Capt. James O'Hara carrying supplies to Kentucky.

The flotilla ground ashore on Corn Island at the Falls of the Ohio on May 27. Clark ordered a fort and supply depot established there and unveiled their true mission. The men greeted the news with varying degrees of enthusiasm or despondency. A score of the latter deserted. The pursuit hauled back seven or eight whom Clark granted clemency for their promise never again to desert. For another month, Clark had the men drill and smoke the meat of game the hunters dragged in.

Clark and his 178 men embarked on June 24, successfully shot the rapids, and rowed the swift current to Fort Massac's ruins opposite the Tennessee River mouth in three days. There, Clark hid the boats and extra supplies. Word of the expedition rowing slowly up the Mississippi would allow Kaskaskia's militia to ready their defense. Clark wanted a total surprise, which could be achieved only by a march through the wilderness to Kaskaskia's rear.

Luck favored Clark. A canoe with hunters ground ashore. Those men had recently visited Kaskaskia and shared word that the town was lightly defended and the population terrified of the Americans. Clark enlisted them as guides. Then a courier arrived with even more vital information—France had allied with the United States. The Americans could now approach Kaskaskia and the other settlements as friends rather than enemies. Once those French settlers learned that Versailles was warring with the Americans, most would likely follow.[98]

On June 28, Clark led his men northwest for a week's trek across the southern Illinois prairies and forests. A crisis arose about midway when the guide got lost. According to Clark, "Never in my life felt such a flow of Rage, to be wandering in a Country where every Nation of Indians could raise three or four times our number and a certain loss of our enterprise by the Enemy's timely notice. I could not bear the thoughts of returning; in Short every idea of the sort served to put me in that passion that I did not master for some time . . . I was . . . determined to put the guide to Death, if he did not find his way."[99] Fortunately for all concerned, the guide picked up the trail several hours later.

Appropriately, they reached Kaskaskia on the evening of July 4. Clark split his small force in two, one to take the town and the other Fort Gage. The Americans overran Kaskaskia without firing a shot. Not a guard was posted to challenge the frontiersmen as they slipped through the dark streets. At Clark's signal, they raised a war whoop, banged on doors, and ordered the terrified people to stay put. Clark burst in on the sole British official in town, Lt. Gov. Philip Francois du Rastel de Rocheblave. When Rocheblave defiantly denounced the rebels, Clark had him handcuffed and his wife and seven children guarded.

Clark swiftly consolidated his rule. The following morning, he gathered Kaskaskia's men at the church, explained the American cause and French alliance, and promised them their lives and property would be safe as long as they supported him and his troops; to a man they agreed. He barracked his men in Fort Gage, which was renamed Fort Clark. He sent Capt. Joseph Bowman and thirty troops fifty miles up the Mississippi valley to occupy Cahokia and gather loyalty oaths from the inhabitants. Bowman accomplished his mission without violence. The Americans and French militia repaired Cahokia's abandoned post and named it Fort Bowman. Daniel Maurice Godefroy de Linctot was named militia captain.

Spanish aid was crucial to the campaign's success. Clark sent Levi Todd up to St. Louis to ask for supplies, information, and the allegiance of the Indians. Once again, Clark could not have been luckier. Lt. Gov. Fernando de Leyba thoroughly sympathized with the Americans and was eager to help. He had been appointed lieutenant governor of upper Louisiana on March 8, 1778, and reached St. Louis on July 10, just after Clark captured Kaskaskia. When Bowman's force took over Cahokia, a couple hundred Cahokia, Sauk, Mascouten, and Kickapoo who were camped nearby fled across the Mississippi to St. Louis and told Leyba that the Americans had taken over Illinois. Leyba reassured them that Spain supported the Americans and encouraged the Indians to stay at peace.

The logic of geopolitics rather than sentiment determined Leyba's position. He shared Madrid's view that American rebellion undermined a British threat to New Spain. British subjects who were mostly French Canadians dominated the upper Mississippi and middle Missouri River fur trade. Leyba was determined to win that trade back for the inhabitants of upper Louisiana, who were also mostly French. To strengthen Spain's stake on the upper Mississippi, he advised abandoning what he deemed the useless and wasteful Fort Carlos III at the Arkansas

River mouth and instead advocated erecting a fort at the Des Moines River mouth to counter British influence at Prairie de Chien at the Wisconsin River mouth farther north.

Vincennes passed into American hands not by soldiers but by Fr. Pierre Gibault and Dr. Jean Laffont, whom Clark sent on July 14 to win over that distant village. Luck once again played a role. Lt. Gov. Edward Abbott had left Vincennes for Detroit only a month before. Shortly after arriving on July 20, Gibault and Laffont gathered the village's men, explained what happened, and got them to swear allegiance to the United States. Jean Marie Philippe Legras accepted a commission as the militia's major. Upon learning of Vincennes' acquiescence to American rule, Clark dispatched Capt. Leonard Helm and four men to raise the flag at Fort Sackville, which they renamed Patrick Henry.

Indian support was also crucial to the campaign's success. Clark spent much of the summer at Cahokia, where he hosted a series of councils with Indian delegations from the region. He eschewed diplomacy for harsh demands and threats. He had no gifts to give and wisely promised none. He offered them nothing but a choice between war and peace. "I am a man and a Warrior and not a councillor," he would proclaim to each delegation as he extended a white peace belt in one hand and red war belt in the other. "Behave like men . . . If you take the bloody path, you shall leave the town in safety . . . We will then try, like warriors, to see who can put the most stumbling blocks in each other's way, and keep our clothes long stained in blood."[100]

Clark's diplomacy was all bluff and bluster that breached etiquette. He lacked both the troops to intimidate the tribes and the money to buy their allegiance. The quick conversion of the French along with Spanish support strengthened his hand. Without French and Spanish allegiance, the tribes would likely have stood firmly against, rather than bowed to, Clark. But Clark's diplomacy worked. None dared raise the war hatchet against him.

At Vincennes, Captain Helm's diplomacy got off to a rocky start when he followed Clark's policy of presenting the chiefs with the stark choice of war or peace. A disgusted and angered Chief Old Tobacco retorted that "you speak in a manner not to be understood. I never yet saw, nor have I heard from my ancestors that it was customary to place good and bad things in the same dish. You talk as if you meant us well, yet you speak of war and peace in the same minute. Thus I treat the speeches . . . with a violent kick."[101] Yet after several days of deliberation among themselves, Old Tobacco and the other chiefs accepted the peace belt. Other tribes in the lower Wabash region—like the White River Delaware, Kickapoo, Mascouten, and Peoria—followed.

Enterprise, audacity, and luck enabled Clark to overcome every challenge. When his men's three-month enlistment was about to expire, he persuaded about 100 to reenlist for another eight months. Those who refused headed back on July 30 toward the upper Ohio, accompanied by Capt. John Montgomery with Rochblave and letters for Gov. Patrick Henry. Clark filled the gaps with French Canadians and Capt. Robert George and sixty men who broke free of Captain

Willing at New Orleans. Though he reveled in the reinforcements, the rumors they carried of Willing's malfeasance disturbed Clark. He confessed to Leyba that "the Intelligence from New Orleans is bad . . . I have long suspected the bad Conduct of an American officer in that Quarter. When plunder is the prevailing Passion of any body of Troops whether Great or Small, their Cuntrey can Expect but little service from them."[102]

Clark's diminishing supplies were replenished just before they ran out. On August 6, he received a boatload from Oliver Pollock in New Orleans. Clark asked for $5,000 worth more. On August 26, Pollock cashed a Virginia draft for $79,087, and from that dispatched $7,200 worth of supplies, including 500 pounds of gunpowder and some swivels upriver. In all, Pollock got Governor Galvez to honor $136,466.85 worth of essentially worthless Virginia credit. Neither Pollock nor Virginia would ever pay off these bills. That money bought desperately needed supplies not just for Clark and other frontier commanders in the Ohio valley, but also for the American armies on the eastern seaboard. For these vital contributions, Oliver Pollock has been called the Robert Morris of the West.[103]

Clark was determined to advance as far up the Wabash as possible before winter. After Vincennes, the next significant settlement upstream was Ouiatenon. There Clark sent Capt. Leonard Helm, Lt. John Bailey, and 100 militia and Indians. They arrived amidst a council between the local Indians and Chippewa. The British agent, Pierre Joseph Celoron de Blainville, escaped capture. He would be the latest of several to bring word to Detroit of the American invasion.

HAMILTON'S CAMPAIGN

The stunning word of Clark's campaign first reached Hamilton at Detroit on August 6 via Francis Maisonville, who was in Illinois when the Americans arrived. But after the shock wore off, Hamilton and his officers assessed the coup's significance. Conquest was too strong a word to describe Clark's initial campaign. His bloodless occupation of the Illinois and Vicennes settlements did shut off the Mississippi valley from the Great Lakes, although the little traffic that circulated on that artery was commercial rather than military. Viewing the British presence there as a financial liability rather than a strategic asset, Gov. Guy Carleton had earlier essentially abandoned the region. Not only did he strip away the regulars, but he also refused to honor any bills of the Royal caretakers left behind, Lieutenant Governors Abbott and Rocheblave. The local French Canadian militia could not be relied upon, especially once they learned that France had allied with the United States. Nor could the region's tribes be expected to resist the invaders; after all, few of their warriors had bothered raiding the Kentucky settlements. So Clark's expedition was hardly a great victory over anything other than fear and want of imagination. Nor did that ragtag handful of Americans threaten Detroit—they were too few and too far away. Even if that clearly audacious leader pulled his followers on to Detroit, they would simply deliver themselves into a death trap sprung by overwhelming numbers of regulars, militia, and Indians. Detroit's militia alone numbered about 575 men split among six companies.[104]

Nonetheless, the American occupation was important. It reduced the danger for American supply and emigrant boats on the upper Mississippi and lower Ohio. From now on, as Hamilton dispatched war parties beyond the Ohio, he would have to keep one eye focused on the lower Wabash. Finally, the takeover drove an American stake into the region that strengthened the rebel bargaining position at the negotiating table. In all, Clark's coup complicated and weakened Britain's strategic position through the Mississippi and Ohio valleys. But more than anything, Clark had inflicted a stinging blow to British pride.

Hamilton resolved to avenge his nation on that upstart and his motley gang. He would first retake Vincennes early that winter and then the Illinois country the following spring. He wrote full reports of what had happened and his intentions to both Canada's governor and the American secretary. Gov. Frederick Haldimand approved Hamilton's plan, urged him "to employ every means" of expelling the invaders, authorized him to recruit volunteers from among Fort Niagara's regulars to his campaign, and wrote Captain De Peyster at Fort Michilimackinac, asking him to assist his colleague in every possible way.[105]

Preparing a wilderness campaign was never an easy task. Complicating Hamilton's effort was his position as Detroit's civil rather than military leader; he had no troops immediately under his command. Capt. Richard Lernoult graciously allowed three officers and thirty soldiers of the 8th Regiment to join Hamilton. To fill the void, Capt. Henry Bird and fifty troops were summoned from Niagara; they arrived on the eve of Hamilton's departure. Indians were essential for the expedition's success. Hamilton sent runners with war belts to distant tribes, especially those on his journey. He held council with the Chippewa, Ottawa, Wyandot, and Potawatomi on September 23 and 29, and induced a number of those warriors to join him. As for supplies, Detroit's warehouses held all that he needed. In late September, he sent ahead ten oxen, ten horses, three pairs of wheels, and 33,000 pounds of supplies to the Miami-Wabash portage.

Rains delayed by days his departure. The expedition finally embarked at two-thirty in the afternoon of October 7. Crammed aboard the bateaux were 232 armed men, including 3 officers and 30 regulars, 14 officers and 71 militia, 3 gunners, and 14 officers and 70 Indians, along with supplies. Other Indians would join his force en route.[106] The expedition sailed and rowed to Grand Rapids, fourteen miles up the Maumee. There, everything had to be unloaded and carried around eight different rapids, which together fell around fifty-five feet, while the boats were dragged upstream. That took five arduous days.

On October 21, Hamilton got word of McIntosh's campaign toward Detroit. Should Hamilton forge on to Vincennes or withdraw to Detroit's defense? He chose to push on, hoping that hundreds of wilderness miles and the late season would stall the American campaign. He judged correctly.

The expedition reached the juncture of the St. Mary and St. Joseph Rivers, which form the Maumee, on October 24. The following day, Hamilton held council with a mélange of different tribes, including the Miami, Wea, Wyandot, Ottawa, Chippewa, Cherokee, Shawnee, and Mascouten. Many joined his expedition. Then the British began the backbreaking labor of carrying the mountain of supplies and bateaux on that nine-mile-long portage. After reembarking, the next important stop was at Ouiatenon. There, Hamilton tried to undo any diplomatic damage caused by Helm's envoys to those tribes. On December 1, he made his plea before the gathered chiefs and was able to elicit assertions of their loyalty. From Ouiatenon, there were no significant Indian villages or white settlements until Vincennes. Hoping to achieve a surprise, Hamilton urged his rowers down the Wabash's swift current.

So far, Hamilton's first independent command was making steady progress. What kind of chief was Hamilton? The leadership necessary to shine on a European parade ground could not differ more from that of a wilderness post let alone a campaign. Hamilton never truly abandoned the former nor embraced the latter. On the march to Vincennes, he insisted on military discipline even though only a handful of redcoats brightened the mix of frontiersmen and Indians. That stirred some resentment among the Indians. Against advice, he positioned the Miami at the column's rear rather than at the head with their war bundles leveled toward the enemy. He grudgingly relented when they protested. Fearful that alcohol would demonize his Indians, he pointedly withheld its use from all ceremonies, even refusing to wet the grindstone with rum when he presented the war hatchet. These minor breaches of etiquette aside, Hamilton strove sincerely and largely succeeded in mastering Indian diplomacy. During councils, he spoke with poetry, metaphorically "buried" the dead with gifts, and sang the songs and danced the steps of war.

Like many more sensitive whites, Hamilton harbored a contemptuous fascination for the Indians. At times, he succumbed to the powerful sensuous mystery of being among them. Night after night, he thrilled at the "various tunes in various languages bellowed aloud by these heralds of the night, the thickness of the Wood and darkness of the Weather with the blaze of a great many large fires extending along the Savage camp for a considerable length, the intervals of silence from time to time broken by these horrible Songs, sometimes by a Chorus of Wolves in full cry after the Deer, formed a very strange but striking medley."[107]

Hamilton was harsher toward white "savages" who presumably should know better: "The characters of most of the Europeans who have dealings with them are not likely to improve the morals, or remove the jealousies of the Indians, as in all remote posts are to be found the most faithless and abandoned among the Traders—Men of that stamp will naturally attempt to push their fortune where they are least known."[108]

The expedition camped within a few hours' hike of Vincennes on December 16. Hamilton sent out two scouting parties, that of Lieutenant Vernet and some chiefs over land and that of Maj. Jehu Hay, Capt. William La Mothe, and his militia company downstream by canoe. Their mission was to gather intelligence and secure a landing above town for the rest of the expedition the next morning. Hay's departure sparked a ruckus as "the young Indians fearing they should not share in the busyness, got in a violent hurry into their canoes with design to accompany him, some of the Chiefs with the interpreters came in haste to inform me [Hamilton] of it. I ran directly to the waterside and with some difficulty pacified them. In the evening went to their camp and represented to the Chiefs, the absolute necessity of their young men being obedient and attentive to order."[109] Such were the constant demands on frontier commanders.

Snow and frigid winds filled the sky the next day, December 17. The expedition landed a mile above town and joined with Hay's command. Together they swiftly marched toward the fort. The 6-pounder was loaded and pointed toward the gate. Hamilton called on Helm to surrender.[110]

Despite Hamilton's speed and precautions, Captain Helm got wind of the enemy's approach. When the British appeared before the fort, he was able to dash off a letter to Clark: "I heard of their coming several days before hand, I sent spies . . . I never got intelligence until they got within 3 miles of the town, as I had called the militia & had all assurance of their integrity I order, at the fireing of the Cannon, every man to appear but I saw but few . . . My determination is to defend the Garrison though I have but 21 men . . . not four men that I can really depend on, but am determined to act brave."[111]

With that six-pounder leveled toward his fort and several hundred enemies eager for combat, Helm decided to negotiate for the best possible terms. Hamilton promised to protect his garrison from the Indians but nothing else. Upon accepting, Helms ordered the flag hauled down and gate opened. Despite Hamilton's attempt at restraining them, the Indians swarmed into the fort and looted but did not harm any of the defenders. No shot was fired; the only casualty was an Indian who broke his arm trying to squeeze through a storehouse window.

Hamilton chose to winter at Vincennes rather than continue on to attack Clark in Illinois. It was a prudent choice. The winter rains were drowning the lowlands. The militia and many Indians were petitioning to go home. The French Canadians had pledged loyalty to the Americans and had to be enticed back to British rule. Supplies were limited. Intelligence of the enemy was nonexistent. Reinforcements, provisions, and information would arrive no sooner than the spring.

For now, the British had to consolidate their hold on Vincennes. Hamilton forced all the French inhabitants to gather in the church at noon on December 19. There he warned them "that they could not expect protection unless they adjured their attachment to the Rebels, and returned to their Allegiance to their rightful Sovereign, renewing their Oath . . . Two hundred and fifty men capable of bearing arms signed their names to this oath, having first kissed a silver crucifix at the foot of the altar." Hamilton had no illusions that the French oaths were much more than a charade: "I have no reason to doubt their having immediately after turned their thoughts to the accomplishment of their treacherous designs."[112] Nonetheless, he organized them into militia companies and drilled them beyond Fort Sackville's walls. He could then release for home the Detroit militia and those Indians who demanded it.

On December 20, scouts under Lieutenant De Quindre brought in two suspects, Canadian Antoine Renard and Spaniard Francis Vigo, whom they arrested on the trail from Kaskaskia. After interrogating them, Hamilton was convinced they were merely merchants. He freed the two with their promise that they would not reveal the British had retaken Vincennes. That proved to be a fatal mistake.

Hamilton then dispatched war parties to gather intelligence and ideally capture Clark. About thirty Ottawa and Canadians left on December 24 toward Kaskaskia. The next day, thirteen Indians led by the Potawatomi chiefs Wyndeego and Eskibee followed. Five Kickapoo left on December 27. Nineteen Ouiatenon headed by Petite Face and Charles Beaubien departed the next day.

There was little more that Hamilton could do besides keep his garrison busy drilling and repairing the fort. Before them was the long, dull wait until the spring. Then supplies and reinforcements would allow them to reembark for the reconquest of the Illinois.

CHAPTER 7

"The Nests Are Destroyed": 1779

Our hard trials are now near at an end—Our great Friend the King of
France & we have tied the hands and the feet of the King of England &
laid him on his back—he bites & kicks & scolds like a drunken mad-
man, but it is our business to keep him tied.
                                        —George Morgan
                                          to Delaware Indians

We have put new Strings to your Bows and straiten'd your Arrows. That
when you see your Enemies at a great distance you may be able to
shoot thro' them.
                                        —Indian women to men

By 1779, the war on the northeastern seaboard had deadlocked. Neither
side was able to crush the other. It was a David and Goliath struggle where
the giant was too ponderous to catch the nimble weakling who lacked a killing
sling and rock. Wearied from the futility of chasing Washington's small, elusive
army, the British hunkered down in New York. But Washington was no more
capable of taking that city than the British were of taking him. Not only were the
Americans outgunned four to one, but British supply vessels sailed unmolested if
not fearlessly to and from New York's harbor. The appearance of a French fleet
off Sandy Hook was always possible ever since Versailles had embraced the
rebels. A want of audacity among French admirals and captains, however, made
that unlikely.

The deadlock heartened rather than discouraged the Americans. If arms could
not defeat the redcoats, time would. Command of the sea might allow the British
to stay indefinitely and land an army anywhere, but as the unwinnable war ground
on, ever more prominent Britons asked why. The national debt piled ever higher
while the economy sputtered along, all to no purpose. Squeezed creditors and
merchants pressured Whitehall to cut the nation's losses and restore British prosperity and dynamism. Even if the Americans won political independence, they
would remain dependent on British goods, credit, and markets. If all the king's
soldiers and sailors could not destroy the Revolution, British counting houses and
factory floors could. Or so the reasoning went.

If independence was a matter of time, what became independent was not. A United States contained east of the Appalachian watershed would be a nation permanently stunted and trod upon by Britain and other great powers. A new nation stretching from the Atlantic to the Mississippi would have the elbow room to grow in population, wealth, and power, and thus someday, argued some visionaries, be able to push its frontiers beyond, perhaps to the Pacific itself.

Nearly all patriots understood that. But the priorities and details were up for grabs. Regional, state, mercantile, ethnic, and occupation groups battled each other and pressured Congress to champion their respective interests. Those states with land claims west of the Appalachians were most adamant in demanding that the United States unroll to the Mississippi River. Those who had already settled in that region sought unimpeded navigation on the Mississippi River all the way to the Gulf of Mexico, with the right to deposit goods in New Orleans. On the seaboard, mercantile interests desired free trade with Britain and other countries. Nascent industrialists demanded high tariffs against competitive foreign goods. New England fishermen fought for continued access to the Newfoundland fishing banks.

Those interests complemented rather than conflicted with one another. It was not difficult to forge a consensus that embraced all those ambitions. On February 23, the foreign affairs committee issued a proposal to Congress that the United States assert boundaries that embraced the entire Great Lakes region as far north as Lake Nipissing, extended as far west as the Mississippi River, and rested along the thirty-first parallel with the Floridas, which would go to Spain in return for an alliance. The United States would insist on the rights to navigate the Mississippi River, lease space in New Orleans warehouses, and fish off Newfoundland. The proposals satisfied the major interest groups that fed off the frontier—fishermen, hunters, peddlers, farmers, speculators, and vagabonds. Congress voted overwhelmingly in favor of those goals on March 19.

Only the most expansive visionaries lost out. Notably absent from the wish list were Canada, Nova Scotia, and the Floridas. With varying degrees of regret or relief, the congressmen acknowledged that they were unlikely to gain diplomatically what they could not take militarily. America's invasion of Canada had been a fiasco that cost a mountain of dead and debt. As for the Floridas, the immediate need for an ally outweighed whatever future economic potential was locked in those distant swamplands. But by abandoning a claim to the Floridas, the United States effectively walled itself off from the Gulf of Mexico.

Agreeing on war aims was the easy part. A far greater challenge for the infant republic was to wring acceptance of those boundaries from the great powers— Britain, France, and Spain. On September 25, Congress expanded its diplomatic missions by appointing John Adams to negotiate a peace treaty with Britain and John Jay an alliance with Spain, while fresh instructions were sent to the envoys already in Paris to secure French recognition of that desired frontier.

Possession was nine-tenths of international as well as national law. America's case for those frontiers was only as good as its grip over them. Congress authorized a two-pronged strategy to win the West, with one campaign capturing Detroit and the other Niagara. As for the Mississippi, Clark had to cling to Kaskaskia and a new fort to be erected near where the Ohio flows into that river. At a glance, the plan made sense, but a plan is only as sound as the power to fulfill it. Lacking adequate means, both campaigns would ultimately fail while America's presence on the upper Mississippi would eventually recede.

THE FRONTIER AND INTERNATIONAL DIPLOMACY
American diplomacy with Spain failed. John Jay was a poor choice for envoy to that proud kingdom. Foreign Minister Jose Monino y Redondo de Floridablanca brushed off the request for recognition of American independence and alliance from the arrogant, extravagant, brash, and demanding Jay, who personified all that the Spanish imagined, despised, and feared in Americans. Although it was in Spain's interests to join the war against Britain, the foreign minister scoffed at any notion of recognizing the rebels, let alone allying with them.

Floridablanca wielded more subtle diplomacy with his French counterpart, Charles Gravier de Vergennes, who continued his frustrating efforts to woo Spain into the war. Vergennes grounded his appeals in sentiment, honor, law, and greed, often called national interests. By sentiment, honor, and law, France and Spain had been allies since 1762, when they signed a family compact between the Bourbon family rulers of the two kingdoms. It was past time for the Spanish to dust off and fulfill the letter and spirit of that treaty. More powerfully motivating was the lengthening list of possible new possessions Vergennes's dangled before the Spanish. But Floridablanca stayed coy despite Vergennes offer to help Spain recover Jamaica, Gibraltar, Minorca, the Floridas, and British settlements on the Caribbean coasts of Nicaragua and Honduras. To this list, Floridablanca demanded a joint armada to invade England and no separate peace. Vergennes reluctantly agreed after eliciting a Spanish promise to assist France in regaining the Newfoundland fisheries, Senegal, and the Caribbean island of Dominica. Since the United States treaty with France also stipulated no separate peace, American independence and frontier expansion were straitjacketed within the war aims of Versailles and Madrid. Despite this, Spain continued to spurn recognizing or allying with the United States.

With considerable trepidation, the Spanish renewed the family compact on April 12. The first pact seventeen years earlier had been a debacle for both kingdoms. Would the reassertion of Bourbon solidarity be any less disastrous than the previous venture? There was reason to be optimistic about their prospects. On paper, the marriage of French and Spanish naval power overshadowed that of Britain in quantity if not quality. That year, the French fleet numbered 63 ships of the line and the Spanish 58, for a combined 121 to the British 90. Victory, however, would grace the side with superior strategy, tactics, seamanship, and gunnery rather than sheer numbers.[1]

Spain withdrew its ambassador from London on June 21 and formally declared war against Britain on July 8. Word of the pending declaration had been dispatched to Spain's envoys and colonial administrators a month earlier, on May 18. Messages, of course, traveled only as fast as sails or steeds could propel them. It was not until late July that the news reached Louisiana governor Bernardo de Galvez in New Orleans. A warning to West Florida's commanding general, John Campbell, was not far behind. The British considered themselves at war when diplomatic relations were cut. Lord Germain promptly wrote Campbell on June 25 of the event and ordered him to prepare a campaign against New Orleans and upper Louisiana. Which governor would first learn of his kingdom's new enemy? Which would land the first punch?

THE SOUTHWEST FRONTIER

For Louisiana governor Bernardo de Galvez, the war declaration was hardly unexpected. He had done what he could to prepare for war. Ever since the American Revolution had begun, tensions had risen steadily between Louisiana and West Florida. Throughout 1779, the governors exchanged letters condemning the other's aggressions and defending their own. Galvez's courier was Capt. Jacinto Panis, who returned with intelligence that West Florida's defenses were but a shadow of what the Spanish had feared. The several hundred troops scattered among West Florida's garrisons suffered from a dearth of supplies and morale; the crumbling forts mounted only a few of their cannons. Panis presented a plan to Galvez on August 16, 1779, that argued West Florida was ripe for conquest if Spain could muster enough ships, troops, munitions, provisions, and, above all, will.

Galvez nodded in agreement. The first blow, however, should be struck not against the Gulf, but at British settlements up the Mississippi River. Galvez had just enough troops to do that and defend New Orleans against a surprise British attack from Pensacola. By the summer of 1779, Galvez's 437 regulars had been augmented by 153 troops from the Canary Islands and 106 from Mexico.

Galvez had hoped to embark up the Mississippi on August 22, but a hurricane blasted through four days before and wrecked much of the flotilla of boats. This would not be the last time that nature disrupted his timetable, but Galvez's will always prevailed over that of the gods. With characteristic energy, he put his men to work salvaging the wrecks. On August 27, the expedition headed upstream. It numbered 667 troops, including 500 regulars, 20 carabiniers, 60 militia, 80 free blacks and mulattoes, and Oliver Pollock and seven other Americans, along with ten cannons. As they slowly ascended the river, that force became a magnet for militia and Indians who wished to enjoy the plunder and glory that they hoped lay ahead. Galvez's army numbered 1,427 when it reached Fort Manchac on September 6. At dawn the next morning, the governor ordered an assault on the decrepit, ill-manned fort. It was a near bloodless victory, with one defender killed and twenty taken prisoner. Six others escaped to carry word to Baton Rouge.[2]

The Spanish army arrived before Baton Rouge four days later. With about 400 regulars, 150 militia, and eighteen cannons surrounded by earthen walls and a moat eighteen feet wide and nine feet deep, Fort Baton Rouge would have to be bombarded into surrender. The trenches zigzagged forward. By September 21, a battery was emplaced and opened fire. The shots killed or wounded a score of defenders. Capt. Alexander Dickson asked for terms. Galvez demanded he surrender not just his fort, but Natchez as well. Dickson agreed. While the militia was disarmed and sent home, 375 regulars became Spanish prisoners. Capt. Juan de la Villebeuvre led fifty troops north to take Natchez. On October 5, he occupied Fort Panmure on that town's edge.

Galvez meanwhile returned with the bulk of his army to New Orleans. His ability to hold Britain's Mississippi settlements depended on clearing British vessels from the maze of lakes and bayous connecting the river and Gulf above New Orleans. Here American operations were decisive. Dominating Lake Pontchartrain was the HMS *West Florida,* with two 6-pounders, two 4-pounders, one 9 $\frac{1}{2}$-inch mortar, and a thirty-man crew. Undaunted, American captain William Pickles weighed anchor aboard his sloop the *Morris* with four 2 $\frac{1}{2}$-pounders, one 1 $\frac{1}{2}$-pounder, and a twenty-man crew against the better-armed British ship. On September 11, the two closed for combat and exchanged shots. The *Morris* rammed the *West Florida.* The Americans swarmed aboard, killing the British captain and three others. Within minutes, the British had struck their colors. Pickles then sailed to the small settlements around the lake and forced the inhabitants to take loyalty oaths to the United States. By September 26, the *Morris* was on the Gulf, where it captured a merchant ship with $2,660 worth of slaves. Around the same time, Spanish ships in the Gulf took three galleys and a barge. The largest prize went to Capt. Vizente Rillieux, who ambushed a British transport bound for Manchac at a narrow passage. The shock of the unexpected gunfire cowed the fifty-six-man crew and soldiers, who surrendered when Rillieux and his dozen men boarded.

Galvez's conquests were so swift and decisive that the British had no time to react. Indeed, word of his attacks came shortly after Germain's letter announcing Spain's war declaration and ordering Brig. Gen. John Campbell to attack New Orleans reached Pensacola on September 9. Two days later, the general replied that he lacked the means to do so. Though he had stepped ashore at Pensacola in January at the head of 1,200 troops, mostly Germans from Waldeck and loyalists from Pennsylvania and Maryland, disease and desertion had steadily whittled his army's ranks. Transport and supplies needed for campaign were short. Nor could the Choctaw or Creek Indians be relied upon. The British could not think of taking New Orleans, but only of defending West Florida against a possible Spanish attack from Havana or New Orleans. At best, Campbell could strengthen his own defenses, but inexplicably he failed to do even that.[3]

THE SOUTHEAST FRONTIER

That year's British losses in West Florida were offset by gains in Georgia.[4] Having captured Savannah on December 29, Lt. Col. Archibald Campbell awaited the arrival of Brig. Gen. Augustine Prevost's 900 troops. On January 6, Prevost landed his army at Colonel's Island, a few miles from Sunbury, the state's second largest port, and marched on that town. Guarding Sunbury's southern approach was Fort Morris, with its 210-man garrison commanded by Maj. Joseph Lane.

Prevost emplaced batteries around Fort Morris and ordered them to open fire. After a short bombardment, Prevost issued a surrender demand. Faced with overwhelming odds, Lane gave up on January 9. Leaving behind a garrison at Sunbury, Prevost marched the bulk of his army to Savannah on January 15.

The first phase of the British campaign was a dazzling success. Within three weeks, they had captured the seaports of Savannah and Sunbury, and killed, wounded, or captured nearly 800 Americans. The campaign's second stage of conquering Georgia's interior could now begin. With Lt. Col. Thomas Brown and his Florida Scouts ranging far ahead, Campbell set off with 3,000 troops up the Savannah River valley toward Augusta on January 23. Brown was determined to seize Augusta, the site of his horrible and humiliating torture four years earlier. Awaiting Brown's arrival at Augusta were Lt. Col. James Ingram and 250 men. The rangers first attacked a log fort on Augusta's outskirts but were driven back, leaving five dead; a musket ball plowed through Brown's arm. The rangers withdrew to Campbell. Hours before the steady advance of Campbell's army, the Americans abandoned Fort Henderson on Spirit Creek on January 30 and then Augusta on January 31. Eleven hundred loyalists from the region flocked to Augusta to enlist in twenty militia companies. The British hold on Augusta seemed unshakable. It was not.

Gen. Andrew Williamson gathered an American army at Fort Moore's Bluff. By mid-February, 1,600 reinforcements, including 1,200 North Carolina militia, had joined his 800 troops. Williamson prepared to march on Augusta. Believing he was outnumbered and would be cut off, Campbell abandoned Augusta on February 14 and retreated back down the Savannah River valley. That same day, Colonels Andrew Pickens and John Dooley and Lieutenant Colonels Elijah Clarke and John Twiggs led the 300 Carolina and Georgia militia to rout 700 loyalists commanded by Col. John Boyd at Kettle Creek on February 13. At a loss of only 9 killed and 23 wounded, the patriots mortally wounded Boyd, killed 40 Tories, captured 70, and scattered most, while only 270 loyalists managed to reach Campbell's army on February 18. The Americans hanged 5 loyalist leaders who had broken their oath and released the rest with their promise to go home and sit out the war.

The British got their revenge. Gen. John Ashe had shadowed Campbell's retreat down the Savannah River valley. Campbell halted when Prevost joined him from Savannah. The two men devised a daring plan. While Campbell dug in, Prevost would embark on a fifty-mile trek around the enemy lines. That trek ended on February 28, when Prevost trapped Ashe's troops with their backs to Briar Creek, sixty miles from Savannah. At a loss of only 5 killed and 11 wounded, the British killed nearly 200 Americans and captured 170. The victorious army then withdrew to Savannah. Campbell sailed off to England, leaving Prevost in civil as well as military command until Gov. James Wright stepped ashore from exile.

The British campaign against Georgia was supposed to coincide with Indian attacks against the frontier, but the Cherokee and Creek war parties were tardy. Had warriors pinned down the American settlers, the British most likely would have held Augusta. As usual, the British found it impossible to coordinate their far-flung offensives. It was not until February 1 that John Stuart wrote his deputies David Tait and Alexander Cameron to rally respectively the Upper Creek and Cherokee, and fight their way to Campbell at Augusta. Stuart added a caveat that his deputies insist that the Indians not murder women, children, or loyalists. By February 10, Tait had gathered 400 Creek and headed east. Meanwhile, Alexander Cameron collected only 100 Cherokee and started toward the settlements.

Learning that a large Creek war party was heading toward the British lines, Gen. Andrew Williamson sent 600 militia under Col. Andrew Pickens and LeRoy Hammond of South Carolina and Col. John Dooley of Georgia to intercept them. Hammond and his men collided with an advance party of Creek on March 22, charged, and killed eight and captured six, including three whites. The next day, Colonel Pickens scattered a different Creek party.

Word of these defeats and Campbell's retreat from Augusta disheartened most Creek, who returned sullenly to their villages. Only Chief Emistisiguo would lead 100 Creek into Savannah. The Indian discouragement deepened when they learned that Superintendent John Stuart had died on March 21. A large war party of Cherokee advancing toward the frontier would soon turn back.

While the previous year's campaigns had devastated most Cherokee villages and forced the chiefs to sue for peace, Dragging Canoe and his followers stayed defiant. Earlier that year, Gov. Patrick Henry had organized an expedition against the Chickamauga. On April 10, Col. Evan Shelby, Col. John Montgomery, and Maj. Charles Robertson led 900 Virginia and North Carolina militia from Fort Patrick Henry on Long Island down the Holston and Tennessee Rivers to attack Dragging Canoe's villages along Chickamauga Creek. Reaching the mouth on April 20, they advanced upstream, burning eleven villages but killing only a half-dozen warriors. Dragging Canoe and his followers disappeared into the Chattanooga Mountains. With nothing left to destroy, Shelby led the bulk of the troops back up the Tennessee, while Montgomery and 100 troops continued downstream to reinforce Clark in Kentucky.

It was a difficult year for the British to raise war parties against the frontier. The worst challenge was to keep mass starvation at bay, or even worse, to prevent their bitter supplicants from turning on their patrons. That winter, smallpox had burned through the southeastern Indians, killing off hundreds of hunters and sowers. Most Indians were eating their seed corn. Cameron bluntly admitted this to Germain, extolling Stuart, who had done "so well for the Country that he lived so long, for had he died in any period for these two years past when no Troops of ours were to be seen to the Southward the very Measures now Adopted by his Excellency Governor Chester would have prompted the Indians to fall upon us; and the present Commissioners might talk to no manner of Purpose."[5] David Tait reported that the Creek and Cherokee "came to Pensacola in the winter and spring which Occasions a very great Expence in provisions and presents, especially to the Cherokees who had nothing to subsist upon in their own Country . . . being so much harassed in their nation as to prevent them making a sufficient Quantity of Provisions."[6]

Hoping to block further Creek incursions, Maj. Gen. Benjamin Lincoln crossed his army over the upper Savannah River on April 20. Maj. Gen. Augustine Prevost countered by sidestepping Lincoln and quick-marching toward Charles Town. Responding to an urgent plea by South Carolina governor John Rutledge, Lincoln pursued on May 6. Prevost drew up his army before Charles Town on May 12 and demanded that Rutledge surrender. The governor and other prominent South Carolinians conferred and then issued a response—they promised neutrality for the war's duration if the British army did not occupy the city. With Lincoln threatening his rear, Prevost withdrew his army back to Savannah. Along the way, his rear guard fought off Lincoln's attack at the Stono River crossing on June 20, with each side suffering about 150 casualties. Prevost and the bulk of his army fortified themselves in Savannah while the general ringed the seaport with the advanced posts of Brown's Florida Scouts at Ebenezer, Delancey's New York brigade at Sunbury, the New Jersey volunteers at Ogeechee, and the 71st at Beaufort.

Indians puzzled Prevost as they did most officers. In June, David Holmes led in 140 Creek, bringing that tribe's total with Prevost to over 300 warriors. But what was Prevost to do with that savage horde other than feed it and try to avoid its incessant demands for councils and gifts? What he did not do was send them back to join other war parties harassing the frontier. Rather than kill or be killed on the frontier, scores of those warriors squatting in Savannah's squalid trenches would perish from an enemy they could not fight—disease. More Indians were on the way.

In midsummer, 300 Lower and Middle Cherokee rallied by Alexander Cameron strode toward Augusta. Aware of their approach, Gen. Andrew Williamson used psychology rather than his 750 troops to defeat them. He sent word by Cherokee messengers that he would let them go home if they handed over Cameron and other loyalist leaders. While the warriors refused to surrender the agents, their ferocity wilted before the bold demand, exaggerated accounts of the number of American troops before them, and true word of the smallpox epidemic raging in Savannah. After assuring Williamson that they would not fight, the Cherokee returned morosely to their villages. Williamson then marched his army through their land and beyond to those Chickamauga villages that had escaped the earlier expedition and torched them.

Britain's Indian policy in the region was in complete disarray in the months following John Stuart's death. His deputies Alexander Cameron and Charles Stuart, along with West Florida governor Peter Chester, vied for the superintendent's position while awaiting orders from Whitehall. On June 25, Germain issued orders to split the Southern Indian Department between the two Florida colonies, with an Atlantic division embracing the Creek, Seminole, and Cherokee, headed by Thomas Brown at St. Augustine, and a Mississippi division that included the Choctaw and Chickasaw under Cameron at Pensacola. That division may have made sense to Germain, glancing at an inaccurate map of the region in faraway London, but for the Creek, Pensacola was much more accessible than St. Augustine. In an attempt to rein in ever rising costs, each division would be annually allocated only 1,955 pounds sterling, while the region's ranking commander would divvy out from his discretionary fund other necessary expenses as they arose. The superintendents would definitely earn every pence of their meager salaries. Rather than hole up in the relative comforts of a colonial port and await the visits of their charges, as did John Stuart, the agents were expected to spend nearly all their time on the trail from one village to the next. In the budget, Germain was just following Parliament's bidding. The legislators were appalled that Stuart's expenses had soared from 19,000 to 77,000 pounds sterling in just three years, with nothing more than a handful of scattered Indian attacks let alone an overwhelming alliance and offensive to show for it.[7]

Good economy was not necessarily good politics. Indians were mercenaries. They tended to sell either tribal nonaggression or a more expensive alliance to the highest bidder. Regardless, they expected a patron to supply them enough munitions and other provisions to deter starvation. As a Choctaw chief put it, if "two People love us whoever gives us the most will be the most Regarded."[8] Never firm, the affections of the southern Indians for the British would steadily corrode as the Great Father's generosity turned to stinginess.

The Americans tried to fill the gap, at least with the Cherokee. The southern colonies split the duty for nurturing relations, with Virginia caring for the Overhill, North Carolina the Middle, and South Carolina the Lower villages. But the Americans could give nothing but platitudes, promises, and threats.

By late summer, the war in the southeast had stalemated. The British bridgehead around Savannah was too strong to be overrun and too weak and slow to chase down and destroy the hovering rebel forces. Then, on September 8, Admiral d'Estaing, with 3,000 troops aboard twenty-five ships of the line and five frigates, dropped anchor at the Savannah River mouth. By September 12, d'Estaing and his army joined 7,000 American troops led by Benjamin Lincoln before Savannah. It was not until September 15 that d'Estaing demanded that Prevost surrender his 2,500 troops and 100 cannons. Prevost delayed answering a day and then rejected the demand. The allies began zigzagging trenches and planting batteries ever closer to the British lines. The siege guns opened fire on October 4. It seemed that time was on the allied side, but d'Estaing was nervous for his fleet's safety from hurricanes or prowling British squadrons. When Prevost spurned yet another surrender demand, d'Estaing persuaded Lincoln to force the issue. On October 9, the two generals led their troops in a grand assault against the Spring Hill redoubt guarding the Augusta road. The attackers were repelled after 700 French and 450 Americans fell dead or wounded while inflicting a mere 150 casualties on the British. A slightly wounded d'Estaing reembarked with his army's remnants and sailed away. Lincoln and his troops withdrew up the Savannah River valley.

That failure was decisive. Had d'Estaing been patient, Savannah most likely would have fallen within weeks, and with it, Britain's southern strategy. Instead, that reckless assault tipped the region's precarious power balance. The following year, a more massive British army would burst through the Savannah bridgehead into the Carolinas while the Creek and Cherokee were emboldened to raid the frontiers. An admiral's prudence might have spared the four southern states the agony of three years of brutal warfare that devastated the region.

THE NORTHERN SEABOARD

Aside from the campaign in Georgia and South Carolina, which receded to a bridgehead at Savannah by late summer, the British elsewhere on the seaboard launched raids rather than offensives. They captured Stony Point and Verplanck, fifty miles up the Hudson River. Entrenched in Castine, Maine, they repelled a rebel flotilla that was later scuttled when a British squadron appeared. Wielding their sea power, they raided and burned Portsmouth and Suffolk in Virginia, and Danbury, Fairfield, and New Haven in Connecticut. The local militia could at best only conduct a fighting withdrawal before the overwhelming invaders and then march into the smoldering ruins left behind by British looters and arsonists.

The Americans did win two minor victories that raised their spirits. On July 16, a bayonet assault by Maj. Gen. Anthony Wayne's light infantry on Stony Point netted 543 prisoners, of whom 74 were wounded, and 20 dead redcoats at a cost of 15 dead and 84 wounded. At a cost of 10 killed and wounded, Maj. Henry Lee captured 158 troops and killed 50 in an attack on Paulus Hook on August 19.[9] But while the Americans could nibble away at British outposts, Gen. Henry Clinton and his army nestled securely beyond reach within impregnable New York. That city's capture was as much an impossible dream for George Washington as Detroit's would prove to be for George Rogers Clark.

CLARK VERSUS HAMILTON

The Americans occupying the Illinois villages were ignorant that Henry Hamilton had reconquered Vincennes in December and sent war parties to spy on them. One of those war parties reached Kaskaskia in early January. For days, Ottawa chief Egushawai, thirty warriors, and six Canadians lurked dangerously nearby, biding their time for a coup. Learning from someone at Kaskaskia that Clark planned to visit Cahokia, they set an ambush about three miles north of the village.

Sure enough, Clark set forth in a carriage escorted by a few men. As fate would have it, the carriage got stuck in the snow not far from where a half-dozen scouts from the war party lay in wait, but they were too far to fire accurately at Clark and his men and too close to slip away unseen and bring back the others. They had no choice but to stay hidden. Clark and his men finally pushed the carriage from the snowdrift and headed on to Prairie du Rocher that night. Only later did they learn of the unsprung ambush. A hunter found the raiders' main camp and hurried back to sound the alarm. That same day, the Indians also captured two black woodcutters but foolishly let them go with the promise they would not reveal the natives' presence. Clark organized a pursuit, but the raiders slipped away back to Vincennes.[10]

That lurking war party was the first sign that Vincennes might have fallen. The suspicion was confirmed on January 29, when Francisco Vigo arrived from there and told all to Clark. That spring, Hamilton would gather an Indian army and first retake Illinois, then crush the Kentucky settlements, and finally head up the Ohio River and capture every fort until the British had conquered the entire region west of the Appalachians.

Most commanders would have sat tight, strengthened their defense, called for reinforcements, and awaited Hamilton's attack later that year. Clark chose a far bolder path. He would attack first: "Being sensible that without a reinforcement which at present I have hardly a right to Expect that I shall be obliged to give up this Cuntrey to Mr. Hamilton without a turn of Fortune in my favour, I am resolved to . . . Risque the whole on a Single Battle . . . Great things have been affected by a few Men well Conducted."[11] Surprise was essential to his campaign's success. Clark reckoned that "the enemy could not suppose that we should be so mad as to attempt to march eighty leagues through a drowned country in the depths of winter."[12]

Not only would Clark attack, but he would also split his already meager number of troops before an enemy that Vigo reported outnumbered his. One party would journey by river and the other overland to converge at Vincennes in about three weeks. On February 5, Lt. John Rogers, forty-two men, two 4-pounders, four swivels, and supplies crowded aboard the keelboat *Willing* for the roundabout river route. Rogers's mission was not to join the attack on Vincennes, but to intercept Hamilton should he attempt to escape downriver or protect Clark and his men should they be repulsed. The following day, February 6, Clark led 171 men and a dozen packhorses east on the 180-mile trek from Kaskaskia to Fort Sackville at Vincennes. What followed was one of the more epic marches in military history.[13]

At times, the land party would wonder whether they had not mistakenly taken the river route instead. The unusually heavy winter rains had transformed the ground into saturated mud or shallow lakes. The trek was miserable, with the men constantly soaked and freezing. But Clark was a brilliant leader who kept their spirits high: "I suffered them to shoot game on all occasions and feast on it like Indians war dances—each company by turns inviting the other to their feasts—which was the case every night."[14] Those men were hardened not just by years of surviving in the wilderness, but also by a lust for vengeance: "Never [were] Men so animated with thoughts of revenging the wrongs done to their Settlements as this small Army was."[15] The misery and hardships strengthened rather than weakened them: "They really began to think themselves superior to other men, and that neither the rivers nor the season could stop their progress. Their whole conversation now was concerning what they would do when they got about the enemy."[16] To that grim end, they stoically pushed on.

On February 13, they reached the Little Wabash River. Miles of seemingly bottomless brown waters drowned the forests and meadows beyond. Clark ordered a halt while they built a pirogue and rested their exhausted bodies and spirits. They crossed the river two days later, plying the sick and supplies in the pirogue until all were across. They slogged on another twenty miles to the Little Embarrass River, which had swelled into a vast lake. Encamped on a small sodden island, they were only a half-dozen miles from Vincennes. Clark had his men hollow out another pirogue.

Snug in their fort, Hamilton and his men were oblivious to Clark's approach. Who would have imagined the enemy would be so crazy as to try the seemingly impossible? Patrols prowled for miles beyond Fort Sackville, and a war party occasionally strode in or out of the gates, but none bothered scouting the flooded lands west of the Wabash.

Hamilton tasked himself with administration and diplomacy. On January 13, he wrote Gov. Bernardo de Galvez, asking him to prohibit and cut off any gunpowder shipments from New Orleans to the Americans. He counciled many times with the local tribes and visiting Indian delegations. Meanwhile, his force melted through January and February. Most of the Indians drifted back to their distant villages for the winter hunt, while the militia received permission to return to Detroit. But Hamilton released the militia and Indians with their promise they would return in the spring. By late February, the British force that had once numbered 232 was reduced to 79 men, of whom only 33 were regulars.[17]

With some trepidation, Hamilton filled that void with the local militia while rightfully suspecting their loyalty. The better part of valor prompted the militia to abandon Capt. Leonard Helm when Hamilton appeared, and then go through the motions of British loyalty oaths and militia drills. Most would happily reembrace the Americans once Clark appeared. Expediency was a minor reason. Most important was news of the France's declaration of war against Britain and alliance with America. Hamilton had gotten no direct word of France's war declaration, only troubling rumors. On February 22, when he warned the chiefs of the possibility, "They appeared a little struck by the news, tho . . . they had intimation of it from the French, as I had heard of rejoicings having been made at the Illinois, & even at St. Vincennes."[18]

Clark and his men resumed their journey on February 18, sloshing through the Little Embarrass's backwaters until it met the Wabash nine miles south of Vincennes. The waters here stretched for a mile across. They found a rise of land that was damp rather than soaked and shivered away another seemingly endless night before smoky fires. At this point, "many of our volunteers began, for the first time, to despair."[19] Clark risked discovery in permitting fires so close to the enemy. He had weighed the odds of an enemy patrol spotting him against hypothermia killing some of his exhausted, malnourished men, and reasoned the latter was more likely.

Against the odds, a patrol did indeed approach. Capt. Francis Maisonville was leading a dozen militia in pursuit of two escaped prisoners when they spied fourteen fires glowing low in the dark night beyond the Wabash's western shore. With the river dividing them, they could not get close enough to tell whether Americans or Indians ringed those smoky fires. They hurried back to Fort Sackville. After hearing the report, Hamilton ordered Capt. William La Mothe, an officer, a sergeant, fourteen militia, and six regulars, all guided by Maisonville, to investigate. They trekked down to the site and peered across the inland sea but saw no one in the woods on the far shore. Where and who were those mysterious intruders?

At daybreak, Clark sent out a patrol in the pirogue. They accosted five Canadians in a canoe and brought them back to camp. The Canadians eagerly informed Clark that no one knew of the American presence. Clark began ferrying his force across the Wabash in the two canoes. By midday, they were all on the eastern bank and began slogging north through the flooded woods.

After a mile or so, the water deepened to chest high. Exhausted and disheartened, the men retreated to shore and slumped against trees. Clark sat alone, wet some powder, and blackened his face. Then suddenly he leapt to his feet, "gave the warhoop and marched into the water without saying a word."[20] Holding their rifles above their heads, the men followed. The water deepened to the necks of the shorter men but no higher. Those too spent to wade were conveyed in the two canoes. That evening, they reached a patch of high ground a couple of miles below Fort Sackville. Clark allowed no fires that night. The men huddled together in their soaked blankets.

The distant thump of Fort Sackville's morning cannon greeted the Americans on the frosty dawn of February 23. The men were eager to advance, but Clark restrained them. Securing the Canadians' neutrality or alliance was essential before the Americans could attack. Clark composed a declaration that announced his presence and demanded that the Canadians choose to either stand aside, fight with him, or "repair to the fort and join his troops and fight like men."[21] He sent the swiftest of the Canadians ahead with the declaration. Then after night fell, with the other four Canadians as guides, Clark led his men forward. When they scattered and slipped through Vincennes, the doors were firmly shut. The Americans crept up to within rifle range of Fort Sackville and opened fire.

Hamilton first attributed the gunfire "to some drunken frolic of the inhabitants." That thought died when a bullet plowed into Sergeant Chapman's stomach. Hamilton ordered his men to the firing platforms and blockhouses. Clark's men surrounded the fort and fired at any shadow against the dark. Bullets struck three other redcoats. The firing continued all that night.

Where were La Mothe and his men? They hurried back to the sound of the guns but found themselves cut off. The party hid in a barn that night as American patrols passed about sixty paces away. About four in the morning, they dashed for the fort. Fortunately, none of the sentries opened fire. Francis Maisonville was not with them. He had volunteered to remain behind in the village to solicit French aid. That was a near fatal mistake.

The American sniping intensified after light blossomed on the morning of February 24. At eleven o'clock, Clark sent a letter to the fort under a truce flag. He called upon Hamilton to "immediately surrender yourself with your Garrison prisoners at discretion—If any of the stores be destroyed or any letters or papers burned, you may expect no mercy, for by Heavens you shall be treated as a murtherer."[22]

Hamilton gathered his officers, read them the letter, and declared, "I was determined if they and the Men were of my mind to hold out to the last." The officers "all declared themselves willing." Hamilton then gathered his troops on the parade ground and voiced his defiance. The redcoats cheered; "the French hung their heads, and . . . said it was hard they should fight against their own Friends and relations who they could see had joined the Americans and fired against the fort."[23] With his force split, Hamilton had no choice but to seek the best possible terms. He rejected Clark's initial demand and deployed his troops while he awaited what he hoped was a more favorable offer.

Two unexpected events allowed Clark to raise the fire at Hamilton's feet. His men captured Francis Maisonville and brought him before Clark. Maisonville admitted to Clark's stern charge that he had joined war parties. Clark decreed that Maisonville would suffer the same fate as the slaughtered pioneers. A frontiersman drew his knife and hacked off two scalp locks the size of sixpence from Maisonville's head. While not life threatening, the pain must have been excruciating.

Shortly thereafter, a volley of musket fire and war whoops sounded at the town's edge. It was a party of nine Indians and two Canadians celebrating their return from a successful scalp raid. They had no idea that Americans were besieging Fort Sackville. Clark charged about seventy of his men under Capt. John Williams against them. The Americans killed one and wounded two; the rest they captured. Clark ordered the captives dragged just beyond musket shot of the fort.

What happened next horrified the fort's defenders. Hamilton watched as "one of them a young Indian about 18 years of age the son of [Pontiac], was saved at the intercession of one Macarty, a Captain of Colo. Clarkes Banditi, who said he formerly owed his life to the Indian's father—One of the others was tomahawked either by Clark or one of his Officers, the other three foreseeing their fate, began to sing their Death song, and were butchered in succession, tho at the very time a flag of Truce was hanging out at the fort and the firing had ceased on both sides . . . The blood of the victims was still visible for days afterwards, a testimony of the courage and Humanity of Colonel Clarke."[24] Clark and his compatriots could just as sneeringly refer to the "courage and humanity" of the "hair buyer" Hamilton. To survive emotionally in any war, especially a frontier war, soldiers tend to sanctify themselves and demonize their enemies for committing the same horrors.

One of the condemned had a Rasputin-like power to sidestep death: "A young chief of the Ottawa nation called Macutte Mong . . . having received the fatal stroke of a Tomahawk in the head, took it out and gave it again into the hands of his executioner who repeated the stroke a second and third time, after which the miserable being, not entirely deprived of life was dragged to the river and thrown in with the rope about his neck where he ended his life and tortures."[25]

The sight of the murdered Indians powerfully shook Hamilton. Clark sensed this and sought to enhance the effect. He demanded that if the "hair buyer" did not surrender, "not a single man should be spared" if the Americans attacked. Hamilton folded. Under a truce flag, he strode through the gate to meet Clark. The lieutenant governor shuddered as Clark approached, his "hands and face still reeking from the human sacrifice in which he had acted as chief priest, he told me with great exaltation how he had been employed."[26]

Locking eyes with Hamilton, Clark loudly repeated his demand that the British surrender with "discretion" or unconditionally. Hamilton swore he would "never make a step so disgraceful and unprecedented while I have ammunition and provision." "You will," Clark replied, "be answerable for the lives lost by your obstinancy."[27] With that, they broke off their talk to consult their officers. A half hour later, Clark and Bowman joined Hamilton and Hay. After more American threats, the British finally succumbed to what Hamilton called "an unprincipled motley banditi."

The formal surrender was postponed until the next morning, February 25. Hamilton marched at the head of seventy-nine men, leaving within the fort stores of munitions, provisions, and trade goods. The post's name changed back to Fort Patrick Henry.[28] A ghastly accident marred the American victory celebration. While firing a thirteen-gun salute from the 6-pounder in a blockhouse, sparks ignited a barrel of cartridges. The explosion burned the exposed skin off Bowman, Captain Widdington, and a British private. Those men would survive but were horribly disfigured.

Clark sought vengeance for all the hundreds of Americans butchered along the frontier. He ordered Hamilton to identify any of his men who had joined in those raids. Hamilton replied that those who did so could answer for themselves. Over Hamilton's angry protests, Clark ordered irons clamped on those who confessed. He then ordered the scalps just brought in by the Indians hung on the tent where Hamilton and the raiding leaders were guarded. One of those accused of leading war parties against Kentucky, the French trader Raimbalt, was nearly executed. He was actually stretching rope when his compatriots intervened with protestations of his innocence. Clark "smiled contemptuously" when Hamilton asserted that by his actions, "he must denounce all pretension to the character of an officer or gentlemen."[29]

Clark followed up his victory by sending Captain Helm with a company of troops on February 26 up the Wabash to capture an expected supply convoy of ten bateaux. Helm's expedition brought down the captured supply boats on March 5. Meanwhile, Lieutenant Rogers arrived with the keelboat on February 27. On March 8, Clark paroled the Detroit militia but ordered Hamilton and the twenty-seven regulars escorted by twenty-three guards to imprisonment in Virginia. Shortly thereafter, he left James Shelby with a small garrison at Vincennes and returned with the rest of his men to Kaskaskia.

Rather than consolidate his defenses, why did Clark not immediately set forth with his men to Detroit? Any immediate expedition not only would be outnumbered and outsupplied by Detroit's regular troops and militia, along with hundreds of warriors, but also would lack the advantage of surprise. Though the dream of doing so persisted, the Americans would never muster enough men, supplies, and transport to make a serious thrust against Detroit. Clark's capture of

Vincennes and the "hair buyer" was the zenith of America's war effort north of the Ohio River.

Nonetheless, that campaign was brilliant by any measure. George Rogers Clark was as much a master psychologist as he was a master wilderness fighter; a shrewd understanding of human nature reinforced his formidable skills at strategy and tactics. Clark's initial campaign occupied rather than conquered the Illinois country and Vincennes; the population of French and Indians was sympathetic and collaborative rather than hostile. But those Canadians and Indians might well have resisted and even defeated a lesser enemy. It was Clark's deft use of surprise and fear that made his takeover and occupation bloodless. Likewise, a weaker leader who embarked in the dead of winter across that drowned land might have provoked a mutiny among his troops. Instead, Clark inspired those freezing, soaked, starving men to push on for weeks of miserable days and nights until they could aim their muskets at Fort Sackville. There, too, Clark paraded his gifts, using psychology to neutralize the Canadians and wring a surrender from Hamilton. His murder of the Indian captives within sight of the British mingled cold calculation with long pent-up rage. But, try as he might, Clark could not finish what he started. Detroit would remain beyond his grasp.

Clark's dreams foundered as much from lack of money as bullets, beans, and men. Like other frontier commanders, he bought on credit with the hope of congressional reimbursement. By late 1779, he owed over $25,000 to various creditors. At New Orleans, Oliver Pollock, Clark's chief backer, finally exhausted his own money and credit.

Jealousy, corruption, and arrogance weakened the American grip on Illinois. When Clark later departed for Fort Nelson at the Ohio falls, he left Col. John Montgomery to command the Illinois country militia, John Todd as county lieutenant, and John Dodge its Indian agent. Those men quarreled noisily among themselves. The French inhabitants wearied of American requisitions and the worthless scrip with which they insisted on paying.

Clark's campaigns secured Kentucky rather than the Illinois and Wabash regions. That year, Kentucky's population swelled with its greatest influx yet. Within a dozen miles of Fort Nelson arose a cluster of hamlets, including Sullivan's Station, Lynn's Station on Beargrass Creek, and Brashears Station at Floyd's Fork. In central Kentucky, settlers founded Lexington, Martin's Station, Old Hickston, Whiteby's Station, Worthington's Station, Pittman's Station, Field's Station, and Bryant's Station.

Daniel Boone led the year's largest party, nearly 100 settlers he had recruited during the spring and summer in North Carolina's Yadkin valley. Embittered by his treason trial and longing for his family, Boone had turned his back on Kentucky after his acquittal the previous year. Following a joyful reunion, he spent the winter hunting and easing his hurt feelings in the Blue Ridge Mountains. At some point, he decided to retest his fate in Kentucky with his family and anyone else he could entice, but he refused to live in Boonesborough. Instead, he founded Boone's Station a half-dozen miles to the northwest.

Virginian policies were as important as Clark's military feats in drawing the migration. On July 23, Virginia's government took an important step toward defending its frontier. It split its thirty-two western counties into a southwestern frontier and northwestern frontier of sixteen counties each. A lieutenant colonel would be named to raise and lead a battalion in each district. Each county would contribute at least 250 men to the battalion. That same month, Virginia's assembly passed a land law that recognized three types of claims: settlement and preemption rights; warrants bought from the state; and military warrants. Three types of settlers were recognized: those who had arrived before January 1, 1778, could buy up to 400 acres at a token price and preempt an additional 1,000 acres at the regular price of 40 pounds sterling for 100 acres; those who had settled after that date until the July 1779 law could preempt up to 400 acres at the regular price; and those who arrived after the new law was enacted enjoyed no preemption right and paid the regular price for land. Finally, the government rejected the tangled claims of the Walpole, Indiana, and United Wabash and Illinois Companies for western lands. Hundreds of settlers arrived in Kentucky that year and thereafter to shelter under the enhanced military and legal protection.[30]

As Kentucky's number of armed men swelled, so too did the confidence to strike back against the enemy. In May, Col. John Bowman led almost 300 men north of the Ohio against Chillicothe, burned the town, and killed Blackfish and another warrior, but lost nine dead. Each man brought back an average of $500 worth of recovered loot.[31]

By autumn, British and Indians had retaken the initiative along the Ohio valley. Capt. Henry Bird and Simon Girty led several raids in the region. They were especially eager to intercept supplies from New Orleans, which took months to reach the upper Ohio. On October 10, the Girty brothers, Matthew Elliott, and 130 Indians ambushed Col. David Rogers and the sixty men oaring several boats. They killed Rogers and forty men and captured Col. John Campbell and five men. The men in one boat escaped.

What fate befell Hamilton and his men? They endured an arduous, humiliating two-and-a-half-month trek to Virginia. Though Hamilton praised his guards for their civility, the hatred of many Americans toward him was a shock: "The poor people saw us with some horror, as being of kindred manners with the Savages . . . we were accosted by the females especially in pretty coarse terms."[32] Most of those "poor people" undoubtedly mourned the lives of loved ones butchered or dragged off, sometimes before their very eyes, by savages dispatched by the "hair buyer." Without his guard, Hamilton might well have been tarred or feathered and even lynched by an enraged mob bent on vengeance.

Gov. Thomas Jefferson ordered the soldiers imprisoned in Chesterfield while Hamilton, Philip Dejean, and William La Mothe were fettered with eighteen pounds of ankle and wrist irons, brought to Williamsburg, and squeezed into the tiny jail. There they would await trial as war criminals and be hanged if found guilty. Later, Maj. Jehu Hay and four other officers were brought to Williamsburg and jailed with the others. George Washington thoroughly approved of Jefferson's action: "I have no doubt of the propriety of the proceedings . . . Their cruelties to our unhappy people who have fallen into their hands and the measures they have pursued to excite the savages to acts of the most wanton barbarity, discriminate them from common prisoners."[33]

British officials protested when they learned that Hamilton and his underlings were being treated as criminals rather than prisoners of war. The British commissary of prisoners threatened to retaliate against an equal number of select American officers, including Capt. James Willing. That threat deterred Jefferson. All but Hamilton were paroled but had to remain in Virginia. So what became of the "hair buyer" and his officers? None ever stood trial. While the other officers remained true to their parole, Lt. Jacob Schiefflin and Phillippe Francois Rastel, Sieur de Rocheblave, escaped in April 1780. Capt. Alexis Maisonville committed suicide on June 1. Hamilton was exchanged on March 4, 1781.

THE UPPER OHIO FRONTIER

Fort Laurens' presence on the Tuscarora's west bank enraged nearly all the region's tribes. Ever more Shawnee, Wyandot, Chippewa, Mingo, and warriors from other tribes appeared in surrounding woods and peppered the fort's walls with musket balls. The soldiers were even exhausting their welcome among the Delaware. Rejecting their chief's admonitions, young Delaware joined warriors from other tribes to skulk nearby and steal any stray property or lives. It was a Delaware that drew that year's first blood, killing and scalping a soldier of the 13th Virginia. The next day, Delaware Indians "shot three of the best horses and carried off two more, then bags, some bells, two saddles and some blankets."[34] A week later, the Americans scored a rare though Pyrrhic victory. On January 30, three miles from Fort Laurens, Simon Girty and a small Mingo party ambushed Capt. John Clark and fourteen troops of the 8th Pennsylvania as they returned from a supply escort. The volley killed two and wounded four Americans. Clark quelled any panic among his troops and led a bayonet charge before the enemy could reload. Girty and the Mingo Indians fled, dragging one of the Americans with them.[35] A month later, the Americans suffered a calamity within sight of the palisade on February 23. By ringing bells, a war party lured into an ambush nineteen men who had been sent out to gather in the horses and slaughtered all but two, whom they dragged away into captivity.

By March, Fort Laurens' defenders teetered at starvation's brink and were reduced to boiling and eating their moccasins and any other leather. To the defenders' relief, an expedition of 200 Virginia militia and 300 troops of the 8th Pennsylvania and 13th Virginia led by Maj. Frederick Vernon appeared on March 20. What happened next would have been comic had the results not been tragic. The defenders joyfully fired a volley to celebrate. The explosion spooked the supply-laden packhorses; bags of flour and other provisions were strewn as the animals bolted through the forest. The starving men would not wait for bread to rise from the flour and instead devoured it raw, a folly that killed three and sickened most. The supplies alleviated the starvation, but the reinforcements did not deter the incessant enemy sniping and ambushes. Indians shot and scalped the sentinel and ensign of a forty-man woodcutting party on March 28. [36]

A debate arose over whether Fort Laurens should be abandoned. That isolated post was clearly a liability that consumed huge amounts of troops and supplies. The Indians slaughtered the fort's cattle and horses grazing in the meadows and attacked those soldiers who ventured forth to gather the livestock or cut wood. With its understrength, malnourished garrison, the fort posed no offensive threat to the hostiles, but instead became a magnet for war parties. Despite all that, the frontier commanders refused to abandon it for fear the Indians could then concentrate their fury on the Ohio valley forts and encourage hitherto neutrals to join. George Washington still saw Fort Laurens as a springboard for attacking the hostile tribes and possibly Detroit, even though no plans, let alone efforts, then existed to do either. The enthusiasm for holding the fort diminished steadily.[37]

As the days grew warmer, Fort Laurens became a rock in a stream of war parties striding past along the trail to the upper Ohio valley. On February 26, Indians killed or captured eighteen settlers on Turtle Creek, twenty miles east of Pittsburgh. In April, raiders struck throughout the Monongahela and Youghiogheny valleys; the news was not always but usually tragic:

> A woman on the Cheat River after killing one Indian and wounding another made her escape. Mr. Sampson's son was taken at his plantation, and another man and woman of that neighborhood were captured. About April 9, four men sent express from Fort Pitt to Hannastown were found dead and scalped about fifteen miles from the former post on the Great Road. April 13 David Morgan of Monongahela County discovered two Indians creeping upon some young people in the field. Morgan had a personal encounter with one whom he finally disabled. April 14 near Cavell's mill two skulking Indians were seen, one was killed, the other escaped. On April 16, David Maxwell and his wife were killed and scalped at Brush Run, near Braddock's old road. Their daughter had been previously captured.[38]

That spring's largest battle in the region opened on April 26, when 100 Indians and British surrounded and fired at Fort Hand. Bullets killed one and wounded three defenders, but the others held out: "The men firing out of the fort, the women were busily employed in running bullets for them."[39] Learning of the siege, Col. Achibald Lochry led the militia from Hannastown, drove off the raiders, and recovered 1,000 pounds sterling worth of plunder. The British and Indians returned to Fort Hand after the militia withdrew. They found a weakness: "Philip McGraw, a sergeant, an old Irishman, was in a sentry box in which was a crack, through which the Indians shot & killed him; & afterward Sergeant McCauley was slightly wounded at the same spot—after which that sentry box was abandoned." [40] The raiders could pick off defenders, but without cannons, they could not take the fort. Within days, they headed back to their villages to replenish their munitions and other supplies.

Among the Americans, few matched Capt. Samuel Brady as a legendary frontier fighter. He and his men dressed, fought, and tried to think like Indians. In June, a Munsee war party killed a soldier between Forts Crawford and Hand and then strode to Sewickley, where they murdered a mother and four children and took prisoner a twelve-year-old boy and ten-year-old girl. Learning of the atrocities, Brady set forth with twenty 8th Pennsylvania veterans and the Delaware tracker Nanowland, or George Wilson. They caught up with the Munsee about fifteen miles above Kittanning. At dawn, after a tense night of waiting, he formed his men in a crescent and they crept forward. At Brady's command, they fired and then sprinted through their gunsmoke toward the survivors. Eight Munsee warriors died, of whom the chief fell across the campfire and lay smoldering. The boy asked for a tomahawk and hacked off the head of his family's murderer.[41] And so the frontier was stained deeper with the blood from ever more sporadic random bursts of brutality.

This year, like the previous, Congress approved and then canceled a campaign into the region, this time up the Allegheny rather than west to the Scioto. On February 15, Washington wrote Gen. Lachlan McIntosh, "The more I contemplate on an expedition from Fort Pitt, the more persuaded I am of the superior advantages that will result."[42] Perhaps the worst obstacle was the lack of intelligence about the land and peoples that awaited them on the Allegheny River's upper reaches. Washington ordered McIntosh to gather that vital intelligence.

But the frustrations of commanding in that region finally overwhelmed McIntosh, and he requested a transfer. His officers and men were even more frustrated with their commander's ineptness and cheered his departure. Col. Daniel Brodhead reckoned McIntosh "to be almost universally Hated by every man in this department both Civil & Military . . . There is not an officer who does not appear to be exceedingly disgusted, and I am much deceived if they serve under his immediate Command another Campaign."[43] Somewhat apologetically, Washington defended his decision for that western command: "The sole reason for appointing General McIntosh to his present command was an opinion of his being in every view qualified for it, and I must observe that while under me, his conduct gave me the most favorable impressions of him in every respect."[44] He then promised to investigate the charges against McIntosh. On February 20, Congress resolved that Washington should accept that request and appoint a successor.[45]

Within a week, Washington chose Daniel Brodhead to be the new western commander, citing "your abilities, your former acquaintance with the back country, and the knowledge you must have acquired upon this last tour of duty . . . in preference to a stranger, who would not have time to gain the necessary information between that of assuming the command and the commencement of operations." [46] Brodhead was about fifty-two when the War Board approved

Washington's recommendation to give him the western command. Despite his age, he was a vigorous and well-respected officer. He was the Berks County delegate to Pennsylvania's provincial convention in July 1775, was commissioned a lieutenant colonel in Colonel Miles's rifle regiment in March 1776, fought in the battle of Long Island in August, and was transferred to the 4th Pennsylvania line in October. On March 12, 1777, he was promoted to colonel and given command of the 8th Pennsylvania. John Morgan spoke for most when he shared his hope that Brodhead would be "the salvation of this unhappy country if it be in the power of man to save it after the blunders and absurdities already committed."[47]

Upon taking command, Brodhead soon found that diplomacy was an essential duty. On April 8, he sent a stern biblical warning to the Wyandot to accept peace or else: "When God intends to save a Nation from destruction he opens the eyes of its Rulers and discovers to them the Danger it is in. So when a Nation is grown too wicked and God is determined to destroy it he suffers it to go on in its Wickedness and continues it in blindness and Destruction comes on it like a whirlwind. Nations are like men when they grow too old they enter into another Childhood their Councils are Foolish & they must soon die."[48] The Wyandot did not bother to reply. With his strong rhetoric and bearing, Brodhead impressed the Delaware, if no other nation. They conferred upon him the name Maghingua Keeshoch, or Great Moon. Those good feelings nearly died on May 3, when a private murdered a Delaware. Brodhead defused the crisis by "covering the dead" with presents to his relatives and chiefs.[49]

The British increasingly evidenced signs of faring even worse. Their niggardly gifts combined with the prolonged war to sap tribal enthusiasms. During a council at Sandusky with Capt. Henry Bird, the chiefs threw down the war hatchet and warned that they might turn to the Americans. The dramatic gesture mingled frustration, bluff, exhaustion, and defiance. Their loyalty hung in the balance. A cowardly reaction would lose them to neutrality and some possibly even to the enemy.

The captain knew this. Only a bold front would save the Indians as allies: "You are welcome to do so. You know that I am not afraid of you. I have fought before now with you & I have conquered, & am able to fight you again, and even both you and the Americans together."[50] One by one, most chiefs reluctantly folded. Half King was the first to rally to Bird's side, and together they swayed other chiefs. Bird and the war chiefs then journeyed to the villages to embolden the warriors against Fort Laurens, but most wanted a reprieve from the warpath to hunt and enjoy their families. Bird could not find enough men willing to paint their faces and head toward the Ohio valley once again.

A few chiefs remained rebellious; they sent word to Brodhead that they were interested in peace. Chief Raven was the most prominent chief to parley with the Americans that year. On July 18, he led a Cherokee delegation to Fort Pitt, after having previously visited the hostile Ohio tribes. The council lasted from July 18 until it concluded with a treaty on July 22. The treaty united the Cherokee and Americans in war against the British, buried all past animosities and crimes between them, allowed American troops to pass through Cherokee territory, promised fair trials for any accused, allowed well-regulated trade, and protected all Cherokee lands from theft.[51] The Americans waved this model treaty like a flag to attract the other chiefs.

Brodhead was a fighter first and diplomat second. He worked feverishly to prepare an expedition to ascend the Allegheny and strike the Seneca and other tribes nestled along shore. In order to gather enough troops, he ordered the garrisons to evacuate Forts McIntosh, Laurens, and Randolph in July. On August 10, his expedition headed up the Allegheny. He and 650 troops with a month's provisions embarked in bateaux at Fort Pitt while 100 soldiers drove herds of cattle and horses along the shore. Stockaded depots were set up at Kittanning and Mahoning. The low water at Mahoning forced Brodhead to transfer his supplies to the pack animals.

Though Brodhead's campaign unfolded with military precision, the enemy remained beyond reach. His scouts could only report the tracks of refugees and the abandoned villages ahead, which his troops later burned. The largest destruction was at Yahrungwago, where his troops torched 165 homes and the corn crop. But the enemy nearly always managed to evade him.

The lucky exception occurred one day when Lieutenant Hardin's scouting party of fifteen troops from the 8th Pennsylvania and eight Delaware warriors spotted a war party of forty Indians in seven canoes descending the Allegheny River. Hardin deployed his men and ordered them to fire at will. Brodhead hurried to the sound of the guns and arrived in time to "discover the Enemy, & six of them retreating across the River without arms, at the same time the rest ran away leaving their Canoes, Blankets, Shirts, provisions and eight Guns, Besides five dead and by the signs of Blood, several went off wounded, only two of my men and one of the Delaware . . . were wounded & so slightly that they are recovered and fit for action."[52]

Brodhead pushed his troops on to Buckloons, where he ordered built a small stockade garrisoned with forty men and the extra supplies packed within. The troops marched on to Canawago and then Yahrungwago, where they camped three days. This was the campaign's zenith. They returned to Fort Pitt without incident.

Brodhead lauded his troops' spirit. Though "many of them returned barefooted and naked they disdained to complain, and to my great mortification I have neither Shoes, Blankets, Hats, Stockings, nor leggins to relieve their necessities."[53] Congress and the states also owed the troops nine months in back pay. Brodhead was forced to discharge most of the 8th Pennsylvania along with two ranger companies of Westmoreland County. Nonetheless, he insisted to Washington that although "I shall be weak in Troops to prosecute an expedition which by your permission I should be happy to make against Detroit, taking the Shawnese in my way. I should be happy to have your permission to make occasional excursions against any of the Indian nations."[54] To this, Washington would give his enthusiastic consent.

THE NEW YORK FRONTIER

The first campaign on the New York frontier began with the budding leaves. On April 19, Colonels Goose Van Schaick and Marinus Willet led 558 troops of the 1st New York from Fort Schuyler into the Onondaga heartland. They took their first prisoner the next day, a warrior. But as they approached a cluster of three villages, Indians spotted them and sounded the alarm. Most Onondaga got away. The troops burned three villages, captured thirty-four Onondaga and one Tory, and killed twelve Indians. On April 24, Van Schaick led these troops back into Fort Schuyler. During that 180-mile expedition, they lost only one man killed. Van Schaick's brief, low-cost raid may have inflicted more casualties on the Indians, if not more destruction, than Sullivan's huge campaign later that year.[55]

As if New York's challenges with the British and Indians were not grievous enough, Gov. George Clinton provoked a showdown with Vermont. Though the Crown had granted Vermont to New York in 1764, most of the settlers supported the creation of their own colony and later state, whose independence they declared in January 1777. All along, New York asserted its unenforceable claim to that region. In early 1779, Clinton dispatched militia officers to rally men on Vermont territory. In February, Vermont governor Crittenden and the legislature countered with a law empowering the state's militia officers to draft any local men to their units. When Putney's captain ordered two New York officers to serve his unit, they refused and were arrested. Clinton dispatched Col. Eleazor Patterson and 100 militia to free those men. Crittenden replied with Ethan Allen and the Green Mountain Boys. On May 24, Allen's troops encircled and captured forty-one New Yorkers and 100 pounds of gunpowder, while the others fled back to their state. After a trial of the prisoners found them guilty of various offenses, Crittenden offered a pardon for all on June 3. New York never again tried to use military force to assert its claim to Vermont.

After Van Schaick's triumph against the Onondaga and Patterson's humiliation by the Vermonters, the New York frontier remained largely quiet until summer. Then the war's largest frontier campaign against the Indians would burn through western New York.

SULLIVAN'S CAMPAIGN

George Washington had a vision and brooked no delay in realizing it. On March 6, he penned a letter to Major Generals Horatio Gates and John Sullivan asking each to command a campaign that would cut through the heart of the Iroquois. The letter would go first to Gates, who, if he declined, was to pass it immediately on to Sullivan. If the latter was not interested, Washington would have to look elsewhere, but at least he had saved some time.[56]

Why was Washington in such a hurry? Even the most limited of campaigns in troops and goals cost weeks to prepare. It would take months to mobilize all the men, supplies, finances, and transport for a campaign targeted against Iroquoia, hundreds of wilderness miles away from the eastern cities.

As Washington expected and hoped, Gates turned up his nose at the offer. Washington and Gates despised each other; neither fancied working together on such an elaborate campaign. Sullivan was no more eager for the command. He received Washington's offer on March 16, mulled over what to do for a day, and then penned a reply to Gates explaining that illness, debts, family worries, and the duty to his present command prevented him from immediately accepting. It was not until March 23 that Sullivan finally agreed to journey to Washington's headquarters at Middle Brook, New Jersey, and discuss the matter.[57]

However reluctant Sullivan was to accept the mission, he quickly gave in once he was ushered before Washington's august presence. Washington was confident that Sullivan was a sensible choice. Few matched the man in battle experiences or patriotic fervor. Of course, experience and fervor are not inseparable from competence, let alone brilliance.

Brilliance was not a word associated with John Sullivan. Among American generals, he was ploddingly efficient and a stoic if uninspired presence in the field. He joined the cause early as a New Hampshire delegate to Congress in 1774 and 1775, fought at the siege of Boston through March 1776, assumed command of the northern army's remnants after the invasion of Canada, returned to fight on Long Island where he was captured, was exchanged in time for that winter's Trenton and Princeton campaigns, commanded an aborted raid on Staten Island in 1777, mismanaged the right wing at Brandywine later that year, performed little better at Germantown in October, and since April 1778 had led the American forces in shadowing the British at Newport, Rhode Island. By early 1779, the stress of war and a chronic illness had aged him far beyond his thirty-nine years, exacerbating a naturally cantankerous disposition that provoked him into jealous squabbles with other generals.

It was not until May 31 that Washington formalized the campaign's strategy, which had been debated and hammered out over the previous months. Two armies would converge in Iroquoia and catch the Indians in a cross fire, with Sullivan's army coming up the Susquehanna River and Brig. Gen. James Clinton's brigade coming down the east branch. Upon uniting at Tioga, they would march north and then west through the remaining Iroquois country. The objective was "the total destruction and devastation of their settlements and the capture of as many prisoners of every age and sex as possible. It will be essential to ruin their crops now in the ground and prevent their planting more . . . The country may not be merely overrun but destroyed." [58]

Sullivan was empowered to make peace with the Indians but should "not by any means listen to any overture of peace before the total ruin of their settlements." Even then, peace would depend on the Indians agreeing to ally with the Americans against the British. The Indians' sincerity would be measured by their willingness "to surprise the Garrison of Niagara and the shipping on the lakes and put them into our possession. This may be demanded as a condition of our friendship." [59] So Fort Niagara was a secondary objective, to be won by Indian rather than American arms. However, "should Niagara fall into your hands in the manner I have mentioned—you will do every thing in your power for preserving and maintaining it, by establishing a chain of forts."[60]

As for battle, Washington encouraged his commanders "to make rather than receive attacks, attended with as much impetuosity, shouting, and noise as possible, and to make the troops act in as loose and dispersed a way as is consistent with a proper degree of government concert and mutual support—It should be previously impressed upon the minds of the men wherever they have an opportunity, to rush on with the war whoop and fixed bayonets—Nothing will disconcert and terrify the Indians more."[61]

By May 7, Sullivan was at Easton, Pennsylvania, where he gathered troops and supplies before marching over the Pocono Mountains to the town of Wyoming. He first sent to Wyoming Gen. Edward Hand, who arrived with his troops on May 8 to take command of the mélange of regulars and militia already there and supervise the supply buildup. Sullivan's next step was to widen the path from Easton to Wyoming so that wagons could easily traverse it. Though the regiments of Spencer and Courtlandt accomplished that duty by May 31, it proved difficult to execute: "The Indian path was no kind of advantage nor does the Road now Cut follow it half a mile in the whole way—the Road is now Cut the whole Distance & through a Country the most Difficult I Ever Saw—it is not possible for a Country to be Thicker with wood among which the Laurels are so thick that a man cannot get through them but on his hands and knees."[62] Finally, on June 18, Sullivan led the brigade of Poor and Maxwell and Proctor's artillery on the five-day march from Easton to Wyoming.

What Sullivan and his men found at the march's end filled them with melancholy. Wyoming was literally a ghost town. The valley's beauty was marred by hundreds of burned houses and the strewn bones of the unburied. Astonishingly, about 250 settlers, mostly widows, children, and the elderly, still eked out their survival amidst the charred ruins and ill-tended fields. Most mournful of all was the gruesome battlefield on the river's west shore. Lieutenant Colonel Dearborn was among those who visited the site, where "we found a great number of bones at & near the field of battle. Among a number of skull bones that we found none was without the mark of the tomahawk. I saw one Grave where 73 of our men were buried & was shown a place where 17 of our men after being taken were made to set down in a ring 16 of whom they Immediately tommahawk'd the other leapt over the ring and made his escape."[63]

Blood had been spilled more recently. On April 23, a war party killed or captured a five-man detachment of the German regiment led by Captain Davis and Lieutenant Jones. Those taken alive were tortured to death. Their comrades erected a stone cairn over the graves. Troops passing by that site invariably shuddered.

The Fourth of July celebration lightened some of the gloom. Since it fell on a Sunday, Independence Day was remembered with long sermons. The party was delayed until the next day. An extra gill of whiskey was issued to each soldier and a quart for officers. As was customary, thirteen toasts were made to such notables as Congress, George Washington, and the French allies. The tenth proposed,

"Civilization or death to all American savages." The last toast appropriately took a longer view: "May this New World be the last Asylum for Freedom and the Arts."[64]

As in any campaign, logistics determined the number of troops and the time and distance they marched. After receiving his orders, Sullivan would need five months to gather enough troops and supplies to launch his campaign. Accomplishing that nightmarish task almost made the actual march seem relatively routine. Supplies converged at Wyoming overland by wagon and packhorse from Easton and upriver by bateaux from Sunbury. Low water and a lack of boats curtailed supplies on the river route.

Pennsylvania was supposed to provide most of the campaign's logistics. Unfortunately, the state was short not just of food, munitions, and clothing, but also of boats, wagons, draft animals, boatmen, and teamsters. Sullivan fired off letters to the state's council urging them to supply his army's needs. The council was sympathetic but discouraging: "Be assured sir, nothing would give us more pleasure than to see the expedition go forward." But the war had drained Pennsylvania to the dregs of its manpower, wealth, supplies, and transportation. Resources were nearly exhausted, given "the great supplies drawn from this state for the wagon service to the Continental army, the Invasion of the enemy, the disaffection of too many among us, and the disgust arising from irregularities of the staff Officers, and the necessary tillage of the Country."[65] The state's supply system was organized by county like the militia. Each county had a wagon master who mobilized its wagons, teamsters, draft animals, and supplies. The task of supplying Sullivan fell mostly on the wagon masters of Berks, Bucks, and Northhampton Counties.[66]

Washington and the War Board were able to gather and send supplies from other states. On May 24, Washington wrote that he was forwarding to Easton 2,000 overalls and 2,000 pairs of shoes from his headquarters at Middle Brook, New Jersey, and 3,400 hunting shirts and 2,000 pairs of shoes from the magazine at Fishkill, New York. But for now, Sullivan would have to go begging. Washington admitted that "so empty are our Arsenals that the Board of War had it not in their power to comply with your requisition for the thousand arms in addition to the two hundred already furnished."[67]

As if the transportation were not bad enough, guards for the supplies were few or nonexistent. Especially vulnerable were the magazines at Middleton and Harris Ferry, which, lacking "a single man to guard them, one or two disaffected persons might in one night destroy the whole, & many such are suspected being about the river."[68] No one ever inflicted that dreaded sabotage, but the fear lingered, along with the inertia to prevent it from happening. Sullivan implored Pennsylvania to mobilize its militia to guard the magazines, but there was always some excuse not to do so. Pennsylvania president Joseph Reed blamed the high monthly wages of $120 for the 450 boatmen which also drained the ranks of the militia.[69]

After all the exertions necessary to get those barrels of meat or flour to the troops, the provisions were often unfit to eat. To the men's rage, thirteen of twenty barrels were filled with rotten food. A lack of salt for the meat or use of green-wood for the barrels was the chief cause.[70]

Although the immediate concern was stockpiling enough provisions for the campaign, every man in the army could not but contemplate what lay ahead. Iroquoia was a blank swatch of map for Sullivan. The general had no idea what he was marching into and asked Gen. Edward Hand for intelligence. Hand reckoned "no difficulty in finding guides to Chemung; beyond that it will be difficult to procure them . . . Spies cannot be had at any rate, at least such as could be depended on."[71]

As for the number of British troops in the region, reports trickled in from escaped prisoners and friendly Indians. In July Nathan Kingsley limped into Albany, having been captured at Wyoming in October 1777. He heard that only 120 troops from Sir John Johnson's regiment and 40 Indians had headed from Montreal to Niagara to join about 300 troops there.[72]

Sullivan figured the campaign would kick over a hornet's nest of 1,400 warriors, and feared even that might be an underestimate. Despite massing three times the manpower, Sullivan had no illusions about fighting the Indians in their homeland. The Indians were "capable of Seizing Every Advantage which the ground can possibly afford perfectly Acquainted with the use of Arms Inured to war from their youth & from the manner of Living Capable of Enduring Every kind of Fatigue are no Despicable Enemy when opposed to three thousand Troops Totally unacquainted with the Country & Indian manner of fighting."[73]

The general issued the campaign's order of march and battle on May 24. The design was a moving and fighting square composed of four brigades, one to a side, protecting the artillery, wagons, and packhorses in the center. Brig. Gen. Edward Hand would command the 3rd or Light Brigade, composed of Lt. Col. William Butler's 4th Pennsylvania, Lt. Col. Adam Hubley's 11th Pennsylvania, Maj. Daniel Burchardt's German Battalion, Maj. James Pharr's Morgan's Riflemen, and Capt. Anthony Selin's Independent Rifle Company. On the right would be Brig. Gen. William Maxwell's 1st Brigade, including Col. Matthias Ogden's 1st New Jersey, Col. Israel Shreve's 2nd New Jersey, Col. Elias Dayton's 3rd New Jersey, and Col. Oliver Spencer's 4th New Jersey. On the left would be Brig. Gen. Enoch Poor's 2nd Brigade of Col. Joseph Cilly's 1st New Hampshire, Lt. Col. George Reid's 2nd New Hampshire, Lt. Col. Henry Dearborn's 3rd New Hampshire, and Maj. Daniel Whiting's 6th Massachusetts. The rear would be protected by Brig. Gen. James Clinton's 4th Brigade of Col. Philip Van Courtlandt's 2nd New York, Col. Peter Gansevoort's 3rd New York, Lt. Col. Frederic Weissenfels's 4th New York, Col. Lewis Dubois's 5th New York, and Capt. Isaiah Wool's New York artillery detachment. Col. Thomas Proctor commanded Sullivan's artillery, which included 250 gunners; eight brass guns, including two 6-pounders, four 3-pounders, and two 5 $1/2$- inch howitzers; and a hand-carried coehorn mortar. Until Clinton's brigade joined the army, the rear guard would alternate between regiments contributed by Maxwell or Poor.[74]

Sullivan's battle plan was simple but effective. In any battle, Hand's light corps would engage and pin down the enemy while the brigades of Maxwell and Poor would try to outflank them and Clinton's brigade marched forward to reinforce the center. Should an attack occur on either flank or the rear, the same tactics would prevail, although the brigades would have different missions.

Discipline was essential to preventing any disaster. Sullivan tolerated no insubordination from the ranks. Courts-martial in June found three privates from the 2nd New York guilty of desertion, but they were issued different sentences because of extenuating circumstances. Oliver Arnold was shot by a firing squad before the army drawn up on three sides. Edward Tyler was forced to run the gauntlet through two regiments of troops wielding ramrods. John Stevens received 100 lashes. On July 1, a court-martial found Privates Michael Rosebury and Lawrence Miller of the Jersey Brigade guilty of trying to induce soldiers to desert. They were condemned to the gallows. The unrepentant Rosebury swung, but Sullivan pardoned Miller in the noose's shadow. On July 21, two soldiers of the 4th Pennsylvania were caught deserting. The penalty was harsh. One got 500 lashes and the other was executed. The worst breach of discipline occurred on July 13, when thirty-three troops of the German regiment deserted, claiming their enlistments had expired. Sullivan sent troops in pursuit. The Germans were soon caught and returned to camp. There the Germans wrote and submitted a petition justifying their behavior but also apologizing and asking for leniency in return for their promise to serve loyally. Sullivan used psychology rather than corporal punishment to restore order. He agreed to pardon them but promised all future desertions would be treated with the utmost severity.[75]

As Sullivan literally whipped his army into shape, runners brought word to Fort Niagara of the American armies massing at Wyoming and Canajoharie. What should be done? Should the British rush to help defend Iroquoia? If so, how could the lack of men, supplies, and transport be overcome? Should the British sit tight at Fort Niagara as the Americans stumbled along the tether of their ever lengthening and fraying supply line? A combined British and Indian force might be able to bag the entire enemy army. But that strategy, however sound, wrote off Iroquoia. How would their red allies react if the British stood by as the Americans burned and looted their way through the Six Nations' heartland? Would they hurl accusations of betrayal and bad faith against the British? Would the desire to save their homes and crops tempt them into neutrality, assuming the Americans demanded it? And then the nightmare scenario loomed—would the Iroquois switch to the seemingly invincible side?

A harassing retreat before Sullivan and Clinton was the most sensible strategy, but until the enemy armies arrived, the British and Indians would try to inflict as much damage on the frontier as possible. On July 28, a force of about 160 Indians and 80 Tories led by Captain MacDonald surrounded Fort Freeland on the West Susquehanna River fifteen miles above Northumberland. Outnumbered and terrified that it would suffer massacre, the thirty-two-man garrison surrendered when MacDonald promised them that the men would become prisoners of war and the women and children set free. MacDonald's word was good. The Indians contented themselves with burning and looting. Meanwhile, Capt. Hawkins Boone and thirty troops were on a scout a few miles away when they heard the distant firing. Boone hurried his troops toward the fort. Indian scouts brought word to MacDonald of their approach. MacDonald prepared an ambush. As Hawkins and his men wearily filed toward the fort, war cries and musket shots exploded on both sides. Within minutes, fourteen of Boone's men were dead and scalped, while the rest became prisoners.[76]

That same week, the Americans suffered another disaster. Joseph Brant led sixty Indians and twenty-seven loyalists to attack Minisink on the Delaware River. They struck on July 20, killing four settlers and capturing others, while losing one dead and another wounded, and then burned the settlement. As usual, they were unable to take the post from which most of the population had fled. Word reached Goshen ten miles east. Militia colonel John Hathorn called out his 120 men and marched to Minisink. Two companies of New Jersey militia joined him. Hathorn led his 150 men in pursuit and caught up to Brant's expedition as it was crossing the Delaware River twenty-seven miles north. Brant turned his men and attacked. In a four-hour forest battle, the Indians and British took forty scalps while losing three dead and ten wounded. Hathorn and his militia retreated back to Minisink. Flushed with victory, Brant led his men to Lackawaxen but was repulsed.[77]

As word of one massacre after another filtered back from distant frontier valleys, generals and congressmen back east grew increasingly impatient with Sullivan's slow preparations. Well aware that his colleague was more methodical than decisive and easily stalled by circumstances, Gen. Nathanael Greene sent Sullivan a rousing pep talk: "The expedition you have the honor to direct will fix the Eyes of the whole Continent upon you . . . People's hopes and expectations being very high, a disappointment will be the more disagreeable. Great preparations and great exertions have been made to pave the way for your success. I hope therefore the little obstacles that may arise in the execution will not retard the progress of the operations and waste the precious moments."[78]

Sullivan would eventually take Greene's advice to heart but would take his time doing so. A frustrated Board of War felt compelled to write Sullivan on July 21 that they regretted "exceedingly the delay of the expedition whose success greatly depended on secrecy and dispatch." They did acknowledge the supply problems beyond Sullivan's ability to remedy. Sullivan shot back: "My duty to the publick & regard to my own reputation compel me to state to congress the reason of the army under my command being so long delayed at this post."[79] He placed the blame squarely on corruption and incompetence in the supply corps. To the president of Congress, Sullivan exclaimed his "mortification to find I shall be oblig'd to leave this post, without the necessary Clothing, for the distressed Soldiers who, I have the honor to command."[80]

Just as Sullivan was about to launch his campaign, Washington threw a monkey wrench into its gears. The commander in chief feared that Gen. James Clinton was massing more supplies than he could carry and thus would never get under way. Washington asked Sullivan to convey supplies for Clinton's army as well as his own. With ill-concealed frustration, Sullivan replied: "I was so far from having a prospect of Supplying General Clintons Detachment with provisions that I have not Even now the most Distant prospect of keeping that part of the Army which is with me from Starving Long Enough to Compleat the Expedition. This I early foresaw & Endeavored to Guard against—Notwithstanding the flattering Accounts given by those Employed by Quartermasters & Commissaries which they are fond of giving when near your person."[81] Sullivan fired off a warning to Clinton: "In case you depended on our magazine for Stores we must all starve together as the Commissaries have deceived us in every article."[82]

Sullivan finally completed his essential preparations by July 31. With Col. Zebulon Butler left behind to command the local garrison and protect the supply line, his army marched from Wyoming at noon on that day. The army arrived that evening at Lackawanna Creek ten miles away. General Hand's light corps led the way, with an elite force of twenty-four riflemen well in front. General Poor's brigade followed, then the seventy-eight wagons, 500 cattle, and 1,200 pack-horses, all prodded and pulled by the drovers and wranglers, with Maxwell's brigade bringing up the rear. All three brigades had flanking parties moving through the woods 100 yards or so from the main body on the road. In all, Sullivan's army numbered 2,312 troops. Nearly a quarter of those men would be detached to guard supply depots en route to Iroquoia. The 214-bateau flotilla with Proctor's artillery and supplies tried to keep abreast of the troops. Captain Gifford and sixty troops of the 3rd New Jersey scouted ahead on the west bank; four light boats kept pace with them, ready to pull ashore and take them off if they ran into a superior enemy force.[83]

It was relatively easy going. A broad, mostly level trail ran all the way from Wyoming to Tioga through a mostly no-man's-land of burned white and Indian hamlets and abandoned fields. The army reached its first intact Indian village, Newtycharming, on August 9. The inhabitants fled well before the Americans could reach them. The troops torched the twenty-eight houses, uprooted the crops, and chopped down the fruit trees, a vandalism they would repeat at every village they reached over the next six weeks.

Nearly all reveled in the destruction. With callous indifference, Lt. Col. Henry Dearborn wrote that "this evening the town of Owagea was made a bonfire of to grace our meeting."[84] Unable to pin down the elusive enemy, some troops desecrated graves and scattered the bones of the dead. Maj. James Norris reported that "whether through principle of Avarice or Curiosity, our Soldiers dug up several of their graves and found a good many laughable relics."[85]

A few expressed a twinge of regret at destroying such bountiful fields and attractive houses. Dr. Jabez Campfield, enlisted as a field surgeon, "very heartily wish these rusticks may be reduced to reason, by the approach of this army, without suffering the extremes of war. There is something so cruel, in destroying the habitations of any people, (however mean they may be, being their all) that I might say the prospect hurts my feelings."[86] Such idealism was in limited supply throughout the colonies, and nearly nonexistent on the frontier.

The revelation that the Iroquois lived as comfortably and prosperously as most Americans astounded all the troops. The corn in some fields rose fifteen feet. Orchards of peaches and apples stretched for many acres. Yet there were differences. Instead of chimneys, Indian cabins had smoke holes in the roof. Hygiene was even less evident than in American towns. The Iroquois drew their water from polluted streams rather than wells. Campfield complained that the "Indians are very dirty; the rubbish of one of their houses is enough to stink a whole country."[87] The troops seized on such distinctions to justify their belief that the Indians were savages to be eradicated.

On the evening of August 11, Sullivan's army marched into Tioga at the juncture of the Susquehanna and Chemung Rivers. Scouts reported that the enemy still occupied Chemung, a half-dozen miles ahead. Sullivan ordered Generals Hand and Poor to lead their troops on a night march to strike either side of Chemung, while Maxwell encamped with his brigade to protect the supplies, wagons, and livestock. It took all night for the brigades of Poor and Hand to stumble their way through the dark and reach the town's outskirts.

The Indians learned of Sullivan's approach. Under cover of a heavy fog, they slipped out of the trap. Only Hand caught up to them. Before his relentless advance, the Indians and British "decamp'd with such precipitation as to leave their Blankets, & some skins behind them."[88]

> [Hand] followed them up the road about half a mile, when a party of about thirty rose and fired upon his advanced party; the General, with his troops, immediately moved up to charge them upon which they fled with precipitation. They were pursued a little further up, but, there appearing no prospect of overtaking them, the troops returned and destroyed the town . . . A small party fired upon our people when destroying their corn but was soon forced to fly. We had in the course of the day seven men killed and thirteen wounded . . . I cannot say what loss the enemy sustained but it must have been inconsiderable as their flight was too sudden to admit of their receiving such injury. Some of their hats were found, one with a ball through the crown, but no dead body, which induces me to believe that none of them were killed outright.

Sullivan lauded his troops: "their conduct was exceedingly praiseworthy; if there was any fault it was their too great eagerness to rush upon the enemy at first sight."[89]

All that could be done was to destroy Chemung. Maj. James Norris gleefully wrote that on the morning of September 12, "about Sun rise the Gen. gave orders for the Town to be illuminated & according we had a glorious Bonfire of upwards of 30 Buildings at once, a melancholy & desperate Spectacle to the Savages many of whom must have beheld it from a Neighboring hill, near which we found a party of them had encamped last night."[90]

The general withdrew his army to Tioga, where he set the troops to work on all the digging, cutting, hauling, and emplacing needed to erect a fort with a palisade, abatis, and ditch linking four blockhouses. Two 6-pounders were mounted on the walls. Over 1,200 people huddled within and just beyond its walls, including the 250 troops of Col. Israel Shreve's 2nd New Jersey, and the sick, wounded, and camp followers, along with hundreds of barrels packed with supplies. The rest of the army pitched their tents in nearby fields.

The farther up the Susquehanna valley Sullivan's army marched, the harder an essential question pressed: where was General Clinton? To Sullivan and his officers, the dearth of enemy resistance on their march might well mean that the Indians and British had stalked off to ambush the lesser of the two American armies. On August 16, Sullivan dispatched General Poor with 900 troops up the Susquehanna to find Clinton and escort him down.

So just where was Clinton? Throughout the summer, Maj. Gen. James Clinton had readied his army to join Sullivan's. Canajoharie, seventy river miles from Albany, was his campaign's staging ground. By May 27, Clinton had massed 3,511 troops there. Twenty-five Oneida would join Clinton's army.[91] Enemy scouts would hurry back with word of the army's presence at Canajoharie and assume it would soon thrust westward against Lake Ontario and most likely Fort Niagara, replaying the 1759 campaign. Who could imagine that the Americans would actually head in a starkly different direction?

Getting the troops, bateaux, and mountain of provisions to Canajoharie up the Mohawk River was routine enough. Transporting them south to Lake Otsego over twenty miles of rutted roads was a Herculean challenge that took weeks to accomplish. Throughout the summer, Clinton sent troops and boats down that land and lake path. As his army diminished at Canajoharie, it increased at Lake Otsego's south end. There the troops dammed the Susquehanna River's head, which raised the lake level three feet. By August 8, both tasks were complete. The army was ready to move. Clinton ordered the dam demolished.

The next morning, August 9, the 207-bateau flotilla rushed downstream with the flood, while the 4th Pennsylvania and 3rd New York marched along the riverbank. They entered and burned their first Indian village on August 14 and thereafter daily destroyed others, including the notorious Oquaga, as they descended the river. On August 19, Clinton's brigade joined with Poor's forces. Together they headed downstream. A salute of thirteen cannon shots greeted them as they reached Tioga on August 22.[92]

Sullivan's army now numbered about 5,000 troops. The general reshuffled some of his regiments. Poor lost Alden's regiment to Clinton but gained in return Van Courtlandt's. Hand received the 4th Pennsylvania and all rifleman companies. The German regiment was organized into four companies of twenty-five men each and split equally between the march and battle flanks.

From Wyoming to Chemung, the trail was mapped, if not before traveled by anyone on the expedition. Beyond that, the wilderness was a great, seemingly endless mystery that hid and randomly disgorged wild savages and beasts. On August 26, Sullivan ordered his army forward into that vast unknown for an extended march of vandalism and, ideally, decisive battle. Though their inability to seize and crush the enemy would disappoint them, the Americans would satiate themselves with destruction.

On this campaign, a lack of food was not usually among the troops' grumbles. They could enliven their daily rations of beef and flour with a cornucopia of vegetables and fruits, along with stray livestock and meat carved from expired draft animals. Though game filled the forest, hunting was prohibited. That did not inhibit some enterprising and bored soldiers from trying to diversify the food brought to their palates. Maj. Jeremiah Fogg recalled that one evening after they had pitched camp, "we were alarmed by the unusual cry of the army caused by the appearance of a doe running through the lines; she happening to run near our quarters, we attempted to seize and confine her, but found her too full of springs! The first salutation I met with was her head against my forehead which knocked me down, stunned me, and prevented my further pursuit. She ran over me treading on me in several places."[93] The doe got away. Other creatures did not escape the kettle or skillet. The troops did not hesitate to smash any animal literally underfoot, especially if it was dangerous. Lt. Col. Henry Dearborn wrote, "I eat part of a fryed Rattle Snake to day which would have tasted very well had it not been snake."[94]

Most of the campaign was day after day of sheer hard marching, cutting, and digging, varied when the troops were loosed with torches in villages, their hands in fields to uproot crops, or with hatchets in orchards to hack down trees. But the hardest work was widening and leveling the trail into a road for the wagon train, an exertion that provoked "a universal cry against the artillery."[95] Sgt. Moses Fellows grumbled that "we marched much Impeded by the artillery and ammunition wagons through thick woods and difficult defiles, such Cursing, Cutting, and Digging, oversetting wagons and Pack Horses into the river."[96]

The campaign was even harder on the draft animals and livestock. One day the horse of Maj. Jeremiah Fogg "stumbled under me and broke its neck."[97] Dead and dying horses and oxen littered the army's wake. On September 24, Sullivan ordered all lame or faltering pack animals killed to prevent the Indians from later rounding up and restoring them; the scene of carnage was appropriately thereafter known as Horseheads. The attrition was mostly due to the hard pace, killing burdens of hauling or pulling, and lack of forage and fodder, but the drovers and wranglers contributed as they bungled their duties. During the campaign, nearly 140 cattle wandered off into the forest. Heavily armed patrols could have rounded up many of the strays, but the men stayed in camp. Nor did the packers evidence greater competence: "Much of our flour is carried in bags & often falling off, and striking against trees, sometimes falling into mud & sometimes into water, as we pass many streams . . . & 5 horses are committed to the management of one clumsy driver."[98] Careless orders contributed to the losses. When the army was ordered to clear its muskets by a general discharge the explosions of musket fire "dispersed our cattle and horses, and eighteen of the latter were never found. This accident detained us until 2 o'clock, so that this day's march has only been two miles."[99]

Danger lurked along the trail. During the campaign, ambushes and accidents killed or injured a score of soldiers. On August 15, Indians killed and scalped one soldier and wounded four privates and a corporal who were rounding up horses. Two days later, Indians killed a soldier and wounded another who had strayed from camp. On September 13, Indians killed a soldier from a scouting party. The scouts charged after the Indians, but they disappeared into the forest. Some careless soldiers were just as dangerous to themselves and their comrades. On August 5, a boatman fell into the river and drowned. Two soldiers died on August 5, one from disease, while the other, Sgt. Martin Johnson of the 3rd New Jersey, keeled over dead after marching all day. On August 23, Pvt. Samuel Gordon pulled the trigger on what he thought was an unloaded musket. The ball and three buckshot wounded one soldier in the leg and hit Captain Kimball, "who was standing at some distance in a tent with several other officers in such a manner that he expired within 10 or 15 minutes as universally lamented as he was esteem'd by all who knew him."[100] On August 24, another soldier wounded himself with his musket.

On August 25, several Oneida reached camp. It was hardly the number that Sullivan had hoped would turn out to guide his army through the wilderness. The general could not restrain his disappointment that "I have far advanced into the enemy's country [and] only four of you warriors have joined me, and they are totally unacquainted with every part of the country through which I have passed." With irony, he told them, "I would not wish to suspect your declarations of friendship to the American states." He then asserted, "I shall expect shortly to be joined by those of your people who are friendly to the American cause."[101] In this Sullivan would bear further disappointment.

The British and Indians blocked Sullivan's path on a half-mile-long ridge before the Indian village of Newtown or Chuknut. There, Col. John Butler had his 60 rangers, 14 troops of the 8th, and about 200 loyalists, along with 500 Indians led by Sayenqueraghta, Cornplanter, and Joseph Brant, build a breastwork masked with cut brush. Their right flank was anchored on a bend of the Chemung River and their left on a large hill. A stream and marshes ran before the ridge, offering clear fields of fire on the Americans if they waded across.

Sullivan's army had spent the night of August 28 about five miles south of Newtown. By eight o'clock on the morning of August 29, the troops had broken camp, formed up, and begun to march brigade by brigade. Hand's advance guard soon spotted Indians sprinting away through the forest. By eleven o'clock, Hand's brigade had gingerly advanced to about 300 yards from the ridge. Scouts reported that an unknown number of the enemy was entrenched up there. Hand deployed his riflemen in a skirmish line and behind them the rest of his brigade in six columns.

Butler wanted the Americans to attack him piecemeal, to feed one regiment after another into the mouths of his massed muskets along the ridge. Ideally, the enemy would attack in columns that could be pinned and then surrounded. Shortly after Hand's troops deployed, Butler sent about 400 British and Indians down the ridge to the creek. Their mission was not to attack, but to entice. They slipped through the woods, firing occasionally. Hand did not take the bait. His riflemen lurked behind trees and sniped at the enemy dodging through the woods across the creek. After about an hour, Butler ordered his men back up the slope. The ruse had failed.

Sullivan and the other generals joined Hand, and together they appraised the situation. A direct assault on the ridge would be suicidal. With the enemy's right protected by the river, the only sensible strategy was to encircle the enemy's left. Hand's brigade, supported by Maxwell in his rear and the artillery—six 3-pounders, two 5 1/2-inch howitzers, and a coehorn mortar—in the center would pin down the enemy, while Poor followed by Clinton would cut through the forest, take that distant hill, and then charge into the enemy's rear.

In a thick forest, even the simplest of plans takes hours for an army the size of Sullivan's to execute. It was nearly three o'clock before all the troops were in position. Hand's riflemen led the advance, stalking slowly through the woods up to the creek; from there, they riddled the breastworks with one carefully aimed shot after another, but they did little damage to the enemy. The only targets were tantalizing glimpses of flesh, uniform, or puffs of musket smoke.

Proctor's cannon shots were more effective, at least psychologically. If the Indians kept low, the long rifle shots would not hit them, but the 3-pound iron balls and 5 1/2-inch shells that crashed through the treetops, raining down splinters and branches, terrified them.

Other than the riflemen, most of Hand's brigade and all of Maxwell's had little to do but wait in long lines before the ridge. The battle was much more laborious for the brigades of Poor and Clinton, who were stumbling through the wilderness toward the hill. It took several hours to get there, the troops marching through thick woods, skirting swamps, splashing through creeks, and passing by cabins in a small clearing. As Poor's troops finally began climbing the hill, Indians posted atop it opened fire. Poor ordered his troops to charge with fixed bayonets, and then fired a volley at short range. The Indians scattered. Poor's men paused briefly to catch their breath and nerve at the summit, and then descended toward the rear of the enemy's line. A group of Indians attacked Poor's right flank but was driven off.

Threatened with encirclement, the Indians and British "fled in the greatest disorder, leaving eleven of their Indian warriors and one female dead on the ground . . . We took two prisoners, one a Tory, the other an enlisted negro in one of the Tory companies . . . Our loss was three killed and thirty-nine wounded, principally of General Poor's brigade."[102] Five of the Americans would later die of their wounds. How many the British and Indian lost was undetermined. The Americans reckoned they had killed or mortally wounded many more but could only curse the Indian practice of carrying off their dead. Those enamored of the custom had to content themselves with scalping the dozen left on the field. Hand's light brigade pursued the enemy for three miles but failed to catch up.

The battle of Newtown would be the campaign's only significant clash of arms. Although thousands of men participated, casualties were light, and the fighting decided little. Outnumbered more than five to one and short of munitions, Butler could at best only delay Sullivan's advance. Sullivan's goal too was stymied. A decisive battle was beyond his grasp. The American army was a slow, blind giant that the Tories and Indians could always sidestep. If only Sullivan could match the enemy with Indian allies of his own, then he could discover their whereabouts in that tangled wilderness and launch those nonexistent Indians with Hand's riflemen against them for a true battle, like Oriskany. But that was not to be. All either side could do was shadowbox with the other.

The following day, after the burning and uprooting at Newtown were done, Sullivan ordered his army to parade. Upon congratulating them for their valor and exhorting them to ever more glorious efforts, he revealed some bad news. Only by immediately accepting daily half rations of a half pound each of flour and beef could the campaign proceed for another two weeks. He left it for them to decide. Still hot from the easy victory and caressed by their commander's flattery, the troops heartily applauded the diet. Maj. Jeremiah Fogg noted that "so great and noble was their spirit that scarce a dissenting voice was heard in camp, while manifesting their consent by an universal hurrah! A wag observed that he had seen men shout for joy in a time of plenty but not for half allowance."[103]

On August 30, Sullivan sent back to Fort Sullivan all the wounded, sick, and lame, and his artillery, except for four 3-pounders and a howitzer. He ordered a fort built at Newtown that would be named after its commander, Lt. Col. George Reid of the 2nd New Hampshire. Sullivan then ordered his army due north from the Chemung River valley along the trail over the low swampy divide to Seneca Lake, whose waters eventually drained into Lake Ontario.

Just where was the enemy? While the Americans imagined hordes of Tories and Indians lurking just out of sight, Butler had withdrawn his force to the Seneca village of Canawauga, twelve miles north of Genesee and the last before Fort Niagara sixty miles away. There they awaited more troops, Indians, munitions, and supplies.

Sullivan's army would not face an Indian for another three days after the Newtown battle. On September 2 at Catherine's Town, a couple of miles from Seneca Lake, a soldier found hidden in bushes "Madam Sacho, one of the Tuscarowa tribe, whose silver locks, wrinkled face, dim eyes, and curvitude of body denoted her to be a full blood antediluvian hag! Her language was very little understood by our interpreters. However, one of our Oneidas could understand her."[104] Maj. John Burrowes was more sympathetic, noting the "poor old creature was just ready to die with fear, thinking she was to be killed."[105] Learning of the discovery, Sullivan had her brought to his marquee. Humanitarianism aside, the woman was the only source of information available on the enemy since the two Tories captured at Newtown. "She informed the General that there was a great debate between the warriors, their squaws and children. The squaws had a mind to stay at home with their children. It was carried to such a length that the warriors were obliged to threaten to scalp the women if they did not go. They sent them off about the middle of the afternoon. The warriors themselves stayed till after sunset the evening we got it."[106]

Sullivan had the woman taken to a house and given provisions and a document informing the reader that she should not be harmed. Though she survived, a gruesome sight awaited Sullivan's army when it later marched back through Catherine's Town. A young woman, possibly a granddaughter, who came to care for Sacho, lay dead in a mud hole. By the stench and decay, she had likely been shot three or four days earlier.

There were other atrocities. Lt. William Barton recalled that at a Cayuga Lake village, soldiers found four Indians, a crippled boy, an old, infirm woman, and two younger women. Sullivan ordered the boy and old woman left unmolested in their house and brought out the other women, but some troops defied the general and gleefully "set the house on fire, after securing and making the door fast. The troops having got in motion and marched some distance, the house was consumed together with the savages, in spite of all exertions."[107]

The Americans committed few such atrocities because so few Indians fell into their hands. All the troops could do was destroy the abandoned villages, crops, and orchards. On September 7 at Kanadasega, they found a naked, sickly white child aged about three years who could "understand English and talked Indian."[108] The mother's fate remained unknown.

The army marched along Lake Seneca's east bank to its north end, and then headed due west toward the Genesee valley. By September 12, the army camped a dozen miles from Genesee Castle or Little Beard's Town. That night, Sullivan dispatched Lt. Thomas Boyd, twenty-six riflemen, the Oneida guide Hanyost, and Stockbridge Mahican Captain Jehoiakim to scout a village a few miles ahead. What Boyd could not know was that Butler's army was on a parallel trail only a mile away. Boyd's men searched the abandoned town. Four Indians on horseback appeared. The Americans opened fire but killed only one, whom they scalped. The others fled back to Butler's camp. Boyd sent back four runners to report to Sullivan and followed more slowly with the rest of his command. Butler dispatched a war party of 200 or 300 toward Boyd. Those warriors caught up to and surrounded Boyd and his men about halfway back to camp. Only seven men escaped; one was wounded. Cut off, Boyd and the others formed a circle and fought on, but the Indians quickly overwhelmed them.

The next day, Capt. William Henderson and sixty troops of the 4th Pennsylvania found fourteen of Boyd's dead clumped together. The fighting was so close that powder burns charred some of the stripped and mutilated bodies. Two men were missing—Boyd and Sgt. Michael Parker. Their horrific fate was discovered on September 14, when Sullivan's army marched into Genesee Castle, which, with 128 houses, was the largest Seneca village.

Boyd and Parker were dragged to Genesee after they surrendered. The Indians unleashed all their pent-up rage on their captives, puncturing their bodies with spears and knives, yanking out tongues, ripping out fingernails, gouging out eyes, and tearing off genitals, stuffing them in the bloody, silently screaming mouths, skinning the muscle off the men's ribs, and finally hacking off their heads. Dogs knawed on the corpses as the troops approached. Lt. Col. Henry Dearborn's reaction to the sight was typical: "This was a most horrid spectacle to behold & from which we are taught the necessity of fighting those more than devils to the last moment rather than fall into their hands alive."[109]

At Genesee and several other towns, the Americans witnessed the macabre sight of dogs with wampum necklaces killed and hanging from carved and painted trees. The sacrifice the Indians hoped would appease the gods who allowed the enemy to ravage their country.

The following day, a white woman named Mrs. Lester, with a child at her breast, stumbled into the American camp. At Nanticoke the previous November, the Indians had murdered and scalped her husband and five children before her eyes and dragged her away into captivity. She had escaped in the confusion as the Seneca abandoned Genesee. A few days after being reunited with her countrymen, tragedy inflicted more wounds when her child died. Capt. Roswell Franklin took the grieving woman under his wing and would later marry her.

When questioned, she revealed that Sullivan's campaign was taking its toll on the enemy's unity and morale. Dissension split the enemy ranks: "The women were constantly begging the warriors to sue for peace & that one of the Indians had attempted to shoot Colonel Johnson for the falsehood by which he had deceived & ruined them, that she overheard Butler telling Johnson it was impossible to keep the Indians together after the battle of Newtown."[110] Nonetheless, Butler and Johnson held firm against those Indians who wanted to negotiate with the Americans.

The campaign reached its zenith with the burning of Genesee Castle and the rescue of the white woman and child. That day, the soldiers joyfully received the order to begin the long march home. They retraced their route toward Seneca Lake's north end. En route, a delegation of three Oneida met the army on September 19. The Oneida had come not to fight or guide, but to plead for mercy on behalf of the Cayuga, whose homeland was as yet untorched. Sullivan criticized the Oneida for trying to shield the Cayuga, whose warriors had ravaged the New York and Pennsylvania frontiers.[111]

At the head of Seneca Lake, Sullivan split his army into four on September 20. He would march with the bulk of the army south down Seneca Lake's east side, over the divide to the Chemung valley, and down it to Fort Reid. Two expeditions, meanwhile, would ravage the Lake Cayuga country, with Lt. Col. William Butler leading his 4th Pennsylvania down the east shore and Col. Henry Dearborn leading the 3rd New Hampshire down the west shore. They would then cut southwest and rejoin the main army at Fort Reid. For the fourth expedition, Sullivan ordered Col. Peter Gansevoort to take a "chosen party" of 100 troops and march northeast beyond Cayuga Lake, through the ruined Onondaga country to Oneida Lake, and then east to Fort Schuyler and down the Mohawk valley until he reached the lower Mohawk Castle, which he was to destroy.

Each expedition fulfilled its mission without sight of, let alone resistance from, hostile Indians. Sullivan's column reached Fort Reid on September 24, serenaded by thirteen cannon shots. There the troops rested and rejoiced at the news that Spain had declared war on Britain. The sick and wounded were embarked on bateaux and sent downriver. Dearborn's command reached Fort Reid on September 26 and Butler's two days later; between them, they had destroyed eight Cayuga villages. Though they had a much longer hike, Gansevoort and his hardy 100 men made rapid time. They reached Fort Schuyler on September 25 and surprised the lower Mohawk Castle on September 29. It was hardly a great victory—the "castle" was a mere hamlet of four houses and a few families. Gansevoort took the prisoners with him to Albany but left the houses intact for local settlers to confiscate.[112]

Sullivan led his army downstream on September 29, as Reid's troops demolished the fort and then followed. The army tarried three days at Fort Sullivan before, on October 3, that post was dismantled and the troops headed down the Susquehanna. They reached Wyoming on October 7. After a brief rest, the army marched over the Poconos, entering Easton on October 15. There, Sullivan offered his troops final congratulations and then dispersed the regiments to their various winter quarters.[113]

It was to be Sullivan's last campaign. On November 6, he confessed to Washington, "My health is too much impair'd to be recover'd, but by a total release from the Business, and though the Physicians give me encouragement that this will restore me, I am myself convinced to the contrary, and fear that I must content myself with enjoying the reflection of having used my utmost to serve my Country."[114] He then asked for a leave of indefinite absence. Three days later, he expressed the same sentiments in a letter to the president of Congress. Congress voted to accepted Sullivan's request on November 30.

So just what did Sullivan's campaign accomplish? While they killed only a handful of the enemy, the troops destroyed the homes, crops, and orchards of forty villages. In all, an estimated 160,000 bushels of corn were uprooted or burned, and thousands of fruit trees hacked down or girdled. The campaigns of Sullivan, Clinton, and Brodhead had destroyed nearly every hostile Six Nations village. By autumn, nearly 3,700 refugees had converged on Fort Niagara to demand the food and clothing of the Great Father. The British lacked the supplies or money to buy such necessities. They encouraged the Indians to winter at Montreal, with its more abundant supplies. Regardless of where they took refuge, the Indians suffered greatly that winter. Compounding the Indian misery was one of the worst winters in memory, with the region blanketed at times beneath six feet of snow.[115]

Sullivan and his men could congratulate themselves on devastating the Six Nations, but they left the most important prize of all untouched. Having reached the western end of Iroquoia at Genesee Castle, why did Sullivan not push on to Fort Niagara? The season was still young, his troops outnumbered the enemy by at least three to one, and the fort was only sixty miles away. Sullivan claimed he would "have ventured to have paid Niagara a visit had I been supplied with 15 days provisions in addition to what I had, which I am persuaded from the bravery & ardor of our Troops would have fallen into our hands."[116] Here the general is flat wrong. A want of siege guns and will rather than food kept the Americans from Fort Niagara. Had Sullivan ordered his men to save a portion of the food they destroyed, his army would have enjoyed the sustenance necessary to reach Fort Niagara. Once there, however, his four 3-pounders and howitzer could merely chip away at the fort's stone walls. Sullivan sent back his two 6-pounders after the battle of Newtown, not that those guns would have made much difference at Niagara.

Yet Sullivan still could have taken Niagara for the same reason he disdained from journeying there—food. The British would have been able to muster only about 500 troops from various regiments. The fort could have adequately sheltered them. But what of those 3,700 Indians? Most likely they, would have had to flee across the Niagara River to Canada or else suffer horrendous carnage from Sullivan's guns if they crowded into Fort Niagara's parade ground. How then could they get enough to eat? How could the warriors easily get more powder and shot? Most likely would have deserted the British. The Union Jack probably would have fluttered down its flagpole within a week or two after Sullivan's army appeared. The frontier war in New York and upper Pennsylvania might well have ended then and there for the war's duration, freeing those troops for other fronts.

That, of course, did not happen. What did happen only briefly relieved the northern frontier. Sullivan's troops kicked in a hornet's nest that stung the upper Susquehanna frontier alone with thirty-five raids from 1780 to 1782 and the New York frontier as often.[117] Rather than cow the Indians, the American campaign inspired them to vengeance. Butler was "happy to acquaint your Excellency [Haldimand] that they seem still unshaken in their Attachment to his Majesty's Cause, and declare as soon as they have placed their Women & Children in Security they will go and take Revenge of the Enemy."[118] In all, Maj. Jeremiah Fogg best summed up the campaign: "The nests are destroyed but the birds are still on the wing."[119]

CHAPTER 8

"They Must Soon Die": 1780

*Nations are like men when they grow too old they enter into another
Childhood their Councils are Foolish & they must soon die.*
—Daniel Brodhead
to Wyandot Indians

*They shot them all down and followed them chin-deep in the water to
get their scalps.*
—Alexander Cameron

Time was America's greatest ally. The Revolution succeeded as long as the
British failed to crush it. In the northern and middle colonies, the British
lacked the wit and will to prevail. The war there had stalemated, with the British
holed up in New York City and the Americans dominant elsewhere along the
seaboard. No British political or military leader could devise a plan to break that
impasse. The rebels were content simply to contain the redcoats in their impregnable Manhattan stronghold, confident that the British would defeat themselves,
buried beneath ever soaring debts, deaths, and lassitude. American diplomacy and
allied victories on other fronts would administer the coup de grace.

With no evident means to crack the northern standoff, Whitehall rallied
around the plan of American secretary George Sackville, Viscount Germain, to
hold in the north and methodically conquer one southern colony after another. But
that demanded thousands more troops. Britain's military commitment to North
America peaked in May 1779 with 37,500 troops. Of those, 17,324 troops were in
New York, including 7,711 British, 7,451 Germans, and 2,162 loyalists, and 3,500
regulars were in Canada. The rest were in the south: there were 12,847 troops in
Charles Town, including 7,041 British, 3,018 Germans, and 2,788 loyalists; 862
Germans and 1,016 loyalists in Savannah; 1,452 troops in West Florida; and 536 in
East Florida.[1]

But could all those king's horses and men prevail? For nearly two years after
Savannah's capture in December 1779, the southern strategy appeared to be work-

ing as the British won a string of victories and overran much of Georgia and the Carolinas. True, that record was clouded by outright defeats at Kings Mountain and Cowpens, and Pyrrhic victories like Guilford Courthouse. Yet overall, the British were winning the war along the seaboard and piedmont. On the frontier, too, the Crown's agents and Indian allies won more than they lost as measured by the hundreds of charred cabins and rotting corpses fouling clearings from Canada to Florida. And then came Yorktown.[2]

INTERNATIONAL DIPLOMACY AND THE FRONTIER

British naval and army power was being stretched to the snapping point by war or the threat of war. A growing threat loomed in the Baltic region, a vital source of British naval supplies. On February 28, Empress Catherine II of Russia declared the creation of the League of Armed Neutrality to deter Britain from seizing ships carrying contraband of war to the belligerents. Denmark and Sweden soon joined. On December 20, Britain declared war against the Netherlands to prevent that country's acceptance into the league, which would embrace only neutrals. With only thirteen ships of the line, the Netherlands was a second-rate power with an immense merchant fleet that was highly vulnerable to attacks by the Royal Navy and British privateers. King George's warships would indeed reap a profitable harvest from Dutch shipping, but at the expense of that many fewer American ships bottled up in port or seized on the high seas. The losses suffered by the French, Spanish, and Dutch all contributed to America's success in winning independence and the frontiers it demanded.[3]

In key European capitals, American envoys tried to conquer at diplomatic tables what the new nation's soldiers failed to secure on the battlefields. At Madrid, John Jay failed utterly. The news that Louisiana governor Bernardo de Galvez had captured Mobile prompted Spain to adamantly reject not only Jay's call for an alliance, but also his insistence that the American frontier ended on the Mississippi River and the rights of free navigation down that stream to the Gulf of Mexico. The Spanish countered that America's western frontier rested on the Appalachian watershed, and called for a peace based on uti possidetis, or those lands then held by military forces. Jay threw up his hands in disgust at notions that would have straitjacketed the United States between the Appalachians and the Atlantic, shorn of New York, Savannah, and Charles Town, then in British hands.

Jay's report of Spain's demands provoked outrage among many delegates when it reached Congress. But America's bargaining position was at a low ebb. The British were conquering the southern colonies while Galvez was taking West Florida. Might made territorial right. Nonetheless, Congress voted on October 4 to reassert its previous frontier claims. The foreign affairs committee appointed James Madison to write a defense of those claims for Jay to use in his reply to the Spanish court. Madison penned a powerful, lawyerly essay that rooted American frontier and Mississippi navigation claims in the 1763 Treaty of Paris, under which those lands and rights were transferred from France to Britain. Thus, the

Americans had to win those rights from Britain, not Spain. On October 17, the foreign affairs committee submitted its report to Congress, which enthusiastically approved it and sent it to Jay.

THE SOUTHEAST FRONTIER: FIRST PHASE

Determined to deal a knockout blow to the southern rebels, Maj. Gen. Henry Clinton set sail with 8,500 troops from New York City on December 26, 1779. Six weeks later, on February 11, 1780, the armada dropped anchor off John's Island in Charles Town Bay and Clinton landed his army. Leaving a few hundred men with Gen. Andrew Williamson at Augusta, Benjamin Lincoln hurried with his army to join Gen. William Moultrie in holding Charles Town. Clinton was happy to allow Lincoln to slip into that trap of a city. While Clinton bottled up Lincoln, cavalry forces led by Col. Banastre Tarleton and Maj. Patrick Ferguson ravaged the surrounding region. The siege lines crept ever closer. British warships sailed past twin forts Moultrie and Sullivan into Charles Town's inner bay. The combined naval and land guns systematically destroyed the city as the defenders' food and munitions steadily dwindled. Then on May 12, the United States suffered its worst defeat of the war when Lincoln ignominiously surrendered his 5,500 troops.

Clinton followed up his victory with related political and military strategies. He issued a proclamation granting amnesty to all rebels who signed an oath of allegiance before June 20. He fanned forces out from Charles Town and Savannah to overrun South Carolina and Georgia all the way to the frontier. As troops garrisoned Augusta, Ninety-Six, Camden, Rocky Mount, Cheraw, and Georgetown in the piedmont, the legions of Colonel Tarleton and Major Ferguson rampaged through the countryside, wiping out pockets of rebels and gathering loyalists as they rode. With this work done, Clinton set sail on June 8 and headed back to the New York stalemate, leaving Maj. Gen. Edward Cornwallis to command the southern theater.

Tarleton struck first blood, killing or capturing nearly all 380 troops under Col. Abraham Buford at Waxhaw Creek on May 29. That "Waxhaw massacre" was the first instance of "Tarleton's quarter" that would terrorize the south for another two and a half years and intimidate many erstwhile patriots into meekly taking the king's pardon. Andrew Williamson and Andrew Pickens were the most prominent patriots among hundreds who swore allegiance to George III before the June 20 deadline.

Meanwhile, several thousand loyalists who had lain low for years joined the British forces overrunning Georgia and South Carolina. Not all those who tried reached the British camp. Over 1,300 North Carolina piedmont loyalists gathered under Col. John Moore at Ramour's Mill and prepared to march south. Gen. Griffith Rutherford with 800 troops at Charlotte and Col. Francis Locke with 400 at Mountain Creek converged to attack the loyalists. Locke reached Moore's men on June 20. About 800 of the loyalists had already slipped away, so the two forces were nearly even. Both sides suffered about 110 casualties, but the patriots took the field: most loyalists scattered to their homes, and Moore fled with only 30 followers to Camden.

Loyalists suffered even heavier losses later that summer. During June and July, Ferguson's legion ravaged western South Carolina and was poised to canter into North Carolina. Col. Charles McDowell, the western North Carolina commander, sent an appeal for help to the "Overmountain Men" of Washington County. With a couple hundred men each, Isaac Shelby and James Robertson joined McDowell's camp at Cherokee Ford on the Broad River. McDowell combined those troops with Elijah Clarke's and under his command rode to Thickety Fort. Without firing a shot, they forced the surrender of its ninety-three loyalist defenders commanded by Col. Patrick Moses on July 30.

Ferguson sent Maj, James Dunlop in pursuit. Dunlop and his troopers caught up with the Americans at Fairforest on August 7. The frontiersmen stood their ground and fired steadily, killing or wounding roughly thirty and capturing fifty of the enemy while losing only four dead and twenty wounded. This was Ferguson's first repulse. Ferguson then sent Col. Alexander Innes against the rebels. Innes attacked with 300 men at Musgrove Mill on August 17. The Americans enticed the British into a trap, killing sixty-three, wounding ninety, and capturing seventy, while losing only four killed and nine wounded.

These gains were wiped out by the fumbling general that Congress sent to replace Lincoln. Although Horatio Gates was timid in battle, his inhibitions magically cleared when it came to politics. While he had presided over the victory at Saratoga, he maneuvered openly for George Washington's job. Upon joining the starving, ragged shards of the southern Continental army at Hillsboro, North Carolina, he conceived an uncharacteristically bold stroke, quick-marching his 1,000 regulars and 2,000 militia to Camden, the British supply depot for western South Carolina. Cornwallis learned of his advance and gathered 2,500 regulars to await Gates there. On the morning of August 16, the day after the weary Americans arrived, Cornwallis ordered his army to attack. The battle did not last long. First the militia and then the Continentals broke before the bayonets and huzzahs of the redcoats. "They ran like a torrent," Gates admitted.[4] While losing 325 men, the British inflicted more than 1,000 casualties on the Americans at Camden and in the pursuit all the way to Hanging Rock, twenty-two miles away. They also captured more than 150 supply-filled wagons. The southern army was shattered. North Carolina lay open to British occupation. Cornwallis marched the bulk of his army on to Charlotte, while Tarleton's legion swept all to the west and Ferguson's troopers cantered even farther into the frontier.[5]

Frontiersmen offered the only significant resistance left in the region. Those men would eventually reap their revenge, but not before some setbacks of their own. Clarke, Shelby, and Williams followed up their Musgrove Mill victory by marching with 600 men against Augusta. With a little more luck and skill, they might have bagged Brown and his command. The timing was poor. Nearly 1,000 Creek led by David Taitt were striding toward Augusta to attend a council called by Brown. En route, Taitt sickened and died. The death was a bad omen to most Creek, who returned home. Little Prince of the Tuckabatchee continued with about 250 Creek. Those Creek combined with Lt. Col. Thomas Brown's audacity to save Augusta.

The battle of Augusta on September 14 was one of the war's more fluid. Clarke split his troops for a simultaneous assault, with Maj. Samuel Taylor attacking the Creek camp and Lt. Col. James McCall assaulting the town from the east. Taylor charged and scattered the Creek, but McCall was repulsed. Brown gathered his men and surged out against Taylor, who retreated. Clarke slipped in behind Brown and captured Fort Grierson and the MacKay house, two strongholds on the town's outskirts. Brown was determined to push back Clarke. He anchored a 1-pounder cannon at each end of his line and had them open fire. Then he ordered the Creek to hit Clarke's left flank while he led his troops against the enemy's right. The Americans retreated in good order, with a portion dashing around to capture a cannon. Brown withdrew into Augusta with his soldiers and Creek warriors. Clarke had his men hem in the town.

The following morning, the Americans dragged the 4-pounder and 6-pounder cannons captured at Fort Grierson to Garden Hill outside Augusta. Riflemen sniped at glimpses of flesh and uniforms within the town's entrenchments as other men built makeshift breastworks for the cannons. A bullet tore through Brown's thighs. A British bullet killed Clarke's best gunner, Capt. William Martin. That evening, Brown spurned Clarke's demand to surrender.

Relief was on the way. Brown had sent a plea for reinforcements to Col. John Harris Cruger, commanding Fort Ninety-Six. Leaving 100 militia in the fort, Cruger marched with Delancey's New York brigade, Col. Alexander Innes's South Carolina royalists, and Col. Isaac Allen's New Jersey volunteers. Learning of that approaching force, Clarke ordered a withdrawal. Brown charged his troops against the Americans, capturing scores of stragglers. When Brown discovered that thirteen of the prisoners had broken their parole, he ordered them hanged together on the MacKay house's veranda. Cruger meanwhile chased Clarke's diminishing force to the Broad River, taking 100 along the way. Then Ferguson learned of Clarke's flight and galloped his men west for the kill.

THE GULF OF MEXICO FRONTIER
The elation of Clinton's capture of Charles Town was partly undercut by disturbing news from the Gulf of Mexico. For months, Maj. Gen. John Campbell had received reports that Gov. Bernardo de Galvez was preparing a campaign against Mobile and Pensacola. On January 11, that threat was made good when Galvez set sail from New Orleans with 754 troops, including 43 of the Regiment Principe of the 2nd Battalion, 50 from the Havana Regiment, 141 from the Louisiana Regiment, 26 carabiniers, 323 white militia, 107 free blacks and mulattoes, 14 gunners, 24 slaves, and 26 Americans, packed aboard one unarmed frigate, four settees, a packet, the war frigate *Volante,* the galliot *Valenzuela,* and four, including *Galvez* and *Kaulican.*[6]

As always, nature was cruel to Galvez. Harsh winds and seas grounded six ships at Mobile Bay's entrance on February 10. After refloating them, it took two weeks to disembark the troops and supplies in the heavy surf and move them just beyond cannon shot of Mobile. On February 20, five ships carrying 1,412 troops sailing from Havana joined Galvez.

By March 1, all of Galvez's troops, supplies, and guns were ashore, protected by the fleet's massed cannons. That day, the governor called on Mobile's commander, Capt. Elias Dunford, to surrender. Dunford politely declined. The laborious process of undertaking a siege began. On March 12, a battery of eight 18-pounders and one 24-pounder was completed and opened fire on Fort Charlotte. Dunford struck his flag that evening. In all, ninety-eight troops of the 60th, sixteen gunners, four Maryland loyalists, two surgeons, sixty sailors, fifty-four civilians, and fifty-one slaves went into captivity.[7]

Campbell first got wind of Galvez's expedition on February 12. In an unusual burst of initiative, he quickly gathered 413 regulars and militia, 105 Indians, two cannons, and a howitzer, and set off overland for Mobile. But the relief army was still far away when word arrived of Dunford's capitulation. Campbell hurried his army back to Pensacola. Galvez found out about Campbell's expedition only after it turned tail. On March 15, a Spanish detachment brought in seventeen British dragoons captured ten leagues from Mobile.

After taking Mobile, Galvez wanted to sail to Pensacola. While awaiting reinforcements from Havana, he received an exaggerated account that Campbell could muster about 3,500 troops. When the Havana reinforcements failed to arrive, Galvez prudently chose to return to New Orleans and prepare a stronger expedition. That effort would take half a year.

Assuming that Galvez was on his way, Campbell ordered Alexander Cameron to rally the Indians to Pensacola's defense. Cameron dispatched his deputies, Alexander McGillvray and William McIntosh for the Creek, and Farquhar Bethune for the Choctaw, to convene councils, distribute gifts, and urge the natives to war. The deputies found very different responses to their pleas. Indian loyalties shifted with the news that the Spanish had taken Mobile. The Choctaw now favored neutrality rather than alliance with Britain. The Creek, however, were far enough away to defy Spain's resurgent power. Those views affected the number of Indians rallied to the warpath. By April 16, there were 1,235 Creek, 236 Choctaw, and 31 Chickasaw at Pensacola ready to defend that citadel or surge against Mobile.[8]

But all those efforts were for naught. When word arrived that Spain's invasion force had dispersed, Campbell saw no need to feed his Indian defenders and ordered them to return to their distant villages. The abrupt and rather contemptuous manner with which he dismissed them dismayed the Indians and angered the agents who had worked so hard to rally them. Alexander Cameron blasted Campbell for knowing nothing "of Indians or their affairs; he thinks they are to be used like slaves or a people void of natural sense."[9]

Not all the Indians were content to leave peacefully. Chickasaw chief Opay-mataha and his warriors scouted around Mobile and took a Spanish scalp and three prisoners home. The 1,500 or more other Indians who had heeded Camp-bell's plea trudged home void of booty or battle tales, bitter at the general's dis-dain. Like the boy who cried wolf, Campbell would miss many of those Indians the following year when he really needed them.

Having joined the war, King Carlos III gave his commanders enough ships, troops, and supplies to win. On April 26, 1780, Vice Adm. Jose Solano sailed from Cadiz with a fleet of 17 warships and 140 transports packed with 11,752 troops under Gen. Victorio de Navia. Solano managed to dodge Adm. George Romney's British fleet in the Caribbean and drop anchor in Havana's harbor on August 4. Galvez joined a portion of that army with his own troops for a try at Pensacola. On October 16, he set sail with 3,829 troops and 164 officers squeezed aboard a fleet of seven warships, six frigates, and fifty-one transports from Havana for Pensacola.[10]

Once again, the weather allied with Britain. A hurricane hit shortly after the expedition reached the open sea. For five days, the raging winds and waves bat-tered and scattered the fleet. Though miraculously no ships were lost, it took weeks before they returned to Havana. Invaluable time and supplies had been consumed. Galvez reluctantly postponed the operation until the next year.

Learning of the armada, Campbell again sought to rally the Indians. Cameron and his deputies journeyed to the councils across the region. This time, far fewer warriors were enticed from the hunt to converge on Mobile for scalps and loot. Cameron reported that the Indians "are daily out in small parties about Mobile and not a Spaniard can venture out of sight of the fort but they knock up and carry off his scalp . . . The Spanish are in greatest distress being cooped up by the Indi-ans."[11] The largest coup was when the Indians killed three and captured fourteen. The victims, however, were French and thus officially British subjects rather than Spanish. Annoying and occasionally tragic as the Indian raids were, they did not threaten Spain's grip on Mobile.

THE TENNESSEE FRONTIER
Amidst the war, a new cluster of American settlements sprouted on the frontier. Following the Cherokee land sessions at the 1777 Long Island treaty, James Robertson and John Donelson combined with Richard Henderson to scheme a settlement at French Creek on the Cumberland River. Settlers would arrive before the 1780 planting season from two directions. Robertson's party would trudge overland, while Donelson's would voyage by flatboat down the Tennessee and up the Cumberland River. Both parties departed in late December 1779.

In January, Robertson's party plodded its way through the frosty wilderness to French Lick without serious incident. They were not the first whites to exploit that site. Casper Mansker and Michael Stoner together and Jacques Timothe Boucher de Montbrun alone had hunted and trapped that region for years, sheltering in crude huts. During the rebellion, about thirty Tory families had fled to the area. The newcomers and old-timers tried to work out disputes over land and authority.

The Donelson party, meanwhile, faced a gauntlet of dangers that might have challenged Odysseus. With high hopes, the argonauts departed Fort Blackmore on the Clinch River on December 22, 1779, but could only inch their way downstream as their boats grounded continually on shallow stretches and hung up on rocks amidst the enveloping hellish cold. Three boats with twenty-eight Wataugans joined the Donelson party's misery on February 20. So far, frustration and frostbite were the worst challenges.

A genuine danger lurked where the river squeezed fast between the Cumberland Mountains. There the party frenziedly poled their awkward flatboats around the notorious boiling pot that devoured and spat out the wreckage of poorly handled craft. It was here that the pioneers entered a shooting gallery of musket balls from Cherokee concealed among trees and boulders on either shore. The firing worsened for the score or so of miles below those rapids where Chickamauga villages dotted the banks. The cost of passage was high. A musket ball killed one man. A slave drowned. Warriors seized two men who stepped ashore, killing one and enslaving the other. A baby was crushed as an outburst of firing provoked a rush to cover on a crowded boat. Smallpox broke out among the Wataugans, and Donelson forced them to drop far behind to lessen the chance of spreading infection. Reaching the Tennessee River mouth on March 15, they laboriously poled their way up the dozen miles of racing Ohio River floodwaters to the Cumberland River mouth and then up it. They did not reach the Red River mouth until April 12. Here Moses Renfroe's family and friends announced they would pole no farther. They went ashore to clear land and raise cabins. In their dying moments, they would mourn that decision. The Donelson party reached Amos Station on April 23 and the next day ended their journey at the Salt River mouth, where they scattered to build homes in the wilderness. Ever the killjoy, Richard Henderson arrived with a party to assert the claims of his Transylvania Company on April 24.

The danger of Indian attack overshadowed the inevitable conflicts over land. A boat crammed with a dozen men and four families ground ashore with a horrifying tale of a Chickasaw attack down the Tennessee River. They repelled the Indians, but another boat with eight men and one family was overwhelmed and never seen again. Then terrified survivors from the Renfroe settlement stumbled into French Lick, having lost twenty of their loved ones and neighbors in a surprise Chickasaw attack.

To meet that threat and resolve conflicting land claims, the settlers engaged in a classic example of frontier democracy by negotiating and signing the Cumberland Compact on May 1. Twelve judges or triers would be elected from among the eight stations, which included around 300 settlers, with three for Nashborough, two for Mankser's, and one each for Bledsoe's, Asher's, Stone's River, Freeland's, Easton's, and Fort Union. All freemen over twenty-one years old could vote. All men from sixteen to sixty had to muster.

Others, meanwhile, sought vengeance for the Chickamauga attacks on Donelson's party. In June, Virginia governor Thomas Jefferson ordered Col. William Campbell to rally the militia and march on the Chickamauga. With 500 men, Campbell reached the Nolachucky by late August. There, Campbell's campaign ground to a halt as word arrived of the disastrous battle of Camden. The troops demanded they be released to defend their families.

That freed the Chickamauga to try to rid the cluster of squatters around French Lick. A war party stalked through the Cumberland settlements in November. Within days, the warriors killed two men at Clover Bottom, three at the Stone River mouth, and two at Mansker's Station, and they shot down a man and captured his daughter making salt at Neeley's Lick. Fed up with a year of horrors, most of the Donelson party fled to the relative safety of Kentucky. Most other settlers clung to their rude cabins and palisades, their only worldly possessions.[12]

THE NEW YORK FRONTIER: FIRST PHASE

The winter was harsh for the thousands of Indians huddled in crowded refugee camps around Fort Niagara and those villages that had escaped destruction from Sullivan's campaign. Disease killed scores of Indians enfeebled by malnutrition. The deprivation and misery, however, cowed few men; most warriors were eager for vengeance.

Not surprisingly, Joseph Brant led the year's first raid. On February 11, he strode east with six whites and about 230 Mohawk, Cayuga, Nanticoke, Delaware, Onondaga, Seneca, and Tutelo toward the Mohawk valley. En route, they ran into a delegation of two Mohawk and two Cayuga heading toward Fort Niagara. Leading those envoys was venerable Mohawk sachem Little Abraham, who carried two letters from Philip Schuyler, one to Guy Johnson calling for a prisoner exchange and the other from Congress beseeching all Indians to return to their homes and neutrality. Brant detached some warriors to escort the envoys to Niagara, and then hurried with the rest of his men toward the Mohawk valley.

Johnson received the envoys and convened a council of Iroquois sachems on February 17 to discuss their message. The sachems spurned the offer and reaffirmed their allegiance to the Crown. Then, in a blatant violation of Indian diplomatic immunity, Johnson jailed the four on charges of subversion. He did, however, agree to Schuyler's suggestion for a prisoner exchange. His harsh treatment of the envoys would prevent him from finding any willing go-betweens to arrange a deal.[13]

Brant's war party, meanwhile, reached the Schoharie valley on April 7. Scouts discovered fourteen troops led by Capt. Alexander Harper who were boiling down sap for maple syrup. Brant and his men crept up, opened fire, and charged, killing three and capturing the rest. Harper claimed that 300 regulars would soon come to their rescue. Brant believed that lie and broke off his raid, herding all but one of the prisoners to Niagara. But before leaving, he sent back a captive with a message for the Americans. Although Brant always tried to restrain his warriors from committing atrocities, he had acquired a reputation as a merciless murderer. That unfair charge ate at his mind. In his message, he explained that while he was fierce in battle, as for captives, "I released many. Neither were the weak and the helpless subjected to death. It is a shame to destroy those who are defenseless. This has uniformly been my conduct during the War." He then condemned those who committed atrocities against the Indians, and promised he would seek vengeance on those who did.[14]

Other war parties that strode from Niagara and elsewhere to attack the frontier were not so restrained. Captain Shinop led twenty-five out on February 16. Sixteen warriors trailed Little Beard and Tanaghkewas on February 26. The next day, three war parties left: Chew Tobacco and eight warriors, Rowland Montour also with eight, and Fish Hook with fifteen. That was just one month's worth. From February 11 through July 1, 498 Indians departed on the warpath from Fort Niagara. Beyond July 1 to late autumn, over 400 warriors would stalk, murder, and loot along the New York frontier.[15]

Those war parties usually succeeded. In early April, war parties raided Cherry Valley, Harpersfield, and Riemendsnyder's Bush. Many did not get that far and instead harassed the closest enemy position, Fort Schuyler. Not all raids originated at Fort Niagara. Many war parties strode south from Crown Point. On March 21, a force of 300 British and Indians captured Skenesborough and its thirteen defenders, but that was the prelude to an even larger raid.

John Johnson must have burned with more than usual anticipation when he led 528 men from Crown Point on May 12. He sought more than destruction, booty, and scalps. He hoped to fight his way through to the mansion he was forced to flee four years earlier. On the evening of May 21, he and his men wearily sprawled in the forest just beyond Johnstown, not far from his estate. As his officers and chiefs crouched around him, Sir John presented his plan for a two-pronged attack. Scouts disrupted his discourse with reports of converging rebel columns that most likely outnumbered his own. The chiefs spoke among themselves and then punctured any elation Johnson may have felt at being poised to avenge himself on those who had driven him from his home. The British could attack Johnstown if they wished, but the Indians would wait for them at Tribe Hill.

Like so many frontier commanders, Sir John found himself at the Indians' mercy. Grudgingly, he scrapped his plan, bypassed Johnstown, and burned Caughnawaga the next day. Johnson proposed heading to Stone Arabia. The chiefs objected once again, complaining of fatigue. Instead, they turned back to Johnstown, pillaging and burning all the way. In all, they destroyed 120 houses and barns, killed eleven settlers, and captured twenty-seven others, of which Sir John later released fourteen who were too old or sick. At Johnstown, 143 loyalists joined his party. Col. John Harper and 300 militia shadowed the raid's progress and a portion of its withdrawal but dared not attack. Johnson's marauders straggled into Crown Point on June 3.[16]

After resting briefly at Fort Niagara, Joseph Brant recruited another war party, this time with 300 warriors and 13 whites. They departed on July 11, bound for the Oneida and Tuscarora villages. In each village, Brant condemned the people for supporting the Americans, had his men torch all the homes, and then ordered everyone to journey to Fort Niagara and pledge allegiance to the Crown. The Oneida and Tuscarora splintered, with some heading to Niagara and others to Albany. This raid completed the destruction of the traditional homeland of the Six Nations. By now, nearly every village was charred ruins and its people huddled in distant refugee camps.

Brant then headed north to the Mohawk valley, where he joined a war party of Sayenqueraghta and Cornplanter. Together they had 400 warriors and a score of whites. They destroyed fifty-three homes and other buildings in the Canajoharie district. While most headed back toward Fort Niagara, two parties split off for more raiding. Cornplanter led about thirty warriors east along the Mohawk valley's southern side; they killed eight settlers and took two. Brant and his men hit the Schoharie valley, killing three and taking fourteen. Then they turned their backs on their swaths of desolation and strode west, but they would soon haunt the frontier again.[17]

THE NORTHWEST FRONTIER

With Henry Hamilton languishing in a Virginia jail, Gov. Patrick Sinclair took command of war in the northwest. At Fort Michilimackinac, Sinclair set in motion his part of a grand five-pronged strategy devised by Lord Germain for sweeping the Mississippi and Ohio valleys of the Americans and Spanish. From Michilimackinac, Capt. Charles Langlade would lead a campaign against St. Louis via the Illinois River and link up with Wabasha's Sioux descending the Mississippi. Upon taking St. Louis, Langlade would head downriver all the way to Natchez. Detroit's new lieutenant governor, Maj. Arent De Peyster, would rally, equip, and dispatch two large war parties, one led by Capt. Henry Bird to harass Fort Nelson at the falls of the Ohio, and another to shadow and possibly retake Fort Patrick Henry at Vincennes if it proved to be ill defended. Meanwhile, in the Gulf of Mexico, Gen. John Campbell would launch an attack from Pensacola against New Orleans, and then advance up the Mississippi River to join Langlade.

No British plan for the west was ever more comprehensive, complicated, and wide ranging. In comparison, the 1777 campaign in New York, however grandiose it seemed at the time, fell short of Sinclair's in everything but the number of troops involved. But like the 1777 plan, Sinclair's would fail miserably.

One problem was that the enemy learned of the plan shortly after Sinclair began to implement it. Details trickled back through the Indian grapevine to George Rogers Clark at Fort Nelson, Fernando de Leyba at St. Louis, and Bernardo de Galvez in New Orleans. Leyba and Clark would repel the attacks on St. Louis and Cahokia, respectively, while Galvez broke the Gulf strategy by his own campaign that captured Mobile.

Before Clark rushed up the Mississippi, he would fulfill orders to build a fort that, in retrospect, was a waste of money, men, and energies that might have been better invested elsewhere. At the time, however, planting a fort near the confluence of the Ohio and Mississippi Rivers seemed like a good idea. That fort would at once help protect navigation on those waters and cement Virginia's stake to the region and America's to the Mississippi River. Upon receiving Gov. Thomas Jefferson's orders, Clark fulfilled the mission with his usual energy and resourcefulness. In April, he led a party to the bluff known as Iron Bank on Kentucky's west end, a half-dozen miles south of the confluence of the Mississippi and Ohio Rivers; purchased the land from the Chickasaw; and by May had erected Fort Jefferson. That lonely outpost was the westernmost extension of American power. It would not last long.[18]

Early that year, Sinclair organized the expedition to sweep down the Mississippi valley. Lacking regulars, he would rely on Indian hordes leavened by militia volunteers and officers. He appointed the Prairie du Chien merchant Emanuel Hesse to command the St. Louis campaign. Hesse was no novice, having fought as a lieutenant in the 60th Royal Americans during the French and Indian War. In February, he spread word for the tribes to rendezvous at the portage linking the Fox and Wisconsin Rivers. In March, two couriers with dispatches along with Chippewa chief Matchekewis and his warriors reached Hesse after a grueling winter journey from Michilimackinac. The word was to advance to Prairie du Chien and rally the Sioux above and Sauk and Fox below along the Mississippi. By May 1, over 750 Indians, mostly Chippewa, Winnebago, and Menominee, leavened by 200 Santee Sioux led by Wabasha and smaller parties of Ottawa, Kickapoo, Mascouten, and Potawatomi, had eagerly gathered to destroy St. Louis. They departed Prairie du Chien on May 2. At Rock Island, Hesse and the chiefs convinced nearly 250 Sauk and Fox to join the expedition. En route to St. Louis, they captured forty-six Spanish subjects. They pushed on to take what Hesse had promised was an undefended town filled with cowardly Spanish. In that, they would find they had been grossly deceived.[19]

The lieutenant governor of upper Louisiana, Capt. Fernando de Leyba, had energetically prepared St. Louis for defense ever since he got word on February 20 that Spain had declared war on Britain. He ordered flood-plagued Fort Carlos, at the confluence of the Missouri and Mississippi Rivers, abandoned and its handful of defenders and rusty cannons brought back to St. Louis. He set to work parties to dig entrenchments linking four circular stone towers on the town's outskirts. Those efforts were spurred in late March, when a trader descending from Prairie du Chien brought word of the expedition. By the time the enemy appeared, entrenchments spiked with abatis arched around the town. Though only one of the towers was completed, its two 6-pounder and three 4-pounder cannons could cover any approach. Manning those defenses were 34 Spanish regulars, 168 foot militia commanded by Lt. Jean Baptiste Martiguy, and 50 mounted militia led by Capt. Eugene Poure. Meanwhile, George Rogers Clark at Fort Jefferson learned of the invasion, gathered all but a handful of defenders, and headed upriver to Cahokia; he arrived on May 25.

The Indian and British flotilla ground ashore on the Mississippi's eastern shore several miles above Cahokia on the evening of May 24. After a day of scouting, Hesse split his force in two. He would lead 650 Indians against St.

Louis, while Jean Marie Ducharme led the rest in a simultaneous attack on Cahokia. They moved out early on May 26. Around one o'clock that afternoon, the Winnebago and Wapasha's Sioux, followed timidly by the Sauk and Fox, swarmed through the fields north of St. Louis, killing or capturing a score of people foolish enough to venture beyond the fortifications. As the Indians moved within range, the Spanish opened fire first with cannons and then muskets, killing a Winnebago chief and three of his warriors and wounding four others. As the Sauk and Fox slunk away to loot and burn outlying farms, the Winnebago and Sioux took cover and fired on the entrenchments. Across the river at Cahokia, Ducharme's Indians hung back when they learned that Clark was before them. They opened a long-range musket fire, and then withdrew when they heard Hesse's repulse before St. Louis. In all, the Indians killed fourteen whites and seven slaves, wounded six whites and one slave, and captured twelve whites and thirteen slaves. Lacking cannons for a siege, and with his Indians' lust for scalps, captives, and plunder satisfied, Hesse had no choice but to withdraw.[20]

Clark crossed the river to celebrate with Leyba their victory and to plan an expedition up the Mississippi. Clark would not join that campaign. Learning of pending British and Indian attacks on Kentucky, he hurried with a portion of his men to Fort Nelson. On June 13, Capt. John Montgomery, with 250 Americans and Illinois militia, and Lt. Picote de Belestre, with 100 Spanish militia, headed upriver. As with most western campaigns, the grasp fell short of the goal. Montgomery's expedition advanced up the Mississippi and Illinois Rivers to Peoria, and then headed overland west to the Rock River's mouth on the Mississippi. There they burned the abandoned Sauk and Fox village of Saukenuk and returned to St. Louis.[21]

Fate granted Fernando de Leyba little time to savor triumph. Stress and illness combined to kill him on June 28. Capt. Franciso Cartabona took over temporary command and sent word back to New Orleans. On July 25, Galvez appointed Franciso Cruzat to replace him. Cruzat arrived at St. Louis on September 24.[22]

In the summer of 1780, the British launched their most destructive raid against Kentucky, and the Kentuckians countered with their largest campaign against the Ohio villages. In June, Lt. Henry Bird headed south from Detroit with about 600 Indians and Canadians, along with a 6-pounder and 3-pounder. His objective was Fort Nelson at the Ohio falls, but when his Indians learned that Clark was there, they demanded that Bird lead them instead toward the Kentucky settlements. Bird had no choice but to comply. They crossed the Ohio River at the Licking River mouth and advanced up that valley until they approached Ruddle's Station on June 22. The 3-pounder was unlimbered and fired only twice before the defenders surrendered. Bird led most of his men on to Martin's Station, whose inhabitants gave up when they saw the cannon. Bird's victory was not only bloodless, but also the war's largest in the Ohio valley. His men herded nearly 300 captives and loyalists back to Detroit.[23]

Another raid occurred a month later, this time against Fort Jefferson. On July 17, a Chickasaw war party led by James Colbert surged through the cabins beyond the fort and killed two settlers and tomahawked another, who staggered away to shelter with other refugees in a detached blockhouse. The defenders opened fire and believed they killed or wounded several Indians and drove off the rest. The Chickasaw slaughtered the livestock and sniped at the fort and block-house. A shot from the garrison wounded Colbert as he approached with a surren-der demand. After six days, the war party withdrew with their loot to the Chickasaw villages.[24]

Meanwhile, Clark labored to gather enough supplies and men to retaliate for Bird's raid. He ordered the vulnerable garrisons of Fort Clark at Kaskaskia and Fort Patrick Henry at Vincennes withdrawn to Fort Nelson. Capt. Valentine Dal-ton and his men were relieved to abandon Fort Patrick Henry. On June 17, they skirmished with a war party of 80 to 100 warriors, killed 2, and scattered the rest. Though they could rejoice at repelling that raid, they dreaded being overrun by a larger war party. From the summer of 1780, no American forts stood north of the Ohio River.[25]

Clark viewed that withdrawal as temporary. If he could severely punish the Ohio Indians, the posts could be reoccupied. It was not until mid-July that he gathered enough supplies to launch his campaign.[26] He spread word to the Ken-tucky militia to meet him as he advanced up the Ohio River, with no one arriving later than July 31 at the Licking River mouth. Each settlement's militia mustered, and four out of five men headed to meet Clark, with half joining at the Kentucky River mouth and the rest at the Licking River mouth. The first blood flowed about a half-dozen miles above the Kentucky River. While Clark led the main force along the south shore, Capt. Hugh McGary and thirty men hunted along the north shore. An Indian party jumped them, killing or wounding nine; McGary and the survivors paddled to safety on the south shore.

On August 1, the men who had ascended the Ohio and those who descended the Licking met where the two waters mingled. The day was spent ferrying those 998 men and their supplies across the Ohio River and constructing a blockhouse on the north shore. In the blockhouse, Clark left his sick, wounded, and a small guard. On August 2, the frontier army advanced with 970 men, a 6-pounder, two 4-pounders, and a supply wagon, each drawn by four horses up the Little Miami val-ley toward Chillicothe. He split his troops into two divisions, with each in turn divided into four parallel columns forty yards apart with flankers and front and rear guards. Daniel Boone was among the scouts who ranged miles ahead of the army.

The Shawnee had ample warning of the Kentuckians' approach. As the enemy neared on August 6, the Indians torched Chillicothe and disappeared into the forest. The frontiersmen gleefully looted what they could and uprooted the crops. Clark then led them northwest to Piqua. A rainstorm stalled their advance a dozen miles short. Without tents or any shelter, the frontiersmen were soon soaked and suf-fered the storm's incessant pelting all night. The next morning, when Clark ordered his troops to clear their guns by company, the volleys spooked the horses, which cost hours to gather.

When they pushed forward on August 8, the Kentuckians encountered the first Indians several miles from Piqua. The warriors delayed the enemy advance by sniping and slipping back through the trees. Clark's army did not reach sight of the village until around two o'clock. Piqua was an unwieldy target with its lodges stretching in clumps for nearly three miles along the Mad River.

Assessing the situation, Clark devised a plan to seize either end of Piqua and crush it like a giant accordion. He ordered the troops of William Linn, John Floyd, and James Harrod to hit the village's southwest end, while Benjamin Logan and his men arced around the village's northeastern end. After those troops began their attacks, Clark would march with Col. George Slaughter's eighty Virginia regulars and the cannon forward against the enemy's heart. It was nearly five o'clock before his left flank got into position and began their attack. Stymied by thick forest, a steep ridge, and a deep river beyond, Logan's men would never reach their objective. When Clark heard the rifle shots break out toward his left, he ordered his cannon to open fire on the village, and then his men to advance. About seventy warriors remained to defend their homes. Most Shawnee took careful aim, fired, and withdrew slowly before the enemy advance. A few Indians holed up in a blockhouse until Clark directed cannon shots against it. The defenders fled as the Americans surged into the village and began burning and plundering.

Estimates of casualties varied even more wildly than usual. Clark accurately reported his own losses of fourteen killed and thirteen wounded but claimed to have inflicted three times that number on the Indians. One Kentuckian cheerfully boasted the expedition carved over seventy-three scalps. If so, all but a half-dozen of those Indians were unable to put up a fight. William Homan, a British gunner with the Shawnee, offered the sober account that "the Indians in the different skirmishes had six men killed and one man & one woman captured . . . The Rebels kill'd the Woman by ripping up her Belly & otherwise mangling her—they also opened the graves of the Indians that had been buried several months, and scalp'd them."[27]

Among the Kentucky casualties was Clark's nephew, Joseph Rogers, who was captured in December 1776 with a party trying to bring gunpowder to the settlements. During the battle, he foolishly sprinted toward the approaching Kentuckians, who mistook him for an Indian and shot him dead.

The frontiersmen spent the night in a hollow square in the meadows outside Piqua, with half the troops alert the night's first half, relieved by the other half until dawn. The next morning, to prevent the Shawnee from scalping their dead, they buried their men within a few remaining houses and then burned them. They then headed south down the trail. After recrossing the Ohio at the Licking River mouth, they disbanded. That campaign was the largest that actually attacked the enemy villages in the Ohio valley during the war. Like so many similar raids elsewhere, it destroyed a hornet's nest. Those enraged hornets would swarm back across the Ohio.

THE NEW YORK FRONTIER: SECOND PHASE

Gov. Frederick Haldimand devised a four-pronged attack against the northern frontier that autumn, three of which would fall on New York and the fourth on Vermont. The aim was to divert troops and destroy supplies that would otherwise flow to American forces on other fronts, as well as liberating and escorting back to Canada as many loyalists as possible.[28]

Two expeditions would sail down Lake Champlain and then diverge on different missions. Maj. Christopher Carleton's 776 men included 201 of the 29th, 113 of the 34th, 113 of the 53rd, 57 of the 84th, 34 Jaegers, 150 loyalists, and 108 mostly Caughnawagha. Capt. John Munro's 195 men included 131 of the King's Royal Regiment, 34 of Capt. William Fraser's independent ranger company, and 30 Mohawk warriors and rangers. On September 28, they set forth from Isle aux Noix aboard eight ships and twenty-six bateaux. Upon reaching Crown Point's ruins on October 6, they separated.[29]

Carleton's expedition continued south to Lake Champlain's end, where they disembarked and marched up the Wood Creek trail. On October 9, they surrounded Fort Ann, whose commander, Capt. Abe Sherwood, quickly capitulated his seventy-four men, who had only four rounds each. Carleton and his men burned the Kingsbury settlements, bypassed Fort Edward, and continued their destruction for another fourteen miles on both sides of the Hudson River. Upon their return, they veered off toward Fort George, guarding Lake George's southern end. On October 11, word of their approach reached Fort George's commander, Capt. John Chipman, who sent out Capt. Thomas Sill with forty-eight troops, to reconnoiter. Carleton's troops ambushed the Americans, killing twenty-seven, capturing eight, and scattering the rest, while suffering no casualties. Carleton and his victorious troops marched up to Fort George's clearing and received Chipman's surrender. Carleton embarked his men and prisoners aboard captured bateaux and headed north up Lake George. By October 16, the exhausted men were back at Crown Point awaiting Munro. The expedition had brilliantly achieved its mission. In seventeen days, those men captured and burned two forts, took 148 captives, and destroyed several score buildings while losing 1 killed, 1 wounded, and 2 deserters.[30]

Meanwhile, Munro and his men hiked over to the Scroon River and followed it south to the Hudson. They left the Hudson where it angles east and continued south to Ballston. On the night of October 12, Munro scattered his men through the town. Without losing a man, they took thirty prisoners and burned most dwellings. They departed the next morning, easily evading the militia's half-hearted pursuit. Six days later, Munro and his weary men rejoined Carleton.[31]

Sir John Johnson would command the largest and most destructive of the expeditions.[32] On September 21, he arrived at Oswego to gather men for his second campaign of the year. When he set off up the Onondaga River on October 1, he led 893 men, including 35 men each of the 8th's and 34th's light companies, 80 line infantry from those two regiments, 10 gunners with a coehorn mortar and a 3-pounder "grasshopper" cannon, 156 loyalists, and a mélange of 265 Indians led by Sayenqueraghta, Cornplanter, and Joseph Brant. To avoid detection, they passed south of Lake Oneida and through the destroyed Onondaga and Oneida villages until they reached the Susquehanna River at Unadilla; then they went up the Charlotte River and over the pass to the Schoharie valley. Here, thirty Indians decided to head north and raid the Mohawk valley; Johnson had trouble keeping the rest with him.

They reached the Schoharie valley's Upper Fort on October 17. Johnson had hoped to bypass that fort, but an alert guard spotted them, and its commander, Capt. Jacob Hager, ordered a three-cannon-shot alarm, which echoed down the valley. With their surprise lost, the British and Indians began pillaging and burning. The raiders reached Middle Fort later that day. Johnson's gunners opened fire with the coehorn and grasshopper, while his troops sniped at its defenders. The fort's commander, Maj. Melanchton Woolsey, wanted to surrender but his officers overruled him. With the coehorn and 3-pounder too weak to cause any serious damage to the fort, Johnson had no choice but to continue down the valley. The guns were unlimbered again to fire on the Lower Fort, but the fire was ineffective, and the garrison, under Lt. Col. Volkert Veeder, was defiant. Johnson's men had shot and burned and strode their way fifteen miles down the valley that day, tarrying briefly before three different forts. It was now late afternoon. Sir John pushed his exhausted men another half-dozen miles north down the valley before camping for the night.

On the morning of October 18, Johnson split his forces. He dispatched Brant and 150 Indians down the Schoharie River's east side, while he marched his main force down the west bank. Both forces looted and burned all dwellings in their path. Brant was unable to intimidate the surrender of Fort Hunter, which was commanded by Gen. Robert Van Rensselaer and 600 troops, so he crossed over the Schoharie and rejoined Johnson. Van Rensselaer pursued slowly with most of his troops. Johnson pointed his men west and unleashed them to destroy their way up the Mohawk valley. They collapsed in exhaustion that night at Anthony's Nose on the north bank, where ridges on both sides hem in the river. Van Rensselaer's force was only a few miles away.

Although the "Noses" would have offered a good position from which to defend against Van Rensselaer, Johnson feared being trapped there by American forces advancing from both sides. On the morning of October 19, he pushed his men northwest a half-dozen miles from the river toward the district around Stone Arabia, protected by Fort Keyser with 152 men and Fort Paris crammed with 350 men commanded by Col. John Brown. The sight of the scattered British and Indians burning homes enraged Brown and his men. Believing that his forces outnumbered the raiders and that Van Rensselaer and his militia would soon arrive, Brown sallied forth with his troops. Johnson's men swarmed against the attack, double-enveloped it, and routed the Americans, killing Brown and forty others, at a loss of one private and three Indians dead and three rangers and Brant wounded. Johnson could induce neither fort's commander to capitulate, so he gathered his troops and continued westward, attacking Forts Hess and Klock along the way.

Van Rensselaer caught up to Johnson late that afternoon near Fort Klock. Reinforcements had raised the American force to around 1,000 men, although two-thirds were militia. Van Rensselaer sent his troops forward, but the enemy's fire threw back first his left and then his center. In the confused fighting, Col. Lewis Dubois slipped his New York levies around the British flank and opened fire, but unsupported, he had to fall back. Both sides withdrew as darkness devoured the battlefield. Despite all the gunsmoke, casualties were light on both sides.

Johnson hurried his worn-out men westward on October 20. Near Fort Herkimer, they attacked a company of militia marching to join Van Rensselaer, killing and capturing ten with no loss to themselves. Van Rensselaer's advance guard under Dubois reached Fort Herkimer early that afternoon, a few hours after Johnson's men had disappeared. On October 21, New York governor George Clinton arrived and took command of the 1,500 troops gathered at Fort Herkimer. By the time Clinton led his troops out the following morning, Johnson and his men were far beyond his grasp.

When the raiders reached Oswego on October 26, they could congratulate themselves on a mission brilliantly realized. At a loss of only 9 killed, 2 wounded, and 52 missing, the raiders had killed over 100 of the enemy and destroyed over 1,000 homes, 1,000 barns, and 600,000 bushels of grain. Few homesteads survived in the Mohawk valley above Schenectady.[33]

What effect did those raids have on the war? George Washington admitted that "the destruction of the grain on the western frontier of New York" presented "the most alarming consequences . . . The settlement of Schoharie alone would have delivered eighty thousand bushels of grain but that fine district is now totally destroyed. I should view this calamity with less concern did I not see the least prospect of obtaining the necessary supplies from the States of Pennsylvania, Delaware, and Maryland previous to the interruption of transportation by frost and bad weather."[34]

THE VERMONT FRONTIER

Vermonters had declared their independence and enacted the world's most liberal constitution in 1779, actions that horrified rather than inspired Congress and the other states. Congress condemned Vermont's independence bid, ordered that government to submit to New York's rule, and all but declared the Vermonters rebels, an ironic policy indeed. Vermont's rugged settlers refused to bow to the will of Congress, New York, or anyone else, especially the British, who remained the state's worst threat.

The fourth raiding party launched by Haldimand that October attacked Vermont. Capt. Joseph Marie La Motte led 300 mostly Seven Nations Indians ashore at the Onion River mouth on Lake Champlain on October 3. They trekked east across Vermont and crossed the divide onto the White River. Down that valley they hurried silently, capturing all who stood stunned before them, murdering all who fled, and leaving a trail of burnt buildings and corpses behind. They destroyed Orange, Washington, Chelsea, Tunbridge, Royalton, and Sharon before returning via Randolph, over the divide to the Dog River, down it to the Onion, and back to their bateaux on October 19. The militia mustered in their wake but was too frightened to follow. In all, La Motte's Indians captured thirty-two and killed perhaps a dozen.[35]

That raid would be the war's last major thrust against Vermont, although minor raids would still wreak havoc. A British and Indian raid on Royalton in October 1780 killed two people and took thirty-two captive from the destroyed town. Rather than intimidate the Vermonters, violence stiffened their defiance. So the British tried a different strategy to subdue Vermont, one that substituted the carrot for the stick.

By late 1779, all British efforts to smother the rebellion had failed. Four years of warfare had drained ever more blood and treasury from the British empire while netting only New York City. An increasingly desperate American secretary George Germain seized upon a new tack. Perhaps greed could succeed where arms failed in crushing the rebels. He wrote General Clinton that "gaining respectable members of Congress or officers of influence or reputation is, next to destroying Washington's army, the speediest way of ending the rebellion."[36] Clinton agreed and targeted Continental army generals Israel Putnam and Benedict Arnold and Vermont militia general Ethan Allen as especially susceptible to the lure of riches. The seduction of Putnam failed, of Arnold succeeded, and of Allen backfired.

To promote Vermont's independence, Ethan Allen quite happily worked both sides of the diplomatic fence from 1780 to 1783. He gleefully played hard to get to offers ventured by various agents of Gen. Frederick Haldimand. Allen contemptuously dismissed any fears that he might turn coat like his hated nemesis of 1775, Benedict Arnold, who betrayed his nation in September 1780. The British tempted not just Allen, but also Vermont. In June 1780, Haldimand envoy Col. Beverly Robinson promised that Vermont "may obtain a separate government under the king and constitution of England."[37]

Vermont's government informed Congress of the offer, hinted broadly at how tempting it was, and again requested recognition. Congress was unyielding despite the implication that Vermont might switch sides. Fortunately for the American cause, Vermont's threat was all bluff. To the British, Allen promised only neutrality in return for recognition of Vermont's independence.

Haldimand spurned the demand but continued trying to entice the Vermonters. Until the war's end and beyond, he repeated his offer and curtailed most attacks on that rebel state's soil. After Robinson's efforts failed, Haldimand dispatched Justus Sherwood to negotiate with Allen, but the only result was a gnawing frustration for Haldimand, who hated the object of his diplomacy: "[Allen's] character is well known and his Followers or dependents are a Collection of the most abandoned Wretches that ever lived, to be bound by no Laws or Ties."[38]

Meanwhile, the attitude of Congress toward Vermont shifted with the war's fortunes. In early 1781, Congress offered Vermont recognition in exchange for the state's withdrawal from towns in New York that it had annexed. Congress then withdrew that offer for various reasons, including a swelling confidence after Yorktown and pressure from New York. New York would remain belligerent in words unmatched by action. It threatened to invade Vermont in 1782 and 1783 but never crossed the border. In 1783, it persuaded Congress to conquer Vermont, but George Washington prudently vetoed the plan. The standoff would smolder another eight years until Vermont was finally accepted into the United States in 1791.

THE SOUTHEAST FRONTIER: SECOND PHASE

The British were about to inflict the coup de grace to the last resistance on the frontier when a near miracle occurred. Rather than cower in their remote settlements, the frontiersmen chose to rally against the approaching enemy. At Sycamore Shoals on September 25, Col. Arthur Campbell and John Sevier each brought 200 men, while Isaac Shelby rode in with 240 men. Col. Benjamin Cleveland and Maj. Joseph Winston meanwhile gathered 350 men from Surrey and Wilkes Counties. The two forces converged at Quaker Meadows and rode hard after Ferguson, who retreated before them. Col. James Williams joined the patriots with 400 men on October 6. With the men and mounts alike exhausted, the commanders decided to prune their force to 910 of the fittest horsemen and 85 of the toughest men afoot.

They finally cornered Ferguson at Kings Mountain on the afternoon of October 7. The frontiersmen surrounded the wooded plateau and crept through the trees, picking off Ferguson's men silhouetted against the sky as they rose to fire down the steep slope. While losing only 28 dead and 64 wounded, the Americans killed 157, wounded 163, and captured 689; Ferguson was among the dead. The frontiersmen had destroyed the western arm of Cornwallis's advance.[39]

Cornwallis responded by calling on the Cherokee to attack the frontier. That forced the overmountain men hastily to return home. They were no sooner preparing for one campaign when they received an appeal on November 20 from Generals William Davidson and William Smallwood. Those men presented a plan to lure Gen. Banastre Tarleton to his destruction early the next year. The leaders chose to split their forces, with some advancing against the Cherokee and the rest against Tarleton.

Col. John Sevier led one thrust against the Cherokee. His men and an Indian war party collided at Boyd's Creek on December 16. Sevier skillfully flanked and routed the Indians, killing twenty-eight and wounding many others, while not suffering any casualties except for a slight wound himself. Sevier was about to follow up his victory with a march on the Chickamauga villages when an express arrived from Col. William Campbell that he awaited the latter's arrival.

The rendezvous was at Big Island. By December 22, about 750 men of Washington, Sullivan, and Fincastle Counties led by Sevier, Campbell, Joseph Martin, and Elijah Clarke had gathered. They headed downstream toward the Little Tennessee River and then up it. Running short of provisions, they got a Christmas present on December 25 when they reached and looted Chota, killed a lurking Indian, and took seventeen horses. Maj. Jonathan Tipton crossed the river with 150 men and burned Chilhowee the next day. They moved farther upriver, destroying

Tellico, Little Tuskegee, Hiwasee, Chestowee, and Kaiatee. They decided to head home on New Year's Day. In all, they killed twenty-nine Indians, wounded many, and captured seventeen.[40]

America's fortunes in the three southern states had plunged to a nadir by late 1780. British garrisons controlled most of Georgia and South Carolina, while Cornwallis readied his army at Camden to invade North Carolina. In the low country and piedmont, American resistance had dwindled to tiny partisan bands led by Francis Marion, Thomas Sumter, and Andrew Pickens, lurking in the swamps. Hundreds of patriot troops could be mustered only in the frontier settlements. A ray of hope penetrated the gloom with the destruction of Ferguson's 1,100-man loyalist army at King's Mountain, but if that victory were not followed by others, the British would inevitably destroy America's feeble grip on the south.

Congress had appointed Maj. Gen. Nathanael Greene on October 7 to replace Horatio Gates after his disastrous defeat at Camden. Greene arrived at Charlotte on December 2. Though badly outnumbered, he chose to split his army to stretch Cornwallis even farther and find fresh sources of supplies for his troops, which had denuded the Charlotte region. On December 26, he led most of the army east to Cheraw on the Peedee River, while he sent Gen. Daniel Morgan into western South Carolina to gather supplies and then march against Fort Ninety-Six.

Upon reaching Cheraw, Greene deployed most of his army to gather supplies, while he dispatched Gen. Henry Lee and his dragoons down the Peedee River to link with Francis Marion and attack British posts. The British repulsed the American attacks on Georgetown on December 28 and Fort Watson the next day. Lee and Marion withdrew back to Cheraw.

Morgan moved swiftly once he joined his 600-man rifle brigade with Gen. William Davidson's 120 North Carolina militia and Andrew Pickens's 350 mounted South Carolina men. On December 30, his advance guard of 85 dragoons and 200 picked mounted militia under Col. William Washington killed or captured 150 loyalists at Hammond's Store and then rode to occupy Fort William, whose defenders fled.

Cornwallis was at Winnsboro, fifty-five miles east of Fort Ninety-Six. When he learned of Morgan's advance toward that post, he took the bait. He ordered Banastre Tarleton and his legion to head off Morgan's force, while Cornwallis led the rest of the army up the Broad River to cut off the enemy's retreat. Maj. Gen. Alexander Leslie with 2,500 troops would march against Greene. The shoot-out between Tarleton and Morgan would take place shortly after the new year dawned.

CHAPTER 9

"Opening Wide Their Jaws":
1781

It is not known how many more may perish before Your war will be at end!

—Captain Pipe

My chain appears to have run out.

—George Rogers Clark

THE GULF OF MEXICO FRONTIER

Emboldened by the dispersal of Gov. Bernardo de Galvez's armada the previous October, Maj. Gen. John Campbell ventured a campaign against Mobile in the new year. That port's Achilles' heel was the Village on the bay's east shore, from which Mobile got its drinking water. If that post fell, Mobile's defense would quickly wither. But the Spanish defense was too strong to be taken by the Indians who had sniped and skulked nearby for the last month or two. Only a European-style siege had any chance of success. In late December, Campbell organized an expedition to destroy the Village sixty-two miles from Pensacola.

Col. J. L. W. von Hanxleden appeared before the Village on January 6, 1780, accompanied by 60 troops of his Waldeck regiment, 100 of the 60th, 250 Pennsylvania and Maryland loyalists, 11 militia horsemen, and 420 Indians, mostly Choctaw, led by Farquhar Bethune and John McIntosh. The British and Indians attacked at dawn the next morning. About 40 of the 200 Spanish troops panicked and rushed toward a boat tied on shore. The Indians "shot them all down and followed them chin-deep in the water to get their scalps."[1] But the other Spaniards coolly lowered their muskets and fired a volley into the attackers, killing von Hanxleden and nineteen others. Disheartened by the loss, the British and Indians withdrew. The Spaniards held the Village at a cost of fourteen killed and twenty-three wounded.[2]

Meanwhile, Galvez gathered another expedition against Pensacola. Five warships and thirty-one transports carrying 1,315 troops sailed from Havana on

February 28 and reached Pensacola Bay on March 10. It took weeks to disembark all the troops, cannons, and supplies, and move them just beyond range of Pensacola's guns. Contingents of troops from Mobile, Havana, and New Orleans arrived to swell the Spanish force. By late April, the Spanish outnumbered the British by four to one. Galvez commanded 7,803 men, including 3,701 Spanish troops with contingents from the Noble, Navarra, Principe, King's, Soria, Hibernian, Cataluan, Espana, Guadalajara, Mallorca, Aragon, Toledo, and Naples Regiments, along with 725 troops of the French Regiment du Cap and 1,504 sailors armed and ashore. Campbell commanded 1,302 troops, including 135 of the 16th, 200 of the 60th, 351 of the Waldeck Regiment, 242 Pennsylvania loyalists, 242 Maryland loyalists, 7 of the 57th, and 62 gunners, along with 600 militia, 300 sailors, 300 armed blacks, and about 120 Creek and 400 Choctaw led by Chief Frenchumastabe. Campbell could not expect any relief. By April 22, Adm. Jose de Solano commanded a fleet of fifteen warships and seven frigates in Pensacola Bay, while a combined Spanish and French fleet of fifteen warships and two frigates cruised the straits between Havana and the Florida Keys to intercept Adm. George Romney's fleet. The Spanish had sealed off Pensacola from the world. Campbell's surrender was just a matter of time.[3]

The British Indian contingent was a fraction of earlier numbers. Alexander Cameron later complained that "had my advice been regarded by General Campbell in time, instead of 500 I should have had 2,000 Indians to oppose the Spaniards at the siege of Pensacola."[4] Just what advice had Campbell spurned? Cameron had pleaded for more gifts to distribute, but Campbell refused to provide them. It is questionable whether many more would have shown up even had generosity prevailed. Campbell had displayed palpable disdain for the Indians after "crying wolf" on three previous occasions. Many of those who had responded to earlier alarms now stayed home or went hunting.

Campbell would alienate many of those who had rallied. On March 30, the Indians joined regulars in an attack on a Spanish detachment. However, the British hung back, forcing the Indians to carry the fight's burden. The next day, Choctaw chief Frenchumastabe complained that the British regulars had not vigorously supported his men. Campbell dismissed the charge. The general's arrogance caused even more Indians to grow disenchanted and abandon Pensacola's defense. Some switched sides. About seventy dissident Choctaw joined the Spanish on April 15 and tried to persuade Frenchumastabe and his men to retreat into neutrality. A few days later, Galvez was able to entice two Tallapoosa chiefs to defect and urge other Creek Indians to follow.[5]

Nonetheless, more Indians arrived to replace them. On April 8, Alexander McGillivray arrived with eighty Creek. On April 15, Benjamin James and Alexander Frazer appeared with ninety Choctaw. On April 27, James Colbert's half-breed son and fifty-four Choctaw joined the siege.[6] But Indians were of little use in a formal siege, and it mattered not to Pensacola's fate how many crouched behind its parapets.

Three strongholds defended Pensacola—Fort George, the Prince of Wales Redoubt, and the Queen's Redoubt. Galvez's siege lines steadily crept toward those forts. On April 26, Campbell ordered an attack on the Spanish lines, but it was repulsed. On April 29, four mortars of the first battery were emplaced and opened fire on the Queen's Redoubt. On May 4, Campbell ordered an attack that briefly captured the battery and spiked the guns before being driven off, but the mortars were simply replaced and the bombardment resumed. On May 8, a lucky shot on the Queen's Redoubt blew up the magazine, killing forty-eight Pennsylvania loyalists, twenty-seven sailors, and a slave, and wounding twenty-four soldiers and sailors.[7] Col. Jose de Ezpeleta led a charge of 800 troops into the redoubt's smoldering ruins and tensely awaited the expected British counterattack. It never came.

With his defense perimeter breached, Campbell faced the stark choice of driving out the Spaniards or asking for terms. After debating the issue with the officers, he hoisted a white flag for negotiations later that afternoon. On May 10, after two days of tough bargaining, Campbell signed a document whereby he ceded not just Pensacola but all of West Florida and its defenders. At Pensacola alone, in addition to all the troops, Galvez captured 143 cannons, 6 howitzers, and large amounts of gunpowder, muskets, and other equipment. The siege cost the Spanish 74 killed and 198 wounded and the British 90 killed, 46 wounded, and 83 deserters. The troops were paroled and shipped to New York. After receiving Spanish speeches and gifts promoting peace between them, the Indians were sent home. Those loyalists who refused to surrender fled northwest to the Chickasaw. In all, Galvez scored a glorious victory, which Madrid would later reward by promoting him to lieutenant general and governor of West Florida along with Louisiana.[8]

But the fighting on the southern frontier did not end with Pensacola's fall. In April, Campbell had sent a runner to Natchez leader John Blommart to persuade all British sympathizers to break their loyalty oaths to Spain and revolt. This presented a moral dilemma to the loyalists, since by doing so they could be treated as criminals and traitors rather than soldiers. Nonetheless, on April 22, Blommart and his followers attacked Fort Panmure, commanded by Capt. Juan Delaville beuvre. The Spanish valiantly held out until exhausted supplies forced them to capitulate on May 4.

The rebels had little time to cherish their triumph. Word soon arrived that Campbell had surrendered all of West Florida to Spain. Continued resistance would certainly brand them as brigands who could swing from gallows if captured. The loyalists split, with many returning home or fleeing. A portion, however, remained nervously defiant.

Galvez first tried to quell the revolt with diplomacy. He dispatched to Natchez Capt. Estevan Robert de la Morandiere with forty militia and word that if the rebels resubmitted to Spanish rule, only their leaders would be punished, with the rest allowed to return peacefully to their homes. Morandiere advanced to Point Coupee and from there on June 14 circulated a decree promising amnesty for all but the ringleaders. The loyalists lost heart and gave up. Morandiere and his troops arrived at Natchez on June 22, occupied Fort Panmure, and sent Blommart and three confederates to New Orleans for trial. The Spanish would partially break their promise. After an investigation that lasted the entire summer, the government arrested seventeen more loyalists.[9]

With all of West Florida surrendered and the revolt's leaders captured, one extraordinary loyalist leader held out. James Colbert had lived nearly all of his sixty years among the Chickasaw and a mélange of 300 or so hardened whites, mulattoes, and slaves in the region. Learning that the revolt was crushed, Colbert sent word to Natchez that Blommart and the other leaders had better be freed or else he would close the Mississippi. The Spanish authorities ignored his demand. It would take Colbert nearly a year before he would act on his threat, but he would do so spectacularly.

THE SOUTHEAST FRONTIER: FIRST PHASE

Nathanael Greene's strategy was working. He had split his army and sent the meager halves to threaten the eastern and western flanks of British forces in South Carolina. It was quite a gamble. His plan's success depended on Gen. Charles Cornwallis delaying his invasion and chasing after Morgan's force, which was marching against Fort Ninety-Six. Greene knew his enemy. That was exactly how Cornwallis reacted.

When Morgan learned that Gen. Banastre Tarleton's 1,100-man legion had cantered after him from Winnsboro on January 6, he slowly withdrew north up the Broad River. Every step toward his own supply depots was a step the enemy distanced from his. Heavy rains slowed and exhausted the British troopers, but under their ruthless commander's exhortations, they steadily gained on the Americans. Rather than continue north up the Broad River, Morgan veered northwest up Thickety Creek to a prairie known as the Cowpens.

Morgan carefully chose his ground. As Tarleton neared on the morning of January 17, Morgan organized a defense up a slope wedged between two low hills. Sharpshooters screened his militia, which stood 100 yards before his Continentals, whose flanks were protected by dragoons. Upon arriving late that morning, Tarleton deployed his troops and ordered an attack. Morgan's troops perfectly fulfilled his plan. The sharpshooters picked off dozens of British before falling back. The militia fired two well-aimed volleys and withdrew through the ranks of the Continentals, who fired several devastating volleys and then surged down the hill against the British. The dragoons meanwhile charged the British cavalry, scattered it, and then galloped into the enemy flanks. The British broke and fled. Daniel Morgan had executed the most perfect double envelopment since Cannae. In all, the Americans killed about 100, wounded about 229, and captured 525 soldiers, 100 horses, and 35 wagons, while suffering 12 dead and 60 wounded. Tarleton escaped with several hundred men.[10]

The Americans had devastated Cornwallis's second expedition into the frontier, but the British still had four times more troops than the Americans across

South Carolina. Cornwallis with his main army was only a few miles behind Tarleton, while Maj. Gen. Alexander Leslie with 2,500 troops was advancing against Greene at Cheraw. Morgan and Greene had no choice but to withdraw. Col. Henry Lee with his dragoons and the partisan leaders Andrew Pickens, Thomas Sumter, and Francis Marion hit and bled the steady British march northward. Cornwallis had to drop off more troops to guard his lengthening supply line. Leslie's troops were split among Charles Town, Wilmington, and several supply centers en route to Cornwallis's army.

Greene halted his 4,500 troops at Guilford Courthouse and awaited the enemy's arrival. On ground well chosen to funnel the British attacks, Greene emulated Morgan's tactics at Cowpens. With Tarleton's diminished legion leading the way, 2,000 British troops paraded on the field around noon on March 15. Lee's cavalry charged and pushed back Tarleton before withdrawing as the infantry approached. After surveying the enemy lines, Cornwallis deployed his regiments and ordered an attack. The British routed the first line of North Carolina militia and then the second line of Virginia militia, but the third line of 1,400 Continentals poured a devastating fire into the massed British ranks and then counterattacked while Lee's cavalry hit the enemy's right flank. The British retreated, regrouped, and charged again. This time they punched through the Americans. Greene ordered a retreat. The British pursued closely for several miles, rounding up many militia stragglers. Cornwallis won a Pyrrhic victory. He had taken the field and inflicted 261 casualties on the Continentals, 461 on the North Carolinians, and 562 on the Virginians, but he had lost 93 killed and 413 wounded—one-fourth of his army.[11]

The armies turned their backs on one another. Cornwallis withdrew to the supplies and fleet at Wilmington. After several months of enjoying rest and reinforcements, Cornwallis would lead his troops north on a road that would end at Yorktown. Greene meanwhile advanced with 1,200 Continentals and 300 North Carolina militia on Camden. Col. Francis Rawdon blocked his way with 900 regulars on Hobkirk's Hill. After a day in which both sides eyed each other, Rawdon decided to attack on the morning of April 25. The Americans fired volleys into the advancing British and then charged. The British held, fired, and then counterattacked. One American regiment after another faltered and then retreated. The losses were relatively even, with the Americans suffering 25 killed, 108 wounded, and 136 missing and the British 258 casualties. Rawdon called off the pursuit and withdrew his men into Camden.[12]

Once again, Greene lost tactically but won strategically. Hearing that Rawdon had withdrawn, he turned his troops around and occupied the field that evening. Marion and Lee had captured Forts Watson and Motte in the meantime and shortly thereafter took Forts Granby and Orangeburg. Those forts held 800 men and heaps of supplies. Rawdon withdrew his army to Monck's Corner, thirty miles northwest of Charles Town. South Carolina and even Georgia were now open for the Americans to retake. Augusta and Fort Ninety-Six were the last British strongholds on the frontier. Greene headed toward Ninety-Six while dispatching Col. Henry Lee with his legion to reinforce Americans already besieging Augusta.

Augusta was the more important of the two. From his headquarters there, Indian Superintendent Thomas Brown tried to rally the Creek and Cherokee, but with little success. The Indian will to raid was steadily diminishing. Repeated American invasions had devastated the Cherokee. Though the Creek warriors had so far escaped an enemy attack, they could not dodge the plagues of smallpox and other diseases that ravaged them. On top of these disasters came news of the British defeats at Kings Mountain and Cowpens, capped by Pensacola's surrender in May.

Despite, or more likely because of, all these horrors, some warriors still raided the frontier. Though most of their villages were charred ruins, the Cherokee attacked again in February. That provoked yet another round of American counterattacks. John Sevier led 150 men against the Middle Cherokee, killing two score Indians and capturing 200 horses, while losing only two dead. Joseph Martin led 200 troops against the Overhill towns, causing similar damage.

With the Indian frontier quiet for now, Augusta became the magnet for rebel forces. In April, Andrew Pickens and Elijah Clarke joined forces and headed that way. Greene reinforced them with Lt. Col. Micajah Williamson. When he learned of the rebel advance, Brown as usual did not passively sit tight. He sent John Douglass and his men to raid Williamson's rear. The raiders captured 400 horses and galloped back into Augusta. Upon learning that the rebels were besieging Augusta, Gov. James Wright ordered Maj. Philip Dill to gather the Savannah valley's loyalist militia and march to Brown's relief. Capt. Isaac Shelby defeated Dill at Walker's Bridge on Briar Creek.

Lee's legion approached Augusta in mid-May. Short of supplies, Lee decided to capture the depot at Fort Galphin. He concealed his regulars and ordered his militia to attack and then retreat. The British took the bait and surged out in pursuit. Lee then charged all his men against the British, who surrendered. With that rich store of munitions and provisions, Lee could then conduct a prolonged siege of Augusta.

He and his men rode into the siege lines on May 22. After surveying the situation, Lee concentrated his forces for an assault on Fort Grierson, the key to Augusta's defense. The Americans overran the fort, but Brown rejected Lee's surrender demand. Lee had his men construct a thirty-foot tower strong enough to support a 6-pounder cannon. Nonplussed, Brown had his men build a tower big enough to hold two cannons. It would be another week before either tower was ready. Meanwhile, on May 28, Brown ordered a sortie on the militia manning the west trenches. His men routed the militia but were driven off by an American bayonet charge. On the night of the twenty-ninth, Brown sent out yet another sortie, but it too was repulsed. The American tower was completed on June 2. The cannon opened fire and knocked out the two British guns. Still, Brown refused to give up. On June 4, Lee sent in yet another demand to surrender or else his troops would launch an assault. Brown began negotiations and finally capitulated on June 5 with the promise that officers would be paroled while the soldiers would remain captives.

On May 22, Greene encircled Fort Ninety-Six, defended by Col. John Cruger and 550 New York, New Jersey, and South Carolina loyalists. Cruger conducted as spirited a defense as Brown, launching several sorties against the siege lines zigzagging toward the fort. Lee and Pickens joined Greene on June 8, bringing American forces to around 1,500 men. The fort's fate seemed sealed, but then on June 11, Greene received the ominous news that Rawdon had received 2,000 fresh troops and was marching to Fort Ninety-Six's relief. Greene ordered Sumter and Marion to gather the militia and block Rawdon's advance. On June 18, Greene ordered an assault on the fort. The loyalists fought off the attack, killing or wounding 127 rebels while suffering 85 casualties. With word that Rawdon was less than thirty miles away, Greene ordered the siege lifted and a retreat to Charlotte.

Once again, Greene won a strategic victory while enduring a tactical setback. Upon reaching Fort Ninety-Six, Rawdon ordered it abandoned. He then chased after Greene. The heat was so withering that fifty British dropped dead from sunstroke. Supplies were nearly spent. Rawdon withdrew his exhausted army to Charles Town.

After massing supplies and filling empty ranks, Greene followed with 2,400 men, including 1,200 Continentals, 300 dragoons under Colonels Harry Lee and William Washington, 150 militia each from North and South Carolina, and 300 rangers under Pickens and 250 under Marion. Blocking the road to Charles Town at Eutaw Springs was Col. Alexander Steward with 2,000 troops, including 300 grenadiers and light infantry; the 3rd, 63rd, and 64th regulars; Cruger's New York and New Jersey provincials; and Maj. John Coffin's troopers. The Americans marched onto the field the morning of September 8. Steward parried Greene's attack and then counterattacked. Most of the Americans held, poured a withering fire into the British, charged, and broke the enemy. Steward rallied his troops, stood firm, and repelled the American advance. Greene ordered a withdrawal. The battle of Eutaw Springs was the south's bloodiest, with the Americans losing 139 killed, 375 wounded, and 8 missing, while the British suffered 85 killed, 351 wounded, and 430 missing, or 42 percent of the army. Once again, Greene was forced briefly from the field but won a decisive strategic victory. The British shut themselves tight within Charles Town, Savannah, and Wilmington for the war's remainder.[13]

Recently the British had invaded another tidewater region. On December 20, 1780, Brig. Gen. Benedict Arnold had landed at Portsmouth and over the next weeks raided all the way to Richmond, burned it, and then returned to control the Hampton Roads region. That spring, Clinton sent Gen. William Philips with reinforcements to take command. Cornwallis decided to join Philips to either conquer Virginia or withdraw back to New York. In late May, he led his army north from Wilmington and joined Philips at Petersburg on May 22. Together they had 7,200 troops. Opposing them was General Lafayette with 1,000 Continentals and 3,000 militia. Cornwallis pursued but never caught Lafayette, though Tarleton's legion did chase Virginia's assembly and Gov. Thomas Jefferson from Charlottesville, over the Blue Ridge Mountains, to Staunton in the upper Shenandoah Valley.

Upon receiving an order from Clinton for reinforcements, Cornwallis called off the fruitless hunt and withdrew to Hampton Roads. Lafayette nipped at his heels all the way and skirmished with the British rear guard at Green Spring on July 4. At Portsmouth, Cornwallis received orders from Clinton to withdraw to Yorktown and Gloucester straddling the York River mouth and there await reinforcements. Cornwallis fulfilled that order by August 1. From his camp a dozen miles west at Williamsburg, Lafayette sent word to Washington that Cornwallis was bottled up at Yorktown.

Cornwallis's withdrawal to the Hampton Roads region was a fateful choice. He rightfully believed that ports like Portsmouth or Yorktown were the perfect places to defend, receive reinforcements and supplies, or, if need be, escape. That was true as long as the British enjoyed naval superiority, but without the fleet, that peninsula's tip was a dead end.

THE NORTHWEST FRONTIER

Governor Galvez was not the only resourceful commander on Spain's frontier. Francisco Cruzat, upper Louisiana's lieutenant governor, also conceived and launched an offensive against the enemy that year. Cruzat reckoned that the destruction of Fort St. Joseph might forestall any planned British invasion of upper Louisiana, intimidate tribes away from the enemy, and just possibly reinforce Spanish claims to the upper Mississippi valley and western Great Lakes. To lead that mission, Cruzat chose militia captain Don Eugene Ponce, who departed on January 2 at the head of sixty-five soldiers and sixty Sauk, Fox, and Potawatomi. They journeyed through that frozen land first up the Mississippi and Illinois Rivers and then over the divide to the St. Joseph River valley. On February 12, the expedition reached undefended St. Joseph. Ponce gathered the astonished inhabitants and declared Spain the region's rightful owner: "I annex and incorporate with the domains of his Very Catholic Majesty, the King of Spain, my master, from now and forever, this post of St. Joseph and its dependencies, with the river of the same name, and that of Illinois, which flows into the Mississippi River."[14] Ponce then broke open the British storehouse. His men happily grabbed all that they could carry and distributed the rest to the delighted Potawatomi. The raiders turned heel for home.

Ponce's declaration was a spurious claim. Briefly occupying and looting a distant post before hurrying away hardly cemented a legitimate Spanish stake to the region, but such boasts can swell a nation's diplomatic power if well played at the negotiation table. That raid further damaged British prestige and power in the Illinois country.

The dream of snuffing out a distant British stronghold burned incessantly within George Rogers Clark. Capturing Detroit would bring the frontier war in the Ohio valley to a sputtering end. All that was needed were enough men, supplies, and transport, along with Clark's indomitable will. The previous October, he journeyed to Richmond, Virginia's new capital, to make his case before Gov. Thomas Jefferson. The governor sympathized but could spare little because he had little. The state treasury was empty and its credit nearly exhausted. The British had conquered Georgia and South Carolina over the previous two years and now threatened Virginia. Whatever men, provisions, and munitions could be scraped together had to meet Benedict Arnold's invasion.

Clark lent a hand, helping to blunt that traitor's raid in January. Arnold's 1,600 men captured and burned Richmond and then withdrew. During that campaign, Clark commanded several hundred militia that traded shots with Col. John Simoe's Queen's Rangers, a regiment of loyalist light infantry. Thus did fate bring two of the war's fiercest warriors and skilled wilderness leaders, Clark and Arnold, to battle one another far from the frontier.

After Arnold withdrew to Portsmouth, Clark did not tarry for what became the decisive Yorktown campaign later that year. Jefferson and the assembly had granted him a brigadier general's commission and 75,000 pounds credit to lead his cherished expedition. Whatever elation Clark may have felt evaporated shortly after he reached Fort Pitt in March. The paper money printed indiscriminately by Virginia's government had depreciated to a fraction of its face value, while the price of ever scarcer goods had soared to the point where Clark could glean only a sliver of what he needed. Nor was his commission any more useful; he could not rally troops if men were not available or willing to step forward. Then in June, Virginia's assembly resolved to cancel Clark's expedition and gather all troops and supplies to repel Cornwallis's invasion. Although Jefferson did not sign the resolution into law, the uncertainty further crimped recruiting and provisioning.

One other implacable obstacle impeded the expedition: Clark was literally stumbling over his own efforts. He was no longer the hero that had captured the "hair buyer" and Fort Vincennes after an epic winter trek through the Illinois wilderness. Victory had eluded him ever since, a reality he tried to drown in drink. Arthur Campbell reported that Clark "has lost the confidence of the people and it is said becoming a Sot; perhaps something worse."[15] What that "something worse" was can only be imagined.

Meanwhile, the devastation of lives and property in the Ohio valley by British and Indian war parties continued to mount. In January and February alone, forty-seven Kentucky settlers were killed or captured and many more were wounded. Indian attacks were repulsed against Stroud's Station in April and McAfee's Station in May. Kentucky's defenders were stretching to the snapping point.

The Tennessee settlements also suffered Indian depredations in the new year. Chickasaw Indians slipped over the wall of Freeland's Station on the night of January 11. Hearing noises outside, all eleven defenders sprang to their arms and began firing through the chinks at the shadowy figures beyond, killing one and wounding several others. The Chickasaw shot down one man who foolishly rushed out and killed a slave in a cabin. The firing of the fort's swivel gun prompted a reply shot from Nashborough a mile away. The Chickasaw disappeared into the night. That was the last Chickasaw attack on Tennessee. Later that year, Col. James Robertson held council with Chickasaw chief Piomingo, and the two agreed to a permanent truce between their peoples.

The Chickamauga, however, continued to harass the Cumberland settlements. On April 2, Dragging Canoe sent three warriors to fire on Col. James Robertson's station. Robertson fell for the ruse and sortied with twenty other mounted men. They galloped right into the ambush, dismounted, and returned fire. The gunshots spooked the horses. Rather than wipe out Robertson and his men, most of the Cherokee tried to capture the horses. Robertson's wife loosed the fort's dogs on the Indians. That diversion allowed Robertson and the survivors to sprint for the fort. That fight cost the settlers five killed and three wounded, while the Cherokee lost one dead.

Reports of such attacks spurred Clark to hurry his campaign preparations. By early August, he had gathered 400 men and several weeks' worth of supplies at Fort Pitt. He embarked down the Ohio River with nearly 300 men for Fort Nelson. Col. Archibald Lochry and 140 Pennsylvanian riflemen were supposed to have accompanied Clark, but lacking supplies, they got a late start. Lochry sent word to Clark that his men would likely need supplies en route. Clark replied that he would send men and provisions to the Miami River mouth. Indians captured those men rowing the message to Lowry.

Those Indians were led by Joseph Brant. What was the ubiquitous Brant doing in the Ohio valley? Joseph Brant always sought the thick of the action, both on the battlefield and in the war. Hearing rumors of an American thrust against Detroit, he journeyed there with his warriors. From there he headed south with about 100 Indians and whites, including Simon Girty. They reached and set an ambush where the Miami River flows into the Ohio River. It was there that they snared the couriers and learned that an even larger prey was nearing. They would not have long to wait. Shortly after Lochry and his men ground ashore on August 26, Brant ordered an attack. The Indians and British killed thirty-seven, including Lochry, and captured the rest, along with thirty-two horses and flatboats filled with supplies.[16]

The loss of Lochry's command was the fatal blow to Clark's campaign. Upon learning of the disaster, Clark convened a council of war. He and his officers bitterly agreed that any expedition against Detroit would have to be postponed until the following year at least, but that was not all. Word of the destruction of Lochry's command and cancellation of Clark's campaign had "thrown the people of this country into great consternation, especially Westmoreland county where the loss of so many of their best men has thinned and weakened their frontier exceedingly. Many are preparing to retreat to the east side of the mountains early in the spring."[17]

Each successful raid or defeat of an American military force inspired the hordes of hostile warriors and alienated those few Indians who still tried to stay neutral. America's diplomatic efforts with the Indians were as stymied by uncontrollable forces as by military efforts. Daniel Brodhead contrasted the British and American means of nurturing their allies: while the "Indian captains appointed by the British commander at Detroit are clothed in the most elegant manner, and have many valuable presents made them . . . the captains I have appointed by authority of Congress are naked and receive nothing but a little whiskey, for which they are reviled by the Indians in general."[18]

These distinctions were not lost on the Delaware. A mix of American neglect, poverty, arrogance, and blundering lost any lingering Delaware affections that year. The pressures mounted on the Coshocton council to abandon neutrality and embrace the British. The council agreed to do so in 1781 and joined at Detroit Chief White Pipe and his people, who had defected the previous year. Killbuck resigned as chief of the Turtle phratry and stayed behind with a handful of followers. They would remain loyal to the Americans for the war's duration and beyond.[19]

But the honeymoon of the Coshocton Delaware with the redcoats was short-lived. While a mound of presents rewarded those Delaware who switched sides, it was accompanied by ever more egregious British contempt. At a Detroit council in November 1781, Delaware chief Captain Pipe unleashed his bitterness on the British: "Father! Many lives have already been lost on your account! Nations have suffered and been weakened! Children have lost Parents, brothers, and relatives! Wives have lost Husbands! It is not known how many more may perish before Your war will be at end!"[20] With such sentiments, most Delaware would simply leech off what British largesse they could while shunning the warpath.

Another tribe that was under more pressure was the Delaware's neighbors, the Moravians. Their villages straddled the war trail linking Detroit and Pittsburgh, but were much closer geographically and economically to the latter. The example of those people making love not war enticed few passing raiders from their missions. The hearts of the Moravians themselves were stirred by the sight of warriors arrogantly stalking back from the American settlements with bloody scalps dangling from their belts or shoving captives before them. While nearly all Moravians tried to stay aloof from the titanic struggle that engulfed them, a few passed on intelligence of the warriors' intentions and actions to Fort Pitt.

Detroit officials were well aware of those sympathies, trade ties, and leaks. By 1781, they decided to eliminate those seemingly pro-American islands in an otherwise British Indian sea. On August 16, Capt. Matthew Elliott, Wyandot chief Half King, Delaware chief Captain Pipe, and about 300 warriors descended on Gnadenhutten to fatten off the crops and try to cow the Moravians into warring with them against the Americans. At a council on August 20, Half King issued a prophetic warning that the Moravians must join or die: "I see you live in a dangerous place. Two powerful and mighty spirits or gods are standing and opening wide their jaws where you are placed . . . therefore it is not advisable for you to remain here longer . . . for here must you all die. I therefore take you by the hand, raise you up, and settle you . . . where I dwell . . . where you will be safe and live in quiet."[21]

Speaking on their flock's behalf, David Zeisberger and John Heckewelder wielded all their powers of diplomacy and Christian pacifism. They thanked Half

King for what they called his concern and generous offer, reasoned that such a momentous choice required considerable time to decide, and promised to answer him next spring. This satisfied Half King but angered Elliott, who tried to incite the Wyandot and other chiefs to threaten the Moravians if they did not succumb immediately.

Although Half King dismissed the Englishman's bluster, he and the other chiefs could not control their warriors. The "rough, wild men," as Zeisberger called them, slaughtered livestock, devoured food, sacked homes, intimidated men, and seduced women. On September 3, Indians seized and stripped the missionaries, looted and burned their homes, and dragged them before Elliott. Warriors committed the same crimes in Schonbrunn and Salem. Their "Indian brethren stood quite amazed, wept aloud, and knew not what to do; some wished to make defense, others deemed this inadvisable, and prevented them. They plundered not only our things, but also what belonged to the church."[22] Like Jesus, the missionaries continued to turn the other cheek to these indignities while refusing to abandon the ruins of their settlements. Finally, however, they surrendered to the threat of violence. On September 11, the British and Indians herded away the missionaries and their flock first to the Delaware capital at Coshocton and then to the Wyandot villages at Sandusky.

A few Moravians escaped to Pittsburgh with word of their plight. The captive Moravians learned that their fate was known "when a war party came back from the settlements with two prisoners, from whom we heard that when the news of our being taken captives reached Pittsburgh, they wished at first to follow after us and rescue us from the hands of the warriors, but that they afterwards gave up. This had hitherto been our greatest concern, that if this should happen we should be placed in the greatest danger, and with our Indian brethren come between two fires."[23]

Though now removed from the immediate threat of violence, the Moravians faced a slow cultural genocide. Half King remained superficially generous and friendly to the Moravians, assuring them continually that he had taken the "believers" in protective custody from pending violence and ruin. Rejecting that excuse, Zeisberger asserted that Half King's efforts to mesh the Moravians with his own people stemmed "from political motives, thinking that his nation, which was very weak, would thereby become strong, for he is hardly in condition to raise over a hundred men."[24] Through constant exhortation, intermarriage, and the isolation or even elimination of the missionaries, Half King hoped to force the Moravians to abandon their faith's pacifism and embrace the Wyandot cause, culture, and language.

But the Moravian fate remained the subject of debate. In November, Zeisberger, Heckewelder, and several prominent Moravian Indians were taken to Detroit to meet with Capt. Arent Schuyler De Peyster and the chiefs. At a council on November 9, the chiefs mulled over not only their conflicting feelings over dragging the Moravians into captivity, but also their raids against the American settlements. Delaware chief Captain Pipe spoke for the chiefs when he presented

De Peyster with some fresh scalps but then questioned "whether the deeds he had done were praiseworthy, and whether he had done right . . . The commandant himself took the scalps from him, and had them put aside. In the same way the other captains acted and delivered their scalps, for which they . . . demanded their pay . . . Thereupon the prisoners also were given over to him."[25] With those transactions done, the council then debated what to do about the Moravians. Should they be released to their former homes, passed on to the Chippewa, or remain with the Wyandot? It was finally decided to keep the Moravians in their makeshift huts on the Sandusky for now.

Those Americans on the northwest frontier had their own reasons to despair. Each year brought seemingly endless destruction of lives and property by invincible warriors. The region was the military graveyard of American generals. Each would arrive with grandiose plans to quell the hostiles and then depart embittered by failure. Like his predecessors, Gen. Daniel Brodhead finally threw up his hands in dismay and begged for a transfer.

On September 25, Gen. William Irvine received an order from Congress to take command at Fort Pitt, Then forty years old, Irvine was born in Ireland, served as a ship's surgeon, and settled in Carlisle, whose propertied inhabitants elected him to Pennsylvania's assembly. In January 1776, the assembly granted him a colonel's commission to raise the 6th Pennsylvania. He was captured in that year's Lake Champlain campaign and not exchanged until August 1778. He was promoted to brigadier general of the 2nd Pennsylvania brigade in May 1779. He arrived at Pittsburgh in November.

What Irvine found appalled him. The 300 troops were "in so wretched a state, that there is very little in my power. I never saw troops cut so truly a deplorable, and at the same time so despicable, a figure. Indeed, when I arrived, no man would believe from their appearance that they were soldiers; nay, it would be difficult to determine whether they were white men."[26] As for Fort Pitt, it was "a heap of ruins." Annual flooding periodically washed away or rotted the fortifications. Irvine recommended abandoning that untenable site and building a fort four miles downstream at the mouth of Chartiers Creek. A bankrupt Congress ignored those and other suggestions.[27]

Irvine was not content to sit tight with his wretched troops and supplies. He saw the "great necessity . . . for adopting speedily some regular plan of action, or this country had better be entirely evacuated and given up at once; as there are at present but small prospects of saving the few troops and stores that are here should the enemy push us in April." The general never explained why he believed his choice was to either attack the enemy or abandon the region. Nor did he submit a detailed plan to carry the war to the enemy. Giving him the benefit of the doubt, Irvine most likely was exaggerating the enemy threat to provoke Congress into sending him enough troops and supplies to do something. Regardless, Congress had nothing to spare. And Irvine would be the fourth Western Department commander whose career was sullied by the near impossibility of acting decisively in that theater.

Washington agreed with Irvine and other advocates that "the possession or destruction of Detroit is the only means of giving peace and security to the western frontier."[28] The question, of course, was how. Washington and his commanders were going about it literally the wrong way. The best way to Detroit was not via the Wabash or Miami River to an arduous portage to the Maumee watershed as Clark proposed, nor was it a long march from Pittsburgh across Ohio to Lake Erie as four Continental commanders had failed to execute. The best way to threaten Detroit was to take Niagara. The second best was an expedition up the Allegheny and over the twenty-five-mile portage to Presque Isle. But inexplicably, neither of those routes was ever seriously considered.

THE NEW YORK FRONTIER

For the British and American Indian commissioners alike, succoring refugees was a more persistent headache than fending off raids. As always, the British enjoyed more money, better administration, and greater sympathy for Indian affairs. Nearly two years after Sullivan's army had destroyed Iroquoia, over 1,500 Indians still huddled in squalid camps outside Fort Niagara's walls to exist off British handouts. Guy Johnson ordered them organized into separate camps of related villages and tribes, and assigned an administrator to see that their minimal needs were met. As if he were not busy enough, Joseph Brant was given responsibility for the Oneida, Mahican, and Cayuga in their cluster of huts. Capt. Robert Lottridge was given the Cayuga. Capt. Gilbert Tice was in charge of the Onondaga and Tuscarorara. Captain Henry Nelles oversaw the Delaware, Nanticoke, Shawnee, and Mahican.[29]

Philip Schuyler was Johnson's American counterpart and faced his own refugee problem. He had fewer charges—93 men, 54 women, and 259 children in scattered hovels near Schenectady—but struggled with far less material or humanitarian means to care for them. The Board of War did appropriate $6,464 to supply food and clothing for those Indians, but only a fraction of that reached those camps. Schuyler tried housing the refugees in Schenectady's fort but had to evacuate them after a soldier murdered one of them after weeks of harassment. They erected a shantytown in the nearby woods. Then smallpox broke out and killed dozens.[30]

The conditions were almost as wretched at Fort Schuyler. With the Mohawk valley devastated and abandoned in its rear, the fort now protected only its dwindling, imperiled garrison packed within crumbling walls and the charred ruins of barracks burned by an accidental fire. The commander, Colonel Cochran, sent a detailed report to Gen. James Clinton. Clinton ordered Cochran to destroy the fort and then march his troops to Fort Herkimer, which would now serve as the westernmost American post in New York. The American frontier had receded. Fort Herkimer, like any frontier post, could not intercept the war parties that haughtily strode past.

This year may have been a record for war parties on the northern frontier. Britain's northern frontier commanders collectively helped launch 64 different parties with 2,945 warriors that killed 54 men; took 127 captives; released 44 women briefly taken; burned 102 houses, 4 small forts, 60 granaries, and 10 mills; and slaughtered or herded away 327 head of livestock. In New York and Pennsylvania, those war parties had an ever longer trail to tread, with years of previous raids having punched back the frontier nearly to the Hudson and far down the Susquehanna. In early January, Mahican Philip Hough led fourteen Delaware on a prolonged raid that eventually hit homesteads east of the Hudson. Not long after, Mohawk David Karaghqunty led his men into the same region. Late that spring, Mohawk David Hill led eighty-three warriors of various tribes to attack Durlach near Otsego Lake. Chief John Deserontyon led forty-four mostly Tuscarora against Canajoharie. Sayenqueraghta trekked with thirty-six warriors down the Allegheny toward Fort Pitt.[31]

One of those raids almost nailed Philip Schuyler at his beautiful mansion atop a hill on Albany's outskirts. One evening, as Schuyler and his family sat in the parlor, the guards outside shouted a warning. Schuyler ordered his family to hurry upstairs as he grabbed a weapon. Warriors burst in. One threw a tomahawk as daughter Margaret ran upstairs with her baby sister in her arms. The tomahawk missed her and stuck in the railing. Schuyler fired and called to imaginary reinforcements. The attackers fled, having wounded one guard and led off another captive. The hatchet mark still scars the railing.[32]

Col. Marinus Willet had the dauntless task of defending the Mohawk valley, whose settlers had nearly all fled, been killed, or been carried off after years of war. From his headquarters at Canajoharie, Willet reported that the valley's muster rolls had plummeted from 2,500 five years earlier to less than 800. Of those losses, one-third had been killed, wounded, or captured, one-third had deserted, and the final third had fled from the frontier. Nearly twenty-four forts were constructed along the sixty-three miles between Schenectady and German Flats, an average of one fort for every two and a half miles. Thus did Willet try to use more forts to make up for less men.[33]

The largest raid occurred late that year. By October's first week, Maj. John Ross gathered at Oswego 607 men, including 25 men of the 8th, 100 of the 34th, 30 of the 84th, 120 of Sir John's Royal Yorkers, 150 of Butler's Rangers, 40 of Lake's loyalist company, 12 of Yeager's loyalist company, and 130 Indians. That small army headed east on October 11. Scores more Indians joined them en route. On October 25, they reached Warren's Bush and began burning and looting. In all, they destroyed 23 homes, 28 barns, 5,411 bushels of grain, 109 tons of hay, and 205 head of livestock. Then they withdrew. Colonel Willet and the militia caught up with them near Johnstown. The British and Indians turned and attacked, forcing Willet and his men to retreat, but the Americans regrouped and continued their pursuit. Other units joined Willet until his troops numbered over 400 whites and 60 Indians. On October 29, the Americans caught the British rear guard on West Canada Creek. In the battle, the Americans lost 13 killed and 24 wounded but did kill the notorious Capt. Walter Butler. Having checked the American pursuit, Ross and his troops escaped, but that raid was costly for the British. In all, they lost about 60 men captured and an unrecorded number of dead and wounded in the various skirmishes.[34]

THE CONFEDERATION, WESTERN LANDS, AND INTERNATIONAL DIPLOMACY

This year Congress finally resolved a bitter five-year battle over the interrelated fates of the national government and the western lands. On March 1, 1781, Congress ratified the Articles of Confederation. The struggle to create America's first constitution began in the summer of 1776, when a draft was introduced in Congress. It took eighteen months of debate for the delegates to decide the confederation's structure and powers before the articles were approved and submitted to the states on November 15, 1777. Then a deadlock arose over conflicting claims to western lands and delayed the confederation's inauguration. Ten states ratified the articles by June 1778. The holdouts were New Jersey, Maryland, and Delaware, which insisted that all those states with western claims surrender them to the national government.

Congress echoed that demand on September 6, 1780, and then resolved on October 10 that it would hold that territory as a public trust, generate revenues from land sales, and eventually carve new states from that realm. Congress based its claim on the 1763 proclamation by which the Crown asserted its control to all lands beyond the Appalachian divide. In declaring independence, Congress automatically inherited those lands from the Crown.

Those assertions of Congress backed by the three holdouts provoked fierce debates within Massachusetts, New York, Connecticut, Virginia, North Carolina, and Georgia, all of which had extensive western land claims and speculators lobbying to exploit them. One by one, the nationalists in those states overcame those with financial or ideological stakes in clinging to their claims, some of which reached all the way across the continent to the Pacific Ocean. Many of those claims overlapped and had bred antagonisms between the colonies and later the states. To Pennsylvania, Connecticut finally gave up its pretensions to the war-devastated Wyoming valley of the upper Susquehanna, thus ending a struggle that had persisted for two decades. Two states, New York and Virginia, ceded only their claims to lands north of the Ohio River. New York, however, retained its claim to Vermont, while Virginia maintained its control over Kentucky. Those claims would not be resolved until 1791 and 1792, when Vermont and Kentucky respectively entered the United States.

The Confederation of the United States enjoyed more powers than the makeshift administration and financial bankruptcy of the Continental Congress, but remained the world's weakest national government. The states retained sovereignty in theory but granted considerable powers to the national government, including war declarations, military operations and appointments, foreign relations, the borrowing of funds, and the allocation of payments and troop quotas among the states. Congress would meet annually in a unicameral legislature with each state allocated one vote. A president with a one-year renewable term was elected by Congress. Notably missing was any independent source of revenue other than western land sales. Taxes and tariffs remained in state hands. Nonetheless, it was a major step forward in America's revolution. Having finally won the tug-of-war with the states for the western lands, Congress then almost ceded much of them to a foreign power.

American envoy John Jay and Foreign Minister Jose Monino y Redondo de Floridablanca continued to butt heads in Madrid. The Spaniard rejected Jay's repeated requests for recognition, alliance, a frontier on the Mississippi south to the thirty-first parallel, free navigation down that river to the sea, and the right to deposit goods at New Orleans. Indeed, the Spaniard dug in his heels deeper with each audience.

For Spain, the war had gone surprisingly well. His Majesty's troops had captured Minorca and West Florida, repulsed a British attack on Central America, and even briefly possessed St. Joseph near Lake Michigan. What war booty in North America should Spain demand? The "logic" of empire dictated that new lands must be conquered to shield previous conquests. With that, Spain demanded the Floridas and exclusive navigation on the Mississippi River as buffers to protect Louisiana, which in turn shielded Texas, which provided a forward defense for Mexico. That logic was solely theoretical. Only Mexico produced more wealth than it cost to administer; the other colonies were financial black holes for Madrid.

Thus did the fate of the western frontier lie in Spain's hands, at least for the near future. By right of might, Spain could choke off America's western claims. Time, of course, favored the Americans, who, as they grew more restless and numerous, eventually swelled into that territory regardless of who claimed it. The Spanish understood that. They tried to cement Spain's claims in treaty now but knew they would have to watch helplessly as American immigrants and intrigues steadily eroded their control in the generations ahead.

If the Americans could not move the Spanish, perhaps the French could with their great military and diplomatic power undergirded by family ties. In Paris, Benjamin Franklin tried to enlist Foreign Minister Vergennes behind America's bid for a Mississippi River frontier and navigation, but Vergennes knew and cared little about that vast vague wilderness beyond the Appalachians. All that mattered was how that region's frontier affected the European and global power balance. Interests rather than sentiments determine one's allies and enemies. An ally today could be a rival tomorrow and an implacable foe the next. French interests were thus best advanced by exacerbating a power balance and rivalry in North America among Britain, the United States, and Spain in which none was predominant and each checked the other. The more each of those powers feared the others and acted on those fears, the less resources any or all of them could muster to challenge French ambitions in Europe and elsewhere. Thus Versailles pursued a triple containment strategy in North America. If the United States were allowed to stretch to the Mississippi, it would amass the power to expand beyond; eventually the Americans might be powerful enough to expel the British and Spanish from the continent. To prevent that perhaps not so distant possibility, France had to prop up Spain's sagging empire in North America. Spain must retake not only the Floridas, but the entire northern Mississippi valley. Yet it would be bad diplomacy to bluntly dismiss the earnest Americans. Whenever the issue arose, Vergennes demurred at taking sides but encouraged the Americans to be flexible. The American dreams would shatter against the realities of Spanish power soon enough. France must stand aloof from that inevitable impact.

For America's envoys, the frustrations of dealing with such wily Old World statesmen would be exacerbated by startling instructions from their own government. As Spain's fortunes rose, America's plunged. By mid-1781, the British had overrun most of Georgia and the Carolinas. The Americans were losing their grip on their outposts in the upper Mississippi and lower Ohio valleys. That worsening crisis panicked Congress. With southern delegates taking the lead, Congress sought help from any quarter no matter what the diplomatic price. Spain had secretly extended military aid to the rebels since 1776 and in 1779 joined the war as a French ally. That was not enough for Congress. To curry recognition, an alliance, and even more aid, Congress agreed to drop what was once thought to be an essential foreign policy goal—free navigation of the Mississippi River. Word of that concession left the envoys aghast in Paris and Madrid. Fortunately for American power, its diplomats ignored their instructions. And then news of Yorktown arrived, which changed everything.

THE SOUTHEAST FRONTIER: SECOND PHASE
When the fire of war was smothered in one place on the frontier, it burst into flames elsewhere. Despite suffering five years of repeated invasions, destruction, and death, some Cherokee continued to resist the Americans. Dragging Canoe and several hundred followers remained holed up in Chickamauga valley, nervously ready to disappear into the mountains when the next American army rampaged through. In late August, Raven and several score warriors slipped through a couple hundred miles of enemy territory and into the British lines at Savannah. Raven angrily explained that he and his warriors sought vengeance against the Americans who "dyed their hands in the blood of many of our Women and Children."[35]

But defiance and hatred only provoked more Cherokee deaths and disasters. Learning of another Cherokee party headed toward Savannah, Gen. John Twiggs and his troops tracked it down, killed 20, and captured 7 women, 2 children, 199 horses, 15,000 pounds of deerskins, and 1,500 beaver pelts.[36] Andrew Pickens led several mounted companies in a raid against the lower towns that autumn. The year ended ominously when disease killed the Cherokee's beloved agent Alexander Cameron on December 27.

The war was crushing the spirit of ever more Cherokee. While the war's victor remained uncertain, most Cherokee acknowledged with mingled bitterness and resignation that they were among its losers. That autumn, Virginia agent Joseph Martin escorted Oconostota and three other chiefs to Williamsburg to plead for peace with Gov. Benjamin Harrison. However, as devastating as these events were to the participants, the year's most decisive struggle occurred far away from the Cherokee homelands.

The northeastern stalemate was in its third year. No major battles had scarred the region since Monmouth in 1778. At most, Gen. Henry Clinton authorized an occasional large-scale raid into New Jersey, Connecticut, up the Hudson, or even to distant Chesapeake Bay. But the effects of those raids, while destructive, were fleeting. The Northeast was spared the incessant guerrilla fighting and civil war ravaging the southern states. During these years, George Washington's greatest challenge was simply holding his army together as disease and desertion steadily depleted the ranks. Then came the thunderbolt of Benedict Arnold's defection in September 1780 after his plan to kidnap Washington and deliver West Point to the enemy was thwarted. The army's survival was tested in the new year when the Pennsylvania regiments went on strike for back pay and discharges. Washington finally defused the crisis by issuing those troops money and provisions while promising to set up a committee to investigate their grievances. He dealt more harshly with a strike by New Jersey troops by having the ringleaders shot for mutiny.

The Revolution's vitality was ebbing away. Only a major victory could boost the faltering morale of the army and nation, and perhaps even bring the war to an abrupt end. The Crown would surely sue for peace if the Americans captured another British army. But that decisive clash could not be joined in the northeast. Clinton showed no signs of stirring from his New York fortress. For that great battle, Washington would eventually look to Virginia, which was the only state then suffering a British army loose on its earth. For the time, however, he was obsessed with besieging New York. For that, he needed more troops, munitions, and the heaviest of siege guns.

Washington journeyed to Wethersfield, Connecticut, and on May 21 met with Maj. Gen. Jean Baptiste de Vineur Rochambeau, who commanded the 4,800 French troops that had been stationed in Rhode Island since the previous July. For the last nine months, Rochambeau had refused repeated pleas from Washington to join him near New York. Earlier that year, he had agreed to allow Capt. Charles Rene Dominique Sochet Destouches to sail with 1,500 troops on transports guarded by two ships of the line to the Chesapeake and cut off Benedict Arnold, who was ravaging the region. Destouches arrived there only to sail away before a superior British squadron. Washington now again implored Rochambeau to join him for an attack on Clinton's 14,500 troops at New York. Rochambeau countered with the idea of joining Lafayette in Virginia against Cornwallis. Washington stood firm. Rochambeau gave in. In June, he marched his army to join Washington's at Dobbs Ferry north of New York. For weeks after Rochambeau's arrival on July 6, the allied commanders reconnoitered the British lines and pondered attack plans. Washington finally admitted that New York City appeared impregnable. Was the war unwinnable?

That gnawing dread lifted on August 14 when Washington and Rochambeau received word from Adm. Francois Joseph Paul de Grasse that he would soon arrive with twenty-eight ships of the line and 3,000 troops. If the eight ships of the line commanded by Jacques Melchior de Laurent de Barras at Newport joined de Grasse, the French would achieve numerical superiority over any fleet the British could then muster in American waters. Washington and Rochambeau swiftly agreed to march against Cornwallis at Yorktown and sent word to Barras and de Grasse to rendezvous with them there.

The allies began their march south on August 21. They paused in New Jersey to give Clinton the impression that they were planning an attack on Staten Island and then resumed their march and received a hero's welcome at Philadelphia on August 30. After pausing briefly, they pushed on to Head of Elk. There they hoped to receive word from de Grasse. That word soon arrived.

De Grasse's fleet reached the Chesapeake capes on August 26 and sent transports up to Head of Elk to retrieve the army. He disembarked the 4,000 troops with his fleet on September 2 to join Lafayette's troops at Williamsburg. On September 5, the combined fleet of Admirals Samuel Graves and Samuel Hood appeared between Cape Henry and Cape Charles, the respective southern and northern lands shouldering Chesapeake Bay's entrance. De Grasse promptly sailed out against the British fleet.

What followed was one of history's most decisive battles. The fleets closed and exchanged broadsides. Though the losses were relatively light, with only one British warship sunk and 336 casualties among the crews, compared with 209 among the French, Graves ordered his fleet to sail south. De Grasse shadowed him for two days and then returned to blockade the British army entrenched at Yorktown and Gloucester. Barras soon arrived from Newport with the siege guns. The battle of the Capes sealed the fate of Cornwallis and thus the American Revolution.

Transports brought the army of Washington and Rochambeau from Head of Elk to Williamsburg on September 18. That army of 8,800 Americans and 7,800 French marched to hem in Cornwallis at the peninsula tips of Yorktown and Gloucester. The allies conducted a classic siege. Trenches were zigzagged forward, batteries emplaced, and sorties repelled. On October 9, the bombardment began and continued steadily. On October 17, Cornwallis asked for a parley. He would surrender only if he received honors of war and passage home with the promise not to serve against France or America for the war's duration. Washington insisted that all troops become prisoners of war. With his munitions and nerves nearly exhausted, Cornwallis agreed.

The surrender took place on October 19. It was an extraordinary victory with the capitulation of 7,171 troops, 1,140 sailors, 191 field cannons and mortars, 31 siege guns, 4 frigates, 39 transports, two score lesser vessels, and 5,000 pounds sterling. Claiming ill health, Cornwallis did not lead his troops from Yorktown down the road to captivity lined by American and French troops presenting arms as a band played with verve and irony "The World Turned Upside Down."[37] Though the war was not yet over, especially on the frontier, it was the beginning of the end.

CHAPTER 10

"The Tomahawks Struck": 1782

They prayed and sang until the tomahawks struck into their heads.
—Missionary David Zeisberger
on the fate of Moravian Indians

We will destroy everything with fire and blood.
—James Colbert

After the blood shed at Lexington and Concord, American independence was just a matter of time. The central questions were when and how. Yorktown provided the answers. Though a peace treaty was still two years off and hundreds more would die gruesome premature deaths on the frontier before then, the Americans won the war at Yorktown. Now the key question was what kind of peace would follow, or, more specifically, what would be the new republic's frontiers.

News of Cornwallis's surrender left King George III unbowed. With bitter defiance, he promised that "by the concurrence and support of my parliament, by the valour of my fleets and armies, and by the vigorous, animated and united exertion of the faculties and resources of my people, I shall be able to restore the blessings of a safe and honorable peace to all my dominions."[1]

While all the king's men might still obey their marching orders, Britain's political elite now gloomily recognized that victory was an impossible dream. After several weeks of acrimonious debate, Parliament finally voted on February 27 to end all offensive warfare in North America. Henceforth, Parliament would "consider as enemies to his Majesty and the Country all those who should advise or by any means attempt to further prosecution of the offensive war on the continent of North America."[2]

Prime Minister Frederick North took the not so subtle hint and resigned on March 20. The king asked Charles Watson-Wentworth Rockingham to form a new government. Rockingham had long favored concessions with the Americans. During his previous stint as chief minister, from 1765 to 1766, he revoked the Stamp

Act, which had provoked the initial round of colonial protests. Like North, Rock-ingham left foreign policy for others to sort out, in his case, the northern secretary Charles Fox and American secretary William Petty Fitzmaurice Shelburne. Those ministers split over concessions to the rebels, with Fox happy to grant uncondi-tional independence while Shelburne held firm to keeping symbolic ties between Britain and America.

That distinction was lost on the American diplomats in Paris. They might have brought the war to a speedier end had they negotiated more with eager Fox than cautious Shelburne, but Franklin knew and liked Shelburne from his days as a colonial agent in London. Shortly after Shelburne settled into his ministry, Franklin wrote him a request that Britain grant the United States independence and Canada in exchange for peace. Shelburne dispatched Richard Oswald to Paris for negotiations. Not to be outdone, Fox sent Thomas Grenville. Because of vari-ous illnesses and diplomatic forays of the other ministers, John Jay and John Adams, Franklin conducted most of the amiable but tough talks. This simplifed American team was mirrored by the British in the summer. Fox was forced to resign on June 30 after losing a political maneuver. Rockingham died the next day, and Shelburne took his chair as prime minister.

The first negotiation round lasted from April until early July. Franklin issued a list of primary peace conditions, including British recognition of American independence, Quebec's borders of 1763 ending on the Ottawa River rather than those of 1774 extending to the Ohio River, American frontiers that embraced the Great Lakes and the Mississippi River's eastern bank with unimpeded navigation rights, and access to the Newfoundland fisheries. The secondary demands included the cession of all of Quebec and Nova Scotia in return for compensating loyalists for their property losses.

Oswald dismissed these and their rationale. Franklin justified America's claims by the various royal charters issued to the colonies and by right of con-quest. Oswald countered that the Americans lost their charter rights when they revolted against the king, and they had hardly set foot in let alone conquered the lands they claimed. Franklin replied that the Americans had inherited the rights to that land from a king whose rapacious acts had forever alienated his former sub-jects. As for the right of conquest, Franklin tended to divert the discussion. That assertion might have applied to the Kentucky and Tennessee settlements, but the Americans had receded from Illinois and Vincennes nearly as thoroughly as the earlier retreat from Canada; the only difference was that British arms had not filled the power void. Oswald brushed aside any notion of Canada's cession and demanded compensation for loyalists forced to flee their homes. He also insisted that the Ohio River rather than the Great Lakes form the frontier west of the Appalachians.

Shelburne's hard-line position was boosted when word arrived of the shatter-ing victory of the battle of the Saintes in the Caribbean, when a British fleet under Adm. George Rodney destroyed seven French ships of the line and captured that fleet's commander, Adm. Francois Joseph Paul de Grasse, on April 12. France and

Spain extended their own peace feelers. During the summer, Shelburne was conducting simultaneous talks with all of Britain's enemies.

Franklin was nonplussed at the rebuff. He merely repackaged and resubmitted his demands to Oswald on July 10. The necessary concessions included independence; boundaries embracing the Great Lakes, Mississippi River, and the thirty-first parallel; and the right to navigate the Mississippi and fish off Newfoundland. The advisable concessions were Canada, compensation for war damages, and free trade without duties with the British isles and its remaining empire.

It took a month and a half before Oswald could reply since the British ministers hotly debated the issue. On September 1, Oswald passed on word from Shelburne that Britain accepted Franklin's necessary demands but rejected his advisable ones. Why was Whitehall suddenly so generous? The talks with France and Spain had stalemated. Shelburne and his ministers hoped to redeploy Britain's army and navy from North America for decisive blows against France and Spain in the West Indes.

But then John Jay joined the negotiations and ended up disrupting and delaying them because of a technicality. He argued that Oswald could not make a legally binding deal since he was not officially accredited a diplomat to the United States. Either Oswald must acquire accreditation, Jay insisted, or the negotiations would end. In so doing, Jay wanted Britain to grant official recognition to the United States before a peace treaty.

Jay was just as suspicious of France. Joseph-Mathias Gerard de Rayneval, first secretary of the French foreign ministry, pretended to act as an impartial broker between Jay and Conde de Aranda, Spain's ambassador to France. Rayneval pressed Jay to accept a boundary that began between Mobile and Pensacola and ran north to the Ohio River, thus keeping the United States far from the Mississippi River. Jay rejected the proposal and insisted on a Mississippi frontier above the thirty-first parallel, free navigation of that river to its source, and the right to deposit goods at New Orleans. In November, Madrid finally agreed to the thirty-first parallel line to the Mississippi River and conceded the northwest territories beyond the Ohio River in return for the Floridas, but the Spanish adamantly dismissed the notion of free navigation or deposit of goods at New Orleans.

Meanwhile, Jay's paranoia that the Great Powers were ganging up on the United States worsened in August when Rayneval left for London. Jay loudly voiced his suspicion that Rayneval would cut a separate peace at America's cost. Franklin thought Jay's points and fears were frivolous, but he was distracted by illness. Valuable time to negotiate was squandered as the talks broke off. The impasse ended on September 28, when Shelburne finally relented and sent Oswald accreditation along with Undersecretary of State Henry Strachey to lead negotiations. Jay was reinforced too as Franklin recovered and Adams returned from a long mission to the Netherlands.

In October, Jay drafted another position. America's boundary would run west along 45 degrees latitude to the St. Lawrence River; then along its southern bank to the Great Lakes, and through the center of Lakes Ontario, Erie, Huron, and

Superior to Lake Nipissing; straight down it to the Mississippi River to 31 degrees latitude; and then due east to the Atlantic Ocean. On October 17, the cabinet agreed to these frontiers if the Americans conceded the rights of both nations to navigate the Mississippi River and promised to repay its debts to British creditors and compensate loyalists. That was mostly fine with the Americans.

On November 30, the United States and Britain signed a preliminary peace treaty that included America's demands for recognition of independence, boundaries, navigation, and fishing in return for promising to pay its debts. They agreed to defer issues of compensation for war damages to Americans and loyalists for later talks. The peace treaty with America, however, depended on Britain securing peace with France, Spain, and the Netherlands. Talks with France and Spain opened and would continue into the next year.

Parliament's resolution in February to end the war did so on the eastern seaboard and led to the November preliminary peace treaty, but the resolution took over a year to stem violence beyond the Appalachians. Though Gen. Frederick Haldimand received word in April to call off any planned offensives and sit tight, that order would not reach the frontier commanders and the warriors until it was too late to recall many of them. Indeed, during 1782, the British seemed to field as many Indians and win as many wilderness battles as ever. Hundreds more decaying corpses and charred ruins would foul the frontier. But all that death and destruction was for nought. The Crown had grudgingly given up the fight.

THE MISSISSIPPI VALLEY FRONTIER

Having conquered West Florida and joined it to Louisiana, the Spanish consolidated their rule. Ideally, that colony would be an economic asset rather than a burden to the empire. To facilitate that end, King Carlos III issued a decree on January 22 that relaxed Spanish mercantilism. For the next decade, Louisiana could trade with the French Caribbean islands, all excess production could be exported, slaves could be imported duty-free from any source, and duties were eliminated for two years on the sales of foreign ships.[3]

Louisiana received a new governor on March 1, when Col. Esteban Miro replaced Bernardo de Galvez, who was recalled to Madrid to receive new honors and duties for his brilliant leadership. Miro's priority was to resolve the trials of the Natchez rebels. The wheels of Spanish justice creaked slowly. It was not until May 6, 1782, a year after the Natchez revolt was crushed, that a verdict of guilty was issued against the twenty-one accused. The governor ordered their property confiscated, a decision that enriched Louisiana's coffers by 3,121 piastres. But the fate of the rebels themselves remained a complex question. Should the traitors be executed as Spanish law demanded? Was such a harsh retribution just, with the war nearly over? Should the governor simply send them into exile or pardon them in return for another loyalty oath?[4]

These questions pressed ever harder on Governor Miro as John Colbert finally made good on his promise to close the Mississippi if the Natchez rebels were not liberated. The loyalists' first act, however, miscarried badly. On April 25, about eight miles above the Yazoo River mouth, a group consisting of the leader, John Turner, eight whites, and three blacks ambushed a Spanish keelboat heading slowly up the Mississippi. Eugene Poure surrendered his men and boat without a fight, but Poure was just biding his time. Four hours later, as the captives were forced to row the boat to a British safe haven, Poure ordered his men to attack. The Spanish swung their oars and bashed in the skulls of six whites and two blacks; Turner and the others jumped into the river and swam to safety. Poure and his men returned to Natchez, joined the expedition of Francois Valle and Eugenio Alvarez, and rowed upriver to Arkansas Post.

Another Spanish keelboat was not so lucky. In March, its nine-man crew set its poles and oars against the Mississippi River's current before New Orleans. In addition to its crew, the boat carried Capt. Silvestre L'Abbadie, Madame Anicanova Ramos de Cruzat, the lieutenant governor's wife, her four sons, supplies, and 4,500 pesos of government funds. At Natchez, they learned of the attack on Poure, but L'Abbadie ordered the men onward without escort. He would soon regret that choice. A British spy in Natchez, Francois La Grange, passed on word of the voyage.

The keelboat reached Chickasaw Bluffs on May 2 and hugged the west bank to avoid any gunshots from loyalists on the far side. Through the nearby foliage, a voice hailed them, claiming his name was Thomas and that he had letters from Governor Cruzat for his wife. Though suspicious, L'Abbadie headed the boat for shore. As the boat touched bottom, forty armed men burst from hiding and leveled their muskets. L'Abbadie surrendered without resistance. The loyalist leader was James Colbert. The British bound their captives, crossed the Mississippi, and then rowed about a mile up the Chickasaw River. They disembarked at a fortified camp.

Colbert's capture of the Spanish was easy. It took him three weeks of tough negotiations, however, before he and his captives agreed on the terms of their release. All along, Colbert displayed "good health, with a strong constitution, active and capable of enduring the greatest hardship in war and possessing a violent temper." He was also a gregarious if not gracious host, regaling his captives with his plans to destroy Spanish rule in the region. He warned that "we will destroy everything with fire and blood." At one point, Colbert's lieutenant, William McGillivray, "interrupted him by saying, 'You talk very freely, and are making our projects known to a man who, if he is given his liberty . . . will not forget to publish our intention.' This reproof immediately closed the mouth of Colbert."[5]

Fierce as Colbert was, he seems to have met his match with Señora Cruzat. The experience must have been especially harrowing for the lieutenant governor's wife, who detested the wilderness and feared for her virtue and the lives of her children. But the señora proved to be a woman of steely mettle. During the ambush, "one of the inhuman brigands ran towards Madame Cruzat with his tomahawk raised . . . as though to cleave in her skull, which the scoundrel was miraculously prevented from doing so by the lady, who, with a courage truly heroic in a woman of her quality and delicate constitution, arrested the arm of her cruel adversary." L'Abbadie attributes their eventual release to Señora Cruzat, who "through repeated and constant requests . . . daily tired the ears of their enemies."[6] On May 22, probably with a deep sigh of relief, Colbert ransomed L'Abbadie, Madame Cruzat, her children, nine crewmen, and the boat, looted of its cargo, when they promised to pay an additional 400 pesos for themselves and 250 pesos for the slaves, and seek to gain the release of the rebels. They reached New Orleans on May 30.

Though Governor Miro refused to set the convicts free, he could do little about the rebels on the middle Mississippi; those bandits would retreat before any large expedition, attack a smaller one, and besiege any fort erected in the region. Both an expedition and a fort would be extremely expensive. How could Miro fulfill his duty to protect Spanish traffic on the Mississippi River?

The governor reasoned that where arms failed, diplomacy might succeed. The Chickasaw had very mixed feelings toward Colbert and his followers. They benefited from the trade goods the whites brought but suffered the infection of the debauchery and drunkenness in Colbert's village only five miles away. Miro sent word to their chief, Payamataha, to drive Colbert from the region or else face Spanish retaliation. He later dispatched Choctaw chief Palous to council with Payamataha. On June 17, the governor then headed to Natchez to supervise Spain's diplomatic and, if need be, military initiatives. From there, he dispatched Lt. Antonio Soler and thirty-three troops to reinforce Arkansas Post. Finally, he sent word to the enterprising Capt. Jacobo Dubreuil to take command of Fort Carlos III.[7]

Unbeknownst to Miro, Cruzat had initiated similar measures from St. Louis. On May 30, word reached him at St. Louis of the approaching keelboat with his family and the supplies. Cruzat dispatched Lt. Diego Blanco, nine soldiers, and fourteen militia downstream to meet the keelboat and escort it to St. Louis. On June 5, Indians informed Cruzat that bandits had captured the keelboat and his family. Cruzat sent Capt. Jacobo Dubreuil and soldiers to St. Genevieve to council with local Kaskaskia, Peoria, Mascouten, and Kickapoo, and ask for any help they could give. Those tribes sent a delegation of twenty-two warriors to the Chickasaw, warning them to curtail Colbert and free the hostages or risk war. Dubreuil then hurried militia lieutenant Carlos Valle with eight men down the Mississippi to inform Blanco. On June 12, Valle ran into Blanco eighteen miles below St. Genevieve as the latter was returning from his fruitless mission. Together they descended the Mississippi to Chickasaw Bluffs, found Colbert's deserted camp, which they burned, and then withdrew to St. Louis. On July 25, Dubreuil's Indian delegation reached St. Louis with six British prisoners and some Chickasaw envoys, who pleaded with Cruzat not to go to war and promised to suppress Colbert.[8]

The standoff persisted for the year's remainder and into the next. Squeezed between the northern tribes and Choctaw, the Chickasaw sent word to Miro of their promise to expel Colbert and align with Spain. An alleged illness kept Chief Payamataha from attending a council with Governor Miro in Natchez. Apparently it also inhibited him from getting rid of Colbert, whose men continued to loot boats on the Mississippi. On October 6, Colbert wrote Miro defending his actions, thanking the governor for not unleashing the Indians against him, and offering to exchange his hostages for Blommart and the other Natchez rebels. Colbert had little to fear from Spain's Indian allies, which were lukewarm at best. Typical was the Choctaw complaint that "we are trembling with fear, and that Spain was not good, because it killed them with hunger and did not give them anything to eat thus making it necessary to steal in order to live."[9] All the Spanish could do before these mingled threats and challenges was shore up their forts in the region and hope for the best.

If Colbert believed he had little to fear from the Spanish, the Americans posed no threat. America's stake to the lower Mississippi seemed to evaporate with the Spanish conquest of West Florida. James Willing's filibustering expedition of 1778 was the only American effort to win the region. After a string of dazzling victories that disarmed Britain's land and naval forces along the Mississippi and adjacent waters, Willing and most of his men immersed themselves into the decadent lure of New Orleans' brothels, grogshops, and gaming tables. All that had been won was lost, and those losses compounded as Willing ran up huge bills on credit.

Willing's extravagances only heaped higher the debt accrued by America's man in New Orleans, Oliver Pollock. The financier for America's Revolution in the west bankrupted himself in his zeal to serve his country. By 1782, he faced impatient creditors. Into the cause he had poured his personal fortune with no return other than the satisfaction that it was just and succeeding. His sole significant asset was his New Orleans home, beset by financiers eager to evict him and his family. Even victories could cut both ways. After the loyalist John Blommart led the Natchez revolt in 1781, he was captured and his property confiscated; Blommart owed Pollock 472 pesos and now had no way to repay it.[10]

Pollock's debt was not as bad as it seemed. He had borrowed most of the money as the official agent for Virginia and Congress. But while those governments might be legally liable, they were far beyond the easy reach of lawsuits. Lenders instead challenged Pollock's credentials and threatened to have him jailed until he repaid his debts, which would have confined him for his life's remainder. It was only the governor's stalwart protection that kept Pollock a free man. Some of the pressure on Pollock eased on April 27, when he submitted documents that proved Gov. Thomas Jefferson had appointed him Virginia's agent.[11]

To clear his and his country's sullied honor, Pollock journeyed to Congress and Virginia and pleaded that they repay the debts he had contracted on their behalf. He arrived in August for what would be months of lobbying. Congress did not take up his petition until October 22, when it issued an ambiguous statement lauding Pollock's "zeal and industry" but deferring any settlement until the accounts could be clearly sorted out and the liabilities assessed. On December 27, Virginia promised to liquidate Pollock's account. These were vital steps toward Pollock's financial rehabilitation, but his creditors would not release him until they got the money. All concerned would wait years for partial or, in many cases, no compensation.[12]

What sort of collateral did Pollock leave behind? All his worldly possessions were gone except his home and his pregnant wife, Margaret, who was a virtual hostage to those creditors who feared he was trying to escape their clutches. The creditor with the best claim to the residence did not hesitate to pressure Mrs. Pollock to surrender it. Margaret complained to Governor Miro that Mr. Macarty "has thought Proper to Infest me here with a Coopers Shop in the front of my Lodgings, and a band of Negroes, that has Insulted me and beat my Servants. In the office under my room he has Constantly either a bandity of Whites or a number of Insupportable Savages the noise of which no human Creature can bear . . . He likewise sent his Negroe Wench to Insult me openly in the street & tell me it was her Masters Orders that I should go out of his House . . . It is true I did strike a Negroe boy of his, tho' it is not half the Punishment he Merited."[13]

Who was the victim and who the victimizer? There may well have been an element of both in all parties to the dispute. Judging from her letters, Margaret Pollock may have been as haughty and ill-tempered as her husband was diplomatic and self-effacing. Eventually Governor Miro himself would turn against Pollock, perhaps as much because of his insufferable wife as the unpaid bills.

The Pollocks were not the only Americans living under the cloud of deepening suspicion and resentment in Spanish territory. With the loyalists defeated and West Florida conquered by Spain, enterprising or desperate Americans descended the Ohio and Mississippi Rivers to acquire land, start businesses, or make trouble. One Spanish official worried that "the Americans recently arrived here . . . appear to have bad intentions, or at least to have fled to this post on account of some crime committed in their own country . . . [Many] are Americans by birth but not sentiment. Their conduct in America was always that of people who place themselves on the stronger side, now one, now the other, according to the success of the belligerent powers. They had profited by everything they could pillage from their countrymen . . . They showed by their remarks the aversion they had to be living under the Spanish government."[14]

Spain faced an imperial dilemma. Its empire suffered from a dearth of pioneers with skills and enterprise. America abounded with such individuals. Thus Madrid encouraged Americans and other foreigners to immigrate to its empire in return for an oath of allegiance to the Spanish king and Catholic Church. The trouble was that along with law-abiding settlers, the policy attracted too many miscreants who, like termites, ate away at rather than bolstered Spanish rule. American settlers would infiltrate Spanish and later Mexican lands; soon surpass in numbers, wealth, and power the Hispanic population; and eventually clamor for annexation by the United States.

While the complaints of American intrigues on the distant frontier trickled into New Orleans, a much more serious incident occurred in adjacent waters. Capt. William Hayden of the privateer *Paty* seized a former British ship, now owned by Don Antonio Argote, set a skeleton crew aboard, and sailed for Boston with his prize. Capt. Martin Navarro chartered a French schooner, *L'Aimable Julie,* to join the Spanish sloop *La Maneta* in pursuit, but they could not catch up to the Americans. That American seizure of a Spanish ship would wound relations between the two nations for several years, distracting diplomats from much more vital issues.[15]

Spanish claims to the upper Mississippi valley were disputed not by desperadoes, but merchants. That year alone, Montreal issued licenses for 120 canoes and 250 bateaux with goods worth 184,000 pounds sterling to trade in the region. Prairie du Chien was the upper Mississippi River's trade center, just as Michilimackinac was for the upper Great Lakes. From there, traders not only fanned out up and down the upper Mississippi watershed, but an intrepid few even trekked west to trade with the middle Missouri River tribes.[16]

To counter that economic invasion, Lieutenant Governor Cruzat sent Pierre Dorion to entice the Sioux from British influence. Surprisingly, though he had few gifts to distribute, Dorion won over every band except Chief Oja's. Those proclaimed ties, however, were so much pipe smoke. Like other tribes, the Sioux simply used the threat of turning to the Spanish to shake down more gifts from the British.

Though the trade threat to Spain's hold on the upper Mississippi was disturbing enough, in early July word reached St. Louis of a pending attack. Cruzat held a war council with his officers on July 9 to decide what to do. The assessment was bleak. The Americans across the river in Illinois were "in a defenseless state, without any garrison or store of munitions of war or provisions sufficient to . . . resist for any time those who may attack them." But St. Louis was just as vulnerable, with its fortifications crumbling or eroded and munitions nearly expended. The Spaniards were not at all confident they could repeat last year's repulse of a massive British and Indian attack. While the rumored attack proved to be illusory, the more insidious threat of foreign merchants prevailed and worsened in the years and decades ahead. Increasingly, those fierce foreign competitors who reaped wealth from Spanish territory and tribes would be American rather than British.[17]

THE SOUTHEAST FRONTIER
The fighting between Americans and British had ended along the southern seaboard. Content to run out the clock, the Americans chose not to besiege Savannah, Charles Town, or Wilmington. Two of America's best generals, Nathanael Greene and Anthony Wayne, commanded the armies watching rather than formally besieging those seaports.

In doing so, the Americans severed the last supply lines to the southern Indians. The tribes withered on their cut vines. The choice was to either submit to the Americans or perish. Mixing pride and fatalism, some Indians chose to go down fighting. In January, a Creek war party headed toward the frontier. Informants passed on word. Elijah Clarke led his men across the Oconee and routed the Creek warriors. That same month, another party of 300 Creek made it all the way to Savannah's outskirts only to stumble into the American lines. An American officer tricked the chiefs into believing he would take them to British headquarters. Instead he brought them before General Wayne. Exhausted and starving, the chiefs and their men faced extermination, but Wayne was conciliatory. He liberally provisioned the Creek Indians and pointed them home. Meekly they returned. From the Creek, Wayne learned that a Choctaw party was approaching and sent troops to intercept them. But the Choctaw evaded the Americans and eventually snuck into Savannah. In May, an even larger war party, a couple hundred Creek led by Chief Emistisiguo, reached the British lines.[18]

In Savannah, Emistisiguo presided over several hundred Creek, Cherokee, and Choctaw whose ranks thinned steadily from disease. The fighting spirit may have seeped from the British, but a measure lingered within the warriors. On the night of June 23, Emistisiguo led his men against Wayne's camp. The surprise scattered the troops, but Wayne rallied them and led a bayonet charge that killed a score of Indians, including Emistisiguo, captured a dozen, and routed the rest. Wayne ordered all twelve captives executed.

The British surrendered Savannah on July 11. General Wayne and a portion of his army marched in to take formal possession, but it would be several weeks before all the loyal British could be evacuated. One by one the regular and loyalist regiments set sail for Charles Town and New York. Then there were the 2,500 civilian loyalists, 4,000 liberated blacks, and couple hundred mostly Creek. By agreement, they too were allowed safe passage. The Indians embarked on July 20 for St. Augustine. It would take until August 9 before the British completed their evacuation of Savannah.

The Cherokee finally sued for peace, but only after enduring more suffering. In September, the Americans launched their last campaign of the frontier war for American independence. The indefatigable John Sevier set out with 250 men from Big Island of the French Broad River on September 20. Upon reaching Chota, he accepted Chief Hanging Maw's plea for peace. Sevier then headed into the Chickamauga country, skirmishing and burning four villages. Dragging Canoe led his people to what became known as the Five Lower Towns below the Cumberland Mountains on the Tennessee River. Sevier returned to Chota for a council with Chiefs Hanging Maw, Tassel, and Oconostota. Meanwhile, Andrew Pickens, Elijah Clarke, and several hundred South Carolina and Georgia troops burned more Cherokee villages but left word that they were willing to talk. The Cherokee accepted the offer. On October 17, Pickens and Clarke counciled with envoys from the lower, middle, and Chickamauga towns. The chiefs bowed to the American demand to surrender all lands between the headwaters of the Savannah and Chattahoochee Rivers to South Carolina.

Most of those lands were claimed by the Overhill Cherokee, who had refused to attend the council. Instead, they appealed to Governors Benjamin Harrison of Virginia and Alexander Martin of North Carolina for a less sweeping theft of their land. Martin, whose state stood to gain territory from the treaty, shunned the plea. Harrison, whose state would get no land, was more conciliatory. The Virginia governor wrote his neighbor that the "Indians have their rights and our Justice is called on to support them. Whilst we are nobly contending for liberty, will it not be an eternal blot on our National character if we deprive others of it who ought to be as free as ourselves."[19] With perhaps a snicker or cynical shrug, Martin rejected the notion. Harrison would never conceive of applying that same principle to Virginia's claim to Kentucky.

The Cherokee were not the only tribe that grudgingly agreed to peace and land concessions. Georgia's governor John Martin had counciled with the Lower Creek led by Tallassee King at Augusta in September. Martin demanded that the Creek surrender all lands east of the Oconee River. Tallassee King skillfully deflected the demand. He denied being able to speak for all Creek, but did promise he would try to bring the rest of his people and the other southern tribes to talks over peace and specific land concessions. For these promises, he and his delegation were amply awarded.

Although nearly everyone else had given up, including the British government, Thomas Brown carried on the losing war from St. Augustine. He sent word to the Creek and Cherokee to join him. Several hundred Creek and several score Cherokee eventually made the long trek. That swelling tide of Indian refugees along with loyalists and slaves into East Florida created an ever worsening humanitarian nightmare rather than a strategic asset. The newcomers' need to be fed was incessant, while their fighting strength was purely potential. By late 1782, there were 2,428 whites, 3,609 blacks, and 2,000 Indians in the colony.[20]

Gov. Patrick Tonyn and Superintendent Thomas Brown conducted their last Indian council of the war in December. Nearly 3,000 Indians crowded into St. Augustine, mostly Creek but also Cherokee and Choctaw, along with a few Mohawk, Seneca, Delaware, Shawnee, Mingo, and Tuscarora. A call for peace rather than war was dispensed with the presents. The war had finally ended on the southeast frontier.[21]

THE NEW YORK FRONTIER

On the New York frontier, only the ubiquitous, tireless Joseph Brant led an expedition that year. Frederick Haldimand's order for a cease-fire reached Maj. John Ross at Fort Niagara only after Brant, 460 warriors, and 43 loyalists under Capt. George Singleton stalked off from Oswego on July 5. Ross dutifully relayed the order to desist, but the raiders marched swiftly and the courier never caught up in time. On July 15, Brant and his men approached Fort Herkimer, which defended the Mohawk valley's west end. While Brant dispersed nearly his entire force in the surrounding woods, he dashed a score of warriors toward the fort to stampede the cattle herd and raise a ruckus with musket shots and war whoops. The decoy worked. Forty Americans sortied in pursuit. When they had advanced far enough, Brant sprang the trap. His men killed nine, including an Oneida. The entire force then closed on Fort Herkimer, pelting its walls with musket balls. The fort's cannon opened fire, hitting no one but deterring an assault. Brant then led his men down to Fort Dayton, whose garrison had heard the distant shots. Troops hurried out of the fort to herd back the livestock. When Brant's force arrived, the Americans were shut up tight within their palisade. Cannons fired toward the woods concealing the enemy, keeping them at bay. The raiders headed to German Flats next, where they gathered the cattle and drove the herd back to Oswego and then along Lake Ontario's shore to feed the starving refugees around Fort Niagara. So ended the war's last British raid on the New York frontier.

Sir John Johnson had set sail in autumn 1781 for London, where he lobbied for a higher rank and office. That effort paid off. On March 14, 1782, the Crown appointed him superintendent and inspector general of Indian affairs and promoted him to colonel with the rank of brigadier general in North America. In doing so, he replaced his cousin Guy Johnson. The Crown had finally tired of Guy's indolence, corruption, and mismanagement.[22]

The new superintendent assumed command on August 15, when he stepped ashore at Quebec. Controversy soon arose. Among Sir John's first acts was to affirm Guy's earlier decision to replace John Butler with their first cousin John Dease. Gov. Frederick Haldimand protested the decision. The superintendent and governor would squabble over that and other issues for another year.

THE OHIO VALLEY FRONTIER

The war in the Ohio valley burned on with all its merciless ferocity. Killers shrugged off word of the distant peace. Those least able or willing to defend themselves tended to suffer the most in America's frontier wars. For seven years, the pacifist Moravians in the Muskingum valley had somehow evaded destruction. That sanctity would end with genocide in 1782. Though they had been herded away to the Sandusky, nearly 100 were allowed to return in March to cull valuables from the homes they were forced to abandon. Tragically, their return coincided with the arrival of an American force bent on reaping as much death and destruction of Indians as possible.

In March, Col. David Williamson led 300 frontiersmen into Gnadenhutten and later Salem. Those Americans were determined to avenge with biblical fury and "justice" the recent murders of settlers. Unable to find the murderers, they vented their rage on the purely innocent. Two teenage boys who witnessed but escaped the massacre revealed to missionary David Zeisberger the horrendous details: "A mile from town they met young Schebosh in the bush, whom they at once killed and scalped, and nearby . . . two friendly Indians, not belonging to us . . . also perished. Our Indians were mostly on the plantations and saw the militia come, but no one thought of fleeing, for they suspected no ill. The militia came to them and bade them come into town, telling them no harm should befall them. They trusted and went, but were all bound, the men being put into one house, the women into another." The Moravians now understood that death was their likely fate and "they began to sing hymns and spoke words of encouragement and consolation to [one] another until they were all slain . . . Christiana, the Mohican who well understood German and English, fell upon her knees before the captain, begging for life, but got for answer that he could not help her."[23]

The American militia's murderous lust was not satiated. At Salem, "the brethern and the sisters alike were bound, led into town, and slain. They made our Indians bring all their hidden goods out of the brush, and then they took them away; they had to tell them where in the brush the bees were, help get the honey out; other things also they had to do for them before they were killed. Prisoners said that the militia themselves acknowledged . . . they had been good Indians. They prayed and sang until the tomahawks struck into the heads. The boy who was scalped and got away said the blood flowed in streams in the house. They burned the dead bodies, together with the houses."[24]

In all, those heroes ripped ninety-six scalps, of which eighty-six were Moravians and the remainder from other tribes who sought refuge from war among those peaceful Indians. Among the known victims were twenty-nine men, twenty-seven women, and thirty-four children.[25]

Had the Moravians been less trusting in their faith, they might never have been massacred. A war party of Wyandot and Delaware "came to Gnadenhutten with a prisoner whose wife and child they killed near Gnadenhutten, and had impaled. The prisoner talked with our Indians and warned them to be off, for the whites were already assembled, would follow up the warriors, and fall upon them if they did not go away." But Zeisberger blamed the tragedy not on misguided faith, but on the British Indians, who "have always labored to bring upon us the whites, and whenever they came back from murdering they came through our towns in order that, if they were pursued the white people might fall upon us."[26]

Where word of the Moravian Indian holocaust spread, vengeance followed. Zeisberger learned that "many white people from the States, who have been taken prisoners, have been tortured and burnt alive in Sandusky and among the Shawanese for killing our Indians in Gnadenhutten. As soon as it is known that any prisoner had part in that affair, he is forthwith bound, tortured, and burnt."[27]

Though the Moravians in Wyandot captivity on the Sandusky had escaped massacre, they remained imperiled. War parties passing through on the trail to the American settlements abused the Moravians: "The savages are pleased now that things go hard with us, that we suffer famine and anxiety, and our cattle all perish, and they say we have now become like them, we should be no better off than they, and so it was."[28]

Even Half King turned openly against the Moravians. He blamed Moravian informants for the recent deaths of his two sons on a raid and stirred hatred among his people toward "the believers." Zeisberger worried that "they are now our greatest foes; for they have brought us and our Indians into the greatest misery, and have us . . . in their power; they would like to extirpate us and our Indians, had they nothing to fear from other nations."[29]

Zeisberger lamented that "nowhere is a place to be found to which we can retire with our Indians and be secure. The world is already too narrow. From the white people, or so-called Christians, we can hope for no protection, and among the heathen nations also we have no friends left, such outlaws are we!" But the missionary refused to succumb to the existential despair that such a succession of mindless tragedies might provoke. His faith explained all: "But praise be to God, the Lord, our God yet lives, who will not forsake us. He will punish us if we deserve punishment, that afterwards he may be the more merciful to us."[30] "God's mercy" was never bestowed upon those people—the Moravian Indians would eventually suffer extinction. Later that year, the remnants were herded to the Chippewa and there assimilated.

While some frontiersmen were content to butcher pacifists, Gen. William Irvine planned to assault the enemy stronghold at Detroit. The plan he sent to George Washington on February 7 envisioned a 2,000-man army split evenly between regulars and militia, marching from Fort Pitt northwest along existing trails to Detroit. At least two 12-pounders, two 6-pounders, and one 3-pounder would be needed to breach Detroit's walls and break up any enemy attacks. The campaign would take at least three months and was best launched during late summer and early autumn, when the foliage thinned and grass remained thick. Supplies would be conveyed by 1,000 horses and 25 wagons. A cattle herd would provide fresh beef. Irvine estimated that the enemy at Detroit included 300 regulars and 1,000 militia, a formidable opposition to the 2,000 Americans marching through the heart of Indian country.[31]

It was a good plan, but Washington discouraged it by explaining Congress's bankruptcy, the need for economy, and the progress of peace negotiations. Irvine had little time or resources to prepare for the expedition. Nearly all his talents were challenged with overcoming supply shortages, desertion, and diplomacy, not just with the Indians, but also with fellow Americans. Although they had decided their border three years earlier, Pennsylvanians and Virginians still squabbled over who was to defend what. It took all of Irvine's diplomatic skills to knit even the most tenuous cooperation between the militias of those states in defending their mutual frontier.[32]

Unable for now to mount his own offensive, Irvine eagerly granted permission for several hundred volunteers to conduct their own. On May 21, nearly 500 men gathered with thirty days' provisions at Mingo Bottom on the Ohio River. There they elected Col. William Crawford their commander. Crawford was seemingly a good choice, having campaigned through part of the region in 1774 during Dunmore's war. He served as lieutenant colonel of the 5th Virginia in 1776 and then transferred to become colonel of the 7th Virginia in 1777. He fought at Brandywine and Germantown that year before heading to Pittsburgh to serve under General Hand. In August 1778, he took command of the region's Virginia militia. He marched with McIntosh's campaign to build Fort Laurens that November, and the next spring marched again with McIntosh to relieve that beleaguered post. Yet not everyone was impressed. While admitting Crawford's bravery, Capt. John Rose despaired that during "a council he speaks incoherent, proposes matters confusedly, and is incapable of persuading people into his opinion, or making use of their weak sides for his argument."[33] Crawford was no Clark. His weak leadership and tactics would doom not just the campaign, but his own life as well.

The little army of 480 mounted frontiersmen rode off on May 25 along trails toward the Sandusky valley 150 miles away. At first they advanced in four columns, but the underbrush was so thick that they bunched together. Along the way, they would have to bypass clusters of villages. It was inevitable that Indians would spot the expedition. It happened at the Tuscarora River. Indian scouts shadowed the expedition as it rode northwest across Ohio, while runners spread the alarm throughout the region.

Crawford and his men got within two miles of the upper Sandusky village when a mélange of about 200 Wyandot, Mingo, Delaware, and rangers led by Capt. William Caldwell attacked about two o'clock on June 4. The fighting persisted until dark. By one account, many of the Americans "were cowardly; no more than about one hundred having fought the Indians."[34] The Indian strategy was to pin down the Americans and provoke them to waste their ammunition until reinforcements arrived to administer the coup de grace. That strategy succeeded.

The Indians kept the Americans awake all night with sporadic firing, probes, and bloodcurdling war cries. The firing intensified with dawn on June 5 and continued throughout the morning. Around noon, about 150 Shawnee joined the battle. The Americans kept the enemy at bay with long-range shots, but by the day's end had spent most of their powder and spirit. In two days, the Americans lost five killed and nineteen wounded, while they killed a ranger and wounded two, including Caldwell, who was shot through the knees, and killed four and wounded eight Indians.

As the gunfire died with the dusk, Crawford gathered his officers to debate what to do. They decided to retreat under cloak of darkness. The Indian pursuers caught up the next morning. Musket balls killed three more Americans and wounded eleven. The expedition fragmented under the relentless pursuit and sniping. An "every man for himself" mentality seized the fleeing frontiersmen. Individual survival depended on getting ahead of others. Wounded compatriots, neighbors, and even friends were abandoned to distract the savages. Captain Rose explained the psychology: "Our men had conceived the most hideous notions of the enemy's multitude . . . Consternation always accompanies a flying Body, whereas the pursuer feels his own superiority and is flushed with success. His very appearance strikes terror and dejection into the pursued . . . the moment we halted we were fired on . . . the larger part was quite bewildered and by the dread that hung upon their souls, incapacitated for action . . . deserted—the smallest body fought heroically."[35]

Crawford and nine others, including his son-in-law William Harrison, disgusted at the militia's refusal to obey orders, chose to avoid the dangerous trail and instead cut through the forest. Had they remained there, they might have escaped, but inexplicably, believing that the pursuit had ended, they angled back to the trail. That was a fatal mistake. A war party was stalking the expedition's rear and soon discovered Crawford and his men behind them. The warriors surged back and surrounded the hapless Americans, who, exhausted of munitions, energy, and will, surrendered.

Frenzied to avenge the Gnadenhutten massacre, the Indians gruesomely tortured to death Crawford and six other men. They were especially eager to prolong Crawford's agony:

> They were taken out, blacked again, and their hands tied behind their backs, when Colonel Crawford was led by a long rope to a high stake, to the top of which the rope about the colonel was tied. All around the stake a great quantity of red hot coals were laid, on which the poor colonel was obliged to walk barefoot, and at the same time the Indians firing squibs of powder at him, while others poked sticks on fire into every part of his body; thus they continued torturing him for about two hours, when he begged of Simon Girty, a white renegade, who was standing by, to shoot him, when the fellow said, "Don't you see I have no gun?" Some little time after this they scalped him, and struck him on the bare skull several times with sticks, and being nearly exhausted he lay down upon the burning embers, when the squaws put shovelfuls of coals on his body, which, dying as he was, made him move and creep a little.[36]

Two men escaped. Dr. John Knight was guarded by only one Indian, who led him to another village for torture. When the Indian untied and ordered him to gather wood for a fire, Knight whacked him with a log, grabbed up the warrior's musket, pointed it, and pulled the trigger. Though the gun misfired, the Indian fled. Knight headed the opposite way and twenty-one days later emerged from the wilderness to Fort Pitt's safety. The other escapee, John Slover, had been one of the expedition's guides.

The expedition's remnants staggered back in small groups or as individuals to Mingo Bottom. In all, the Americans may have left a trail of as many as seventy dead men from the Sandusky plain back to the Ohio River. What caused the fiasco? For Captain Rose, hubris best explained the disaster: "It seems we left home to conquer ourselves by imaginary suppositions. Could we expect to frighten all the nations of Indians with 400 men into tame submission—could we expect to destroy them without any opposition, and carry off their property?"[37] With battle, that hubris turned to terror and rout.

The Indians followed up their victory with a counterattack on the frontier. In July, about 100 Indians with several British volunteers of the 8th Regiment overran and burned Hannastown, the Westmoreland County seat, killed nine and captured twelve settlers, and slaughtered or drove off the livestock. Most people escaped to the town's Fort Reed and watched in fear and fury as the enemy burned all but two houses in the town. Indians crept up and fired on the stockade, whose defenders shot back. No one was hit in the exchange except a small girl in the fort. A portion of the attackers strode to Fort Miller four miles distant and took it.[38]

To deter or, if that failed, defeat future Indian raids, Kentucky's government ordered George Rogers Clark to build forts at the mouths of the Kentucky, Limestone, and Licking Rivers, along with two row galleys with cannons to patrol the

Ohio River. That order was impossible to fulfill, given the dearth of men, equipment, provisions, and money. Although no forts were erected, workmen did construct at the Licking River mouth the *Miami*, an eighty-foot-long, twenty-foot-wide galley with twenty oars on each side and a swivel at the prow. In the summer, thirty-eight militia under Col. Robert Patterson reinforced the gun crew commanded by Capt. Robert George. The militia did not fancy rowing that huge craft up and down the Ohio River and demanded twice their promised pay. That strike ensured the already unlikely chance that the *Miami*'s crew would ever sight, let alone close with, an enemy canoe.

The enemy was coming, this time several hundred warriors led by Simon Girty, William Caldwell, and Alexander McKee. They slipped across the Ohio and crept up to the clearing around Bryan's Station on August 15, but scouts warned the settlers, and they forted up while a rider galloped off to carry the alarm to the other settlements. While the station's walls were stout enough to allow the riflemen to repel an assault, there was no well. A prolonged siege would force the defenders to yield for lack of water. Pretending they were unaware of the lurking enemy, the women ventured forth with buckets in hand to the creek 100 yards beyond the gate. Although the men lining the palisade likely would have killed a number of Indians if they rushed the women, more than enough would have survived to capture the bucket brigade. With tomahawks raised over their loved ones, the men undoubtedly would have capitulated. But the Indians refrained, and the women struggled back with water-filled buckets into the fort. Not long after, the Indians opened fire but did not dare charge. While some continued sniping at the walls, other Indians scattered out to burn the surrounding cabins and crops and slaughter livestock.

Help was on its way. On August 17, scouts reported that the militia had mustered and was hurrying toward them. The Indians gathered their loot and headed north. To the settlers' cheers, the militia arrived a little later. The combined forces numbered 182 men. The senior officers, including head colonel John Todd, subordinate colonels Daniel Boone and Stephen Trigg, and Maj. Hugh McGary, debated whether to pursue or await the arrival of Col. Benjamin Logan and his contingent. Todd and Trigg persuaded a cautious Boone and McGary to give chase before the enemy got away. By now it was evening, so they delayed their departure to daybreak the next morning. They strode hard on the enemy's tracks through the hilly forests all day on August 18 but never caught up. Though exhausted, they slept little that night, with half the men on guard half the night. They resumed their pursuit at dawn on August 19.

A few hours later, they reached the lip of Licking River valley near Blue Licks Spring and spotted the enemy splashing across the ford a half mile below. The officers heatedly debated what to do. McGary now was eager for battle and shouted down as cowardice Boone's warning that the Indians were trying to entice them into an ambush. While the others hesitated, McGary leapt on his horse and yelled, "Them that ain't cowards follow me."[39] Stung by the taunt, Todd, Trigg, and Boone joined him. By one account, Boone burst into tears from the stress, smear, and madness of the attack. As he led his company, including his son Israel, forward, he remarked bitterly, "We are all slaughtered men."[40]

Boone was right. The Kentuckians surged across the river and up the hill into a trap and were butchered. The Indian fusillade and charge killed sixty-six and wounded scores more within a few minutes; to Boone's horror, a bullet took his son's life. The survivors panicked and fled back across the river. Boone emerged unscathed along with, as irony would have it, McGary, who had urged them to their destruction. Although the battle of Blue Licks is often called the American Revolution's last battle, hundreds more would die before peace was finally restored to the frontier.[41]

The latest bloodbath spooked many settlers into another stampede east. General Clark ordered troops to block the Wilderness Road and Cumberland Gap, thus penning up scores of frightened, disheartened pioneers in Kentucky against their will. He promised the settlers that he would avenge their loss with a campaign against the Ohio villages. It would be another two months before he kept his promise.

General Irvine, meanwhile, prepared his own campaign against the Ohio tribes. Not only did he get permission to do so, but Secretary at War Benjamin Lincoln authorized an expedition of 1,200 troops, of which 350 men would be regulars and the rest militia. However, to Irvine's disgust, the mission was downgraded from destroying Detroit to attacking the hostile villages on the Scioto. At least he would have enough men. The governments of Virginia and Pennsylvania promised to send troops and supplies.[42]

Then a scare rippled across the frontier. In the two months since the destruction of Hannastown, the upper Ohio region had been fairly quiet. That calm was shattered on the evening of September 11, when an expedition of 238 Indians and 40 rangers opened fired on Fort Henry at Wheeling and kept up the fire through the next day. No one on either side was hit. As the British and Indians left, two men deserted to the Americans.[43]

While most on the frontier were eager for vengeance, Irvine's campaign fizzled out, defeated by the whiff of peace. General Irvine informed Washington: "I would have marched the 20th of September into the Indian country with about eight hundred militia and a small detachment from this post, had I not received letters on the eighteenth from the secretary at war and council of Pennsylvania." The word was that peace was pending, the British had called off the Indians, and the national and state coffers were empty. When that word spread, most of the militia stayed home with their families. Irvine's army failed to materialize.[44]

The expedition's cancellation was actually a relief to Irvine, who "never could see any great advantages gained by excursions of this kind . . . nothing short of destroying the British post at Detroit from which they receive the means to carry on the war or establishing posts in their country will effectually answer the end." He then proposed an expedition heading up the Allegheny and over the portage to Lake Erie, establishing a fort and "two stout row galleys, each for one hundred men, and to mount two twelve pounders with other smaller guns. These, from the accounts I have, would be quite equal to destroy all their fleet."

How did the news and proposal strike Washington? He thought "it best the expedition was laid aside. Your reasoning on the subject is very just—such excursions serve only to draw the resentment of the savages." As for the plan for taking Lake Erie, it "is far beyond any means we have in our power. We cannot advance a single farthing, and . . . it would be impossible for us to build vessels there without the enemy's knowledge; and then they could, and doubtless would, build vessels with heavier metal as fast as we."[45]

Irvine's strategic sense was sound. Vast sums of money, men, supplies, and energy had been squandered on campaigns into the Ohio country that petered out like McIntosh's or were bloodily repulsed like Crawford's. Alas for the American cause, the war was nearly spent before someone realized that Detroit's fate rested on who mastered Lake Erie. That scheme of asserting naval supremacy would have to await the next war with Britain. By late 1782, the Revolution had scraped the bottom of nearly all American resources.

The cancellation of Irvine's expedition was yet another obstacle to Clark as he tried to assemble his own army at the Licking River mouth. It was not until early November that he was ready to go, but this time he commanded his largest force yet. On November 4, Clark led 1,050 Kentuckians north across the Ohio River. With him were many of the Blue Licks survivors primed for vengeance, including Daniel Boone. On the march, Clark deployed his troops in a way that minimized the chance of a surprise attack and allowed them to swiftly reinforce each other. An advance guard of fifty men was followed by four companies in Indian file 100 yards apart that in turn led the main body, which was trailed by four files of twenty-five men each. After a hard six-day march, they reached the small hamlet of Willstown on November 10; skirmished with the warriors, who fled; and captured some squaws. They pushed on to Piqua that same day. Those who fought at Willstown had not spread the alarm. Clark's advance guard was moving through Piqua's cornfields before the Shawnee spotted them. The warriors snatched up their arms and fought long enough to allow their women, children, and old men to escape across the river, and then they followed. Clark's men killed ten Indians, took seven prisoners, and freed two captives, while losing only one man killed and one wounded. While the rest of Clark's men were looting and burning Piqua, Col. Benjamin Logan led his men to the nearby trading post of the Canadian Lorimier and did the same.

That evening, Clark heard the just liberated John Sovereign, who spoke Shawnee, call out to the Indians sheltering in the forest across the river. When a voice answered through the dark, Clark proposed a prisoner exchange to take place at the Ohio falls near Fort Nelson in half a moon. When the Shawnee seemed conciliatory, Clark dispatched Lt. James McCulloch into their midst. McCulloch disappeared for the next five days. Daniel Boone meanwhile led ninety men in a raid that destroyed the village of Stillwater a dozen miles away.

Warriors slipped around the American camp, sniping and trying to decoy the enemy into ambushes. They killed two men who foolishly strayed from camp. McCulloch's peace mission failed, but he remained with the Indians another three months and continued to negotiate. Clark led his army back to the Licking, and from there the troops dispersed to their homes for the winter. Clark's holy grail, the capture of Detroit, remained as illusory as ever.[46]

CHAPTER 11

"Is the Great King Conquered?": 1783 and Beyond

With our fate will be the destiny of unborn millions.
—George Washington

The Country is large enough to contain us all.
—George Washington

W ord of the preliminary treaty did not reach the United States until March 12. Whatever elation animated the American troops faded quickly. They could not disperse until the official treaty was ratified. Until then, the officers and troops would simply idle away their dreary days as they awaited news and longed for home.

Congress and the states were just as eager for a genuine peace. Expenses buried those governments deeper every day the war continued. How could they dig themselves out from that avalanche of debt? The debate over that question would rage for another decade. Meanwhile, they whittled down the army's troops and officers, sending them home with nothing more than promises of future compensation.

Those that departed and the skeleton army that stayed with George Washington were incensed at the injustice of it all. At Newburgh up the Hudson, fear spread through the army that Congress might never honor its pledges to them. Washington sympathized with the plight of his soldiers, "goaded by a thousand stings . . . soured by penury and what they call the ingratitude of the public . . . without one farthing of money to carry them home, after having spent the flowers of their days . . . in establishing the freedom and independence of their country, and suffered everything human nature is capable of enduring on this side of death . . . I cannot avoid apprehending that a train of evils will follow."[1] On March 15, Washington was able to quell an eruption of those "evils" among his officers, who threatened not to disband until Congress paid them in full for their services. With that crisis defused, he could only wonder when the next would explode.

The British troops too had to bide their time until the official peace treaty was ratified. Their only remaining ground after eight years of war was the stronghold of New York City, which they would evacuate by the summer's end. For the troops, it was a relatively easy matter to pack their loot and stomp aboard the transports, but that could happen any time or never. At least the killing had stopped on the seaboard. The records reveal no casualties from the numbing boredom and senselessness of it all.

The Americans would not be gracious winners. Conciliation with their former loyalist neighbors was unthinkable for most after years of vicious warfare, especially on the frontier. An editorial in the *New Jersey Journal,* reprinted in other newspapers, condemned the "return of those abominable Wretches, those Robbers, Murderers, and Incendiaries even to come near us, no method is left us to prevent this great Calamity but by a general Association to render their Situation by every means in our power so unhappy that they will prefer a voluntary Banishment to the proposed return, let it be a Crime abhorred by Nature to have any communication with them—Like Cain of old they will carry the mark on their foreheads, let them be avoided like persons contaminated by the most deadly contagion and remain as their just demerits as Vagabonds on the face of the Earth."[2]

And that is exactly what most Americans did. Perhaps 80,000 loyalists fled the United States during the war. Most were long gone to other colonies or England itself before the peace treaty; Nova Scotia was the most popular refuge, with nearly 25,000 loyalists settling there. But many loyalists clung to the Crown's handful of toeholds in the United States, hoping that Britain would win the war and they could return to their homes. That, of course, failed to happen. Nearly 8,000 loyalists would depart with the British fleet from New York, including the Queen's Rangers, De Lancey's Volunteers, the Loyal Americans, the King's American Regiment, Tarleton's British Legion, and the New York Volunteers. Almost as many sailed with fleets from Charles Town and Savannah. The largest exodus originated in St. Augustine, where refugees swelled East Florida's population to 17,375, including 6,090 whites and 11,285 blacks. Britain's treaty with Spain allowed those people eighteen months to emigrate or become Spanish subjects. Nearly all chose a life elsewhere, with about 4,000 stoically returning to the United States while 10,000 dispersed themselves among various British possessions.[3]

THE FRONTIER WAR

For the frontier, there was no peace, only a tense bitter truce. Upon receiving word of the preliminary treaty, Britain's frontier commanders sent runners to distant villages to recall or cancel raiding parties. They reached nearly every council in time. Only a scattering of small raids shattered the frontier war's lull that winter and spring. Yet as long as peace hovered uncertain beyond the horizon, the temptation lingered for warriors to seek glory and vengeance.

The Americans actually launched that year's first raid. All too typically the rebel effort mingled farce with tragedy. After months of lobbying, Col. Marinius Willet got George Washington's approval for his proposed winter raid on Oswego. On February 8, Willet and 600 troops set forth from Fort Herkimer. They trudged by sleigh to Fort Brewerton's ruins and then donned snowshoes and pushed on. With their Oneida guide John Otaawighton at their head, they made swift progress; by February 13, they were only a few miles from Oswego. Willet had hoped for a dawn attack, but they plowed through the drifts with no sight of Oswego as the sky lightened and the sun rose ever higher to glisten off the snowbound wilderness. The guide had gotten lost. Unlike George Rogers Clark in a similar fix, Willet did not threaten to execute him if he could not find the way.

A Seneca patrol spotted them, fired, and dashed back to sound the alarm. With the chance of a surprise attack lost, Willet ordered his men to head back to Fort Herkimer. Around the same time, another scouting party arrived at Oswego with word that the expedition's sleighs were lightly guarded. Capt. John Ross hurried thirty men out to catch up and slip around the enemy and then burn those sleighs. Though the pursuit never caught up to Willet's swift withdrawal, it did capture two stragglers, receive two deserters, and find a man dead from exertion on the trail. Ross was quite scathing in his assessment of the enemy's operation: "Nothing but a frantic zeal or a misinformation of our situation could have induced them to have undertaken so ridiculous an enterprise . . . particularly in the fullness of the moon, when every object was as discernable as at noonday."[4]

Though his effort failed, Willet at least could console himself with having tried. Commanders elsewhere on the 1,500-mile frontier were impotent to do even that. The squalor and despair permeating Fort Pitt's garrison would have deadened most commanders to few thoughts other than securing a transfer back east as soon as possible. In his two and a half years commanding the Western Department, Gen. William Irvine had experienced all the frustrations, ignominy, and powerlessness of his predecessors. Unlike McIntosh and Brodhead, but like Hand, Irvine himself had not taken the field. Instead, he had organized and dispatched expeditions commanded by others who met disaster in the Ohio wilderness. Perhaps because peace was so near, Irvine was eager to inflict a last strike on the enemy and score an elusive victory. In March, he shared with Washington a scheme for an expedition against Fort Schlosser, which guarded Lake Erie's discharge into the Niagara River. As he had with Irvine's previous schemes, Washington disillusioned him.[5]

In between reveries, Irvine worried not about the enemy, but about his soldiers' reaction to peace. Having gone without pay for months, the regulars might well loot Fort Pitt of anything they could carry off and burn the rest. Irvine toyed with the idea of subduing the regulars with militia but concluded it might worsen an already foul situation.[6]

George Rogers Clark also called for a last campaign. With the war won, his rationale for more fighting was to follow up the diplomatic victory with a show of strength to intimidate the tribes: "We shall be Eternally Involved in a war with some nation or other of them until we shall at last in order to save blood and treasure be Reduced to the necessity of convincing them that we are always able to crush them at pleasure, and determined to do it when Ever they misbehave . . . A greater opportunity can never offer to Reduce them to Obedience than the present moment."[7] But Congress and the states had scraped the barrel of money, recruits, and enthusiasm for fighting Indians—at least for now.

The tribal elders were just as eager for peace and determined to hold back those warriors who still lusted for vengeance. Only one major Indian raid bloodied the northern frontier that year. Seventeen settlers were slaughtered at Wheeling Creek, a "stroke . . . very unexpected; numbers of people were returning to their places in confidence that these wretches would not dare to continue the war unsupported."[8]

Violence still festered in the lower Mississippi valley. Word that Gov. Esteban Miro would not free the Natchez rebels enraged James Colbert. To bolster his bargaining power, he led 100 whites and 40 Indians against Fort Carlos III on the Arkansas River and captured Lt. Luis Villars, ten soldiers, and four civilians outside the fort on April 17. Capt. Jacobo Dubreuil held the fort with forty troops and four Indians. Colbert's men ambushed a Spanish sally and killed two soldiers, wounded one, and took six more prisoners. Colbert then sent Villars's wife, Maria Luisa Valle de Villars, with one of his officers under a flag of truce to demand that Dubreuil surrender. Once the two stepped beyond gunshot of Colbert's men, Dubreuil sent eleven soldiers and four Quapaws charging from the fort. Colbert's officer fled, Mrs. Villars was rescued, and Quapaw war cries spooked the British. Realizing it would be impossible to capture the fort and fearing the 120 Quapaw warriors in the nearby village could wipe him out, Colbert gave up the siege on April 24. Releasing all but Villars, three soldiers, three slaves, and a civilian among the hostages, he retreated to his lair across the Mississippi. There he freed Villars with his promise to return with 2,000 piastres ransom for himself and the others if he did not gain the release of the five Natchez rebels awaiting sentence in New Orleans.[9]

Shortly thereafter, Capt. Joseph Valliere arrived at Fort Carlos III with an escort for a supply convoy heading upriver. Dubreuil asked him to organize a pursuit of Colbert. On May 10, Valliere led 100 whites and 24 Quapaw across the Mississippi and up the Chickasaw River. Three miles upstream, the Spanish caught up to the British, killed Colbert's lieutenant, William McGillivray, scattered the rest, and captured the enemy's supplies. Colbert's resistance on the Mississippi effectively ended on that day.

The trial of John Blommart and the four other Natchez rebel leaders ended at New Orleans in July with judgments of guilty as charged. The rebels sailed rather than swung for their crimes; with Miro's pardons, they were exiled to Jamaica. When Colbert learned that the rebels were freed, he decided to head to St. Augustine to receive official instructions on whether to continue his struggle. Upon his arrival on October 5, the governor informed him that the war was over. Though disappointed, Colbert retained his captured slaves and other loot. Sometime in December en route home, Colbert broke his neck when his horse threw him. His followers buried him in an unmarked wilderness grave. So ended the last British resistance on the southern frontier.

British diplomats to the Indians would have a lot of explaining to do as the news spread of American independence and the king's defeat. Those agents were as much worried about the native reaction to peace as they were about not reaching the warriors before they strode off to the frontier. The tribes had sacrificed enormously in a war they ultimately lost. Would the savages turn their rage on their British allies? Canadian governor Frederick Haldimand warned that the Indians "will soon . . . become acquainted with this unpleasant information and the Effect it will have upon them may be easily conceived. It will therefore be highly necessary that you narrowly watch the Conduct of the Indians and without seeming to suspect them taking every Precaution against their surprising any small Posts or Detachments you may have abroad for there is no saying what their Resentment may tempt them to do."[10]

Sir John Johnson had the disagreeable task of journeying to Niagara and informing the Indians that not only had King George III admitted defeated, but he also had surrendered the Indian lands south of the Great Lakes to the Americans. When the Niagara council opened on July 23, 1,685 Indians had gathered. During the fifteen-day talks, Johnson tried to assuage their rage by permitting the several thousand displaced Iroquois refugees to stay in Canada. But on whose land? Eventually those tribes claiming the north shores of the St. Lawrence River and Lake Ontario were bribed to allow the Iroquois along with thousands of loyalists to resettle there.

St. Augustine was for the southern frontier what Niagara was for the northern—a magnet for refugees and councils. In the spring, over 600 Chickasaw, Choctaw, and Creek gathered there to meet with Gov. Patrick Tonyn, Superintendent Thomas Brown, and General McArthur. Rumors circulated that the British were going to abandon the Indians to the Americans and Spanish. Lower Creek chief Okaiegige angrily retorted: "We have heard that the Great King intends to throw away this land. We . . . took up the Hatchet for the English at a time we cou'd scarce distinguish our friends from our foes. We joined the Kings warriors and have lossed in the Service a number of our people. The King and his Warriors have told us they never wou'd forsake us. Is the Great King conquered? Or does he mean to abandon us? Or does he intend to treat his Friends as slaves, or only give our lands to his and our Enemies. Do you think we can turn our faces to our Enemies, and ask a favor from them."[11] At a council later that year, Cherokee chief Raven bitterly reminded his hosts: "We never turned our backs on the Enemy but remembered your talks. We subsisted our Women and Children on acorns . . . and were determined to hold the English fast by the arm and like Men stand or fall with our friends . . . we have heard . . . that the English have given up

our lands . . . to be divided amongst our Enemies. The Peacemakers and our Enemies have talked away our land at a Rum drinking."[12] To such accusations, the
British could make no satisfying reply. All they could do was commiserate and try
to bury Indian sorrows under piles of presents.

THE TREATY OF PARIS

So what had become of the final peace treaty that most people so eagerly awaited?
When the year opened, the peace process seemed to be progressing steadily. On
January 20, Britain concluded preliminary treaties with France and Spain. Shelburne was as generous with those countries as he had been with the United States.
He agreed that Spain could have West and East Florida along with Minorca in
return for the Bahamas and acceptance of British Gibraltar, while France could
enjoy the rights to fish off Newfoundland, fortify Dunkirk, and get back Senegal,
St. Lucia, and its former colonies in India. All that remained was to convert the
three preliminary treaties into final agreements, but then the unexpected happened.

A last-minute protest arose within Parliament against the preliminary treaties
with the United States, France, and Spain. On February 21, the opposition introduced a contradictory motion accepting peace and American independence but
denouncing the concessions. Chief Minister William Petty Shelburne resigned in
disgust. It took seven weeks before the factions could trade enough political
horses to agree on a new government, this one a coalition with William Henry
Cavendish Bentinck Portland as chief minister and Charles James Fox and Frederick North as northern and southern secretaries, respectively. After years of
championing American independence, Fox abruptly took a hard line. Britain
would exclude American goods from its home market and overseas colonies.

To the frustration of nearly all concerned, the war's official end would be
delayed another half year. On September 3, the United States and Britain signed
a peace treaty that differed little from the preliminary agreement. That same day,
Britain signed treaties with France and Spain. Congress received the treaty on
October 10, but it took until January 15, 1784, before enough delegates could
gather at Annapolis, then the capital for America's peripatetic government, to ratify the peace. Ratifications were finally exchanged between the United States and
Britain on May 12, 1784. News of that final gesture was anticlimactic after years
of destruction, death, and deprivation, followed by months of inaction waiting for
it all to end.

On the heels of the departing redcoats, Washington marched his ghost of an
army into New York City on November 25, 1783. He had finally liberated the
scenes of his most humiliating defeats seven years earlier. After an emotional
farewell to his officers during a banquet at Faunces Tavern, he left New York on
December 4 for Annapolis. There on December 23, Washington appeared before
Congress and received the ecstatic appreciation of the delegates. And then,
exhausted from eight years of war, he retired to his Mount Vernon plantation. His
retirement would be short-lived.

WINNING THE PEACE

The Americans had won their war for independence, but the consequences of that peace for the United States were vague politically, economically, and geographically. That was especially true for the frontier. Sovereignty over that land may have changed, but territorial disputes were as contentious as ever. Americans had to win clear title from the tribes, the British and Spanish empires, and each other. That Herculean task would dominate much of the new republic's policies for the next sixty years.

Peace allowed American diplomacy with the Indians to begin in earnest. The war had shattered most relations with the tribes. The new Great Father would inherit Britain's frontier problems and role of negotiating, protecting, and nurturing the Indians while regulating trade, land sales, and migration. Like the British overlords, the Americans wanted to avoid expensive wars with the tribes. But while the crown tried to protect the Indians from the ravages of the whites, the United States government ultimately sided with the settlers, merchants, and speculators.

The rationale behind these policies was simple. The Americans considered themselves the war's winners and expected the Indians to pay with land for all the murderous destruction they had committed on the frontier. That attitude became official policy in October 1783 when Congress concluded that the tribes were the war's aggressors, had rejected repeated entreaties by the Americans to remain neutral, and "had wantonly destroyed our villages and destroyed our citizens."[13] Yet the delegates were not naive. They understood that just because those tribes were on the losing side, this did not make them vanquished. The committee admitted that the Indians were "not in a temper to relinquish their territorial claims without further struggles." What should be the government's policy toward the tribes?

Wisely the congressmen realized that the United States was then too weak militarily and financially to impose its rule by force. Time favored the Americans against the Indians along with the neighboring British and Spanish empires. America's population would steadily expand indefinitely, with the excess spilling over the Appalachians and spreading across the wilderness beyond. Diplomacy and, if necessary, war could expel the tribes from those lands as settlers inevitably pushed the remnants farther west.

Not everyone was willing for time and settlements to crowd away those tribes from their lands. Gen. William Irvine at Fort Pitt expressed the general belief on the frontier that "nothing short of a total extirpation of all the western tribes of Indians, or at least driving them over the Mississippi and the lakes, will insure peace."[14] That almost happened.

How could westward expansion be reconciled with keeping peace with the Indians? How could rival claims be reconciled? How could the Indians be mollified? The United States government failed to resolve these related conundrums. The result was unremitting landgrabs and violence punctuated sporadically by devastating wars, which included the chronic raids and deaths of 1,500 settlers in the Ohio valley from 1783 to 1790, which bled into the war against Little Turtle's alliance from 1790 to 1795; skirmishes with the Sauk and Fox in 1804; Black Hawk's resistance of 1808, 1811, 1815, 1830, and 1832; the wars against Tecumseh's alliance of 1811 and 1812 to 1814, and the Creek from 1813 to 1814; skirmishes with Kickapoo in 1819, and Winnebago in 1826 to 1827; and fighting with the Seminole in 1816, 1817, 1818, 1835 to 1842, 1855, and 1858.[15]

Treaties bracketed the wars, each one trimming or hacking away more Indian lands. The tribes diminished and broke up; the fragments fled farther west until they crossed the Mississippi River, but that barrier only fleetingly stemmed America's frontier advance. The 1830 Indian Removal Act provoked the largest exodus, with nearly all the southeast tribes except pockets of Cherokee in the Smoky Mountains and Seminole in the Everglades forced at bayonet point to migrate to the Indian territory on the Oklahoma prairies. During a decade, thousands died of disease, starvation, exhaustion, and brutality on the "trail of tears."

These struggles with the Indians paralleled and overlapped with conflicts, negotiations, and violence between the United States and Britain and Spain. The 1783 Treaty of Paris did not resolve all of the war's frontier disputes with those great powers. Some conflicts would take years to settle, while others festered for decades. The British refused to evacuate the northwest forts and deadlocked over just where Maine's boundary should be drawn. The Spanish denied the Americans navigation on the Mississippi River and deposit of goods at New Orleans. Some tribes used the territory and trade of both great powers to war against the Americans.

It took the United States a dozen years before it resolved a portion of these disputes. On November 19, 1794, John Jay signed the Treaty of Amity, Commerce, and Navigation, by which Britain agreed to surrender the forts it occupied in American territory. That, combined with Gen. Anthony Wayne's decisive victory over Little Turtle's alliance at the battle of Fallen Timbers on August 20, 1794, and the subsequent Treaty of Greenville on August 3, 1795, helped maintain a troubled peace in the Old Northwest until 1811.

Thomas Pinckney signed the Treaty of San Lorenzo on October 27, 1795, by which Spain allowed Americans free navigation on the Mississippi River and the right to deposit goods at New Orleans for the next three years while reaffirming the border at the thirty-first parallel. That only briefly alleviated the conflict. In 1800, Spain secretly traded New Orleans, the Louisiana Territory, and its half of Hispaniola to France for the Duchy of Tuscany. Spain would hold those lands in trust until the French could militarily assert ownership. In 1802, Spain revoked the American right of navigation and deposit at New Orleans.

In response, President Thomas Jefferson sent James Monroe to Paris to probe Napoleon for the truth of that rumored transfer and offer him as much as $10 million for New Orleans. With his dream of a New World empire stymied by the British fleet and tropical diseases, Napoleon offered the entire Louisiana Territory for $15 million. Monroe snatched the deal, signing a treaty on April 30, 1803, that doubled the nation's territory by expanding over the entire western Mississippi River watershed all the way to the crest of the central and northern Rocky Mountains, for three pennies an acre. In doing so, the United States at once resolved one festering diplomatic problem with Spain and inherited countless others with hundreds of tribes, Britain, Spain, Mexico, and Russia across those new lands over the next nine decades.

The new diplomatic challenges piled atop those lingering from the American Revolution. While the British may have finally withdrawn from the Old Northwest, the Americans believed that they poached trade from that territory while arming and instigating Indian attacks on the frontier. Those accusations combined with British depredations of American shipping and impressment of sailors provoked President James Madison to ask Congress for a war declaration on June 14, 1812. The fighting, which lasted until Gen. Andrew Jackson's defeat of a British attack on New Orleans on January 8, 1815, raged almost entirely on the frontiers. Though no territory changed hands with the Treaty of Ghent, signed on December 24, 1814, the war did spur American nationalism and assertiveness.

Four years later, the United States won East and West Florida after an effort that mingled violence and diplomacy. Tensions along the border worsened as slaves escaped to the Seminole and Creek living in the Floridas. After inconclusive fighting between the Americans and those tribes in 1816 and 1817, Gen. Andrew Jackson launched an invasion in March 1818 that seized and hanged British agents to the Indians and captured Pensacola from the Spanish. Though Jackson's invasion was a clear cause for war, the Spanish were outgunned by the Americans, so they swallowed their pride and negotiated. On February 22, 1819, John Quincy Adams signed the Transcontinental Treaty, by which Spain granted the Floridas and recognized the 1803 acquisition of the Louisiana Territory with boundaries from the Sabine River to the forty-second parallel and then west to the Pacific Ocean, in return for the United States assuming responsibility for $5 million in claims against Spain by American merchants.

While America's southern and western borders were now clearly delimited, the northern frontier with Canada remained disputed. Negotiations unshadowed by the threat of war managed those disputes for two decades. The 1817 Rush-Bagot Treaty resulted in an unguarded frontier between the United States and Canada, while the 1818 convention allowed for the joint exploitation and ownership of the Oregon Territory. But then violence flared, first in 1837 when sympathetic Americans aided and aborted the Canadian independence struggle, and more seriously from 1839 to 1842 as Americans and British struggled over the rich timberlands of the still undelineated frontier between Maine and New Brunswick in the Aroostock River valley and elsewhere. The frontier between the United States and Canada finally received its current border from the Atlantic Ocean to the Rocky Mountain watershed by the Webster-Ashburton Treaty of 1842. That concluded the last international territorial dispute of the American Revolution's frontier war.

One other great challenge accompanied American efforts to assert clear title to the Revolution's frontiers from the tribes, Britain, and Spain. How would the Americans divvy up and govern those frontiers? Though the states had granted much of that land to the United States government when they ratified the Articles of Confederation, the process by which that territory would be split into states remained unclear in 1783.

The new republic's legitimacy and solvency depended on frontier lands. With a worthless currency, frontier land was the only valuable resource available to Congress. The government would try to pay off its debts by selling off land to demanding soldiers and speculators alike. Deciding that policy was easy; implementing it would be much more difficult. The promised land that enticed countless soldiers to war was awarded by the government to very few in peace. Speculators gobbled up vast tracts and sold them to veterans and nonveterans alike.

Congress took the first step with the 1785 Land Act. The government would survey the territory into townships of thirty-six square miles, subdivided into thirty-six sections of one square mile each. The sixteenth section of each township would be allocated for public education. Anyone could buy that land for a minimal 640 acres at one dollar an acre. Of course, only rich speculators could afford that much land, but that was the point. Congress at once rewarded those influential and generous lobbyists while avoiding the tedium of selling off smaller portions to poor, needy settlers.

What seemed like a viable policy actually exacerbated long-standing frontier tensions, especially the tug-of-war between creditors and debtors. The poor could acquire land only by borrowing money from speculators. Though inflation eroded some of that burden, hard currency became ever more elusive. Thousands could not maintain payments and lost their land. A stream of petitions requesting debt relief and outright forgiveness issued from the frontier and lodged in the distant tidewater state capitals. But debt relief reflected the larger issue of imbalanced political power. To varying degrees among the states during the Revolution, they had alleviated a portion of the gross malapportionment of representatives among the seaboard, piedmont, and frontier. However, that was not enough to satisfy the frontiersmen, who demanded either more representation or their own government.

These grievances exploded into violence in August 1786 across most of central and western Massachusetts when thousands of "regulators" rose to shut down the courts and issue decrees canceling debts. The Massachusetts assembly appointed Gen. Benjamin Lincoln to gather an army of volunteers to disperse what became known as Shay's Rebellion after its most prominent leader, Capt. Daniel Shays, a Revolutionary War veteran. By January 1787, Lincoln had succeeded in dispersing the rebels through several skirmishes and promises of pardon. Shay's Rebellion shook not just Massachusetts, but also Congress and nearly all the states, where similar regulator revolts might well erupt against soaring debts, land speculators, taxes, and lack of representation. Congress responded decisively in two ways, one with a model for disposing of western lands and the other with a new constitution, which strengthened the national government.

The 1787 Northwest Ordinance established guidelines for settling and governing that vast wilderness embraced by the Ohio River, Great Lakes, and Mississippi River. That territory would eventually be broken up into not less than three or more than five states. Before then, Congress would appoint the governor and three judges to administer the territory until 5,000 free male settlers spread over that land. Then an elected legislature and an appointed council of five would join the governor and judges in administration. Residents had to own 50 acres to vote and 200 to serve in the legislature. That territory could also send a nonvoting representative to Congress. When the territory's voting population reached 60,000, the people could write a constitution and apply for statehood. The ordinance also outlawed slavery and promoted public education. One clause of the ordinance stated that "the utmost good faith shall always be observed towards the Indians; their land and property shall never be taken without their consent; and in their property, rights and liberty, they shall never be invaded or disturbed, unless in just and lawful wars authorized by Congress." Somehow that principle got obscured in the dust churned by the land rush. As for land prices, those of the 1785 Land Act prevailed. Thus did the fate of subsistence farmers remain in the hard hands of speculators and creditors. But tens of thousands of hopeful pioneers flooded into the territory anyway over the next few years alone.

The 1787 Constitution significantly boosted the new republic's powers, including those for the president to wage war and negotiate treaties, and for Congress to ratify treaties, regulate trade, raise and appropriate money, and declare war. To varying degrees, all those duties affected America's frontier policies. The tug-of-war between the national and state governments over frontier policy was decisively shifted to the former with Article IV, Section 3, which granted "Congress . . . Power to dispose of and make all needful Rules and Regulations respecting the territory or other property belonging to the United States."

Wielding those powers, the United States asserted an administration over the territories won by the Treaty of Paris and subsequent treaties from the Appalachians to the Mississippi River, and Great Lakes to Gulf of Mexico until those lands reached the 60,000-settler threshold, whereupon statehoods were granted. That process in the revolutionary frontier led to statehood for Vermont (1791), Kentucky (1792), Tennessee (1796), Ohio (1803), Indiana (1816), Mississippi (1817), Illinois (1818), Alabama (1819), Maine (1820), Michigan (1837), Florida (1845), and Wisconsin (1845).

The frontier war for American independence settled or exacerbated many conflicts. Perhaps the most crucial question of all was rhetorically asked by colonial immigrant J. Hector St. John de Crevecoeur in his classic book *Letters from an American Farmer,* published in 1782: "What then, is the American, this new man?" Crevecoeur answered by defining an American as someone "who, leaving behind him all his ancient prejudices and manners, receives new ones from the new mode of life he has embraced, the new government he obeys, and the new rank he holds. He becomes an American by being received in the broad lap of our great Alma Mater. Here individuals of all nations are melted into a new race of men, whose labours and posterity will one day cause great changes in the world . . . Here the rewards of his industry follow with equal steps the progress of his labour . . . Here religion demands but little of him . . . The American is a new man who acts upon new principles."[16] Crevecoeur was unerringly accurate in his observations and prescient in his predictions.

The American nation emerged and developed soon after the first English colonies took root in the New World. The ocean dividing the British Isles and other European countries from the Americans was vast. The colonies and especially the frontier offered challenges and chances for wealth and freedom unparalleled in the Old World. Those who peopled the colonies came from diverse origins, but mostly shared a spirit of enterprise, independence, and curiosity unprecedented in the lands they left behind. The emotional ties to their ancestral countries weakened with each generation, consumed by the love for the new land and assimilation within American culture.

American culture was distinct not just in political philosophy, but also in literature, architecture, painting, music, furniture, and all other measures of artistic and material culture. That ever more vigorous and prolific high culture at once reflected and reinforced the American mindset. But American political philosophy was and remains the most powerful expression of the nation's culture. The American mind was forged from a century and a half of political development that both mirrored and shaped abstract republican principles.

The frontier war for independence bolstered that nationalism. Frederick Jackson Turner was right—American culture and democracy were partially forged on the anvil of frontier hardships, opportunities, excesses, freedoms, and exploitations, all fired by war and a common enemy.[17] The great irony, of course, was that American ideals and ambitions were attained by extirpating the freedoms, lands, and very existence of the native peoples in their path.

George Washington anticipated and rued that bleak future for the Indians and frontier Americans alike. He knew the frontier well, having endured countless hardships and horrors during his younger years in the wilderness as a surveyor, diplomat, soldier, and speculator. All too many who fought for or profited from the frontier harbored nothing but loathing or outright hatred for the Indians. Washington was among the few whose experiences aroused sympathy rather than bitterness toward both frontier natives and newcomers. With the war finally ended in 1783, he could shift his efforts from ensuring his army's survival to building his nation, for which settling the frontier was an essential element. He penned his thoughts on that great enterprise in many a letter that year and thereafter to Congress and influential Americans. In one such letter, after detailing all the wise steps for nurturing mutually just and prosperous relations between Americans and Indians, he concluded: "The Country is large enough to contain us all."[18]

NOTES

CHAPTER 1

1. George Rogers Clark to Patrick Henry, February 1, 1779, in Kathrine Wagner Seineke, ed., *The George Rogers Clark Adventure in the Illinois, and Selected Documents of the American Revolution at the Frontier Posts* (New Orleans: Polyanthos, 1981), 348–49 (hereafter cited as *Clark Adventure*).
2. Milton W. Hamilton, ed., "Guy Johnson's Opinions on the American Indian," *Pennsylvania Magazine of History and Biography* 77 (July 1952): 321.
3. Quoted in John D. Barnhart, ed., *Henry Hamilton and George Rogers Clark in the American Revolution, with the Unpublished Letters of Lieutenant Governor Henry Hamilton* (Clarkfordsville, Ind.: R. E. Banta, 1951), 137 (hereafter cited as Hamilton journal).
4. See the outstanding analysis of Paul Lawrence Stevens, *"His Majesty's 'Savage' Allies": British Policy and the Northern Indians during the Revolutionary War* (Buffalo: State University of New York at Buffalo, 1984), 1:72–151. Stevens bases his analysis on numerous primary and secondary sources, some of the more important of which include Sir William Johnson's memorandum on Six Nations and other confederacies, in James Sullivan and A. C. Flick, eds., *The Papers of William Johnson,* 14 vols. (Albany, N.Y.: State University of New York, 1921–65), 4:240–46 (hereafter cited as Johnson papers); a list of different nations in the northern district and their fighting strength in George Croghan, "A Selection of Letters and Journals Relating to Tour into the Western Country," in *Early Western Travels,* ed. Reuben Gold Thwaites, 32 vols. (Cleveland: The Arthur H. Clark Company, 1904–7), 1:167–69; William Johnson to Charles Inglis, November 1770, in E. B. O'Callaghan, ed., *The Documentary History of the State of New York,* 4 vols. (Albany, N.Y.: Weed, Parsons, and Company, 1850–1), 4: 267–69 (cited hereafter as DHSNY); William Johnson to William Tryon, October 22, 1773, in E. B. O'Callaghan and Berthold Fernow, eds., *Documents Relative to the Colonial History of the State of New York,* 15 vols. (Albany, N.Y.: Weed, Parsons, and Company, 1853–87), 8: 458–59 (hereafter cited as NYCD); Guy Johnson to Thomas Gage, November 24, 1774, Johnson papers, 8:694–97; estimate of Indian warriors made by George Morgan, March 27, 1778, in Evarts B. Greene and Virginia D. Harrington, *American Population before the Federal Census of 1790* (New York: Columbia University Press, 1932), 199.
5. Robert M. Calhoon, "Loyalism and Neutrality," in *The Blackwell Encyclopedia of the American Revolution,* ed. Jack P. Greene and J. R. Pole (Cambridge, Mass.: Basil Blackwell, 1994), 247–59.
6. Dunmore to Dartmouth, December 24, 1774, in Reuben Gold Thwaites and Louise Phelps Kellogg, eds., *Documentary History of Dunmore's War* (Madison: Wisconsin Historical Society, 1905), 371 (hereafter cited as *Dunmore's War*); Seneca chief Sayengeraghta, Haldimand papers, 21779:21, Public Archives of Canada (hereafter cited as PAC).

7. Haldimand to Clinton, September 29, 1781, Clinton papers, 5:176, Clement Library, University of Michigan.
8. White Mingo, October 18, 1776, Morgan letter book, book 2, Clement Library, University of Michigan.
9. William Knox to Grey Cooper, April 27, 1779, in K. G. Davies, ed., *Documents of the American Revolution, 1770–1783,* 21 vols., Colonial Office Series (Shannon, Ireland: Irish University Press, 1972–82), 17:112–13 (hereafter cited as DAR).
10. For a good overview, see Patrick M. Malone, *The Skulking Way of War: Technology and Tactics among the Indians of New England* (Lanham, Md.: Madison, 1991).
11. James Smith, *An Account of the Remarkable Occurrences of Col. James Smith during His Captivity with the Indians, in the Years 1755, '56, '57, '58, & '59* (Cincinnati: Robert Clark & Company, 1870), 140.
12. Barnhart, Hamilton journal, 127.
13. Ibid., 122.
14. Ewel Jeffries, *A Short Biography of John Leeth* (Cleveland: The Burrows Brothers Company, 1904), 38–39.

CHAPTER 2

1. See William Nester, *The Great Frontier War: Britain, France, and the Struggle for North America, 1607 to 1755* (Westport, Conn.: Praeger Publishers, 2000); *The First Global War: Britain, France, and the Conquest of North America, 1756–1775* (Westport, Conn.: Praeger, 2000); *"Haughty Conquerors": Amherst and the Great Indian Uprising of 1763 and 1764* (Westport, Conn.: Praeger Publishers, 2000).
2. Order in Council, May 15, 1761, Colonial Office Records (hereafter cited as C.O.) 5.23:26, British Public Record Office.
3. Board of Trade report, November 11, 1761, Aspinwall papers, Massachusetts Historical Society Collections, 4th series, 9:441–47.
4. Verner W. Crane, ed., "Hints Relative to the Division and Government of the Newly Acquired Countries in America," *Mississippi Valley Historical Review* 8 (1922): 10–12; Egremont to Board of Trade, May 5, 1763, Shelburne papers, 49:283–90, William Clements Library, University of Michigan (hereafter cited as WCL); NYCD 7:519–20.
5. R. A. Humphreys, "Lord Shelburne and the Proclamation of 1763," *English Historical Review* 49 (1934): 241–64.
6. Board of Trade to Stuart, July 10, 1764, C.O. 324/17:417–19; Plan of 1764, NYCD, 7:637–41.
7. Peter D. G. Thomas, "The Greenville Program, 1763–1765," Greene and Pole, *Encyclopedia of the American Revolution,* 107; Jack Sosin, *Whitehall and the Wilderness: The Middle West in British Colonial Policy, 1760–1774* (Lincoln: University of Nebraska Press, 1961), 81–83.
8. Peter D. G. Thomas, "Stamp Act," in Greene and Pole, *Encyclopedia of the American Revolution,* 122; Thomas, "The Stamp Act Crisis and Its Repercussions Including the Quartering Act Controversy," Ibid., 113.
9. Quoted in Carl Van Doren, ed., *Benjamin Franklin's Autobiographical Writings* (New York: The Viking Press, 1945), 153.
10. Statistics and quote from Sosin, *Whitehall and Wilderness,* 130–32.

11. David L. Jacobson, *John Dickinson and the Revolution in Pennsylvania, 1764–1776* (Berkeley: University of California Press, 1965).
12. Page Smith, *A New Age Begins: A People's History of the American Revolution* (New York: Penguin Books, 1976), 1:293–96.
13. James Munro, ed., *Acts of the Privy Council of England,* Colonial Series, 6 vols. (London: Anthony Brotheus, 1908–12), 4:729–30 (hereafter cited as *Acts of the Privy Council*).
14. Francis Fauquier to Board of Trade, July 26, 1766, C.O. 5.133:306.
15. Shelburne to Johnson, September 13, 1766, Johnson papers, 5:374–75; Shelburne to Gage, September 13, 1766, in Clarence Edwin Carter, ed., *The Correspondence of General Thomas Gage with the Secretaries of State, 1763–1775,* 2 vols. (Hamden, Conn.: Archon Books, 1969), 2:45 (hereafter cited as Gage correspondence); Gage to Shelburne, November 11, 1766, Gage correspondence, 1:112; Johnson to Shelburne, December 16, 1766, NYCD, 7:880–83.
16. Johnson to Banyar, March 10, 17, 1770, Johnson papers, 12:787–88, 794; Albert T. Volwiler, *George Croghan and the Westward Movement, 1741–1782* (Cleveland: Arthur Clark, 1926), 249, 251; Peter C. Mancall, *Valley of Opportunity: Economic Culture along the Upper Susquehanna, 1700–1800* (Ithaca, N.Y.: Cornell University Press, 1991), 97–105.
17. Volwiler, *Croghan,* 271, 279–87.
18. Croghan to Trade Board, June 8, 1764, NYCD 7:602; Croghan to Benjamin Franklin, February 25, 1766, Johnson papers, 5:37; Johnson to Croghan, March 28, 1766, Johnson papers, 5:119; Croghan to Johnson, December 12, 1766, Johnson papers, 4:886–89; Croghan to Johnson, March 30, 1766, in Clarence W. Alvord and Clarence E. Carter, eds., *The New Regime, 1765–1767* (Springfield: Illinois State Historical Library, 1916), 205; Articles of Agreement, March 29, 1766, *New Regime,* 203–4; Croghan to Johnson, March 20, 1766, *New Regime,* 205–6; Benjamin Franklin to William Franklin, May 3, 1766, *New Regime,* 224–25; Benjamin Franklin to William Franklin, May 10, September 12, 27, 30, October 11, November 8, 1766, June 13, 1767, in Leonard Labaree, ed., *The Papers of Benjamin Franklin* (New Haven, Conn.: Yale University Press, 1969), 13:276, 414, 424, 430, 454, 486; "Reasons for establishing a British colony at the Illinois with some proposals for carrying the same into immediate execution," Shelburne papers, 48:95–112; Croghan to Benjamin Franklin, January 27, 1767, Shelburne papers, 48:135–43.
19. "Plan proposed by General Lyman, for Settling Louisiana and for erecting New Colonies between West Florida and the Falls of St. Anthony," Lyman to Shelburne, October 28, 1766, Shelburne papers, 48:35–46, 113, 121–22, WCL.
20. Cabinet minutes, September 11, 1767, Shelburne papers, vol. 161, unfoliated, WCL; Shelburne to Board of Trade, October 5, 1767, Shelburne papers, 50:185–217.
21. Board of Trade to Shelburne, December 23, 1767, NYDC, 7:1004–6; Shelburne to Johnson, January 5, 1768, NYCD, 8:2; Trade Board report, March 7, 1768, NYCD, 8:19–31; Barrington to Gage, April 4, 1768, Gage papers, WCL; Hillsborough to Gage, April 15, 1768, Gage correspondence, 2:64.
22. Shelburne to Carleton, November 14, 1767, C.O. 42/27:210, PAC transcript.
23. Gage to Johnson, May 16, 1764, Johnson papers, 4:424.
24. Gage to Conway, May 8, 1766, Gage correspondence, 1:90.
25. First quote from Gage to Barrington, September 8, 1770, Gage correspondence, 2:557; second quote from Gage to Barrington, March 4, 1772, Gage correspondence,

2:601; see also Cabinet Minutes, March 18, 1768, C.O. 5/1088:156; Gage to Johnson, April 4, August 7, 1768, Johnson papers, 4:177, 313; Gage to Hillsborough, June 16, 1768, Gage correspondence, 1:175–79; Gage to Barrington, March 4, 1769, Gage correspondence, 2:502; Hillsborough to Gage, December 4, 1771, Gage correspondence, 2:137; Conway to Gage, May 20, 1766, C.O. 5/84:249; Barrington to Gage, October 10, 1765, May 7, September 12, 1766, Gage papers, WCL.

26. Hillsborough to Johnson, March 12, 1768, NYCD, 8:36.

27. Stuart to Fauquier, February 10, 1766, C.O. 5/66:783–85; Stuart to Trade Board, December 2, 1766, C.O. 5/67:399; Fauquier to Stuart, September 17, 1767, C.O. 5/69:265; Shelburne to Fauquier, November 14, 1767, C.O. 5/1345:391–92.

28. Jack M. Sosin, *The Revolutionary Frontier, 1763–1783* (Albuquerque: University of New Mexico Press, 1967), 56.

29. Johnson to Hillsborough, November 18, 1768, NYCD, 8:110; Hillsborough to Johnson, January 4, 1769, NYCD, 8:145; Trade Board's Instructions, April 25, 1769, C.O. 5/70:375–98; Hillsborough to Johnson, May 13, 1769, NYCD, 8:168; Stuart to Hillsborough, February 12, 1769, C.O. 5/70:249–53; Hillsborough to Stuart, May 13, 1769, C.O. 5/70:407–8.

30. Croghan to Wharton, November 2, 1771, Croghan papers, box 37, Cadwallader Collection, Historical Society of Pennsylvania, Philadelphia (hereafter cited as HSP).

31. Johnson report on council, July 21, 1770, NYCD, 8:237; Stuart journal of Lochaber congress, C.O. 5.72:59.

32. Dunmore to Hillsborough, March [20], 1772, C.O. 5/1350:37–41.

33. Cadwallader Colden to John Penn, February 6, 1770, Minutes, Provincial Council of Pennsylvania, 9:656; John Penn to Botetourt, March 5, 1770, C.O. 5/1349:115; Botetourt to Penn, March 24, 1770, C.O. 5/1349:115; Carleton to Colden, March 13, 1770, C.O. 5/1349:112–13; Eden to Colden, May 9, 1770, Pennsylvania Archives, Philadelphia: Joseph Severn; Harrisburg: Commonwealth of Pennsylvania, 1852–1949, 1st series, 4:369 (hereafter cited as PA); Penn to Colden, June 28, 1770, C.O. 5/1349:155; Carlton to Colden, May 30, 1770, C.O. 5/1349:153; Colden to Bland and Henry, July 11, 1770, C.O. 5/1349:149.

34. Hillsborough to Colden, April 14, 1770, NYCD, 8:210; Colden to Hillsborough, July 7, 1770, NYCD, 8:216; Johnson to Hillsborough, August 14, 1770, NYCD, 8:225; Hillsborough circular letter, November 11, 1770, C.O. 5/71:441–44.

35. Dunmore to Hillsborough, January 18, 1771, NYCD, 8:261; Tryon to Hillsborough, January 9, 1772, NYCD, 8:288.

36. Wharton memorandum to Trent, in Kenneth P. Bailey, ed., *The Ohio Company Papers, 1747–1817, Being Primarily Papers of the "Suffering Traders" of Pennsylvania* (Arcata, Calif.: Arthur H. Clark, 1947) (hereafter cited as Ohio Company papers); Robert Callender to William Trent, November 24, 1768, "Papers Relating to Indian Losses, 1766–1770," Indian Records Collection, 1716–1856, HSP, 2:16; Trent to [Callender], December 1, 1768, Ohio Company papers, HSP, 2:53; Article of agreement, December 30, 1768, Ohio Company papers, 205–10; 1754 committee of suffering traders to Moses Franks, January 4, 1769, Ohio Company papers, HSP, 1:57; Samuel Wharton to George Croghan, April 3, May 18, 27, June 16, 1769, Croghan papers; William Trent to Croghan, June 10, 1769, Croghan papers; Wharton to Johnson, June 14, 1769, Johnson papers, 7:18–19.

37. Wharton to Croghan, September 4, December 6, 1769, Croghan papers; Trent to Croghan, April 11, 1770, Croghan papers; Petition by Walpole Company, C.O. 5/1332:285–887.

38. Montague to Virginia Committee of Correspondence, January 15, 1770, *Virginia Magazine of History and Biography* 7 (1904–5): 159; Journal of the Board of Trade, 1768–1775, 170–71; William Lee petition, January 24, 1770, C.O. 5/1332:319; James Mercer to Ohio Company committee, January 9, 1772, Mulkearn, Mercer papers, WCL, 312.

39. Mercer to Washington, December 18, 1770, in Stanislaus Hamilton, ed., *Letters to Washington, and Accompanying Papers,* 5 vols. (Boston: Houghton Mifflin and Co., 1902), 4:40; Thomas Lee to James Mercer, January 13, Mercer papers, 318; Wharton to Croghan, September 4, 1770, Croghan papers; Journal of the Board of Trade, 1768–1775, 188; Thomas Walpole to Hillsborough, July 16, 1770, C.O. 5/1332:403.

40. Dunmore to Hillsborough, November 12, 1770, NYCD, 8:253.

41. DAR, 3:254–55.

42. Ibid., 5:202–4, 9–90; Gage correspondence, 1:334–36.

43. Thomas Perkins Abernethy, *Western Lands and the American Revolution* (New York: Russell and Russell, 1959).

44. Suffolk to King George III, July 21, 1772, in John Fortescue, ed., *The Correspondence of King George the Third, from 1760 to December 1783,* 6 vols. (London: Macmillan, 1927–28), 2:369 (hereafter cited as correspondence of George III); George III to Suffolk, July 21, 1772, correspondence of George III, 2:369–70; Gage to Barrington, August 5, 1772, Gage correspondence, 2:615–16; Barrington to Gage, September 2, 1772, Gage papers, WCL; Barrington to Gage, September 18, 1772, Gage papers, WCL.

45. Board of Trade report, May 6, 1773, C.O. 5/1368:326–55, 575; Act of the Privy Council, in *Acts of the Privy Council,* 6:541–43.

46. William Murray to Gratz brothers, May 15, 1773, Ohio Company papers, HSP, 1:102; Lord to Gage, July 3, 1773, Add. mss. 21730, f. 132; Lord to Haldimand, September 3, 1773, Add. mss. 21731, f. 7; Dartmouth to Haldimand, December 1, 1773, Add. mss. 21695, f. 53. Haldimand to Lord, March 8, 1774, and Proclamation, both enclosed in Haldimand to Gage, June 10, 1774, Johnson papers, 8:1074–75.

47. Dunmore to Dartmouth, May 16, 1774, C.O. 5/1352:141; Dartmouth to Dunmore, September 8, 1774, C.O. 5/1352:231–38.

48. Washington to Crawford, September 21, 1767, in Consul W. Butterfield, ed., *Washington-Crawford Letters: Being the Correspondence between George Washington and William Crawford, from 1767 to 1781, Concerning Western Lands* (Cincinnati: Robert Clarke and Company, 1877), 3–4, 8–9.

49. John C. Fitzpatrick, ed., *The Diaries of George Washington, 1748–1794,* 4 vols. (Boston: Houghton Mifflin, 1925), 2:9, 37, 84–87; Washington to Croghan, November 24, 1770, in John C. Fitzpatrick, ed., *The Writings of George Washington,* 39 vols. (Washington, D.C.: Government Printing Office, 1931–44), 3:30; Croghan to Washington, August 18, 1771, in Hamilton, *Letters to Washington,* 4:79.

50. Journal of Alexander McKee, October 7–8, 1773, Johnson papers, 7:1032–36; see also McKee to William Johnson, October 16, 1773, March 3, 1774, Johnson papers, 7:1032–36.

51. Order in Council, April 7, 1773, NYCD, 8:357–58; Dartmouth circular letter, February 5, 1774, C.O. 5/75:53–54.

52. For the key policy documents, see John Stuart to Thomas Gage, May 12, 1774, Gage papers, WCL; Stuart to Frederick Haldimand, February 10, 1774, Gage papers; James Wright to Haldimand, May 20, 1774, Gage papers; Stuart to Haldimand, Feb-

ruary 3, 1774, Haldimand papers, PAC, 12:261–67; Alexander Cameron to Stuart, February 4, 1774, Haldimand papers, 12:282. For good overviews of this issue, see John Richard Alden, *John Stuart and the Southern Colonial Frontier: A Study of Indian Relations, War, Trade, and Land Problems in the Southern Wilderness, 1754–1775* (Ann Arbor: University of Michigan Press, 1944), 294–313; J. Russel Snapp, *John Stuart and the Struggle for Empire on the Southern Frontier* (Baton Rouge: Louisiana State University Press, 1996), 39.

53. Alan Gallay, *The Formation of a Planter Elite: Jonathan Bryan and the Southern Colonial Frontier* (Athens: University of Georgia Press, 1989), 141–45.

54. Proceedings of the Governor and Council of Georgia, June 11, 1773, Colonial Records of the State of Georgia, 12:361–63.

55. For varying accounts, see recollections of Henry Jolly, Michael Cresap, Jr., Bazaleel Wells, George Edington, and Michael Myers in *Dunmore's War*, 9–14, 15, 16, 16–17, 17–19.

56. Dunmore reply to Iroquois and Delaware chiefs, May 29, 1774, in Nicolas B. Wainwright, ed., "Turmoil at Pittsburgh: Diary of Augustine Prevost, 1774," *Pennsylvania Magazine of History and Biography* 85 (April 1961): 154–55.

57. Alexander McKee Journal, June 10, 1774, NYCD, 8:464.

58. Letter from Carlisle, July 4, 1774, *Dunmore's War*, 67.

59. Dunmore circular letter, June 10, 1774, Dunmore to Connolly, June 20, 1774, Dunmore to William Preston, July 3, 1774, Dunmore to Andrew Lewis, July 12, 24, 1774, *Dunmore's War*, 33–35, 37–38, 61–63, 97–98.

60. William Preston circular letter, July 20, 1774, *Dunmore's War*, 91–93.

61. Angus McDonald to John Connolly, [August 1774], Maryland Journal, September 7, 1774, *Dunmore's War*, 151–54, 155–56.

62. Dunmore to Dartmouth, December 24, 1774, *Dunmore's War*, 368–95; Augustine Prevost diary, April to September 1774, "Turmoil at Pittsburgh," 133–39.

63. Augustine Prevost diary, April to September 1774, "Turmoil at Pittsburgh," 140–43; Andrew Lewis to William Preston, September 8, 1774, "Dunmore's War," 190–92.

64. Quoted in Thomas Jefferson, *Notes on the State of Virginia* (Chapel Hill: University of North Carolina Press, 1955), 63.

65. Thomas Gage to Frederick Haldimand, August 18, 1774, Haldimand papers, 21,665, folder 298.

66. Thomas Gage to Guy Johnson, November 28, 1774, Johnson papers, 8:687–99.

67. Dartmouth to Dunmore, September 8, 1774, DAR, 8:194–96; Dunmore to Dartmouth, December 24, 1774, *Dunmore's War*, 368–95.

68. Dunmore to Dartmouth, December 24, 1774, *Dunmore's War*, 369.

69. Indian council, July 11, 1774, NYCD, 8:476; Congress proceedings, Johnson Hall, June 19 to July 16, 1774, NYCD, 8:474–84; William Johnson to Dartmouth, June 20, 1774, NYCD, 8:459–61; William Johnson to Thomas Gage, July 4, 1774, Johnson papers, 7:1113–16; Guy Johnson to Thomas Gage, July 12, 1774, Johnson papers, 7:1121–24.

70. William Johnson to Dartmouth, April 17, 1774, NYCD, 8:419–21; William Johnson to Thomas Gage, April 20, 1774, Johnson papers, 8:1128–30; Daniel Claus to Thomas Gage, July 28, 1774, Johnson papers, 8:643–46; William Johnson will [January 27, 1774], (probated July 25, 1774), Johnson papers, 7:1062–76.

71. Guy Johnson to Dartmouth, July 12, 26, 1774, NYCD, 8:471–72, 472–74; Guy Johnson to Thomas Gage, July 12, 26, 1774, Johnson papers, 7:1121–24, 8:640–43;

Thomas Gage to Dartmouth, July 18, 1774, Carter, Gage correspondence, 1:360; Dartmouth to William Johnson, July 6, 1774, NYCD, 8:468–69; Dartmouth to Guy Johnson, September 8, 1774, NYCD, 8:489; Dartmouth to Thomas Gage, September 8, 1774, Gage correspondence, 2:173.

72. George III to Frederick North, September 11, November 18, 1774, correspondence of George III, 3:131, 153.
73. Thomas Gage to William Barrington, October 3, 1774, Gage correspondence, 2:655–56.
74. Thomas Gage to Dartmouth, November 14, 1774, Gage correspondence, 1:383–84; Thomas Gage to Guy Johnson, December 28, 1774, Johnson papers, 8:703–4.

CHAPTER 3

1. Dartmouth to Thomas Gage, January 27, 1775, Gage correspondence 2:181, 179–84.
2. Don Higginbotham, *The War of American Independence: Military Attitudes, Policies, and Practice, 1763–1789* (Boston: Northeastern University Press, 1971), 65.
3. For excellent summaries, see James Kirby Martin, *Benedict Arnold: Revolutionary Hero, An American Warrior Reconsidered* (New York: New York University Press, 1997); Michael A. Belleisles, *Revolutionary Outlaws: Ethan Allan and the Struggle for Independence on the Early American Frontier* (Charlottesville: University of Virginia Press, 1993).
4. J. Kevin Graffagnino, ed., *Ethan and Ira Allen: Collected Works,* 3 vols. (Benson: 1992), 2:3.
5. Congressional resolution, May 31, 1775, in Worthington Chauncey Ford, Guillard Hunt, John C. Fitzpatrick, and Roscoe R. Hill, eds., *Journals of the Continental Congress, 1774–1789,* 34 vols. (Washington, D.C.: Government Printing Office, 1904–37), 2:73–74 (hereafter cited as JCC).
6. Congressional resolution, June 16, 1775, JCC, 2:91–92.
7. Page Smith, *A New Age Now Begins: A People's History of the American Revolution* (New York: Penguin Books, 1989), 1:532.
8. Massachusetts Provincial Congress to Samuel Kirkland, April 4, 1775 (enclosure a speech to the Mohawks), American Archives, 4–1:1349–50.
9. JCC, 2:182, 174–83.
10. Committee report on Caughnawaga, Massachusetts House of Representatives, August 3, 1775, in Peter Force, ed., *American Archives: Consisting of a Collection of Authentic Records, State Papers, Debates, and Letters,* 3 vols. (Washington, D.C.: M. St. Clair Clarke and Peter Force, 1837–46, 1848–53) 4–3: 301 (hereafter cited as American Archives); George Washington to President of Congress, August 4, 1775, in John F. Fitzpatrick, ed., *The Writings of George Washington,* 39 vols. (Washington, D.C.: Government Printing Office, 1931–44), 3:397–98; George Washington to Philip Schuyler, August 15 and 20, 1775, *Washington Writings,* 3:423–44, 436–39.
11. Thomas Gage to Guy Carleton, April 21, 1775, Gage papers, American Series, vol. 127.
12. Thomas Gage to Guy Carleton, May 20, 1775, enclosing extract of letter from Thomas Gage to Guy Johnson, May 10, 1775, Gage papers, American Series, vol. 129.
13. Thomas Gage to John Caldwell, May 10, 1775, Gage papers, American Series, vol. 128.
14. Thomas Gage to John Stuart, September 12, 1775, DAR, 11:105.

15. Thomas Gage to Barrington, June 12, 1775, Gage correspondence, 2:684–85.
16. Dartmouth to Thomas Gage, July 5, 1776, NYCD, 8:592.
17. King George III to Dartmouth, July 17, 1775, in *Great Britain, Historical Manuscripts Commission, The Manuscripts of the Earl of Dartmouth,* 3 vols. (London: Her Majesty's Stationery Office, 1887–96), 1:440.
18. Dartmouth to Guy Johnson, July 24, 1775, NYCD 8:596; Dartmouth to Thomas Gage, August 2, 1775, Gage correspondence, 2:204–6; Dartmouth to Guy Carleton, July 24, 1775, C.O. 42/34, folder 140–14.
19. For the most detailed accounts of this struggle, see Guy Johnson journal, May to November 1775, NYCD, 8: Minute Book of Tryon County.
20. Walter Pilkington, ed., *The Journals of Samuel Kirkland: 18th Century Missionary to the Iroquois, Government Agent, Father of Hamilton College* (Clinton, N.Y.: Hamilton College, 1980), 100–2 (hereafter cited as *Kirkland Journals*).
21. Guy Johnson to Samuel Kirkland, February 14, 1775, Pilkington, *Kirkland Journals,* 105.
22. Samuel Kirkland to Guy Johnson, February 21, 1775, *Kirkland Journals,* 106–10; Oneida chiefs to Guy Johnson, February 23, 1775, *Kirkland Journals,* 111.
23. Guy Johnson to Thomas Gage, March 31, 1775, Gage papers, WCL, 127.
24. Guy Johnson journal, May to November 1775, NYCD, 8:658.
25. Guy Johnson to committee, May 20, 1775, in Samuel Frey, ed., *Minute Book of the Committee of Safety, Tryon County* (New York: Dodd, Mead and Co., 1905), 125.
26. Little Abraham to Albany Committee, May 20, 1775, American Archives, 4–2:664–65; Albany Committee to Mohawks, May 25, 1775, American Archives, 4–2:842.
27. Guy Johnson journal, May to September 1775, NYCD, 8:635–37, 658–59; Gage to Carleton, August 18, 1775, Gage papers, WCL, 134.
28. Philip Schuyler to Albany Committee, July 15, 1775, in *Minutes of the Albany Committee of Correspondence, 1775–1778,* 2 vols. (Albany, N.Y.: J. B. Lyon Company, 1923–25), 158.
29. Oneida chiefs to New England provinces, June 19, 1775, American Archives, 4–2:1116–17.
30. Oneida and Tuscarora answer, July 1, 1775, Minutes of the Albany Committee of Correspondence, 1:122–24.
31. German Flats Indian council, August 14–16, 1775, NYCD, 8:617–20; Twelve United Colonies and Six Nations, August 15 to 16, August 23 to September 2, 1775, NYCD, 8:605–8, 608–31.
32. Arendt de Peyster to Thomas Gage, June 16, 1775, Gage papers, American Series, vol. 130.
33. John Caldwell to Thomas Gage, May 5, 1775, Richard Lernoult to Thomas Gage, May 14, 1775, Gage papers, American series, vol. 128; John D. Barnhart and Dorothy L. Riker, *Indiana to 1816: The Colonial Period, The History of Indiana,* vol. 1 (Indianapolis: Indiana Historical Bureau and Indiana Historical Society, 1971), 174–75.
34. Frederick Louis Billon, ed., *Annals of St. Louis,* 2 vols. (St. Louis: printed for the author, 1886 and 1888), 1:129–30.
35. Indian speech, Shawney Towns, June 26, 1775, Haldimand papers, 21,845, folder 483, 40.

36. Dunmore to Dartmouth, May 1, 1775, DAR, 8:107–10.
37. Indian speech, Shawney Towns, June 26, 1775, Haldimand papers, 21,845, folder 483, 41.
38. Ibid., 39.
39. Ibid., 38.
40. Ibid., 44, 47.
41. Ibid., 49.
42. Ibid., 56.
43. Ibid., 58.
44. Ibid., 52.
45. Edward G. Williams, ed., "The Journal of Richard Butler, 1775: Continental Congress' Envoy to the Western Indians," *Western Pennsylvania Historical Magazine* 46 (October 1963): 381–95; 47 (January 1964): 31–46; 47 (April 1964): 144–56.
46. Quoted in John Dodge, *An Entertaining Narrative of the Cruel and barbarous Treatment and extreme Sufferings of Mr. John Dodge during his Captivity of Many Months among the British at Detroit* (Cedar Rapids, Iowa: The Torch Press, 1907), 29–31.
47. Treaty of Pittsburgh, 1775, in Reuben Gold Thwaites and Louise P. Kellogg, eds., *The Revolution on the Upper Ohio, 1775–1777* (Madison: Wisconsin State Historical Society, 1908), 25–43, 70–127.
48. Ibid., 85–89
49. Ibid., 96.
50. Henry Hamilton to Guy Carleton, November 30, 1775, *Upper Ohio, 1775–1777,* 130.
51. William Preston to Dunmore, March 10, 1775, *Upper Ohio, 1775–1777,* 1–6.
52. John Brown to William Preston, May 5, 1775, *Upper Ohio, 1775–1777,* 10.
53. George W. Ranck, *Boonesborough: Its Founding, Pioneer Struggles, Indian Experiences, Transylvania Days, and Revolutionary Annals* (New York: New York Times and Arno Press, 1971), 232–49.
54. Dunmore to Thomas Gage, [n.d., ca. August 22, 1775; received September 6, 1775], Gage to Dunmore, September 10, 1775, Gage papers, American series, vols. 134 and 135; Proposals for raising an Army to the Westward, for alarming the Frontiers of Virginia, Maryland, Pennsylvania, and New York, & for obstructing a communication between the Southern & Northern governments, September 11, 1775, Gage papers, American Series, vol. 135; Thomas Gage to Dunmore and John Connolly, September 10, 1775, Gage answer to Connolly proposal, September 11, 1775, separate letters from Thomas Gage to Guy Carleton, Alexander McKee, and Hugh Lord, September 11, 1775, Gage papers, American series, vol. 135; Thomas Gage to Dartmouth, September 20, 1775, Gage correspondence, 1:414–16; John Connolly, "A Narrative of the Transactions, Imprisonment, and Sufferings of John Connolly, an American Loyalist and Lieutenant-Colonel in His Majesty's Service," *Pennsylvania Magazine of History and Biography* 12 (1888): 310–24, 407–20; 13 (1889): 61–70, 153–67, 281–91; Percy B. Caley, "The Life Adventures of Lieutenant-Colonel John Connolly: The Story of a Tory," *Western Pennsylvania Historical Magazine* 11 (April 1928): 101–6; Connolly's Plot, *Upper Ohio, 1775–1777,* 136–42; Connolly to Gage, September 11, 1775, Gage papers, Clement Library; Gage reply, September 11, 1775, Gage papers, Clement Library; Gage to Lernoult, September 11, 1775, Gage papers, Clement Library; Gage to Carleton, September 11, 1775, Gage papers,

Clement Library; Gage to Captain Hugh Lord (at Kaskaskia), September 12, 1775, Gage papers, Clement library.

55. Henry Laurens to John Laurens, June 23, 1775, in Philip M. Hamer, et al., eds., *The Papers of Henry Laurens,* 14 vols. (Columbia: University of South Carolina Press, 1958), 10:188–89.

56. John Stuart to South Carolina Committee of Intelligence, July 18, 1775, C.O. 5/76/155.

57. John Stuart to Thomas Gage, July 9, 1775, Gage papers, WCL.

58. John Stuart to Dartmouth, July 21, 1775, C.O. 5/76/151.

59. Charles Loch Mowat, *East Florida as a British Province, 1763–1784* (Berkeley: University of California Press, 1943), 108.

60. William Knox to Grey Cooper, April 27, 1779, DAR, 17:112–13; Helen L. Shaw, *British Administration of the Southern Indians, 1756–1783* (New York: AMS Press, 1981), 175–77; John Stuart to Thomas Gage, October 3, 1775, in John Drayton, *Memoirs of the American Revolution,* 2 vols. (New York: New York Times and Arno Press, 1969), 1:296–98.

61. George Washington to Philip Schuyler, December 24, 1775, *The Writings of George Washington* 4:178–80.

62. Provincial congress to eastern Indians, May 15, 1776, in Frederic Kidder, ed., *Military Operations in Eastern Maine during the Revolution, Chiefly Compiled from the Journals and Letters of Colonel John Allan, with Notes and a Memoir of Col. John Allan* (1867; reprint, New York: Kraus Reprint Company, 1971), 51–52.

63. Provincial congress, June 21, 1775, *Military Operations,* 53.

64. John Allan report, November 21, 1776, *Military Operations,* 170, 175.

65. See Petition of Bejamin Foster and others for Machias, August 18, 1775; Petition of Jeremiah O'Brien, February 2, 1776; Resolve to man two vessels at Machias, n.d., *Military Operations,* 43–46. For the best book on the subject, see James S. Leamon, *Revolution Downeast: The War for American Independence in Maine* (Amherst: University of Massachusetts Press, 1994).

66. Joseph Hamon, *Le Chevalier de Bonvouloir, premier emissaire secret de la France aupres du Congres de Philadelphie avant l'independence americaine* (Paris: Jouve, 1953); Orville T. Murphy, *Charles Gravier, Comte de Vergennes: French Diplomacy in the Age of Revolution, 1719–1787* (Albany: State University of New York, 1982).

67. Allen and others to Congress, June 10, 1775, American Archives, 4th series, 2:957–58; Benedict Arnold to Congress, June 13, 1775, American Archives, 4th series, 2:976–77; Congressional resolution, June 27, 1775, JCC, 2:108–10. For good accounts of the campaign, see Robert McConnell Hatch, *Thrust for Canada: The American Attempt on Quebec in 1775–1776* (Boston: Houghton Mifflin Company, 1979); Kenneth Roberts, ed., *March to Quebec: Journals of the Members of Arnold's Expedition* (New York: Doubleday, 1938); Fred C. Wurtele, ed., *Blockade of Quebec in 1775–1776 by the American Revolutionists* (New York: Kennikat Press, 1970).

68. State of His Majesty's Troops in the Province of Quebec, June 24, 1775, C.O. 42/34, folder 157.

69. Thomas Gage to Guy Carleton, June 15, and June 3, 1775, Gage papers, American Series, vols. 130 and 129.

70. Guy Carleton to Dartmouth, August 14, 1775, C.O. 42/34, folders 174–76; Guy Johnson journal, May to November 1775, NYCD, 8:659–60.

71. Record of Indian transactions, 1775, NYCD, 8:636, 659–60.

72. Ray Stannard Baker, "Remember Baker," *New England Quarterly* 4 (October 1931): 620–28.

73. Lorimier, "Mes Services," in Hospice Anthelme J. B. Verreau, ed., *Invasion du Canada, collection de memoires recueilles et annote par M. l'abbe Verreau, pretre* (Montreal: Societe Historique de Montreal, 1873), 248–49; Guy Johnson journal, May to September 1775, NYCD, 8:660–61; Philip Schuyler to John Hancock, September 8, 1775, Philip Schuyler to Congress, September 19, 1775, Philip Schuyler to George Washington, September 30, 1775, American Archives, 4–3:669–70, 738–40, 751–54.

74. Ethan Allen, *A Narrative of Colonel Ethan Allen's Captivity Containing His Voyage & Travels* (New York: Richard W. Ellis [The Georgia Press] for Fort Ticonderoga, 1930).

75. Benedict Arnold to Congress, June 23, 1775, American Archives, 4th series, 2:1066–67.

76. Benedict Arnold to Reuben Colburn, August 21, 1775, in Philander D. Chase, ed., *The Papers of George Washington: Revolutionary War Series,* 6 vols. (Charlottesville: University of Virginia Press, 1985–), 1:409–10.

77. James Kirby Martin, *Benedict Arnold, Revolutionary Hero: An American Warrior Reconsidered* (New York: New York University Press, 1997), 155.

78. Return of Rebel casualties, December 31, 1775, C.O. 42/35, folder 32; Guy Carleton to William Howe, January 12, 1776, American Archives, 4th series, 4:656.

CHAPTER 4

1. Alan Valentine, *Lord George Germain* (New York: Oxford University Press, 1962); Gerald S. Brown, *The American Secretary: The Colonial Policy of Lord George Germain, 1775–1778* (Ann Arbor: University of Michigan Press, 1963).

2. Richard Howe to Germain, September 26, 1775, Germain papers, 3, WCL; William Howe to Dartmouth, October 9, 1775, American Archives, 4–3:991–93; Extract of Burgoyne letters, August 10 and 18, 1775, correspondence of George III, 3:242–45; Ira D. Gruber, *The Howe Brothers and the American Revolution* (Chapel Hill: University of North Carolina Press, 1972); Troyer Steele Anderson, *The Command of the Howe Brothers during the American Revolution* (New York: Oxford University Press, 1936); William B. Willcox, *The Portrait of a General: Sir Henry Clinton in the War of Independence* (New York: Alfred A. Knopf, 1964).

3. Lord North to House of Commons, November 20, 1775, in William Corbett and J. Wright, eds., *The Parliamentary History of England, from the Earliest Period to the Year 1803,* 36 vols. (London: T. C. Hansard, 1806–1820), 18:94.

4. Guy Johnson to Germain, January 26, 1776, and Journal of Guy Johnson from May to November 1775, NYCD, 8:654–57, 658–62.

5. Germain to John Burgoyne, August 23, 1776, in *Report on the Manuscripts of Mrs. Stopford-Sackville of Drayton House, Northhampshire,* 2 vols. (London: H.M. Stationery Office, 1904 and 1910), 2:40; see also George Germain to John Burgoyne, March 28, 1776, Germain papers, DAR, 10:252; George Germain to Guy Carleton, June 21, 1776, C.O. 42/35, folders 40–44; George Germain to Guy Carleton, August 22, 1776, American Archives, 5–1:1105.

6. For his definitive biography, see Isabel Thompson Kelsay, *Joseph Brant, 1743–1807: Man of Two Worlds* (Syracuse, N.Y.: Syracuse University Press, 1984).

7. George Washington to Philip Schuyler, June 7, 20, 27, 1776, George Washington to John Hancock, June 21, 1776, John Hancock to George Washington, June 25, 1776, American Archives, 4–6:742, 992, 1011, 1011–12, 1065–66.
8. Congressional resolution, May 10, 1776, Journal of Congress, 2:342.
9. For the best work on this, see Pauline Maier, *American Scripture: Making the Declaration of Independence* (New York: Vintage, 1998).
10. Philip Schuyler to John Johnson, January 16, 1776, American Archives, 4:823–24.
11. Journal of James Dean, March 21 to April 3, 1776, American Archives, 4–5:1100–4.
12. Council proceedings, April 29 to May 10, 1776, Maryly B. Penrose, comp., *Indian Affairs Papers: American Revolution* (Franklin Park, N.J.: Liberty Bell Associates, 1981), 40–55; George Washington to Philip Schuyler, June 9 and 16, 1776, American Archives, 4–6:769, 926–27.
13. There are no extant British records of these councils. The best account is by the American spy Paul Long, [Paul Long] to George Morgan, July 1776, George Morgan Letter Book, 1776, 43–49, Carnegie Library, Pittsburgh (hereafter cited as GMLB), from which come the preceding quote and statistics on warriors two paragraphs down.
14. This quote and the following are from Meeting with Kayashuta, [July 6, 1776], GMLB, 1776, 37–39.
15. Simon Girty's report to George Morgan, July 26, 1776, GMLB, 1775, 52–58.
16. Philip Schuyler to John Johnson, May 10, 1776, American Archives, 4th series, 5:643.
17. Minutes of meeting between Volkert Douw, Elias Dayton, and the Mohawks, Fort Hunter, May 19, 1776, Johnstown, May 20–21, 1776, Schuyler papers, box 13, New York Public Library.
18. Orville W. Carroll, *Fort Stanwix: History, Historic Furnishing, and Historic Structure Report* (Washington, D.C.: Office of Park Historic Preservation, National Park Service, U.S. Department of the Interior, 1976).
19. Schuyler council with Indians, August 8–13, 1776, American Archives, 5–1:1035–49.
20. Intelligence from an [Seneca] Indian, September 3, 1776, GMLB II; William Pilkington, ed., *The Journals of Samuel Kirkland* (Clinton, N.Y.: Hamilton College, 1980), 112–13.
21. Elias Dayton to Philip Schuyler, August 15, September 4, 11, 22, 1776, American Archives, 5–1:1033–35; 5–2:245–48.
22. Martin, *Benedict Arnold,* 189. For other accounts of the campaign, see George F. G. Stanley, ed., *For Want of a Horse: Being a Journal of the Campaigns against the Americans in 1776 and 1777 Conducted from Canada, by an Officer Who Served with Lt. Gen. Burgoyne* (Sackville, N.B.: The Tribune Press Limited, 1961); James Phinney Baxter, ed., *The British Invasion from the North: The Campaigns of Generals Carleton and Burgoyne from Canada, 1776–1777, with the Journal of Lieut. William Digby of the 53rd, or Shropshire Regiment of Foot* (New York: Da Capo Press, 1970); Max von Eelking, ed., *Memoirs and Letters of Major General Riedesel during His Residence in America* (New York: The New York Times & Arno Press, 1969); Horatio Rogers, ed., *Hadden's Journal and Orderly Books: A Journal Kept in Canada and upon Burgoyne's Campaign in 1776 and 1777, by Lieutenant James Murray Hadden; Also Orders Kept by Him and Issued by Sir Guy Carleton, Lieut.*

General Burgoyne, and Major General William Phillips in 1776, 1777, and 1778 (Albany, N.Y.: Joel Munsell's Sons, 1884); Thomas Baldwin, ed., *The Revolutionary Journal of Col. Jedutan Baldwin, 1775–1778* (Bangor, Maine: Printed for the De Burians, 1906); Robert McConnell Hatch, *Thrust for Canada: The American Attempt on Quebec in 1775–1776* (Boston: Houghton Mifflin Company, 1979).

23. Andrew Park, Jacob Mauer, and Hugh MacKay, "Account of Events at the Cedars," Chevalier de Lorimier, "Mes Services," in Anthelme J. B. Verreau, ed., *Invasion du Canada, collection des memoires recuilles et annote par M. l'abbe Verreau, pretre* (Montreal: Societe Historique de Montreal, 1873), 19–31, 268–83; Benjamin Stevens, "Diary of Benjamin Stevens, of Canaan, Connecticut," *Daughters of the American Revolution Magazine* 45 (July–December 1914), 137–40; Capitulation at the Cedars, July 10, 1776, American Archives, 5–1:158–69.

24. Guy Carleton to George Germain, June 20, 1776, American Archives, 4–6:1002–3; John Sullivan to George Washington, June 7–12, 24, 1776, American Archives, 4–6:1036–38, 1201–21.

25. Richard Ketchum, *Saratoga: Turning Point of America's Revolutionary War* (New York: Henry Holt and Co., 1997), 71, 105, 136–138.

26. Randolph C. Downes, *Council Fires on the Upper Ohio: A Narrative of Indian Affairs in the Upper Ohio Valley until 1795* (Pittsburgh: University of Pittsburgh Press, 1969), 186.

27. Dartmouth to Thomas Gage, August 2, 1775, Gage correspondence, 2:204–6; Guy Carleton to John Caldwell, July 19, 1776, and Guy Carleton to Hugh Lord, July 19, 1776, HP/BM 21,699:19 and 20; James Andrews to John Blackburn, July 23, 1776, DAR, 10:340; Captain Hugh Lord memorial to Board of Trade, n.d., received December 3, 1776, DAR, 10:417; Kathryn Harrod Mason, *James Harrod of Kentucky* (Baton Rouge: Louisiana State University Press, 1971), 95–96.

28. E. Fabre Surveyer, "Philippe Francois de Rastel de Rocheblave," in Percy J. Robinson, ed., *Toronto during the French Regime: A History of the Toronto Region from Brule to Simcoe, 1615–1793* (Chicago: University of Chicago Press, 1933), 233–42; Guy Carleton to George Germain, August 13, 1777, and Philippe Francois de Rocheblave to Germain, January 22 and February 28, 1778, in Edward Mason, ed., *Rocheblave Papers, 1776–1778, Vol. 4* (Chicago: Chicago Historical Society, 1890), 394–95, 395–97, 407–8.

29. J. Watt De Peyster, *Miscellancies by an Officer: By Colonel Arent Schuyler De Peyster, 1774–1813* (New York: Chasmar, 1888, vol. 1; New York: C. H. Ludwig, 1888, vol. 2), 2–3, 1:5–15; Guy Carleton to De Peyster, June 25, 1776, HP/BM 21,699:10; Guy Carleton to Christopher Carleton, August 21, 1776, HP/BM 21,699:27.

30. Summary of conditions on the frontiers in the first months of 1776, *Upper Ohio, 1775–1777*, 143.

31. Anonymous report, April 2, 1776, *Upper Ohio, 1775–1777*, 147–51.

32. George Morgan to Henry Hamilton, May 31, 1776, GMLB 1776, 15–16; Commissioners for Middle Department . . . for Indian Affairs, August 18, 1776, GMLB II.

33. George Morgan to Indian commissioners, July 26, 1776, GMLB 1776, 59–63; John Heckewelder, *A Narrative of the Mission of the United Brethern among the Delaware and Mohegan Indians* (Philadelphia: McCary and Davis, 1820), 144–46.

34. Morgan Letterbook, July 24, 1776, 38, reprinted in John Almon, *The Remembrancer; or, Impartial Repository of Public Events,* 17 vols. (London: n.p., 1775–84), 3:53–54; Meeting with Kayashuta, some Shawnee and Delaware, [July 6, 1776], GMLB, 1776, 37–39.
35. William Wilson to Indian commissioners, September 26, 1776, American Archives, 5–2: 514–18; Henry Hamilton to Dartmouth, August 29 to September 2, 1776, MPHSC, 10:264–70.
36. William Wilson to Indian commissioners, September 26, 1776, American Archives, 5–2:518; Henry Hamilton to Dartmouth, August 29 to September 2, 1776, in *Michigan Pioneer Historical Society: Collections and Researches* (Lansing, Mich.: The Society, 1877–1929), 10:264–70.
37. John Floyd to William Preston, July 21, 1776, in George W. Ranck, *Boonesborough: Its Founding, Pioneer Struggles, Indian Experiences, Transylvania Days, and Revolutionary Annals* (New York: New York Times and Arno Press, 1971), 349–51.
38. John Mack Faragher, *Daniel Boone: The Life and Legend of an American Pioneer* (New York: Henry Holt and Company, 1992), 144.
39. Louise Phelps Kellogg, *The British Regime in Wisconsin and the Northwest* (New York: Da Capo Press, 1971), 139, 146.
40. Speech of Cornstalk, November 7, 1776, Morgan Letterbook, reproduced in Francis Jennings et al., eds., *Iroquois Diplomacy: A Documentary History of the Diplomacy of the Six Nations and Their League,* 50 reels (Woodbridge, Conn.: Research Publications, 1985), reel 32, Revolution and Confederation, 147.
41. George Morgan to President of Congress, November 8, 1776, *Upper Ohio, 1775–1777,* 217; Minutes of the Pittsburgh council, October 15 to November 6, 1776, Jasper Yeates papers, Correspondence 1762–80, Manuscript Room, The Historical Society of Pennyslvania, Philadelphia.
42. Dorsey Pentecost to Patrick Henry, November 5, 1776, *Upper Ohio, 1775–1777,* 213.
43. Matthew Arbuckle to John Neville, December 26, 1776, GMLB I.
44. Patrick Tonyn to Henry Clinton, May 21, 1776, C.O. 5/556338. For accounts of this year's southern diplomacy and campaigns, see James H. O'Donnell, *The Cherokees of North Carolina in the American Revolution* (Raleigh, N.C.: Department of Cultural Resources, 1976), 12–20; Edward J. Cashin, *The King's Ranger: Thomas Brown and the American Revolution on the Southern Frontier* (Athens: University of Georgia Press, 1989), 40–58; James H. O'Donnell, *Southern Indians in the American Revolution* (Knoxville: University of Tennessee Press, 1973), 34–53.
45. Patrick Tonyn to Henry Clinton, June 11, 1776, C.O. 5/556340.
46. William Howe to John Stuart, May 23, 1776, quoted in Maldwyn A. Jones, "Sir William Howe: Conventional Strategist," in George Athan Billias, ed., *George Washington's Opponents: British Generals and Admirals in the American Revolution* (New York: William Morrow and Company, 1969), 56–57.
47. William Knox to Grey Cooper, April 27, 1779, DAR, 17:112–13.
48. Patrick Tonyn to Henry Clinton, June 11, 1776, C.O. 5/556/340.
49. John Stuart to Germain, August 23, 1776, Henry Stuart to John Stuart, August 23, 1776, Peter Chester to Germain, September 1, 1776, DAR, 7:188–91, 191–208, 214–16.
50. William McClenechan to William Fleming, July 24, 1776, *Upper Ohio, 1775–1777,* 170.

51. "To General Lee: Petition of Parish of St. George and St. Paul, including the Ceded Lands," July 31, 1776, New York Historical Society Collections, 2:181–82 (hereafter cited as NYHSC).

52. Page Smith, *A New Age Now Begins: A People's History of the America Revolution* (New York: Penguin, 1989), 1:634.

53. Charles Loch Mowat, *East Florida as a British Province, 1763–1784* (Berkeley: University of California, 1943), 108, 110.

54. William Drayton to Francis Salvador, July 24, 1776, in Robert Wilson Gibbes, *Documentary History of the American Revolution* (New York: Appleton and Company, 1853–57), 2:29.

55. Thomas Jefferson, 1776.

56. North Carolina delegates letter to provincial council, n.d., in Williams Saunders and Walter Clark, eds., *The State Papers of North Carolina* (New York: AMS Press, 1968–78), vol. 10, part 2, pp. 730–32.

57. Quoted in O'Donnell, *Southern Indians,* ix.

58. John Stuart to Germain, August 23, 1776, C.O. 5/77:128.

59. Paul Chrisler Phillips, *The West in the Diplomacy of the American Revolution* (Urbana: University of Illinois Press, 1913); Jonathan R. Dull, *The French Navy and American Independence: A Study of Arms and Diplomacy, 1774–1787* (Princeton, N.J.: Princeton University Press, 1975); William C. Stinchcombe, *The American Revolution and the French Alliance* (Syracuse, N.Y.: Syracuse University Press, 1969); Ronald Hoffman and Peter J. Albert, eds., *Peace and Peacemakers: The Treaty of 1783* (Charlottesville: University of Virginia Press, 1986); Jonathan R. Dull, *A Diplomatic History of the American Revolution* (New Haven, Conn.: Yale University Press, 1985).

60. "Considerations sur l'affaire des Colonies anglois de l'Amerique," March 12, 1776, Etats Unis, Memoires et Documents, 1:9; "Reflexions Sur la Conduite qu'il convient a la France de tenir a l'egard des Colonies Angloisses, par M. Gerard de Rayneval," Etats Unis, Memoires et Documents, 1:4, folder 59; See also Orville T. Murphy, *Charles Gravier, Comte de Vergennes: French Diplomacy in the Age of Revolution, 1719–1787* (Albany, N.Y.: State University of New York Press, 1982).

61. John Walton Caughey, *Bernardo de Galvez in Louisiana, 1776–1783* (Berkeley: University of California Press, 1934), 86.

62. Ibid., 87; Gibson to Unzaga, September 30, 1776, *Galvez,* 135.

63. Dale Van Every, *A Company of Heroes: The American Frontier, 1775–1783* (New York: Mentor Books, 1963), 119–20.

64. Horatio Gates to President of Congress and George Washington, July 16, 1776, American Archives, 5–1:376.

65. Benjamin Whitcomb scouting report, July 14–August 6, 1776, American Archives, 5–1:828–29; Guy Carleton to Christopher Carleton, August 21, 1776, HP/BM 21,699:27.

66. Guy Carleton to John Burgoyne, August 7, 1776, HP/BM 21,699:24; [Guy Carleton] to Arent De Peyster, August 21, 1776, HP/BM 21,699:27.

67. Stanley, *Want of a Horse,* 80–81; Baxter, *British Invasion,* 122–26; Eelking, *Riedesel,* 1:55–57.

68. William Philips to Sion Fraser, September 10, 1776, in C. T. Atkinson, "Some Evidence for Burgoyne's Expedition," *Journal of the Society for Army Historical Research* 26 (Winter 1948): 132–42.

69. Joshua Pell, "Diary of Joshua Pell, Junior: An Officer of the British Army in America, 1776–1777," *The Magazine of American History* 2 (January–February 1878): 46; Benedict Arnold to Horatio Gates, September 7, 1776, American Archives, 5–2:223–24.
70. J. Robert Maguire, ed., "Dr. Robert Knox's Account of the Battle of Valcour, October 11–13, 1776," *Vermont History* 46 (Summer 1978): 141–50.
71. Elizabeth Commetti, ed., *The American Journals of Lt. John Enys* (Syracuse, N.Y.: Syracuse University Press, 1976), 29–30.
72. Ibid., 31.
73. Alexander Fraser to Frederick Haldimand, June 11, 1779, HP/BM 21,780, folders 38–40.
74. Petition, February 5, 1776, Reply to petition, February 9, 1776, in *Military Operations*, 55–56, 56–57.
75. Indian declined, September 19, 1776, *Military Operations*, 58.
76. George Washington to eastern Indians, December 24, 1776, *Military Operations*, 59.
77. Jonathan Eddy surrender demand to Joseph Gorham, November 10, 1776; Gorham reply, November 10, 1776; Jonathan Eddy appeal, January 5, 1777, *Military Operations*, 67–72, 72–73, 73–74.
78. Don Higginbotham, *The War of American Independence: Military Attitudes, Policies, and Practice, 1763–1789* (Boston: Northeastern University Press, 1983), 151.
79. Smith, *New Age*, 1:742.
80. Ibid., 1:754–89.
81. Ibid., 1:790–810.
82. Ibid., 1:811–27.

CHAPTER 5

1. Page Smith, *A New Age Now Begins: A People's History of the American Revolution* (New York: Penguin, 1989), 1:828–38.
2. For advice on the general campaign, see William Howe to George Germain, November 30, 1776, DAR, 12:264–66; Germain to King, December 10, 1776, King to North, December 13, 1776, Correspondence of George III 3:405–6, 406–7. For excellent secondary accounts of the campaign planning, see Gerald S. Brown, *The American Secretary: The Colonial Policy of Lord George Germain, 1775–1778* (Ann Arbor: University of Michigan Press, 1963), 62, 83–85; Ira D. Gruber, *The Howe Brothers and the American Revolution* (Chapel Hill: University of North Carolina, 1972), 174–84; Piers Mackey, *The War for America, 1775–1783* (Cambridge: Harvard University Press, 1965), 103–20; John S. Pancake, *1777: The Year of the Hangman* (University, Ala.: The University of Alabama Press, 1977), 87–94; William B. Willcox, *The Portrait of a General: Sir Henry Clinton in the War of Independence* (New York: Alfred A. Knopf, 1964), 130–53; William B. Willcox, "Too Many Cooks: British Planning before Saratoga," *The Journal of British Studies* 3 (November 1962): 45–90. For the definitive work on Burgoyne's campaign, see Richard Ketchum, *Saratoga: Turning Point of America's Revolutionary War* (New York: Henry Holt and Company, 1997).
3. Guy Carleton to Germain, September 28, November 17, 1776, DAR, 10:380, #2148; John Burgoyne to Germain, containing memorandum on next year's campaign, January 1, 1777, DAR, 8:13, #1 and i–ii; James Murray to George Germain, August 27,

September 6, 1776, Historical Manuscripts Commission, *Report on the Manuscripts of Mrs. Stopford Sackville of Drayton House, Northhampshire,* 2 vols. (London: H.M. Stationery Office, 1904 and 1910), 1:370, 370–71; Dunmore to William Knox, March 22, 1777, DAR, 8:62, #337 and 337i.

4. For advice on Indians, see Dunmore to William Knox, March 22, 1777, DAR, 8:62, #337 and 337i; Henry Hamilton to Dartmouth, August 29–September 2, 1776, DAR, 10:365, #2035; John Stuart to George Germain, August 23, September 16 (three letters), 1776, DAR, 11:188–91, 12:223, n. 1; William Howe to George Germain, November 30, 1776, DAR, 12:264–66; Guy Johnson to George Germain, August 6, 9, November 25, 1776, NYCD, 8:682–83, 683–84, 687–88.

5. Gerald Howson, *Burgoyne of Saratoga: A Biography* (New York: Times Books, 1979); James Lunt, *John Burgoyne of Saratoga* (New York: Harcourt Brace Jovanovich, 1975).

6. William Howe to George Germain, December 20, 1776, DAR, 12:268–69.

7. King to North, February 24, 1777, correspondence of George III, 3:421; John Burgoyne, Thoughts on war from Canada, C.O. 42/36, folders 19–26.

8. William Howe to George Germain, January 17, 20, 1777, DAR, 14:28–30, 33.

9. For the official but unsigned evaluation of Burgoyne's plan, see Remarks on the Conduct of the War from Canada, March 5, 1777, and Remarks on the Requisition & observations, March 5, 1777, correspondence of George III, 3:443–44, 444–45; George Germain to William Howe, March 3, 1777, DAR, 14:46–47, 47–49; George Germain to King George III, March 18, 1777, correspondence of George III, 3:427.

10. Germain to Carleton, March 26, 1777, DAR, 14:53–56.

11. George Germain to Guy Carleton, February 19, 1777, C.O. 42/36, follows 41–42.

12. Carleton to Hamilton, September 26, 1777, MPHC, 9:351.

13. Guy Carleton to Richard Lernoult, February 1777, HP/PAC 21,678, follows 191; Guy Carleton to John Butler, February 9, 1777, HP/PAC 21,699:87.

14. Michael A. Belleiles, *Revolutionary Outlaws: Ethan Allen and the Struggle for Independence on the Early American Frontier* (Charlottesville: University of Virginia Press, 1993).

15. Oneida chiefs to Samuel Elmore, January 19, 1777, PCC, Item 153:59–60.

16. Barbara Graymount, *The Iroquois in the American Revolution* (Syracuse, N.Y.: Syracuse University Press, 1972), 113–14.

17. Samuel Kirkland to Philip Schuyler, January 19, 1777, Philip Schuyler to John Hancock, January 25, 1777, Samuel Elmore to Philip Schuyler, April 22, 1777, PCC, Item 153:71–73, 43–51, 124.

18. Philip Schuyler to Timothy Bedel, January 6, 1777, NYHSC for 1879, 59; Philip Schuyler to James Dean, February 6, 7, 1777, NYHSC for 1879, 72–73, 73–74; Timothy Bedel to Philip Schuyler, February 6, 16, 1777, N.H. Provincial Papers, 17:128–29, 129–30.

19. Samuel Kirkland to Indian commissioners, November 23, 1776, to April 1777, Philip Schuyler papers, box 13, New York Public Library.

20. Journal of New York Committee of Safety, February 10, 1777, New York convention to chiefs at Oneoghquaga, February 11, 1777, chiefs of Oneoghquaga to president and Great Council at Kingston, March 1, 1777, John Harper to New York convention, March 10, 1777, Journals of Provincial Congress, April 14, 1777, Journals of the Provincial Congress, 1:801–2, 802–3, 2:419, 1:879–80.

21. Daniel Claus, observations of Joseph Brant, [1780], Claus papers, 2:207–14; Daniel Claus, anecdotes of Joseph Brant, September 1778, Claus papers, 2:53–62; Philip Schuyler to Pierre Van Courtlandt, February 15, 1777, Journals of the Provincial Congress, 2:357.

22. John Butler to Guy Carleton, April 8, 1777, Captain Richard Lernoult to Guy Carleton, April 11, 1777, C.O. 42/36, folders 117, 133–34.

23. Eelking, *Riedesel,* 1:91–92; Samuel Mackay's report, March 31, 1777, HP/PAC 21,841, folders 42–45.

24. Robert Yates for Northern Department Indian commissioners to Henry Laurens, January 18, 1778, PPC, Item 166:377–80; Minutes of Northern Department Indian affairs commission, April 15, 1778, Papers of the Continental Congress, Item 153, 3:298–303.

25. Philip Schuyler to John Hancock, June 8, June 14, 1777, PCC, Item 153, 3:144–50, 152–58; Philip Schuyler to Peter Gansevoort, June 9, 1777, Philip Schuyler to James Dean, June 10, 1777, James Dean to Philip Schuyler, June 25, 1777, NYHSC for 1879, 100, 101–2, 118–19.

26. Claus, anecdotes of Joseph Brant, Claus papers, 2:53–62; Philip Schuyler to Goose Van Schaick, June 14, 1777, NYHSC for 1879, 107–9.

27. Nicolas Herkimer to Philip Schuyler, July 2, 1777, PCC, Item 63, 58–61; Philip Schuyler to Nicolas Herkimer, July 4, 1777, NYHSC for 1879, 134–36.

28. A Message from Iroquois to Virginians and Pennsylvanians, February 2, 1777, GMLB I.

29. William M. Darlington, ed., *Christopher Gist's Journals, with Historical, Geographical, and Ethnological Notes and Biographies of His Contemporaries* (Pittsburgh: J. R. Weldin & Co., 1893), 214–16.

30. Delaware council messages to George Morgan, February 26, March 29, 1777, George Morgan to Delaware council, March 6, 1777, GMLB I.

31. Heckewelder, *United Brethern among the Delaware and Mohegan,* 141–42.

32. George Rogers Clark diary, entries January 30 to April 23, 1777, George Rogers Clark memoir, 1773–1779, Clark papers, Collections of the Illinois Historical Library (IHC), 8:20–22, 215–16.

33. William Crawford to John Hancock, April 22, 1777, *Upper Ohio, 1775–1777,* 250–51.

34. John Mack Faragher, *Daniel Boone: The Life and Legend of an American Pioneer* (New York: Henry Holt, 1992), 147–49.

35. George Rogers Clark diary, April 24 to May 30, 1777, Clark papers, IHC, 8:20–22.

36. John Killbuck to George Morgan, June 7, 1777, Samuel Meason to Edward Hand, June 8, 1777, PA, 1, 5:444–45; George Rogers Clark diary, December 25, 1776, to March 30, 1778, Clark papers, IHC, 8:22.

37. Account of trade licenses for 1777, HP/PAC 21,722, folders 38; Louis Phelps Kellogg, *The British Regime in Wisconsin and the Northwest* (New York: Da Capo Press, 1971), 144; Harold Innis, *The Fur Trade in Canada* (New Haven, Conn.: Yale University Press, 1930), 186.

38. Henry Hamilton to Guy Carleton, March 22, 31, May 11, 1777, HP/PAC 21,841, folders 57–59; Reginald Horsman, *Matthew Elliott, British Indian Agent* (Detroit: Wayne State University, 1964), 14–17.

39. Guy Carleton to Arendt De Peyster, October 6, 1776, MPHSC, 10:270; Arendt De Peyster to Guy Carleton, May 26, June 9, July 12, 1777, C.O. 42/37, folders 37–38, 45–46, 51.

40. Petition of Daniel Murray, agent for contractors Patrick Kennedy and Thomas Bentley, March 31, 1777, in Clarence W. Alvord, ed., "Kaskaskia Records, 1778–1790," *Collections of the Illinois Historical Society* 5 (1909), 4–6; Rocheblave to Henry Hamilton, May 8, 1777, C.O. 42/37, folders 41–42; Edward Mason, ed., *Rocheblave Papers, 1776–1778, Vol. 4* (Chicago: Chicago Historical Society, 1890), 391–92.

41. Francisco Cruzat to Don Bernardo de Galvez, November 26, 1777, in Louis Houck, ed., *The Spanish Regime in Missouri: A Collection of Papers and Documents Relating to Upper Louisiana Principally within the Present Limits of Missouri during the Dominion of Spain, from the Archives of the Indies at Seville,* 2 vols. (Chicago: R. R. Donnelly & Sons Company, 1909), 1:134–36.

42. Mason, *Rocheblave Papers,* 389–90, 391–92.

43. Guy Carleton to Philippe de Rocheblave, October 28, 1776, in Edward Mason, ed., "Rocheblave Papers (1776–1778)," *Chicago Historical Society Collections* 4 (Chicago: Chicago Historical Society, 1890), 382–93; Guy Carleton to Henry Hamilton, May 16, 1777, MPHSC, 12:307–8.

44. Edward Abbott to Guy Carleton, April 15, May 4, May 26, 1777, June 9, C.O. 42/37, folders 35–36, C.O. 42/36, folders 302–3, C.O. 42/37, folders 37–38, C.O. 42/37, folders 45–46; Guy Carleton to Edward Abbott, September 2, 1777, HP/BM 21,699:172–73.

45. Dorsey Pentecost to William Harrod, January 28, 1777, *Upper Ohio, 1775–1777,* 226–27.

46. Zackwell Morgan to William Harrod, May 7, 1777, *Upper Ohio, 1775–1777,* 252 53.

47. For the definitive account of the Saratoga campaign, see Ketchum, *Saratoga.* See also George Athan Billias, ed., *George Washington's Opponents: British Generals and Admirals in the American Revolution* (New York: William Morrow and Company, 1969), 158–61, 174–75, 182–83; Brian Burns, "Massacre or Muster?: Burgoyne's Indians and the Militia at Bennington," *Vermont History* 45 (Summer 1777): 136–37; John R. Elting, *The Battles of Saratoga* (Monmouth Beach, N.J.: Philip Freneau Press, 1977).

48. Germain to Carleton, March 26, 1777 (no. 14), HP/BM 21,698, folders 3–4; Guy Carleton to Germain, May 20 (no. 19), May 22 (no. 20), May 23 (no. 21), June 27 (no. 25), 1777, C.O. 42/36, folders 94–106, 136–38, 140–41, 290–92.

49. William Howe to Guy Johnson, April 5, 1777, BAHQP, #476; Johnson to Howe, April 5, 1777, BAHQP, #477; Howe to Johnson, April 7, 1777, BAHQP, #479; Johnson to Howe, April 6, 1777, BAHQP, #478; Howe to Johnson, April 7, 1777, BAHQP, #480; Guy Johnson to George Germain, April 7, 1777, NYCD, 8:707.

50. Review of Guy Johnson's proceedings from the end of 1775, July 20, 1779, HP/BM 21,767, folders 133–15; Guy Johnson to George Germain, July 7, 1777, NYCD, 8:713–14.

51. William Howe to George Germain, April 2, 1777 (secret), DAR, 14:64–65; see also William Howe to Guy Carleton, April 5, 1777 (confidential), DAR, 14:66; for insights into Howe's character, see Levin Friedrich Ernst von Muenchhausen, *At General Howe's Side, 1776–1778: The Diary of General William Howe's Aide de*

Camp, Captain Friedrich von Muenchhausen, translated by Ernst Kipping and annotated by Samuel Smith (Monmouth, N.J.: Philip Freneau Press, 1974); Edward H. Tatum, ed., *The American Journal of Ambrose Serle, Secretary to Lord Howe, 1776–1778* (San Marino, Calif.: The Huntington Library, 1940).

52. Gen. John Burgoyne, *A State of the Expedition from Canada as Laid before the House of Commons by Lieutenant General Burgoyne* (London: Printed for J. Almon, 1780), 97, vi ff.; John Burgoyne to William Howe, July 2, 1777, DAR, 14:125. Burgoyne, *State of the Expedition,* 10–11, 97; John Burgoyne to George Germain, June 22, 1777, C.O. 42/36, folders 279–83.

53. Arthur St. Clair to Philip Schuyler, June 18 and 24, 1777, NYHSC for 1879, 12–13, 14–16.

54. John Burgoyne to George Germain, June 22, 1777, enclosing speech to Indians and their response, June 21, 1777, C.O. 42/36, folders 279–83, 285–87.

55. Arthur St. Clair to Philip Schuyler, June 26, 28, 30, July 2, 1777, NYHSC for 1879, 17–18, 18–19, 19–20, 69–70.

56. Elting, *The Battles of Saratoga,* 32–33.

57. Martin, *Benedict Arnold,* 350.

58. Burgoyne, *State of the Expedition,* 81; Stanley, *Want of a Horse,* 110–12.

59. John Burgoyne to William Howe, August 6, 1777, DAR, 14:156–57. See also Ketchum, *Saratoga,* 103, 163, 265–66.

60. Horatio Gates to John Burgoyne, September 2, 1777, John Burgoyne to Horatio Gates, September 6, 1777, in Henry Steele Commager and Richard B. Morris, eds., *The Spirit of Seventy-Six* (New York: Bonanza Books, 1983), 560–61; for the best account of the Jane McCrea tragedy, see June Namias, *White Captives: Gender and Ethnicity on the American Frontier* (Chapel Hill: University of North Carolina Press, 1993), chapter 4; see also James Austin Holden, "The Influence of the Death of Jane McCrea on Burgoyne's Campaign," *Proceedings of the New York State Historical Association* 12 (1913): 249–310; John Burgoyne to Simon Fraser, July 26, 1777, in C. T. Atkinson, ed., "Some Evidence for Burgoyne's Expedition," *Journal of the Society for Army Historical Research* 26 (Winter 1948): 132–42.

61. Smith, *New Age,* 2:948–62.

62. Ibid., 2:962–71.

63. Ibid., 2:978–91.

64. Extract from Detroit council, June 17, 1777, in Reuben Gold Thwaites and Louise P. Kellogg, eds., *Frontier Defense on the Upper Ohio, 1777–1778* (Madison: Wisconsin State Historical Society, 1912), 7–13 (hereafter cited as *Upper Ohio, 1777–1778*); Council at Detroit, June 17–24, 1777, C.O. 42/37, folders 70–77; George Germain to Guy Carleton, March 26, 1777, DAR, 14:51–53; Guy Carleton to Henry Hamilton, May 16 and May 21, 1777, MPHSC, 12:307–8.

65. Henry Hamilton to Guy Carleton, June 16 to July 3, 1777, Henry Hamilton to George Germain, June 17 to July 3, 1777, C.O. 42/37, folders 24–25, 57–66; David Zeisberger to Edward Hand, September 23, 1777, *Upper Ohio, 1777–1778*, 101–3.

66. Henry Hamilton to George Germain, September 5, 1777, C.O. 42/37, folders 172.

67. Henry Hamilton to Guy Carleton, n.d. [December 5, 1777], n.d. [January 15, 1778], MPHSC, 9:440–42.

68. Henry Hamilton to Guy Carleton, June 16 to July 3, 1777, Henry Hamilton to George Germain, June 17 to July 3, C.O., 42/37, folders 24–25, 57–66.

69. Guy Carleton to Henry Hamilton, September 15, 1777, MPC, 9:530.
70. Guy Carleton to George Germain, August 11, 1777, DAR, 14:157–58.
71. Quoted in Louise Phelps Kellogg, *Frontier Advance on the Upper Ohio* (Madison: University of Wisconsin Press, 1916), 18.
72. Clark diary, December 25, 1776, to March 30, 1778, Clark papers, IHC, 8:23.
73. Otis Rice, *The Allegheny Frontier: West Virginia Beginnings, 1730–1830* (Lexington: University of Kentucky Press, 1970), 96–97.
74. Heckewelder, *Narrative,* 165–66.
75. Henry Hamilton to Guy Carleton, n.d. [December 5, 1777], MPHSC, 19:440–42.
76. James Smith, *An Account of the Remarkable Occurances in the Life and Travels of Col. James Smith, during His Captivity with the Indians, in the Years 1755, '56, '57, '58, & '59* (Cincinnati: Robert Clarke & Co., 1870), 134–35.
77. Matthew Arbuckle to Edward Hand, October 6, November 7, 1777, Captain John Stuart narrative and Cornstalk murder deposition, November 10, 1777, David Zeisberger to Edward Hand, November 16, 1777, Edward Hand to Patrick Henry, December 9, 1777, Edward Hand to War Secretary, December 24, 1777, *Upper Ohio, 1777–1778,* 125–28, 149–50, 157–62, 164–67, 175–77, 189–90.
78. For accounts of that year's military operations, see Edward J. Cashin, *The King's Ranger: Thomas Brown and the American Revolution on the Southern Frontier* (Athens: University of Georgia Press, 1989), 58–72; O'Donnell, *Southern Indians,* 54–68.
79. George Germain to John Stuart, February 7, 1777, DAR, 14:35–37; see also George Germain to John Stuart, April 2, October 11, 1777, DAR, 14:63–64, 209–10.
80. John Stuart to Germain, January 24, 1777, C.O. 5/78/83–84.
81. William Knox to Grey Cooper, April 27, 1779, DAR, 17:112–13.
82. Charles Stuart to John Stuart, March 4, April 8, 1777, C.O. 5/78:126, 128.
83. John Stuart to Patrick Tonyn, July 21, 1777, DAR, 13:173.
84. John Stuart to Augustine Prevost, July 24, 1777, Public Record Office 30/55/6/629.
85. Quoted in O'Donnell, *Southern Indians,* 60.
86. Samuel Elbert to Creek leaders, August 13, 1777, C.O. 5/557/364–66.
87. John Stuart to Philotouchie and other Lower Creek deputies, October 20, 1777, PRO 30/55/710.
88. Augustine Prevost to Patrick Tonyn, December 20, 1777, C.O. 5/558:25–27; Patrick Tonyn to Augustine Prevost, December 24, 1777, C.O. 5/558:30–34; Patrick Tonyn to Germain, December 29, 1777, C.O. 5/558:102.
89. Barry St. Leger to John Burgoyne, n.p. [likely May 25, 1777], C.O. 42/36, follows 209–10; note on real size of St. Leger's force, 1777, Germain papers, 8 WCL; Daniel Claus to William Knox, October 16, 1777, NYCD, 8:719–21; John Butler, list of Indian Department officers, June 15, 1777, John Butler, list of rangers, June 15, 1777, C.O. 42/36, folders 321–22, 323; John Albert Scott, *Fort Stanwix (Fort Schuyler) and Oriskany* (Rome, N.Y.: Rome Sentinel Company, 1927); William W. Campbell, *The Border Warfare of New York during the Revolution; or, The Annals of Tryon County* (New York: Baker & Scribner, 1894); William Max Reid, *The Story of Old Fort Johnson* (New York: G. P. Putnam's Sons, 1906); Barry St. Leger to John Burgoyne, August 27, 1777, *The Spirit of Seventy-Six,* 564–65; Journal of William Colbraith, August 1 to August 6, 1777, *The Spirit of Seventy-Six,* 556–64, 566–57; Col. Marius Willet narrative, August 11, *The Spirit of Seventy-Six,* 565.

90. Guy Carleton to Mason Bolton, May 18, 1777, Guy Carleton to John Butler, May 18, 1777, C.O. 42/36, folders 193–94, 197–87.

91. Daniel Claus to William Knox, October 16, 1777, NYCD, 8:719.

92. Ibid., 8:720–21; John Butler to Guy Carleton, June 16, July 28, 1777, C.O. 42/36, follows 341–42; C.O. 42/37, folders 97–97.

93. Barbara Graymount, *The Iroquois and the American Revolution* (Syracuse, N.Y.: Syracuse University Press, 1972), 119–24, 126–28.

94. Barry St. Leger to Guy Carleton, n.d., NYCD, 8:721.

95. Barry St. Leger to Guy Carleton, August 27, 1777 (two letters), C.O. 42/37, folders 89–90, 91–95.

96. Barry St. Leger to Guy Carleton, August 27, DAR, 14:171–74; Daniel Claus to William Knox, October 16, 1777, NYCD, 8:720–21.

97. Frederick Cook, ed., *Journals of the Military Expedition of Major General John Sullivan against the Six Nations of Indians in 1779* (Auburn, N.Y.: Knapp, Peck, and Thompson, 1887), 479 (hereafter cited as *Sullivan's Journals*).

98. Barry St. Leger to Peter Gansevoort, August 9, 1777, DAR, 14:171–74.

99. Peter Gansevoort to Barry St. Leger, August 9, 1777, quoted in John F. Luzander, Louis Torres, and Orville W. Carroll, *Fort Stanwix: History, Historic Furnishings, and Historic Structure Reports* (Washington, D.C.: Office of Park Historic Preservation, National Park Service, U.S. Department of Interior, 1976), 48.

100. Adam Crysler journal, in James J. Talman, ed., *Loyalist Narratives from Upper Canada* (Toronto: The Champlain Society, 1946), 56–57.

101. Ernest A. Cruikshank, *The King's Royal Regiment of New York* (Toronto: Ontario Historical Society, 1984), 20.

102. John Burgoyne to William Howe, August 6, 1777, DAR, 14:156–67.

103. John Burgoyne to Friedrich Baum, August 9, 1777, Friedrich Baum to John Burgoyne, August 12, 13, 1777, Burgoyne, *State of the Expedition,* reprinted in Karl J. R. Arndt, "New Hampshire and the Battle of Bennington: Colonel Baum's Mission and Bennington Defeat as Reported by a German Officer under General Burgoyne's Command," *Historical New Hampshire* 32 (Winter 1977): 202–7.

104. Hoffman Nickerson, *The Turning Point of the Revolution; or, Burgoyne in America* (Boston: Houghton Mifflin, 1928), 2:224–63; Elting, *The Battles of Saratoga,* 196–200.

105. John Burgoyne to George Germain, August 20, 1777 (two letters), DAR, 14:162–65.

106. Nickerson, *Turning Point,* 322–26; Elting, *Battles of Saratoga,* 47, 68.

107. Elting, *Battles of Saratoga,* 50–55.

108. Beating orders to John Butler, appointed major, September 15, 1777, HP/BM 21,700:2–4; Daniel Claus to William Knox, October 16, November 6, 1777, NYCD, 8:719–23, 723–26.

109. Graymount, *Iroquois in the American Revolution,* 163.

110. Daniel Claus to William Knox, November 6, 1777, NYCD, 8:723–26.

111. John Butler to Guy Carleton, February 2, 1777 [with enclosure of December council notes], C.O. 42/38, folders 108–11; John Butler to Guy Carleton, December 14, 1777 (no. 2), MPHSC, 19:340.

112. Caughey, *Galvez,* 91–92; Robert V. Haynes, *The Natchez District and the American Revolution* (Jackson: University of Mississippi Press, 1976), 38–49.

113. Caughey, *Galvez,* 91.

114. Ibid., 136.

CHAPTER 6

1. Jonathan Dull, *The French Navy and American Independence: A Study of Arms and Diplomacy, 1774–1787* (Princeton, N.J.: Princeton University Press, 1975), 359–60.

2. Piers Mackesy, *The War for America, 1775–1783* (Cambridge: Harvard University Press, 1965), 139–40; Gruber, *The Howe Brothers,* 252–61, 268–77; Willcox, *The Portrait of a General,* 197–210; Eric Robson, *The American Revolution in Its Political and Military Aspects, 1763–1783* (New York: W. W. Norton and Company, 1966), 177–78.

3. The Parliamentary Register, 1st series, 9 (1777–78), 145–49.

4. Ibid.

5. Return of troops in Canada, July 30, 1778, correspondence George III, 4:182; see also Gustave Lanctot, *Canada and the American Revolution, 1774–1783* (Cambridge: Harvard University Press, 1967), 176–77.

6. George Washington to Congress committee, January 29, 1778, Jared Sparks, ed., *Correspondence of the American Revolution, Being Letters of Eminent Men to Washington, 1775–1789,* 4 vols. (Boston: Russell, 1834–37), 10:400–1.

7. Johnstown treaty minutes, March 7–10, 1778, Philip Schuyler papers, box 14, NYPL; Philip Schuyler to Henry Laurens, March 15, 1778, NYHSC for 1879, 200–2.

8. Mary Beacock Fryer, *King's Men: The Soldier Founders of Ontario* (Toronto: Dundurn Press Limited, 1980), 224.

9. John Butler to Guy Carleton, April 10, 1778, C.O. 42/38, folder 112. Paul A. W. Wallace, *Indians in Pennsylvania* (Harrisburg: Pennsylvania Historical and Museum Commission, 1981), 161–62.

10. Daniel Claus, anecdotes of Joseph Brant, Claus papers, 2:53–63; Guy Johnson to George Germain, September 10, 1778, NYCD, 8:752; Taylor and Duffin to Daniel Claus, October 26, 1778, MPHSC, 19:360–62; Ernest Cruikshank, *The Story of Butler's Rangers and the Settlement of Niagara* (Niagara Falls, Ont.: Reknown, 1988), 43; Graymount, *Iroquois in the Revolution,* 165–66.

11. Graymount, *Iroquois in the Revolution,* 166–67.

12. Henry Hamilton to Guy Carleton, January 15, 1778, MPC, 9:430–33; Proclamation of Henry Hamilton, January 5, 1778, GMLB III; Henry Hamilton to Guy Carleton, [January 15, 1778], HP/MPHSC, 9:430–33.

13. Henry Hamilton to Guy Carleton, April 25, 1778, HP/MPHSC 9:433–37; John Filson, *The Discovery, Settlement, and Present State of Kentucke* (New York: Readex Microprint Corporation, 1966), 64–65. For an excellent secondary account, see John Mack Faragher, *Daniel Boone: The Life and Legend of an American Pioneer* (New York: Henry Holt and Company, 1992), 154–65.

14. Lyman Copeland Draper interview with Nathan and Olive Boone, 1851, Draper manuscript 6S122, University of Wisconsin, Madison.

15. Henry Hamilton to Guy Carleton, April 25, 1778, MPC, 9:433–37.

16. Henry Hamilton to Guy Carleton [January 15, 1778], MPC, 9:430–33; Guy Carleton to Henry Hamilton, March 14, 1778, MPC, 9:351–52.

17. Edward Hand to William Crawford, February 5, 1778, Edward Hand to Jasper Ewing, March 7, 1778, *Upper Ohio, 1777–1778* 202–4, 215–20.

18. George Morgan to Captain White Eyes, March 20, 1778, commissioners to Captain White Eyes, March 27, 1778, George Morgan to Delaware chiefs, March 27, 1778, *Upper Ohio, 1777–1778,* 228–29, 234–37, 241–44.

19. Heckewelder, *Narrative,* 170–71; David Zeisberger to George Morgan, April 6, 1778, GMLB III.
20. Heckewelder, *Narrative,* 170–82.
21. William McKee to Edward Hand, June 21, 1778, *Frontier Advance,* 98.
22. Paul Taylor, notes, *Frontier Advance,* 69, 67–70.
23. Matthew Arbuckle to Edward Hand, June 2, 1778, *Frontier Advance,* 64–65; John Stuart narrative, *Frontier Advance,* 70–73; David Zeisberger to George Morgan, June 9, 1778, *Frontier Advance,* 82–83; Arthur Campbell to Charles Cummings, June 10, 1778, *Frontier Advance,* 85–87.
24. Edward Hand to the Delawares, June 16, 1778, *Frontier Advance,* 92.
25. Detroit council minutes, June 14–20, 1778, MPHSC, 9:442–52; Detroit council, June 29–July 3, 1778, MPHSC, 9:452–58.
26. White Eyes to George Morgan, July 19, 1778, *Frontier Advance,* 18.
27. David Zeisberger to George Morgan, July 19, 1778, *Frontier Advance,* 119.
28. Henry Hamilton to Hector Cramahe, August 17, 1778, Henry Hamilton to Frederick Haldimand, n.d. [September 1778], MPHSC, 9:463–64, 464–69; Jehu Hay to Dederick Brehm, n.d. [August 17, 1778], HP/BM 21,841, folders 89–90; accounts of bills drawn by Henry Hamilton, MPHSC, 20:206–7; Petition of Committee, Harrodsburg, June 20, 1776, IHC, 8:15.
29. Hamilton to Cramahe, August 12, 1778, second of two letters, MPC, 9:462, 461–62.
30. Henry Hamilton to Hector Cramahe, August 12, 1778, HP/MPSHC, 9:462.
31. Edward Abbott to Guy Carleton, June 8, 1778, MPC, 9:488–89.
32. Raport general des sauvages arrive d'enhaut . . . printemps, 1778, Haldimand papers, 21779; Wayne E. Stevens, *The Northwest Fur Trade, 1763–1800* (Urbana: University of Illinois Press, 1928), 57–65.
33. Arendt De Peyster to Guy Carleton, May 30, June 29, 1778, HP/MPSHC, 9:365–66, 366–67; David A. Armour and Keith R. Wilder, *At the Crossroads: Michilimackinac during the Revolution* (Mackinac Island, Mich.: Mackinac Island State Park Commission, 1978), 217.
34. Haldimand to Hamilton, August 6, 1778, MPC, 9:399–402; Jean N. McIlwraith, *Sir Frederick Haldimand* (Toronto: Morang & Co., 1905).
35. Faragher, *Daniel Boone,* 198.
36. For the best accounts of the campaign, see memorandum of Indian operations from 1778 to 1780, in C. E. Cartwright, ed., *The Life and Letters of the Late Honorable Richard Cartwright* (Toronto: Belford Brothers, 1876), 30–32; John Butler to Mason Bolton, July 8, 1778, HP/BM 21,760, folders 31–34; Journal of Adam Chrysler, in James J. Talman, ed., *Loyalist Narratives from Upper Canada* (Toronto: The Champlain Society, 1946), 58; Carl F. Klinck and James J. Talman, eds., *The Journal of John Norton, 1815* (Toronto: The Champlain Society, 1970), 275–76; Journal of Richard McGinnis, *The Spirit of Seventy-Six,* 1006–7; Zebulon Butler to Board of War, July 10, 1778, in Henry B. Dawson, *Battles of the United States, by Sea and Land: Embracing Those of the Revolutionary and Indian Wars, the War of 1812, and the Mexican War; with Important Official Documents,* 2 vols. (New York: Johnson, Fry, and Company, 1859), 1:429–30; Nathan Denison to Jonathan Trumball, July 28, 1778, in Julian P. Boyd and Robert J. Taylor, eds., *The Susquehanna Company Papers,* 11 vols. (Ithaca, N.Y.: Cornell University Press, 1930–71), 7:47–48; Graymont, *Iroquois in the Revolution,* 168–72; Cruikshank, *Butler's Rangers,* 46–51.

37. Mr. Slocum's account related to Lt. Col. Henry Dearborn, journal, in Frederick Cook, ed., *Journals of the Military Expedition of Major General John Sullivan against the Six Nations* (Auburn, N.Y.: Knapp, Peck, Thompson, 1887), 65 (hereafter cited as *Journals*).

38. Butler to Mason Bolton, July 8, 1776, C.O. 42/38, folder 169–70.

39. "John Burrowes Journal," *Journals,* 50.

40. Peter Bellinger to Peter Gansevoort, July 19, 1778, General Military Papers, 4, NYPL; Henry Glen to Peter Gansevoort, July 24, 1778, General Military Papers, Clinton papers, 3:475–76, 559, 581–82.

41. Graymont, *Iroquois in the Revolution,* 178–80.

42. Ibid., 174, 179, 180, 181–82.

43. Ibid., 184–91.

44. "Diary of Captain Benjamin Warren in 1778," ed. David E. Alexander, *Journal of American History* 3 (1909): 383.

45. Clinton to Jay, November 17, 1778, *Public Papers of George Clinton,* ed. Hugh Hastings and J. A. Holden, 10 vols. (New York: AMS Press, 1968–78), 4:289–90.

46. Allan's Report, November 21, 1776, *Military Operations,* 166–79.

47. Allan's first report to Massachusetts Council [1777], Allan report, November 21, 1776, *Military Operations,* 165–66, 166–79.

48. Alexander Campbell report, July 13, 1777, *Military Operations,* 197–99.

49. John Allan journal, British account, *Military Operations,* 134, 26–34, 224–28.

50. Germain to Henry Clinton, March 8, 1778, Commager and Morris, *Spirit of Seventy-Six,* 1075.

51. John Stuart to Patrick Tonyn, July 10, 1778, C.O. 5/80/235–38.

52. K. G. Davies, ed., *Documents of the American Revolution,* 21 vols. (Shannon: Irish University Press, 1972–81), 15:13; O'Donnell, *Southern Indians,* 77.

53. O'Donnell, *Southern Indians,* 71–72; Saunders and Clark, eds., *State Papers of North Carolina,* 24:15.

54. Much of this section's information comes from the at times contradictory accounts of Wilbur Henry Siebert, *Loyalists in East Florida, 1774 to 1785: The Most Important Documents Pertaining Thereto, Edited with an Accompanying Narrative* (Boston: Gregg Press, 1972); Edward Cashin, *The King's Ranger: Thomas Brown and the American Revolution* (Athens: University of Georgia Press, 1989).

55. Siebert, *East Florida Loyalists,* 52–54, 60–61.

56. Cashin, *King's Ranger,* 80.

57. Smith, *New Age,* 2:1306–7.

58. Robert V. Haynes, *The Natchez District and the American Revolution* (Jackson: University of Mississippi Press, 1976), 51–75.

59. Ibid., 73.

60. Caughey, *Galvez,* 137.

61. Ibid., 123–24.

62. Ibid., 129.

63. Ibid.

64. Ibid., 130.

65. Congressional Resolution, June 11, 1778, *Frontier Advance,* 88; Report of Board of War, June 10, 1778, C.O. Item 147, 2:81–85.

66. Edward Hand to Horatio Gates, May 14, 1778, *Frontier Advance,* 50.

67. Timothy Pickering to George Washington, May 19, 1778, *Frontier Advance*, 55.
68. Edward Hand to Horatio Gates, April 28, 1778, *Frontier Advance*, 49.
69. Washington to Congress, May 12, 1778, George Washington to Lachlan McIntosh, May 26, 1778, *Frontier Advance*, 60.
70. George Washington to Timothy Pickering, May 23, 1778, *Frontier Advance*, 57–59; George Washington to Richard Campbell, May 24, 1778, *Frontier Advance*, 59–60; George Washington to William Russell, May 28, 1778, *Frontier Advance*, 61; Henry Laurens to Horatio Gates, June 6, 1778, CC, Item 13, 1:366.
71. Virginia council resolution, July 7, 1778, *Frontier Advance*, 104.
72. George Morgan to War Board, July 17, 1778, *Frontier Advance*, 12–13.
73. George Morgan to Delawares, July 12, 1778, *Frontier Advance*, 112, 110–12.
74. Congress resolution, July 25, 1778, *Frontier Advance*, 121.
75. Edward Hand to Mrs. Hand, August 6, 1778, *Frontier Advance*, 125.
76. John Leith to George Morgan, August 19, 1778, *Frontier Advance*, 130, 129–31.
77. Baubee to George Morgan, August 16, 1778, *Frontier Advance*, 129.
78. David Zeisberger to Fort Pitt commissioners, August 25, 1778, *Frontier Advance*, 133.
79. Treaty at Fort Pitt, September 12, 1778, *Frontier Advance*, 141, 138–45.
80. Headquarters order, September 21, 1778, *Frontier Advance*, 433.
81. David Zeisberger to George Morgan, January 20, 1779, *Frontier Advance*, 201–2.
82. John Killbuck to George Morgan, January 20, 1779, *Frontier Advance*, 203; Delaware chiefs to Washington and Congress, May 10, 1779, *Frontier Advance*, 320.
83. Headquarters orders, October 21, 1778, *Frontier Advance*, 436.
84. Headquarters orders, November 12, 1778, *Frontier Advance*, 443.
85. Court martials, June 6–20, 1778, *Frontier Advance*, 415–20.
86. Headquarters orders, August 9, 1778, *Frontier Advance*, 425.
87. Headquarters orders, October 9, 1778, *Frontier Advance*, 435.
88. General orders, October 26, 1778, *Frontier Advance*, 438.
89. Headquarters order, October 22, 1778, *Frontier Advance*, 437.
90. Lachlan McIntosh to William Fleming, October 30, 1778, *Frontier Advance*, 154–55; Youghiogany Magistrates to Lachlan McIntosh, October 27, 1778, *Frontier Advance*, 151–52.
91. John Cuppy recollections, *Frontier Advance*, 159.
92. Lachlan McIntosh to Delawares, November 22, 1778, *Frontier Advance*, 179.
93. John Cuppy recollections, *Frontier Advance*, 160.
94. Jacob White recollections, *Frontier Advance*, 163.
95. Lachlan McIntosh to War Board, January 11, 1779, *Frontier Advance*, 197–99.
96. William Christian to Stephen Trigg, November 22, 1778, *Frontier Advance*, 177–78; Lachlan McIntosh to George Bryan, official report, December 29, 1778, *Frontier Advance*, 183.
97. Patrick Henry to George Rogers Clark, January 2, 1778 (two letters), in Seineke, *Clark Adventure*, 214–15; Wythe, Mason, and Jefferson to Clark, January 3, 1776, *Clark Adventure*, 216.
98. John Campbell to George Rogers Clark, June 8, 1778, *Clark Adventure*, 242–43.
99. George Rogers Clark, *Clark's Memoir from English's Conquest of the Country* (Ann Arbor, Mich.: University Microfilms, 1966), 475–76.
100. Clark, *Clark Memoir*, 492–503.

101. Barnhart, Hamilton journal, 111; Beaubin's account, September 27, 1778, Haldimand papers, 21782.
102. Clark to Leyba, November 6, 1778, *Galvez,* 133.
103. Caughey, *Galvez,* 98–101.
104. Rapport general des milices & de la Compagnie des Volontaires du Detroit, 30 Aout, 1778, HP/BM 21,782, folders 92.
105. Hamilton to Germain via Carleton, August 8, 1778, IHC, 1:330–31; De Peyster to Haldimand, August 15, 1778, IHC, 1:334–35; De Peyster to Haldimand, August 31, 1778, MPC, 9:369–70; Haldimand to Hamilton, August, 26, 27, 1778, MPC, 9:402–4, 404; Haldimand to De Peyster, August 30, 1778, MPC, 9:353–34; Hamilton to Dartmouth, September 2, 1776, MPHSC, 10:264–70; Hamilton to Haldimand, September 16, 1778, MPC, 9:475–77; De Peyster to Haldimand, September 21, 1778, MPC, 9:371–73; Henry Hamilton to Frederick Haldimand, September 22 to October 3, 1778, HP/MPHSC, 9:477–82.
106. Hamilton to Haldimand, October 7, 1778, MPC, 9:486–87.
107. Barnhart, Hamilton journal, 128.
108. Ibid., 131.
109. Ibid., 147.
110. Ibid., December 17, 1778, 147–49, December 30, 1778, 159; Hamilton to Haldimand, December 18, 1778, Haldimand papers, 21781.
111. Leonard Helm to George Clark, December [17], 1778, IHC, 1:226.
112. Barnhart, Hamilton journal, 150–51.

CHAPTER 7
1. Jonathan R. Dull, *A Diplomatic History of the American Revolution* (New Haven, Conn.: Yale University Press, 1985), 110.
2. For the campaign, see Caughey, *Galvez,* 137, 153–62.
3. Caughey, *Galvez;* William Coker and Robert Rhea, eds., *Anglo-Spanish Confrontation on the Gulf Coast during the Revolution* (Pensacola, Fla.: Gulf Coast History and Humanities Conference, 1982).
4. Cashin, *King's Ranger,* 101; O'Donnell, *Southern Indians,* 80–94.
5. Alexander Cameron to Germain, May 10, 1779, C.O. 5/80/171–74.
6. David Taitt to Germain, August 6, 1778, C.O. 5/80/235 38.
7. Germain to Alexander Cameron and Thomas Brown, June 25, 1779, C.O. 5/81:123; Germain to John Campbell, August 5, 1779, C.O. 5/597, pt. 1:224.
8. Quoted in O'Donnell, *Southern Indians,* 92.
9. Smith, *New Age,* 1343–47, 1353–58.
10. Clark, *Clark's Memoir,* 516–17.
11. George Rogers Clark to Patrick Henry, February 3, 1779, *Clark Adventure,* 348–49.
12. Clark, *Clark Memoir,* 519.
13. George Rogers Clark to John Rogers, February 3, 1779, *Clark Adventure,* 349.
14. Clark, *Clark Memoir,* 521; Clark to Mason, November 19, 1779, IHC, 8:139, 142; Bowman journal, IHC, 8:156.
15. Bowman journal, February 23, 1779, IHC, 8:159.
16. Clark, *Clark Memoir,* 522.
17. Hamilton troop returns, December 24, 1778, January 30, 1779, Canadian Archives, B 122:253, 287–88.

18. Barnhardt, Hamilton journal, 176–77.
19. Clark, *Clark Memoir,* 524.
20. Bowman journal, February 23, 1779, IHC, 8:159.
21. Clark, *Clark Memoir,* 528.
22. Barnhart, Hamilton journal, 180.
23. Ibid., 180, 181.
24. Ibid., 182–83.
25. Ibid.
26. Ibid., 183.
27. Ibid., 184.
28. Inventory at Fort William Henry, March 9, 1779, *Clark Adventure,* 358–60.
29. Barnhart, Hamilton journal, 187–88.
30. Virginia Council, July 23, 1778, *Frontier Advance,* 40–44.
31. Faragher, *Daniel Boone,* 209.
32. Barnhart, Hamilton journal, 200, 196.
33. Washington to Jefferson, July 10, 1779, Fitzpatrick, *Writings of Washington,* 15:401.
34. John Gibson to Lachlan McIntosh, February 13, 1779, *Frontier Advance,* 224–25.
35. Lachlan McIntosh to Archibald Lochry, January 29, 1779, *Frontier Advance,* 210; Henry Jolly reminiscences, *Frontier Advance,* 211.
36. Benjamin Biggs recollections, *Frontier Advance,* 257.
37. George Washington to Daniel Brodhead, May 10, 1779, *Frontier Advance,* 315–17.
38. Anonymous letter, April 20, 1779, *Frontier Advance,* 292; Lachlan McIntosh to George Washington, March 12, 1779, *Frontier Advance,* 240–42; Benjamin Biggs recollections, *Frontier Advance,* 256–57; John Heckewelder to Daniel Brodhead, April 9, 1779, *Frontier Advance,* 282–83.
39. Archibald Lochry to Daniel Brodhead, May 1, 1779, *Frontier Advance,* 299.
40. James Chambers recollections, *Frontier Advance,* 300; Samuel Moorhead to Daniel Brodhead, April 27, 1779, *Frontier Advance,* 295.
41. Brodhead letter, June 24, 1779, *Frontier Advance,* 373–74; Henry Jolly recollections, *Frontier Advance,* 374–75; Peter Henry recollections, *Frontier Advance,* 376–78.
42. George Washington to Lachlan McIntosh, February 15, 1779, *Frontier Advance,* 226–27.
43. Daniel Brodhead to George Washington, January 16, 1779, *Frontier Advance,* 200; John Dodge to Congress, January 25, 1779, *Frontier Advance,* 206–10.
44. George Washington to Daniel Brodhead, February 15, 1779, *Frontier Advance,* 230–31.
45. Congress resolution, February 20, 1779, *Frontier Advance,* 233.
46. George Washington to Daniel Brodhead, March 5, 1779, *Frontier Advance,* 238–40.
47. John Morgan to Daniel Brodhead, January 31, 1779, Morgan papers, GMLB, book 3.
48. Daniel Brodhead to Wyandots, April 8, 1779, *Frontier Advance,* 278.
49. Delaware chiefs to Brodhead, April 9, 1779, *Frontier Advance,* 282; Daniel Brodhead to George Washington, May 3, 1779, *Frontier Advance,* 306; George Washington to Daniel Brodhead, May 21, 1779, *Frontier Advance,* 332–33.
50. Delaware chiefs to Brodhead, June 17, 1779, *Frontier Advance,* 363.
51. Cherokee and Daniel Brodhead council, July 18, 1779, *Frontier Advance,* 392, 400.

52. Daniel Brodhead to Washington, September 16, 1779, *Sullivan's Journals,* 307–8; Daniel Brodhead to Sullivan, August 6, October 10, 1779, *Sullivan's Journals,* 3:93–94, 147–48.
53. Brodhead to Washington, September 10, 1779, *Sullivan's Journals,* 308.
54. Ibid., 309.
55. Capt. Thomas Machin journal, *Sullivan's Journals,* 192–94; Alexander Scrammel, Middle Brook headquarters, Capt. Thomas Machin journal, *Sullivan's Journals,* 193–94.
56. George Washington to John Sullivan, March 6, 1779, in Otis G. Hammond, ed., *The Letters and Papers of Major-General John Sullivan, Continental Army,* 3 vols. (Concord, N.H.: New Hampshire Historical Society, 1931), 2:530–31 (hereafter cited as Sullivan papers).
57. John Sullivan to Horatio Gates, March 17, 23, 1779, Sullivan papers, 2:535–36, 542.
58. Washington instructions to Sullivan, May 31, 1779, Sullivan papers, 3:49.
59. Ibid., 3:51.
60. Ibid., 3:52.
61. Ibid., 3:50.
62. Sullivan to Washington, May 31, Sullivan papers, 3:47.
63. Lt. Col. Henry Dearborn journal, Sullivan papers, 64.
64. Ibid.
65. Pennsylvania Council to Sullivan, May 21, 1779, Sullivan papers, 3:31; Sullivan to Pennsylvania president Joseph Reed, May 11, June 3, 1779, Sullivan papers, 3:19, 54–56.
66. Sullivan to Washington, May 26, 1779, Sullivan papers, 3:42–43; Sullivan to Washington, June 29, 1779, Sullivan papers, 3:65–66; Adam Hubley to Sullivan, July 2, 1779, Sullivan papers, 3:69–71.
67. Washington to Sullivan, May 28, 1779, Sullivan papers, 3:44; Washington to Sullivan, May 24, 1779, Sullivan papers, 3:40–41.
68. Ephraim Blaine to Sullivan, May 24, 1779, Sullivan papers, 3:39.
69. Sullivan to Joseph Reed, May 31, 1779, Sullivan papers, 3:46–47; Joseph Reed to Sullivan, June 3, 1779, Sullivan papers, 3:54–56.
70. Sullivan to Washington, July 10, 1779, Sullivan papers, 3:76; Board of War to Sullivan, July 21, 1779, Sullivan papers, 3:78–80.
71. Edward Hand to John Sullivan, May 20, 1779, Sullivan papers, 3:26–27.
72. Extracts of letters from Philip Schuyler and Volckert Douw, July 24 and 27, 1779, Sullivan papers, 3:84–85.
73. Sullivan to Washington, April 16, 1779, Sullivan papers, 3:6.
74. Sullivan order of march, May 24, 1779, Sullivan papers, 3:36–38; Sullivan's officer roster, 1779, *Sullivan's Journals,* 315–29.
75. Sullivan orders, headquarters, Wyoming, June 25, *Sullivan's Journals,* 118.
76. Major James Norris journal, *Sullivan's Journals,* 227.
77. Washington to Sullivan, August 1, 1779, *Sullivan's Journals,* 3:90.
78. Nathaniel Greene to Sullivan, June 21, 1779, *Sullivan's Journals,* 3:64.
79. Sullivan to John Jay, July 21, *Sullivan's Journals,* 80.
80. Sullivan to President of Congress, July 26, 1779, *Sullivan's Journals,* 3:86.
81. Sullivan to Washington, July 10, 1779, *Sullivan's Journals,* 3:75; Washington to Sullivan, July 1, 1779, *Sullivan's Journals,* 66–69.

82. Sullivan to James Clinton, July 11, 1779, *Sullivan's Journals*, 3:78.

83. For these dispositions, see Sullivan to John Jay, July 21, 1779, *Sullivan's Journals*, 3:83.

84. "Diary of Lieutenant Colonel Henry Dearborn," *Sullivan's Journals*, 71.

85. Maj. James Norris journal, *Sullivan's Journals*, 229.

86. "Jabez Campfield Journal," *Sullivan's Journals*, 54.

87. Ibid., 60.

88. Sullivan to President of Congress, August 15, 1779, *Sullivan's Journals*, 3:95–98.

89. Sullivan to Washington, August 15, 1779, *Sullivan's Journals*, 3:99, 100.

90. Maj. James Norris journal, *Sullivan's Journals*, 229.

91. Sullivan to Washington, June 29, 1779, *Sullivan's Journals*, 3:66; Reverend William Rogers letter, *Sullivan's Journals*, 252.

92. Lt. William McKendry journal, *Sullivan's Journals*, 198–212.

93. Maj. Jeremiah Fogg journal, *Sullivan's Journals*, 94.

94. Lt. Col. Henry Dearborn journal, *Sullivan's Journals*, 64.

95. Maj. Jeremiah Fogg journal, *Sullivan's Journals*, 94.

96. Sgt. Moses Fellows journal, *Sullivan's Journals*, 87.

97. Maj. Jeremiah Fogg journal, *Sullivan's Journals*, 95.

98. "Jabez Campfield Journal," *Sullivan's Journals*, 60.

99. Maj. Jeremiah Fogg journal, *Sullivan's Journals*, 97.

100. Lt. Col. Henry Dearborn journal, *Sullivan's Journals*, 71.

101. Sullivan to Oneida Indians, September 1, 1779, *Sullivan's Journals*, 3:114.

102. Sullivan to Washington, August 30, 1779, *Sullivan's Journals*, 3:110–11, 107–12.

103. Maj. Jeremiah Fogg journal, *Sullivan's Journals*, 95.

104. Ibid., 96.

105. Maj. John Burrowes journal, *Sullivan's Journals*, 45.

106. Ibid., 45.

107. "Lieutenant William Barton Journal," *Sullivan's Journals*, 13.

108. Maj. John Burrowes journal, *Sullivan's Journals*, 47.

109. Lt. Col. Henry Dearborn journal, *Sullivan's Journals*, 75.

110. Sullivan to John Jay, September 30, 1779, *Sullivan's Journals*, 3:132.

111. Sullivan to Oneida, 1779, *Sullivan's Journals*, 117:116–19.

112. Sullivan to Peter Gansevoort, September 20, 1779, *Sullivan's Journals*, 3:122–23; Peter Gansevoort to Sullivan, October 8, 1779, *Sullivan's Journals*, 3:145–46.

113. Sullivan to John Jay, September 30, 1779, *Sullivan's Journals*, 123–37.

114. Sullivan to Washington, November 6, 1779, *Sullivan's Journals*, 158; Sullivan to President of Congress, November 6, 1779, *Sullivan's Journals*, 3:161–62; Action of Congress, November 15, 1779, *Sullivan's Journals*, 3:162–63; Sullivan's resignation accepted by Congress, November 30, 1779, *Sullivan's Journals*, 3:163–66.

115. Donald R. McAdams, "The Sullivan Expedition: Success or Failure?" *New York Historical Society Quarterly* 54 (1970): 62–75; Sullivan to John Jay, September 30, 1779, *Sullivan's Journals*, 3:134; Bolton to Haldimand, October 2, November 10, 1779, Add. mss., 21,760, folder 226, 244.

116. Sullivan to John Jay, September 30, 1779, *Sullivan's Journals*, 3:135.

117. McAdams, "Sullivan Expedition," 70–73; John H. Carter, "Indian Incursions in Old Northumberland County during the Revolutionary War, 1777–1782," in Snyder, ed., *Northumberland County*, 373–80.

118. Butler to Haldimand, September 20, 1779, Haldimand papers, Add. mss., 21,765, folders 140–41.
119. Maj. Jeremiah Fogg journal, *Sullivan's Journals,* 101.

CHAPTER 8
1. Smith, *New Age,* 2:1392.
2. Clark to Todd, March 1780, IHC, 8:404; Dodge to Jefferson, August 1, 1780, IHC, 8:437–38; De Peyster to Bolton, June 27, 1780, MPHC, 19:536–37; Le Gras to Clark, December 1, 1780, IHC, 8:469; Cruzat to Galvez, November 14, 1780, Lawrence Kinnaird, *Spain in the Mississippi Valley, 1765–95* (Washington, D.C.: Government Printing Office, 1949), 2:398–99 (hereafter cited as *Spain in the Mississippi Valley); Speeches to Crozat, 1780, Spain,* 2:401–2.
3. Jonathan R. Dull, *A Diplomatic History of the American Revolution* (New Haven, Conn.: Yale University Press, 1985), 110.
4. Horatio Gates to George Washington, August 20, 1780, Gates papers, NYHS.
5. Smith, *New Age,* 2:1415–16.
6. Caughey, *Galvez,* 174–86.
7. Ibid.; Robert Haynes, *The Natchez District and the American Revolution* (Jackson: University of Mississippi Press, 1976), 127–29.
8. James H. O'Donnell III, "Hamstrung by Penury: Alexander Cameron's Failure at Pensacola," in Coker and Rhea, *Anglo-Spanish Confrontation on the Gulf Coast,* 82.
9. Alexander Cameron to Germain, October 31, 1780, May 27, 1781, DAR, 18:221–22, 20:150.
10. Eric Beerman, "Jose Solano and the Spanish Navy at the Siege of Pensacola," in Coker and Rhea, *Anglo-Spanish Confrontation on the Gulf Coast,* 125–26.
11. Cameron to Germain, October 31, 1780, C.O. 5/82, folder 111.
12. Samuel Cole Willams, *Tennessee during the Revolutionary War* (Knoxville: University of Tennesse Press, 1974), 104–16, 167–79.
13. Graymont, *Iroquois in the Revolution,* 224–29.
14. Brant letter, April 10, 1780, CC, Item 67, 258.
15. Graymont, *Iroquois in the Revolution,* 229.
16. Earle Thomas, *Sir John Johnson, Loyalist Baronet* (Toronto: Dundurn Press, 1986), 88.
17. Graymont, *Iroquois in the Revolution,* 234–37.
18. Thomas Jefferson to George Rogers Clark, January 1, 29, 1780, John Montgomery to George Rogers Clark, May 1780, *Clark Adventure,* 418, 418–20, 439–40.
19. James Neal Primm, *Lion of the Valley: St. Louis, Missouri* (Boulder, Colo.: Pruett Publishing, 1981), 45.
20. Don Rickey, "The British-Indian Attack on St. Louis, May 26, 1780," *Missouri Historical Review* 55 (1960): 44, 35–45; John Rogers to George Rogers Clark, May 15, 1780, *Clark Adventure,* 434.
21. John Rogers to George Rogers Clark, July 22, 1780, *Clark Adventure,* 445.
22. Sinclair to Haldimand, July 8, 1780, WHC, 11:155–57; Calve to Haldimand, August 23, 1780, MPHC, 10:442; Sinclair to Haldimand, August 3, 1780, MPHC, 9:572–73.
23. Haldimand to De Peyster, August 10, MPHC, 10:416; Bird to De Peyster, July 1, 1780, MPHC, 19:538; McKee to De Peyster, July 8, 1780, MPHC, 19:541–43.

24. Robert George to George Rogers Clark, July 31, 1780, *Clark Adventure,* 448–49.
25. John Todd to Thomas Jefferson, June 2, 1780, Valentine Dalton to George Rogers Clark, June 25, July 29, 1780, *Clark Adventure,* 440, 443–44, 447–48.
26. For the most accessible source of essential documents on this campaign, see J. Martin West, ed., *Clark's Shawnee Campaign of 1780: Contemporary Accounts* (Springfield, Ohio: Clark County Historical Society, 1975) (hereafter cited as *Clark's Campaign*); Homan to Bird, August 15, 1780, MPHC, 10:418–19.
27. William Homan to Henry Bird, August 15, 1780, *Clark's Campaign,* 9; for the seventy-three scalp number, see Henry Wilson account, *Clark's Campaign,* 35.
28. For an excellent account of these campaigns, see Gavin Watt, *The Burning of the Valleys: Daring Raids from Canada against the New York Frontier in the Fall of 1780* (Toronto: Dundurn Press, 1997).
29. Ibid., 95.
30. Ibid., 96–109.
31. Ibid., 119–36.
32. Ibid., 157–67.
33. Howard Swiggert, *War out of Niagara: Walter Butler and the Tory Rangers* (New York: Columbia University Press, 1933), 204–20.
34. George Washington to President of Congress, November 7, 1780, in John Fitzpatrick, ed., *The Writings of George Washington* (Washington, D.C.: Government Printing Office, 1937), 20:311–15.
35. Watt, *Burning of Valleys,* 137–49.
36. George Germain to Henry Clinton, September 27, 1779, Clinton papers, WCL.
37. Michael A. Bellesiles, *Revolutionary Outlaws: Ethan Allen and the Struggle for Independence on the Early American Frontier* (Charlottesville: University of Virginia Press, 1993), 195, 195–96.
38. Quoted in Watt, *Burning of Valleys,* 92; Mary Beacock Fryer, *Buckskin Pimpernel: The Exploits of Justus Sherwood, Loyalist Spy* (Toronto: Dundurn Press, 1981).
39. Smith, *New Age,* 1431.
40. Williams, *Tennessee during the Revolutionary War,* 182–92; O'Donnell, *Southern Indians,* 107–8.

CHAPTER 9

1. Cameron to Germain, February 10, 1781, C.O. 5/82, folder 130.
2. Caughey, *Galvez,* 193–96.
3. Jack D. L. Holmes, "French and Spanish Military Units in the 1781 Pensacola Campaign," *Anglo-Spanish Confrontation on the Gulf Coast,* 148.
4. Alexander Cameron to Germain, May 27, 1781, DAR, 20:150; Alexander Cameron, Return of Indians, February 1, 1781, DAR, 19:39; James A. Servies, *The Siege of Pensacola, 1781: A Bibliography* (Pensacola, Fla.: The John C. Pace Library, 1981).
5. Kathryn Holland, "The Anglo-Spanish Contest for the Gulf Coast as Viewed from the Townsquare," *Anglo-Spanish Confrontation on the Gulf Coast,* 101.
6. Holland, "Anglo-Spanish Contest," 100–1.
7. Campbell to Clinton, May 12, 1781, Carleton papers, PRO 30/55, folder 89.
8. Caughey, *Galvez,* 187, 206–14; Holmes, "French and Spanish Military," 148.
9. Haynes, *Natchez District,* 139–43.
10. Smith, *New Age,* 2:1457.

11. John Pancake, *This Destructive War: The British Campaign in the Carolinas, 1780–1782* (Tuscaloosa: University of Alabama Press, 1985), 185; Higginbotham, *War of American Independence,* 370.

12. Pancake, *Destructive War,* 198.

13. Ibid., 216–21.

14. Poure proclamation, February 12, 1781, *Galvez,* 169; De Quindre a De Peyster, 14 juin 1780, Haldimand papers, 21782; De Peyster to Bolton, July 6, 1780, MPHC, 19:540; Sinclair to Haldimand, July 8, 1780, MPHC, 19:560; Memorial and Petition, n.d., MPHC, 10:367; Cruzat to Galvez, January 10, 1781, *Spain,* 2:415; De Peyster to Haldimand, January 8, 1781, MPHC, 10:450–51; Cruzat to Galvez, August 6, 1781, *Spain,* 2:431–34; R. David Edmunds, *The Potawatomis: Keepers of the Fire* (Norman: University of Oklahoma Press, 1978), 109–12.

15. Campbell to Davies, October 3, 1782, in William P. Palmer, ed., *Calendar of Virginia State Papers and Other Manuscripts Preserved in the Capitol at Richmond,* 11 vols. (New York: Kraus Reprint, 1968), 3:337.

16. A. Thompson and Alexander McKee to De Peyster, August 29, 1781, extract of letter from Kentucky, December 6, 1781, reprinted Pennsylvania Packet, March 12, 1782, in C. W. Butterfield, *Washington-Irvine Correspondence: The Official Letters* (Madison: David Atwood, 1882), 229 (hereafter cited as *Washington-Irvine*); Isabel Thompson Kelsay, *Joseph Brant, 1743–1807: Man of Two Worlds* (Syracuse, N.Y.: Syracuse University Press, 1984), 309–15.

17. William Irvine to President of Congress, December 3, 1781, *Washington-Irvine,* 154–55; Thompson to De Peyster, September 26, 1781, MPHC, 10:515–16; McKee to De Peyster, September 26, 1781, MPHC, 10:517–18; William Irvine to George Washington, December 2, 1781, *Washington-Irvine,* 77; A. Thompson and Alexander McKee to unknown, August 29, 1781, *Washington-Irvine,* 230.

18. Brodhead to Reed, January 22, 1781, *The Olden Times,* 2:383.

19. William Penn and Cooshockung council to Brodhead, January 13, 1781, WHC, 24:314–15; Heckewelder to Brodhead, February 26, 1781, WHC, 24:337–38; Brodhead to Shepherd, March 8, 1781, WHC 24:342; Brodhead to Washington, March 27, 1781, PA, series 1, 9:39; Brodhead to Reed, May 22, 1781, PA, series 1, 9:161–62; Speech of Cochocton Delaware, June 7, 1781, in De Peyster, *Miscellancies,* 2:8–9.

20. James H. O'Donnell III, ed., "Captain Pipe's Speech: A Commentary on the Delaware Experience, 1775–1781," *Northwest Ohio Quarterly* 64 (1992), 126–33.

21. Eugene T. Bliss, ed., *Diary of David Zeisberger, A Moravian Missionary among the Indians of Ohio,* 2 vols. (Cincinnati: R. Clarke, 1885).

22. Ibid., 13.

23. Ibid., 17–18.

24. Ibid., 25.

25. Ibid., 37.

26. William Irvine to George Washington, December 2, 1781, *Washington-Irvine,* 75.

27. William Irvine to President of Congress, December 8, 1781, *Washington-Irvine,* 155.

28. George Washington to William Irvine, December 18, 1781, *Washington-Irvine,* 83.

29. "Distribution of Corn and Hoes for the Indians of Colonel Johnson's Department, planting at Buffaloe Creek," May 13, 1781, Haldimand papers, Add. mss., 21,760, folder 120.

30. Philip Schuyler to Congress, March 29, 1781, CC, Item 153, 3:547–48.

31. "Return of Indian War Parties of Guy Johnson's Department Now on Service," April 21, 1781, B109:146, PAC; Return of several war parties of Guy Johnson's department from January 1 to October 24, 1781, B109:203A, PAC.
32. Philip Schuyler to Henry Glen, Schuyler papers, acc. 67, box 2, no. 11158, NYPL.
33. Ernest A. Cruikshank, *The King's Royal Regiment of New York* (Toronto: T. H. Best Printing, 1984), 79–80.
34. Graymont, *Iroquois in the Revolution,* 248–52.
35. Raven at Savannah, September 1, 1781, C.O. 5/82:287.
36. John Twiggs to Nathaniel Greene, December 15, 1781, PCC, no. 155, 2:409–11.
37. Smith, *New Age,* 2:1708.

CHAPTER 10
1. Smith, *New Age,* 2:1718.
2. Higginbotham, *War of American Independence,* 383.
3. Royal edict on Louisiana, January 22, 1782, in Lawrence Kinnaird, trans. and ed., *Translations of Materials from the Spanish Archives in the Bancroft Library, University of California, Berkeley, American Historical Association, Annual Report for the Year 1945* (Washington, D.C.: Government Printing Office) 1946–49), Part 2, *The Postwar Period, 1782–1791,* 1–4.
4. Property sale from English prisoners, May 6, 1782, Kinnaird, *Spain in the Mississippi Valley,* 2:12–13.
5. L'Abaddie declaration, July 5, 1782, *Spain in the Mississippi Valley,* 2:31, 29.
6. Ibid., 2:25, 27, 21–34; L'Abbadie to Miro, May 22, 1782, *Spain in the Mississippi Valley,* 2:15–16; Navarro to Galvez, June 4, 1782, *Spain in the Mississippi Valley,* 2:18–20.
7. Girmarest to Payemataha, June 11, 1782, *Spain in the Mississippi Valley,* 2:20; Report on Palous mission, September 1782, *Spain in the Mississippi Valley,* 2:57–58.
8. Cruzat to Miro, August 8, 1782, *Spain in the Mississippi Valley,* 2:49–54.
9. Maxent to Bouligny, September 24, 1782, *Spain in the Mississippi Valley,* 2:59; Colbert to Miro, October 6, 1782, *Spain in the Mississippi Valley,* 2:60; Spanish overtures to Chickasaws, October 24, 1782, *Spain in the Mississippi Valley,* 2:61–62; Penas to Miro, November 23, 1782, *Spain in the Mississippi Valley,* 2:65; Maxent to Miro, December 5, 1782, *Spain in the Mississippi Valley,* 2:67–68.
10. Pollock affidavit, [1782], *Translations of Materials from the Spanish Archives,* 8.
11. Examination of Pollock's commission from Jefferson, April 20, 1782, *Spain in the Mississippi Valley,* 2:8–11; Pollock to Miro, April 27, 1782, *Spain in the Mississippi Valley,* 2:11–12.
12. Pollock to Miro, September 4, 1782, *Spain in the Mississippi Valley,* 2:55–56; Resolution of Congress on Pollock's accounts, October 22, 1782, *Spain in the Mississippi Valley,* 2:61; Virginia House of Delegates Resolution, December 27, 1782, *Spain in the Mississippi Valley,* 2:68–69.
13. Margaret Pollock to Miro, November 23, 1782, *Spain in the Mississippi Valley,* 2:64–65; Hanson to Miro, October 31, 1782, *Spain in the Mississippi Valley,* 2:63–64.
14. Grand-Pre to Miro, May 26, 1782, *Spain in the Mississippi Valley,* 2:16–17.
15. Navarro to Galvez, December 4, 1782, *Spain in the Mississippi Valley,* 2:66–67.
16. A. P. Nasatir, "The Legacy of Spain," *Anglo-Spanish Confrontation on the Gulf Coast,* 12.

17. Reports of British plans to attack Spanish Illinois, July 8, 1782, *Spain in the Mississippi Valley,* 2:34–35; Council of war at St. Louis, July 9, 1782, *Spain in the Mississippi Valley,* 2:39–47.

18. Anthony Wayne to Nathaniel Greene, February 11, 28, 1782, in Richard K. Showman, ed. *Papers of General Nathanael Greene* (Chapel Hill: University of North Carolina Press, 1976), vol. 54.

19. Benjamin Harrison to Alexander Martin, November 12, 1782, North Carolina Colonial Records, 16:457–58.

20. Cashin, *King's Ranger,* 157.

21. Ibid., 157–58.

22. John Johnson to Daniel Claus, March 31, 1782, Claus papers, 3:115, PAC.

23. Bliss, *Zeisberger Diary,* 79–80.

24. Ibid., 80–81.

25. Ibid., 85.

26. Ibid., 82.

27. Ibid., 133; Heckewelder, *Narrative,* 223–306; for the massacre, see Heckewelder, *Narrative,* 310–25; Frederick Lineback, 1782, PA, series 1, 9:524–25; letter from Fort Pitt, March 30, 1782, *Olden Times,* 2:478–79; Cook to Moore, September 2, 1782, PA, series 1, 9:629; Croghan to Dorsey, April 28, 1782, GRC papers, Draper mss., 30–41; William Irvine to George Washington, *Washington-Irvine,* 99–102.

28. Bliss, *Zeisberger Diary,* 67.

29. Ibid., 77.

30. Ibid., 86.

31. William Irvine to George Washington, February 2, 1782, *Washington-Irvine,* 92–94.

32. William Irvine to Benjamin Harrison, April 20, 1782, *Washington-Irvine,* 266–67.

33. Baron Rosenthal "John Rose," *Eyewitness Accounts of the American Revolution, Journal of a Volunteer Expedition to Sandusky* (New York: Arno Press, 1969), 293 (hereafter cited as *Rose Journal*).

34. William Croghan to William Davies, July 6, 1782, *Washington-Irvine,* 292–93.

35. *Rose Journal,* 307, 309.

36. William Croghan to William Davies, July 6, 1782, *Washington-Irvine,* 293.

37. *Rose Journal,* 307.

38. William Irvine to Benjamin Lincoln, July 16, 1782, Michael Huffnagle to William Moore, July 1782, Ephraim Douglas letter extract, July 28, 1782, David Duncan to James Cunningham, July 30, 1782, *Washington-Irvine,* 176–77, 251, 251–52, 252–53.

39. John Dabney Shane interview with Jacob Stevens, c. 1840, Draper manuscript 248212–15.

40. Quoted by Rebecca Boone Lamond to Lyman Copeland Draper, August 23, 1845, Draper manuscript 22C36; for tears, see Lyman Copeland Draper interview with Joseph Scholl, 1868, Draper manuscript 238212–15.

41. Extract of letter of Captain Caldwell, August 26, 1782, Haldimand papers, 21783.

42. Benjamin Lincoln to William Irvine, September 7, 14, 1782, *Washington-Irvine,* 181–82, 183–84.

43. James Marshall to William Irvine, September 15, 1782, *Washington-Irvine,* 313.

44. William Irvine to George Washington, October 29, 1782, *Washington-Irvine,* 134–340.

45. George Washington to William Irvine, December 11, 1782, *Washington-Irvine,* 141.

46. McKee to De Peyster, August 28, 1782, Haldimand papers, 102:154–57; George Rogers Clark to Benjamin Harrison, November 27, 1782, *Washington-Irvine*, 401–2; McKee to De Peyster, November 15, 1782, Haldimand papers, 21783.

CHAPTER 11

1. George Washington to Secretary of State, October 2, 1782, in Fitzpatrick, *Writings of George Washington*, 25:227–28.
2. *New Jersey Journal*, reprinted by the New York Packet or American Advertiser, April 17, 1783.
3. Smith, *New Age*, 2:1760; Wilbur Henry Siebert, *Loyalists in East Florida: The Most Important Documents Pertaining Thereto, Edited with an Accompanying Narrative* (Boston: Gregg Press, 1972), 1:131; Wilber H. Siebert, "The Loyalists in West Florida and the Natchez District," *Mississippi Valley Historical Association Proceedings* 8 (1916): 102–22; Thelma Peters, "The Loyalist Migration from East Florida to the Bahama Islands," *Florida Historical Quarterly* 40 (October 1961): 123–41.
4. John Ross to Frederick Haldimand, February 17, 1782, Haldimand Papers, PAC; George Washington to Marinius Willet, December 18, 1782, March 5, 1783, *Writings of Washington*, 25:499–51, 26:190.
5. William Irvine to George Washington, March 6, 1783, *Washington-Irvine*, 142–44.
6. William Irvine to George Washington, March 28, 1782, *Washington-Irvine*, 144–48.
7. Clark to Harrison, May 22, 1783, IHC, 19:237.
8. William Irvine to George Washington, *Washington-Irvine*, 149.
9. D. C. Corbitt, "James Colbert and the Spanish Claims to the East Bank of the Mississippi," *Mississippi Valley Historical Review* 24 (1938): 457–72; Robert Haynes, *The Natchez District and the American Revolution* (Jackson: University Press of Mississippi, 1976); Jack Holmes, Spanish-American Rivalry over the Chickasaw Bluffs, 1780–1795," *East Tennessee Historical Society Publication* 34 (1962); Gilbert Din, "Arkansas Post in the American Revolution," *Arkansas Historical Quarterly* 40 (1981): 3–30.
10. John Ross to Frederick Haldimand, April 25, 1783, Haldimand Papers, PAC.
11. Talks of Indians to British officials, C.O. 5/8/415–16.
12. Talks by chiefs to Thomas Brown, November 17, 1783, PRO T 1/601/298–306.
13. Congressional committee report, October 1783, 25:681–83.
14. William Irvine to Benjamin Lincoln, April 10, 1783, *Washington-Irvine*, 187.
15. Reginald Horsman, *Expansion and American Indian Policy, 1783–1812* (Lansing: Michigan State University Press, 1967), 1–15.
16. J. Hector St. John de Crevecoeur, *Letters from an American Farmer and Sketches of Eighteenth Century America* (New York: Penguin Classics, 1986), 69, 70.
17. Frederick Jackson Turner, *The Frontier in American History* (New York: Dover Publications, 1996).
18. George Washington to James Duane, in Fitzpatrick, *Writings of George Washington*, 27:134.

BIBLIOGRAPHY

ABBREVIATIONS

Am. Arch. *American Archives.*

BAHQP   British Army Headquarters' Papers (sometimes called Carleton papers), PRO 30/55, vols. 1–10 (London: Public Record Office). Microfilm copy at State University of New York at Buffalo.

DHSNY   *Documentary History of the State of New York.*

HSP   Historical Society of Pennsylvania.

IHC   Collections of the Illinois Historical Library.

JCC   Journals of the Continental Congress.

JR   Jesuit Relations.

LC   Library of Congress.

MHS   Massachusetts Historical Society.

MPA   Mississippi Provincial Archives (Jackson: Press of the Mississippi Department of Archives and History, 1921–84).

MPHSC   Michigan Pioneer Historical Society, Collections and Research (Lansing, Mich.: The Society, 1877–1929).

NYCD   *Documents Relative to the Colonial History of New York.*

NYHS   New York Historical Society.

NYPL   New York Public Library.

PA   Pennsylvania Archives (Philadelphia: Joseph Severn; Harrisburg: Commonwealth of Pennsylvania, 1852–1949).

PAC   Provincial Archives of Canada.

PCC   Papers of the Continental Congress.

PCR   Minutes of Provincial Council of Pennsylvania from the Organization to the Termination of Proprietary Government, ed. Samuel Hazard (Harrisburg, PA: Theophilus Fenn, 1838–53).

WHC   Collections of the State Historical Society of Wisconsin, ed. Lyman C. Draper and Reuben G. Thwaites (Madison, Wis.: The Society, 1855–1911).

WLCL   William L. Clements Library.

ARCHIVES AND INSTITUTIONS

American Philosophical Society, Philadelphia: Benjamin Franklin papers.

Archives des Affaires Etrangeres, Correspondance Politique, Angleterre; Espagne; Memoirs et Documents, Amerique; Angleterre.

Archivio General de Indias, Seville: Papeles Procedentes de Cuba.

Beinecke Library, Yale University, New Haven, Conn.

British Museum: Philipe Yorke, Earl of Hardwicke papers; Thomas Pelham-Holles, Duke of Newcastle.

Canadian Archives: General Frederick Haldimand papers, Add. mss. nos. 21,661–21,982.

Carnegie Library, Pittsburgh: Colonel George Morgan letterbooks, 3 vols., 1775–79.

Collections of the Michigan Pioneer and Historical Society, Lansing: 40 vols., 1874–1929; vols. 9 and 10, 1886 and 1908.

Connecticut Historical Society: William Samuel Johnson papers.

David Library of the American Revolution, Washington Crossing, Pennsylvania.

David Library of the American Revolution, Brown University.

Henry Huntington Library, San Marino, California: James Campbell, Earl of Loudoun papers; George Grenville letter books.

Historical Society of Pennsylvania, Philadelphia: George Croghan papers, Cadwallader collection; Board of Trade papers, Plantations General (copies); George Morgan letter book, 1767–1768; Ohio Company papers; William Trent papers; Wharton letter book.

Houghton Library, Harvard University, Cambridge, Massachusetts: "Henry Hamilton Drawings of North American Scenes and American Indians, 1769–1778."

Illinois Historical Collections, Springfield: 1903–; 1903, vols. 1, 8, and 9.

Illinois Historical Survey, Urbana: William Legge, Earl of Dartmouth papers; Sir William Johnson papers; Wharton manuscript (transcripts).

Institute of Early American History and Culture, University of North Carolina, Chapel Hill, North Carolina.

Library of Congress: British Public Records Office (C.O. 5), transcripts of the Library of Congress (L.C., C.O. 5); Peter Force transcripts, series 7e, reels 13–14, items 55–57; Edward Hand papers, 1775–1846; Benjamin Franklin papers.

Massachusetts Historical Society, Boston: "An Estimate of the Indian Nations Employed by the British during the Revolutionary War," 1st series, 10 (1809).

Newberry Center for the History of the American Indians, Chicago: Edward Ayers papers.

The Newberry Library Center for the History of the American Indian Biographical Series, University of Indiana, Bloomington, Indiana.

New York Public Library: Philip Schuyler Papers, Indian papers, 1710–96, boxes 13–15, reel 7; the Indian Affairs Collection; Connelly, John, "Journal of My Proceedings &ca Commencing from the Late Disturbances with the Cherokees upon the Ohio," April 14–May 27, 1774 (18 pages); Chalmers Collection, Indians 1750–75, folders 34–39.

Papers of the Continental Congress, 1774–89, National Archives Microfilm, no. M247.

P. K. Yonge Library, University of Florida: microfilm of Papeles Procedentes de Cuba.

Public Archives of Canada, Ottawa: Records Relating to Indian Affairs (R.G. 10), second series, microfilm reel C-1223; Minutes of Indian Affairs, 1755–90; Claus papers; Colonial Office, Public Record Office (copies); Henry Bouquet papers (copies); Frederick Haldimand papers (transcripts).

Public Record Office, Britain: Colonial Office; William Pitt, Earl of Chatham papers; Charles Egremont, Earl of Egremont papers; Treasury Board papers.

Southern Historical Collection, University of North Carolina, Chapel Hill: Rutherford papers.

William L. Clements Library, University of Michigan, Ann Arbor: Sir Jeffery Amherst; Henry Clinton papers; Thomas Gage papers; William Knox papers; William Petty, Earl of Shelburne papers; George Germain papers.

Wisconsin Historical Society: Lyman Copeland Draper Collection.

PUBLISHED ORIGINAL DOCUMENTS AND SOURCES

Abbott, W. W. ed. *The Papers of George Washington.* Charlottesville: University Press of Virginia, 1983.

Abler, Thomas S., ed. *Chainbreaker: The Revolutionary War Memoirs of Governor Blacksnake, as Told to Benjamin Williams.* Lincoln: University of Nebraska Press, 1989.

Adams, Randolph G. *The Papers of Lord George Germain.* Ann Arbor: University of Michigan Press, 1928.

Adams, Thomas R., ed. *American Independence, the Growth of an Idea: A Bibliographical Study of the American Political Pamphlets Printed between 1764 and 1776, Dealing with the Dispute between Great Britain and Her Colonies.* Providence, R.I.: Brown University Press, 1965.

Alexander, David E., ed. "Diary of Captain Benjamin Warren in 1778." *Journal of American History* 3 (1909).

Allen, Ethan. *A Narrative of Colonel Ethan Allen's Captivity Containing His Voyage & Travels.* New York: Richard W. Ellis [The Georgia Press] for Fort Ticonderoga, 1930.

Alvord, Clarence W., ed. "Kaskaskia Records, 1778–1790." *Collections of the Illinois Historical Society* 5 (1909).

Alvord, Clarence W., and Clarence E. Carter, eds. *The Critical Period, 1763–1765.* Springfield, Ill.: Illinois State Historical Library, 1916.

Alvord, Clarence W., and Clarence E. Carter, eds. *The New Regime, 1765–1767.* Springfield: Illinois State Historical Library, 1916.

Alvord, Clarence W., and Clarence E. Carter, eds. *Trade and Politics, 1767–1769.* Springfield, Ill.: Illinois State Historical Library, 1921.

Ambler, Charles, ed. "Some Letters and Papers of General Thomas Gage." *The John P. Branch Historical Papers of Randolph-Macon College* 4 (1914): 86–111.

Arndt, Karl J. R. "New Hampshire and the Battle of Bennington: Colonel Baum's Mission and Bennington Defeat as Reported by a German Officer under General Burgoyne's Command." *Historical New Hampshire* 32 (Winter 1977): 202–7.

Atkinson, C. T., ed. "Some Evidence for Burgoyne's Expedition." *Journal of the Society for Army Historical Research* 26 (Winter 1948): 132–42.

Bailey, Kenneth P., ed. *The Ohio Company Papers, 1747–1817, Being Primarily Papers of the "Suffering Traders" of Pennsylvania.* Arcata, Calif.: The Arthur Clark Company, 1947.

Baldwin, Thomas, ed. *The Revolutionary Journal of Col. Jeduthan Baldwin, 1775–1778.* Bangor, Maine: Printed for the De Burians, 1906.

Barnhart, John D., ed. *Henry Hamilton and George Rogers Clark in the American Revolution, with the Unpublished Letters of Lieutenant Governor Henry Hamilton.* Crawfordsville, Ind.: Banta, 1951.

Bateson, Mary, ed. *A Narrative of the Changes in the Ministry, 1765–1768, Told by the Duke of Newcastle in a Series of Letters to John White.* London: M. P. Camden Society Publications, new series, 59, 1898.

Baxter, James Phinney, ed. *The British Invasion from the North: The Campaigns of Generals Carleton and Burgoyne from Canada, 1776–1777, with the Journal of Lieut. William Digby of the 53rd, or Shropshire Regiment of Foot (1887).* New York: Da Capo Press, 1970.

Beecher, Raymond, ed. *Letters from a Revolution, 1775–1783: A Selection from the Bronck Family Papers at the Greene County Historical Society.* Albany: The New York State American Revolution Bicentennial Commission, 1973.

Billon, Frederick Louis, ed. *Annals of St. Louis.* 2 vols. St. Louis: printed for the author, 1886 and 1888.

Blair, Emma Helen. *The Indian Tribes of the Upper Mississippi Valley & Region of the Great Lakes (1911).* Lincoln: University of Nebraska Press, 1996.

Bliss, Eugene T. *Diary of David Zeisberger, A Moravian Missionary among the Indians of Ohio.* 2 vols. Cincinnati: R. Clarke, 1885.

Bolton, Herbert E., ed. *Athanase de Mezieres and the Louisiana-Texas Frontier, 1768–1780.* 2 vols. Cleveland: Clark, 1983.

Bourdin, H. L., and S. T. Williams, eds. "Crevecoeur on the Susquehanna, 1774–1776." *Yale Review* 14 (1925): 581–82.

"Bowdoin and Temple Papers." *Massachusetts Historical Society, Collections.* 6th series. Vol. 9.

Boyd, Julian P., ed. *The Papers of Thomas Jefferson.* Princeton, N.J.: Princeton University Press, 1950.

Boyd, Julian P., et al., eds. *The Susquehanna Company Papers.* 4 vols. Wilkes-Barre, Pa.: Sheldon Reynolds Memorial Publications of the Wyoming Historical and Genealogical Society, 1930–33.

Boyd, Julian P., and Robert J. Taylor, eds. *The Susquehanna Company Papers.* 11 vols. Ithaca, N.Y.: Cornell University Press, 1930–71.

Brigham, Clarence S., ed. *British Royal Proclamations Relating to America, 1603–1783.* Vol. 12. Worcester, Mass.: Transactions and Collection of the American Antiquarian Society, 1911.

Brown, William, et al., eds. *Archives of Maryland.* 60 vols. Baltimore: Maryland Historical Society, 1883–.

Burgoyne, John. *A State of the Expedition from Canada . . .* Albany, N.Y.: J. Munsell, 1860.

Burnett, Edmund C. *Letters of Members of the Continental Congress, 1774–1789.* 8 vols. Washington, D.C.: Government Printing Office, 1921–36.

Burt, A. L. *The United States, Great Britain, and British North America from the Revolution to the Establishment of Peace after the War of 1812.* New Haven, Conn.: Yale University Press, 1940.

Butterfield, Consul W., ed. *The Washington-Crawford Letters: Being the Correspondence between George Washington and William Crawford, from 1767 to 1781, Concerning Western Lands.* Cincinnati: Robert Clarke & Co., 1877.

Campbell, William W. *The Border Warfare of New York during the Revolution; or, The Annals of Tryon County.* New York: Baker & Scribner, 1845.

Cappon, Lester, ed. *The Adams-Jefferson Letters.* 2 vols. Chapel Hill: University of North Carolina Press, 1959.

"Captain [Harry] Gordon's Views of the British Military Establishment in America." *Mississippi Valley Historical Review* 15 (1928): 92–95.

Cardy, Michael, ed. "The Iroquois in the Eighteenth Century: A Neglected Source." *Man in the Northeast* 38 (Fall 1989): 1–20.

Carter, Clarence, ed. "Observations of Superintendent John Stuart and Governor James Grant of East Florida on the Proposed Plan of 1764, for the Future Management of Indian Affairs." *American Historical Society* 20 (1915): 815–31.

Carter, Clarence, ed. *The Territorial Papers of the United States.* 28 vols. Washington, D.C.: Government Printing Office, 1934–75.

Carter, Clarence E., ed. "Documents Relating to the Mississippi Land Company, 1763–1774." *American Historical Review* 16 (1911): 311–19.

Carter, Clarence Edwin, ed. *The Correspondence of General Thomas Gage with the Secretaries of State, 1763–1775.* 2 vols. Hamden, CT: Archon Books, 1969.

Cartwright, C. E., ed. *The Life and Letters of the Late Honorable Richard Cartwright.* Toronto: Belford Brothers, 1876.

Clark, Thomas O., ed. *Travels in the Old South: A Bibliography.* 2 vols. Norman: University of Oklahoma Press, 1956.

"Clark's Conquest of the Illinois." *Collections of the Illinois State Historical Society* 1 (1903).

Commager, Henry Steele, ed. *Documents of American History,* 7th ed. 2 vols. New York: Appleton-Century-Crofts, 1963.

Commager, Henry Steele, and Richard B. Morris, eds. *The Spirit of Seventy-Six: The Story of the American Revolution as Told by Participants (1958).* New York: Bonanza Books, 1983.

Commetti, Elizabeth, ed. *The American Journals of Lt. John Enys.* Syracuse, N.Y.: Syracuse University Press, 1976.

Connolly, John. "A Narrative of the Transactions, Imprisonment, and Sufferings of John Connolly, an American Loyalist and Lieutenant-Colonel in His Majesty's Service," *Pennsylvania Magazine of History and Biography* 12 (1888): 310–24, 407–20; 13 (1889): 61–70, 153–67, 281–91.

Cook, Frederick, ed. *Journals of the Military Expedition of Major General John Sullivan against the Six Nations.* Auburn, N.Y.: Knapp, Peck, Thompson, 1887.

Corbett, William, and J. Wright, eds. *The Parliamentary History of England, from the Earliest Period to the Year 1803.* 36 vols. London: T. C. Hansard, 1806–1820.

Corbitt, D. S., and Roberta Corbitt, eds. "Papers from the Spanish Archives Relating to Tennessee and the Old Southwest, 1783–1800." *Tennessee Historical Society Publications* 9 (1937).

Corbitt, D. S., and Roberta Corbitt, eds. "Papers from the Spanish Archives Relating to Tennessee and the Old Southwest." *Tennessee Historical Society Publications* 40 (1968).

Craig, Neville B., ed. *The Olden Time.* 2 vols. New York: Kraus Reprint Co., 1976.

Crane, Vernon, ed. "Hint Relative to the Division and Government of the Conquered and Newly Acquired Countries in America" [attributed to Henry Ellis]. *Mississippi Valley Historical Review* 8 (1922): 367–73.

Darlington, William M., ed. *Christopher Gist's Journals, with Historical, Geographical, and Ethnological Notes and Biographies of His Contemporaries.* Pittsburgh: J. R. Weldin & Co., 1893.

Darlington, William M., ed. *Fort Pitt and Letters from the Frontier.* New York: The New York Times and Arno Press, 1971.

Davies, K. G., ed. *Documents of the American Revolution, 1770–1783.* Colonial Office Series. 21 vols. Shannon, Ireland: Irish University Press, 1972–82.

Dawson, Henry B. *Battles of the United States, by Sea and Land: Embracing Those of the Revolutionary and Indian Wars, the War of 1812, and the Mexican War; with Important Official Documents.* 2 vols. New York: Johnson, Fry, and Company, 1859.

de Chastellux, Francois Jean. *Travels in North America, in the Years 1780, 1781, and 1782.* 2 vols. London: G. F. J. and J. Robinson, 1787.

de Crevecoeur, J. Hector St. John. *Letters from an American Farmer, and Sketches of Eighteenth Century America.* New York: Penguin, 1981.

De Peyster, J. Watt. *Miscellanies by an Officer: By Colonel Arent Schuyler De Peyster, 1774–1813.* New York: Chasmar, 1888, vol. 1. New York: C. H. Ludwig, 1888, vol. 2.

De Vorsey, Louis, ed. *De Brahm's Report of the General Survey in the Southern District of North America.* Columbia: University of South Carolina Press, 1971.

Dodge, John. *An Entertaining Narrative of Mr. John Dodge during His Captivity and Barbarous Treatment and Extreme Suffering among the British at Detroit.* Reprint, Cedar Rapids, Iowa: The Torch Press, 1907.

Doughty, Arthur C., ed. *Documents Relating to the Constitutional History of Canada, 1759–1791.* Ottawa: 1907.

Eelking, Max von, ed. *Memoirs and Letters of Major General Riedesel during His Residence in America.* (New York: The New York Times & Arno Press, 1969.

Evans, William A., ed. *Detroit to Sackville, 1778–1779: The Journal of Normand MacLeod.* Detroit: Burton Historical Society, 1978.

Feller, Seymour, trans. and ed. *Jean-Bernard Bossu's Travels in the Interior of North America, 1751–1762.* Norman: University of Oklahoma Press, 1962.

Filson, John. *The Discovery, Settlement, and Present State of Kentucke.* New York: Readex Microprint Corporation, 1966.

Fitzpatrick, John C., ed. *The Diaries of George Washington, 1748–1794.* 4 vols. Boston: Houghton Mifflin, 1925.

Fitzpatrick, John C. ed. *The Writings of George Washington.* 39 vols. Washington, D.C.: Government Printing Office, 1931–44.

Flick, Alexander C., ed. "New Sources on the Sullivan-Clinton Campaign in 1779." *Quarterly Journal of the New York State Historical Association* 10 (1929): 185–224, 265–317.

Force, Peter, ed. *American Archives.* 4th series. 6 vols. Washington, D.C.: 1837–46.

Force, Peter, ed. *American Archives.* 5th series. 3 vols. Washington, D.C.: 1848–53.

Ford, Worthington C., and Gaillard Hunt, eds. *Journals of the Continental Congress, 1774–1789.* 34 vols. Washington, D.C.: Government Printing Office, 1904–37.

Fortescue, John, ed. *The Correspondence of King George Third from 1760 to December 1783, Printed from the Original Papers in the Royal Archives at Windsor Castle.* 6 vols. London: Macmillan, 1927–28.

Frey, Samuel, ed. *Minute Book of the Committee of Safety.* Tryon County, New York: Dodd Mead, 1906.

Fryer, Mary Beacock. *King's Men: The Soldier Founders of Ontario.* Toronto: Dundurn Press Limited, 1980.

Galvez, Bernard de. "Diary of the Operations against Pensacola, 1781." *Louisiana Historical Quarterly* 1 (1917).

Gelb, Norman, ed. *Jonathan Carver's Travels through America, 1766–1768: An Explorer's Portrait of the American Wilderness.* New York: John Wiley & Sons, 1993.

Gibbes, Robert Wilson, ed. *Documentary History of the American Revolution.* 3 vols. New York: Appleton, 1853–57.

Goodman, Nathan G., ed. *A Benjamin Franklin Reader.* New York: Thomas Y. Crowell Company, 1945.

Hamer, Philip M., ed. "Correspondence of Henry Stuart and Alexander Cameron with the Wautaugans." *Mississippi Valley Historical Review* 17 (1930–1): 451–59.

Hamilton, J. G. de Roulhac, ed. "Revolutionary Diary of William Lenoir." *Journal of Southern History* 6 (1968): 247–57.

Hamilton, Milton W., ed. "Guy Johnson's Opinions on the American Indian." *Pennsylvania Magazine of History and Biography* 77 (1953): 311–27.

Hamilton, Stanislaus, ed. *Letters to Washington, and Accompanying Papers.* 5 vols. Boston: Houghton, Mifflin, and Company, 1898–1902.

Hammond, Otis G., ed. *Letters and Papers of Major-General John Sullivan.* 3 vols. Concord: University of New Hampshire Historical Society, 1930–39.

Harpster, John W., ed. *Pen Pictures of Early Western Pennsylvania.* Pittsburgh: University of Pittsburgh, 1938.

Hastings, Hugh, and J. A. Holden, ed. *Public Papers of Governor George Clinton.* 10 vols. Albany, N.Y.: State Printers, 1899–1914.

Hawes, Lilla M., ed. "The Papers of Lachlan McIntosh, 1774–1779." *Collections of the Georgia Historical Society* 12 (1957): 56–60.

Hazard, Samuel, ed. *Minutes of the Provincial Council of Pennsylvania from the Organization to the Termination of the Proprietary Government.* Harrisburg and Philadelphia: Theophilus Fenn,1838–53.

Heckewelder, John. *History, Manners, and Customs of the Indian Nations Who Once Inhabited Pennsylvania and the Neighboring States.* New York: Arno, 1971.

Heckewelder, John. *A Narrative of the Mission of the United Brethren among the Delaware and Mohegan Indians, from Its Commencement in the Year 1740 to the Close of the Year 1808.* Philadelphia: McCary & Davis, 1820; New York: Arno, 1971.

Hervey, S. H. A., ed. *Journals of the Hon. William Hervey, in North America and Europe, from 1755 to 1814; with Order Books at Montreal, 1760–1763.* London: Bury St. Edmund's, Paul and Mathew, 1906.

Historical Manuscripts Commission. *Report on the Manuscripts of Mrs. Stopford-Sackville of Drayton House, Northhampshire.* 2 vols. London: H.M. Stationery Office, 1904 and 1910.

Historical Manuscripts Commission. *Report on the Manuscripts of Mrs. Stopford-Sackville.* 2 vols. London: His Majesty's Stationery Office, 1920.

Houck, Louis, ed. *The Spanish Regime in Missouri: A Collection of Papers and Documents Relating to Upper Louisiana Principally within the Present Limits of Missouri during the Dominion of Spain, from the Archives of the Indies at Seville.* 2 vols. Chicago: R. R. Donnelly & Sons Company, 1909.

Hughes, Thomas. *A Journal by Thos. Hughes for His Amusement & Designed Only for His Perusal by the Time He Attains the Age of 50 If He Lives So Long (1778–89).* Port Washington, N.Y.: Kennikat Press, 1970.

Hulbert, Archer Butler, and William N. Schwarzte, eds. *David Zeisberger's History of the Northern American Indians.* Columbus: Ohio State Archaelogical and Historical Society, 1910.

Humphries, R. A., ed. "Governor James Murray's Views on the Plan of 1764 for the Management of Indian Affairs." *Canadian Historical Review* 16 (1935): 162–69.

Hutchinson, Peter O., ed. *The Diary and Letters of His Excellency Thomas Hutchinson, Esq.* 2 vols. New York: Lenox Hill Publishing Co., 1971.

"Illustrative Letters from the Sir William Johnson Manuscripts." *American Antiquarian Society Proceedings* 18 (1906–07), 404–10.

Jacobs, Wilbur R., ed. *Indians of the Southern Colonial Frontier: The Edmond Atkin Report and Plan of 1755.* Columbia: University of South Carolina Press, 1954.

James, James Alton, ed. *George Rogers Clark Papers, 1771–1781.* Springfield: Illinois State Historical Society, 1912.

James, James Alton, ed. *George Rogers Clark Papers, 1781–1784.* Springfield: Illinois State Historical Society, 1926.

Jennings, Francis, et al. *The History and Culture of Iroquois Diplomacy: An Interdisciplinary Guide to the Treaties of the Six Nations and Their League.* Syracuse, N.Y.: Syracuse University Press, 1985.

Jennings, Francis, William N. Fenton, Mary A. Druke, and David R. Miller, eds. *Iroquois Indians: A Documentary History of the Six Indians and Their League.* Woodbridge, Conn.: Research Publications, 1985.

Johnston, Charles M., ed. *Valley of the Six Nations: A Collection of Documents on the Indians Lands of the Grand River.* Toronto: Champlain Society, 1964.

"Journal of Daniel Boone." *Ohio Archaeological and Historical Publications* 13 (1904).

The Journal of Nicolas Cresswell, 1774–1777. New York: Dial, 1924.

Kellogg, Louise P., ed. *Frontier Advance on the Upper Ohio, 1778–1779.* Madison: Wisconsin State Historical Society, 1916.

Kidder, Frederic, ed. *Military Operations in Eastern Maine and Nova Scotia during the Revolution, Chiefly Compiled from the Journals and Letters of Colonel John Allen.* Albany, N.Y.: Munsell, 1867.

Kiernon, George C. H., trans. "Documents Concerning the History of the Indians of the Eastern Region of Louisiana." *Louisiana Historical Quarterly* 8 (1925).

Kimball, Gertrude Selwyn, ed. *Correspondence of William Pitt When Secretary of State with Colonial Governors and Military and Naval Commissioners in America.* London: Macmillan, 1906.

Kinietz, Vernon, and Erminie W. Voeglin, eds. *Shawnese Traditions: C. C. Trowbridge's Account, Occasional Contributions from the Museum of Anthropology of the University of Michigan.* No. 9. Ann Arbor: University of Michigan Press, 1939.

Kinnaird, Lawrence, ed. "Clark-Leyba Papers." *American Historical Review* 41 (1935–36).

Kinnaird, Lawrence, trans. and ed. *Translations of Materials from the Spanish Archives in the Bancroft Library, University of California, Berkeley, American Historical Association, Annual Report for the Year 1945.* Washington D.C.: Government Printing Office, 1946–49. Vols. 2–4: Part 1: *The Revolutionary Period, 1765–1781*; Part 2: *The Postwar Period, 1782–1791*; Part 3: *Problems of Colonial Defense, 1792–1794.*

Klinck, Carl F., and James J. Talman, eds. *The Journal of Major John Norton.* Toronto: Champlain Society, 1970.

Labaree, Leonard W., ed. *Royal Instructions to British Colonial Governors, 1670–1776.* 2 vols. New York: D. Appleton-Century Company, 1935.

Labaree, Leonard W., et al. *The Papers of Benjamin Franklin.* New Haven, Conn.: Yale University Press, 1959–.

Lamb, R. *An Original and Authentic Journal of Occurrences during the Late American War.* Reprint, New York: Arno Press, 1968.

Legg, L. G. Wickham, ed. *British Diplomatic Instructions, 1689–1789.* Vols. 35, 38, 43, and 49. London: Royal Historical Society New Series, 1927.

"Letter of Sir William Johnson to William Franklin." *American Antiquarian Society Transactions* 27 (1934): 1–27.

"Letters from the Canadian Archives." *Collections of the Illinois State Historical Society* 1 (1903).

Loskiel, George Henry. *History of the Mission the United Brethren among the Indians in North America.* London: The Brethren's Society for the Furtherance of the Gospel, 1779.

Loudon, Archibald, ed. *Selection of Some of the Most Interesting Narratives of Outrages Committed by the Indians, in Their Wars with the White People.* Reprint, New York: Times and Arno, 1971.

Lowie, Walter, and Matthew St. Clair Clarke, eds. *American State Papers, Documents, Legislative and Executive, of the Congress of the United States (1789–1815), Class II, Indian Affairs.* Washington D.C.: Gales & Seaton, 1832.

Maguire, J. Robert, ed. "Dr. Robert Knox's Account of the Battle of Valcour, October 11–13, 1776." *Vermont History* 46 (Summer 1979): 141–50.

Mason, Edward, ed. "Rocheblave Papers (1776–1778)." Chicago: Chicago Historical Society, 1890.

Mathews, Albert, ed. "Letters of Dennys De Berdt, 1757–1770." *Publications of the Colonial Society of Massachusetts* 8 (1910): 293–461.

McCormick, Cyrus H., ed. *The Illinois-Wabash Land Company Manuscript.* With an Introduction by Clarence W. Alvord. Privately printed, 1915.

McDowell, William L., ed. *Documents Relating to Indian Affairs, 1754–1756.* Columbia: University of South Carolina Press, 1970.

McIlwain, C. H., ed. *Peter Wraxall's Abridgement of the New York Indian Records.* Cambridge: Harvard University Press, 1915.

McWilliams, Richebourg Gailliard, ed. *Iberville's Gulf Journals.* University, Ala.: University of Alabama Press, 1981.

Minutes of the Albany Committee of Correspondence, 1775–1778. 2 vols. Albany, N.Y.: J. B. Lyon Company, 1923–25.

Moore, Alexander, ed. *Nairne's Muskhogean Journals: The 1708 Expedition to the Mississippi River.* Jackson: University Press of Mississippi, 1988.

Morrison, Alfred, trans. and ed. *Travels in the Confederation, by John David Schoept.* 2 vols. New York: Bergman, 1968.

Mulkearn, Lois, ed. *George Mercer Papers Relating to the Ohio Company of Virginia.* Pittsburgh: University of Pittsburgh Press, 1954.

Munro, James, ed. *Acts of the Privy Council of England*, Council Series, 6 vols. London: Anthony Brothers Limited, 1908–1912.

Murdoch, David H., ed. *Rebellion in America: A Contemporary British Viewpoint, 1765–1783.* Santa Barbara, Calif.: Clio, 1979.

Namias, June. "Jane McCrea and the American Revolution." In June Namias, ed. *White Captives: Gender and Ethnicity on the American Frontier.* Chapel Hill: University of North Carolina Press, 1993.

Namias, June, ed. *A Narrative of the Life of Mary Jemison: By James Seaver.* Norman: University of Oklahoma Press, 1992.

Naumier, Lewis B., ed. "Charles Garth, Agent for South Carolina." *English Historical Review* 54 (1939): 632–52.

O'Callaghan, Edmund Bailey, ed. *Orderly Book of Lieutenant General John Burgoyne, from His Entry into the States of New York until His Surrender at Saratoga, 16th October 1777.* Albany: J. Munsell, 1860.

O'Callaghan, E. B., ed. *The Documentary History of the State of New York.* 4 vols. Albany, N.Y.: Weed, Parsons, and Co., 1849–51.

O'Callaghan, E. B., and Berthold Fernow, eds. *Documents Relative to the Colonial History of the State of New York.* 15 vols. Albany, N.Y.: Weed, Parsons, and Co., 1856–87.

O'Donnell, James H., ed. "Captain Pipe's Speech: A Commentary on the Delaware Experience, 1775–1781." *Northwest Ohio Quarterly* 64 (1992): 126–33.

Palmer, William P., ed. *Calendar of Virginia State Papers and other Manuscripts Preserved in the Capitol at Richmond.* 11 vols. Reprint, New York: Kraus Reprint Corporation, 1968.

Pease, Theodore Calvin, ed. *Anglo-French Boundary Disputes in the West, 1749–1763*. Springfield: Illinois State Historical Library, 27, French Series 2, 1936.

Pell, Joshua. "Diary of Joshua Pell, Junior: An Officer of the British Army in America, 1776–1777." *The Magazine of American History* 2 (January–February 1878): 43–47, 107–12.

Penrose, Maryly B., ed. *Mohawk Valley in the Revolution: Committee of Public Safety Papers & Genealogical Compendium*. Franklin Park, N.J.: Liberty Bell Associates, 1978.

Penrose, Maryly, comp. *Indian Affairs Papers: American Revolution*. Franklin Park, N.J.: Liberty Bell Associates, 1981.

Peyser, Joseph L., ed. *Letters from New France: The Upper Country, 1686–1783*. Urbana: University of Illinois Press, 1992.

Pilkingham, Walter, ed. *The Journals of Samuel Kirkland*. Clinton, N.Y.: Hamilton College, 1980.

Prucha, Francis Paul, ed. *Documents of United States Indian Policy*. Lincoln: University of Nebraska Press, 1975.

Quaife, Milo Milton, ed. *Alexander Henry's Travels and Adventures in the Years 1760–1776*. Chicago: Lakeside Press, R. R. Donnelly & Sons, 1921.

Quaife, Milo M., ed. *The Capture of Old Vincennes, the Original Narratives of George Rogers Clark and of His Opponent Gov. Henry Hamilton*. Indianapolis, Ind.: The Bobbs-Merrill Company, 1927.

Quaife, Milo Milton, ed. *The Conquest of the Illinois*. Chicago: Donnelly, 1920.

Ranck, George W. *Boonesborough: Its Founding, Pioneer Struggles, Indian Experiences, Transylvania Days, and Revolutionary Annals*. New York: New York Times and Arno Press, 1971.

Redington, Joseph, and Richard A. Roberts, eds. *Calendar of Home Office Papers of the Reign of George III, 1760–1775*. 4 vols. Reprint, Nendeln, Liechtenstein: Kraus Reprint Ltd., 1967.

Robert, Kenneth, ed. *March to Quebec: Journals of the Members of Arnold's Expedition*. New York: Doubleday, 1938.

Robinson, Percy J., ed. *Toronto during the French Regime: A History of the Toronto Region from Brule to Simcoe, 1615–1793*. Chicago: University of Chicago Press, 1933.

Rogers, Horatio, ed. *Hadden's Journal and Orderly Books: A Journal Kept in Canada and upon Burgoyne's Campaign in 1776 and 1777, by Lieutenant James Murray Hadden; Also Orders Kept by Him and Issued by Sir Guy Carleton, Lieut. General Burgoyne, and Major General William Phillips in 1776, 1777, and 1778*. Albany, N.Y.: Joel Munsell's Sons, 1884.

Russell, Nelson Vance. "The Indian Policy of Henry Hamilton: A Reevaluation." *Canadian Historical Review* 11 (1930): 20–37.

Saunders, William L., and Walter Clark, eds. *The Colonial and State Records of North Carolina*. 30 vols. Raleigh: Secretary of State, 1886–1914.

Schoolcraft, Henry Rowe, ed. *Historical and Statistical Information Respecting the History, Condition, and Prospects of the Indian Tribes of the United States.* 6 vols. Philadelphia: Lippincott, Grumbo, 1851–57.

Scott, John Albert. *Fort Stanwix (Fort Schuyler) and Oriskany.* Rome, N.Y.: Rome Sentinel Company, 1927.

Scribner, Robert L., et al., eds. *Revolutionary Virginia, the Road to Independence: A Documentary Record.* 7 vols. Charlottesville: University Press of Virginia, 1973–83.

Seineke, Kathrine Wagner, ed. *The George Rogers Clark Adventure in the Illinois, and Selected Documents of the American Revolution at the Frontier Posts.* New Orleans: Polyanthos, 1981.

Sheehan, Bernard. "The Problem of the Indian in the American Revolution." In Philip Weeks, ed. *The American Indian Experience.* Arlington Heights, Ill.: Forum, 1988.

Showman, Richard K., ed. *Papers of General Nathanael Greene.* Vol. 54. Chapel Hill: University of North Carolina Press, 1976.

Shortt, Adam, and Arthur G. Doughty, eds. *Documents Relating to the Constitutional History of Canada.* 2 vols. Ottawa: S. E. Dawson, 1907.

Simcoe, J. G. *Simcoe's Military Journal: A History of the Operations of a Partisan Corps Called the Queen's Rangers.* New York: Barlett & Welford, 1844.

Simmons, R. C., and P. D. G. Thomas, eds. *Proceedings and Debates of the British Parliaments Respecting North America.* Millwoood, N.Y.: Kraus International Publications, 1982.

Smith, James. *An Account of the Remarkable Occurrences of Col. James Smith during His Captivity with the Indians, in the Years 1755, '56, '57, '58, & '59.* Cincinnati: Robert Clark & Company, 1870.

Smith, William Henry, ed. *St. Clair Papers: The Life and Public Services of Arthur St. Clair . . . with His Correspondence and Other Papers.* 2 vols. Cincinnati: Clarke, 1882.

Sparks, Jared, ed. *Correspondence of the American Revolution: Being Letters of Eminent Men to George Washington from the Time of his Taking Command of the Army to the End of His Presidency.* 4 vols. Boston: Little, Brown, and Company, 1853.

Stanley, George F. G., ed. *For Want of a Horse: Being a Journal of the Campaigns against the Americans in 1776 and 1777 Conducted from Canada, by an Officer Who Served with Lt. Gen. Burgoyne.* Sackville, N.B.: The Tribune Press Limited, 1961.

Stevens, Benjamin. "Diary of Benjamin Stevens, of Canaan, Connecticut." *Daughters of the American Revolution Magazine* 45 (July–December 1914): 137–40.

Stevens, Sylvester K., and Donald H. Kent, eds. *Wilderness Chronicles of Northwestern Pennsylvania.* Harrisburg: Pennsylvania Historical Commission, 1941.

Stevens, Sylvester, Donald Kent, and Emma Woods, eds. *Travels in New France by JCB.* Harrisburg: Pennsylvania Historical Survey, Pennsylvania Historical Commission, 1941.

Stock, Leo Francis, ed. *Proceedings and Debates of the British Parliaments Respecting North America.* 5 vols. Washington, D.C.: Carnegie Institute, 1924–41.

Stone, William S., ed. *Journal of Captain Pausch, Chief of the Hanau Artillery during the Burgoyne Campaign.* Albany, N.Y.: Joel Munsell & Sons, 1886.

Stuart, Charles, ed. *Memoir of Indian Wars and Other Occurrences: By the Late Colonel Stuart, of Greenbriar.* New York: Arno, 1971.

Sullivan, James, ed. *Minutes of the Albany Committee of Correspondence, 1775–1778.* 2 vols. Albany: The University of the State of New York, 1923 and 1925.

Sullivan, James, and A. C. Flick, eds. *The Papers of William Johnson.* 14 vols. Albany: State University of New York, 1921–65.

Surrey, N. M. Miller, ed. *Calendar of Manuscripts in Paris Archives and Libraries Relating to the History of the Mississippi Valley to 1803.* 2 vols. Washington D.C.: Carnegie Institution, Department of Historical Research, 1926–28.

Swettland, Luke. *A Narrative of the Captivity of Luke Swettland, in 1778 and 1779, among the Seneca Indians.* Waterville, N.Y.: Guernsey, 1875.

Talman, James J., ed. *Loyalist Narratives from Upper Canada.* Toronto: Champlain Society, 1946.

Tatum, Edward E., ed. *The American Journal of Ambrose Serle, Secretary to Lord Howe, 1776–1778.* San Marino, Calif.: The Huntington Library, 1940.

Thwaites, Reuben Gold, ed. *Early Western Travels, 1748–1846.* 32 vols. Cleveland: The Arthur H. Clarke Company, 1904–7.

Thwaites, Reuben Gold, ed. *The Jesuit Relations and Allied Documents: Travels and Explorations of the Jesuit Missionaries in New France, 1610–1791.* 73 vols. Reprint, New York: Pageant Book Co., 1959.

Thwaites, Reuben Gold, and Louise P. Kellogg, eds. *Documentary History of Dunmore's War.* Madison: Wisconsin State Historical Society, 1905.

Thwaites, Reuben Gold, and Louise P. Kellogg, eds. *Frontier Defense on the Upper Ohio, 1777–1778.* Madison: Wisconsin State Historical Society, 1912.

Thwaites, Reuben Gold, and Louise P. Kellogg, eds. *Frontier Retreat on the Upper Ohio, 1779–1782.* Madison: Wisconsin State Historical Society, 1917.

Thwaites, Reuben Gold, and Louise P. Kellogg, eds. *The Revolution on the Upper Ohio, 1775–1777.* Madison: Wisconsin State Historical Society, 1908.

"Trumball Papers." *Massachusetts Historical Society, Collections.* 5th series. Vols. 9–10.

Van Der Beets, Richard, ed. *Held Captive by the Indians: Selected Narratives, 1642–1836.* Knoxville: University of Tennessee Press, 1973.

Vaughan, Alden T., ed. *Early American Indian Documents: Laws and Treaties, 1607–1789.* Frederick, Md.: University Publications of America, 1979.

Verreau, Anthelme J. B., ed. *Invasion du Canada, collection des memoires recuilles et annote par M. l'abbe Verreau, pretre.* Montreal: Societe Historique de Montreal, 1873.

Von Muenchhausen, Levin Friedrich Ernst. *At General Howe's Side, 1776–1778: The Diary of General William Howe's Aide de Camp, Captain Friedrich von Muenchhausen.* Translated by Ernst Kipping and annotated by Samuel Smith. Monmouth, N.J.: Philip Freneau Press, 1974.

Wainwright, Nicolas B., ed. "Turmoil at Pittsburgh: Diary of Augustine Prevost, 1774." *Pennsylvania Magazine of History and Biography* 85 (April 1961): 111–62.

Washburn, Wilcomb E., ed. *The Garland Library of Narratives of North American Indian Captivities.* 111 vols. New York: Garland Publishing Co., 1975–79.

Watts, Florence G. "Some Vincennes Documents of 1772." *Indiana Magazine of History* 334 (1938): 199–212.

Webster, John Clarence, ed. *The Journal of Jeffrey Amherst, Recording the Military Career of General Amherst in America from 1758 to 1763.* Chicago: Ryerson Press, 1931.

West, J. Martin, ed. *Clark's Shawnee Campaign of 1780: Contemporary Accounts.* Springfield, Ohio: Clark County Historical Society, 1975.

Williams, Edward G., ed. "The Journal of Richard Butler, 1775: Continental Congress' Envoy to the Western Indians." *Western Pennsylvania Historical Magazine* 46 (October 1963): 381–95; 47 (January 1964): 31–46; 47 (April 1964): 144–45.

Wright, Albert Hazen, ed. *The Sullivan Expedition of 1779: Contemporary Newspaper Comment and Letters, Studies in History.* Nos. 5–8. Ithaca, N.Y.: A. H. Wright, 1943.

Wurtele, Fred C., ed. *Blockade of Quebec in 1775–1776 by the American Revolutionists.* New York: Kennikat Press, 1970.

SECONDARY SOURCES: BOOKS AND ARTICLES

Abby, Kathryn T. "Peter Chester's Defense of the Mississippi after the Willing Raid." *Mississippi Valley Historical Review* 22 (1935): 17–35.

Abernethy, Thomas Perkins. *Western Lands and the American Revolution.* Reprint, New York: Russell and Russell, 1959.

Abler, Thomas S. "Iroquois Cannibalism: Fact Not Fiction." *Ethnohistory* 27 (1980): 309–16.

Abler, Thomas S., and Michael H. Logan. "The Florescence and Demise of Iroquoian Cannibalism: Human Sacrifice and Malinowski's Hypothesis." *Man in the Northeast* 35 (Spring 1988): 1–26.

Alden, John Richard. *General Gage in America.* Baton Rouge: University of Louisiana, 1948.

Alden, John Richard. *John Stuart and the Southern Colonial Frontier: A Study of Indian Relations, War, Trade, and Land Problems in the Southern Wilderness, 1754–1775.* Ann Arbor: University of Michigan Press, 1944.

Alford, Thomas Wildcat. *Civilization and the Story of the Absentee Shawnees.* Norman: University of Oklahoma Press, 1936.

Allen, Robert S. *His Majesty's Indian Allies: British Policy in the Defense of Canada, 1774–1815.* Toronto: Dundurn, 1992.

Alvord, Clarence W. "Genesis of the Proclamation of 1763." *Michigan Pioneer and Historical Collections* 36 (1908): 20–32.

Alvord, Clarence W. "Lord Shelburne and the Founding of British American Goodwill." *Proceedings of the British Academy* 11 (1924–1925): 369–96.

Alvord, Clarence W. "Party Politics and the British Empire." *Nineteenth Century* 97 (1925): 326–33.

Alvord, Clarence W. "Virginia and the West: An Interpretation." *Mississippi Valley Historical Review* 3 (1934): 19–38.

Alvord, Clarence Walworth. *The Mississippi Valley in British Politics: A Study of the Trade, Land Speculation, and Experiments in Imperialism Culminating in the American Revolution.* 2 vols. New York: Russell and Russell, 1959.

Ambler, Charles H. *George Washington and the West.* Reprint, New York: Russell and Russell, 1971.

The American Historical Association's Guide to Historical Literature. New York: American Historical Association, 1961.

Anderson, Gary Clayton. "Early Dakota Migration and Intertribal War: A Revision." *The Western Historical Quarterly* 11 (January 1980): 17–36.

Anderson, Gary Clayton. *Kinsmen of Another Kind: Dakota-White Relations in the Upper Mississippi Valley, 1650–1862.* Lincoln: University of Nebraska Press, 1984.

Anderson, Troyer Steele. *The Command of the Howe Brothers during the American Revolution.* New York: Oxford University Press, 1936.

Anson, Bert. *The Miami Indians.* Norman: University of Oklahoma Press, 1970.

Armour, David, and Keith R. Widder. *At the Crossroads: Michilimackinac during the American Revolution.* Mackinac Island, Mich.: Mackinac Island State Park Commission, 1986.

Aron, Stephen. "Pioneers and Profiteers: Land Speculation and the Homestead Ethic in Frontier Kentucky." *Western Historical Quarterly* 27 (1992): 179–98.

Atkinson, C. T. "Some Evidence for Burgoyne's Expedition." *Journal of the Society for Army Historical Rearch* 26 (Winter 1948): 132–42.

Auth, Stephen F. *The Ten Years' War: Indian-White Relations in Pennsylvania, 1755–1765.* New York: Garland Publishers, 1989.

Axtell, James. "Colonial America without the Indians: Counterfactual Reflections." *Journal of American History* 73 (1986–87): 981–96.

Axtell, James. *The European and the Indian: Essays in the Ethnohistory of Colonial North America.* New York: Oxford University Press, 1981.

Axtell, James, and William C. Sturtevant. "The Unkindest Cut; or, Who Invented Scalping?" *William and Mary Quarterly* 37 (1980): 451–72.

Bailey, Edith A. *Influence toward Radicalism in Connecticut, 1754–1775.* Northampton, Mass.: Smith College Studies in History, Vol. 4. 1920.

Bailey, Kenneth P. *The Ohio Company of Virginia and the Westward Movement, 1748–1792.* Glendale, Calif.: The Arthur H. Clark Company, 1939.

Bailyn, Bernard. *Faces of Revolution: Personalities and Themes in the Struggle for American Independence.* New York: Knopf, 1990.

Bailyn, Bernard. *The Ideological Origins of the American Revolution.* Cambridge, Mass.: Belknap Press, 1967.

Bailyn, Bernard, and Philip D. Morgan, eds. *Strangers within the Realm: Cultural Margins of the First British Empire.* Chapel Hill: University of North Carolina Press, 1991.

Baird, W. David. *The Quapaw Indians: A History of the Downstream People.* Norman: University of Oklahoma Press, 1980.

Bakeless, John. *Background to Glory: The Life of George Rogers Clark.* Lincoln: University of Nebraska Press, 1992.

Baker, Ray Stannard. "Remember Baker." *New England Quarterly* 4 (October 1931): 620–28.

Balingham, Emily J. "The Depopulation of the Illinois Indians." *Ethnohistory* 3 (Summer–Fall 1956): 193–217, 381–412.

Barnhart, John D. "A New Evaluation of Henry Hamilton and George Rogers Clark." *Mississippi Valley Historical Review* 37 (1951): 643–52.

Barnhart, John D., and Dorothy L. Riker. *Indiana to 1816: The Colonial Period, The History of Indiana.* Vol. 1. Indianapolis: Indiana Historical Bureau and Indian Historical Society, 1971.

Barsh, Russell Lawrence. "Native American Loyalists and Patriots: Reflections on the American Revolution in Native America History." *Indian Historian* 10 (Summer 1977): 9–19.

Basye, Arthur Herbert. *The Lords Commissioners of Trade and Plantations, Commonly Known as the Board of Trade, 1748–1782.* New Haven, Conn.: Yale University Press, 1925.

Bauman, Richard. *For the Reputation of Truth: Politics, Religion, and Conflict among the Pennsylvania Quakers, 1750–1800.* Baltimore: Johns Hopkins Press, 1971.

Beattie, Daniel J. "The Adaptation of the British Army to Wilderness Warfare, 1755–1763." In Maarten Ultree, ed. *Adapting to Conditions: War and Society in the Eighteenth Century.* Tuscaloosa: University of Alabama Press, 1986.

Bellesiles, Michael A. *Revolutionary Outlaws: Ethan Allen and the Struggle for Independence on the Early American Frontier.* Charlottesville: University of Virginia Press, 1993.

Bennett, John. *Blue Jacket, War Chief of the Shawnees and His Part in Ohio's History.* Chillicothe, Ohio: n.p., 1943.

Berger, Carl, ed. *Broadsides and Bayonets: The Propaganda War of the American Revolution.* Philadelphia: University of Pennsylvania Press, 1961.

Berkhofer, Robert F. *The White Man's Indian: Images of the American Indian from Columbus to the Present.* New York: Knopf, 1977.

Billias, George Athan, ed. *George Washington's Opponents: British Generals and Admirals in the American Revolution.* New York: William Morrow and Company, 1969.

Billington, Ray A. "The Ft. Stanwix Treaty of 1768." *New York History* 25 (1944): 182–94.

Blanco, Richard L., ed. *The American Revolution, 1775–1783: An Encyclopedia.* 2 vols. New York: Garland, 1993.

Bowden, Henry Warner. *American Indians and Christian Missions.* Chicago: University of Chicago Press, 1981.

Bowler, R. Arthur. *Logistics and the Failure of the British Army in America, 1775–1783.* Princeton, N.J.: Princeton University Press, 1975.

Boyd, Julian P. *The Susquehanna Company.* New Haven, Conn.: Yale University Press, 1935.

Braund, Kathryn E. Holland. *Deerskins and Duffels: Creek Indian Trade with Anglo-America, 1685–1815.* Lincoln: University of Nebraska Press, 1993.

Brebner, John B. *North Atlantic Triangle.* New Haven, Conn.: Yale University Press, 1945.

Brewer, John. *Sinews of Power: War, Money, and the English State, 1688–1783.* New York: Unwin Hyman, 1989.

Brown, Douglas. *The Catawba Indians: The People of the River.* Columbia, S.C.: University of South Carolina Press, 1966.

Brown, George, et al., eds. *Dictionary of Canadian Biography.* Toronto: University of Toronto Press, 1966–.

Brown, Gerald S. *The American Secretary: The Colonial Policy of Lord George Germain, 1775–1778.* Ann Arbor: University of Michigan Press, 1963.

Buck, Solon J. and Elizabeth Hawthorn Buck. *The Planting of Civilization in Western Pennsylvania.* Pittsburgh: University of Pittsburgh Press, 1939.

Burrows, Edwin, and Michael Wallace. "The American Revolution: The Ideology and Psychology of National Liberation." *Perspectives on American History* 6 (1972): 208–15.

Burt, Alfred A. *Guy Carleton, Lord Dorchester, 1727–1803.* Ottawa: The Canadian Historical Association, 1968.

Butterfield, Herbert. *George III and the Historians.* Rev. ed. New York: Macmillan, 1969.

Caley, Percy B. "The Life Adventures of Lieutenant-Colonel John Connolly: The Story of a Tory." *Western Pennsylvania Historical Magazine* 11 (April 1928): 101–6.

Calloway, Colin G. *The American Revolution in Indian Country: Crisis and Diversity in Native American Communities.* New York: Cambridge University Press, 1995.

Calloway, Colin G. *Crown and Calumet: British-Indian Relations, 1783–1815.* Norman: University of Oklahoma Press, 1987.

Calloway, Colin G. "New England: Algonkians in the American Revolution." *Annual Proceedings of the Dublin Seminar for New England Folklore* (1991): 51–62.

Calloway, Colin G. "Sentinels of the Revolution: Bedel's New Hampshire Rangers and the Abenakis on the Upper Connecticut." *Historical New Hampshire* 4 (1990): 271–95.

Calloway, Colin G. "Simon Girty: Interpreter and Intermediary." In James A. Clifton, ed. *Being and Becoming Indian: Biographical Studies of North American Frontiers.* Chicago: Dorsey, 1989.

Calloway, Colin G. "Suspicion and Self-Interest: British-Indian Relations and the Peace of Paris." *Historian* 48 (November 1985): 41–60.

Calloway, Colin G. "'We Have Always Been the Frontier': The American Revolution in Shawnee Country." *American Indian Quarterly* 16 (1992): 39–52.

Calloway, Colin G. *The Western Abenaki of Vermon, 1600–1800: War, Migration, and the Survival of an Indian People.* Norman: University of Oklahoma Press, 1991.

Cappon, Lester J., Barbara Bartz Petchenik, and John Hamilton Long, eds. *Atlas of Early American History: The Revolutionary Era, 1760–1790.* Princeton, N.J.: Princeton University Press, 1977.

Carey, Lewis J. "Franklin Is Informed of Clark's Activities in the Old Northwest." *Mississippi Valley Historical Review* 21 (1934): 375–78.

Carroll, Orville W. *Fort Stanwix: History, Historic Furnishing, and Historic Structure Report.* Washington, D.C.: Office of Park Historic Preservation, National Park Service, U.S. Department of the Interior, 1976.

Carstens, Kenneth C. "The 1780 William Clark Map of Fort Jefferson." *Filson Club History Quarterly* 67 (1993): 23–43.

Cashin, Edward J. "'But Brothers, This Is Our Land We Are Talking About': Winners and Losers in Georgia's Backcountry." In Ronald Hoffman, Thad W. Tate, and Peter J. Albert, eds. *An Uncivil War: The Southern Backcountry during the American Revolution.* Charlottesville: University of Virginia Press, 1985.

Cashin, Edward J. *The King's Ranger: Thomas Brown and the American Revolution on the Southern Frontier.* Athens: University of Georgia Press, 1989.

Cashin, Edward J. *Lachlan McGillivray, Indian Trader: The Shaping of the Southern Colonial Frontier.* Athens: University of Georgia Press, 1992.

Cashin, Edward J. "Sowing the Wind: Governor Wright and the Georgia Backcountry on the Eve of the Revolution." In Harvey H. Jackson and Phinizy Spaulding, eds. *Forty Years of Diversity: Essays on Colonial Georgia.* Athens: University of Georgia Press, 1984.

Caughey, John Walton. *Bernado de Galvez in Louisiana, 1776–1783.* Gretna, La.: Pelican, 1972.

Caughey, John Walton. *McGillivray of the Creeks.* Norman: University of Oklahoma Press, 1938.

Caughey, John Walton. "The Natchez Rebellion of 1781 and Its Aftermath." *Louisiana Historical Quarterly* 16 (1933): 57–83.

Caughey, John Walton. "Willing's Expedition down the Mississippi, 1778." *Louisiana Historical Quarterly* 15 (1932): 5–36.

Chalou, George C. "George Rogers Clark and Indian America, 1778–1780." In *The French, the Indians, and George Rogers Clark in the Illinois Country.* Indianapolis: Indiana Historical Society, 1977.

Cleland, Hugh. *George Washington in the Ohio Valley.* Pittsburgh: University of Pittsburgh Press, 1955.

Clifton, James A. *The Prairie People: Continuity and Change in Potawatomi Indian Culture, 1665–1965.* Lawrence: Regents Press of Kansas, 1977.

Clifton, James A., ed. *Being and Becoming Indian: Biographical Studies of North American Frontiers.* Chicago: Dorsey, 1989.

Coker, William S., and Robert R. Rea, eds. *Anglo-Spanish Confrontation on the Gulf Coast during the American Revolution.* Pensacola, Fla.: Gulf Coast History and Humanities Conference, 1982.

Coker, William S., and Thomas D. Watson. *Indian Traders of the Southeastern Spanish Borderlands: Panton, Leslie, & Company and John Forbes & Company, 1783–1847.* Pensacola: University of West Florida Press, 1986.

Coleman, Kenneth. *The American Revolution in Georgia, 1763–1789.* Athens: University of Georgia Press, 1959.

Connor, George E. "The Politics of Insurrection: A Comparative Analysis of the Shay's, Whiskey, and Fries' Rebellion." *Social Science Journal* 29 (1992): 259–81.

Cook, Roy Bird. "Virginia Frontier Defenses, 1719–1795." *West Virginia History* 1 (1940): 119–30.

Corbitt, D. C. "James Colbert and the Spanish Claims to the East Bank of the Mississippi." *Mississippi Valley Historical Review* 24 (1938): 457–72.

Corkran, David H. *The Cherokee Frontier: Conflict and Survival, 1740–1762.* Norman: University of Oklahoma Press, 1962.

Corkran, David H. *The Creek Frontier, 1540–1783.* Norman: University of Oklahoma Press, 1967.

Cotterill, R. S. *The Southern Indians: The Story of the Civilized Tribes before Removal.* Norman: University of Oklahoma Press, 1954.

Cotterill, Robert S. "The Virginia-Chickasaw Treaty of 1783." *Journal of Southern History* 8 (1942): 483–96.

Coupland, Sir Reginald. *The Quebec Act: A Study in Statemanship.* Oxford: Clarendon Press, 1925.

Cruikshank, Ernest. *The Story of Butler's Rangers and the Settlement of Niagara.* Niagara Fall, Ont.: Reknown, 1988.

Dabney, William, and Marion Dargon. *William Henry Drayton and the American Revolution.* Albuquerque: University of New Mexico Press, 1962.

Davis, Andrew Mcfarland. "The Indians and the Border Warfare of the Revolution." In Justin Winsor, ed. *Narrative and Critical History of America.* 8 vols. Boston: Houghton Mifflin, 1884–89.

Davis, Robert Scott, Jr. "George Galphin and the Creek Congress of 1777." *Proceedings and Papers of the Georgia of Historians* (1982): 13–20.

De Vorsey, Louis. *The Indian Boundary in the Southern Colonies, 1763–1775.* Chapel Hill: University of North Carolina Press, 1961.

Din, Gilbert C. "Arkansas Post in the American Revolution." *Arkansas Historical Quarterly 40* (1981): 3–30.

Din, Gilbert C. "Loyalist Resistance after Pensacola: The Case of James Colbert." In William S. Coker and Roberta Rea, eds. *Anglo-Spanish Confrontation on the Gulf Coast during the American Revolution.* Pensacola, Fla.: Gulf Coast History and Humanities Conference, 1982.

Din, Gilbert C., and A. P. Nasatir. *The Imperial Osages: Spanish-Indian Diplomacy in the Mississippi Valley.* Norman: University of Oklahoma Press, 1983.

Dixon, Max. *The Wataugans.* Johnson City, Tenn.: Overmountain Press, 1976.

Dobyns, Henry F. *Their Number Become Thinned: Native American Population Dynamics in Eastern North America.* Knoxville: University of Tennessee Press, 1983.

Dowd, Gregory Evans. *A Spirited Resistance: The North American Indian Struggle for Unity, 1745–1815.* Baltimore: Johns Hopkins Press, 1992.

Downes, Randolph C. "Cherokee-American Relations in the Upper Tennessee Valley, 1776–1791." *East Tennessee Historical Society Publications* 8 (1936).

Downes, Randolph C. *Council Fires on the Upper Ohio: A Narrative of Indian Affairs in the Upper Ohio Valley until 1795.* Pittsburgh: University of Pittsburgh Press, 1969.

Downes, Randolph C. "Dunmore's War: An Interpretation." *Mississippi Valley Historical Review* 20 (1934): 311–30.

Downes, Randolph C. "The Indian War on the Upper Ohio, 1779–1782." *Western Pennsylvania Historical Magazine* 17 (1934): 93–115.

Eccles, W. J. "The Fur Trade and Eighteenth Century Imperialism." *William and Mary Quarterly* 40 (1983): 341–62.

Edmunds, R. David. *The Potawatomis: Keepers of the Fire.* Norman: University of Oklahoma Press, 1978.

Eid, Leroy V. "'A Kind of Running Fight': Indian Battlefield Tactics in the Late Eighteenth Century." *Western Pennsylvania Historical Magazine* 71 (1988): 147–71.

Eid, Leroy V. "'National' War among Indians of Northeastern North America." *Canadian Review of American Studies* 16 (1985): 125–54.

Ericson, Fred J. "British Motives for Expansion in 1763: Territory, Commerce, or Security." *Papers of the Michigan Academy of Science, Art, and Letters* 27 (1941): 581–94.

Ernst, Joseph Albert. *Money and Politics in America, 1755–1775: A Study in the Currency Act of 1764 and the Political Economy of Revolution*. Chapel Hill: University of North Carolina Press, 1973.

Evans, Raymond E. "Notable Persons in Cherokee History: Dragging Canoe." *Journal of Cherokee Studies* 2 (1977): 176–89.

Every, Dale Van. *A Company of Heroes: The American Frontier, 1775–1783*. New York: Mentor Books, 1963.

Faragher, John Mack. *Daniel Boone: The Life and Legend of an American Pioneer*. New York: Holt, 1992.

Faux, David K. "Iroquoian Occupation of the Mohawk Valley during and after the Revolution." *Man in the Northeast* 34 (Fall 1987): 27–39.

Faye, Stanley. "Illinois Indians on the Lower Mississippi, 1771–1782." *Journal of the Illinois State Historical Society* 35 (1942): 57–72.

Ferguson, E. James. *The American Revolution: A General History, 1763–1790*. Homewood, Ill.: Dorsey Press, 1979.

Ferling, John E. *A Wilderness of Miseries: War and Warriors in Early America*. Westport, Conn.: 1980.

Ferling, John, ed. *The World Turned Upside Down: The American Victory in the War of Independence*. Westport, Conn.: Greenwood Press, 1988.

Flexner, James Thomas. *Mohawk Baronet: Sir William Johnson of New York*. New York: Harper and Brothers, 1959.

Ford, Worthington Chauncey. *The Minute Book of the Committee of Public Safety of Tryon County*. Brooklyn, N.Y.: Historical Printing Club, 1897.

Fortescue, Sir John W. *A History of the British Army*. 13 vols. London: 1899–1930.

Foster, Michael K., Jack Campisi, and Marianne Mithun, eds. *Extending the Rafters: Interdisciplinary Approaches to Iroquoian Studies*. Albany, N.Y.: 1984.

Franklin, W. Neil. "Pennsylvania-Virginia Rivalry for the Indian Trade of the Ohio Valley." *Mississippi Valley Historical Review* 20 (March 1934): 463–80.

Fraser, Kathryn M. "Fort Jefferson: George Rogers Clark's Fort at the Mouth of the Ohio, 1780–1781." *Register of the Kentucky Historical Society* 81 (1983): 1–24.

Frey, Sylvia R. *The British Soldier in America: A Social History of Military Life in the Revolutionary Period*. Austin, Tex.: University of Texas Press, 1981.

Frey, Sylvia R. *Water from the Rock: Black Resistance in a Revolutionary Age*. Princeton, N.J.: University of Princeton Press, 1991.

Fryer, C. E. "Further Pamphlets for Canada-Guadeloupe Controversy." *Mississippi Valley Historical Review* 5 (1917): 227–30.

Gallay, Alan. *The Formation of a Planter Elite: Jonathan Bryan and the Southern Colonial Frontier*. Athens: University of Georgia Press, 1989.

Galloway, William A. *Old Chillicothe*. Xenia, Ohio: Buckeye, 1934.

Ganyard, Robert L. "Threat from the West: North Carolina and the Cherokee, 1776–1778." *North Carolina Historical Review* 45 (1968): 47–66.

Gephardt, Ronald. *Revolutionary America, 1763–1789: A Bibliography.* 2 vols. Washington, D.C.: Library of Congress, 1984.

Gibson, Arrell M. *The Kickapoos.* Norman, University of Oklahoma Press, 1963.

Gibson, Arrell Morgan. *The Chickasaws.* Norman: University of Oklahoma Press, 1971.

Gilbert, Arthur N. "The Changing Face of British Military Justice, 1757–1783." *Military Affairs* 49 (1979): 80–84.

Gipson, Lawrence Henry. *A Bibliographical Guide to the History of the British Empire, 1748–1776.* New York: Alfred A. Knopf, 1968.

Gipson, Lawrence Henry. *The British Empire before the American Revolution.* 12 vols. New York: Alfred A. Knopf, 1958–70.

Given, Brian J. "The Iroquois Wars and Native Arms." In Bruce A. Cox, ed. *Native Peoples, Natives Lands.* Ottawa: Carleton University Press, 1988.

Gold, Robert L. "The Settlement of the Pensacola Indians in New Spain, 1763–1770." *Hispanic American Historical Review* 45 (1965): 567–76.

Goodwin, Gary C. *Cherokees in Transition: A Study of Changing Culture and Environment Prior to 1775.* Chicago: University of Chicago, Dept. of Geography, 1977.

Grant, William L. "Canada versus Guadeloupe, an Episode of the Seven Years' War." *American Historical Review* 17:4 (July 1912): 735–43.

Gray, Elma E., and Leslie R. Gray, *Wilderness Christians.* Ithaca, N.Y.: Cornell University Press, 1956.

Graymont, Barbara. *The Iroquois and the American Revolution.* Syracuse, N.Y.: Syracuse University Press, 1972.

Graymont, Barbara. "The Oneida and the American Revolution." In Jack Campisi and Laurence M. Hauptman, eds. *The Oneida Indian Experience: Two Perspectives.* Syracuse, N.Y.: Syracuse University Press, 1988.

Green, Michael D. "Alexander McGillivray." In R. David Edmunds, ed. *American Indian Leaders: Studies in Diversity.* Lincoln: University of Nebraska Press, 1980.

Green, Michael D. "The Creek Confederacy in the American Revolution: Cautious Participants." In William S. Coker and Robert R. Rea, eds. *Anglo-Spanish Confrontation on the Gulf Coast during the American Revolution.* Pensacola, Fla.: Gulf Coast History and Humanities Conference, 1982.

Greene, Evarts, and Virginia D. Harrington. *American Population before the Federal Census of 1790.* New York: Columbia University Press, 1932.

Greene, Jack P. "'A Posture of Hostility': A Reconsideration of Some Aspects of the Origins of the American Revolution." *Proceedings of the American Antiquarian Society* 87 (April–October 1977): 27–68.

Greene, Jack P. *The Quest for Power: The Lower Houses of Assembly in the Southern Royal Colonies, 1689–1776.* Reprint, New York: W. W. Norton, 1972.

Greene, Jack P. *The Reinterpretation of the American Revolution, 1763–1789.* New York: Harper & Row, 1968.

Greene, Jack P. "The Seven Years' War and the American Revolution: The Causal Relationship Reconsidered." In Peter Marshall and Glyn Williams, eds. *The British Atlantic Empire before the American Revolution.* London: Frank Cass, 1980.

Greene, Jack P. "The Social Origins of the American Revolution: An Evaluation and Interpretation." *Political Science Quarterly* 88 (1973): 1–14.

Greene, Jack P. "An Uneasy Connection: An Analysis of the Preconditions of the American Revolution." In Stephen G. Kurtz and James H. Hutson, eds. *Essays on the American Revolution.* Chapel Hill: University of North Carolina Press, 1973.

Greene, Jack P., and J. R. Pole, eds. *The Blackwell Encyclopedia of the American Revolution.* Cambridge, Mass.: Blackwell, 1991.

Grinde, Donald A., and Bruce E. Johnson. *Exemplar of Liberty: Native America and the Evolution of Democracy.* Los Angeles: UCLA American Indian Studies Center, 1991.

Gruber, Ira D. *The Howe Brothers and the American Revolution.* Chapel Hill: University of North Carolina, 1972.

Guttridge, G. H. *English Whiggism and the American Revolution.* Berkeley: University of California Press, 1942.

Guzzardo, John C. "The Superintendent and the Ministers: The Battle for Oneida Allegiances." *New York History* 57 (1976).

Haarman, Albert W. "The Spanish Conquest of British West Florida, 1779–1781." *Florida Historical Quarterly* 39 (1960): 107–34.

Hagan, William T. *Longhouse Diplomacy and Frontier Warfare: The Iroquois Confederation in the American Revolution.* Albany, N.Y.: New York State Bicentennial Commission, 1976.

Hale, W. Richard. *The Royal Americans.* Ann Arbor: University of Michigan Press, 1944.

Hamer, Philip M. "Anglo-French Rivalry in the Cherokee Country, 1754–57." *North Carolina Historical Review* 2 (1925): 303–22.

Hamer, Philip M. "John Stuart's Indian Policy during the Early Months of the American Revolution." *Mississippi Valley Historical Review* 17 (1930): 351–66.

Hamer, Philip M. "The Wataugans and the Cherokee Indians in 1776." *East Tennessee Historical Society Publications* 3 (1931): 108–26.

Hanna, Charles A. *The Wilderness Trail; or, the Ventures and Adventures of the Pennsylvania Traders on the Allegheny Path.* 2 vols. New York: Putnam and Sons, 1911.

Hanna, William S. *Benjamin Franklin and Pennsylvania Politics.* Stanford, Calif.: Stanford University Press, 1964.

Hardaway, John A. "Colonial and Revolutionary War Origins of American Military Policy." *Military Review* 56 (1976): 77–89.

Harrison, Lowell. *George Rogers Clark and the War in the West.* Lexington: University of Kentucky Press, 1976.

Hatch, Robert McConnell. *Thrust for Canada: The American Attempt on Quebec in 1775–1776.* Boston: Houghton Mifflin Company, 1979.

Hatley, Tom. *The Dividing Path: Cherokees and South Carolinians through the Era of the Revolution.* New York: Oxford University Press, 1993.

Hauptman, Laurence M. "Refugee Havens: The Iroquois Villages of the Eighteenth Century." In Christopher Vecsey and Robert Venables, eds. *American Indian Environments: Ecological Issues in Native American History.* Syracuse, N.Y.: Syracuse University Press, 1980.

Hauser, Raymond. "The Illinois Indian Tribe: From Autonomy to Self-Sufficiency to Dependency and Depopulation." *Journal of the Illinois State Historical Society* 69 (May 1976): 127–38.

Haynes, Robert V. *The Natchez District and the American Revolution.* Jackson: University Press of Mississippi, 1976.

Helderman, L. C. "The Northwest Expedition of George Rogers Clark, 1786–87." *Mississippi Valley Historical Review* 25 (1938).

Henderson, Archibald. "The Treaty of Long Island of the Holston, 1777." *North Carolina Historical Review* 8 (1931): 76–78.

Henretta, James A. *The Evolution of American Society, 1700 to 1815: An Interdisplinary Analysis.* Lexington, Mass.: D. C. Heath, 1973.

Higginbotham, Don. "The Early American Way of War: Reconnaissance and Appraisal." *William and Mary Quarterly* 44:2 (April 1987): 230–73.

Hoffman, Ronald, Thad W. Tate, and Peter J. Albert, eds. *An Uncivil War: The Southern Backcountry during the American Revolution.* Charlottesville: University of Virginia Press, 1985.

Holden, James Austin. "The Influence of the Death of Jane McCrea on Burgoyne's Campaign." *Proceedings of the New York Historical Association* 12 (1913): 249–310.

Holland, Kathryn. "The Anglo-Spanish Contest for the Gulf as Viewed from the Townsquare." In William S. Coker and Robert Rea, eds. *Anglo-Spanish Confrontation on the Gulf Coast during the American Revolution.* Pensacola, Fla.: Gulf Coast History and Humanities Conference, 1982.

Holmes, Jack D. L. *Gayoso: The Life of a Spanish Governor in the Mississippi Valley, 1789–1799.* Baton Rouge: Louisiana State University Press, 1965.

Holmes, Jack D. L. "Spanish-American Rivarly over the Chickasaw Bluffs, 1780–1795." *East Tennessee Historical Society Publications* 34 (1962).

Holmes, Jack D. L. "Spanish Treaties with West Florida Indians, 1784–1802." *Florida Historical Quarterly* 48 (1969).

Horsman, Reginald. *Expansion and American Indian Policy, 1783–1815.* East Lansing: Michigan State University Press, 1967.

Horsman, Reginald. *Matthew Elliott, British Indian Agent.* Detroit: Wayne State University Press, 1964.

Houck, Louis, ed. *The Spanish Regime in Missouri.* 2 vols. Chicago: Donnelly, 1909.

Houlding, J. A. *Fit for Service: The Training of the British Army, 1715–1795.* New York: Oxford University Press, 1981.

Howard, James H. *Shawnee! Ceremonialism of a Native Indian Tribe and Its Cultural Background.* Athens: Ohio University Press, 1981.

Howard, Robert West. *Thundergate: The Forts at Niagara.* Englewood Cliffs, N.J.: Prentice-Hall, 1968.

Howson, Gerald. *Burgoyne of Saratoga: A Biography.* New York: Times Books, 1979.

Hoxie, Frederick E., ed. *Indians in American History.* Arlington Heights, Ill.: Davidson, 1988.

Humphreys, Robin W. "Lord Shelburne and British Colonial Policy, 1766–1768." *English Historical Review* 50 (1935): 257–77.

Humphreys, Robin W. "Lord Shelburne and the Proclamation of 1763." *English Historical Review* 49 (1934): 241–64.

Humphreys, Robin W. "Lord Shelburne and a Projected Recall of Colonial Governors in 1767." *American Historical Review* 37 (1932): 269–73.

Hunt, George T. *Wars of the Iroquois: A Study of Intertribal Trade Relations.* Madison: University of Wisconsin Press, 1960.

Innis, Harold. *The Fur Trade in Canada.* New Haven, Conn.: Yale University Press, 1930.

Jablow, John. *Indians of Illinois and Indiana.* New York: Garland Publishing, 1974.

Jackman, Sydney, ed. *With Burgoyne from Quebec.* Toronto: Macmillan, 1963.

Jacobs, Wilbur R. *The Appalachian Frontier.* Lincoln: University of Nebraska Press, 1967.

Jacobs, Wilbur R. *Dispossessing the American Indian: Indians and Whites on the Colonial Frontier.* New York: Charles Scribner's Sons, 1972.

Jacobson, David L. *John Dickinson and the Revolution in Pennsylvania, 1764–1776.* Berkeley: University of California Press, 1965.

James, Alfred Procter. *The Ohio Company: Its Inner History.* Pittsburgh: University of Pittsburgh Press, 1959.

James, James A. "An Appraisal of the Contributions of George Rogers Clark to the History of the West." *Mississippi Valley Historical Review* 17 (1930): 98–115.

James, James A. "The Northwest: Gift or Conquest?" *Indiana Magazine of History* 30 (1934): 1–15.

James, James A. "Oliver Pollock Financier of the Revolution in the West." *Mississippi Valley Historical Review* 16 (1929): 67–80.

James, James A. "To What Extent Was George Rogers Clark in Military Control of the Northwest at the Close of the American Revolution?" *American Historical Association, Annual Report for 1917* (1920): 313–29.

Jeffries, Ewel. *A Short Biography of John Leeth.* Reprint with introduction by Reuben Gold Thwaites, Cleveland: The Burrows Brothers Company, 1904.

Jennings, Francis. "The Indians' Revolution." In Alfred F. Young, ed. *Explorations in the History of the American Revolution.* De Kalb: Northern Illinois University Press, 1976.

Johnson, Bruce E., and Elisabeth Tooker. "Commentary on the Iroquois and the U.S. Constitution." *Ethnohistory* 37 (1990): 279–97.

Johnson, Cecil. *British West Florida, 1763–1783.* New Haven, Conn.: Yale University Press, 1947.

Kellogg, Louise Phelps. *The British Regime in Wisconsin and the Northwest.* New York: Da Capo Press, 1971.

Kellogg, Louise Phelps. *Frontier Advance on the Upper Ohio.* Madison: Wisconsin Historical Publications, 1916.

Kellogg, Louise Phelps. "Indian Diplomacy during the Revolution in the West." *Transactions of the Illinois State Historical Society* 36 (1929): 47–57.

Kellogg, Louise Phelps. *Revolution on the Upper Ohio, 1775–1777.* Port Washington: Kennikat Press, 1970.

Kellogg, Louise Phelps. "Wisconsin Indians during the American Revolution." *Transactions of the Wisconsin Academy of Sciences, Arts, and Letters* 24 (1929): 47–57.

Kelsay, Isabel Thompson. *Joseph Brant, 1743–1807: Man of Two Worlds.* Syracuse, N.Y.: Syracuse University Press, 1984.

Kenton, Edna. *Simon Kenton: His Life and Period, 1755–1836.* Garden City, N.Y.: Doubleday, Doran, 1930.

King, Duane H. "Long Island of the Holston: Sacred Cherokee Ground." *Journal of Cherokee Studies* 1 (1976): 113–27.

Kinietz, William Vernon. *The Indians of the Western Great Lakes, 1615–1760.* Ann Arbor: University of Michigan Press, 1940.

Kinnaird, Lawrence. *Spain in the Mississippi Valley, 1765–94.* Part 1: The Revolutionary Period, 1765–81. Washington D.C.: Government Printing Office, 1949.

Kinnaird, Lawrence. "The Spanish Expedition against Fort St. Joseph in 1781: A New Interpretation." *Mississippi Valley Historical Review* 19 (1932): 173–91.

Kinnaird, Lawrence. "The Western Fringe of Revolution." *Western Historical Quarterly* 7 (1976): 253–70.

Knollenberg, Bernard. "General Amherst and Germ Warfare." *Mississippi Valley Historical Review* 41 (1954–55): 489–94, 761–73.

Lambert, Robert Stansbury. *South Carolina Loyalists in the American Revolution.* Columbia: University of South Carolina Press, 1987.

Lanctot, Gustave. *Canada and the American Revolution, 1774–1783.* Cambridge: Harvard University Press, 1967.

Leamon, James S. *Revolution Downcast: The War for American Independence.* Amherst: University of Massachusetts Press, 1993.

Levinson, David. "An Explanation of the Oneida-Colonist Alliance in the American Revolution." *Ethnohistory* 23 (1976): 265–89.

Lewis, George E. *The Indiana Company, 1763–1798: A Study in Eighteenth Century Frontier Land Speculation and Business Venture.* Glendale, Calif.: A. H. Clark, 1941.

Lunt, James. *John Burgoyne of Saratoga.* New York: Harcourt Brace Jovanovich, 1975.

Luzander, John F., Louis Torres, and Orville W. Carroll. *Fort Stanwix: History, Historic Furnishing, and Historic Structure Reports.* Washington, D.C.: Office of Park Historic Preservation, National Park Service, U.S. Department of the Interior, 1976.

Mackesy, Piers. *The War for America, 1775–1783.* Cambridge: Harvard University Press, 1965.

MacPherson, K. R. "List of Vessels Employed on British Naval Service on the Great Lakes, 1755–1875." *Ontario History* 55 (September 1963): 72–79.

Mahon, John K. "Anglo-American Methods of Indian Warfare, 1676–1794." *Mississippi Valley Historical Review* 45 (1970): 3–35.

Malone, Patrick M. *The Skulking Way of War: Technology and Tactics among the Indians of New England.* Lanham, Md.: Madison, 1991.

Mancall, Peter C. "The Revolutionary Journal and the Indians of the Upper Susquehanna Valley." *American Indian Culture and Research Journal* 12, no. 1 (1988): 39–57.

Mancall, Peter C. *Valley of Opportunity: Economic Culture along the Upper Susquehanna, 1700–1800.* Chapel Hill: University of North Carolina Press, 1991.

Marshall, Peter. "The West and the Indians, 1756–1776." In Jack P. Greene and J. R. Pole, eds. *The Blackwell History of the American Revolution.* Oxford: Blackwell Publishers, 1991.

Martin, Joel. *Sacred Revolt: The Muskogees' Struggle for a New World.* Boston: Beacon, 1991.

Marx, Leo. *The Machine in the Garden: Technology and the Pastoral Ideal in America.* New York: Oxford University Press, 1964.

Mason, Kathyrn Harrod. *James Herrod of Kentucky.* Baton Rouge: Louisiana State University Press, 1971.

McAdams, Donald R. "The Sullivan Expedition: Success or Failure?" *New York Historical Society Quarterly* 54 (1970): 62–73.

McArthur, Duncan. "The British Board of Trade and Canada, 1760–1774; I, The Proclamation of 1773 [sic]." *Canadian Historical Association, Annual Report for 1932* (1932): 97–113.

McConnell, Michael N. *A Country Between: The Upper Ohio Valley and Its People, 1724–1774.* Lincoln: University of Nebraska Press, 1992.

McIlwraith, Jean N. *Sir Frederick Haldimand.* Toronto: Morang & Co., 1905.

Merrell, James H. "Indians and the New Republic." In Jack P. Greene and J. R. Pole, eds. *The Blackwell History of the American Revolution.* Oxford: Blackwell Publishers, 1991.

Merrell, James H. "Some Thoughts on Colonial Historians and American Indians." *William and Mary Quarterly* 46 (1989): 94–119.

Metzger, Charles H. "An Appraisal of Shelburne's Western Policy." *Mid-America* 9 (1937): 169–81.

Metzger, Charles H. *The Quebec Act: A Primary Cause of the American Revolution.* Monograph Series 16. New York: United States Catholic Historical Society, 1936.

Mitchell, Robert D., ed. *Appalachian Frontier: Settlement, Society, and Development in the Preindustrial Era.* Lexington: University Press of Kentucky, 1991.

Mohr, Walter H. *Federal-Indian Relations, 1774–1788.* Philadelphia: University of Pennsylvania Press, 1933.

Moore, Arthur K. *The Frontier Mind: A Cultural Analysis of the Kentucky Frontiersman.* Lexington: University of Kentucky Press, 1957.

Morgan, Edmund S. *The Birth of the Republic, 1763–1789.* Chicago: University of Chicago Press, 1977.

Morgan, Edmund S., and Helen M. Morgan. *The Stamp Act Crisis: Prologue to Revolution.* Rev. ed. New York: Alfred A. Knopf, 1963.

Morrison, Kenneth M. "Native Americans and the American Revolution: Historic Sources and Shifting Frontier Conflict." In Frederick E. Hoxie, ed. *Indians in American History.* Arlington Heights, Ill.: Davidson, 1988.

Mowatt, Charles Loch. *East Florida as a British Province, 1763–1784.* Gainesville: University Presses of Florida, 1964.

Murrin, John M. "The French and Indian War, the American Revolution and the Counterfactual Hypothesis: Reflections on Lawrence Henry Gipson and John Shy." *Reviews in American History* 1 (1973): 307–18.

Namier, Sir Lewis. *England at the Time of the American Revolution.* 2nd ed. London: Macmillan and Co., 1961.

Nasatir, Abraham P. "The Anglo-Spanish Frontier in Illinois Country during the Revolution, 1779–1783." *Journal of the Illinois State Historical Society* 212 (1928): 343–50.

Nasatir, A. P. *Borderland in Retreat: From Spanish Louisiana to the Far Southwest.* Albuquerque: University of New Mexico Press, 1976.

Nash, Gary B. "The Forgotten Experience: Indians, Blacks, and the American Revolution." Reprinted in Richard D. Brown, ed. *Major Problems in the Era of the American Revolution.* Lexington, Mass.: Heath, 1992.

Nash, Gary B. *Race, Class, and Politics: Essays on American Colonial and Revolutionary Society.* Urbana: University of Illinois Press, 1986.

Nelson, Paul David. *General Horatio Gates: A Biography.* Baton Rouge: Louisiana State University, 1976.

Norton, Mary Beth. *The British-Americans: Loyalist Exiles in England, 1774–1782.* Boston: Little, Brown, and Company, 1972.

Norton, Thomas Elliot. *The Fur Trade in Colonial New York, 1686–1776.* Madison: University of Wisconsin, 1974.

O'Callaghan, Edmund, and Berthold Fernow, eds. *Documentary History of the State of New York*. 4 vols. Albany, N.Y.: Weed, Parsons, and Company, 1850–1851.

O'Callaghan, Edmund, and Berthold Fernow, eds. *Documentary Relative of the Colonial History of New York*. 15 vols. Albany, N.Y.: Weed, Parsons, and Company, 1853–1887.

O'Donnell, James H. "Captain Pipe's Speech: A Commentary on the Delaware Experience, 1775–1781." *Northwest Ohio Quarterly* 64 (1992): 126–33.

O'Donnell, James H. *The Cherokees of North Carolina in the American Revolution*. Raleigh, N.C.: Department of Cultural Resources, 1976.

O'Donnell, James H. "The Florida Revolutionary Indian Frontier: Abode of the Blessed or Field of Battle?" In Samuel Proctor, ed. *Eighteenth Century Florida: Life on the Frontier*. Gainesville: University Presses of Florida, 1976.

O'Donnell, James H. "Frontier Warfare and the American Victory." In John Ferling, ed. *The World Turned Upside Down: The American Victory in the War of Independence*. Westport, Conn.: Greenwood Press, 1988.

O'Donnell, James H. *The Southern Indians and the American Revolution*. Knoxville: University of Tennessee Press, 1972.

O'Donnell, James H. *"The Virginia Expedition against the Overhill Cherokee, 1776."* *East Tennessee Historical Society* 39 (1967): 13–25.

Olmstead, Earl P. *Blackcoats among the Delawares: David Zeisberger on the Ohio*. Kent, Ohio: Kent State University Press, 1991.

Olson, Gary D. "Thomas Brown, the East Florida Rangers, and the Defense of East Florida." In Samuel Proctor, ed. *Eighteenth Century Florida and the Revolutionary South*. Gainesville: University Presses of Florida, 1978.

Olson, Gary D. "Thomas Brown, Loyalist Partisan, and His Revolutionary War in Georgia, 1778–1782." *Georgia Historical Quarterly* 54 (1970): 1–19.

Osborne, George C. "Major General John Campbell in British West Florida." *Florida Historical Quarterly* 27 (1949): 317–39.

Ourada, Patricia K. *The Menominee Indians: A History*. Norman: University of Oklahoma Press, 1979.

Pancake, John S. *1777: The Year of the Hangman*. Tuscaloosa, Ala.: The University of Alabama Press, 1977.

Pancake, John S. *This Destructive War: The British Campaign in the Carolinas, 1780–1782*. Tuscaloosa: University of Alabama Press, 1985.

Pares, Richard. "American versus Continental Warfare, 1739–1763." English Historical Review 51 (1936): 429–65.

Pares, Richard. *War and Trade in the West Indes, 1739–1763*. London: F. Cass, 1963.

Parker, Arthur C. "The Indian Interpretation of the Sullivan-Clinton Campaign." *Rochester Historical Society Publications Fund Series B* (1929): 45–59.

Pearce, Roy Harvey. *The Savages of America: A Study of the Indian and the Idea of Civilization*. Baltimore, Md.: Johns Hopkins Press, 1965.

Peckham, Howard. *The Toll of Independence: Engagements and Battle Casualties of the American Revolution.* Chicago: University of Chicago Press, 1974.

Peters, Thelma. "The Loyalist Migration from East Florida to the Bahama Islands." *Florida Historical Quarterly* 40 (October 1961): 123–41.

Pieper, Thomas I., and James B. Gidney. *Fort Laurens, 1778–1779: The Revolutionary War in Ohio.* Kent, Ohio: Kent State University Press, 1976.

Porter, Kenneth W. "The Founder of the 'Seminole Nation': Secoffee or Cowkeeper." *Florida Historical Quarterly* 27 (1949): 362–84.

Procter, James. *The Ohio Company: Its Inner History.* Pittsburgh: University of Pittsburgh Press, 1959.

Proctor, Samuel, ed. *Eighteenth Century Florida: The Impact of the American Revolution.* Gainesville: University Presses of Florida, 1978.

Proctor, Samuel, ed. *Eighteenth Century Florida and Its Borderlands.* Gainesville: University Presses of Florida, 1975.

Proctor, Samuel, ed. *Eighteenth Century Florida: Life on the Frontier.* Gainesville: University Presses of Florida, 1976.

Proctor, Samuel, ed. *Eighteenth Century Florida and the Revolutionary South.* Gainesville: University Presses of Florida, 1978.

Prucha, Francis Paul. *The Great Father: The United States and the American Indians.* Lincoln: University of Nebraska Press, 1984.

Quaife, Milo M. "Detroit Battles: The Blue Licks." *Burton Historical Collection* 6 (1927): 17–32.

Quaife, Milo M. "The Ohio Campaigns of 1782." *Mississippi Valley Historical Review* 17 (1931): 515–29.

Quaife, Milo M. "When Detroit Invaded Kentucky." *Burton Historical Collection, Leaflet* 4 (1925): 17–32.

Reid, John Philip. *A Better Kind of Hatchet: Law, Trade, and Diplomacy in the Cherokee Nation during the Early Years of European Contact.* University Park: Pennsylvania State University Press, 1976.

Reid, John Philip. *In Defiance of the Law: The Standing Army Controversy, the Two Constitutions, and the Coming of the American Revolution.* Chapel Hill: University of North Carolina Press, 1981.

Reid, William Max. *The Story of Old Fort Johnson.* New York: G. P. Putnam's Sons, 1906.

Rice, Otis K. *The Allegheny Frontier: West Virginia Beginnings, 1730–1830.* Lexington: University Press of Kentucky, 1970.

Rice, Otis K. *Frontier Kentucky.* Lexington: University Press of Kentucky, 1975.

Richter, Daniel K., and James H. Merrill, eds. *Beyond the Covenant Chain: The Iroquois and Their Neighbors in Indian North America, 1600–1800.* Syracuse, N.Y.: Syracuse University Press, 1987.

Rickey, Don. "The British-American Attack on St. Louis, May 26, 1780." *Missouri Historical Review* 55 (1960): 35–45.

Ritcheson, Charles R. *British Politics and the American Revolution.* Norman: University of Oklahoma Press, 1954.

Robson, Eric. *The American Revolution in Its Political and Military Aspects, 1763–1783*. New York: W. W. Norton and Company, 1966.

Robson, Eric. "British Light Infantry in the Mid-Eighteenth Century: The Effect of American Conditions." *Army Quarterly* 62 (1952): 209–22.

Russell, Nelson V. *The British Regime in Michigan and the Old Northwest, 1760–1796*. Northfield, Minn.: Carleton College, 1939.

Savelle, Max. *The Diplomatic History of the Canadian Boundary, 1749–63*. New Haven, Conn.: Yale University Press, 1940.

Savelle, Max. "Diplomatic Preliminaries of the Seven Years' War in America." *Canadian Historical Review* 20 (1939): 1–43.

Savelle, Max. *George Morgan: Empire Builder*. New York: Columbia University Press, 1932.

Savelle, Max. *Seeds of Liberty: The Genesis of the American Mind*. New York: Alfred A. Knopf, 1948.

Schaaf, Gregory. *Wampum Belts and Peace Trees: George Morgan, Native Americans, and Revolutionary Diplomacy*. Golden, Colo.: Fulcrum, 1990.

Schweintz, Edmund de. *Life and Times of David Zeisberger*. Philadelphia: Lippincott, 1870.

Searcy, Martha Condray. *The Georgia-Florida Contest in the American Revolution, 1776–1778*. Tuscaloosa: University of Alabama Press, 1985.

Servies, James A. *The Siege of Pensacola, 1781: A Bibliography*. Pensacola, Fla.: The John C. Pace Library, 1981.

Shaw, Helen L. *British Administration of the Southern Indians, 1756–1783*. Lancaster, Pa.: Lancaster Press, Inc., 1931.

Sheehan, Bernard. "The Famous Hair Buyer General: Henry Hamilton, George Rogers Clark, and the American Indian." *Indiana Magazine of History 79* (1983): 1–28.

Sheehan, Bernard. "The Problem of the Indian in the American Revolution." In Philip Weeks, ed. *The American Indian Experience*. Arlington Heights, Ill.: Forum, 1988.

Shy, John. *A People Numerous and Armed: Reflections on the Military Struggle of American Independence*. New York: Oxford University Press, 1976.

Shy, John. *Toward Lexington: The Role of the British Army in the Coming of the American Revolution*. Princeton, N.J.: Princeton University Press, 1965.

Siebert, Wilbur H. *Loyalists in East Florida, 1774 to 1785*. 2 vols. Deland: Florida State Historical Society, 1929.

Siebert, Wilbur H. "The Loyalists and the Six Nations in the Niagara Peninsula." *Transactions of the Royal Society of Canada* 9 (1915): section 11.

Siebert, Wilbur H. "The Loyalists in West Florida and the Natchez District." *Proceedings of the Mississippi Valley Historical Association* 8 (1916): 102–22.

Silverman, Kenneth. *A Cultural History of the American Revolution: Painting, Music, Literature, and the Theatre in the Colonies and the United States from the Treaty of Paris to the Inauguration of George Washington*. New York: Thomas Y. Crowell Company, 1976.

Slaughter, Thomas P. *The Whiskey Rebellion: Frontier Epilogue to the American Revolution.* New York: Oxford University Press, 1986.

Slotkin, Richard. *Regeneration through Violence: The Mythology of the American Revolution, 1660–1860.* Middleton, Conn.: Wesleyan University Press, 1973.

Snapp, J. Russell. *John Stuart and the Issue of Empire on the Southern Frontier.* Baton Rouge: Louisiana State University, 1998.

Snapp, J. Russell. "William Henry Drayton: The Making of a Conservative Revolutionary." *Journal of Southern History* 57 (1991): 637–58.

Sosin, Jack M. "The British Indian Department and Dunmore's War. *Virginia Magazine of History and Biography* 74 (January 1966): 34–50.

Sosin, Jack M. *The Revolutionary Frontier, 1763–1783.* Albuquerque: University of New Mexico Press, 1967.

Sosin, Jack M. "The Use of Indians in the War of the American Revolution: A Reassessment of Responsibility." *Canadian Historical Review* 46 (1965): 101–21.

Sosin, Jack M. *Whitehall and the Wilderness: The Middle West in British Colonial Policy, 1760–1775.* Lincoln: University of Nebraska Press, 1961.

Stanley, George F. "The Six Nations and the American Revolution." *Ontario History* 56 (1964): 217–32.

Star, J. Barton. *Tories, Dons, and Rebels: The American Revolution in West Florida.* Gainesville: University Press of Florida, 1976.

Stevens, Paul L. "His Majesty's 'Savage' Allies": British Policy and the Northern Indians during the Revolutionary War. Buffalo: State University of New York at Buffalo, 1984.

Stevens, Paul L. *A King's Colonel at Niagara, 1774–1776: Lt. Col. John Caldwell and the Beginnings of the American Revolution on the New York Frontier.* Youngstown, N.Y.: Old Fort Niagara Association, 1987.

Stevens, Paul L. "'To Invade the Frontiers of Kentucky?': The Indian Diplomacy of Philippe de Rocheblave, Britain's Acting Commandant at Kaskaskia, 1776–1778." *Filson Club History Quarterly* 64 (1990): 205–46.

Stevens, Paul L. "'To Keep the Indians of the Wabache in His Majesty's Interest': The Indian Diplomacy of Edward Abbott, British Lieutenant Governor of Vincennes, 1776–1778." *Indiana Magazine of History* 83 (1987): 141–70.

Stevens, Paul L. "Wabasha Visits Governor Carleton, 1776: New Light on a Legendary Episode of Dakota-British Diplomacy on the Great Lakes Frontier." *Michigan Historical Review* 16 (1990): 21–48.

Stevens, Wayne E. *The Northwest Fur Trade, 1763–1800.* Urbana, Ill.: University of Illinois Press, 1928.

Sullivan, James, and A. C. Flick, eds. The Papers of William Johnson. Albany, N.Y.: State University of New York, 1921–1969.

Swiggert, Howard. *War out of Niagara: Walter Butler and the Tory Rangers.* New York: Columbia University Press, 1933.

Sword, Wiley. *President Washington's Indian War.* Norman: University of Oklahoma Press, 1986.

Szatmary, David. *Shay's Rebellion: The Making of an Agrarian Insurrection.* Amherst: University of Massachusetts Press, 1980.

Talbert, Charles Gann. *Benjamin Logan: Kentucky Frontiersman.* Lexington: University of Kentucky, 1952.

Tanner, Helen, Adele Hast, and Jacqueline Peterson. *Atlas of Great Lakes Indian History.* Norman: University of Oklahoma Press, 1987.

Taylor, Alan. *Liberty Men and Great Proprietors: The Revolutionary Settlement on the Maine Frontier.* Chapel Hill: University of North Carolina Press, 1990.

Thayer, Theodore. *Pennsylvania Politics and the Growth of Democracy, 1740–1776.* Harrisburg: Pennsylvania Historical and Museum Commission, 1953.

Thomas, Earle. *Sir John Johnson, Loyalist Baronet.* Toronto: Dundurn, 1986.

Thwaites, Reuben Gold. *Daniel Boone.* New York: D. Appleton, 1991.

Tucker, Robert W., and David C. Hendrickson. *The Fall of the First British Empire: Origins of the War of American Independence.* Baltimore: Johns Hopkins Press, 1981.

Turner, Frederick Jackson. *The Frontier in American History.* New York: Dover Publications, 1996.

Usner, Daniel H. *Indians, Settlers, and Slaves in a Frontier Exchange Economy: The Lower Mississippi Valley before 1783.* Chapel Hill: University of North Carolina Press, 1992.

Valentine, Alan. *Lord George Germain.* New York: Oxford University Press, 1962.

Van Every, Dale. *A Company of Heros: The American Frontier, 1777–1783,* New York: Mentor Books, 1963.

Venables, Robert W. "The Indians' Revolutionary War in the Hudson Valley, 1775–1783." In Lawrence M. Hauptman and Jack Campisi, eds. *Neighbors and Intruders: An Ethnohistorical Exploration of the Indians of the Hudson's River.* Ottawa: National Museum of Man, 1978.

Vernes, H. A. "Medical Crisis at Fort Niagara, 1779–80." *Niagara Frontier* 24 (Winter 1977): 89–94.

Vivian, James F., and Jean H. Vivian "Congressional Indian Policy during the War for Independence: The Northern Department." *Maryland Historical Magazine* 63 (1968): 241–74.

Volwiler, Albert T. *George Croghan and the Westward Movement, 1741–1782.* Cleveland: Arthur H. Clark, 1926.

Wainwright, Nicholas B. *George Croghan: Wilderness Diplomat.* Chapel Hill: University of North Carolina Press, 1959.

Walker, James W. St. G. *The Black Loyalists: The Search for the Promised Land in Nova Scotia and Sierra Leone, 1783–1870.* New York: Holmes and Meier, 1976.

Wallace, Anthony F. C., with Sheila C. Steen. *The Death and Rebirth of the Seneca.* New York: Alfred A. Knopf, 1970.

Wallace, Paul A. W. *Indians in Pennsylvania.* Harrisburg: Pennsylvania Historical and Museum Commission, 1981.

Waller, George. *The American Revolution in the West.* Chicago: Nelson-Hall, 1976.

Watt, Calvin. *Burning of the Valleys.* Toronto: Dundurn Press, 1997.

Weber, David. *The Spanish Frontier in North America.* New Haven, Conn.: Yale University Press, 1993.

Weeks, Stephen B. "General Joseph Martin and the War of Revolution in the West." *Annual Report of the American Historical Association* (1893).

Weisman, Brent Richards. *Like Beads on a String: A Culture History of the Seminole Indians in Northern Peninsula Florida.* Tuscaloosa: University of Alabama Press, 1989.

Wells, Robert. *The Population of the British Colonies in America before 1776: A Survey of Census Data.* Princeton, N.J.: Princeton University Press, 1975.

Weslager, C. A. *The Delaware Indians: A History.* New Brunswick, N.J.: Rutgers University Press, 1991.

Wheeler-Vogelin, Ermine, and Helen Hornbeck Tanner, eds. *Indians of Ohio and Indiana Prior to 1795.* 2 vols. New York: Garland, 1974.

Whitaker, A. P. "Spain and the Cherokee Indians, 1783–1791." *North Carolina Historical Review* 4 (1927): 2525–69.

Whitaker, Arthur Preston. *The Spanish-American Frontier, 1783–1795.* Lincoln: University of Nebraska Press, 1969.

White, Richard. *The Middle Ground: Indians, Empires, and Republics in the Great Lakes Region.* New York: Cambridge University Press, 1994.

White, Richard. "The Winning of the West: The Expansion of the Western Sioux in the Eighteenth and Nineteenth Centuries." *The Journal of American History* 65 (September 1978): 319–43.

Willcox, William B. *The Portrait of a General: Sir Henry Clinton in the War of Independence.* New York: Alford A. Knopf, 1964.

Willcox, William B. "Too Many Cooks: British Planning before Saratoga." *The Journal of British Studies* 3 (November 1962): 45–90.

Williams, Edward G. "Fort Pitt and the Revolution on the Western Frontier." *Western Pennsylvania Historical Magazine* 59 (1976): 1–37, 129–52, 251–87, 379–444.

Williams, Samuel Cole. *History of the Lost State of Franklin.* Rev. ed. New York: Press of the Pioneers, 1931.

Williams, Samuel Cole. *Tennessee during the American Revolution.* Knoxville: University of Tennessee Press, 1974.

Wilson, Bruce. "The Struggle for Wealth and Power at Fort Niagara, 1775–1783." *Ontario History* 68 (1970): 137–54.

Wise, S. F. "The American Revolution and Indian History." In John S. Moir, ed. *Character and Circumstance: Essays in Honor of Donald Grant Creighton.* Toronto: Macmillan, 1970.

Wood, Gordon. *The Radicalism of the American Revolution.* New York: Vintage, 1991.

Wood, Peter H., Gregory A. Waselkov, and M. Thomas Hatley, eds. *Powhatan's Mantle: Indians in the Colonial Southeast.* Lincoln: University of Nebraska Press, 1989.

Wright, J. Leitch, Jr. "British East Florida: Loyalist Bastion." In Samuel Proctor, ed. *Eighteenth Century Florida: The Impact of the American Revolution.* Gainesville: University Presses of Florida, 1978.

Wright, J. Leitch, Jr. *Creeks and Seminoles: Destruction and Regeneration of the Muscogulge People.* Lincoln: University of Nebraska Press, 1986.

Young, Alfred F. *The American Indian and the American Revolution.* Chicago: Occasional Papers of the Newberry Center for the History of the American Indians, 1983.

Young, Alfred F. *The American Revolution: Explorations in the History of American Radicalism.* DeKalb: Northern Illinois University Press, 1976.

INDEX